Unfinished Democracy

Unfinished Democracy
The American Political System

Harrell R. Rodgers, Jr.
The University of Houston

Michael Harrington
Queens College–City University of New York

Scott, Foresman and Company   Glenview, Illinois
Dallas, Texas   Oakland, New Jersey   Palo Alto, California   Tucker, Georgia
London, England

Library of Congress Cataloging in Publication Data

Rodgers, Harrell R
  Unfinished democracy.

  Includes index.
  1. United States—Politics and government—1945-
2. Political participation—United States. 3. United
States—Economic conditions—1945-   4. United
States—Social conditions—1945-   I. Harrington,
Michael, joint author. II. Title.
JK274.R74   320.973   80-21795
ISBN 0-673-15458-0
ISBN 0-673-15415-7 (pbk.)

  2 3 4 5 6-RRC-85 84 83 82 81

Acknowledgments

pp. 119–122: Excerpt from article by Paul Anderson describing the film of Memorial Day in
Chicago, June 16, 1937. Reprinted by permission of the St. Louis *Post Dispatch*.

pp. 129–130: Excerpt of events of August 12, 1965, compiled by the McCone Commission:
California Governor's Commission on the Los Angeles Riots: Transcripts, Depositions, Consultant's
Reports, and Selected Documents. Reprinted by permission of Honorable Edmund G. "Pat" Brown,
Governor of California 1959–1966.

p. 151: From "How to Buy a Bill," The Washington Post, September 1, 1977. Copyright the
Washington *Post*.

pp. 265–267: Excerpt from "Ralph Nader Takes on Congress as Well as Big Business," interview
by Linda E. Demkovich. *National Journal,* March 11, 1978, No. 10. Reprinted by permission.

Credits for photographs, charts, and cartoons appear on pp. 609–611.

Much of the public and most politicians today are frustrated, perplexed, and perhaps even a little angry and frightened by a government that seems to defy comprehension and control, an economy that seems determined to malfunction, and social problems that appear to grow worse every day. We are not immodest enough to suggest that this book constitutes a blueprint for understanding and solving all these problems. We have, however, tried to show students why the task of self-government has grown so complex, and why economic and social problems have reached the stage where they defy easy solution. We have also raised some of the issues that will have to be debated and identified the types of reform that will have to be instituted to deal with our current problems.

Preface

In introducing students to American government in this troubled period, we have tried to be positive but realistic and honest about both the strengths and weaknesses of the political and economic systems. We have not been afraid to raise controversial issues, but we hope we have presented them fairly and constructively. We believe that even though our problems are substantial, they are correctable and manageable. In fact, we put the current malaise in historical context to show that the nation has survived many periods of unrest and turmoil. Often these periods have produced new political coalitions and reforms that have reshaped and revitalized the political process for a time. Reassessments and adjustments, we note, are inevitable and potentially positive.

The book is divided into three major sections. Part 1 examines the public's role in the political process. It addresses such questions as: "Can the public influence and control the political process?" "What are the causes of low political participation?" "Can political participation be increased?" and "Who rules the American political process?" Part 1 concludes with an in-depth analysis of the economic system, emphasizing the increasing role that the government plays in the economy. We attempt to show that the economic and political systems are so inalterably linked that unless the public can have some influence over certain types of economic decisions, it cannot really control the political process.

Part 2, which consists of Chapters 8 through 14, is concerned with American political institutions and politics. The underlying theme is that neither American political institutions nor parties are optimally designed to facilitate policy-making, thus making it difficult for the system to adequately deal with many social problems. We discuss the Congress, the Presidency, the bureaucracy, and the courts in separate chapters. These chapters demonstrate how the institutions interact, and how each institution has affected each of the other branches of government. Finally, we show how the design and the performance of the major institutions affect political parties and interest groups, and how the institutional and political processes interact to affect public policy.

Part 3, consisting of Chapters 15 through 20, provides an in-depth analysis of American foreign policy and several areas of domestic policy. The domestic policy chapters examine four of America's most severe social problems—poverty, crime, racial discrimination, and urban decline. We explain how the economic and political systems (and the ideologies that underlie these systems) separately and interactively helped cause the particular problem and how they contribute to the continuation of the problem. For example, we show how weaknesses in the economic system contribute to these problems and how political and institutional priorities erect barriers to their resolution. These chapters are also designed to give the student further insight into the political process by examining the evolution of major public policies. Each chapter discusses and critiques the reforms that are generally thought to be necessary to resolve these and other domestic ills.

Chapter 21 assesses the progress the American system has made in creating a truly democratic, creative, and prosperous nation and suggests some of the continuing barriers to fulfilling our basic goals. While the direction the nation will take in the next ten years or so is not certain, we have tried to review the basic alternatives and their implications for the nation.

Finally, a brief postscript discusses and analyzes the 1980 presidential campaign and election.

To aid the student, Professor Richard Payne of Sam Houston State University has prepared a *Study Guide* to accompany *Unfinished Democracy*. The Guide includes chapter outlines, key terms, and sample fill-in-the-blank, essay, and multiple-choice questions. Professors James Carter (who swears that he has no relatives serving in high office) and Beryl Pettus of Sam Houston State University have prepared an *Instructor's Manual* for the volume. The Manual contains chapter overviews, suggested lecture topics, sample questions, and numerous test items.

Working with the team from Scott, Foresman and Company has been both a personal and professional pleasure. The Scott, Foresman staff is quite simply the most professional and astute that we have ever worked with. From the beginning, the staff accepted this book as a team effort, and every member did his or her job with great energy and skill. Bruce Borland's enthusiasm, insights, and indefatigable efforts on behalf of this book were an inspiration and comfort from beginning to end. Robert Johnson surprised us not only by demonstrating superb publishing acumen, but also by proving to be exceptionally well informed politically. This inspired combination of talents was especially helpful. Charlie Schaff also did a superb job of untangling our syntax, helping us write in a more lean and comprehensive style, and selecting the right pictures and cartoons to emphasize and reinforce our thoughts. His attention to detail was as welcome as it was characteristic of the team to which he belonged. Barbara Schneider did an excellent job on the design of the book, and Mary Moss and Nina Biskinis pleased us with their fine picture research. Greg Odjakjian, the Scott, Foresman representative in Houston, helped us in our initial negotiations with his company, provided us with dozens of helpful suggestions, and inspired us with his enthusiastic support for this project.

As any author knows, the most underrated contributor to any book is the typist. In this case the heroine is Sandy McMurtry, who labored long and hard to convert handwritten pages into legible type. Her excellent work made our burden much lighter, and to her we owe a considerable debt.

A number of scholars provided us with invaluable critiques, including Edward Dreyer of the University of Tulsa and Donald Lamkin of St. Louis Community College at Meramec. Al Watkins of the University of Texas convinced us to rewrite one of the chapters and provided valuable points throughout the text. Benjamin Page of the University of Chicago also provided us with an excellent critique that led to many important improvements.

Harrell Rodgers would like to express a special thanks to his wife, Lynne, for her uncommonly beautiful love and for her constant encouragement and unwavering faith that a belief in the fundamental decency and value of people is the only real faith—the only real salvation for all of us.

H. R.

M. H.

Overview

Contents

2 AMERICAN POLITICAL INSTITUTIONS AND POLITICS *212*

3 SOCIAL PROBLEMS, POLITICS, AND ECONOMICS 404

> He that goeth about to persuade a multitude that they are not so
> well governed as they ought to be, shall never want attentive and
> favourable hearers.
>
> Richard Hooker

1

Throughout history most governments have been failures. Unsuccessful governments, sometimes overthrown by their populace or by foreign invaders but often merely collapsing on their own, are piled high through the pages of world history. Most of them have failed because they have not been based on the consent of their citizens, have not been attuned to the public's needs, and have been too inept to establish a prosperous, reasonably stable political system in which people could live safely and happily.

Prologue
"We Are the Greatest!"

In some parts of the world, change is not only frequent but violent:

> Between the end of the [Second World War] and 1969, forty of the approximately
> 100 states in Asia, Africa, and Latin America experienced at least one successful
> military seizure of power. Between 1948 and 1967, almost all the countries of
> Latin America, two-thirds of the countries of Asia, and one-half of those coun-
> tries in Africa independent by 1962 recorded one or more successful or unsuc-
> cessful attempts to change their governments by unconstitutional means. Over a
> shorter time span (1946 to 1959), but including a wider range of type of political
> instability, Eckstein cites the *New York Times* as reporting more than 1,200 clear
> cases of "internal war," including "civil wars, guerrilla wars, localized terror-
> ism, mutinies, coups d'etat."[1]

Indeed, failure is so prevalent among governments that only a relatively small percentage of all the people in history have had the good fortune to live in even modest prosperity and peace. By any standards, most humans even today do not enjoy political freedom, and most are illiterate and poor.

By historical standards, the American people have indeed been fortunate. Our political system is celebrated by many as one of the most enduring and enlightened of all *social contracts* among a free people. Indeed, the American Constitution, which is the embodiment of the public contract, is widely considered to be a work of great genius. As testimony, it is the oldest *constitution*

The "tall ships" sailed into New York harbor to celebrate America's Bicentennial on July 4, 1976.

in existence. Through political crisis, internal and external wars, depressions, and civil revolt, the Constitution has persevered.

The American political system is therefore one of the most successful on earth. While most observers would acknowledge that it is not without flaws, it does represent one of the most open, democratic, and progressive forms of government in existence. In a complex way, most Americans appreciate this fact. For the most part, Americans would not swap places with the people of any other country. Americans tend to believe that they have one of the most enlightened political systems, one of the strongest economies, the finest educational systems, the most sophisticated medical technologies, the strongest military, and the most opportunity. Many feel, in fact, that Americans are the chosen few.

Yet Americans have always harbored serious grievances against their government, and lately these have intensified. The reason is that in recent years American society has labored through an extremely unsettling period. Americans have been deeply troubled by abuse of power and corruption in government, high inflation and high unemployment, severe crime and juvenile delinquency, urban blight, struggles over civil rights, conflict and agony over a lost war, and dozens of other social ills. As a result, surveys reveal serious tensions in the public's attitude toward the society, the political system, and political leaders.

Indeed, many of these problems may be related to a larger shift in American life, one which will have a profound impact upon our political institutions. That transition became visible in the 1970s.

Franklin Roosevelt's *New Deal*—the reform movement which created the welfare state in response to the Great Depression in the 1930s—became the "public philosophy" of the United States for an entire generation. Political debate primarily took place within the confines of this "philosophy." As Samuel H. Beer, who coined that phrase, notes:

> To say that a public philosophy is crucial to a democratic polity is not to say that its presence will eliminate, or even reduce, political conflict. Quite the contrary. Even when a public philosophy prevails within a nation, its assertions will provoke counter-assertions, as the 'liberalism' of the 1930s called forth the 'conservatism' of the 1940s. Yet such a conflict too has its coherence: one side says 'yes,' the other 'no,' but both are trying to answer the same question.[2]

In the 1970s, and now in the 1980s, that unanimity of the political antagonists with regard to the question being debated has disappeared. As a result, many of the traditional labels in American politics—like liberal and conservative—have become problematic.

One of the reasons for this change has to do with the American economy. Under the New Deal, the federal government accepted the responsibility of intervening in the economy in order to promote full employment and economic prosperity and stability. The Republican Presidents—Eisenhower, Nixon, and Ford—accepted that obligation and so did Roosevelt's Democratic heirs, Tru-

The Democratic Presidents pictured above at the 1964 Democratic Party Convention—Kennedy (top center), Truman (top right), and Johnson (bottom)—were all political heirs of Franklin D. Roosevelt (pictured top left). FDR's New Deal shaped government policies and political debate in America for a generation.

man, Kennedy, Johnson, and Carter. The public philosophy of the New Deal, in keeping with capitalist principles, assumed that private corporations would make the fundamental decisions about the allocation of resources. Washington was to use *fiscal policy* (determining whether the federal budget would be in surplus or deficit) and *monetary policy* (controlling the supply of money) to ensure that there would be adequate buying power to absorb the output of the corporations and thereby to keep Americans at work, mainly in the private sector.

In theory, if buying power was insufficient, the government would operate at a deficit and put money into people's pockets so that they could purchase what the private corporations produced. If buying power was excessive, with too much money competing for too few goods and consequently creating *inflation*, Washington would raise taxes and/or interest rates to cut down demand. According to the theory, unemployment could be eliminated by small bursts of controlled inflation, and inflation could be reduced by slight increases in unemployment. In the long run, the economy would then operate on an even keel. The deficits needed to combat joblessness would be compensated for by the surpluses required to deal with inflation.

6

The theory never worked that neatly in practice, but it did operate as a guide for Republicans and Democrats, for conservatives and liberals. To be sure, the conservatives tended to emphasize the problem of inflation, and the liberals focused on unemployment, but both were operating within a common framework. The highwater mark of confidence in this public philosophy occurred in the 1960s, the longest prosperous period in American history. As Lyndon Johnson left the Presidency in January 1969, he proudly told the Congress that his record in office

> demonstrates the vitality of a free economy and its capacity for steady growth. No longer do we view our economic life as a relentless tide of ups and downs. No longer do we fear that automation and technical progress will rob workers of jobs rather than help us to achieve greater abundance. No longer do we consider poverty and unemployment permanent landmarks on our economic scene.[3]

In the years since President Johnson made that statement, the American economy has experienced three recessions with chronically high levels of unemployment, persistent poverty, and soaring prices. Even more troubling, the assumption that unemployment and inflation were counterposed to one another, and therefore that joblessness would bring down prices or that inflation would reduce unemployment, has been contradicted by a new economic reality. During the years 1969–70, 1974–75, and 1979–80, inflation and unemployment moved in the same direction at the same time, creating a phenomenon that has been labeled *stagflation*. Clearly, the economic strategies which had been followed for almost half a century no longer applied.

The public philosophy of the New Deal assumed that private corporations would make the fundamental decisions about the allocation of resources. Washington was to use fiscal policy and monetary policy to ensure that there would be adequate buying power to absorb the output of the corporations and thereby to keep Americans at work, mainly in the private sector.

But this situation did not simply affect the economy, the unemployment rate, and the consumer price index. If there were constant growth in the Gross National Product (GNP) under conditions of price stability, then every group in the society would see its position improve at the same time. Economics, it was said in the sixties, was no longer a "zero sum game" like poker, in which the winners take from the losers. Now there would be a "positive sum game" in which everyone would win. Therefore, there could be a new politics of cooperation between business, labor, the government, and the rest of society. The booming economy which paid for helping the poor or creating a decent life for the aging simultaneously made the nonpoor and the young better off.

Thus, when the public philosophy of the New Deal began to disintegrate in the seventies, it profoundly affected social policy and political life as well

The U.S. Marathon.

as the economy. Real income went up—and then went down. There were huge deficits—like the $64 billion shortfall in Washington's accounts in 1975—to pay for the highest unemployment rates since the Great Depression. Leaders of both parties began to talk of the need of cutting back benefits for the poor and the aging. Political life in general became more atomized and, in many cases, more mean as groups fought one another over scarce resources rather than working together to produce a widely shared abundance.

When the public philosophy of the New Deal began to disintegrate in the seventies, it profoundly affected social policy and political life as well as the economy.

These events also profoundly affected America's position in the world. When one wanted to say that something was truly stable, the popular adage held that it was "sound as a dollar." But the economic troubles at home in the United States made the dollar less desirable abroad. And that meant that Washington had less leverage on a global scale, both politically and militarily. In the fall of 1979, for instance, the *Federal Reserve system* drastically restricted the money supply, a move that would increase unemployment, make it impossible for many Americans to buy a house, and in general have a deep impact upon the average citizen. This was done largely in response to pressures from West Germany and other European nations who demanded that America bring inflation under control. At this point, *Business Week* commented, "International economic forces began to play an unprecedented major role in the formulation of domestic economic policy" in the United States.[4]

In this book we must confront the political consequences of these major economic, social, and even global shifts. This is why our analysis will not treat political structures and trends in isolation from this larger context. For we may well be living in a time of change that will transform all aspects of American society in the same momentous way the New Deal did in the 1930s.

This is not to suggest that there has already been a clear political response to these developments. Faced with economic problems that refused to obey the old rules, living in the aftermath of the Vietnam War and the Watergate scandal, the U.S. government experienced one of the most severe erosions of public confidence in modern times. The figures below, taken from the Harris Poll, are illustrative. Note the precipitous drop between 1966 and 1977 in the public's confidence in the political system and political leaders. Equally important, the figures show that the effects of Watergate have been longstanding. While the public's confidence improved some in 1977, the changes were quite minor.

Percent in Agreement	Dec. 1977	Sept. 1976	Sept. 1966
"The people running the country don't really care what happens to you."	60	64	26
"What I think doesn't count much anymore."	61	63	37
"The rich get richer and the poor get poorer."	77	78	45
"I feel left out of things going on around me."	35	45	9

Figure 1.1 also shows the serious decline in public confidence in recent years. The figures show that between 1958 and 1978 the public became much more inclined to believe that the government wastes a lot of money, that the government is run for the benefit of the few, that there are a lot of crooks in government, and that you cannot trust the government to do right.

Four items in a November 1978 Harris Poll reflect the public's belief that politicians are not honest and that the government disproportionately represents special interests to the detriment of average citizens.[5] Eighty-four percent of the public agreed with the statement: "We do not have a federal government which is almost wholly free of corruption and pay-offs." Sixty-one percent

FIGURE 1.1
Confidence in Government: 1958–1978

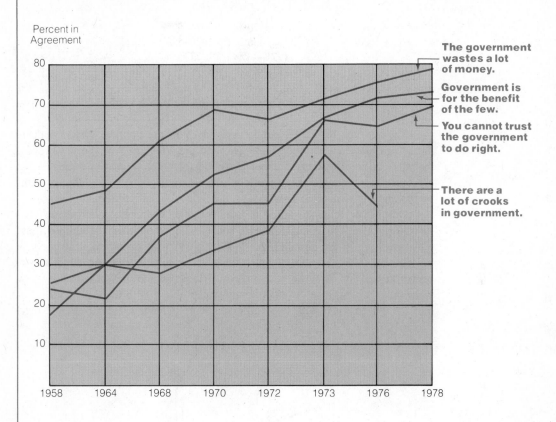

Percent in
Agreement

The government wastes a lot of money.

Government is for the benefit of the few.

You cannot trust the government to do right.

There are a lot of crooks in government.

Source: University of Michigan Center for Political Studies/Survey Research Center.

disagreed with the statement: "We have a federal government in which the good of the country is placed above special interests." Sixty-nine percent believed that the best people are not attracted to serve in government, and 59 percent believed that public officials are more interested in helping themselves than the country.

A number of recent Gallup polls also reveal that the public does not give politicians very high marks for honesty and ethical standards. In 1976 only 14 percent of the public gave members of the House of Representatives a rating of high or very high. Nineteen percent gave senators a high or very high rating.[6]

As a summary measure, the Harris Poll calculates a yearly alienation index. Between 1966 and 1978 the Harris Index of Alienation showed that the percentage of the public that could be labeled alienated rose from 29 percent to 58 percent. The yearly figures were as follows:

1966–20%	1974–57%
1969–36%	1976–59%
1971–40%	1977–58%
1973–55%	1978–59%

Thus, beginning in 1973, a clear majority of the public could be labeled "politically alienated."

The serious decline in public confidence in the political system reflects more than just concern over Watergate and the Vietnam War. Surveys reveal that the public is distressed about a number of other serious problems. Most prominently, the public expresses concern about stagflation—simultaneous inflation and high unemployment.[7]

Despite tax cuts designed to stimulate the economy, job training programs, and even programs to create some public service jobs, unemployment remained high in the mid and late 1970s. In 1975 the unemployment rate was 8.7 percent; after dropping slightly for several years it averaged about 6 percent in 1979. While these rates exceeded those of the previous decade, they were only an exaggeration of a continuing problem with the American economy. Between 1950 and 1974 official unemployment averaged about 5 per-

"I'd just like to know what in hell is happening, that's all! I'd like to know what in hell is happening! Do *you* know what in hell is happening?"

cent; during this period unemployment dropped below 3 percent only once (2.9 percent in 1953).

Along with serious unemployment, inflation has been high enough to erode the public's buying power and savings. The inflation rate was 11 percent in 1975, 5.7 percent in 1976, 6.5 percent in 1977, and 7.6 percent in 1978. In 1979 the inflation rate was an astounding 13.3 percent. Economists predicted similar rates for the early 1980s. In 1975 the buying power of families fell 2.6 percent, even though median family income rose by $818, to $13,720. This followed a 3.5 percent decline in 1974 and was the fourth drop in six years.

We may well be living in a time of change that will transform all aspects of American society in the same momentous way that the New Deal did in the 1930s.

In 1976 there was a small recovery. Median family income increased to $14,960, an after-inflation increase of about 3 percent.[8] In 1977 median family income ($16,010) increased at the same rate as inflation, yielding no increase in purchasing power. In 1978 median family income increased by 9.6 percent (to $17,640), but inflation reduced the real gain to 2 percent.

These economic problems are somewhat ironic because America has one of the strongest economies in the world; in 1979, the *Gross National Product* (GNP) was 2.3 trillion dollars. However, while our GNP towers over the rest of the world (more than double the Soviet Union's GNP), America no longer has the highest per capita GNP, a figure derived from dividing total GNP by population. Kuwait, the United Arab Emirates, Qatar, Switzerland, Sweden, and Canada all now have a higher per capita GNP than the United States.[9] Nor does America any longer rank first in per capita income, the total income earned in one year divided by the total population, including children and nonworking adults. In 1978 per capita income was $7,810, which according to various studies would rank America from fifth to seventh place in the world.[10]

While America's per capita income is not the highest in the world, it is high enough to provide all citizens with a decent living standard. As a hypothetical example, if income were equally divided across the population, all four-person families would have had an annual income of $31,240 ($7,810 × 4) in 1978. But, of course, income is not equally divided, or even close to it (as will be seen in Chapter 7). Thus, some citizens receive extremely high incomes, while many others have little or no income.

This creates another severe problem—poverty. America has always had a great deal of poverty. In 1975, according to the federal government's official poverty count, there were 25.9 million American poor. The poverty count in 1975 increased by 2.5 million poor over 1974, and exceeded poverty for every year back to 1967. In 1976, 1977, and 1978, the official count declined to 25 million, 24.7 million, and 24.5 million, respectively—still about 12 percent of the total population. As Chapter 15 will detail, as many as 40 to 60 million

The American public is concerned about the high rate of crime and frustrated by the government's inability to curb it. In 1980, a group of young people in New York City formed the "Guardian Angels," a volunteer organization that patrols the city's subway system to help prevent crime.

Americans actually live in poverty by some estimates. In polls, the public ranks reforming welfare and providing more and better jobs as a high priority.

Another problem the public expresses continuing concern about is crime. Among the major industrialized nations of the world, America definitely has the highest rate of violent crime. In 1977 the FBI catalogued 11 million serious crimes, 21 per minute. In the same year, the Census Bureau counted 41.1 million reported and unreported serious crimes.[11] Surveys reveal that the public is frightened and angered by high crime and does not believe that the government is doing enough to control and prevent it.

Along with these problems, Americans reported concern over such other problems as air and water pollution, urban congestion and blight, the quality of consumer goods, and the high cost of medical care. While some progress has been made against pollution, the air in most urban areas is not healthy and most major bodies of water in America suffer from pollution. Urban congestion is also severe in all major American cities, primarily because of a failure to develop viable public transportation systems. In the Midwest and North, most of the major cities suffer from serious blight, a problem that affects all major cities to one degree or another. American medicine, while highly sophisticated, is essentially a high-priced commodity, one that many Americans cannot afford. In the mid-1970s the cost of medical care was increasing at a rate that exceeded one million dollars an hour.[12]

While all these problems are very real and do cause the public serious distress, the annoyance and even concern of the American people do not necessarily mean that a majority has begun to doubt the basic legitimacy of the American political system. The public can be unhappy with current officeholders and policies but still believe that the political system is essentially viable, even if it is temporarily mismanaged or corrupted. The data, in fact, reveal that even during the most critical stages of the Watergate scandal the public basically retained an attachment to the American political system. For example, in 1976 the Survey Research Center asked the following two questions:

A. Some people believe a change in our whole form of government is needed to solve the problems facing our country, while others feel no real change is necessary. Do you think a big change is needed in our form of government, or should it be left pretty much as it is?
   1. Need a big change, 25%
   2. Need some change, 28%
   3. Keep as is, 47%

B. There has been some talk recently about how people have lost faith and confidence in the government in Washington. Do you think this lack of trust in the government is just because of the individuals in office or is there something more seriously wrong with government in general and the way it operates?
   1. Individuals in office, 67%
   2. Something wrong with government, 31%
   3. Both, 2%

Notice that on the first question only 25 percent of the public express an interest in major changes in the political system, with another 28 percent preferring some change. The second question shows that most citizens (67 percent) blame political ills on officeholders, with 31 percent expressing a belief that the system itself is flawed. While the percentage of citizens who perceive fundamental problems with the political system is not small, the data do reveal that a majority of the American public has not given up on the political system and is at least reluctant to support drastic alterations of it.

This evidence, however, should not be interpreted to minimize the importance of the public's current dissatisfaction or the seriousness of the social problems which affect them. Still, the data indicate that if politicians established and enforced high standards for their own conduct, and if a period free of substantial corruption came to pass, public faith would probably improve considerably.

Improvements in public confidence would probably be accompanied by improvements in the public's feelings of *political efficacy*. Citizens who are efficacious feel that they can control and influence the political system. During the 1950s and early 1960s the American public had fairly high levels of political efficacy,[13] but these feelings declined in the mid-1970s. The following questions from the Survey Research Center's 1978 nationwide study provide good examples:

A. People like me don't have any real say about what the government does.
   1. Agree, 46%
   2. Disagree, 54%

B. Sometimes politics and government seem so complicated that a person like me can't really understand what's going on.
   1. Agree, 73%
   2. Disagree, 27%

C. Generally speaking, those we elect to Congress in Washington lose touch with the people pretty quickly.
   1. Agree, 73%
   2. Disagree, 27%

D. I don't think public officials care much what people like me think.
   1. Agree, 53%
   2. Disagree, 47%

E. Parties are only interested in people's votes but not in their opinions.
   1. Agree, 65%
   2. Disagree, 35%

These data indicate that at least a majority of the population in 1978 did not feel that they had much voice in the government and that politicians do not really represent people like themselves. These feelings may have resulted from a number of factors other than Watergate: average citizens may feel a bit overwhelmed by the size and complexity of modern governments; the value of one vote in elections in which thousands and even millions are cast may seem insignificant; many of the public issues may seem remote and beyond citizen influence; the people may feel that public policies are too rarely beneficial to persons like themselves. For whatever reasons, a substantial proportion of the public clearly does not feel in control of, or even to some extent in contact with, the government. There is also a pervasive feeling that government disproportionately represents special interests and the rich.

These attitudes emerge within the larger context defined earlier in this chapter: the exhaustion of the "public philosophy" which has dominated American life for half a century. That development is, in turn, the consequence of an unprecedented economic problem which defies the conventional wisdom of both liberals and conservatives. So the student of the American political system in the 1980s has the difficult task of analyzing and understanding a reality which is in the process of considerable change, of seeing political structures within the context of an economy and society in transition. The purpose of this book is to make that difficult undertaking easier.

ORGANIZATION OF THE BOOK

In a true democracy the public controls the government. The great civilizing innovation of democratic theory is that it requires government to be based on the consent of the governed. In a true democracy every citizen has an equal opportunity to influence his or her government, and collective public influence determines the leaders and direction of government. The theme of this book is that the American public plays an important role in the political system but for many reasons generally does not control political institutions and public officials. As the polls above indicate, the people have considerable insight into their limited powers. This insight helps to lower their evaluations of political institutions and leaders and reduces their estimates of their potential to play a more significant role in the political system.

Assessing the public's influence in the political process, and the barriers to increasing their influence, yields important insights into modern American democracy, American political institutions, and the social problems that result from government failure. The chapters that follow are divided into three sections, each of which considers one of these points. Chapters 2 through 7 constitute Part 1. They examine such topics as the traditional and nontraditional role of the public in the political process and address the question of whether the public's participant role can be increased. Chapters 6 and 7 discuss political corruption and the economic system in terms of their ability to bias the political process and thus lower public influence and control.

The American public plays an important role in the political system but for many reasons does not generally control political institutions and public officials.

Part 2 consists of Chapters 8 through 14, which examine American political institutions and politics. These chapters attempt to show how the mechanics and dynamics of American political institutions both influence and reflect the public's role in the political system. They isolate those factors that bias political influence and show how these biases are reflected in institutional performance and failure. In addition, the chapters explain how institutional roles have changed over the years to meet new environmental changes and to respond to the frequent failure of political institutions to meet their responsibilities.

Chapters 15 through 20 constitute Part 3. These chapters examine some of America's major social problems. They attempt to show how these problems reflect the institutional and political bias resulting from inadequate public influence and control over the political process. Chapter 21 summarizes some of the text's major points and discusses a number of the trends and challenges that will characterize and confront the American political process in the years to come. The final chapter briefly discusses the 1980 presidential election.

Footnotes

1. Thomas H. Greene, *Comparative Revolutionary Movements* (Englewood Cliffs, N.J.: Prentice-Hall, 1974), p. 6.
2. Samuel H. Beer, "In Search of a New Public Philosophy," in *The New American Political System,* ed. Anthony King (Washington, D.C.: American Enterprise Institute, 1978), p. 6.
3. Economic Report of the Presidency, 1969 (Washington, D.C.: Government Printing Office, 1969), p. 4.
4. Gelvin Stevenson, *Business Week,* November 5, 1979.
5. "Most Americans Think System Can Work," *The Houston Post,* November 13, 1978, p. 4C; see also "American Pessimism Over Government Grows," *The Houston Post,* December 8, 1977, p. 4D.
6. "Politicians Rated Low on Honesty," *The Houston Post,* September 1, 1976.
7. See the Gallup result in "Inflation Seen as Most Serious Problem," *The Houston Post,* November 21, 1977, p. 6D; and the Harris survey, "Inflation Heads List of Worries," *The Houston Post,* September 21, 1978, p. 2C.

8. Bureau of the Census, ''Money Income and Poverty Status of Families and Persons in the United States: 1976 (Advance Report),'' *Current Population Reports,* Series P-60, No. 107 (September 1977), p. 1.

9. ''U.S. Rated the Fifth Wealthiest Nation,'' *The Houston Post,* July 7, 1977, p. 2E; ''U.S. Only 7th in GNP Per Capita,'' *The Houston Post,* August 6, 1978, p. 11B.

10. ''Despite the Dollar's Decline, U.S. Retains Top Living Standard Among Major Nations,'' *The Wall Street Journal,* May 1, 1979, p. 40.

11. ''Projections on Crime Released,'' *The Houston Post,* February 20, 1979, p. 7A.

12. Dr. Bernard Winter, ''A Cure for What Ails Us,'' *The Progressive,* December 1970, p. 11.

13. See Gabriel Almond and Sidney Verba, *The Civic Culture: Political Attitudes and Democracy in Five Nations* (Princeton, N.J.: Princeton University Press, 1963).

1

PUBLIC PARTICIPATION AND CONTROL

> **Government is a plain thing, and fitted to the capacity of many heads.**
>
> **Thomas Paine**

2

The data presented in Chapter 1 provide a disturbing portrait of the American public. They reveal that the people certainly do not feel in control of the political system and, in many instances, do not even think they have much influence in a democratic society. In an attempt to determine whether these feelings are justified, we will examine the public's knowledge, interest, and participation in the political system in this chapter and attempt to evaluate its role in the political process. In a brief discussion of the 1976 presidential election, we will probe this theme as it relates to the economic crisis that continues to have a pervasive impact upon the politics of the 1980s.

Political Participation and Political Control

ARE AMERICANS POLITICAL ANIMALS?

Do Americans enjoy, even relish, performing their civic duty? Do they take pride in keeping tabs on public officials, in communicating their thoughts and needs to them, in removing public officials who fail to live up to the public trust? While the democratic image of American citizens would suggest that they do enjoy these tasks, the evidence suggests otherwise. Numerous studies indicate that, for the most part, Americans are reluctant political participants.

Robert Dahl once said that "politics is a remote, alien, and unrewarding activity . . . which lies for most people at the outer periphery of attention, interest, and activity."[1] Studies of political participation suggest that there is more than a grain of truth in this assessment. Figure 2.1 shows data on citizen political participation collected in three major studies. While the studies show differences in rates of participation, none of the studies indicates high rates of civic activity.

The most recent of them, the 1976 Election Study, shows that only 6 percent of the public claimed to have attended a political meeting or rally in 1976; 8 percent reported wearing a campaign button or putting a political sticker on their car; 5 percent reported working for a candidate or party in

Except during presidential campaigns, conventions, and elections, most Americans do not participate in politics.

1976; and 8 percent reported giving money. Only 17 percent claim to have ever written a public official, and only 12 percent reported ever signing a petition.

Studies by Milbrath and by Verba and Nie show findings that are roughly parallel to those of the 1976 study, although the Verba and Nie study reported considerably higher rates of participation on a number of items. One point, however, should be emphasized: all the figures are based on public reports of participation and thus are likely to be exaggerations. Because they are embarrassed by their lack of participation, many people will claim to have engaged more extensively in political acts than they actually have.

Even with these exaggerations, only a relatively small percentage of the American public makes claims of political participation. As Verba and Nie conclude:

> Few, if any, types of political activity beyond the act of voting are performed by more than a third of the American citizenry.
>
> Activities that require the investment of more than trivial amounts of time and energy as well as those that have a short time referent (such as a single election) tend to be performed by no more than 10 to 15 percent of the citizenry.
>
> Less demanding activities as well as those with longer time referents (i.e., longer than a single election campaign) are performed by between 15 and 30 percent of the citizenry.[2]

Voting, another form of political activity, also shows low levels of citizen participation. The most highly organized and publicized elections in our society are presidential elections, which occur every four years. In the twentieth century an average of 59.4 percent of the voting age population has voted in presidential elections (see Figure 2.2). In both 1920 and 1924 less than a majority of eligible voters went to the polls. In 1972 and 1976, respectively, only 55.4 percent and 54.4 percent of the *electorate* voted. These rates of turnout are much lower than those for national elections in other Western democratic countries. In fact, no other established democracy has such a low rate of public voting. For example, in 1976 the voting turnout in Sweden and West Germany was 91 percent. National elections in New Zealand and Ireland in 1975 saw a turnout of 84 and 75 percent, respectively. In 1974 the turnout in Canada was 71 percent; in France, 86 percent; and in Great Britain, 73 percent. None of these countries requires voting.

During the nineteenth century, voter participation in American presidential elections frequently approached or even equaled current voting rates in Western European countries. For example, between 1840 and 1896, voting turnout averaged 77.1 percent.[3] The decline in voter turnout reflects, in part, a very substantial increase in the proportion of American adults eligible to vote. In the nineteenth century, voting was restricted primarily to white males. However, with the ratification of the Nineteenth Amendment in 1920, women gained the right to vote. The civil-rights acts of the 1960s greatly expanded black voting, and eighteen-year-olds gained the *franchise* with the ratification

FIGURE 2.1
Rates of Political Participation

1976 Study

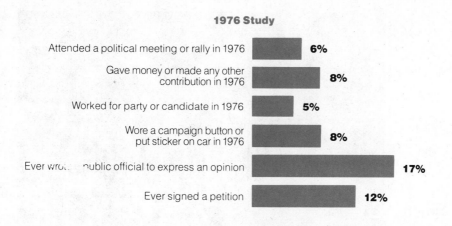

Attended a political meeting or rally in 1976	6%
Gave money or made any other contribution in 1976	8%
Worked for party or candidate in 1976	5%
Wore a campaign button or put sticker on car in 1976	8%
Ever wrote public official to express an opinion	17%
Ever signed a petition	12%

1972 Study

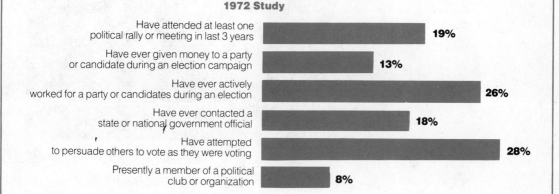

Have attended at least one political rally or meeting in last 3 years	19%
Have ever given money to a party or candidate during an election campaign	13%
Have ever actively worked for a party or candidates during an election	26%
Have ever contacted a state or national government official	18%
Have attempted to persuade others to vote as they were voting	28%
Presently a member of a political club or organization	8%

1965 Study

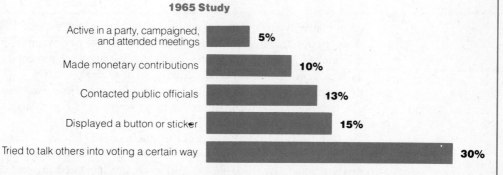

Active in a party, campaigned, and attended meetings	5%
Made monetary contributions	10%
Contacted public officials	13%
Displayed a button or sticker	15%
Tried to talk others into voting a certain way	30%

Source: Figures for 1976 are from 1976 National Election Study, University of Michigan Center For Political Studies; figures for 1972 are from Sidney Verba and Norman H. Nie, *Participation In America* (New York: Harper & Row, 1972), p. 31; and figures for 1965 are from Lester W. Milbrath, *Political Participation* (Chicago: Rand McNally, 1965), p. 16.

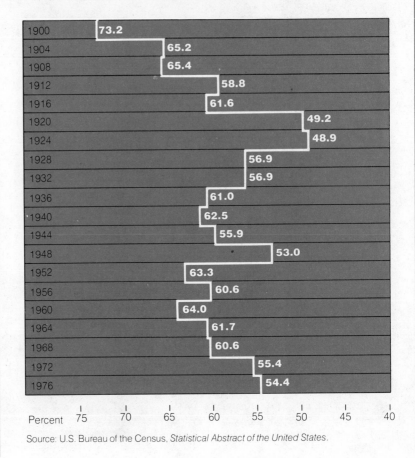

FIGURE 2.2
Voting in Presidential Elections: 1900–1976

Year	Percent
1900	73.2
1904	65.2
1908	65.4
1912	58.8
1916	61.6
1920	49.2
1924	48.9
1928	56.9
1932	56.9
1936	61.0
1940	62.5
1944	55.9
1948	53.0
1952	63.3
1956	60.6
1960	64.0
1964	61.7
1968	60.6
1972	55.4
1976	54.4

Percent 75 70 65 60 55 50 45 40

Source: U.S. Bureau of the Census, *Statistical Abstract of the United States*.

of the Twenty-sixth Amendment in 1971. Voting tends to be lower among those groups traditionally excluded from the ballot. For example, in the 1976 election, 60.9 percent of whites voted, while only 48.7 percent of black and 31.8 percent of Spanish-origin citizens went to the polls. Only 40 percent of the eligible eighteen to twenty-four-year-old voters exercised the franchise. The exception is women. Almost as many women (58.8 percent) as men (59.6 percent) went to the polls in 1976.

While voting rates have declined, the number of voters going to the polls has increased dramatically. In the presidential election of 1824 only 365,833 persons voted. By 1900 the number of voters increased to some 14 million, and it reached about 62 million in 1956. By 1976, 81 million citizens went to the polls out of a total voting age population of about 150 million. Thus, the

This French poster ("Think of the year 2000—Vote") reflects the emphasis placed on voting in that country. Voter turnout rates are much higher in most Western democratic nations than they are in the United States.

voting base has expanded even as rates of participation have declined.

Voter turnout in nonpresidential national elections averaged 17 percentage points less than voting in presidential elections between 1952 and 1976.[4] Every two years, all 435 members of the House of Representatives are elected, along with one-third of the 100 U.S. senators. In nonpresidential election years between 1954 and 1978, these contests attracted about 43 percent of the eligible electorate, with a high turnout of 46.3 percent in 1962 and a low of 36.1 percent in 1974. In 1978 only 37 percent of the eligible electorate voted. Voting for state offices is generally even lower. Most statewide races attract only about 30 percent of eligible voters. City elections and bond elections generally attract between 20 to 30 percent of potential voters and can drop below 10 percent of the eligibles.

Although voting rates in state and local elections are usually low, 67 percent of the California electorate turned out in 1978 to vote on Proposition 13, the proposal to dramatically lower property tax rates. Led by Howard Jarvis (right), the campaign to pass Proposition 13 was successful.

Clearly, there is often a lack of enthusiasm about campaigns among those eligible to vote, and this is true even of many voters. There are two obvious signs of lethargy. First, many citizens admit having little interest in campaigns or in how they turn out. For example, in 1976 the Survey Research Center asked the public how much they personally cared about who might win the 1976 presidential contest. Forty-two percent said they did not care very much who won, making the election something less than an earth-shaking event for almost half of all adults.[5]

In addition, only about one-third of the electorate, on the average, claims to be very interested in presidential campaigns. Figure 2.3 shows the percentage of citizens who reported being very interested in presidential campaigns between 1952 and 1976. The 35 percent of citizens who claimed to be very interested in the 1976 campaign was about average for recent years. Over this same period, anywhere from one-fifth to one-third of all adults admitted that they were really not very interested in the presidential campaign.

The second indication of lethargy is the low level of public knowledge about political events and personalities. Consider the following:

1. Less than half of all adults can name the member of the U.S. House of Representatives who represents them (46 percent) or which party their representative belongs to (41 percent).[6]
2. Less than half realize that their state has two senators in Washington (49 percent).[7]
3. Only 35 percent can name both U.S. senators from their state.[8]
4. Only 28 percent can name their state senator.[9]
5. Barely one-third knows when members of Congress are up for reelection or how many will run.[10]
6. Only 69 percent can name the current Vice-President of the United States.[11]
7. Twenty percent of the American people believe that the U.S. Congress includes the U.S. Supreme Court.[12]

It should be obvious that if citizens are to maintain some control over the public officials who represent them, they must at least know who their repre-

FIGURE 2.3
Interest in Presidential Campaigns: 1952–1976

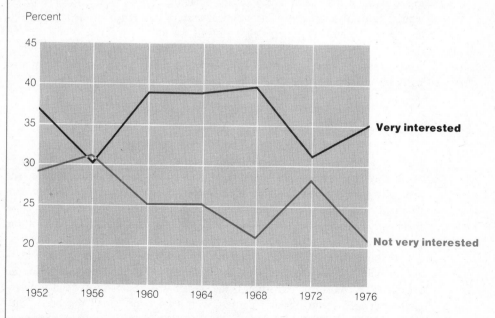

Source: Figures for 1952 through 1972 are from Norman H. Nie, Sidney Verba, and John R. Petrocik, *The Changing American Voter* (Cambridge: Harvard University Press, 1976), p. 273. Figures for 1976 are from the National Election Study, University of Michigan Center for Political Studies.

sentatives are and something about the type of job they do. Yet even among those citizens who can name their representatives, only a small proportion know how their representatives vote on issues, what committees they serve on, or the degree of expertise or dedication they bring to their job.

Clearly, a large proportion of the population is not very preoccupied by politics. And among the citizens who are interested, active, and informed about politics, there is a distinct class bias. As Verba and Nie conclude:

> Political participation is predominantly the activity of the wealthier, better educated citizen with higher-status occupations. Those who need the beneficial outcomes of participation the least—who are already advantaged in social and economic terms—participate the most.[13]

Politically inactive citizens are disproportionately those of lower socioeconomic status, minorities, those without a high school education, and the young (ages eighteen to thirty).

THE CITIZEN'S VOTE

Given their low levels of interest, knowledge, and participation, on what factors do voters base their vote, and of what importance is the vote? In other words, can citizens control the political system through the vote? Social science research has not completely resolved the answer to either question, but the first is easier to answer. Studies have indicated three major factors which seem to be the most important in influencing the public's voting decision—party identification, candidate image, and political issues.

Party identification

Until recent years, party identification seemed to be the most stable and in many ways the most important of these factors. Studies revealed that citizens generally took the party identification of their parents and tended to stay with that party throughout their lifetime.[14] While citizens did not always vote for their party, their party attachment tended to serve as their "window" on the political world and helped to shape their perception of political reality.[15]

Although large numbers of citizens have not abandoned their party identification in recent years, new voters have been less inclined to develop an attachment.[16] As Table 2.1 shows, the public was generally divided until recently between the two major parties, with a relatively small number of citizens thinking of themselves as Independents. Those who identified themselves as Independents tended to be the least informed and most apathetic of citizens.[17]

In the midst of conflict over Vietnam, Watergate, and other problems,

TABLE 2.1
Party Identification 1952–1978

Identification of Respondent	Oct. 1952	Oct. 1954	Oct. 1956	Oct. 1958	Oct. 1960	Nov. 1962	Oct. 1964	Nov. 1966	Nov. 1968	Nov. 1970	Nov. 1972	Nov. 1974	Nov. 1976	Nov. 1978
Strong Democrat	22%	22%	21%	23%	21%	23%	26%	18%	20%	20%	15%	17%	15%	15%
Weak Democrat	25	25	23	24	25	23	25	27	25	23	26	21	25	24
Independent, Democrat	10	9	7	7	8	8	9	9	10	10	11	13	12	14
Independent	5	7	9	8	8	8	8	12	11	13	13	15	14	14
Independent, Republican	7	6	8	4	7	6	6	7	9	8	10	8	10	9
Weak Republican	14	14	14	16	13	16	13	15	14	15	13	14	14	13
Strong Republican	13	13	15	13	14	12	11	10	10	10	10	8	9	8
Apolitical, other	4	4	3	5	4	4	2	2	1	1	2	4	1	3

Source: Data from National Election Studies, University of Michigan Center for Political Studies.

two changes occurred. First, fewer citizens developed solid attachments to the two major parties. As Table 2.1 shows, the ranks of unattached Independents increased from 5 percent in 1952 to 14 percent in 1976. During this same period, the ranks of all Independents, including those leaning toward one of the parties, increased from 22 to 36 percent of the electorate. Those citizens reporting strong attachment to either of the parties also declined substantially. By 1976 only 40 percent of the population was attached strongly or weakly to the Democratic party, and only 23 percent had such attachments to the Republican party. Thus, those who identify themselves as some form of Independent have become the second largest group in the electorate.

Second, those who identify themselves as Independents tend to be reasonably well informed and distrustful toward or even alienated from the political system. This, of course, is the result of the growing distrust produced by conflict and corruption within the political system.[18]

The decline in party attachment in recent years has made other factors such as candidate image and issues more important to the voting choice. But this change should not be exaggerated. Decreased attachment to the parties may be only a temporary phenomenon caused by an unusual level of political tensions in recent years. And although party identification has always helped shape the public's voting decisions, it has never been a complete determinant of the vote for most citizens.

The public's image of the two parties is not very sophisticated and thus may be of limited value. For example, the public tends to think of the Republican party as the representative of big business and the rich, and the Democratic party as the representative of working people and the poor. While these images are exaggerations (see Chapter 8), they are essentially rational. Working on these assumptions, citizens attempt in most elections to vote their pocketbooks; that is, they vote for the party they believe will best look out for their economic interests. Under normal circumstances this means that moderate to lower socioeconomic groups will tend to vote Democratic, while upper socioeconomic groups will favor the Republican party.

But political events are often complex enough to blur this simple distinction. For example, if the party in power has been unable to create healthy economic conditions or unable to deal with pressing social problems, large numbers of citizens may decide to vote for the out-party in the hope that it can do better. Thus, in 1952 and 1956, millions of working people and the poor voted for Eisenhower because they were tired of the long Democratic rule and had lost faith in the ability of the Democrats to solve social problems. The public was also highly attracted to Eisenhower, who seemed kind and honest, even fatherly. Similarly, in 1964 millions of Republican identifiers voted for Lyndon Johnson because he seemed to have a firm grip on the political helm and because they distrusted Barry Goldwater, who was considered by many to be too conservative, even dangerous. A similar phenomenon occurred in 1972 when millions of Democrats voted to give Richard Nixon a second term because he seemed to be in control of the political environment and because they feared George McGovern, who seemed too liberal.

*If citizens are to maintain some control over the public officials who
represent them, they must at least know who their representatives are and
something about the type of job they do. Yet even among those citizens
who can name their representatives, only a small proportion know how
their representatives vote on issues, what committees they serve on, or
the degree of expertise or dedication they bring to their job.*

Thus, a number of conditions have always moderated the effects of party identification. First, the public seems to feel that neither party should rule too long. Any time a party has been in power for two or more terms, the public tends to feel that the other party should have a turn in office.[19] Second, there is a distinct tendency for the public to feel that a President should have two terms in office. President Ford's failure to win another term was the first time a President had been so denied in forty-four years. Third, because the public is so ill informed, it is easily frightened by candidates who give the impression that they will deviate substantially from the status quo. Candidates who are considered to be on the fringes of the political spectrum are in trouble even within their own party.

Ronald Reagan, shown here campaigning outside the Alamo, parlayed his high visibility and conservatism to gain the 1980 Republican presidential nomination.

Candidate image

Candidate image often interacts with party identification to shape the public vote or even on occasion to supplant it. Candidate image is likely to be an important determinant of the vote in any election in which voters have a clear image of the candidates. In most elections, however, the public will be asked to vote on so many candidates that they may have little idea who many of them are. Under these circumstances the voters will generally rely on party identification or name familiarity. If the voter has paid only enough attention to the race to vaguely know who the candidates are, the candidate identified with the voter's party is most likely to be perceived as the most attractive, capable, and trustworthy.

The ability of candidates to make themselves visible to voters depends on the importance of the office, the number of other candidates running, the resources of the candidates, and the candidate's identifiability before the race. A celebrity running for office has an advantage, as does an incumbent politician whose name may be familiar to voters, even if only vaguely familiar. Presidential candidates can generally make themselves known to the public because the elections are long, well financed, and quite visible. Candidates for local office may be able to develop their image, especially in smaller cities and nonpartisan elections where party identification cannot provide an easy voting cue.

Issues

The role of issues in influencing voting behavior is difficult to nail down but does not seem to be as important as party identification or candidate image. Issues are not often critical in an election because the public is often too uninformed to follow issues that are even modestly complex, because most campaigns are not developed around highly articulated issues, and because the parties may not differ on the major issues—or the differences may not be apparent to the public

In *The American Voter,* a classic study of voting behavior, Campbell et al. concluded that four conditions must exist before issues can be critical to voting.[20] First, a voter must have a position on an issue. Second, the voter must have some idea of what government policy is on the issue. Third, the voter must perceive some difference between the parties on the issue. Fourth, the issue must be important enough to the voter to influence his or her vote.

Campbell et al. found that fewer than 30 percent of the public, on the average, could satisfy the first three prerequisites (the range on 16 issues was from 18 to 36 percent).[21] Among those who could meet the first three conditions, issues were not always a clear basis for their voting decision because frequently the party with which they identified agreed with their position on the issue. Thus, the authors concluded that generally issues were not particularly important in predicting voting behavior.

The decline in party attachment in recent years has made other factors such as candidate image and issues more important to the voting choice.

The American Voter reflected conditions in the tranquil 1950s. During the 1960s and 1970s public issues were more intense, but the evidence does not indicate that issues became more important in shaping the public's voting decision. Between 1964 and 1976 some of the most important campaign issues were Vietnam, crime, the civil-rights backlash, unemployment and inflation, and abuse of power. Studies of the 1968 election showed that the public could not distinguish a difference between the stand of Humphrey and Nixon on so critical an issue as Vietnam.[22] Neither could the public distinguish much difference between Humphrey and Nixon on the issue of civil rights, even though Nixon developed a Southern strategy designed to assure the South that if elected he would back off on enforcement of civil rights laws.[23] The issue of crime or law and order has also been too nebulous for party distinctions.

Thus, even during a period of serious strife in American history, the importance of issues in determining public voting did not seem to increase significantly. Margolis calculated that in the 1960s and early 1970s the ability of the public to discern differences between the parties on issues still averaged only about 30 percent, occasionally rising to 50 percent on some issues.[24] However, this does not mean that issues were the determining factor in shaping the voting decision of even these voters because in many instances issue preferences corresponded to party identification. In addition, there may be a wide variation in the issues that each citizen considers most important. Rather than perceiving two or three important issues, citizens may perceive dozens.

Party identification, candidate image, and issues: The 1976 election

In the 1976 presidential campaign and its immediate aftermath, a new and continuing complication may well have affected the relation between issues and politics in this country. That campaign, as we will see in a moment, saw the first debate over the contemporary economic crisis, an attempt to come to grips with the disintegration of the public philosophy of the New Deal and all of its successors. But it is at least possible that *neither* side in the dispute came up with an effective answer to the most bewildering domestic problems in a generation. Under those circumstances, the people's disaffection from political involvement could be determined not by a positive or negative response to a candidate's position but by a suspicion that *no* issue alternative was being offered. If this is the case, it is one more sign that we live in a time in which the old politico-economic synthesis no longer works and a new synthesis has not yet been elaborated.

The critical issues in 1976 were inflation, unemployment, and honesty in government.[25] Carter and Ford took diametrically opposed positions on the first two questions; their differences in this area will be the initial focus of our analysis.

Gerald Ford campaigned in 1976 using a new version of traditional conservative theory. Conservatives have long argued that government should not directly involve itself in the management of the economy. In their reading of the public philosophy of the last generation, Washington had a role to play, but it was distinctly limited to encouraging, or helping through subsidies, wealth-production in the private sector. If the corporations were left alone or given discrete aid, they would create new jobs, expand productivity, generate both profits and wages, and thus increase the tax revenues available to government for helping those left out of this process (the poor, the unemployed, the severely handicapped). Critics of this approach often described it as a *"trickle-down" theory* that favored the rich on the grounds that they would then act in such a way as to benefit everyone else.

During the 1960s, when public support for "Great Society" programs to eliminate poverty, improve education, provide medical care for the aging, and other reform measures was high, many business leaders argued for a partnership between government and the corporations in the pursuit of those social goals. That was a modification of standard conservative principles. But in the 1970s, when simultaneous inflation and high unemployment undermined at least some of the assumptions of the New Deal philosophy, the executives turned away from that social activism. Or more precisely, many of them argued that it was precisely excessive government intervention which was responsible for "double digit" inflation in 1974 (a 12.2 percent increase in consumer prices) and almost 9 percent unemployment in 1975. One of the most articulate proponents of this analysis was Ford's Treasury secretary, William E. Simon. His views—later summarized in a best-selling book, *A Time for Truth*—shaped Ford's views on inflation and unemployment in 1976 and continue to have a considerable influence in the 1980s.

In the 1976 campaign, Ford argued that huge federal deficits had overheated the economy, thus causing inflation. At the same time, federal borrowing to pay for its excessive spending had "crowded out" the private sector, thus preventing it from raising money for new investments, which would increase productivity. By consuming more and more of its wealth, rather than using it to generate more wealth, the United States was losing ground to its advanced industrial competitors. Not only West Germany and Japan were investing more than the United States; so was the United Kingdom, the country widely regarded as the weakest of the advanced capitalist economies.

Therefore, the Ford view continued, it was necessary to hold down federal spending in order to fight inflation and open up the money market to the private sector. Under such circumstances, profits, which were often attacked as if they merely supplied luxuries to the rich, actually performed the important economic and social function of providing investment funds for jobs, productivity, and expansion in general. To be sure, holding down government spending in order to let the genius of free enterprise flourish would involve a short-term increase in unemployment. But in the long run, this strategy would actually combat both joblessness and high prices.

In the period prior to his reelection in 1972, Richard Nixon had publicly proclaimed himself a "Keynesian" and had followed highly stimulative fiscal and monetary policies, which indeed helped him to win a landslide victory over George McGovern. A mere four years later, Nixon's successor, Ford— and with him the entire Republican party—dramatically repudiated that approach. This was one more sign of the deep-seated change taking place in American politics, of that disintegration of the public philosophy of the past half-century.

Jimmy Carter's campaign reaffirmed the traditional Rooseveltian approach that Ford rejected. Unemployment, Carter said, should not be used as a weapon against inflation for two reasons. First, Carter argued that without high demand, industry would have no motive to expand. So using joblessness to fight high prices would lead to stagnation and more joblessness. On the other hand, the increased sales that would result from a full employment strategy would yield profits which could then be reinvested in further expansion. To supplement those profits the Democrats, like the Republicans, would support low-interest loans and tax breaks to help industry with its capital needs.

Issues are not often critical in an election because the public is often too uninformed to follow issues that are even modestly complex, because most campaigns are not developed around highly articulated issues, and because the parties may not differ on the major issues—or the differences may not be apparent to the public.

Second, Carter held that increased unemployment would cause a higher federal deficit and thus subvert any anti-inflation strategy based on controlling government spending. The reason was that the jobless were often entitled to receive food stamps and welfare benefits as well as unemployment compensation. Focusing only on that last program, unemployment payments in 1974 totaled almost $17 billion, compared to about $2 billion in 1968. A study frequently cited by Carter during the 1976 election estimated that every 1 percent of unemployment cost $3 billion in unemployment compensation and $2 billion in welfare. Simultaneously, it produced a loss of $14 billion in tax revenues.

Carter also disputed the usual argument that high employment contributed to inflation by increasing purchasing power and thereby bidding up prices. He pointed out that inflation in the 1970s was most severe precisely when joblessness was high. That inflation, he held, was caused primarily by excessive energy prices and by a lack of competition in rigged markets. On all of these economic issues, Carter took the classic Democratic position. Thus, it might seem wrong to see the 1976 election as the first political response of the American system to its new and unprecedented economic situation. And indeed, if one ended this analysis on election day, 1976, it would simply report a conflict between a traditional Democratic issue position and a considerably more conservative Republican stance.

But as soon as one looks at the Carter Presidency, a critical fact becomes quite obvious: the new chief executive could not deliver on his standard promises, not because he had been dishonest in making them, but because the Keynesian remedies which had enjoyed a certain success from Roosevelt to Lyndon Johnson no longer applied. (This point will be developed at greater length in Chapter 7.) Gerald Ford and the Republicans had their theory about why this happened: government intervention, which had once been seen as the cure for economic ills, was now their prime cause. Carter had rejected that thesis in the name of a traditional Democratic approach but immediately discovered that it did not work as it once had.

Leon Keyserling, who had been chairman of the Council of Economic Advisers under President Truman, criticized Carter from the liberal Left, arguing that his actual policies were as conservative as those of Ford and Richard Nixon. As a result, Keyserling said, Washington's policies were characterized by "inconsistencies, false starts and conflicts. . . . Seldom was confidence by the people lower, even when the government seeks to blame this on the people and asks *them* to provide remedies which they alone cannot provide."[26] If Keyserling is right, then American politics might well be quite volatile and confused until a new economic policy in the eighties, analogous to the New Deal innovations of the thirties, actually proves its worth in practice.

In the period prior to his reelection in 1972, Richard Nixon had publicly proclaimed himself a "Keynesian" and had followed highly stimulative fiscal and monetary policies, which indeed helped him to win a landslide victory over George McGovern. A mere four years later, Nixon's successor, Ford—and with him the entire Republican party—dramatically repudiated that approach.

If a certain bewilderment about unprecedented economic problems played a role in 1976, that trend was reinforced by the issue of honesty in government. That theme was favorable to the Democrats simply because they were the out-party and not tainted by Watergate. While no one accused Ford of participating in that scandal, his pardon of Richard Nixon displeased many citizens and suggested to some a deal in which Ford was made Vice-President contingent upon his agreement to pardon Nixon if Watergate forced him from office. Ford tried to deal with the issue by emphasizing his own reputation for honesty. Carter exploited the issue for everything it was worth. He stressed the necessity of honesty and confidence in government, promised the public he would never tell them a lie, and even cast politics in terms of public love and understanding.

The times clearly favored the out-party. The Republicans had served two terms, the economy was in deep and even bewildering trouble, and scandal had shocked and disappointed the public. The public's faith and trust in their government, and their sense of political efficacy, was lower than at any other time in recent history. Carter's approach to such a troubled citizenry should have been an almost perfect nostrum. But the public seemed too jaded by recent events to trust either candidate very much. Polls showed that neither candidate aroused much enthusiasm in the public.[27] Those citizens who voted seemed to do so more out of a sense of duty and concern rather than because of trust in one of the candidates.

The role of issues in this election is difficult to measure. Given the public's lack of sophistication about political matters, it is highly doubtful that many citizens voted for one of the candidates because they favored the specif-

"However, our poll shows that you rate very high among voters who never heard of you."

ics of the candidate's stand on the economy. With the lack of public information, the best that could be expected is that many citizens voted for Carter in the hope that a change in leadership would result in new efforts to improve the economy. Certainly Watergate and the pardon of Nixon hurt Ford, but clearly the issues were not overwhelming. Given the circumstances of the election, Carter might well have been expected to win by a landslide.

Interestingly, party loyalty seemed to be a major determinant of the vote for the first time since the 1960 election. Eighty percent of all Democrats voted for Carter, while almost 90 percent of all Republicans voted for Ford. Since party identification and social status are correlated, it is not surprising that the socioeconomic division of the electorate was quite pronounced. Carter received two-thirds of the votes cast by the least economically advantaged, while Ford received two-thirds of the votes cast by those with the highest incomes. The vote was also divided by political ideology. Three-fourths of those citizens identifying themselves as liberal cast ballots for Carter, while 70 percent of those labeling themselves conservative voted for Ford.[28]

The most important groups in Carter's victory were blacks and labor union members. Carter received five of every six votes cast by black Americans. One analyst concluded that Carter probably would not "have carried any region, even the South, without black support. Thus, the first true Southerner to be elected President since the pre–Civil War period owed his victory to the descendants of the slaves freed in that war."[29] About one-fifth of all Democrats are now black Americans.[30]

As soon as one looks at the Carter Presidency, a critical fact becomes quite obvious: the new chief executive could not deliver on his promises, not because he had been dishonest in making them, but because the Keynesian remedies which had enjoyed a certain success from Roosevelt to Lyndon Johnson no longer applied.

Continuing a trend of recent years, the election of 1976 made the Democratic party more black, less southern, and less conservative, with a sizeable group of liberal white Anglo-Saxon Protestants (WASPS). While many white Southerners have switched to the Republican party, Catholics and white Protestants of lower socioeconomic status in the North have increasingly switched to the Democratic party. The Republican party has become more conservative, less black, less Catholic, and relatively less the party of white Protestants.[31]

In summary, the major factors influencing the public's vote in national elections are party identification, candidate image, and issues. The circumstances of a particular election determine which of these factors will be most important. Because the public's political knowledge is so low, party identification and candidate image are most likely to be the important variables. Between 1952 and 1976, candidate image was probably the most important factor influencing the vote in presidential elections. Below the national level, where political contests are less likely to capture the public's interest, party identification is generally more important. City elections, however, are frequently nonpartisan, and these contests are much more likely to turn on candidate image.

The Kelly and Mirer argument about public voting behavior has a great deal of appeal. They maintain that since politics is generally not that important to the average citizen, the vote decision is not a very complex one for most citizens:

> The voter canvasses his likes and dislikes of the leading candidates and major parties involved in an election. Weighing each like and dislike equally, he votes for the candidate toward whom he has the greatest net number of favorable attitudes, if there is such a candidate. If no candidate has such an advantage, the voter votes consistently with his party affiliation, if he has one.[32]

Applying this rule, Kelly and Mirer found that they could correctly predict the vote of 85 to 90 percent of their respondents for 1952 through 1964 and 82 percent in 1968.

PUBLIC CONTROL OF PUBLIC LEADERS

Given the public's limited political knowledge, low levels of participation, and limited interest in political events, can the public control politicians and the political system through the vote? Clearly, the public is not able to play the civics-text role of the rational/active citizen who weighs each candidate's qualifications and issue positions, votes for the candidate who passes this test, and then keeps a careful eye on the elected official to determine if his or her performance in office merits reelection. This role simply requires more knowledge, attention, and interest than most citizens devote to the political system.

Even if citizens did try to play this role, it would be very difficult. Between federal, state, and local elections the average citizen is asked to make judgments about literally dozens of public officials and offices. Obtaining adequate information about all the candidates, including incumbents, would be quite difficult. In addition, many campaigns (perhaps most) center around personalities and generalities rather than hard issues. Stanley Kelly, Jr. has said:

> Contemporary campaign discussion is often of such a character that it is unlikely to help voters much in their efforts to arrive at a wise choice of public officials. It may, in fact, have quite the reverse effect. Campaign propagandists obscure the real difference between candidates and parties by distortion, by evasiveness, and by talking generalities.[33]

During the 1976 presidential election, there was considerable controversy about the fuzziness of Jimmy Carter's positions. In the presidential primaries it is undoubtedly true that Carter hid behind generalities. As Carter's evasiveness became something of an issue in the campaign, he took firmer stands on the issues. Still, Carter never quite lived down the label of evader, and this probably accounted for some of his loss of support during the last two months of the election. After ten months as President, Carter complained that during the election everyone had claimed he was too evasive to understand, and now everyone seemed to be arguing that he was not living up to firm campaign promises. The reason, of course, is that as the election neared its climax, Carter did become more specific, and there were firm campaign pledges that his performance could be judged against.

The news media's criticisms of Carter were the major reason he became firmer on the issues. In campaigns of less visibility than a presidential election, there is less likelihood that pressures will be placed on the candidates to be firm on the issues. The public, of course, can only respond to the stimuli presented to it.[34] If issues are well developed in a campaign, they may be more important in shaping the public's vote. If personalities are emphasized, candidate image may be more important. If issues and candidates are both poorly developed, party loyalty becomes more important. Issues, of course, cannot be too technical or the public will not be able to follow the debate.

As a consequence, issues usually are not very specific even when they are clear. Issues such as law and order, the debate over Vietnam, or even

Americans do not tend to support candidates whose positions on the issues are too far from the political center. In 1964, Lyndon Johnson won a landslide victory over Barry Goldwater (above) partly because voters perceived Goldwater as too conservative.

Watergate reflect little in the way of specific policy alternatives. Law and order, for example, is a meaningless issue to the extent that everyone supports it. A law-and-order stand can mean that a candidate will seek harsher punishment for lawbreakers, attack the conditions in society which cause crime, or do both. Most candidates are not, however, even clear about these broad alternatives.

Many politicians are afraid to try to develop issues because it commits them, and because the public is inherently suspicious of candidates who give the impression that they will alter the political system very drastically or deviate substantially from traditional policies. Throughout American history, candidates who have given the impression of being too far from the political middle have suffered at the polls. Prominent examples include William Jennings Bryan, Barry Goldwater, and George McGovern. As Nie, Verba, and Petrocik state: "The public does respond to candidates who offer a choice rather than an echo. But unfortunately for the candidate who offers the choice, the public seems to choose the echo."[35] The public's ignorance of politics and

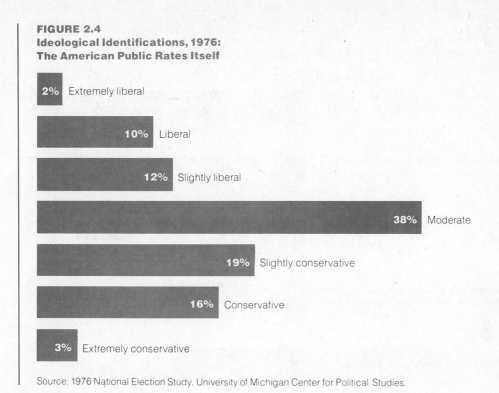

FIGURE 2.4
Ideological Identifications, 1976:
The American Public Rates Itself

2% Extremely liberal

10% Liberal

12% Slightly liberal

38% Moderate

19% Slightly conservative

16% Conservative

3% Extremely conservative

Source: 1976 National Election Study, University of Michigan Center for Political Studies.

public policies contributes to this tendency. Since the public knows little, their natural tendency is to be frightened by any deviation from standard approaches or commitments.

At any given time most American voters consider themselves to be political moderates or conservatives. Figure 2.4 shows the public's self-classified political leanings in 1976. Notice that the most common classification is that of moderate (38 percent). Next most common is slightly conservative (19 percent), followed by conservative (16 percent). Only 24 percent of the public identifies themselves as liberals of some persuasion. Thus it would seem that most Americans are committed ideologically to limited innovations in the political system or none at all. From a practical point of view, however, the labels the public pins on itself have a limited meaning. Most Americans, whether they are liberal, conservative, or moderate, expect the government to play a large role in society and to provide a wide range of specific services. Citizens who label themselves conservative or moderates therefore still support extensive government activities that are distinctly liberal in nature.

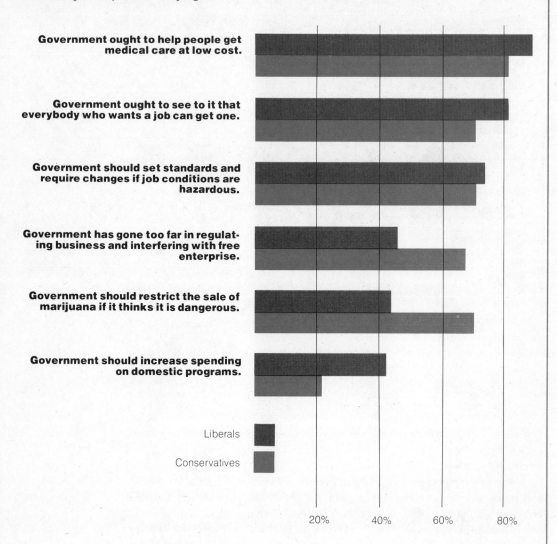

FIGURE 2.5
Liberals and Conservatives:
Where They Differ, Where They Agree

Government ought to help people get
medical care at low cost.

Government ought to see to it that
everybody who wants a job can get one.

Government should set standards and
require changes if job conditions are
hazardous.

Government has gone too far in regulating business and interfering with free
enterprise.

Government should restrict the sale of
marijuana if it thinks it is dangerous.

Government should increase spending
on domestic programs.

Liberals

Conservatives

20%   40%   60%   80%

Figure 2.5 provides some excellent examples. In a 1978 *New York Times* poll, there was a modest difference between professed liberals and conservatives on a number of policy issues, with conservatives taking distinctly liberal positions. For instance, while 90 percent of the liberals thought the government should help people obtain medical care, 80 percent of the conservatives also agreed. Eighty percent of the liberals and 70 percent of the conservatives also thought the government should see that anyone who wants a job gets one. Seventy-three percent of the liberals and 66 percent of the conservatives supported government monitoring of job safety standards. However, when asked if the government should increase spending on domestic programs, only 22 percent of conservatives and 42 percent of liberals agreed. What the poll shows is that in the abstract both conservatives and liberals will often opt for a limited government role, but when specific political issues are raised, both expect the government to play a role in solving them. This is one reason that people who think of themselves as conservatives often vote for Democratic candidates.

Indeed, it is possible that this pattern persists despite apparent shifts to the Left or the Right in the electorate. In 1964, Lloyd A. Free and Hadley Cantril surveyed the political attitudes of Americans. This was in the heyday of the Great Society, in a year when Lyndon Johnson won a landslide victory over the conservative, Barry Goldwater, and when many commentators talked of the end of conservatism itself in America. Yet Free and Cantril discovered that 30 percent of the people in their sample that year described themselves as completely conservative and another 20 percent said they were predominantly conservative. Only 16 percent characterized themselves as completely liberal. However, when one turned from the ideological plane, where one talks about political philosophy, to the question of attitudes about specific legislative proposals, that same sample turned out to be 65 percent ''operational'' liberals.[36]

American politics, then, is complex. In a ''liberal'' period, like the mid-sixties, a majority define themselves as ideological conservatives; in a ''conservative'' period like the late seventies, a majority favor liberal positions with regard to specific legislative proposals. This paradox is another factor undermining the ability of the people to control politicians. The people are of a divided mind about the issues—if they are aware of them at all. So those elected to office hardly receive a mandate on programs and thus have considerable independence from their own electorate.

In many instances the public may not really vote for the winning candidate. They may instead vote against his or her opponent.[37] This negative role is often the one an uninformed population is best qualified to play. They may not know exactly where each candidate stands on the issues, but they know whether they feel comfortable with current political events or their economic prosperity under a particular administration. Voting against one candidate rather than for the other candidate, of course, gives the public little or no control over the winning candidate.

Negative voting is most likely to occur in highly visible elections like a presidential contest, in which a candidate represents a particular administration that can be held responsible for the state of the political and economic systems. Below the Presidency, *incumbency* has generally given a candidate a substantial advantage. The general rule has been that 90 percent or more of all incumbents—those who hold the offices—in the U.S. House and Senate have won reelection. However, in 1974, in the midst of Watergate, forty members of the House were defeated for reelection. Thirty-six of the defeated incumbents were Republicans, and most were considered defenders of Nixon. The effects of Watergate on the House were shortlived. In 1976 only thirteen incumbents were defeated. The Senate, however, felt the effects of public distrust and alienation. Nine of twenty-five members of the Senate running for reelection in 1976 were defeated, a return rate far below normal.[38] In 1978 the defeat level for senators was still much higher than usual as ten incumbents lost reelection bids. Another ten senators retired, producing the largest turnover in Senate seats since 1946. House incumbents were still safe in 1978; only 19 incumbents went down to defeat.

The independence the election process gives officeholders is augmented by two factors. First, most officeholders represent a rather large number of citizens, with fairly diverse opinions on many issues, and they cannot generally determine how their constituents feel about most issues. The average member of the House of Representatives has some 400,000 to 500,000 constituents, and a U.S. senator may represent as many as 20 million persons. Outside of very expensive polling techniques, these elected officials cannot accurately know how their constituents feel about most issues. Polls sent to constituents by officials are not reliable because they reflect the views only of those who return them and because they sometimes contain biased questions.

Second, even if officials could determine their constituents' attitudes toward issues, most members of Congress do not feel that they should be bound by their constituents' opinions. Most senators and representatives feel that they should do what they think is best rather than simply be the agent of their constituents' wishes.[39]

From a practical point of view, however, the labels the public pins on itself have a limited meaning. Most Americans, whether they are liberal, conservative, or moderate, expect the government to play a large role in society and to provide a wide range of specific services.

These factors hardly mean that members of Congress can simply ignore their constituents. All members of Congress have strong ties within their constituency, and they often have special constituent interests that they are concerned with. Without a strong contingent in their district, members of Congress would have no one to organize and run their campaign or raise money for them. Most districts also have some industries or specific concerns that the member of Congress takes a special interest in. These range from textiles in Georgia and oil in Texas to farm products in the Midwest and defense bases in the state of Washington.

Interests of this nature are generally well organized and in a position to keep in touch with their representative in Congress. Since these interests are often critical to the economic well-being of the district, and because they can organize to defeat a representative who ignores them, they are generally given consideration. Citizens who are not represented in such a way, however, may well be largely ignored. This is especially true if the citizens are politically inactive and lack the resources to contribute to campaigns or to organize interest groups.

CONCLUSIONS

The sense of political alienation evident in so many of the polls of recent years seems to be the result of two converging trends, both of which have been documented in this chapter. First, there are the perennial limits to effective citizen participation in the democratic process: political indifference on the part of many citizens, a lack of knowledge about issues, and a tendency to make choices in terms of inherited party identification or candidate images. Even in the most stable periods, when the public seems reasonably content with the way things are going, such trends tend to subvert the American ideal of popular control of leaders.

Second, there are new elements in the current situation: the impact of the Vietnam War, the Watergate scandal, and the continuing perplexity of policy-makers faced with unprecedented economic contradictions. Under "normal" circumstances most political scientists would see these developments as portents of a "realignment" in the party system, as part of the breakdown which precedes a new synthesis. (This proposition will be discussed at greater length in Chapter 8.) But there is no force which guarantees that this situation will end in the near future or that its ending will be a happy one. However, there is no point in indulging in a vague pessimism. So, in the next chapter, we will examine what might be done to increase public control over the political process and thereby reduce the sense of disaffection which has seemed so marked in the recent past.

Footnotes

1. Robert A. Dahl, *Who Governs? Democracy and Power in an American City* (New Haven: Yale University Press, 1961), p. 279.
2. Sidney Verba and Norman H. Nie, *Participation in America: Political Democracy and Social Equality* (New York: Harper & Row, 1972), p. 32.

3. See the *Congressional Quarterly*, 34, no. 44 (1976), p. 3070. All the figures were collected by Walter Dean Burnham of the Massachusetts Institute of Technology.

4. *Ibid.*

5. 1976 National Election Study, University of Michigan Center for Political Science.

6. Subcommittee on Intergovernmental Relations, *Confidence and Concern: Citizens View American Government: A Survey of Public Attitudes* (Washington, D.C.: Government Printing Office, 1973), p. 215.

7. Robert S. Erikson and Norman R. Luttbeg, *American Public Opinion: Its Origins, Content and Import* (New York: Wiley, 1973), p. 25.

8. *Ibid.*

9. *Ibid.*

10. John C. Wahlke, "Policy Demands and System Support: The Role of the Represented," *British Journal of Political Science,* 1 (July 1971): 273.

11. Erikson and Luttbeg, *American Public Opinion,* p. 25.

12. Subcommittee on Intergovernmental Relations, *Confidence and Concern,* p. 215.

13. Verba and Nie, *Participation in America,* p. 150.

14. See Angus Campbell, Philip E. Converse, Warren E. Miller, and Donald E. Stokes, *The American Voter* (New York: Wiley, 1964), pp. 86–96.

15. *Ibid.*, pp. 15–30.

16. On voter abandonment of party identification, see James L. Sundquist, *Dynamics of the Party System: Alignment and Realignment of Political Parties in the United States* (Washington, D.C.: The Brookings Institute, 1973), pp. 332–54.

17. Campbell et al., *The American Voter,* pp. 67–85.

18. See Norman H. Nie, Sidney Verba, and John R. Petrocik, *The Changing American Voter* (Cambridge: Harvard University Press, 1976), p. 279.

19. Donald E. Stokes and Gudmund R. Iversen, "On the Existence of Forces Restoring Party Competition," in Angus Campbell et al., *Elections In The Political Order* (New York: Wiley, 1967), pp. 180–211.

20. Campbell et al., *The American Voter,* pp. 170–74.

21. *Ibid.*, p. 182.

22. Benjamin I. Page and Richard A. Brody, "Policy Voting and the Electoral Process: The Vietnam War Issue," *American Political Science Review* (September 1972): pp. 979–95.

23. See Leon E. Panetta and Peter Gall, *Bring Us Together: The Nixon Team and the Civil Rights Retreat* (Philadelphia: Lippincott, 1971).

24. Michael Margolis, "From Confusion to Confusion: Issues and the American Voter (1956–1972)," *The American Political Science Review,* 71 (March 1977): 31–43.

25. See Henry A. Plotkin, "Issues in the 1976 Presidential Campaign," in Gerald Pomper et al., *The Election of 1976: Reports and Interpretations* (New York: David McKay, 1977), pp. 35–53.

26. Leon Keyserling, "Liberal and Conservative National Economic Policies and their Consequences, 1919–1979," (Conference on Economic Progress, Washington, D.C., 1979), p. 54.

27. Gerald M. Pomper, "The Presidential Election," in Pomper et al., *The Election of 1976,* p. 76.

28. *Ibid.*, p. 74.

29. *Ibid.*, p. 62.

30. Nie, Verba, and Petrocik, *The Changing American Voter,* p. 242.

31. *Ibid.*, pp. 241–42.

32. Stanley Kelly, Jr., and Thad W. Mirer, "The Simple Act of Voting," *American Political Science Review,* 68 (June 1974): 574.

33. Stanley Kelly, Jr., *Political Campaigning: Problems in Creating an Informed Electorate* (Washington, D.C.: The Brookings Institute, 1960), p. 80.

34. Nie, Verba, and Petrocik, *The Changing American Voter*, p. 319.
35. *Ibid.*
36. Lloyd A. Free and Hadley Cantril, *The Political Beliefs of Americans* (New Brunswick: Rutgers University Press, 1967), p. 32.
37. *Ibid.*
38. See Charles E. Jacob, ''The Congressional Elections and Outlooks,'' in Pomper et al., *The Election of 1976*, pp. 83–105.
39. Roger H. Davidson, *The Role of the Congressman* (New York: Pegasus, 1969), p. 117; and John Wahlke et al., *The Legislative System* (New York: Wiley, 1962).

The general spread of the light of science has already laid open to every view the palpable truth, that the mass of mankind has not been born with saddles on their backs, nor a favored few booted and spurred, ready to ride them legitimately, by the grace of God.

T. Jefferson

3 There is no doubt about the apathy of the American public. The data presented in Chapter 2 show convincingly that most Americans vote irregularly and take little interest in the political process. But data from other Western nations reveal a somewhat different pattern. In those countries the public seems better informed and certainly more active. The major question, then, is: Why are American citizens different?

Can Public Knowledge and Participation Be Increased?

In theory, everyone in the United States believes in maximum public participation in the democratic process. In reality, as we will see, various groups and thinkers want to maintain a certain apathy in America. They are fearful of what would happen if the indifferent millions—well over half of the electorate in congressional elections, sometimes 90 percent of the voters in a municipal campaign—would actually get involved in politics. Moreover, some laws discourage public participation, and reforms which might bring a much higher percentage of the electorate to the polls meet considerable resistance.

This is not to suggest that some kind of a plot exists to keep the masses out of our public life. Many factors are at work in this critical area of society. Some observers have suggested that Americans are too affluent, too pampered, too oriented toward play and material possessions to be concerned about the serious side of politics and life. Polls do sometimes suggest that a sizeable proportion of Americans have a horror of serious political inquiry and that a significant number seem too preoccupied to take much notice of politics. Andrew Hacker eloquently discusses these tendencies:

> Much talk is heard . . . of the need for purposive leadership. The argument runs that while the American people may be overly self-centered, this condition could be overcome by the emergence of leaders capable of inspiring citizenry to personal

As more and more citizens become discouraged about participating in the political process, public policies are increasingly influenced by elites and special interests.

sacrifices for public ends. Yet the fact remains that there arrives a time in a nation's history when its people have lost the capacity for being led. Contemporary Americans simply do not want—and will not accept—political leadership that makes more than marginal demands on their emotions or energies. Thus, for all the eloquence about the need for leadership, Americans are temperamentally unsuited for even a partial merger of personality in pursuit of a common cause.[1]

CAUSES OF APATHY

While Hacker is undoubtedly correct when he says that a significant percentage of the American public is difficult to inspire and lead, he is discussing the symptoms of apathy, not its complex causes. An analysis of this problem suggests that the causes of public apathy may come from faults in the system rather than from the people. It further suggests certain political and social changes that could produce a much more politically active and concerned citizenry. We will begin by analyzing some of the causes of public apathy and then examine some reforms that might be undertaken to transform citizens into political activists interested in understanding, controlling, and directing their government.

Political alienation

Polls such as those discussed in Chapter 1 show four public attitudes that discourage public attachment to, and participation in, the political process. They show that significant percentages of the public consider politicians to be:

a. dishonest and untrustworthy;
b. biased toward the needs of the rich;
c. unconcerned about, or unable to deal with, serious social problems which affect average citizens; and
d. out of touch with the needs and interests of average citizens.

As noted in Chapter 1, public distrust of politicians increased considerably in the 1970s and undoubtedly reflected concern and even shock over Watergate and other scandals. The public has long felt that the government is biased in favor of the needs of the rich at the expense of the rest of the public. But these sentiments have also escalated as the public has learned of political corruption in high office. The best indicators of these feelings are items which show that in 1977, 77 percent of the public believed that in our system of government the rich get richer and the poor get poorer; and 71 percent believed that government is for the benefit of the few.

Two studies in recent years report that about half of all nonvoters are in the eighteen to thirty-four age range. Most reveal that they avoid politics because they do not believe that either party will deal with serious social problems such as pollution, unemployment, and unfair tax laws.[2] These trends, in

"Frankly, I don't care one way or the other about voter apathy."

part, seem to reflect specific grievances about both the orientation, values, and priorities of political leaders and their level of competence. Notice that the polls in Chapter 1 show considerable public skepticism about the ability of officials to solve social problems, even if they wanted to.

Polls also indicate that many people are simply bewildered by the size, complexity, and remoteness of the political process. Significant proportions of the public report feeling left out of the system, unable to make their views known or have them taken into consideration. These feelings are understandable: when millions of people vote, many have to wonder how significant their *one* vote is. When politicians represent thousands and even millions of people (e.g., a U.S. senator), they symbolize little more than a name or a picture in the paper to most of their constituents.

Any of the feelings described above, or any combination of them, may motivate some people to opt out of the political process rather than struggle with it. As Berg et al. observe:

> Tilting at windmills might be a popular sport for those who have the resources and the inclination to preserve this form of entertainment, but for a large number of people who must devote their time and money to more pressing concerns, it is not regarded as a profitable activity. Many citizens have not "copped out" of politics; they have "opted out." They simply have decided that the odds against securing their goals through political activity or contributions are too great to justify their involvement in the game.[3]

Ironically, perhaps, opting out of the system aggravates all those conditions which originally discourage public interest and participation. Berg et al. point out:

> The game of politics seems to operate according to an inflexible law: The greater the number of people who refuse to become involved in politics,the greater the influence exercised by those who remain. . . . There are always powerful interests prepared to fill the vacuum that is produced by the absence of the rank-and-file citizen in politics. By abandoning the field of battle, the average voter leaves the political wars to be fought by big contributers and powerful interests.[4]

As politics is left to special interests, then, public policies increasingly favor those who are active in the system. Politicians become more dependent on and indebted to special interests and the rich for contributions. Thus, apathy and antipathy simply create a vicious cycle.

Discrimination and voting barriers

Throughout most of American history, a large percentage of the public was either discouraged or barred from voting. During the early period of American history, property requirements kept many citizens from voting. Women and blacks were not allowed to vote under the original Constitution. Blacks gained the franchise with the Fifteenth Amendment (1870), but by the turn of the century the Southern states were using customs, laws, physical violence, and economic intimidation to effectively nullify the amendment. The civil-rights laws of the 1960s finally made the black franchise a reality. Women gained the franchise with the Nineteenth Amendment, passed in 1920.

The *poll tax* (a small fee for voter registration) long served as a device to keep both poor whites and poor minorities from voting. The Twenty-fourth Amendment in 1964 prohibited states from charging any fee for voting in federal elections, and the Supreme Court prohibited the collection of a fee for registration to vote in *any* election in 1966.[5] Eighteen-year-olds won the right to vote with ratification of the Twenty-sixth Amendment in 1971.

Voter registration requirements also long served to discourage voting. Until the late 1960s many states required citizens to reside in the state for six months to two and a half years before they could vote in either federal or state elections. The Supreme Court struck down these burdensome requirements, removing all residency standards for voting in presidential elections and limiting state residency requirements to short periods. (The Court seems to suggest a limit of about 50 days.)[6] Since 1970 all states but North Dakota (which has no registration requirements) have adopted permanent registration systems in which voters register once and remain on the rolls unless they fail to vote in a number of consecutive elections.

ORIGINAL

TO BE USED FROM FEB. 1, 1964 TO JAN. 31, 1965

POLL TAX *Receipt* ★ COUNTY OF HARRIS No. 10120

★ STATE OF TEXAS DATE *Jan 3* 1964

RECEIVED OF *H. R. RODGERS JR.*

the sum of $1.50 in payment of poll tax, the taxpayer says that:

His ☑ Her ☐ HOME address is *1732 DES JARDINES* ZIP CODE

	YEARS	Occupation is *STUDENT*	PRECINCT NUMBER
He ☑ She ☐ is age	*21+*	White ☑ Colored ☐ Native born ☑	*218*
and has resided in Texas . . .		Naturalized citizen of the U.S. ☐	
in Harris County	*19*		
in City of *Houston*		Birthplace—State of *Miss.*	

Party Affiliation (TO BE FILLED IN BY PRECINCT CLERK WHEN VOTING *DEMOCRAT*

ALL OF WHICH I CERTIFY,

(SEAL OF OFFICE) IF PARTIAL EXEMPTION GIVE REASON

By *Ernest A. Jones* (1)

ASSESSOR AND COLLECTOR OF TAXES, HARRIS COUNTY, TEXAS DEPUTY

Until the Twenty-fourth Amendment outlawed it in 1964, the poll tax kept many poor people in the South—both blacks and whites—from voting.

Though the franchise has been extended in recent years, and though many of the traditional barriers to voting have been lowered or removed, the impact of past discrimination is still substantial. Millions of minority group members and women never developed the voting habit, and some may never adopt a role they were so long excluded from. While women had legally gained the franchise long before it was effectively extended to blacks in the South, social norms defined politics as male business, discouraging many women from voting and from running for public office. Progress against these attitudes has been substantial in recent years, yet some women are still reluctant to vote, and few women run for public office. The lack of female role models still identifies politics as primarily a male profession. Studies show that some blacks are still afraid of physical or economic retaliation if they vote.[7]

Political socialization

The public schools play a large role in introducing students to the mechanics of the political system. They define the conceptual standards which students will use to evaluate the political system and by which they will formulate their own role in the political system.[8] The evidence indicates that what the schools teach students seriously retards their understanding of, and future role in, the political process.

Some of the most persistent charges made against the schools are that they convey a highly idealistic image of the political process, confusing what *ought* to be with what *is;* avoid serious examinations of social problems and their causes; and place emphasis on the general success, wealth, power, and world prestige of American society and government.[9] While social problems may be touched on by the more progressive texts and teachers, the impression is generally given that the problems are relatively minor and easily resolved within the present political and economic structure. Public officials are also presented idealistically as honest, objective, hard-working, and committed to public service.

As politics is left to special interests, public policies increasingly favor those who are active in the system. Politicians become more dependent on and indebted to special interests and the rich for campaign contributions.

Critics of the public school role raise three other serious points.[10] First, they point out that most civics texts and courses not only present a distorted image of the American system, but that other systems are distorted as well. In extreme cases all other political systems are simply dismissed as being highly inferior to the American system. Communist and socialist systems are lumped together and labeled as godless, uncivilized, and tyrannical. While these charges may accurately describe some political systems, they are inaccurate generalizations. Socialism and communism are different systems; countries governed or influenced by socialists, such as the Scandinavian nations, are not godless and uncivilized, and they are firmly democratic and prosperous. Lumping all other systems together, or failing to examine objectively the positive and negative features of various governments, reduces student insight into the diversity of cultures and political and economic approaches.

The evidence indicates that what the schools teach students seriously retards their understanding of, and future role in, the political process.

Second, it is frequently pointed out that the idealistic image of the political system denies students a sophisticated understanding of the clash of interests in American society and the attempts made by these various interests to use the government to achieve their own ends. If students do not understand that the public varies considerably in their interests and needs, and that public policies generally reflect a bias in favor of some groups over others, they will never learn to identify their own interests. Nor will they ever realize that those interests will be considered and fulfilled only if they make their feelings known through voting, memberships in interest groups, or some other methods. And they will never understand that these are necessary but not sufficient conditions. Thus Bachrach and Baratz argue that "citizens do not know their own best interests, but this is because of a 'mobilization of bias' whereby citizens are socialized to be unaware of their own interests and political capabilities."[11]

A third point raised by more radical critics is that the educational process purposefully miseducates students by never allowing them to examine and evaluate the values underlying the social and political system. Milibrand, for example, argues that the "educational system, from the lower grades to graduate schools, inculcates capitalist values in its students and confirms the class destiny and status of most students."[12] Milibrand also points out that when minor social problems are emphasized, the controversy is designed to deflect "attention from the greatest of all problems, namely that here is a social order governed by the search for private profit."[13] It is clear that neither students or adults spend much time examining the values that America's society and political system are based on. And raising these questions can stimulate charges of un-Americanism.

Regardless of their reasons, critics do have a point: students are given an introduction to the political system which is hardly designed to turn them into active, concerned, and sophisticated political participants in their adult years. Certainly it would not be subversive to teach students about the complexity and values of the political system and to explain that no political system is likely to be run in the public interest unless citizens take an active and informed interest in that system. Indeed, democracy is based on the belief that only public vigilance and participation create a good political system and meaningful citizenship.

The implications of the indoctrination that students are given to the political system are quite obvious: it denies many citizens political knowledge and skills. As Lane and Sears note: "The Platonic Code (only the guardians are to be educated for leadership) here, in fact, has its modern incarnation."[14]

Cronin also raises a serious point about the long-term implications of the sugar-coated versions of politics that children receive in the public schools. Using the Presidency as an example, he asks:

> What happens when the citizen who was raised on the sanitized textbook version of the Presidency learns that the presidential establishment sees to it that the government extensively subsidizes corporate farmers, opposition political forces in Chile, Lockheed Aircraft, home-building companies, and the like; or that the Presidency is sensitively deferential to monopolistic organizations such as ITT and the Teamster's Union because of their political and financial clout? What happens when the student learns too about deliberate government suppression of information about massacres of Vietnamese citizens, irregularities in defense contracting; illegal campaign practices, political fixes, Watergate conspiracies, and advertisements and telegram campaigns rigged to give the appearance of public support for devious presidential policies?[15]

What happens was made clear by the Watergate scandal. When the public learned of the scandal, they were shocked and disillusioned. How they reacted to this shock, however, was quite insightful. Rather than becoming more interested in performing the citizen role of throwing out the corrupt and untrustworthy, many citizens decided that the political system was unworthy of public interest and support. Idealism, therefore, led to withdrawal rather than activism. Withdrawal, of course, only left the government in the hands of an even smaller portion of the public.

Class destiny

The prevailing philosophy of a society's social, political, and economic system can determine how people evaluate their role in society and the political process. The prevailing philosophy might cause politically inactive and uninfluential citizens to consider their inactivity wrong and in need of correction. Society itself might view politically apathetic citizens (especially if they numbered in the millions) as a serious societal problem requiring reform. On the other hand, the prevailing philosophy might suggest that public apathy reflects personal rather than societal failure, that, in fact, it reflects the natural order of things.

The latter philosophy exists in America. The "American Creed"—reinforced by a prevailing Protestant ethic and by a capitalistic economic system—maintains that those who are successful and powerful are so because of their superior personal characteristics. Those who are apathetic, suppressed, and powerless are so because of their lack of character. Thus, power and powerlessness reflect the aggregate personal characteristics of society. While something of an exaggeration, this is basically the philosophy that prevails in the American system. Newspaper editors may bemoan public apathy from time to time, but it is not generally considered to be a serious social problem, and certainly the government spends little energy trying to reduce it.

Neither students or adults spend much time examining the values that America's society and political system are based on. And raising these questions can stimulate charges of un-Americanism.

Those without power in the American political system also frequently accept the prevailing philosophy and blame themselves for their condition. Even groups with a long history of discrimination and suppression frequently believe that they deserve their lowly fate. This diverts attention away from factors in the system that promote apathy, away from representation that is biased toward the needs and interests of some at the expense of others.[16]

The failure of savior representatives

Public disappointment with the inability of elected representatives to considerably improve the benefits Americans receive from the political system has caused some recently activated citizens to retreat from politics. This problem is most common among groups like minorities and women who have been able, after a long struggle, to elect a representative to the local, state, or federal government, with the hope that this new public official would significantly alter public policies.

Black politicians, for example, frequently complain that their constituents, who waited so long for black representation, now expect them to change the world overnight. But since the American political system is weighted toward preservation of the status quo, a few black or a few women representatives can generally have little effect on public politics. Constituents with high expectations often react to delays and little sign of progress by denouncing their temporary faith in the system and returning to a state of apathy, cynicism, and hopelessness.

The two-party system

The American party system has a significant impact on public participation. In Europe, where participation is much higher, there are multiple parties, some of which are oriented toward the education and mobilization of the working class. Prewitt and Stone note the impact:

> In each of these latter nations, lower-class citizens have greater opportunities to express themselves politically through the group process than they do in the United States. This discrepancy partly reflects the fact that in Britain, Germany, and Italy there have been deliberate efforts to mobilize and politically involve the lower classes by radical or working-class political parties.[17]

Paradoxically, the fact that workers in Europe in the late twentieth century participate in politics more than their peers in America is at least in part the result of a disadvantage suffered by the Europeans in the nineteenth century. In Europe, the labor and socialist parties all grew out of civil rights, rather than economic, battles. The working class did not have the right to vote, and its original struggles were directed toward gaining the most basic rights of citizenship. When a group is thus forced to wage bitter campaigns for the recognition of its humanity, profound emotions of solidarity often result. So, for instance, the first great political organization of the workers in England was the Chartist movement of the 1830s and 1840s. Its demands all focused on citizen rights, not on wages or hours.

In the United States, workers in New York and Philadelphia organized

Western European workers, like these striking British coal miners, are more politically active and have more class solidarity than their American counterparts.

their own political parties in 1829 and 1830. But those efforts were abandoned very quickly. One reason was that the white male worker in this country had the "free gift of the ballot" almost from the beginning of the Republic. The solidarity based on an angry, wounded sense of exclusion did not exist here on a class basis, though it has played an important role in racial and ethnic movements, like the civil-rights campaigns of the 1950s and 1960s. The workers were integrated into the various American parties and did not organize independently, as a class, in their own party. Strangely, the historic advantage of American workers may be one reason why they have less distinctive political impact today than workers in Europe.

This trend is particularly noticeable in the social class of the politicians elected by working-class districts in this country: they are almost always middle class. Workers choose lawyers, and sometimes even millionaires, to speak for them in the Congress. In Europe, and particularly in Britain, however, it is normal for trade unionists to sit in Parliament and occasionally to become the nation's chief executive (like James Callahan, the Labour prime minister of Great Britain until 1979). Going through those bitter civil-rights struggles in the nineteenth century, European workers often achieved a political legitimacy and pride which the Americans—because they had an easier time of it—did not acquire. So, workers in this country have excluded themselves from much of the political process.

> The "American Creed"—reinforced by a prevailing Protestant ethic and by a capitalistic economic system—maintains that those who are successful and powerful are so because of their superior personal characteristics. Those who are apathetic, suppressed, and powerless are so because of their lack of character.

Indeed, one of the leading scholarly analysts of electoral behavior, Walter Dean Burnham, has suggested that the "hole" in the American electorate—those tens of millions of nonvoters—is composed of people with the same social and economic characteristics as those who vote for labor and socialist parties in Europe.[18] In part, the history just described helps explain this phenomenon. So does the fact that the European welfare states created by labor and socialist parties tend to have much more extensive programs for the people at the bottom of the society than in the United States. (These include such programs as national health systems, family allowances, and four-week vacations.)

In addition, the European political systems in which those labor and socialist parties operate are parliamentary. In America, the government is based on a "winner-take-all" principle. The candidate for President or Congress who wins by one vote gets all of the power of the position he or she gains. In Europe, where there are various forms of *proportional representation,* a small party can still affect the election and policies of a prime minister who is elected by the parliament. In Canada, which is similar to the United States in many ways but has a *parliamentary political system,* a socialist party (the New Democratic Party) received more than two million votes in the 1979 election and thus increased its power as a strong and influential minority. No such party exists in America, in part because of our presidential system. Ironically, the Canadian affiliates of major American unions, like the United Auto Workers and the United Steel Workers, are formally and publicly committed to supporting this openly socialist party.

So, in addition to the unique character of the American working-class experience, our political structures, militating as they do against third parties, tend to dampen tendencies toward innovations which might appeal to disgruntled voters.

INCREASING PARTICIPATION

Can public participation be increased? Reforms could certainly be undertaken to increase voting behavior and participation. Below we will discuss a number of these reforms, some of which were recommended to Congress in 1977 by President Carter.

There are, however, three major reasons why any reform will have difficulty passing Congress. The first is simply that members of Congress and other politicians would have to support the reforms, and generally they are extremely reluctant to alter the system in ways which might reduce their control. Second, increased public participation would disproportionately aid the Democratic party. Most politically apathetic citizens are low-income and young citizens, people who would primarily support the Democratic party. Thus, Republicans see considerable disadvantages in increasing the size of the electorate.

Third, many politicians (both Democrats and Republicans) have considerable fears and biases toward those persons who would be brought into the political process by reforms. Some elites believe that many working-class citizens are unfit for civic duty and would constitute a hazard to the social system. Even some social scientists share these biases. Two political scientists, for example, argue that the public is turbulent, ignorant, and inherently dangerous:

> Democracy is government by the people, but the responsibility for the survival of democracy rests on the shoulders of elites. This is the irony of democracy: Elites must govern wisely if government ''by the people'' is to survive. If the survival of the American system depended upon an active, informed, and enlightened citizenry, then democracy in America would have disappeared long ago; for the masses of America are apathetic and ill-informed about politics and public policy, and they have a surprisingly weak commitment to democratic values—individual dignity, equality of opportunity, the right to dissent, freedom of speech and press, religious toleration, due process of law. But fortunately for these values and for American democracy, the American masses do not lead, they follow.[19]

Such arguments basically assume that for two reasons the public is untrustworthy. First, it is feared that the public does not really support democratic principles. There is undoubtedly an element of truth to this charge. Many citizens will claim to support democratic principles when they are stated in the abstract but will reject specific applications of those rights. For example, some citizens will claim to support freedom of speech and religion, but not for those whom they dislike. A study by Stouffer reported that 68 percent of the public believed that a communist should not be allowed to speak in their community, 60 percent would deny freedom of speech to an atheist, and 31 percent would support censorship of a socialist.[20] More recent studies consistently reveal that a significant proportion of the public does not understand the implications of democratic rights and shows undemocratic attitudes.[21] During periods of war

Many elites believe that the American public harbors antidemocratic attitudes. During the Vietnam War, some citizens seemed intolerant of criticisms of government policy, a right protected by the First Amendment's guarantee of free speech.

or civil strife, the public tends to be even less democratic. A new study by Lawrence reported slight improvements in public support for basic democratic principles, but support was still far from unanimous.[22]

It is important to note that elites are only slightly more supportive of democratic principles than the general public. In the Stouffer study, elites expressed many undemocratic attitudes.[23] McCloskey also studied 3,020 elites and concluded that only 49 percent showed a commitment to democratic rights.[24] Stouffer labeled 31 percent of those in manual occupations and 66 percent of those in professional occupations as being tolerant of the rights of others.[25]

The raw figures undoubtedly suggest a greater difference between elite and public attitudes than actually exists. The studies cited here involved hypothetical situations and certainly overestimated the tolerance of elites, who are more sophisticated in answering such questions. In fact, elites in American history have frequently shown extremely suppressive attitudes toward their critics and those with whom they disagree. Obvious examples include the Alien and Sedition Acts of John Adams' administration, the imprisonment of Japanese Americans during World War II, the suppression of antiwar leaders during both world wars and the Korean and Vietnam wars, the various red scares after both world wars, and most recently the actions of Nixon and his aides during the Watergate scandal. Nixon consistently lied to the American public, attempted to punish his political enemies, and willfully obstructed justice. The depth of Nixon's biases reflects exceptional intolerance. For example, in one of the Watergate tapes Nixon says: "The Italians . . . they're not like us . . . they smell different, they look different, act different . . . of course, the trouble is . . . the trouble is, you can't find one that is honest."[26]

In the final analysis, then, both elites and the public sometimes fail to understand and support democratic principles. The antidemocratic tendencies of the public hardly seem different enough from those of elites to justify excluding the public from the political process. There would also seem to be little reason to consider barring citizens from effective roles in the political process unless there was evidence that their antidemocratic views were unchangeable. Certainly there is no evidence to support this. The studies cited above indicate that the public's antidemocratic attitudes stem from inadequate education, economic inequality, and lack of personal efficacy resulting from too little control over their work environment. These are conditions produced by the political and economic system, not inherent characteristics of the people.

Second, the public is considered to be untrustworthy because it is too easily manipulated by demagogic leaders.[27] Since citizens show some antidemocratic tendencies and some prejudices, they are thought to be vulnerable to unscrupulous politicians and candidates who attempt to build a following on prejudice. In recent years, support for George Wallace has been held up as the prime example of the public's weakness. In fact, the evidence is clear that the general public does not like "extremists" of any sort. For any candidate to be labeled "extremist" is the kiss of death, regardless of the direction of their political orientation. Barry Goldwater, George McGovern, and, indeed, George Wallace all faltered at the polls because the public feared that they were too far from the political center.

One of the most significant elite attacks on "excessive" democracy summarized many of these arguments in sophisticated fashion. In a 1975 report to the Trilateral Commission—a group which counted Jimmy Carter, Cyrus Vance, and Zbigniew Brzezinski among its members before they became, respectively, President, secretary of state and national security adviser—Michael Crozier, Samuel P. Huntington, and Joki Yatanuki analyzed *The Crisis of Democracy*. In Europe, they said, "citizens make incompatible claims. Because they press for more action to meet the problems they have to face, they require more social control. At the same time they resist any kind of social control that is associated with the hierarchical values they have learned to discard and reject."[28]

More broadly, these analysts concluded that on a worldwide basis "the successful operation of democratic government has given rise to tendencies which impede that functioning." Four trends were singled out: democratic egalitarianism and individualism have made authority in general seem less legitimate; "the democratic expansion of political participation and involvement has created an 'overload' on government and the imbalanced expansion of governmental activities, exacerbating inflationary tendencies in the economy; political competition has led to fragmentation of the parties; governments responsive to the electorate have become nationalistic as a result."[29]

So there are many practical and theoretical objections against "too much" democracy. Some elites see the apathy of the American citizen, which is supposed to contradict our basic principles, as a happy fact.

The public's antidemocratic attitudes stem from inadequate education, economic inequality, and lack of personal efficacy resulting from too little control over their work environment. These are conditions produced by the political and economic system, not inherent characteristics of the people.

Instituting reforms to increase public participation and control over the political system may be very difficult, then, but certainly there is no evidence that justifies elite prejudices against public participation. Below we will examine a number of reforms that could be instituted to increase public participation and rule.

Easy reforms

Some reforms would be quite simple and would probably have a positive but modest impact on voter knowledge and turnout. For example, in Europe, election day is often a holiday, and many believe a similar tradition in America would increase voting. The government, business, or both could sponsor television commercials and other activities designed to increase registration and educate and stimulate public voting. One such experiment showed great success. In 1978 California state officials organized a unique campaign to increase voter registration. State officials asked fast-food restaurants (e.g., McDonald's), local stores, the telephone company, and the National Guard to pass out voter registration cards. People who would not take time to go to the courthouse to register were often willing to send the card in if it was given to them. In just 20 days 11,000 new voters were registered in San Diego alone. In future years California state officials hope to expand the program.

For many years some members of Congress have tried to get Congress to pass legislation authorizing an amendment to the Constitution which would abolish the Electoral College and provide direct election of the President and Vice-President by popular vote (see Chapter 8). In 1978 the Harris Poll reported that by a margin of 74 to 13 percent, the public favored such an amendment. Replacing the archaic and complex Electoral College would simplify the process of electing Presidents and might encourage more participation.

"I know it needs fixing, but right at this moment I'm sick of it!"

Simplifying voter registration

Many believe that making voter registration simpler and requiring the states to register qualified voters would increase participation significantly. America is the only major nation in the Western world where the government does not assume the obligation of registering its citizens to vote. In 1977 President Carter recommended a bill designed to simplify registration and to increase the states' interest in registering voters. To encourage all qualified voters to go to the polls, the bill would have required the states to establish a system of election day registration.[30]

Carter's bill would have provided funds for the states to make a better effort to register voters before the election and to establish registration booths at the polls or other conveniently located places on election day. The law would have allowed the states to establish the identification requirements necessary to prove eligibility (e.g., a driver's license). It would also have required voters to sign a form acknowledging that they understood that vote fraud is punishable by a five-year prison term and a $10,000 fine.

The administration's expectation was that election-day registration and improved state efforts to register its voters would increase turnout by about 10 percent. A 10 percent increase in turnout would be a substantial improvement in participation rates. Critics charged that election-day registration would increase fraud, but four states (Maine, Minnesota, Oregon, and Wisconsin) have such registration and have found that it has increased participation without significantly increasing voter fraud. If a state requires normal procedures and burdens of proof to be met, increased fraud does not seem likely. Critics also argued that election-day registration would cause increased congestion at the polls. This would be true if voter registration were held at the polls. However, the proposed law would have allowed registration to be held elsewhere.

The critics of this bill were primarily Republicans and southern Democrats. Republicans tended to dislike the bill because most of the increased turnout would probably consist of Democratic supporters. Experience in the states that have adopted election-day registration shows that those most likely to use it are young people, blacks, and other minorities, and low-income citizens. Thus, in three of the four states which allow election-day registration, the Democratic party has made substantial gains since the reform was adopted. Southern Democrats tended to oppose the bill because it would probably have increased black voting. Republicans and southern Democratic opposition was strong enough to keep the bill from reaching the voting stage in 1978 and 1979, leaving the proposal dead for the time being.

Altering the school's role

Revising the school's approach to the study of the political process could have a substantial impact on the way students relate to that process as adults. A revised curriculum could do a better job of educating students and could teach the necessity, skills, and personal and societal implications of civic participation. Such a curriculum could be positive and nonpartisan while still presenting a realistic view of the political process and social and economic problems. Specific instructions on how to be an activist in the political process could also be included.

Worker democracy

A democracy depends substantially upon a public that is personally efficacious (willing to make decisions for themselves), capable of participation in collective decision-making, and tolerant and respectful of other opinions and lifestyles. Democratic theorists believe that a democratic political system can promote and develop these values in citizens. Many scholars believe that other environmental contexts, such as family and work relationships, can also play a considerable role in the development of a democratic personality. Yet as Jenkins notes, "Despite the obvious parallels, the connection between industrial democracy and political democracy is rarely discussed."[31]

The evidence available on the impact of job environments on workers is insightful. What the studies show is that millions of jobs in America are so dull and oppressive that they make workers nonefficacious, authoritarian, and intolerant. Published in 1973, the investigation of work environments by the Department of Health, Education, and Welfare (HEW) summarized a large number of studies "connecting low status, little autonomy, isolation, and repetitiousness of the job to the low self-esteem, anxiety, tension, passivity, and social alienation of the worker." As Best and Connally point out, "While inequities in income and educational levels attached to various jobs play a role in these correlations, the design of work and the structure of power in the work place are crucial factors as well."[32]

Some elites see the apathy of the American citizen, which is supposed to contradict our basic principles, as a happy fact.

Both supporters and critics of industrial capitalism have long noted the potentially negative impact of many jobs on worker personality. Adam Smith, the founding theorist of capitalism, observed that under the routine, disciplined jobs required by capitalism the individual "generally becomes as stupid and ignorant as it is possible for a human creature to become."[33] Smith thought the advantages of capitalism were so substantial that the price was worth paying. Jenkins, an opponent, argues that "workers subjected to the modern industrial-capitalist world tend to be 'stupid and ignorant' not only on the job, but off it as well."[34] Roger Masters raises a critical but broader point:

> There's every reason to believe that industrial society, a relative innovation, is simply unnatural from a biological point of view. Man got along for 2,000 years in an agricultural society. Then he was following a natural cycle. Now he just works himself to death, breaks it periodically with a vacation and the rest of the time gets bored and has the impression of never getting anywhere.[35]

The critical question, of course, is: What, if anything, can be done to improve the job environment and the impact that environment has on workers? The reforms suggested by some are job democracy, increased worker responsibility, and control over the work environment. Some countries, especially Scandinavian nations, are currently experimenting with worker democracy, and reports of its impact are quite positive.[36] A few American corporations have tried worker democracy, but have placed substantial restraints on worker control.

American companies have found that worker efficacy increased with a democratic job environment, leading employees to eventually raise questions that threatened the freedom of management. This seems to be a general phenomenon; but although it is considered positive in the more managed economies of the Scandinavian countries it often would not be in our economy. Swedish sociologist Bertil Gardell reports:

> In companies where employees believe they have. . . a great degree of influence on the company's operations, there is a relatively large group that wishes to influence larger management questions . . . It is not true, as is often claimed, that self-management and influence over small areas will divert attention from the more important economic questions; it will rather create greater independence . . . and a more highly developed demand for participation in decision-making.[37]

However, corporations can use an appearance of industrial democracy for their own purposes. Peter Drucker, one of the chief theorists of a probusiness point of view in the United States, wrote a book about *The Unseen Revolution* in 1976. In it he showed that pension funds, nominally owned by and operated on behalf of workers, were coming to dominate the American economy. He called this trend "pension fund socialism." It was, Drucker argued, a healthy trend because it would make it possible "for management to regain legitimacy precisely because it re-established a genuine, socially anchored ownership."[38] Yet Drucker himself freely conceded that "nothing has happened to either work or worker. The relations at work between workers, work groups, task and boss have not been affected at all."[39] In Drucker's candid perspective, a seeming democratization of work would give the executives more freedom of maneuver—but not the workers.

But perhaps the most ironic expression of this possibility took place in 1979. In that year, the United Automobile Workers (UAW) Union was involved in an extremely important campaign to organize the plant in Oklahoma

Douglas Fraser, president of the United Automobile Workers' Union, became a member of Chrysler Corporation's board of directors in 1980. Fraser is the first union representative to reach the board of directors of a major U. S. corporation.

City. As one of the most progressive unions in America, the UAW had long cooperated with various experimental programs to increase worker control of the factory environment and decrease alienation. In the Oklahoma City campaign, the UAW discovered that the company used all the techniques developed in those experiments—the abolition of the role of foreman, regular sessions for airing grievances, democratic work groups—as a means of keeping the union out.[40]

In short, within the capitalist boundaries of the American economic structure, there are profound limits on the democratization of work life. Management wants to maintain its freedom. If it senses a loss of legitimacy, it may be willing to make concessions which seem to increase worker control over their lives. It may even utilize anti-alienation measures to fight the union, as in Oklahoma City. But the fact remains that most Americans will continue to spend most of their waking hours at work under authoritarian conditions of discipline. This schooling in the factory or the office may well be one of the sources of apathy in the democratic society. It may teach people on a daily basis that they really cannot influence the decisions which control their lives.

The public initiative

Some believe that the public could be stimulated to participate more if they could have a more direct impact on legislation. One method often suggested to achieve this is the *initiative*. By petition process, the initiative allows citizens to put an issue on the ballot for public approval or rejection. Twenty-three states have the initiative. In 1977, then-Senator James Abourezk (D., S.Dak.) introduced a bill into Congress that would have amended the Constitution to allow a national initiative system.

Abourezk's amendment would have permitted an issue to be placed on the ballot if a number of qualified voters equal to 3 percent of those who voted in the previous presidential election signed a petition. Signatures would have had to be gathered in at least ten states. In the late 1970s this would have required some 2.5 million signatures from qualified voters to put an issue on the ballot. If a majority of the voters approved the issue, it would have become law. Citizens could have passed laws or repealed legislation passed by Congress. The initiative could not have been used to amend the Constitution, to declare war, or to call out federal troops. Any law passed by the initiative would have been subject to judicial review. Congress could have repealed laws passed on initiative, but only by a *roll-call vote* (each member's vote would be recorded and published).

If issues of any importance appeared on the ballot because of the initiative, an increase in public participation would probably result. Public debate would also increase. Critics argue that the initiative would allow Congress to duck controversial issues, but since an initiative campaign would bring the issue to public attention, it seems doubtful that Congress could avoid it. Certainly the initiative would place more responsibility on the public, although its best use would probably be to force Congress to deal with an issue. Most legislation is too complex to be handled adequately by an initiative process.

The Abourezk amendment received little support from Congress, which is unlikely to consider giving up any of its power or risk passing legislation that might make it look bad. But it is certainly an idea that represents citizen democracy, and one that most likely will continue to be an issue.

Other substantial reforms

As noted earlier, a major barrier to participation is public disillusionment and distrust of politicians. Public cynicism about, and alienation from, politicians is so severe that public officials should consider the question of their honesty and competency to be an emergency issue. They should realize that it will require extraordinary measures to demonstrate their personal honesty and determination to unflinchingly uphold high ethical standards for all members of government. Chapter 6 examines the reforms that Congress passed after Watergate and others that are still pending before Congress. Passage and enforcement of these reforms should serve to ensure ethical standards in government, with the potential of substantially increasing public faith and participation.

Studies have long shown that public participation is greatest in those states and localities with strong party competition. Competition between parties increases campaigning and the discusssion of issues and provides voters with more alternatives. In one-party states, citizens who dislike the prevailing party and its candidates have little motivation to vote. Chapter 8 examines the reforms that could be passed to strengthen party competition.

Participation would also be increased if third parties could more easily bring their messages before the public and have a better chance of actually winning contests. Third parties can more easily base their programs on the needs of particular groups, some of which may consist of citizens who feel unrepresented by the two major parties. If a third party can show the popularity of an issue, the major parties will also be likely to respond to that issue and increase their appeal. Chapter 8 discusses the reforms that could be instituted to increase the efficacy of third parties.

CONCLUSIONS

Many Americans have never developed or have even abandoned the democratic role of choosing and attempting to influence and control their political leaders at the polls. Democracy is based on the assumption that citizens should pick and control their political representatives and that as they do so, they will mature as citizens and as individuals. Thus, democracy seeks to establish not only citizen rule, but also mature and prudent citizens.

The theory of democracy is a powerful and attractive one that has not been fully realized in America. In part this is due to elite resistance to public control and in part to factors in the system that discourage citizen participation. Many reforms could be undertaken to remove past and present barriers to voting, to increase public faith and confidence in political leaders, and to give the public more control over public policies.

Many elites can be expected to continue to try to limit public control, but the increasing complexity of public issues—and the promise of democracy—provide powerful reasons for extending and ensuring public rule.

Footnotes

1. Andrew Hacker, *The End of the American Era* (New York: Atheneren, 1970), pp.142–43.
2. Poll data by Peter Hart cited in Joseph Kraft, "Nonvoter Study Cites Disillusion," *The Houston Post,* October 7, 1976, p.D3; Warren Miller and Teresa Levitin, *Leadership and Change* (Cambridge, Mass.: Winthrop, 1976).
3. Larry L. Berg, Harlan Hahn, John R. Schmidhauser, *Corruption in the American Political System* (Morristown, New Jersey: General Learning Press, 1976), p. 49.
4. *Ibid.,* p. 51.
5. *Harper* v. *Board of Elections,* 303 U.S. 663(1966).
6. See Richard Claude, *The Supreme Court and the Electoral Process* (Baltimore, Md.: The John Hopkins Press, 1970).
7. Lester M. Salamon and Stephen Von Evera, "Fear, Apathy, and Discrimination: A Test of Three Explanations of Political Participation," *American Political Science Review* 67 (December 1973): 1288–1306.
8. See David Easton and Jack Dennis, *Children in the Political System: Origins of Political Legitimacy* (New York: McGraw-Hill, 1969); Robert D. Hess and Judith V. Torney, *The Development of Political Attitudes in Children* (Chicago: Aldine, 1967).
9. See Easton and Dennis, *Children in the Political System;* Hess and Torney, *Political Attitudes in Children.*
10. Byron G. Massialas, "American Government: We Are the Greatest," in Benjamin Cox and Byron Massialas, eds., *Social Studies in the U.S.* (N.Y.: Harcourt Brace, 1967); L. Harmon Zeigler and Wayne Peak, "The Political Functions of the Educational System," *Sociology of Education* 43 (Spring 1970): 142–55.
11. Peter Bachrach and Morton S. Baratz, "Decisions and Nondecisions: An Analytic Framework," *American Political Science Review* 57 (September 1963):632–42.
12. Ralph Milibrand, *The State in a Capitalist Society* (New York: Basic Books, 1969), p. 241.
13. *Ibid.,* p. 261.
14. Robert E. Lane and David O. Sears, *Public Opinion* (Englewood Cliffs, N.J.: Prentice-Hall, 1964), p. 27.
15. Thomas E. Cronin, *The State of the Presidency* (Boston: Little, Brown, 1975), pp. 47–48.
16. See Richard Sennet and Jonathan Cobb, *The Hidden Injuries of Class* (New York: Knopf, 1972).
17. Kenneth Prewitt and Alan Stone, *The Ruling Elite: Elite Theory, Power and American Democracy* (New York: Harper & Row, 1973), p. 218.
18. Walter Dean Burnham, "American Politics in the 1980s," *Dissent* (Spring 1980), p. 157.

19. Thomas R. Dye and Harmon Zeigler, *The Irony of Democracy* (North Scituate, Mass.: Duxbury Press, 1975), p. 2.
20. Samuel A. Stouffer, *Communism, Conformity and Civil Liberties* (New York: Wiley, 1966).
21. Herbert McCloskey, "Personality and Attitude Correlates of Foreign Policy Orientation," in J. Rosenau, ed., *Domestic Sources of Foreign Policy* (New York: Free Press, 1967), pp. 51–110; Lewis Lipsitz, "Work Life and Political Attitudes: A Study of Manual Workers," *American Political Science Review* 70 (December 1964): 112–33.
22. David Lawrence, "Procedural Norms and Tolerance: A Reassessment," *American Political Science Review* 70 (March 1976):80–100.
23. Stouffer, *Communism, Conformity and Civil Liberties,* p. 40.
24. McCloskey, "Personality and Attitude Correlates of Foreign Policy Orientation," p. 57.
25. Stouffer, *Communism, Conformity and Civil Liberties,* p. 62.
26. Cited in Jimmy Breslin, *How the Good Guys Finally Won: Notes From An Impeachment Summer* (New York: Ballantine, 1975), p. 44.
27. See Dye and Zeigler, *The Irony of Democracy,* pp. 14–18.
28. Michael Crozier, Samuel P. Huntington, and Joki Yatanuki, *The Crisis of Democracy* (New York: New York University Press, 1975), p. 21.
29. *Ibid.,* p. 161.
30. See Rhodes Cook, "How Election Day Registration Has Worked Out So Far," *The Congressional Quarterly,* May 14, 1977, pp. 912–15.
31. David Jenkins, *Job Power: Blue and White Collar Democracy* (New York: Penguin, 1974), p. 60.
32. See Michael H. Best and William E. Connolly, *The Politicized Economy* (Lexington, Mass.: D.C. Heath, 1976), p. 130.
33. Cited in Jenkins, *Job Power,* p. 2.
34. *Ibid.,* p. 40.
35. Cited in Jenkins, *Job Power,* p. 10.
36. See Jenkins, *Job Power,* pp. 246–81.
37. Bertil Gardell, "Produktionstek nik ock manniskovarde," *Fackjorenings,* November 19, 1970. Cited in Jenkins, *Job Power,* p. 241.
38. Peter Drucker, *The Unseen Revolution* (New York: Harper & Row, 1976), p. 92.
39. *Ibid.,* p. 133.
40. Personal communication to Michael Harrington from Martin Gerber, Director of Organization for the U.A.W.

4

In a democratic society, where does political power lie? The apparent answer is with the people: democracy clearly means self-governance. But what is self-governance? Is a political system democratic if its citizens periodically consent to public policies or if the public selects its political rulers? Or does democracy require more? Does true self-governance mean that citizens must take an active part in running the political process?

Who Rules in America?

Classical democracy, as epitomized by the Greeks, required that a society be organized in a way that maximizes the public's participation in their own governance. To the Greeks, democracy was a system of government designed not only to legitimize political power by public consent, but also to allow average citizens to develop intellectually, morally, and spiritually by directly participating in political decision-making. A critical concept in classical democratic theory was that maximum development of human potential requires popular participation in the political process. As Bachrach has said: "The central theme of classical democratic theory is based on the supposition that man's dignity and indeed his growth and development as a functioning and responsive individual in a free society, is dependent upon an opportunity to participate actively in decisions that affect him."[1]

Of course, classical democracy in Greece had slavery as a precondition. The citizens were able to devote so much time and thought to the affairs of the *polis*, or city-state, only because they were relieved of mundane tasks by workers without political rights. This is an early example of the relationship between political power and economic structure, a point which will be examined later in this chapter.

Even with that very important qualification about the role of slavery in Greece, classical democracy still reflected great faith in the ultimate wisdom, good faith, and character of average citizens. And those who inherited the Greek ideal but rejected the slave substructure of the Greek system were consequently even more hopeful, for they sought to extend participation to everyone in the society. As John Dewey pointed out, democratic theory does not

Is political power in America in the hands of the people? Or is it in the hands of a small group of citizens who are not necessarily accountable to the public?

rest on the assumption that popular rule works only if the public has considerable experience in decision-making, great wealth, or extensive education: "The foundation of democracy is faith in the capacities of human nature, faith in human intelligence and in the power of pooled and cooperative experience. It is not belief that these things are complete but that if given a show they will grow and be able to generate progressively the knowledge and wisdom needed to guide collective action."[2]

DEMOCRACY AND THE CONSTITUTION

Classical democracy symbolizes an ideal state that has been approached in only a limited number of *polities*, or political systems, most of which were experimental. The great majority of the delegates to the Constitutional Convention of 1787 believed that classical democracy was impractical and dangerous and went to considerable extremes to make certain that most citizens would not play a role (direct or indirect) in the political process. The framers of the Constitution were, for the most part, a landed aristocracy—educated, wealthy, and privileged. They were interested in creating a government strong enough to promote private enterprise and to protect private property. At the same time, they wanted to preserve the spirit and form of popular government without indulging in "excess" democracy.[3]

Since most citizens in 1787 were poor and without property, the framers were afraid that if the public had much influence in the government, the majority have-nots would eventually threaten, even seize by force, the great wealth of the propertied few. Thus there was much discussion at the convention about the inevitable leveling that resulted from excesses of democracy.[4] The only safe government, they believed, would be one run by the most educated and wealthy citizens, who could be counted upon to protect the interests of the rich and well born. Alexander Hamilton expressed this antidemocratic spirit quite bluntly:

> All communities divide themselves into the few and the many. The first are the rich and the well born, the other the mass of the people. The voice of the people has been said to be the voice of God; and however generally this maxim has been quoted and believed, it is not true in fact. The people are turbulent and changing; they seldom judge or determine right. Give therefore to the first class a distinct, permanent share in the government. They will check the unsteadiness of the second and as they cannot receive any advantage by a change, they therefore will ever maintain good government.[5]

Not every member of the convention feared popular rule (George Mason and Benjamin Franklin spoke in favor of the people), but those who favored a larger role for the public were in the minority. The majority who feared "excess" democracy were not without noble intentions. They sincerely hoped to create a good political system, but they did not ignore their own self-interest or suspend their prejudices while working out its design. The framers not only feared the public; they also feared that unless precautions were taken the new government might be seized by a small number of persons from their own ranks. To protect against this possibility, the framers utilized the concepts of *separation of powers* and *checks and balances*. The power of the government was divided between three branches (the Presidency, the Congress, and the courts), and each branch was given some checks over the other branches.

Two of the branches of government were designed to be free of public influence, and only one chamber of Congress would be chosen by those citizens who could vote. The President was to be chosen not by popular vote but by the Electoral College, a group of eminent citizens selected by voters in each state. The framers expected this group to make an independent judgment in their selection of the President. This, of course, was an aristocratic theory designed to keep the public from directly electing the President while placing the actual decision in the hands of those whom the framers felt could be trusted. Alexander Hamilton explained in the *Federalist Papers* that the President would be chosen "by those persons capable of analyzing the qualities and adapted to the station and acting under circumstances favorable to deliberation."[6] The rise of political parties eventually democratized the Electoral College somewhat by encouraging electors to support particular candidates.[7]

from Article 1, Section 3: "The Senate of the United States shall be composed of two Senators from each State, chosen by the Legislature thereof, . . ."

from Article 2, Section 1: "The executive Power shall be vested in a President of the United States of America. He shall. . .together with the Vice President, . . .be elected as follows:

Each State shall appoint, in such manner as the Legislature thereof shall direct, a number of Electors, equal to the whole number of Senators and Representatives to which the State may be entitled in Congress . . . .

The Electors shall meet in their respective States, and vote by ballot for two Persons . . . ."

**Limits
on Public
Control**

from Article 2, Section 2: "The President. . .shall nominate, and by and with the Advice and Consent of the Senate, shall appoint Ambassadors, other public Ministers and Consuls, judges of the supreme Court, and all other Officers of the United States, whose appointments are not herein otherwise provided for . . . .

The federal courts were also removed from public influence by placing the selection of judges in the President's hands. The President's selections had to be approved by the Senate, but once approved the judges served for life (during good behavior), and their compensation could not be reduced by a vengeful Congress.

Selection of members of the U.S. Senate was given to state legislatures. This was not changed until the Seventeenth Amendment was ratified in 1913. The public could elect the members of the House of Representatives, but only a limited number of citizens could vote. The framers did not attempt to define voter qualifications: they simply specified that the qualifications for voting in federal elections would be the same as those required to vote for the most numerous branch of the state government (i.e., the state legislature). Voter qualifications, then, were set by the states and excluded most citizens. Women, slaves, and whites held in bondage were not allowed to vote. Various states also excluded whites who did not own property.

POLITICAL POWER IN MODERN AMERICA

Democracy, then, got off to a rather shaky start in America. The issues of extending public control over political leaders and involving the public in political decisions have never ceased to provoke controversy and conflict. While dozens of examples of reforms for increasing public control over public officials can be cited, these changes have never come easily. A civil war had to be fought to give blacks citizenship and the franchise, but in much of the country even these victories were temporary. Not until the 1960s were these rights genuinely extended to millions of black citizens. Women did not gain the right to vote until 1920, and only recently have women become a potent voting force in the political process. During recent years the Supreme Court has struck down burdensome residency requirements and voter registration fees that kept millions of citizens from voting.[8]

The majority who feared "excess" democracy were not without noble intentions. They sincerely hoped to create a good political system, but they did not ignore their own self-interest or suspend their prejudices while working out its design.

Despite the extension of the franchise and reforms such as *sunshine laws*, which increase the citizen's opportunity to know what the government is doing, other factors have made it increasingly difficult for the public to control the government. The most obvious is the phenomenal increase in the complexity of society and governmental functions and roles. In fact, government has become so complex that modern democracy is primarily thought of as a pro-

from the Fifteenth Amendment: "The right of citizens of the United States to vote shall not be denied or abridged by the United States or by any State on account of race, color, or previous condition of servitude."

from the Seventeenth Amendment: "The Senate of the United States shall be composed of two Senators from each State, elected by the people thereof, for six years . . . ."

from the Nineteenth Amendment: "The right of citizens of the United States to vote shall not be denied or abridged by the United States or by any State on account of sex."

from the Twenty-sixth Amendment: "The right of citizens of the United States, who are 18 years of age or older, to vote shall not be denied or abridged by the United States or by any State on account of age."

Expanding Public Control

cess by which the public periodically is given an opportunity to express its approval or disapproval of public officials. As noted earlier, in the American political system little emphasis is placed on citizen participation beyond periodic voting. Most American citizens are not active in the political process; most are not even regular voters. Americans also tend to be poorly informed about the political process, having little knowledge even about those political officials who represent them. What does the public's limited role mean for political power in America? Does it mean that only a small group of citizens are really powerful and influential in the political system? If so, are these citizens accountable to the public?

Social scientists are badly divided over the extent to which political leaders are accountable to the American public. Several theories which have been proposed will be examined below. However, who holds positions of power in the American political system is an empirical question that has been studied extensively. These studies concur that at any given time only a small number of persons control the political system. Dye, for example, reached the following conclusion:

> Great power in America is concentrated in a tiny handful of men. A few thousand individuals out of 200 million Americans decide about war and peace, wages and prices, consumption and investment, employment and production, law and justice, taxes and benefits, education and learning, health and welfare, advertising and communications, life and leisure.[9]

Along with numerous other scholars, Dye concludes that domination of the political system by a small number of persons is part of the general domination of economic and social institutions by a small group of persons. Based on empirical investigation, Dye and Pickering concluded that about 5,500 people

> control half of the nation's industrial assets, half of all assets in communications, transportation and utilities, half of all banking assets, and two-thirds of all insurance assets; they control nearly 40 percent of all the assets of private foundations, half of all private university endowments; they control the most prestigious civic and cultural organizations; they occupy key federal government positions in the executive, legislative, and judicial branches; they occupy all the top command positions in the Army, Navy, Air Force and Marines.[10]

Domination of the economic and political system by a small number of persons may have bad results for society, but on its face these findings are not all that disturbing as far as the political system is concerned. Any political system, regardless of its underlying philosophy, must place political power in the hands of a relatively small number of persons. As Lasswell and Lerner note: "The discovery that in all large-scale societies the decisions at any given time are typically in the hands of a small number of people, confirms a basic fact: Government is always by the few, whether in the name of the few, the one, or the many."[11]

The suffragists' campaign in the early years of the twentieth century led to the adoption of the Nineteenth Amendment in 1920, guaranteeing women the right to vote. But women have only recently become a potent political force in America.

The most important difference between governments is, of course, the extent to which the rulers are controlled by and responsible to the public. But who the rulers are is also important. By examining who the political leaders are, and what occupations and social classes they are drawn from, we can gain insights into the distribution of political power in American society.

Empirical studies agree that political leaders and top governmental officials are not drawn from a very broad class of Americans. Dye points out that "studies consistently show that top business executives and top political decision-makers are atypical of the American public. They are recruited from the well-educated, prestigiously employed, older, successful, affluent, urban, white, Anglo-Saxon, upper and upper-middle class, male population of the nation."[12] Dye studied 286 top political leaders including the President, Cabinet officials, political advisers, ambassadors, and congressional leaders. He found that these officials conformed to the pattern noted in previous studies.[13]

Matthews conducted a similar study limited to Presidents, Vice-Presidents, and Cabinet officials from 1789 to 1934. He found that all but about 4 percent of these officials were drawn from the professional upper-middle class. They also tended to be lawyers by training (especially after 1877) and were overwhelmingly male, white, and Anglo-Saxon. His findings clearly show that the children of manual laborers, small farmers, and other low-income citizens have rarely managed to attain positions of high authority in the executive branch.[14] Matthew's study was confirmed by Mintz, who extended the analysis through the Nixon administration years.[15]

Stanley, Mann, and Doiq conducted an ambitious study of 1,000 administrators who filled 180 top positions in the administrations of Roosevelt through Johnson. They also found that individuals from upper-middle-income backgrounds dominated these positions. They concluded, "Considering how different the jobs are it is astonishing how much alike the men are . . . ; these executives come from big government, big law, big business."[16] Even with recent civil rights laws and the women's movement, these basic findings still stand. Few blacks, women, or persons from working-class backgrounds hold positions of great authority in the federal government.

What do these findings mean? At the very least, they reveal that political power is a class phenomenon in America. With few exceptions, only those persons who attain an upper-middle-income status can realistically expect to hold influential positions in the national government. Such threshold barriers as education, professional attainment, and the ability to attract considerable sums of money to run for office effectively eliminate most citizens from the opportunity to serve in the federal government. The data also reflect an obvious consequence of racial and sexual discrimination in America: during most of our history, only white males, primarily from Anglo-Saxon backgrounds, have had much chance of attaining positions of political power.

In what broader context should these findings be interpreted? Outside of showing a leadership selection process which excludes most Americans, what do these results say about democracy and the political power of average citizens in a democracy? Some influential analysts have argued that the evidence indicates that democracy is essentially a fraud, a guise by which citizens are given the illusion of power while actually being governed by a ruling class. For example, the Italian theorist Gaetano Mosca wrote:

> In all societies—from societies that are very meagerly developed and have barely attained the dawnings of civilization, down to the most advanced and powerful societies—two classes of people appear—a class that rules and a class that is ruled. The first class, always the less numerous, performs all political functions, monopolizes power and enjoys the advantages that power brings, whereas the second, the most numerous class, is directed and controlled by the first.[17]

To Mosca this was a desirable outcome. The chief benefit of society, he thought, was to legitimize rule by a better class of people—an elite with wealth, education, and merit.

Like Mosca, Vilfredo Pareto believed a ruling elite always evolved in a democracy and was necessary because the public lacked the character to rule itself.[18] While Pareto and Mosca believed in elite rule, they also believed that the elite must accept a few of the most talented people from the masses into their ranks. This would renew the ruling elite and limit the chance that a talented nonelite might organize the masses against their rulers. Those people admitted to the ranks of the rulers would pose no threat since they would be quickly socialized to elite values.

Roberto Michel's writings contributed to the belief that societies are always ruled by an isolated elite, regardless of the outside appearance of the government. Michel studied European political parties and concluded that political organization always leads to rule by the few over the many. "He who says organization, says oligarchy,"[19] Michel wrote. Michel labeled his thesis the "iron law of oligarchy." His "law" held that all political organizations resulted in a self-perpetuating elite, which the public ritualistically ratified periodically.

The issues of extending public control over political leaders and involving the public in political decisions have never ceased to provoke controversy and conflict. While dozens of examples of reforms for increasing public control over public officials can be cited, these changes have never come easily.

Michel believed that it was not the public's inherent inferiority that caused their subjugation, but the rulers' ability to use the resources at their disposal (funds, patronage) to ensure their power. While Michel did not accept Mosca and Pareto's explanations for elite rule, he concluded that the result was the same: the public was always controlled by a ruling elite. If the public became restless, the elite could pacify them by enacting modest reforms that did not alter the reality of power, or even grant merely symbolic benefits.

Jose Ortega y Gasset, a Spanish intellectual, also helped to defend elite rule. He argued that a society could not maintain a viable democracy if the public were allowed to participate directly in political decision-making. In *The Revolt of the Masses,* Ortega y Gasset argued that the public was unprepared intellectually and morally to play a significant role in political decision-making.[20] He felt that the public was prone to demagogic appeals by fascists and communists, and he blamed the public, rather than elites, for the rise of fascism in Spain. Ortega y Gasset's main theme was that a wise elite was necessary to protect democracy from the masses. Such theories would later be referred to as democratic elitism.

Political power is a class phenomenon in America. With few exceptions, only those persons who attain an upper-middle-income status can realistically expect to hold influential positions in the national government.

Joseph Schumpeter, an economist, formulated an American version of democratic elitism. Like Ortega y Gasset, Schumpeter believed that the public was inherently unprepared for the responsibility of political participation. Public participation, he thought, could only lead to rule by demagogues: "The electoral mass is incapable of action other than a stampede."[21] Schumpeter saw elections only as a method of accomplishing the circulation of elites. To preserve democracy, he believed that the ruling elite must be insulated from the public's uninformed and emotional influence.

During the 1930s, numerous American scholars argued that an elite—one little controlled or influenced by the public—controlled the American political system.[22] Among academic social scientists, elite rule was the prevailing thesis.[23] Some of these writers were quite critical of elite rule. Some even saw a conspiracy behind elite control. Anna Rochester, for example, argued in *Rulers of America* that finance capital wielded by investment bankers controlled the political system through their financial domination of the political parties.[24] This theory undoubtedly overestimated the unity of business interests and the importance of campaign donations, even large ones, on office holders.[25] In *America's 60 Families,* Ferdinand Lundberg argued that 60 families dominated both American business and government.[26] This study was widely criticized by both friends and foes of elitism. Most conceded that some families had long been very powerful in American business and government but pointed out that many persons who were not members of these families obtained positions of power.

In 1956 C. Wright Mills advanced the most sophisticated theory of elite rule. In *The Power Elite,* he put forth a theory of political power which became the focus of scholarly debate for many years.[27] Mills believed that America had progressed through five distinct periods of power relations. The first period lasted from the Revolution to the end of John Adams' administration. During this period, America was governed by an aristocracy which often in-

THE BOSSES OF THE SENATE.

This satirical cartoon from the 1890s shows business interests in control of the government. Sixty years later, C. Wright Mills labeled the period from 1866 until the New Deal as the era of corporate domination.

terchanged roles in economic, political, military, and social institutions. The second period lasted until the Civil War and involved a political elite in charge of the new party system. The third period, the era of corporate domination, lasted from 1866 until the New Deal. Corporations dominated the political system and used their domination to rationalize the plunder of the public treasury. The fourth period involved the New Deal. During this period, corporate power in the government was not reversed, but competing power groups evolved and began to challenge corporate domination. The fifth period brought us up to the present, a period Mills labeled the era of the power elite.

Contemporary society, Mills argued, was characterized by three levels of power: the power elite, the middle levels of power, and mass society. He did not believe that the public has any meaningful control over the power elite. The middle levels of power (mostly Congress and interest groups) make some important decisions but generally cannot influence decisions concerning the most critical issues, which Mills defined as war and peace, economic slump and prosperity. The critical decisions, Mills argued, were made by a power elite composed of the top political officials, top corporate executives and directors, and the high military. He believed that the middle levels of power were in a state of stalemate, which made it possible for the power elite to maintain its position.

Mills argued that the members of the power elite interlocked in four important ways: (1) they shared common objectives; (2) their career patterns overlapped; (3) their economic origins and educational backgrounds were similar; and (4) they interacted socially. He noted that the members of the power elite did not always agree with one another but believed that they shared common interests which bound them together.

Mills concluded that the common belief that the public changed the political system periodically by becoming agitated over abuses was mostly a myth. The public, Mills argued, were primarily the pawns of elites, and rarely were able to achieve meaningful changes in the political system even when they tried very hard. Like many revisionist historians, Mills believed that history was primarily the result of elite struggles:

> Marx was basically wrong. Look, it is obvious that the proletariat doesn't make history, no matter how much you want to stretch historical facts. At certain points in history it has been more active than others, but clearly an elite has made and still makes the world history. How anyone can deny this in the face of the modern power state is almost unbelievable.[28]

Mills' theory was attacked from both the left and the right. Dahl, for example, argued that Mills could not prove that his power elite really had power.[29] But since Mills defined the elite as those in control of the major institutions of power, Dahl's argument is not well taken. Others maintained that business only has power when the Republicans are in office, and since the Democrats have ruled for long periods during the twentieth century, business could not be part of the power elite.[30] The evidence, however, reveals that businesses are hardly left out of government when the Democrats are in office, nor is business punished and neglected during periods of Democratic rule. Businessmen contribute large sums to Democratic candidates, and they serve in numerous important posts in the government during Democratic administrations. The Democrats have never attempted to nationalize industries or redistribute wealth. In addition, the health of the economy is so important to the success of any government that it is unlikely that business could be ignored. As Prewitt and Stone note:

> The facts do indicate both a community of interest between the political and economic elites, and a role interchangeability and overlapping among them. All of this occurs within the framework of a business society in which the proper functioning of that economic system is one of the prime functions of government. Moreover, it is a society in which the holders of great sums of money enjoy enormous advantages—political and otherwise—more so than the members of any other class. Money is the yardstick of the society and money makes its views known through elite clubs and other institutions as well as through its representatives in the political directorate. In this very complex sense, the corporate elite may be said to form part of the power elite.[31]

"The country's going to the dogs—happily it's the top dogs."

Mills' work and a less important book by Floyd Hunter[32] stimulated considerable debate over who has political power in America and how responsible those in power are to the public. Basically, this debate led to the articulation of two major theories of power—elitism and pluralism. Below we will explain, contrast, and evaluate these two theories and look at a third type of analysis which differs from both.

Elitism vs. pluralism

While elitism and pluralism are quite distinguishable from one another in their interpretations of power in America, they share three points of agreement:

1. Both theories agree that at any given time political power rests in the hands of a small number of people.
2. Both agree that those who rule are different from the general public. Rulers, it is agreed, mostly reflect upper-middle-income backgrounds, are better educated than the public, have better and more prestigious occupations, and are generally white males.

3. Both agree that there is little evidence of classical democracy in America. That is, there is little evidence that the public plays a very large or informed role in most of the decisions made in the political system.

Pluralism, however, is by far the most optimistic of the two theories. It does not maintain that the public directly rules, but it does argue that the public's interests are reflected in the political process and that the public has ample opportunities to influence that process. Since elitism preceded pluralism, and since pluralism is actually a revised form of elitism, we will discuss elitism first.

Elitism can be summarized as follows:[33]

1. American society is divided into two groups—the few who rule and the many who are ruled.

2. While there is competition, and disagreement among the ruling elites, only a narrow range of issues is involved. These issues are never fundamental to the existence of the elite system.

3. Public policies generally reflect elite rather than public values and interests. Changes in public policies generally represent changes in elite values or changes in the elite. Elite change results not from public removal of elites who have disappointed them but from changes in the economic elite in society.

4. Many groups attempt to influence political elites, but some are much more successful than others. Groups that represent labor and the public have some influence in the political system, but big business is the most important interest. Big business is the best organized, wealthiest, and most successful interest during both Democratic and Republican administrations.

5. Only rarely are elites forced to make decisions because of pressure from the public. When elites must respond to public pressures, they can usually deflect them by passing policies that are mostly symbolic—designed primarily to appease the public without substantially altering the distribution of political power or wealth.

6. While some nonelites are admitted to elite ranks, they have little power unless they adopt elite values. Admitting and converting talented nonelites to the elite ranks reduce the chances of revolution.

7. The poor, minorities, and women are mostly excluded from power because of elite biases toward them, because they lack the necessary resources to wield real influence within the political system, and because they are socialized to accept the status quo.

8. The public generally pose little threat to elite power because they are lazy and ignorant about politics and easily manipulated by the elite.

As noted, pluralism is basically a reinterpretation of elitism. Pluralists basically argue that elites are more subject to influence by the public than elitism admits. They claim that political influence is more widespread than elitism suggests, and that elites work within a constitutional framework that preserves basic democratic principles while providing necessary leadership and direction for the political system.

Pluralism can be summarized as follows:[34]

1. While citizens do not directly participate in political decision-making, policies are not made by isolated elites acting by themselves. Public policies result from bargaining, compromise, and accommodation between competing elites who represent and are influenced by many types of groups. Elites function within institutional settings and are restricted by formal laws and informal norms.

2. A chief characteristic of American politics is competition among groups, none of which has a systematic advantage in the political process. Labor and consumer groups have as much power in the political process as do business groups.

3. The government is basically a neutral arbitrator among groups. If some groups become too dominant or abusive of some sectors of the public, the government restores the balance and/or protects the abused group.

4. The frequent election of Democratic administrations shows that business does not dominate the political process. In fact, it shows that business is unrepresented for very long periods of time.

5. Citizens can influence the political process in several ways:
   a. by choosing between competing elites during elections;
   b. by joining groups specifically designed to lobby the government;
   c. by working within a political party and helping to choose the party's candidates for office;
   d. by organizing supporters, raising money, and running for office with the intent of becoming one of the elites.

6. Elites do not completely ignore even those citizens who are not well represented by groups. The needs of the poor, minorities, and women, for example, are given consideration because they are potentially very powerful groups. Of course, these groups can become directly powerful any time they want to become actively involved in politics.

7. The large amount of progressive legislation (civil rights laws, women's franchise, social security, etc.) passed by Congress throughout American history shows that the public has great influence.

8. Elites are best prepared to run the government because they are well educated and from the upper-middle class. This class has a stake in a stable and prosperous society and is more committed than usual to democratic principles. The public is best suited to a limited role in the political process because they are uninformed and subject to being misled by demagogues.

George Meany, the late president of the AFL-CIO, and Senator Edward Kennedy. According to the pluralist theory of power, public policy results from the competition for government influence between interest groups.

Public apathy, then, is not completely bad; it may even be beneficial because it allows elites to have the most influence in the system. Apathy, in fact, may reflect public support for the political system: the public may not be active because they are basically happy with the political process.

Pluralists, then, argue that democratic values are maintained in our society by voters choosing between competing elites who fulfill public needs by making policy through a process of bargaining, compromise, and accommodation. Democratic principles are protected by elite commitment to democratic values, by citizen mobilization through groups and parties, and by democratic rules that can be enforced against abusive elites. Thus, the theory maintains, the system works: it deals with public needs and is still democratic.

The structural theory of power

Both the elitist and pluralist theories focus upon the people who make decisions. They debate whether these elites must be responsive to, or are independent of, popular pressures and movements. The structuralist theory emphasizes the way elites are forced to make their choices within a rather narrow range of options determined by the needs of on-going economic and social structures.

Pluralists basically argue that elites are more subject to influence by the public than elitism admits. They claim that political influence is more widespread than elitism suggests and that elites work within a constitutional framework that preserves basic democratic principles while providing necessary leadership and direction for the political system.

The structural theory can be summarized as follows:[35]

1. In totalitarian societies, like those in the various communist countries, political and economic power are intertwined, since the economic decisions are made by political leaders. In such a system, if members of the bureaucracy lose out in the political power struggle, they simultaneously lose the ability to determine economic policy. (Normally, they also forfeit personal economic privileges, like country houses and the right to shop in special stores, which are reserved for the bureaucracy.)

In the capitalist democracies, the relationship between the political and the economic is much more complex. If the presidential candidate supported by business is defeated, as happened in 1976, that does not mean that the corporate executives are fired. They continue on in their powerful positions. Thus, in analyzing power in a democracy, one must examine the relationship between the private economic sector and the public political sector.

2. On one level, this analysis can be done within the framework of either elitist or pluralist theory. The leaders of the private sector are themselves members of the social upper class and often spend part of their careers in government. Liberal—usually Democratic—administrations consciously seek to win "business confidence" in order to gain the widest possible support for their policies. Thus, Jimmy Carter accepted the Democratic presidential nomination in 1976 with a speech which was somewhat populist and anticorporate but shortly thereafter had a highly publicized luncheon with a group of powerful industrialists at a fashionable New York restaurant.

3. The structural theory, however, focuses upon the influence of private economic structures as it operates independently of political deals and plots within the elite. For instance, in the United States since World War II, the profits retained by corporations have been a major, and usually dominant, source of funds for new investments. As long as this is the case, no government, no matter how liberal or even radical, can tax or otherwise reduce profits to the point that this source of capital would dry up and cause a major crisis of the system.

For example, in the debate over a "windfall profits" tax on the oil companies—a special tax imposed because those corporations benefit from the monopoly prices set by the Organization of Petroleum Exporting Countries (OPEC)—one would expect the oil lobby to argue against a high tax on the grounds that profits were needed for exploration for new oil. They did exactly that. But one part of the tax was also opposed by a liberal journal, the *New Republic,* normally a critic of the oil companies, on the grounds that it would not motivate the industry to behave in a responsible way.[36] Economic necessity, it said, made it wrong to carry out an "act of vengeance" on the companies.

4. The on-going economic structures do not simply define limits within which *any* government must operate; they also form the basis of a hidden agenda. Even those politicians who act upon it are not at all necessarily aware of its existence. In the late fifties, for instance, President Eisenhower proposed a sweeping federal interstate program (which will eventually have cost more than $100 billion). At the time, there was little discussion of how this huge investment in an infrastructure for the private car and the trucking industry would affect the railroads, the location of industry, or the economic attractiveness of the cities of the Northeast and Middle West.

Yet it is clear that the advantages private automobile owners and trucking firms received from this social expenditure also changed some of the most important patterns in American society. The fact that the political leadership did not consider all of these dimensions of their decision was not an accident or the result of their personal ignorance. Rather, it was simply "natural" in a society in which the automobile and oil industries, with all of their suppliers (which, in the case of the auto, includes the steel industry), are central to the entire economy.

5. More broadly, the democratic capitalist state is not itself capitalistic. It promotes income and wealth for the individual and tax revenues for itself by seeing to it that the private economy functions in the most efficient and profitable way. Therefore, the priorities of the corporate leadership tend to be the priorities of the elected officials, even those who are liberal and somewhat anticorporate.

6. In the structuralist analysis, real differences are debated in political campaigns and the two major parties administer the economy, in contrasting ways. However neither party questions the underlying structures—which can be defined as those institutions and arrrangements which operate no matter who is in power—and both adapt to their needs.

With these three theories summarized, we can now probe their respective strengths and weaknesses.

Structuralist theory emphasizes the way elites are forced to make their choices within a rather narrow range of options determined by the needs of on-going economic and social structures.

A critique of pluralism, elitism, and structuralism

An analysis of pluralism reveals serious weaknesses in its interpretation of the American political system and shows that it is essentially rather skeptical of true democracy. Elitism, on the other hand, exaggerates the isolation of elite rule and the influence of certain groups in the system. Both theories will be critiqued to help provide insights into the realities of political rule in the American system.

The following points can be made about pluralism:[37]

1. If groups are the key to political influence, then all sectors of the public would have to be represented by groups and the groups would have to be essentially equal in power. The evidence indicates that this is not true. As Chapter 7 shows, many citizens are not represented by groups, and some groups are considerably more powerful than others. Groups which represent upper socioeconomic interests are the best organized, the most active, have the most money to spend, and are the most likely to be influential.

On the other hand, many citizens have little or no representation. As one critic put it: "The vice in the groupist theory is that it conceals the most significant aspect of the system. The flaw in the pluralist heaven is that the heavenly chorus sings with a strong upper-class accent. Probably about 90 percent of the people cannot get into the pressure system."[38]

2. There is no evidence that business ever lacks political influence. Business executives serve in both Democratic and Republican administrations and contribute money to both parties. Both parties try hard to get along with business while in office and attempt to keep the economy healthy.

3. The existence of competing and multiple elites is not a guarantee of citizen influence. The key to citizen influence is the extent to which the elites hold competing positions on important issues of policy, especially for those that represent the needs of all sectors of the public. The evidence indicates, however, that the needs of many citizens may not be well represented by political elites. When elites do differ on issues, it is much more likely that they will argue over minor policy matters rather than those which involve the distribution of power and wealth in the political system.

4. Pluralism accepts much too easily a limited role for average citizens in the political process. It completely dismisses the option of trying to greatly increase the role of citizens. In many ways pluralism shows a lack of faith and even a suspicion of average citizens that is unjustified by available evidence. The data in Chapter 3 show that there are many sound reasons for citizen apathy, that apathy does not reflect faith and confidence in the political system, and that average citizens are not exceptionally prone to antidemocratic stands or support for demagogues.

5. The emphasis on the potential of citizen influence through political participation is overly optimistic and, to some extent, begs the question. The

fact is that most citizens do not play an active role in the political system, so this influence is not very likely to occur. Some groups also find it much harder to organize, obtain funding, and have their efforts taken seriously. Groups such as women and minorities have much more difficulty being taken seriously by voters and thus find it much more difficult to run for and win election to public office.

In addition, citizen groups find it difficult to influence the system because they generally seek some positive action such as legislation. It is much more difficult to get legislation passed than it is to preserve the status quo. A bill, for example, must go through a dozen stages to be enacted into law. At any one of these stages the bill may be blocked by a small number of legislators. Thus, a group's power often depends upon whether it wants to defend the status quo, or alter it.

6. Pluralism alters the normal democratic role of elites. Rather than being probationary servants who must be carefully observed and controlled, elites are elevated to a trustee or guardianship role over the political process. Democracy survives not because of citizen control of elites but because elites do not have to be influenced too directly by a potentially dangerous public. The evidence does not indicate that this faith in elites or the distrust of average citizens is justified. This concept of elite trust, of course, drastically alters

Since political power is not distributed equally in America, many citizen groups find it difficult to change established policies. The Equal Rights Amendment, for example, still had not been ratified in 1980, even though opinion polls continued to show strong public support for the measure.

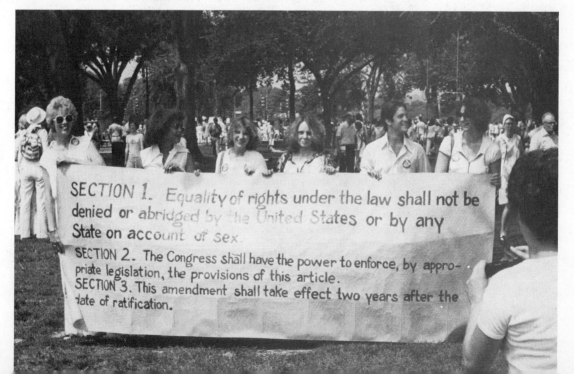

basic democratic theory, changing it from a very liberal to a very conservative, even aristocratic, idea.

7. Pluralism badly exaggerates the influence of groups that are not well represented or very active in the political process. The objective conditions of women and blacks make it clear that elites have not looked after the needs of these groups throughout history because they were potentially powerful. The evidence is clear that these groups were long neglected because of their lack of influence and that they have had great difficulty in influencing the political system even when they have tried very hard to do so. One of Richard Nixon's close advisers made this point very well. Jeb Magruder explained why the Nixon administration was little concerned with certain groups. "We didn't spend time on the disadvantaged for the simple reason that there were no votes there . . . We don't have a democracy of the people. We have a special-interest democracy."[39]

Even Lyndon Johnson in his retirement years believed that special interests were most influential in the American political system and that they had always worked to the detriment of the average citizen. "My grandfather taught me early in life that neither misery nor squalor is inevitable so long as the government assumes the positive role of eliminating the special interests that cause most of our problems in America—particularly the money lenders largely confined to New York, and those who had the money supply and knowledge and possessions in New York, Chicago, and Boston. They'd always been paid proportionately a far higher percentage of the total end product than they deserved. They lived off our sweat, and even before air conditioning they didn't know what sweat was. They just clipped coupons and wrote down debentures we couldn't spell and stole our pants out from under us."[40]

8. Does progressive legislation demonstrate public influence? In fact, it does. It not only shows that the public can influence the political system, but also reflects limitations on public influence. The civil rights bills, social security legislation, and many other pieces of progressive legislation were passed only when long-standing deficiencies or biases in the political process created conditions severe enough to cause public officials to act to offset public demands. Many of these severely needed reforms did not appear until the public resorted to violence or civil disobedience. Few would argue with the conclusion that blacks did not receive relief until generations after they needed it very badly.

In addition, some progressive legislation is mostly symbolic. This was true of many of the civil rights bills, some of the environmental laws, and much of the legislation designed to deal with the needs of the poor. Thus, the public can influence the political system, but it is quite difficult to do so and often requires turbulent conditions.

9. The pluralist argument that the government is only a neutral judge among competing interests is unsupportable. Some groups are much more influential and much more likely to have representatives in the system. Few

would disagree with the assertion that poor people, environmentalists, independent oil operators, and small businesses have much less representation in the system than big businesses.

10. Pluralists undoubtedly place too much faith in the power of the established rules—such as statutes, the Constitution, and informal norms—to restrain elites. Certainly, these rules place real and important constraints on elites (Watergate, in its own way, showed this), but they do not ensure that elites will not abuse their powers. Blacks, women, and other groups were subjugated for long periods in our society despite the Bill of Rights and other laws.

Norms may also serve not to protect but to exclude the public from influence. Norms may dictate that an oil company's request for a subsidy is reasonable, while demands by welfare mothers for jobs and child care aid are considered outrageous. Norms may also specify that some policy options are outside of consideration and thus never placed on the agenda. Some social scientists refer to this as the power to make a nondecision, to exclude some options from debate.[41]

The deficiencies of pluralism, then, are substantial. Elitism also suffers from a number of problems but reflects political reality somewhat better than pluralism. The following critical points can be made about elitism:

1. Elitists are undoubtedly correct that not all groups have equal influence in the political process and that big business is quite influential. However, elitism does not reflect the complexity of the interactions between business interests and policy-makers. While business interests are united in their support of such principles as private property and free enterprise (at least self-serving free enterprise), businesses differ on many individual matters of policy. The legislation one business pursues may be opposed by another equally powerful business. Big business is not always assured of success, therefore, even when it is highly organized and has many supporters in Congress.

Groups with interests counter to those of big business—labor unions or consumers, for example—may be able to influence elites to support their legislative views. But such victories are not easily obtained, rarely if ever fundamentally reduce business influence or power, and generally deal with something like product safety, worker conditions, or pollution. Still, business does not operate in a vacuum and does not always win or find victory easy. Thus, the system may be seriously biased toward business, but the values of other interests prevail on many issues.

2. Elitism exaggerates the unity of elite bias in favor of the status quo. Virtually all elites believe the American political system is one of the best—if not the best—political systems in the world and that it is essentially viable. However many elites believe that the political system suffers from many biases and deficiencies, and favor change.

There are even a sizable number of persons among the elite who favor a considerably more egalitarian system than the present one. These liberal and

Although business interests are highly influential in the political process, labor unions and consumer groups can also have a substantial impact on economic and social policies.

moderate elites support such measures as fundamental tax reform, national health insurance, and dozens of other left-of-center policies. Most of these people represent constituencies with large numbers of union members, minorities, and the poor. Most of them are members of the Democratic party; they number about 100 to 150 in the Congress and have some representation in the bureaucracy. Of course, some Presidents have also been sympathetic to these points of view.

3. The elitist argument that public policies reflect elite rather than public values is generally true but exaggerated. The extent to which elite values will prevail depends upon the issue. If a redistributive issue[42] is involved (one concerning the power, wealth, and prerogatives of the elite), elite values will generally prevail. If, however, more general legislation is involved, the groups that influence the outcome are likely to be more diverse. Of the many groups that lobby Congress, some—such as those which represent labor, and self-styled public interest groups like Common Cause and the Nader groups— are sometimes influential contenders in the political process.

4. It is generally true that the public plays a small role in the political process and consequently places few restraints on elites. Still, most elites rarely feel that they can act with complete impunity toward the public.

Elites know the public is not watching them carefully but tend to be concerned that some act on their part may attract critical public attention. This fear restrains elites to some extent but does not generally keep them from serving or disproportionately representing certain elite interests. Lyndon Johnson, for example, believed that below the public tranquility was the possibility "of a mass stampede, a violent overreaction to fear, an explosion of panic such as . . . had occurred in the heyday of Joseph McCarthy."[43]

Some of the deficiencies of the structuralist theory are listed below:

1. It cannot predict or explain extremely significant policy choices. Since this theory only identifies the limits within which policies are made and the general bias which informs the decisions of both liberals and conservatives (and in Europe, socialists and communists), it has little predictive value in the short run. It is better able to state what cannot be done within a given system—those policies which, since they conflict with basic structural needs, cannot be adopted by any government—than what will be done.

2. There is a related flaw. The structuralist view is not particularly useful in specifying how decisions are made. For instance, President Eisenhower's proposal to develop a federally funded interstate highway system had to be formulated by an administrative bureaucracy, pass through a number of congressional committees, be moved to the floor of Congress, debated, amended, passed into law, and implemented. At each stage of this process, individuals and groups could and did intervene to shape the legislation to their own purposes or their own special conception of the common good.

The structural analysis is silent on this process. It must be complemented by insights derived from the elitist and pluralist views. Elitism would stress the bureaucratic domination of all the individual choices and would describe how the bureaucracy imposed its view on elected officials. The pluralist perspective would underscore the degree to which actual decisions were molded by the conflict and competition of interested parties. As a theory of limits and biases in the political process, the structuralist model is not particularly useful in dealing with the political mechanisms within the system.

3. In much the same way, the structural model does not adequately deal with the impact of individuals upon a system. It is quite right to observe that Franklin Roosevelt's New Deal turned out to be the salvation of American capitalism rather than its destruction, as most of the social upper class thought at the time. It is also important to note, in light of both the elitist and pluralist analyses, that most of the American elite was opposed to what Roosevelt was doing. Paradoxically, forces critical of capitalism, like the organized labor movement and the minorities, were in the forefront of the struggle for reforms which ended up strengthening capitalism.

In all of this, one sees the value of the structural approach. But what of Roosevelt's personal role? He was, Oliver Wendell Holmes is said to have remarked, a "second rate intellect and a first rate temperament." That is, he improvised the New Deal rather than framing it on some ideological basis. What if Roosevelt had not been elected? Would the "system" have automatically produced an individual capable of saving it? That is not at all clear.

F.D.R.

"Come along. We're going to the Trans-Lux to hiss Roosevelt."

4. The structural model can be understood to mean that the whole process of electoral politics is utterly unimportant and that the underlying economic and social institutions are all-determining. Ultimately this notion could lead to the thesis that democracy itself is irrelevant in the United States. This is by no means a *necessary* conclusion of the structuralist method, but it is a possible interpretation and one which has been made by a large number of people. Thus, when communists use the structuralist concept of "bourgeois democracy," they rightly point out that the democratic system is profoundly influenced by the elite concentration of private economic power. But they almost always forget the possibility, and the reality, of democratic incursions and modifications of the private economy.

5. Consider another reading of the structural theory. If the underlying economic and social institutions are basic to the functioning of the system, and if one then wrongly concludes that politics has no impact upon what happens but is merely manipulated by the economic "forces," where is there a principle of change? Since these economic forces constitute the status quo, they will not change voluntarily. Also, politics has been declared impotent.

A complex structural theory can solve this problem readily enough: politics is not impotent even if it is not as independent of the economy as some of the other theories imply. The underlying structures are contradictory and crisis-prone and periodically break down, whether established society likes it or not. Still, it is necessary to make a fairly subtle reading of the structural theory to understand these matters. More than a few people have used it to project a seamless, unchanging economic and social system.

CONCLUSIONS

Where does the critique of these theories leave us? First, although all the theories reject the simplistic view that the "people" rule directly in the United States, all of them see both value and some effectiveness in our democratic institutions. Thus, the elitist and structural theories, which emphasize that decisions are often not under the control of the electorate, or even the politicians voted into office, both recognize that democratic pressures have an impact on both the small group of decision-makers and economic structures.

Second, it is possible to take elements from all three theories, even though one might find one of them as the most useful general framework. There are instances where popular mobilization makes a significant difference: for example, the "tax revolt" of 1978, symbolized by Proposition Thirteen in California, caused legislators to reconsider their policies. Yet at the same time the "professionalization of reform" has given experts and other elites a power they never had before. And even conceding those previous pluralist and elitist points, it is also true that there are limits upon political change and that they are often rooted in on-going economic structures and necessities.

Third, all three theories also recognize the possibility of change. Clearly, the pluralist analysis is most optimistic in this regard. If the people organize themselves for a purpose, they can compel the government to meet their demands. Both the elitist and structural theories are less hopeful, seeing the domination of the people from the top down or the structural determination of policy as powerful impediments to the functioning of a truly popular government. But each of them, as we have seen, holds out the efficacy—even if limited—of democratic control of an officially democratic society.

These optimistic aspects of the theories should not, however, make one complacent. For all of these theories, even the most hopeful of the three, describe a political reality that deviates significantly from the proclaimed ideas of the United States. They tell of a political system in which a small group of citizens holds a disproportionately large share of political power. They describe a political system biased in favor of certain socioeconomic, racial, and sexual groups, a government which favors upper socioeconomic and business interests, but one in which other interests can sometimes be very powerful, especially on nonredistributive issues. In their view of the political system, the public generally plays a limited and indirect role but has the potential to substantially influence the political system if special events spur them to action. However, these theories also suggest a political system in which the public has generally been socialized to accept elite values. Thus, the public is unlikely to attempt to force changes in the political system that would substantially alter the bases of political and economic power in America.

Footnotes

1. Peter Bachrach, *The Theory of Democratic Elitism: A Critque* (Boston: Little, Brown, 1967), p. 98.
2. John Dewey, *The Public and Its Problems* (New York: Holt, 1927), p. 211.
3. See Charles A. Beard, *An Economic Interpretation of the Constitution* (New York: Macmillan, 1913); and Forrest McDonald, *We The People—The Economic Orgins of the Constitution* (Chicago: Chicago University Press, 1958).
4. See Max Farrand, ed., *Records of the Federal Convention* (New Haven: Yale University Press, 1927), Vol. 1.
5. Farrand, ed., *Records of the Federal Convention,* p. 412.
6. Alexander Hamilton, *The Federalist.*
7. Each state requires electors to vote for the candidate who received the most popular votes, but no state has filed criminal or civil charges against electors who have failed to do so. On a number of occasions since World War II, electors have decided to vote their own conscience and ignore the popular vote.
8. *Harper* v. *Board of Elections,* 303 U.S. 663 (1966).
9. Thomas R. Dye, *Who's Running America?* (Englewood Cliffs, New Jersey: Prentice-Hall, 1976), p. 3.
10. Thomas R. Dye and John W. Pickering, "Government and Corporate Elites: Convergence and Differentiation," *Journal of Politics* (November 1974), p. 905. In this source, Dye and Pickering guess that there are some 4,000 critical elites. Dye adjusts the figure in *Who's Running America?*
11. Harold Lasswell and Daniel Lerner, *The Comparative Study of Elites* (Stanford: Stanford University Press, 1952), p. 7.
12. Thomas R. Dye, "Men in Authority: Five Thousand Top Institutional Positions in America and the Men Who Occupy Them" (paper presented to the annual meeting of the American Political Science Association, New Orleans, Sept. 4–8, 1973), p. 23.
13. *Ibid.*
14. Donald Matthews, *Social Background of Political Decision-Makers* (New York: Doubleday, 1954).
15. Beth Mint, "The President's Cabinet: 1897–1972," *The Insurgent Sociologist* (Spring 1975): 144.
16. David Stanley, Dean Mann, and Jameson Doig, *Men Who Govern* (Washington, D.C.: Brookings, 1967), pp. 78–79.
17. Gaetano Mosca, *The Ruling Class* (New York: McGraw-Hill, 1939), p. 50.
18. Vilfredo Pareto, *Mind and Society* (New York: Harcourt Brace Jovanovich, 1935).
19. Roberto Michels, *Political Parties* (New York: Free Press, 1958), p. 418.
20. José Ortega y Gasset, *The Revolt of the Masses* (New York: Norton, 1957).
21. Joseph A. Schumpeter, *Capitalism, Socialism, and Democracy* (New York: Harper and Row, 1960), p. 293.
22. See Theodore J. Lowi's introduction to Kenneth Prewitt and Alan Stone, *The Ruling Elites: Elite Theory, Power, and American Democracy* (New York: Harper and Row, 1973), pp. vii–xii.
23. *Ibid.*
24. Anna Rochester, *Rulers of America* (New York: International Publishers, 1936).
25. See the critique in Prewitt and Stone, *The Ruling Elites,* pp. 54–56.
26. Ferdinand Lundberg, *America's 60 Families* (New York: Van Guard, 1937).
27. C. Wright Mills, *The Power Elite* (New York: Oxford University Press, 1956). This analysis was summarized in part from Prewitt and Stone, *The Ruling Elites,* pp. 83–113.
28. Saul Landau, "C. Wright Mills: The Last Six Months," *Ramparts* (August 1965), p. 48. Quoted in Prewitt and Stone, *The Ruling Elites,* p. 107.
29. Robert A. Dahl, "A Critique of the Ruling Elite Model," in G. William Domhoff

and Hoyt B. Ballard, eds., *C. Wright Mills and the Power Elite* (Boston: Beacon Press, 1968), pp. 25–34.

30. Arnold M. Rose, *The Power Structure* (New York: Oxford University Press, 1967), p. 461.

31. Prewitt and Stone, *The Ruling Elites,* p. 99.

32. Floyd Hunter, *Top Leadership U.S.A.* (Chapel Hill: University of North Carolina Press, 1959).

33. Some excellent statements on elitism are Prewitt and Stone, *The Ruling Elites;* G. David Garson, *Power and Politics in the United States: A Political Economy Approach* (Lexington, Mass.: Heath, 1977), pp. 31–57; G. William Domhoff, *Who Rules America?* (Englewood Cliffs, N.J.: Prentice-Hall, 1967); G. William Domhoff, *The Higher Circles: The Governing Class in America* (New York: Vintage Books, 1971); Gabriel Kolko, *Wealth and Power in America: An Analysis of Social Class and Income Distribution* (New York: Praeger, 1962); and Thomas R. Dye and L. Harman Zeigler, *The Irony of Democracy* (North Scituate, Mass.: Duxbury, 1975).

34. Some excellent statements on pluralism are Earl Latham, *The Group Basis of Politics* (New York: Octagon Books, 1965); Robert A. Dahl, *A Preface to Democratic Theory* (Chicago: University of Chicago Press, 1956); and David B. Truman, *The Governmental Process* (New York: Knopf, 1951).

35. The term "structuralism" can be misleading since it has been widely and variously used in Europe—particularly in France—and has been the subject of debates among anthropologists and philosophers as well as among political scientists and sociologists. Three excellent summaries of the concept as it is used here can be found in Leon Lindberg et al., eds., *Stress and Contradiction in Modern Capitalism* (Lexington, Mass.: Heath, 1975). These essays—"Is Democratic Control of Capitalist Economies Possible" by Andrew Martin; "The Theory of the Capitalist State and the Problem of Policy Formation" by Claus Offe; and "Paradigms of Relations Between State and Society" by Robert R. Alford—were presented at an international conference of social scientists of various schools in 1973. Alford's contribution is particularly valuable since it also examines the elitist and pluralist models from a structuralist perspective. One of the authors of this text has also utilized this methodology: See Part II in Michael Harrington, *Twilight of Capitalism* (New York: Simon and Schuster, 1976). The writings of the late Nicos Poulentzes, a Greek-born French Marxist, offer much that is worthwhile but on a rather sophisticated level of analysis.

36. "How to Tax Oil Companies," *The New Republic,* December 22, 1979.

37. The following provide excellent critiques on pluralism: Henry Kariel, *The Decline of American Pluralism* (Stanford: Stanford University Press, 1961); Charles McCoy and John Ployford, eds., *Apolitical Politics: A Critique of Behavioralism* (New York: Thomas Y. Crowell, 1967); Michael Parenti, "Power and Pluralism: A View From the Bottom," *The Journal of Politics,* 32 (August 1970), pp. 501–30; Jack L. Walker, "A Critique of the Elite Theory of Democracy," *American Political Science Review,* 60 (June 1966); Theodore Lowi, *The End of Liberation* (New York: Norton, 1969).

38. E. E. Schattschneider, *The Semi-Sovereign People* (New York: Holt, Rinehart and Winston, 1960), p. 35.

39. Studs Terkel, "Jeb Magruder Reflects," *Harper's,* October 1973, p. 72.

40. Doris Kearns, *Lyndon Johnson and the American Dream* (New York: New American Library, 1976), p. 96.

41. Peter Bachrach and Morton S. Baratz, "Decisions and Non-Decisions," *American Political Science Review* 57 (September 1963): 632–42.

42. See Theodore Lowi, "American Business, Public Policy, Case Studies, and Political Theory," *World Politics* (July 1964), pp. 677–715.

43. Kearns, *Lyndon Johnson and the American Dream,* p. 148.

A riot is the language of the unheard.
Martin Luther King, Jr.

In earlier chapters we noted that the American public is generally rather politically inactive. But our image of the American public's modest role in the political process is altered somewhat by considering the unorthodox idea that public violence has often served as a substitute for, or supplement to, traditional forms of political participation. Groups who are generally powerless have often adopted violence as a means of influencing the political system when they have found it impossible to change the system peacefully. Such violence has been so frequent, in fact, that one student of American history concluded that "collective violence is part and parcel of the Western political process."[1]

5

Violence as Political Participation and Power

Much of this political violence has resulted from the extreme deprivation of certain groups and from elite resistance to group attempts to improve their condition. In an assessment of American violence, Brown concluded: "All too often unyielding and unsympathetic established political and economic power has incited violence by its refusal to heed and redress just grievances."[2]

Workers' rising expectations of better wages and living conditions and the resistance to such gains by the propertied class and their governmental allies produced some of the most notable periods of political violence in American history. Literally dozens of farmer and labor revolts resulted because businesses and public officials attempted to defend their privileges against have-not groups.

Civil strife throughout history has, in fact, reflected elite reaction to public demands. When elites have reacted sympathetically, violence has been unnecessary. However, elite accommodation to public demands for rapid alteration of the status quo or a more equitable distribution of wealth has been quite rare. Generally, political and business elites have attempted to suppress protesters through use of the state militia, federal troops, hired guards and deputies, economic harassment, legal sanction, and manipulation of the media.

New Orleans streetcar workers overturn a trolley during a 1929 strike. Lacking political influence, disadvantaged groups in America have sometimes resorted to violence to achieve ends that could not be obtained through the political system.

Since the law and definitions of public order have generally reflected elite values, dissenting groups have usually found it very difficult to achieve their goals even when they have resorted to extreme violence.[3]

Along with agrarian and labor violence, racial conflict has been quite prevalent in American history. Basically, three types of racial strife have occurred. First, there were slave revolts. Second, there were race riots. Race riots essentially involved one deprived group using violence against another deprived group that was viewed as a further threat to the first group's already precarious economic condition. The third stage of racial conflict was reached in the 1960s when blacks revolted against their continued suppression by destroying white property in their neighborhoods and by fighting the police and soldiers who were called in.

The use of hired guards, the police, and often the military by elites to protect their position in society indicates another frequent function of violence in American history. Both economic and political elites have often used violence as one aspect of their political power. As the analysis below will show, public violence has often occurred in the form of reprisals or defenses against elite-inspired violence.

In this chapter, we will examine some of the various types of political violence that have occurred in the United States. It should be stressed that the analysis touches only the tip of the iceberg. It would hardly be possible to provide even a modest summary of all the major events of political violence that have happened in our history. The various episodes of violence surveyed are divided by category, but the categories are not exclusive and serve only as a convenience. Some major violent events reflect several of our classifications and could easily be discussed under two or more headings.[4] We will attempt to show some of the dimensions of American political violence, analyze why the violence occurred, and reflect on how the implications of political violence affect our understanding of public participation and power in the American political system.

VIOLENCE AGAINST POLITICAL SUPPRESSION

Colonial opposition to British rule in America provided the impetus for many violent acts by public groups against the British during the period leading up to the Revolutionary War. In fact, acts of violence against the British and their colonial supporters were in some ways the public equivalent of the intellectual attacks on the British waged by more educated and wealthy patriots such as Sam Adams, John Adams, Richard Henry Lee, Thomas Paine, and James Otis.

One of the first attacks on the British resulted from increasing colonial opposition to the British practice of impressing American sailors and laborers into service in the British Navy. British impressment gangs frequently roamed

American ports, forcing Americans to serve on British ships. In 1747 a group of white and black sailors and laborers forcibly rescued one of their allies who had been seized by a British impressment gang commanded by Commodore Charles Knowles. The Americans freed their mate, captured some of the British sailors, including their lieutenant, and assaulted the sheriff and his deputy when they tried to come to the aid of the British. The Americans then marched on the British representative's home, causing him to flee the city. Other impressment riots occurred in New York in 1764, Newport in 1765, Casco Bay, Maine, in 1764, and Norfolk in 1767.[5]

> *Civil strife throughout history has reflected elite reaction to public demands. When elites have reacted sympathetically, violence has been unnecessary. However, elite accommodation to public demands for rapid alteration of the status quo or a more equitable distribution of wealth has been quite rare.*

The Stamp Act riots of 1765 are rather well known. In 1765 Parliament enacted the Stamp Act to raise revenue for the British empire. The act required that all formally written or printed matter such as deeds, bills, diplomas, and newspapers carry a stamp to indicate that the designated taxes had been paid. The colonies were completely opposed to the tax. Merchants refused to sell the stamps, and mobs attacked British tax collectors, destroying some of their homes. Not one stamp was ever sold in America.[6]

The Boston Massacre of 1770 is generally thought of as a classic example of British violence against the colonial population, and in some respects it was. The incident, however, was provoked by an American mob that attacked a British sentry and then used oyster shells and snowballs to pelt the British troops who came to his rescue. The mob was angry about the Townshend Acts—taxes on lead, paint, paper, glass, and tea—and competition with British troops for local jobs. The British troops tried to reason with the mob but eventually panicked and opened fire, killing five and wounding six. The incident was quickly described as a massacre and served as an important event in unifying American resistance to British rule.[7]

American support for the Revolutionary War was solidified by the physical intimidation of British loyalists by colonial mobs. During 1774 and 1775, revolutionaries tarred and feathered loyalists, rode them out of town on rails, branded many, imprisoned some, and hung a number. This prerevolutionary violence clearly represented a form of political participation. Citizens who saw no other means of being politically influential resorted to violence to achieve political ends.

Violence was relied upon hundreds of times thereafter in America. The draft riots that occurred during the Civil War are good examples. The most serious riot occurred in New York in 1863. It reflected racial tensions (between Irish and blacks competing for dwindling jobs) and resentment toward unfair

The Boston Massacre dramatized England's political suppression of colonial America. British troops killed five Bostonians and wounded six others in the incident, which strengthened the colonists' opposition to British rule.

draft laws. The precipitating incident was a law allowing one to avoid the draft by paying a sum of $300. Irish rioters attacked the wealthy and the draft boards first, and then turned on blacks. Over a three-day period the rioters fought the police and the army. Estimates of deaths ranged from 300 to 1200.[8] Riots also occurred in Newark, Jersey City, Troy, Boston, Toledo, and Evansville, but they were not as severe as the one in New York.

VIOLENCE BY OFFICIALS AGAINST PROTESTERS

There are many examples of public officials using violence against public groups who were making demands upon the political system. The often bloody events surrounding the attempts of workers to form labor unions, discussed later in this chapter, offer excellent examples. Three other famous examples are the Tompkin Square incident of 1874, the routing of the Bonus Army in 1932, and the antiwar riot of 1968 in Chicago.

During the depression of 1873, groups of unemployed workers petitioned local governments for public programs to create jobs. In New York one group sought to meet with local officials to make such a request. The officials refused to meet with them. The group then asked the police for a permit to march from Tompkin Square to the City Hall. The police refused to grant the permit. The group then asked for a permit to hold a demonstration at Tompkin Square. The police vacillated but decided the night before the meeting to deny this permit also. The demonstrators were not informed that the permit had been denied until the morning of the meeting.

On that morning, some 7,000 unemployed men, women, and children had gathered at the square. Around 10:30 a.m. mounted and unmounted police charged the unarmed and peaceful demonstrators, indiscriminately clubbing anyone in their path. Samuel Gompers, the famous labor leader, was among those at the square. He described the police attacks as "an orgy of brutality."[9] For the next several days any small group of poorly dressed citizens caught congregating were beaten and mauled by club-wielding police. Hundreds were injured, including, said Gompers, "the sick, the lame, and the innocent by-stander."[10]

The Bonus Army of 1932 was reminiscent of Coxey's Army of 1894, a ragtag host of unemployed poor people who had marched to Washington to plead for help—only to be arrested and run out of town. The Bonus Army numbered in the thousands and also consisted of unemployed citizens; these, however, were veterans of World War I who had been unable to obtain local help for the misery that befell them during the Great Depression. In 1924 Congress had voted to provide all World War I veterans a bonus, which would be paid twenty years later. Thousands of unemployed veterans decided to march to Washington to petition the government for immediate payment of the bonus as a form of relief.

Accompanied by their wives and children, the veterans arrived in Washington. They set up a tent city and spent their days petitioning Congress and the President for the bonus. There were no reports of violence by the Bonus Army. Congress finally considered the request but turned it down. President Hoover refused to meet with the veterans. When the veterans decided to stay in their tent city and make another effort to convince Congress to support its cause, Hoover ordered the U.S. Army to force the veterans from the city.

Three of America's most famous generals directed the operation. General Douglas MacArthur, along with his aides, Dwight D. Eisenhower and George S. Patton, led four troops of cavalry, four companies of infantry with fixed bayonets, and four tanks to the tent city. MacArthur ordered the tent city gassed and then set the city on fire as its occupants were routed. The unarmed men, women, and children fled the city in fear of their lives. The campaign resulted in the death of an eleven-week-old child who had been born in the tent city earlier in the summer; another child was blinded; and many suffered bayonet and saber wounds. Many citizens were proud of the government's work, but some dissented. "What a pitiful spectacle," said the Washington News, "is that of the great American Government, mightiest in the world, chasing unarmed men, women and children with Army tanks. . . . If the

World War I veterans, demanding immediate payment of the deferred bonus promised to them, converged on Washington, D. C., in 1932. After Congress refused to pay the bonus, U. S. Army troops, led by General Douglas MacArthur, destroyed the Bonus Army's tent city (above).

Army must be called out to make war on unarmed citizens, this is no longer America."[11]

The 1960s was a period of great turbulence in America. The ghettos erupted across the nation, and protests against the Vietnam War were numerous. In 1968 thousands of critics of the war decided to stage a massive demonstration in Chicago while the Democratic National Convention was being held there. The protesters were mostly college students consisting of supporters of antiwar candidate Eugene McCarthy, radicals, Yippies, and others who felt that the war was unjust.

The longtime "czar" of Chicago, Mayor Daley, decided not to accommodate the demonstrators in any way. The city refused to issue a permit for the parade and refused to allow the demonstrators to sleep in the public parks. The mayor ordered 6,000 police officers, backed up by Army troops, to enforce the bans. The only choice left to the demonstrators was to leave town or defy city authorities. The demonstrators negotiated with officials for some form

During the 1968 Democratic Party Convention in Chicago, police openly used violence against antiwar protesters who had come to the city to stage a demonstration.

of accommodation but were repeatedly rebuked. The protesters finally decided to ignore orders to leave town and resist police efforts to harass them. During the evenings of August 25, 26, and 27, minor clashes occurred as police chased demonstrators from parks, but the incidents were controlled because most of the protesters followed the protest leaders' pleas for compliance with park curfews.

Tensions grew, however, and then exploded on the night of the 28th as protesters tried to march to the Amphitheater, where the convention was being held. Protesters clashed with the police in city parks and then in the streets of the city. The clashes became brutal when the police lost control and mercilessly clubbed everyone in sight, including journalists, news photographers, and innocent bystanders.

A commission appointed to study the conflict concluded that a police riot had occurred.[12] The commission also concluded that the city administrators' arrogant attitude toward the protesters caused the bloody street battle.

VIOLENCE AGAINST ECONOMIC SUPPRESSION

Throughout American history, a significant part of the population has always had great difficulty in obtaining enough work and income to live decently. This economic distress has been the catalyst for a long history of violent clashes between the general public, on one hand, and wealthier citizens and their governmental supporters, on the other. Conflicts over attempts to form labor unions constitute an example of such clashes, as do a number of nonlabor disputes.

Nonlabor conflicts

The Boston Bread Riot of 1713 was one of the first examples of public violence in response to economic want. The riot resulted from public hunger caused by a severe food shortage. Groups petitioned the government to halt the export of scarce American grains to other countries. Inaction by local officials led to a revolt against grain merchants. In Boston harbor, a mob seized a ship that was loaded with wheat and destined for a foreign market. To pacify the mob, the colonial governor ordered the wheat delivered to local bakers to be turned into loaves and sold to the public.[13]

The New Jersey Tenant Riots of 1745–1754 were considerably more violent. The clashes occurred over the rightful ownership of much of the land area of New Jersey. In the late seventeenth century, the duke of York awarded much of this land to two British lords. At approximately the same time, the duke's appointed governor in America (not knowing of his actions) granted the same land to settlers. Dispute over rightful ownership went on for some 80 years. The lords and their heirs tended to have the most influence with the crown and with American officials and courts and thus won most legal battles with the settlers and their heirs. The settlers appealed to the crown, but to no avail.

In 1745 the clash climaxed when one of the most prominent settlers was jailed for refusal to pay rent to the lords. Other settlers marched on the jail and freed their ally. This led to additional arrests and jail breaks. A decade of riots resulted, many of which were quite bloody. By 1754 an accommodation was reached, and the conflict subsided.

The New York farmers' rebellion of 1776 was one event in another series of landlord-tenant battles that occurred in that state. During the early eighteenth century, a small number of wealthy families succeeded in accumulating massive estates for very small sums of money. Much of the land was actually defrauded from local Indians. Some of the estates involved several hundred thousand acres of land. The wealthy families rented the land to tenants, who often doubted their just title. Tenants frequently attempted to gain legal recognition of their own deeds and sought to challenge the validity of landlord claims. Inevitably, the tenants lost these court challenges because the magistrates were indebted to the property owners; many of the magistrates had been appointed to the bench by the landowners.

After 1750 the tenants increasingly resorted to violence against the landlords. Armed bands of tenants waged a number of pitched battles with posses and militia. Deaths and serious injuries on both sides were frequent. On one occasion a band of 200 tenants marched on their landlord's home with the intent of murdering him and leveling his house unless he signed leases favorable to the tenants. An armed posse routed the group. In another incident, 1700 armed tenants disrupted courts and freed jailed tenants. Another group marched on New York City to burn landowners' homes but lost an engagement with the militia.

The government conceded to landowner appeals for aid and employed the full force of the militia against the tenants. The superior forces of the militia eventually defeated the tenants, killing many and driving others from the state.

Shays' Rebellion is one of the best-known conflicts between public authorities and farmers in American history. The rebellion reached insurrection proportions before it ended. It was caused by high taxes on Massachusetts farmers that were designed to help the state rapidly pay off war debts. The taxes were so burdensome that hundreds of farmers lost their property, some were jailed for debt, and others were even sold into servitude. Between 1785 and 1786 there were 4,000 suits for debt in Worcester County alone.[14]

Farmers, struggling to preserve the fruits of their life's work, began to organize to put pressure on the government for lower assessments and to put an end to the debt proceedings. The farmers petitioned the government for relief, but their requests were ignored and the foreclosures continued. When peaceful methods failed, the farmers decided to close the courts by force. Under the command of former officers of the Continental army, such as Daniel Shays, farmers forcibly closed numerous courts.

> *A significant part of the population has always had great difficulty obtaining enough work and income to live decently. Economic distress has been the catalyst for a long history of violent clashes between the general public, on one hand, and wealthier citizens and their governmental supporters, on the other.*

In late 1786, Secretary of War Henry Knox sent federal troops into Massachusetts to battle the farmers. Numerous clashes resulted. In December Shays' forces, numbering about 1,000, won several victories and were threatening to seize the military garrison at Springfield. Additional troops arrived and artillery weapons were used to rout Shays' troops. Scattered guerrilla bands continued to fight the army for several months, but then resistance collapsed. Daniel Shays died in poverty in New York thirty years later.[15]

The Whiskey Rebellion of 1794 was another uprising of farmers against taxes. In 1791 Congress passed a tax on whiskey. Since whiskey was an important cash crop for frontiersmen who had no method of transporting their grain crop to market, the tax burdened the farmers significantly. The farmers resisted the taxes and began to fight marshals and tax inspectors who attempted to serve them with subpoenas requiring court appearances. Tax inspectors were harassed by mobs, and court proceedings were disrupted.

In one incident a mob of some 500 farmers surrounded the home of a tax inspector and demanded that he surrender his commission. A small contingent of federal troops attempted to defend the house, but was defeated. Upon failing to find the inspector in the house, the mob burned the residence. This and other battles persuaded President Washington to form an army of 12,900 and march on the rebels. The mobs scattered before the advancing army, and the insurrection ended.

A New York riot in 1837 involved mob action as a technique of political influence that was outside the realm of traditional political participation. The panic of 1837 resulted in considerable economic deprivation for many citizens as meat, coal, flour, and rent prices rose two and three times in a two-year period. The Locofoco, a division of the Democratic party opposed to monopolies, called a public meeting to plan a petition campaign calling upon the government for aid and for an end to monopolies.

A large contingent of those who attended the meeting, however, objected to petition and argued for an immediate assault on flour merchants, who, they claimed, were hoarding flour to drive up its price. Many of the crowd agreed, and an assault on merchants proceeded. The assault on the property of the rich severely frightened the propertied class and caused many of them to predict the end of the Republic.

Classic examples of public violence stemming from a lack of other opportunities to influence politics are the eviction riots of the Great Depression. During the Depression, when millions were destitute, landlords and banks evicted and foreclosed on thousands of families per week. Sympathetic crowds were attracted to the pitiful scene of furniture and possessions being deposited on the street as the victims of the Depression were removed from their homes. Stirred to outrage by such scenes, participants in the crowd often restored the possessions to the home and drove the landlord or bank representative from the neighborhood. Sometimes these acts were spontaneous, but the Communist party began to organize group resistance to eviction.

Increasingly, the police were called in to enforce the landlord and bank evictions, and crowds began to clash with them. In one such incident in Chicago in 1931, a large crowd closed in on the police, who fired point blank into the mob. Three persons were killed and numerous others wounded. Their deaths enflamed public resentment. Sixty thousand persons marched in a mass funeral and the anti-eviction movement spread to other northern cities.[16]

During the Depression, farmers had their own version of anti-eviction resistance. While thousands upon thousands of farmers lost their homes because of foreclosure,[17] many others held on to their life's possessions because of organized farmer resistance. Sometimes farmers simply drove sheriffs, bank officials, real estate speculators, and auctioneers away from a threatened farm. More often, however, the farmers armed themselves (sometimes with guns but more often with hoes and scythes) and intimidated anyone who tried to bid on the endangered farm. Farmers often carried a rope with a hangman's noose to the auction scene as another method of discouraging outside bidders. Having frightened off the competition, one farmer would place the high bid of one penny, and then return the farm to its owner.

As our limited survey demonstrates, violence has often been the political tool of farmers. From Bacon's rebellion in the late seventeenth century to the present, farmers have had to struggle mightily in our society. They have generally adopted violence only when other political techniques proved futile. Despite the long-standing economic problems of American farmers, they have had a great impact on American politics. Farmers organized the Grangers, backed the Greenbackers, and formed the heart of the Populist party, which proposed many of the reforms of the Progressive Era.

Since the Great Depression, farmers have turned to violence less frequently and certainly never on the scale of seventeenth- or eighteenth-century violence. But there have been many incidents in which striking farmers have dumped milk, destroyed crops, abused noncooperative farmers, intercepted trucks carrying farm products to market, and blocked access to food-processing plants and offices of state and local officials. In both 1978 and 1979, farmers organized tractorcades to Washington, D.C., where they blocked streets, disrupted traffic, turned farm animals loose at the Capitol, demonstrated, forcibly occupied the secretary of agriculture's office, and engaged in numerous skirmishes with the police. At Hidalgo, Texas, the farmers blocked the International Bridge to disrupt the importation of Mexican crops, fought the police, demonstrated on the courthouse lawn, and used tractors to seal the police and judges inside the local courthouse. None of this suggests that farmers are inherently violent. The contrary seems to be true. But farmers have turned to violence when they have concluded that necessity demanded it.

Labor violence

Throughout American history, only racial violence has produced more deaths, injuries, and general mayhem than labor strife. As Taft and Ross note: "The United States has had the bloodiest and most violent labor history of any industrial nation in the world."[18] Taft and Ross' analysis of labor violence in America, which they say "grossly underestimates the casualties," reveals some 700 deaths, several thousand serious injuries, and 160 occasions on which state and federal troops intervened in labor disputes.[19]

Not all the victims of the violence were workers. While none of the major labor unions ever adopted violence as a philosophy, conditions were frequently so hostile to worker interest and needs that violence was often accepted as necessary. In addition, many of the workers were rugged people, nurtured in environments in which violence was often used to settle conflicts. Thus laborers frequently fought pitched battles with police, militia, and scabs and engaged in sabotage against owners' property. The tension between workers and owners was so intense that both sides often seemed to adopt violence as an integral part of the labor struggle.

The worst incidents of violence occurred when owners refused to accept workers' rights to organize a union or when owners decided to destroy an existing union. Much of the conflict resulted from the owners' attitude that workers were a less-than-human resource to be exploited for personal profit. Owners, especially in nineteenth-century industrial America, tended to believe that they had no obligations to workers and that workers should be paid as little as possible and never have any say about the conditions of their work environment. As one manufacturer put it: "I regard my employees as I do a machine, to be used to my advantage, and when they are old and of no further use I cast them into the street."[20]

From Bacon's rebellion in the late seventeenth century to the present, farmers have had to struggle mightily in our society. They have generally adopted violence only when other political techniques have proved futile.

The second half of the nineteenth century was, of course, the era of the robber baron. Industrialists often had low ethical and moral standards and worshipped nothing above the dollar. They robbed and plundered for profit with impunity, and even stole from one another. But they had great power in the political system. Their combined economic and political powers made them the dominant force in society. In his annual message to Congress in 1888, President Grover Cleveland noted both the power and the abuses of the corporation: "Corporations, which should be the carefully restrained creatures of the law and servants of the people, are fast becoming the people's masters."[21] In 1913 President Woodrow Wilson stated: "The masters of the government of the United States are the combined capitalists and manufacturers of the United States."[22]

In clashes with their workers, the industrialists clearly had the distinct advantage. They could afford to hire private police, who were often little more than thugs, to protect their interests. They could also generally obtain state and federal aid and could import impoverished workers from other areas to take the jobs of striking workers. The police, company guards, and the militia often provoked violent confrontations with workers. Often the hired guards were professional provocateurs who traveled from one union disorder to another, serving the needs of the owners.

Pitting the working class against itself often served to direct attention away from who its common enemy was. Industrialists found it easy to hire guards to fight workers because there were so many people who needed any kind of work. As Jay Gould, one of the most virulent of the robber barons, once bragged: "I can hire one half of the working class to kill the other half."[23] Industrialists and their supporters in public office and the media also sought to defame workers by charging that their demands were un-American, socialist, or even communist. Such propaganda was often quite successful.

Lobbying groups who spoke for the industrialists and for business in general were the enemies of the working people and did much to undermine their struggle for a better life. The two most prominent groups were the Chamber of Commerce and the National Association of Manufacturers. Both groups waged a continuing battle against unions, claiming among other things that they were attempts to "Sovietize" the United States. As late as 1938, the National Association of Manufacturers distributed 2,200,000 copies of a pamphlet entitled *Join the CIO And Help Build A Soviet America.*[24]

While American businessmen sometimes cynically used such propaganda to their advantage, many had a deep-seated hatred of working people. When Hitler came to power in Germany as the spokesperson of industry, many American tycoons and lesser lights openly admired him. Henry Ford, J.T. Wilson, president of IBM, and many other industrialists accepted decorations from Hitler.[25] A past president of the National Association of Manufacturers even went so far as to say that "American business might be forced to turn to some form of disguised Fascistic dictatorship."[26]

The charged atmosphere and the forces on the side of industrialists were so disadvantageous to workers that only intense and prolonged efforts on their part could produce any change. The one factor that drove workers on was their chronic poverty. Millions of workers lived in the most abject poverty. The major industrial cities of the North contained millions of impoverished workers living in crowded, unsanitary, life-sapping tenements. The determination to escape this life continued to give workers courage and determination against almost insuperable odds. Below we will examine a few examples of the terrible conflicts that marred the development and recognition of labor unions.

During the 1840s and 1850s, some of the first violence against workers who attempted to organize labor unions occurred. The struggle involved coal miners who worked six days a week, from dawn to dark, for $11 or $12 a week. The mines were so unsafe that death by accident was common. In one Pennsylvania county, 566 miners were killed and 1,655 seriously injured in one seven-year period.[27] Workers' attempts to form unions were met with bloody retaliation by mine owners. The conflict produced the famous Molly Maguires, a secret organization of Irish miners who fought their employers with guns and bombs. But the owners had superior forces, and the struggling unions were literally "shot out of existence."[28]

The depression of 1873 brought increasingly difficult times for millions of workers and their families. The railroads, like most enterprises, lost business and began to reduce the number of employees. In 1877 the railroads ordered a 10 percent wage cut for all employees. To cut down on employees, they also doubled the number of cars per train. The suffering workers struck immediately. The strike began in Martinsburg, West Virginia, on the Baltimore and Ohio line and spread rapidly to other cities. Railroads in Pennsylvania, New York, and New Jersey were almost completely disrupted by strikers and their supporters.

In Cumberland, Maryland, the local militia refused to attack the strikers, many of whom were their friends and relatives. The governor of Maryland attempted to send state militia from Baltimore to Cumberland, but a huge crowd of strikers refused to allow the troop trains to leave the station. A fight broke out between the militia and workers, resulting in 12 fatalities. The angry mob burned the Baltimore and Ohio station.

Violence was considerably more pronounced in Pittsburgh. Again the local militia refused to fight strikers, so the governor sent in militia from Philadelphia. The strikers, their supporters, and, in many instances, their wives and children fought militia men who advanced on them with fixed bayonets. The crowds mostly stoned the militia, who retaliated by firing into the crowds. Ten to twenty persons were killed, and several times that number were wounded. The enraged mob chased the militia into a railroad roundhouse, which was then set on fire. The militia escaped the burning building but had to retreat under gunfire. Having routed the militia, the strikers burned as much of the railroad property as they could. The depot was destroyed along with 104 locomotives and 2,152 cars.[29]

As the conflict grew, larger and larger numbers of militia and federal troops were employed. The forces against the strikers were overwhelming, and eventually the workers were defeated. At the height of the strike, all railroads except those in New England and the South were idled. Ninety persons were killed, and hundreds were wounded. The events in Pittsburgh could easily be described as an insurrection.

Enraged workers in Pittsburgh destroyed railroad buildings, tracks, and cars after battling with the state militia during the 1877 railroad strike.

The Homestead Strike in 1892 is a classic example of an industry using its superior financial and political clout to crush a union. The general manager of the Pennsylvania steel mills was Henry Clay Frick, an ardent foe of unions. Despite the fact that only 25 percent of all steelworkers were members of the union and that wages were pegged to the price of steel, Frick decided to destroy the union. He began by attempting to impose a new contract on the workers, which cut wages by 22 percent and abolished many jobs. The workers, union and nonunion, refused to accept the contract.

Frick retaliated by closing the huge steel mill at Homestead. Frick's intention was to hire an army of Pinkerton police to guard the plant while he brought in scab labor. The workers anticipated Frick's actions and placed an armed picket around the plant. The workers also hired a launch and patrolled the river in hopes of cutting off any scabs or Pinkertons who might attempt to reach the plant by that route. A small army of 300 Pinkertons, armed with Winchester rifles, arrived on the outskirts of town and then boarded two barges in an attempt to reach the plant. The workers discovered the boats, and a battle ensued. The workers vastly outnumbered the Pinkertons and within a day forced them to surrender. The surviving Pinkertons were abused by the mob and then shipped back home by train.

Undaunted, Frick appealed to the governor for National Guard troops. The governor sent in 8,000 soldiers, who provided the cover for scabs brought in to reopen the plant. Frick then decided to administer the final blow through the courts. He charged the workers with murder, riot, and insurrection, and 185 indictments were handed down. To stay out of jail, the workers had to raise over a half million dollars in bail money. These sums bankrupted the union and the unemployed workers and led to the downfall of the strike. Four months after the strike had begun, Frick had won total victory over the workers.

The Pullman Strike of 1894 was another example of owners' contempt for workers and demonstrated the owners' ability to obtain political support in their battles with employees. During the depression of 1893, half of the employees of the Pullman Palace Car Company were laid off, and the other half were working for 80 percent of their normal wages. Most of the workers lived in a company town owned by Pullman. Their rents averaged some 25 percent higher than those paid for comparable accommodations in surrounding communities.

In May 1894, a committee of workers appealed to the company for a restoration of their wages or a reduction in company rents. The company refused and issued job termination orders for three members of the committee. The workers decided to strike and asked their affiliate, the American Railroad Union (ARU), to support them. The ARU agreed and decided not to handle Pullman cars. The ban on Pullman cars quickly spread across the country. Rail traffic out of Chicago was soon completely halted. Pullman workers also set about sabotaging company property. Freight cars were derailed and damaged, and scabs were forcibly removed from trains.

The railroad owners fought back by hiring special police and persuading

The U. S. Cavalry escorts the first train out of Chicago after the 1894 Pullman strike. Railroad owners were able to use special company police, Chicago police, and U. S. Army troops to help defeat the workers.

the Chicago police to join them in waging skirmishes with strikers. Some 2,000 special police were hired, men described by the Chicago superintendent of Police as "thugs, thieves, and exconvicts."[30] The police fought the strikers but were unable to get the trains moving again.

The railroads turned to the federal government for aid. The attorney general was Richard Olney, an ex-railroad lawyer and board member. Olney obtained an *injunction* against blocking trains on the grounds that the mail was being disrupted. The workers ignored the injunction. This gave President Cleveland the grounds to send in federal troops, even though the governor of Illinois objected. For a number of days, battles between troops, the police, and workers raged. Mobs burned hundreds of railroad cars. By early July, there were 14,000 police officers and troops in Chicago fighting the workers, and these superior numbers finally overwhelmed them. During the strike, violence occurred in at least seven states, thirty-four persons were killed, and property damage ran into the millions.

The violence surrounding miners' attempts to obtain union recognition and decent wages parallels the mayhem that characterized the struggle between industrial management and workers. In an era of violence between capitalists and workers, some of the mine strikes were exceptionally violent, even by the blood-stained standards of the day. Some of the ugliest battles occurred during the strike of silver and lead mines at Coeur d'Alene, Idaho, in 1892. The miners in Idaho were well organized in 1892 and had forced a uniform wage on the mine owners. The owners formed the Mine Owners Protective Association and sought to force a 25 percent cut in miners' pay.

When the miners refused to accept the reduction, the owners locked them out of the mines. To take their employees' places, the owners imported hundreds of scabs. The workers tried to convince the scabs to join their ranks but had little success. Several small clashes occurred between union members and Pinkerton guards, one of which resulted in the death of a striker. Enraged by the killing, the strikers dynamited the Pinkerton barracks at Frisco Mill, killing one guard and wounding 20 others. Becoming increasingly militant, the strikers marched on the local mines and managed to capture each of them after pitched battles. The strikers then drove most of the scabs out of town.

The governor of Idaho reacted by declaring the area in a state of insurrection. He sent in the state militia, backed up by federal troops. The scabs were brought back, and some 600 strikers were arrested and detained in bullpens. All union miners not arrested were fired. The courts eventually ordered the release of most of the miners, and the strike continued. The inability of the owners to run the mines without experienced help caused most of them to accept union workers and give in to their demands. Two owners who refused to accept the unions fought pitched battles with workers again in 1899.[31]

Coeur d'Alene was a minor skirmish compared to the thirty-year war that occurred in the Colorado coal towns between 1884 and 1914. The Colorado violence peaked in 1913–14 when the United Mine Workers (UMW) made another in a long series of attempts to force the owners to recognize their union. The UMW asked the governor to arrange a conference between union representatives and the mine owners. The governor tried, but the owners refused to meet with union representatives. A strike was called, and the union asked the governor to force the owners to obey a number of state laws they had long ignored. Some of the laws involved safety standards; others guaranteed workers certain personal rights, such as the freedom to make purchases at stores of their choice (rather than just at the company-owned stores).

> *In an era of violence between capitalists and workers, some of the mine strikes were exceptionally violent, even by the blood-stained standards of the day.*

The owners decided to use battle tactics to defeat the union. All strikers were evicted from company-owned towns, and a mercenary army was formed by importing agents who were deputized by the local sheriff. Owners hired spies to infiltrate the ranks of the strikers, most of whom now lived in tent cities. Automobiles and a train were fitted with armored plate and machine guns. The company police began to wage war against the strikers. Tent colonies were attacked, and meetings of workers were fired upon. The strikers fought back, and several casualties resulted.

To stem the violence, the governor sent the National Guard into the area, but they quickly became the agents of the mine owners. As an official government report noted, "By April, 1914 the Colorado National Guard no longer offered even a pretense of fairness or impartiality, and its units in the field had degenerated into a force of professional gunmen and adventurers who were economically dependent on and subservient to the will of the coal operators."[32]

Strikers were beaten and harassed, and their wives and daughters molested. The company police and National Guard began to wage more attacks on the tent cities. In an unusually brutal attack, the police and National Guard fired on the tent city at Ludlow with machine guns, killing five strikers and a young boy. The troops then set the tent city on fire, killing two women and eleven children. Three strikers taken prisoner were beaten and executed by the troops.

Enraged by such atrocities, an army of 700 to 1,000 armed strikers went on a rampage. The strikers went from mine to mine, destroying and killing. One historian described the ensuing ten-day rebellion as a period of "anarchy and unrestrained class warfare."[33] President Wilson sent federal troops into the area to bring the violence to an end. Before the fighting ended, seventy-four persons were killed, hundreds wounded, and extensive property damage done. President Wilson tried to help the union negotiate with the owners, but the owners refused to meet even with the President. In December 1914 the miners accepted defeat, and the strike ended.

The period from 1911 to 1916 was perhaps the bloodiest in American history outside of the Civil War era. Hundreds of strikes occurred, many involving violence, some ending in company victories, some being resolved in favor of workers. The strikes ranged across the United States and involved railroads, textiles, timber, iron, coal, and copper mines, oil refineries, longshoremen, streetcar conductors, and farm workers.

During World War I strikes subsided, but after the war workers who had refrained from striking for patriotic reasons decided the time was ripe for advances. Strikes increased but were still met with organized and armed resistance and increasingly with charges of subversion, communism, and bolshevism. Violence by owners and their hired police was increasingly justified by red-baiting propaganda labeling the workers as foreign agents. The increasing use of such propaganda served as a powerful weapon against workers.

A good example of the red-baiting approach was the steel strike of 1919. Steel workers in Indiana and Pennsylvania had tried for years to bargain with management but had been rebuffed. In 1919 the United States Steelworkers tried again to obtain a bargaining conference with management. The owners refused all dealings with the union. Elbert Gary of United States Steel refused to talk with the union, despite pleas from the President of the United States, ministers, and other prominent persons. In response, the union called a general strike, and some 250,000 workers left their jobs.

The owners resorted to immediate brutality. Thousands of special police were hired. The police guarded the plants and waged battles against strikers. Meetings and even casual gatherings of strikers were attacked, and pickets were ridden down by mounted police. Strikebreakers were imported, most of whom were poor and unsuspecting blacks. The strikers attacked the scabs and police on numerous occasions in small skirmishes, which produced a number of casualties. On October 4, a riot broke out in Gary, Indiana, which was dispersed by an army of militia and special police. The next day brought more rioting with strikers fighting scabs and storming the gates of the steel plant.

Federal troops arrived and took up sides against the strikers. The Army Commander, General Leonard Wood, called the strike a red insurrection and vowed to crush it. The Army fought the strikers, broke up their meetings, raided their headquarters, and spread the message that a red plot was in progress. The newspapers, which during the nineteenth and first half of the twentieth centuries were predominantly the enemies of workers, also spread the word that an attempted revolution was in progress. The steel owners' superior forces, plus the loss of public support caused by the propaganda campaign, led to the collapse of the strike. The mills were finally unionized in the 1930s.

Another steel workers' strike provides perhaps the most graphic illustration of the brutality that characterized the struggle between management and workers in the nineteenth and the first half of the twentieth century. In 1937 many steel companies, such as Bethlehem, Republic, Youngstown Sheet and Tube, and Inland, had not yet recognized unions. In 1937 the Congress of Industrial Organization (CIO) struck these plants. Republic decided to crush the strike by hiring and housing scabs within the plants, and by hiring guards to keep the strikers away from the plant. The Chicago police, being hostile to the strikers, protected the strikebreakers and harassed union pickets.

On Memorial Day, 1937, a group of 2,000 to 3,000 strikers decided to throw a massive picket around Republic Steel. The strikers marched toward the plant, but were intercepted by the Chicago police. The police refused to allow the marchers to proceed, and then fired into the ranks without warning. The ensuing melee was filmed by Paramount Pictures. The film captured the horror of the scene so profoundly that it is worth a lengthy description. The following account was written by a *St. Louis Post-Dispatch* reporter who witnessed a number of screenings of the film at a congressional meeting chaired by Senator Robert La Follette.[34]

> The first scenes show police drawn up in a long line across a dirt road which runs diagonally through a large open field before turning into a street which is parallel to, and some 200 yards distant from, the high fence surrounding the Republic mill. The police line extends 40 or 50 yards on each side of the dirt road. Behind the line, and in the street beyond, nearer the mill, are several patrol wagons and numerous reserve squads of police.
>
> Straggling across the field, in a long irregular line, headed by two men carrying American flags, the demonstrators are shown approaching. Many carry placards.

They appear to number about 300—approximately the same as the police—although it is known that some 2,000 strike sympathizers were watching the march from a distance.

A vivid close-up shows the head of the parade being halted at the police line. The flag-bearers are in front. Behind them the placards are massed. They bear such devices as : "Come on Out—Help Win the Strike;" "Republic vs. the People," and "C.I.O."Between the flag-bearers is the marchers' spokesman, a muscular young man in shirtsleeves, with a C.I.O. button on the band of his felt hat.

He is arguing earnestly with a police officer who appears to be in command. His vigorous gestures indicate that he is insisting on permission to continue through the police line but in the general din of yelling and talking his words cannot be distinguished. His expression is serious, but no suggestion of threat or violence is apparent. The police officer, whose back is to the camera, makes one impatient gesture of refusal, and says something which cannot be understood.

Then suddenly, without apparent warning, there is a terrific roar of pistol shots, and men in the front ranks of the marchers go down like grass before a scythe. The camera catches approximately a dozen falling simultaneously in a heap. The massive, sustained roar of the police pistols lasts perhaps two or three seconds.

Instantly the police charge on the marchers with riot sticks flying. At the same time tear gas grenades are seen sailing into the mass of demonstrators, and clouds of gas rise over them. Most of the crowd is now in flight. The only discernible case of resistance is that of a marcher with a placard on a stick, which he uses in an attempt to fend off a charging policeman. He is successful for only an instant. Then he goes down under a shower of blows.

The scenes which follow are among the most harrowing of the picture. Although the ground is strewn with dead and wounded, and the mass of the marchers are in precipitate flight down the dirt road and across the field, a number of individuals, either through foolish hardihood, or because they have not yet realized what grim and deadly business is in progress around them, have remained behind, caught in the midst of the charging police.

In a manner which is appallingly businesslike, groups of policemen close in on these isolated individuals, and go to work on them with their clubs. In several instances, from two to four policemen are seen beating one man. One strikes him horizontally across the face, using his club as he would wield a baseball bat. Another crashes it down on top of his head and still another is whipping him across the back.

These men try to protect their heads with their arms but it is only . matter of a second or two until they go down. In one such scene, directly in the foreground, a policeman gives the fallen man a final smash on the head, before moving on to the next job.

In the front line during the parley with the police is a girl, not more than five feet tall, who can hardly weigh more than 100 pounds. Under one arm she is carrying a purse and some newspapers. After the first deafening volley of shots she turns to find that her path to flight is blocked by a heap of fallen men. She stumbles over them, apparently dazed.

The scene shifts for a moment, then she is seen going down under a quick blow from a policeman's club, delivered from behind. She gets up, and staggers

Police used guns, tear gas, and clubs to stop striking steel workers from forming a picket around the Republic plant on Memorial Day, 1937 Throughout the nineteenth and early twentieth centuries, workers' attempts to strike or unionize frequently resulted in violence between workers and owners and their agents.

around. A few moments later she is shown being shoved into a patrol wagon, as blood cascades down her face and spreads over her clothing.

Preceding this episode, however, is a scene which, for sheer horror, outdoes the rest. A husky, middle-aged, bare-headed man has found himself caught far behind the rear ranks of the fleeing marchers. Between him and the others, policemen are as thick as flies, but he elects to run the gauntlet. Astonishingly agile for one of his age and build, he runs like a deer, leaping a ditch, dodging as he goes. Surprised policemen take hasty swings as he passes them. Some get him on the back, some on the back of the head, but he keeps his feet, and keeps going.

The scene is bursting with a frightful sort of drama. Will he make it? The suspense is almost intolerable to those who watch. It begins to look as if he will get through. But no! The police in front have turned around now, and are waiting for him. Still trying desperately, he swings to the right. He has put his hands up, and is holding them high above his head as he runs.

It is no use. There are police on the right. He is cornered. He turns, still holding high his hands. Quickly the bluecoats close in, and the night sticks fly—above his head, from the side, from the rear. His upraised arms fall limply under the flailing blows, and he slumps to the ground in a twisting fall, as the clubs continue to rain on him. . . .

Ensuing scenes are hardly less poignant. A man shot through the back is paralyzed from the waist. Two policemen try to make him stand up, to get into a patrol wagon, but when they let him go his legs crumple, and he falls with his face in the dirt, almost under the rear step of the wagon. He moves his head and arms, but his legs are limp. He raises his head like a turtle, and claws the ground. . . .

The scene shifts to the patrol wagons in the rear. Men with bloody heads, bloody faces, bloody shirts, are being loaded in. One who apparently has been shot in the leg, drags himself painfully into the picture with the aid of two policemen. An elderly man, bent almost double, holding one hand on the back of his head, clambers painfully up the steps and slumps onto the seat, burying his face in both hands. The shoulders of his white shirt are drenched with blood.

There is continuous talking, but it is difficult to distinguish anything with one exception—out of the babble there rises this clear and distinct ejaculation: "God Almighty!"

The camera shifts back to the central scene. . . . A policeman, somewhat disheveled, his coat open, a scowl on his face, approaches another who is standing in front of the camera. He is sweaty and tired. He says something indistinguishable. Then his face breaks into a sudden grin, he makes a motion of dusting off his hands, and strides away. The film ends.

Labor violence decreased considerably after 1940, but isolated instances of violence resulting from strikes and organizing efforts continue to the present.

RACIAL VIOLENCE

As noted in the introduction, racial violence has taken three major forms: slave revolts, race riots, and ghetto riots. Each in their own way shows groups using violence to achieve ends that could not be gained through conventional political participation. Racial violence has punctuated American history so often, and with such intensity, that deaths and injuries resulting from such conflict dwarf all other forms of violence that have been surveyed here combined. Blacks have overwhelmingly been the victims of this violence.

Slave revolts

The slaves, of course, had no lawful recourse to rectify their grievances. Their only alternatives to passive acceptance were to fight their masters, flee, or engage in limited, mostly masked acts of retaliation against the person or property of slaveholders. The latter options were chosen much more frequently than organized violence against owners. While there were a number of slave revolts, few involved substantial injuries to whites, and none freed large numbers of slaves or improved their treatment. To the contrary, slave insurrections, or even rumors of revolts, were smashed with immediate and brute force. The brutality of white suppression apparently explains why there were fewer slave insurrections in America than in most other slave countries.

The first recorded slave revolt occurred in New York in 1712.[35] A number of slaves organized a conspiracy to set their owners' outhouses on fire and then murder them when they came outside to investigate or fight the blaze. They managed to kill nine whites and wound others before the militia ended the rebellion. Most of the rebels were captured, and twenty-four were sentenced to death. Six of the sentences were reprieved, but the other slaves were hanged or burned. The sentence of one rebel ordered that he be "burned with a slow fire that he may continue in torment for eight or ten hours and continue burning in the said fire until he be dead and consumed to ashes."[36] Twenty-nine years later a slave conspiracy led to death verdicts for 13 other slaves in the same city.

A number of minor revolts occurred in Louisiana between 1790 and the early 1800s, but none was very serious. However, in each case twenty-five to sixty slaves were killed in skirmishes and resulting executions. A more serious uprising occurred in 1811 when 500 slaves wounded their owner, killed his son, and then marched on New Orleans. The slaves burned a few plantations along the way. The slaves were met by a large contingent consisting of militia and federal troops. The troops easily defeated the slaves, killing seventy to eighty of them. Sixteen slave leaders were tried and executed. As a warning, the heads of the sixteen executed leaders were placed on poles along the Mississippi River.

In Charleston, South Carolina, in 1822 a rumor spread that a slave revolt was in the offing. Many blacks were questioned and abused, but most revealed no knowledge of a conspiracy. Finally, two slaves implicated a few others in a supposed plot, and six slaves were hung. The hanging only increased hostility and fears on both sides and caused another round of accusations and trials. This led to the execution of another 35 slaves, and the deportation of many others. Historians are not certain that any plot was ever contemplated.[37]

The most famous of all slave revolts was the Virginia uprising led by Nat Turner in 1831. Turner had taught himself to read and had become a religious leader among local blacks. He came to believe that the Bible willed him to lead a revolt against white slave owners. Turner precipitated his plot, taking an eclipse as God's signal, by leading an attack on his master's family, killing all of them. His forces then marched on surrounding plantations, killing all whites they encountered. Some sixty whites were killed. On the third day of the revolt the rebels were engaged by white militia and were defeated rather easily. After hasty trials, twenty of the rebels were hung, and one hundred other blacks were slaughtered by whites who went on a vicious retaliatory rampage.

Slave revolts were always brutally suppressed, and none succeeded in freeing large numbers of slaves. For many slaves, the only recourse was to escape. The broadside (right) offers a reward for the return of three fugitive slaves.

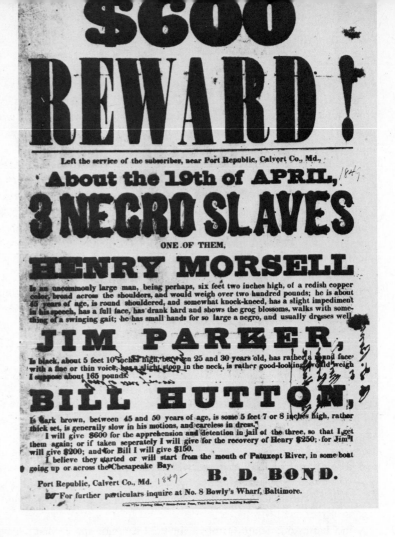

$600 REWARD!

Left the service of the subscriber, near Port Republic, Calvert Co., Md.,

About the 19th of APRIL, 1849

3 NEGRO SLAVES

ONE OF THEM,

HENRY MORSELL

Is an uncommonly large man, being perhaps, six feet two inches high, of a redish copper color, broad across the shoulders, and would weigh over two hundred pounds; he is about 45 years of age, is round shouldered, and somewhat knock-kneed, has a slight impediment in his speech, has a full face, has drank hard and shows the grog blossoms, walks with something of a swinging gait; he has small hands for so large a negro, and usually dresses well.

JIM PARKER,

Is black, about 5 feet 10 inches high, between 25 and 30 years old, has rather a round face with a fine or thin voice, has a slight stoop in the neck, is rather good-looking, would weigh I suppose about 165 pounds.

BILL HUTTON,

Is dark brown, between 45 and 50 years of age, is some 5 feet 7 or 8 inches high, rather thick set, is generally slow in his motions, and careless in dress.
  I will give $600 for the apprehension and detention in jail of the three, so that I get them again; or if taken seperately I will give for the recovery of Henry $250; for Jim I will give $200; and for Bill I will give $150.
  I believe they started or will start from the mouth of Patuxent River, in some boat going up or across the Chesapeake Bay.

B. D. BOND.

Port Republic, Calvert Co., Md. 1849

☞ For further particulars inquire at No. 8 Bowly's Wharf, Baltimore.

From "The Printing Office," Steam-Power Press, Third Story Sun Iron Building Baltimore.

The last major slave insurrection occurred in Texas in 1860. If an actual plot existed, its details are not well known. What is known is that an arsonist burned much of the business sector of Dallas, and seven other cities were seriously damaged by fire all in one day. Over the next few weeks some of these same towns and others suffered serious fires. The rumor spread that abolitionists and slaves were engaged in an insurrection designed to destroy white property and lives. Blacks subjected to torture began to "confess." Vigilantes began to hold trials and hang or burn white abolitionists and their supposed black followers. Seventy-five to one hundred persons were killed. Vigilantes continued to harass and terrorize blacks and abolitionists for several months. Such harsh measures were, of course, typical of white reaction to black resistance or to rumors of contemplated resistance.

The slave rebellions reveal familiar insights. They show suppressed people using extralegal methods in an attempt to achieve ends not obtainable through the political process. And they show official violence being used as a supplement to, or even as an extension of, political power.

Race riots

No group of Americans has suffered more persecution than black citizens. Whether blacks lived in free sections of the country or under the yoke of slavery, whites have tended to be prejudiced toward them ever since colonial days. They have attempted to suppress blacks through legal and extralegal means. Much of the violence had an economic antecedent. Prosperous whites wanted to keep blacks suppressed so that they could be economically exploited and poor whites tried to kill blacks or frighten them out of their community so that they would not have to compete with them for scarce jobs. Black retaliation or resistance to white terror only served as an excuse for whites to unleash maniacal brutality. Meier and Rubruick describe the pattern: "In each of these conflagrations, the typical pattern was initial Negro retaliation to white acts of persecution and violence, and white perception of this resistance as an organized, premeditated conspiracy to 'take over,' thus unleashing the massive armed power of white mobs and police."[38]

Racial violence has punctuated American history so often, and with such intensity, that deaths and injuries resulting from such conflicts dwarf all other forms of violence that have been surveyed here combined.

Black retaliation leading to riots resulted only when the tolerance levels of blacks reached the breaking point. As the sections below will show, white violence against blacks was a consistent pattern, weaving a tapestry of death and injury across American history.

Some of the first notable race riots occurred in Providence, Rhode Island, in the early nineteenth century. Most Providence blacks had been freed in the late eighteenth century, but they were still treated as inferiors, exploited, and often attacked by whites. In 1824 a riot led to the burning of the black section of town, and many blacks left the state. In 1831 whites again attacked the black community, leaving four dead and fourteen wounded.

Like New England, the old Northwest was anti-slavery, but it was also anti-black. In Cincinnati in 1841, for example, black citizens were given sixty days to post a bond of $500 each, or leave the state. Before the deadline was up, whites attacked the black district, murdering and looting. Again in 1841, Irish workers, incensed by black competition for jobs, attacked the black district, destroying property and killing innocent citizens.

The period following the Civil War was one of the most violent in American history. Racists throughout the South and in many border states adopted civil violence as the method of denying blacks the freedom won by the war. Hysterical, fanatical, and merciless whites sought to reestablish slavery in all but name by brute force. Bands of ex-Confederate soldiers frequently acted as vigilantes, killing, beating, and raping blacks.

In 1866 such a group savagely attacked blacks in Memphis and burned their homes, churches, and schools. A similar incident in South Carolina in 1870 left thirteen people dead and hundreds wounded. In Arkansas in 1868 white mobs took over the courts, killed civilian authorities, and murdered hundreds of blacks. One authority estimated that between 1868 and 1870 in Texas alone, one thousand blacks per year were murdered. In Louisiana the estimate was 3,500 casualties between 1866 and 1875; 1,884 of these were deaths and injuries occurring in 1868.[39] Many of these deaths resulted from riots, others from what were termed "nigger hunts." White vigilantes simply went on rampages, killing any blacks that could be found. One such "hunt" resulted in 262 black deaths.[40] Official records show that between 1882 and 1903 lynch mobs hung and burned 1,985 southern blacks.[41] Blacks often fought back, even on occasion forming militias, but were generally no match for the superior numbers and arms of white mobs.

The slave rebellions show suppressed people using extralegal methods in an attempt to achieve ends not obtainable through the political process. And they show official violence being used as a supplement to, or even as an extension of, political power.

One of several instances in which the civil government was overthrown by a mob intent on reestablishing white supremacy occurred in North Carolina in 1898. In 1894 a Republican had been elected governor, and five blacks had been elected to the state legislature. Blacks began to receive some patronage, holding such offices as justice of the peace, alderman, and postmaster. The Democratic party decided to reverse these gains through intimidation. A vigilante committee began to murder blacks and issued a public threat against any black who attempted to vote in the 1898 elections. Blacks were turned away from the polls by armed mobs, and the Democrats won the election.

Two days later a white vigilante committee in Wilmington, North Carolina, went on a rampage, killing blacks indiscriminately, burning a black newspaper, and forcing the mayor (a Republican) and all black officials to resign their offices. The state legislature, now controlled by Democrats, instituted the poll tax and the *grandfather clause* to strip blacks of the franchise. Actions such as these occurred throughout the South, leading to another fifty or sixty years of the suppression of blacks.

Tensions between the races were always intense, even in the Midwest and North. Vigilante groups terrorized blacks, courts frequently were rigged against them, and clashes between the races occurred with some regularity. Between 1900 and 1949 there were thirty-three serious race riots.[42]

Typical of such conflicts was the East St. Louis riot of 1917. This clash resulted from white hostility toward the increasing black community, which provided a pool of low-priced labor—labor which sometimes replaced white workers. When a strike at a local aluminum plant was broken, partly because white and black strikebreakers had been used, the white union decided to drive blacks out of the city. A riot resulted in which bands of whites attacked black property and any blacks they could lay hands on. Over 300 buildings were destroyed, and 100 blacks were killed. A few excerpts from an account of the riot reveal the wholesale savagery that occurred:[43]

> Right here I saw the most sickening incident of the evening. To put the rope around the negro's neck, one of the lynchers stuck his finger inside the gaping scalp and lifted the negro's head by it, literally bathing his hand in the man's blood.

> "Get hold, and pull for East St. Louis!" called a man with a black coat and a new straw hat, as he seized the other end of the rope. . . . This time the negro was lifted to a height of about seven feet from the ground. The body was left hanging there . . . .

> A few negroes, caught on the street, were kicked and shot to death. As flies settled on their terrible wounds, the gaping-mouthed mobsmen forbade the dying blacks to brush them off. Girls with blood on their stockings helped to kick in what had been black faces of the corpses on the street.

> The crowd then turned to Black Valley. Here the greatest fire damage was caused. Flames soon were raging and the shrieking rioters stood about in the streets, made lurid by the flames, and shot and beat negroes as they fled from their burning homes.

> They pursued the women who were driven out of the burning homes, with the idea, not of extinguishing their burning clothing, but of inflicting added pain if possible. They stood around in groups, laughing and jeering, while they witnessed the final writhings of the terror and pain-wracked wretches who crawled to the streets to die after their flesh had been cooked in their own homes.

The Chicago riot of 1919 resulted from many of the same tensions that led to the East St. Louis riot. The black population of Chicago doubled between 1916 and 1919, frightening and alienating many whites who felt blacks would take over their neighborhoods and jobs. Blacks returning from World War I were also more militant and refused to passively accept white harassment. Tensions erupted in numerous small clashes, which resulted in a number of deaths and the bombing of 24 black homes during June and July of 1919.[44] In July a black youth swimming in Lake Michigan drowned after being stoned by a white mob. This touched off a riot that lasted seven days. Some 30 black and white people died, over 500 were injured, and about 1,000 persons were left homeless. Serious race riots also occurred during that year in Omaha, Charleston, Washington, D.C., Longview, Texas and Knoxville, Tennessee. Two years later a riot in Tulsa, Oklahoma, resulted in as many as 150 black deaths. A riot in Detroit in 1943 caused considerable property damage and 34 deaths, 25 of them blacks.[45]

Ghetto riots

The ghetto riots in the 1960s represented a turning point in the long saga of black suppression in America. The riots resulted not from reactions to specific acts of white brutality, but from an accumulation of grievances stemming from the persistent racism that bore down on black citizens day in and day out. Pervasive racism and grinding poverty turned black ghettos into tinder boxes that simply reached the point of combustion and exploded into conflagrations.

The continuing racism and deprivation that blacks suffered became particularly unbearable because of the struggle for racial equality then occurring in the nation. In 1954 the Supreme Court had decreed the end of school segregation,[46] setting off a wave of civil-rights activities. Throughout the South, black and white civil-rights workers struggled against racist police, judges and citizens to end racism in its many forms. Presidents Kennedy and Johnson both expressed sympathy for the goal of black equality, giving blacks hope for a better life. But changes came slowly. Blacks anticipated the fulfillment of promises while struggling daily under racism and its consequences. The contradictions were intolerable, and the resulting frustration led to some 200 black ghetto riots.

At the height of the ghetto conflict, a federal commission studied twenty-three of the most serious riots.[47] Their findings shocked much of the nation. The commission blamed the riots directly on white racism: "White racism is essentially responsible for the explosive mixture which has been accumulating in our cities since the end of World War II. . . . What white Americans have never fully understood—but what the negro can never forget—is that white society is deeply implicated in the ghetto. White institutions created it, white institutions maintain it, and white society condones it."[48] In addition, the commission found that the riots could not be blamed on a small criminal element in each community. They found that a significant proportion of the ghetto residents participated in the riots and that a large segment of the residents supported the riots.[49] The commission also concluded that the riots did not result from communist conspiracies (as some had claimed), nor were they organized.

Among the other reasons for the riots noted by the commission, two should sound familiar at this point in our analysis:[50]

1. A climate that tends toward approval and encouragement of violence as a form of protest has been created by white terrorism directed against nonviolent protest; by the open defiance of law and federal authority by state and local officials resisting desegregation; and by some protest groups engaging in civil disobedience who turn their backs on nonviolence, go beyond the constitutionally protected rights of petition and free assembly, and resort to violence to attempt to compel alteration of laws and policies with which they disagree.
2. The frustrations of powerlessness have led some blacks to the conviction that there is no effective alternative to violence as a means of achieving redress of grievances, and of moving the system.

While the ghetto riots generally happened in the 1960s, one similar riot occurred as early as 1935. In that year Harlem simply erupted. Harlem in the 1930s was a prison for foodless, jobless, and increasingly hopeless people. All the normally severe deprivations of the black population were magnified by the Great Depression. Discrimination was pervasive in Harlem, with white merchants who depended upon blacks for trade refusing to hire black employees. Even city services in Harlem were provided by all-white crews.

Some of the residents began to picket stores that refused to hire black employees. Most of these efforts were frustrated, however, when owners obtained injunctions. The intervention of the courts on the side of white businessmen increased hostility considerably. To add to the tensions, the white police who patrolled Harlem frequently clashed with the black residents. Police brutality became a major grievance of the residents. When a crowd of blacks believed that the police intended to beat a black teenager arrested for shoplifting, they gathered on a corner and began giving speeches condemning police brutality. When these speakers were beaten and arrested by the police, the riot exploded.

Black mobs concentrated not on killing whites, but on destroying white property in the ghetto. Over 200 stores were looted, including many that blacks had been picketing. One black was killed and over 100 other persons were injured.[51]

The riots of the 1960s followed a similar pattern. They occurred in hundreds of cities, and more than one disturbance occurred in some cities. Three of the most severe riots were the Watts riots of 1965 and the Detroit and Newark riots of 1967.

Watts, a black community in Los Angeles, erupted in August, 1965 (the 1960s riots tended to be summer events). During a period of national prosperity and promise, Watts was an island of unemployment and deprivation. Tensions were high, needing only a spark to set them off. The spark came in the form of rumors. The word traveled through Watts that the police had beaten a black taxi driver and a pregnant woman. Bands consisting primarily of teenagers and children began to stone police cars driven by whites. The police tried to disperse the crowds, but they only grew larger. The crowds then began to loot and burn white-owned businesses.

Riot police and the National Guard were called in, and six days of battle ensued. When the battle was over, 600 buildings had been burned or seriously damaged, with estimated damage of $40 million. Thirty-four persons suffered mortal wounds, and another 1,032 were injured. Four thousand persons were arrested. Estimates of resident participation in the riot varied from 7,000 to 10,000.[52]

One of the youths in the initial crowd of rock throwers explained his reasons for joining the riot:

Like why, man, should I go home? These _____ cops have been pushin' me 'round all my life. Kickin' my _____ and things like that. Whitey ain't no good. He talked 'bout law and order, it's his law and his order, it ain't mine. . . .

_____, if I've got to die, I ain't dying in Vietnam, I'm going to die here. . . .

I don't have no job. I ain't worked for two years. _____ He, the white man, got everythin', I ain't got nothin'. What you expect me to do? . . .

They always _____ with the Blood beatin' with sticks, handcuffing women, I saw one of them _____ go up side a cat's head and split it wide open. They've been doin' it for years. Look how they treated us when we were slaves—we still slaves. . . .

Whitey use his cops to keep us here. We are like pigs in a pen. . . .[53]

The summer of 1967 witnessed the peak in ghetto riots. During 1967 some 164 urban disorders occurred, resulting in untold property damage, and some 90 deaths. The two major riots were in Newark and Detroit. The Detroit riot began when the police raided five illegal drinking and gambling spots, arresting some 80 persons. Crowds gathered and began to stone the police cars carrying the patrons to jail. Through the night the crowds increased to thousands, and looting and burning began.

The Detroit riot (below) in 1967 was one of the most serious urban disorders of the 1960s. Forty-three people died, and millions of dollars of property was destroyed.

At first the outnumbered police simply stood by as looting occurred. Then the mayor called in the National Guard, who were backed up by Army paratroopers. The amateurish performance of the National Guard contributed significantly to the death and destruction that followed. Any rumor of snipers or any sound of a gun shot caused the nervous Guardsmen to unleash a torrent of shots, often in the wrong direction. If there was even a rumor of a gun shot from a building, fifty-caliber machine guns were often used to strafe the building. Many innocent bystanders were killed.

Other homicides resulted from real snipers, from police shooting looters, and from store owners and employees fighting looters. The police acted with extreme brutality. Arrested blacks were often beaten and abused, many requiring hospitalization. In one documented instance a black woman under arrest was forced to strip by police who photographed and molested her.[54]

When the riot ended, property damage was in the millions, and forty-three persons were dead.

The riots of the 1960s appear to have served the function of traditional political participation: they increased the policy influence of blacks in the political system. The riots brought attention to the conditions under which black Americans continue to live and forced public officials to deal with some of these problems. Could blacks have achieved these ends without resorting to violence (see Chapter 17)?

CONCLUSIONS

In this chapter, we have surveyed some of the types of violence that have been such a prominent part of American history. We have attempted to show some of the dimensions and intensity of this violence. While the survey is illustrative rather than exhaustive, it shows that American history has been quite violent. It also shows that violence has often been employed by groups who perceived no other way to achieve their political ends. Groups who are greatly disadvantaged in terms of personal wealth and political influence frequently turn to violence to compensate for their lack of influence in the political system.

Those with power, on the other hand, have frequently used violence as a political resource. Privileged groups have often hired agents to use violence against workers or tenants. At times, they have used the police, militia, and the army to do their bidding. The ability of elites to draw on such power resources has often allowed them to overwhelm disadvantaged groups. Thus farmers and workers have had to struggle mightily throughout our history to gain the concessions from elites that have given them a better life-style.

When the public's role in such events as farmer, union, and civil-rights movements is considered, it becomes obvious that the public has played a larger role in shaping American society—politically, economically, and socially—than raw voting scores or other measures of traditional political participation would indicate. On many occasions throughout history, elites have clearly been forced to yield concessions to labor, farmer, and racial groups in order to stop agitation and to regain public allegiance and obedience to government authority. The concessions made may not have fundamentally altered the distribution of political power or wealth, but they have not been inconsequential.

That groups throughout American history have often felt it necessary to resort to violence to overcome their political and economic deprivation indicates, of course, some serious inequities in political power. Slowly, these inequities have been lessened. While probably no one would argue that the public and its allies are as powerful as big business and its supporters, the inequity is not nearly as severe as it was throughout most of American history. Thus, the biases of the political system that have frequently allowed property owners to use state powers to keep the public suppressed have been diminished in more recent years, if not completely alleviated.

Footnotes

1. Charles Tilly, "Collective Violence in European Perspective," in Hugh Davis Graham and Ted Robert Gurr, eds., *The History of Violence in America* (New York: Bantam Books, 1969), p. 42.
2. Richard Maxwell Brown, "Historical Patterns of Violence in America," in Graham and Gurr, *Violence in America*, p. 75.
3. See Ted Robert Gurr, *Rogues, Rebels, and Reformers* (Beverly Hills: Sage Publications, 1976), pp. 77–79.
4. See, for example, the classifications used by Brown in "Historical Patterns of Violence in America," pp. 45–84.
5. See Richard Hofstadter and Michael Wallace, eds., *American Violence: A Documentary History* (New York: Random House, 1970), p. 60.
6. Rebecca Brooks Gruver, *An American History* (Reading, Mass.: Addison-Wesley, 1976), p. 124.
7. *Ibid.*, p. 127.
8. Hofstadter and Wallace, *American Violence*, p. 212.
9. Samuel Gompers, "Seventy Years of Life and Labor," cited in Hofstadter and Wallace, *American Violence*, p. 346–47.
10. *Ibid.*, p. 347.
11. Cited in James David Barber, *The Presidential Character* (Englewood Cliffs, N.J.: Prentice-Hall, 1977), p. 31.
12. *Rights in Conflict: The Violent Confrontation of Demonstrators and Police in the Parks and Streets of Chicago During the Week of the Democratic National Convention of 1968. A Report Submitted by Daniel Walker, Director of the Chicago Study Team, To the National Commission on the Causes and Prevention of Violence (1968).*
13. See Hofstadter and Wallace, *American Violence*, p. 109.
14. *Ibid.*, p. 118.
15. *Ibid.*, p. 119.
16. *Ibid.*, p. 173.
17. Richard O. Boyer and Herbert M. Morais, *Labor's Untold Story* (New York: United Electrical, Radio and Machine Workers of America, 1976), p. 262.

18. Philip Taft and Philip Ross, "American Labor Violence: Its Causes, Character, and Outcome," in Graham and Gurr, *Violence in America,* p. 281.

19. *Ibid.,* p. 380.

20. Boyer and Morais, *Labor's Untold Story,* p. 78.

21. *Ibid.,* p. 65.

22. *Ibid.,* p. 141.

23. *Ibid.,* p. 65.

24. *Ibid.,* p. 317.

25. *Ibid.,* p. 320.

26. *Ibid.,* p. 320.

27. Taft and Ross, "American Labor Violence," p. 300.

28. Boyer and Morais, *Labor's Untold Story,* p. 46.

29. Hofstadter and Wallace, *American Violence,* p. 133.

30. *Ibid.,* pp. 151–52.

31. *Ibid.,* p. 148

32. George P. West, *Report on the Colorado Strike,* United States Commission on Industrial Relations, 1915, p. 101.

33. Brown, "Historical Patterns of Violence in America," pp. 74–75.

34. Donald G. Sofchalk, "The Chicago Memorial Day Incident: An Episode of Mass Action," *Labor History,* 6 (Winter 1965): 3–43.

35. Hofstadter and Wallace, *American Violence,* p. 188.

36. *Ibid.,* p. 188.

37. *Ibid.,* pp. 193–94.

38. August Meier and Elliot Rubwick, "Black Violence in the 20th Century: A Study of Rhetoric and Retaliation," in Graham and Gurr, *Violence in America,* p. 404.

39. Hofstadter and Wallace, *American Violence,* pp. 223–24.

40. *Ibid.,* p. 55.

41. Brown, "Historical Patterns of Violence in America," p. 50.

42. *Ibid.,* p. 55.

43. W. E. B. DuBois and Martha Gruening, "Massacre at East St. Louis," *Crisis* 14(1918): 222–38; cited in Hofstadter and Wallace, *American Violence,* pp. 242–45.

44. Hofstadter and Wallace, *American Violence,* p. 250.

45. *Ibid.,* p. 254.

46. *Brown* v. *Board of Education,* 347 U.S. 483(1954).

47. *Report of the National Advisory Commission on Civil Disorders* (1968).

48. *Ibid.,* pp. 2, 10.

49. *Ibid.,* p. 127. See also Charles S. Bullock, III, and Harrell R. Rodgers, Jr., *Racial Equality in America: In Search of an Unfulfilled Goal* (Pacific Palisades, Ca.: Goodyear Publishing Co., 1975), pp. 141–68.

50. *Ibid.,* pp. 10–11.

51. Hofstadter and Wallace, *American Violence,* pp. 258–62.

52. *Ibid.,* p. 263.

53. Cited in Hofstadter and Wallace, *American Violence,* pp. 264–67.

54. *Ibid.,* p. 267.

Vote early and vote often.
Tammany Hall Slogan

The American people have always been rather suspicious that their political leaders are tainted by corruption. Whether or not most officeholders are honest, there has always been enough evidence of illegal, indiscreet, and immoral acts by government officials to sustain the public's suspicions. A major political scandal such as Watergate, the Bobby Baker affair, or the Teapot Dome incident tends to send public trust plummeting to its depths. Although it slowly recovers, it never soars because of almost constant revelations of minor incidents of corruption.

6

Political Corruption: How Bad Is It?

There has always been a considerable amount of corruption in the American political system. In many states and cities, corruption has been prevalent enough to be a part of the political tradition. During one period in which corruption in state legislatures was rather obvious, Mark Twain quipped: "I think I can say, and say it with pride, that we have legislatures that bring higher prices than any in the world."

During certain eras, political corruption at the national level has been obvious and well documented. The half-century between the end of Reconstruction and the Great Depression has been dubbed by some historians as the "Golden Age of Boodle." For example, in a forgivable overstatement about the period, Thayer charges:

> Never has the American political process been so corrupt. No office was too high to purchase, no man too pure to bribe, no principle too sacred to destroy, no law too fundamental to break. The old Anglo-Saxon belief that public duty required certain personal and financial sacrifice was giving way to the conviction among certain men that politics, at least in part, was a lucrative source of personal enrichment. In Henry Adams's words, "The moral law has expired."[1]

Of course, political corruption began long before this era. In the 1860s, Boss Tweed ran the New York state legislature, an institution in which legislative votes were commonly purchased.[2] Tweed rather openly looted the public treasury and demanded kickbacks from all contractors doing public work. Tweed's power in large measure rested on his ability to use illegal funds to

The days of buying and selling offices and elections in backroom deals are gone, but money still buys political influence in America. The major links between money and political power today are campaign contributions and conflicts of interest.

bribe members of the state legislature. Another big-city boss of this era, Simon Cameron, who later became a member of Lincoln's Cabinet, once described an honest politician as one "who once bribed, stays bribed."[3] Most big cities in the East and Midwest had political machines run by bosses whose power rested at least in part on graft and bribes.

Much of the money needed to run parties or party machines during the nineteenth century came from officeholders who were appointed by the party. Officeholders were routinely assessed a percentage of their city, state, or federal salary. In 1880 President James Garfield asked his national party head to determine how much some of his appointees were contributing, with the implied threat that they should be fired if they were not donating their fair share.[4] In 1882 all state employees in Pennsylvania received the following letter:[5]

> Two percent of your salary is _____. Please remit promptly. At the close of the campaign we shall place a list of those who have not paid in the hands of the department you are in.

In 1883 the Pendleton Act, prohibiting contributions from federal civil servants, was passed. The subsequent scarcity of funds resulted in business becoming the major contributor of campaign funds.

Corruption at the state level often led to two other frequent problems. First, elections were often stolen. The same *political machine* that ran the party generally counted the votes. This often led to ballot stuffing, rigged counts, and paid voters. Senator Boies Penrose, the corrupt Pennsylvania boss, once blatantly explained:

> The fraud of an election does not really begin til night; then in dozens of precincts where the judges and election clerks of both big parties have been "fixed" we put down just what returns we want, or may need to insure us a majority. John Smith may have 500 votes in a given precinct, but if John Smith is the man we want to defeat, we knock off two ciphers and credit him with five votes. This is cheaper than hiring 500 "Indians" to cast illegal ballots. With a five-cent pencil we can in five minutes cast more votes on paper than 5,000 citizens can cast in a ballot box in a whole day.[6]

No one will ever know how many elections have been stolen. It would be safe to say that the number runs into the thousands. The impact of some stolen elections may have been major. There is some evidence that Lyndon Johnson was first elected to the Senate by a razor-thin margin provided by rigged votes. Voting irregularities in Texas and Illinois in 1960 may have given Kennedy his edge over Nixon.[7]

Corruption at the state level during the nineteenth century also frequently caused senatorial elections to be little more than auctions. Until the passage of the Seventeenth Amendment in 1913, U.S. senators were appointed by their respective state legislatures. During their deliberations, money frequently changed hands, contracts and jobs were bartered, and candidates often won because they enriched more members of the state legislature than any other candidate.

CONTEMPORARY CORRUPTION

While there is still evidence of political corruption in the American political system, contemporary corruption is generally more subtle than it was in the "Golden Age of Boodle." Evidence of bribery, kickbacks, and manipulation of contracts at the state level is uncovered with some regularity, but at the federal level such incidents are relatively rare. Vote counts are also much better supervised now, especially since passage of the Voting Rights Act of 1965 and its subsequent extensions.

No one will ever know how many elections have been stolen. It would be safe to say that the number runs into the thousands.

Still, the Watergate scandal (see the analysis in Chapter 11) focused attention on federal officials, and increased scrutiny continues to reveal acts of personal and political misconduct. These incidents tend to surface with just enough regularity to keep corruption and public misconduct in the public eye. The type of misdeeds involving federal officials is indicated by the list of small and large scandals that came to public light after Vice-President Spiro Agnew was forced from office by charges of bribery, conspiracy, and tax evasion, and after Watergate forced President Nixon's resignation.[8]

1. Between 1975 and 1977, over fifty members of Congress admitted accepting illegal campaign contributions. Only one member was indicted by a grand jury.

2. In December 1975, Gulf Oil admitted that over the preceding decade it had given more than $5 million in illegal campaign contributions to dozens of members of Congress. Senator Hugh Scott (R., Pa.), the retiring minority leader, admitted accepting $45,000 in illegal funds, some of which he passed on to other members of Congress.

3. In February 1976, eighteen members of Congress admitted accepting free hunting trips from various defense contractors and failing to report these trips. Among these members were John J. Flynt (D., Ga.), chairman of the House Ethics Committee, and Carl Albert (D., Okla.), the retiring Speaker of the House.

4. Scandals involving sex touched five members of the House. In May 1976 Representative Wayne L. Hays (D., Ohio) was charged by the *Washing-*

ton Post with keeping an aide (Elizabeth Ray) on his staff to serve primarily (or wholly) as his mistress. Representative John Young (D., Tex.) was accused by one of his aides (Colleen Gardner) of having kept her on the payroll primarily to use her for sexual purposes.

Representatives Joe D. Waggonner, Jr., (D., La.) and Allen T. Howe (D., Utah) were arrested in separate incidents for attempting to solicit sex on a public street. Frederick Richmond (R., N.Y.), another member of the House, was arrested for soliciting sex with two young males.

5. Representative Andrew J. Hinshaw (R., Ca.) was convicted of bribery by a federal court. He served seven months of a one-to-fourteen-year term.

6. Representative Henry Helstoski (D., N.J.) was indicted by a federal grand jury on charges that he extorted money from Chilean and Argentinian aliens in return for his help in blocking their deportation.

7. Representative William Clay (D., Mo.) was sued by the Justice Department over allegations that he charged false travel expenses to his congressional budget. Justice dropped the suit after Clay agreed to refund the money. Justice also announced that it was terminating investigations of nine other house members on similar charges, because it would be difficult to prove that their behavior was intentional.

8. Representative Frank Horton (R., N.Y.) was arrested in New York after a high-speed chase in the early morning hours on July 18, 1976. Horton was charged with speeding and drunken driving. He was convicted and sentenced to eleven days in jail.

9. Representative James F. Hastings (R., N.Y.) was indicted by a federal grand jury for operating a kickback scheme involving the salaries of his congressional aides. He served fourteen months of a twenty-month to five-year term.

10. In 1976 the House Ethics Committee* voted to reprimand Representative Robert Sikes (D., Fla.) for his failure to report owning stock in a defense company (Fairchild Industries) that he commonly dealt with and favored as head of the Military Appropriations Construction Subcommittee. He was also found guilty of failing to report ownership of stock in a bank that he used his office to establish. The committee reported that it was concerned about an "obvious and significant conflict of interest" in Sikes' sponsoring a bill that benefited land he owned but took no action on this point because it concluded that his constituents knew about the issue but still reelected him.

11. In the fall of 1976 a major charge of congressional corruption was made by the press. Charges were raised that a Korean businessman (Tong-sun Park), with headquarters in Washington, D.C., had for some twenty years served as an agent of South Korean dictator Park Chung-hee. Allegations were

*The formal name is the House Committee on Standards of Official Conduct.

"Mr. Park, would you refrain from throwing money when a question is asked? A simple yes or no would suffice!"

made that Tong-sun Park had long provided sizable cash gifts to members of Congress in return for their support for the dictatorship in South Korea.

Investigations were eventually launched by the House International Relations Subcommittee and by the Senate Committee on Ethics. The House Ethics Committee voted to reprimand California Democrats Edward Roybal, John J. McFall, and Charles H. Wilson for failing to report campaign contributions from Park. Three House members were indicted by federal grand juries for accepting bribes from Park. Representative Otto E. Passman (D., La.) was accused of accepting between $367,000 and $407,000; Representative Richard T. Hanna (D., Col.), with accepting $262,000; and Representative Cornelius Gallager (D., N.J.), with receiving $211,000. The committee said it had evidence which could not be proven that four other current members of the House received large sums.

Park testified that he passed out $850,000 to representatives and $21,000 to senators between 1969 and 1976. The House International Relations Subcommittee concluded that the money had been used to bribe U.S. officials, buy influence among journalists and professors, extort money from American companies, and rig military procurement contracts to win support for the "authoritarian" government of President Park Chung-hee.

The Senate Committee on Ethics concluded that only two members of the Senate, both deceased, were guilty of accepting illegal contributions from Park: Hubert Humphrey (D., Minn.) had failed to report at least $5,000 in contributions to his 1968 campaign, and John McClellan (D., Ark.) had failed to report a $1,000 contribution. Evidence was submitted that Senator Birch Bayh (D., Ind.) illegally accepted a contribution on federal property. Bayh disputed the charge.

12. In January 1978, charges of bribery and conspiracy were dropped against former Representative Edward A. Garmatz (D., Md.) when a grand jury witness admitted lying and forging documents.

13. In February 1978, former Representative Richard A. Tonry (D., La.) was released from prison after serving six months for violations of the federal election law.

14. In April 1978, Representative Charles Diggs (D., Mich.) was indicted on thirty-five charges of mail fraud and making false statements to the government. Diggs was found guilty by a jury and sentenced to three years in prison. While on appeal, Diggs was overwhelmingly reelected in Nov. 1978. On July 31, 1979, the House voted to censure Diggs, but rejected a movement to expel him from the House. Diggs admitted to the House that he padded his office payroll and accepted kickbacks from five present and former employees. He agreed to repay the House $40,031.66, plus interest.

15. In April 1978, former Representative Hugh J. Addonizio (D., N.J.) completed a five-year sentence for conspiring to extort $235,000 from contractors doing business with the state of New Jersey.

16. In July 1978, Representative J. Herbert Burke (R., Fla.) was indicted after an altercation at a nude go-go bar. He was charged with intoxication, resisting arrest, and trying to convince a witness to lie about the incident.

17. In September 1978, former Representative Frank Clark (D., Pa.) was charged with thirteen counts of mail fraud, perjury, and income tax evasion. The specific allegation was that Clark paid congressional salaries to thirteen people who did personal or campaign work for him.

18. In September 1978, Representative Daniel J. Flood (D., Pa.) was indicted on charges that he accepted bribes in exchange for his assistance in helping businessmen, constituents, and others obtain federal contracts or other special treatment from the federal government. In early 1979, his trial resulted in a hung jury. One juror refused to vote for conviction on the ground that Flood was too old to be sent to jail. Prosecutors announced intentions to retry Flood.

19. In the fall of 1978 the Senate Committee on Ethics launched an investigation of Senator Edward W. Brooke's (R., Mass.) finances when a divorce proceeding revealed discrepancies in his income disclosures. In October 1978, the committee announced that while the evidence showed that finances had been concealed and documents altered, there was no proof that Brooke was personally responsible.

20. In November 1978, Representative Joshua Eilberg (D., Pa.) was indicted for allegedly accepting payment for helping a Philadelphia hospital obtain a federal grant.

21. In December 1978, the Senate Committee on Ethics voted to investigate the financial records of Senator Herman Talmadge (D., Ga.) on charges that he converted campaign contributions to personal use, submitted false expense vouchers to the Senate, filed false reports of campaign receipts and expenditures, failed to report taxes on gifts of stock to his ex-wife, and failed to report gifts received and property owned. In September 1979, the Senate voted to denounce Talmadge's behavior and require him to repay the Senate $12,894.57, plus interest. Denouncement carried no penalty; it was a compromise reached after the Senate voted not to censure him.

22. In December 1979, the House Ethics Committee accused Representative Charles Wilson (D., Ca.) of payroll padding, accepting kickbacks, converting campaign funds to personal use, lying under oath, and accepting gifts from an individual with a direct interest in legislation before Congress. In April 1980 the committee recommended censuring him and forcing him to give up his subcommittee chairmanship for these alleged violations.

23. In February 1980, Congress was again jolted by allegations that eight of its members had accepted bribes from FBI agents posing as representatives of wealthy Arab businessmen. In a sting operation called Abscam, agents reportedly paid members of Congress to introduce bills mandating U.S. citizenship for the Arab businessmen. Several of the congressmen were videotaped

accepting bundles of cash. The eight named by the FBI were Senator Harrison A. Williams, Jr. (D., N.J.) and Representatives John W. Jenrette (D., S.C.), Richard Kelly (R., Fla.), Raymond F. Lederer (D., Pa.), John M. Murphy (D., N.Y.), John P. Murtha (D., Pa.), Michael Myers (D., Pa.), and Frank Thompson (D., N.Y.).

The Department of Justice announced that it would present the evidence to the grand jury, and the ethics panels of both chambers announced intentions to conduct investigations.

Between 1975 and 1977, over fifty members of Congress admitted accepting illegal campaign contributions. Only one member was indicted by a grand jury.

This long series of crimes and scandals touched only a minority of the members of Congress but was substantial enough (especially in the Watergate era) to cast a pall over the whole Congress. The frequency of violations of the public trust contributes to the erosion of public confidence in officials, often leading to public antipathy toward the political process. The reluctance of Congress to set high standards of conduct for its members and investigate charges of corruption also contributes substantially to public distrust.

Even though both houses of Congress have ethics committees, until recently neither chamber showed an interest in establishing or supervising standards of official conduct. The atmosphere created by Watergate allowed a public-interest group, Common Cause, to pressure the House into the investigation of Representative Robert Sikes mentioned above. The investigation was the first ever by the House Ethics Committee, which was created in 1968. The reluctant committee found the evidence against Sikes overwhelming but took the least action it possibly could.

In the early stages of the investigation of Tong-sun Park the Ethics Committee also showed little enthusiasm for its job. The first counsel to the committee resigned after publicly criticizing the committee and its chairperson, John J. Flynt (D., Ga.), for footdragging. The resignation increased pressures for the investigation to be conducted seriously. In response, the House leadership arranged for Leon Jaworski, the Watergate prosecutor, to return to Washington as the new special counsel for the committee.

The frequency of violations of the public trust contributes to the erosion of public confidence in officials, often leading to public antipathy toward the political process.

The investigation of Daniel Flood was launched in early 1978—two years after the press had begun reporting his questionable activities. The House Ethics Committee finally agreed to the investigation but only after the Senate submitted information on Flood's activities to the committee for "any action deemed necessary." It was the first time a complaint against a House member had come from the Senate.

NEW CODES OF ETHICS

The survey of political scandals above reveals that most corruption is tied to money, either through bribes, campaign contributions (which can resemble bribes), or conflicts of interest (where the officeholder has a financial stake in a particular policy alternative). Since it would never be possible to eliminate the chance of a few bad apples being elected to public office, viable reform requires eliminating any factors in the system that lead to corruption. This would primarily mean eliminating the link between money and political power. The Watergate scandal and embarrassment over a few of the incidents noted above led to one such attempt. In early 1977 both the House and the Senate adopted new ethics codes that included financial disclosure.

Prior to 1977, both houses of Congress had financial disclosure rules, but they were not very restrictive. Members of the House were required to report all substantial holdings in companies that do business with the federal government or are regulated by federal agencies. They also had to report all sources of honoraria but not the amounts received, all capital gains in excess of $5,000, and sources of outside income over $5,000 a year but not the amounts received. Senators were only required to report income from speeches, articles, and television appearances if they received $300 or more. They were also required to report political contributions and gifts of more than $50.

In March and April 1977, respectively, the House and Senate adopted codes that require much more thorough financial disclosure. (The codes, which began in January 1979, also apply to top House and Senate employees.) Members are required to annually disclose sources and amounts of income. Office slush funds financed by private contributions are prohibited. Acceptance of gifts worth more than $100 from lobbyists is forbidden, as is the use of public funds for foreign travel by retiring or defeated members. Members are prohibited from using their free mail privileges to send literature to their constituents sixty days before an election in which they are a candidate. The Senate code also stipulates that senators may not be affiliated with a firm or partnership and may not practice any profession during regular Senate office hours.

The codes represent a milestone in congressional supervision of the behavior of members and employees. Disclosure of income and its sources had long been opposed by a majority of the members of Congress. Enactment of the legislation did not come easily. Only the extraordinary events of Watergate created the pressures necessary for passage. Many members of Congress voted for passage not because they liked the codes but because they feared the consequences of opposition. In the House, large numbers of Republicans and southern Democrats tried to cripple the codes with weakening amendments, but these efforts were defeated. In the Senate, the Minority Leader Howard Baker (R., Tenn.) opposed the codes because he felt that they discriminated against the rich. As a last effort he tried to convince the Senate to agree to let the code die in 1981, after the controversy over Watergate had subsided.[9] But the pressures of the times were too severe, and the code became law without his proposed restriction.

YOU'RE A *MODERATE* ON ETHICS?

INDEED...I'M IN FAVOR OF THEM, BUT NOT TO THE EXTENT OF OUTRIGHT *HONESTY.*

At the very least, the codes should reduce the corrupting influences upon members of Congress. Expensive gifts from lobbyists cannot be accepted (most members, though, did not accept expensive personal gifts even before this legislation). Disclosure should also put pressures on members of Congress to at least be cautious about the funds they accept. The Senate prohibition on outside work should also limit senatorial ties with corporations and law firms doing business with the government. The ban on slush funds will remove one incentive for members to accept funds from groups or individuals who hope to influence their vote.

As originally passed, the ethics codes also limited congressional members' outside earnings to no more than 15 percent of their $57,000 salary (this did not include income from investments, interest, etc.). The limitation was particularly unpopular with members but was felt necessary at the time to appease critics and to justify a congressional raise of $12,900. Members chafed under the restriction but were afraid to abolish it for fear of public opposition. In March 1979, however, barely two months after the codes had taken effect, the Senate agreed to alter the restriction, allowing senators to earn $25,000 a year from speaking engagements and placing no limit on other outside earnings.

This alteration said a great deal about the ethics and courage of the members of the Senate. Without notice to the public or the media, the Senate revised the standard while only a few senators were on the floor. Acting on a prearranged plan, all but a few senators left the floor while those remaining introduced and then passed the alteration. Although any senator can ask that a record of voting be kept, no senator made such a request, and certainly no member threatened or staged a filibuster. Once the quick action was taken, senators reentered the chamber and denounced the action, claiming that if they had been on the floor they would have voted against it. None, however, took any steps to have the decision reversed. Common Cause Chairperson David Cohen labeled the masquerade ''an act of greed and cowardice.'' Public reaction forced a recorded vote on the change a few days later, and the charade ended. Many senators who had been claiming that they opposed the change now voted for it, and the revision passed. In August 1979 the Senate also voted to trim back the financial disclosure requirements and limit the requirement to about 300 of their top aides.

In October 1978 another important ethics bill was passed by Congress. The new act codified into federal law the House and Senate ethics standards adopted in 1977 and expanded the coverage to all upper-level federal employees. Under the act, top officials of all three branches are required to disclose their incomes and assets, but, as noted above, the number of officials covered was reduced in 1979. The bill also placed restrictions on the ability of ex-government officials to accept employment with firms they dealt with while holding federal office and limited their ability to represent such business interests before the government. To enforce the standards, an Office of Government Ethics (OGE) was established.

In response to those calling for the creation of a permanent Office of Special Prosecutor, the bill compromised by allowing the attorney general to request the appointment of a special prosecutor to investigate charges of corruption by top executive officials, including the President. A three-person judicial panel from the U.S. court of appeals for the District of Columbia will decide whether the request for a special prosecutor should be granted.

The new code will establish higher ethical standards throughout the government and hopefully will restrain the often incestuous relationship between federal employees and special interests. The special-prosecutor provision is not ideal because the attorney general, an appointee of the President, will probably be very reluctant to provoke an investigation of his or her boss or other top presidential appointees. Still, publicity about abuses should spur the attorney general into action.

While the codes are a positive and very important step, a significant question is whether they are enough. Clearly the answer is no. The codes will have little or no impact on the most important and undoubtedly the most corrupting link between money and public office—campaign contributions. It is also not clear that the codes will be adequate to deal with conflicts of interest. Below we will examine the problems caused by campaign contributions and analyze one proposed solution. Finally, we will examine the evidence on conflict of interest and evaluate the ethics code's probable impact on the problem.

CAMPAIGN CONTRIBUTIONS

John W. McCormack, a former Speaker of the House of Representatives, had a sign over his office door which read ''nothing for nothing.''[10] In Washington most sophisticates could only utter a polite ''Amen.'' Gerald Ford, House minority leader and later President, spelled the message out: "In Washington, money's the name of the game. Without it, you're dead."[11]

There are two major ways that money oils the wheels in Washington. The first is through campaign contributions; the other is through lobbying activities. Most members of Congress must depend upon some large campaign donors to get and stay elected. No member of Congress can escape the highly paid, well-staffed, and persistent lobbyists who provide much of their campaign funds (see Chapter 11).

Getting elected and reelected to public office is generally very expensive. As Will Rogers once noted: "Politics has got so expensive that it takes lots of money even to get beat with." For example, in 1978 candidates for the House spent $88 million in the November general elections (not counting primary expenditures). This was a significant increase over the 1976 expenditure of $60.9 million. In the thirty-five Senate contests in 1978, candidates spent $65.5 million, up from $38.1 million in 1976.[12] Another $41.3 million was spent by House and Senate candidates during the primaries, bringing total expenditures to 194.8 million.[13]

The average candidate for the House spent over $100,000 in the general election in 1978, while the average Senate candidate spent over $900,000. The cost of campaigns varied greatly depending upon whether the candidate was an incumbent or a challenger, the closeness of the contest, and whether the district was located in a rural, urban, or suburban district. Those elected to the House for the first time in 1978 averaged spending $229,000. Nearly a third of all House contests had expenditures of over $250,000. Nine candidates spent over $500,000, with a high of $1,136,112.[14]

Twenty-one Senate candidates spent over $1 million dollars, with a high of $7.5 million spent by North Carolina Republican Jesse Helms. Helms spent $12 per vote against an opponent who spent $.26 per vote. John Tower (R., Tex.) spent $4.3 million, while John W. Warner (R., Va.) spent $2.9 million.[15]

While the codes are a positive and very important step, a significant question is whether they are enough. Clearly the answer is no. The codes will have little or no impact on the most important and undoubtedly the most corrupting link between money and public office—campaign contributions.

The question, of course, is where do candidates get the large sums necessary to run elections, and what effect do the donations have on them? Because of recent laws, the first question can be answered rather precisely. Only a relatively small percentage of the total population provides the funds for campaigns. The *Congressional Quarterly* estimated that about 90 percent of all campaign contributions in 1974 were provided by 1 percent of the population.[16] The evidence indicates that these figures are rather typical. While some middle- and low-income citizens may send a small donation to candidates,

Without public financing for congressional races, campaign costs continue to rise sharply. Senator John Warner (R., Va.), pictured above with his wife, actress Elizabeth Taylor, was one of twenty-one senatorial candidates in 1978 who spent more than $1 million on their campaigns.

most contributions come from a small proportion of the citizens from upper-middle- and upper-income brackets. Businesses and unions cannot provide direct donations, but their employees and members can do this through *Political Action Committees* (PACs). Businesses, unions, medical professions, and farm organizations make the largest contributions to campaigns.

Until the Federal Election Campaign Act of 1974, a significant proportion of all campaign donations consisted of very large contributions from rich individuals. These donations reached unprecedented levels in Nixon's campaigns in 1968 and 1972. One source noted that from 1952 to 1964:

> The number of individual contributors giving more than $10,000 hovered between 95 and 130; they gave between $1.5 million and $2.3 million. But in 1968 there were 424 of the biggest givers, and their contributions totaled more than $12 million. In 1972, about 1,750 Americans contributed or lent sums of $10,000 to political campaigns, their total gifts reached $73 million. The systematic Nixon money canvass in 1972 represented a historic departure from past financing practices: 153 donors gave $50,000 or more, for a total of $19.8 million.[17]

One individual, W. Clement Stone, gave Nixon $2 million in 1972. A wealthy Democratic supporter, Stuart R. Mott, gave McGovern $729,000 in 1972.

Interest-group contributions can also be very lucrative. In 1978 interest groups and private contributors provided congressional candidates with $35.1 million in donations, up from $22.6 million in 1976, $12.5 million in 1974, and $8 million in 1972. The figures below show interest-group contributions by category in 1976.[18]

Interest-Group Category	*Total Contributions*
American Medical Association	$1,790,879
Dairy committees	$1,362,159
AFL-CIO COPES	$ 996,910
Maritime-related unions	$ 979,691
United Auto Workers	$ 845,939
Coal, oil, and natural gas interests	$ 809,508
National educational associations	$ 752,272
Financial institutions	$ 605,973
International Association of Machinists	$ 529,193
United Steelworkers of America	$ 463,033
American Dental Association	$ 409,835

More than two-thirds of these funds were donated by labor and business groups. Most of the remaining funds were contributed by medical and agricultural groups.

In 1976, as always, most campaign contributions went to incumbents, allowing them to substantially outspend challengers. The twenty-four Senate incumbents seeking reelection in 1976 were able to outspend their challengers by a ratio of about 3 to 2. In House races, incumbents outspent challengers by $12.3 million, a ratio of about 1.7 to 1.[19] This financial edge for incumbents was basically consistent with previous years. In 1972 congressional incumbents outspent challengers 2 to 1. In 1974 the Democrats maintained this edge, but the Republican incumbents (because of Watergate) were only able to outspend challengers 3 to 2.[20] The advantage incumbents enjoy in campaign contributions helps them stay in office. Generally, about 90 percent of members of the House and Senate who stand for reelection win.

Do campaign contributions have a negative impact on the political system? Do they prejudice officeholders in favor of donors to the detriment of average citizens? Ironically perhaps, many elected officials will freely admit that they do. In fact, some members of Congress agree with those who believe that campaign contributions constitute the most pervasive form of corruption in the American political system. The reason, of course, is obvious. No one gives large sums to a candidate without expecting something in return. If officeholders must please their large donors to ensure continued contributions, the donors clearly have an unfair advantage. Many members of Congress admit feeling compromised by campaign donations but nevertheless feel compelled to accept them.

Like many other people, Morris K. Udall (D., Ariz.) sees campaign contributions as a corrupting influence on the members of Congress:

> More than anything else, more than sex scandals or junkets or the issues of pay and fringe benefits—I believe the institution of Congress is damaged, both in public perception and the integrity of its functioning, by the escalating costs of campaigning and the massive amounts of special interest money being pumped into election campaigns.[21]

Bobby Baker, one-time secretary of the Senate and fund collector for Senators Lyndon Johnson and Robert Kerr (D., Okla.) saw the corrupting influence from the inside:

> The way in which political campaigns are financed constitutes a national cancer. I've been a part of it so I know. It will destroy this country unless something is done. People are selling their souls. They have to. They are human. There is not a human being who can take money from somebody and not be influenced.[22]

Representative Jim Wright (D., Tex.), majority leader of the House, feels that campaign contributions have both a corrupting and a trivializing effect:

> The price of campaigning has risen so high that it actually imperils the integrity of our political institutions. Big contributions more and more hold the keys to the gate of public service. This is choking off the well springs of fresh men, and thought, and severely limiting the field of choice available to the public. I am convinced, moreover, that the intellectual quality of political campaigns is deteriorating as a result. One curious by-product of big money in politics is the slick, shallow public-relations approach with its nauseating emphasis on "image" at the expense of substance. In the arena where Lincoln and Douglas once debated great issues, advertising agencies last year (1970) hawked candidates like cornflakes.[23]

Bobby Baker, Senate secretary for the majority party during the late 1950s and early 1960s, was forced to resign in 1963 when he was charged with using his political influence to control government contracts and obtain illegal campaign contributions.

Orfield argues that campaign contributions bias the system in favor of wealthy contributors and the status quo:

> Perhaps the grandest distortions in congressional representation came from the extraordinary difficulty of defeating incumbents, and the great dependence of congressional campaigns on large contributions from interests with very specific legislative objectives. The slow turnover of members causes Congress to be always dominated by members with a vested interest in the organizational status quo. Sometimes it also isolates the legislative branch from changes in public attitudes. The members' dependency on business, unions and the more affluent professions greatly increases the difficulty of enacting legislation to reform these institutions.[24]

The charges against campaign contributions, then, are extensive. Many feel that they corrupt members, some feel that they trivialize campaigns, and others feel that they protect incumbents while wedding them to the status quo. Some examples of these kinds of problems are illuminating.

No one gives large sums to a candidate without expecting something in return. If officeholders must please their large donors to ensure continued contributions, the donors clearly have an unfair advantage.

The most persistent charge leveled against the current methods of financing campaigns is that campaign contributions often purchase political influence. Undoubtedly, this is often true. If a group gives a candidate a large donation, that person will be less likely to vote against the group while in office. For example, in 1976 the American Medical Association (AMA) gave one candidate for the House (Ron Paul, R., Tex.) $30,000. It hardly stretches a point to suggest that a donation that large would influence his vote on matters affecting the AMA. One senator from Texas (Lloyd Bentsen) received $265,181 from oil and gas lobbies. Bentsen could hardly be expected to take any actions while in office that might lead to a termination of such funds. Robert Krueger (D., Tex.) received $51,147 from oil and gas lobbies in 1976, and later attempted to spearhead a House drive to deregulate natural gas prices.

In 1977 it was revealed that six senators who were helping to write a compromise energy-tax bill had received contributions totaling $504,123 from oil and gas interests in their last campaigns. Critics charged that the decision they reached on energy would be affected by their contributions. Clearly, if the oil and gas interests did not expect their contributions to have some influence, they would not make them.

Also in 1977 it was reported that the maritime lobby had won a controversial decision from the House Merchant Marine Committee which would require a rising proportion of all oil imports to travel in American ships at rates several times higher than prevailing shipping costs. The Government Accounting Office (GAO) reported that the bill would cost consumers $240 million a year in unnecessary freight charges. President Carter backed the bill even though his secretary of the treasury warned that it would be inflationary, would create unemployment, would invite retaliation from other countries, and would violate treaties with some thirty other countries.[25]

How did such a bill gain so much support? Critics pointed to lavish campaign contributions. During the presidential primaries, the maritime lobby gave Carter $100,000. It also spent another million dollars on contributions to other members of Congress. Twenty-six members of the House Merchant Marine Committee received a total of $83,263 (all but two of whom voted for the bill). The chairperson of the committee, John M. Murphy (D., N.Y.), received $9,950 in 1977, a non-election year. Many charged that the Maritime Union had simply bought itself a bill. The *Washington Post,* for example, observed:

> The Maritime Lobby, with the help of its many friends in the White House and Congress, has invented a different kind of revenue sharing. The system has a certain scientific interest, since it's beginning to look like the political equivalent of the perpetual-motion machine. The Maritime Lobby—the unions, the ship operators and the shipyards—invests wisely in certain elections. The politicians express their gratitude by extending and augmenting the enormous subsidies that go to the U.S. merchant marine. That further enriches the Maritime industry, enabling it to pour still larger contributions into political campaigns the next time around. It's a delightful system for everybody except, of course, the taxpayers and consumers who supply the endless subsidies that keep the wheel turning.[26]

Campaign contributions often cause decisions to be made which create serious financial burdens for the public. One prominent example is the series of events during the Nixon administration that became known as the milk scandal. On March 12, 1971, Agriculture Secretary Clifford Hardin set the milk price support for the coming year at 79 percent of parity. The dairy cooperatives had been seeking 85 percent of parity. The government announced that it had investigated the dairies' request for 85 percent of parity but had concluded that during a period of high prices it would be too hard on consumers.

The dairy cooperatives, however, were not willing to take no for an answer, and they had learned how to wield power in Washington. Several years earlier, William Powell, president of the Mid-American Dairymen, publicly announced that the dairy industry had learned a hard lesson about politics in Washington: "I have become increasingly aware that the soft and sincere voice of the dairy farmer is no match for the jingle of hard currencies in the campaign funds of the politicians . . . ."[27] The dairy industry put together a slush fund of several million dollars and started spreading it around. By the time of parity dispute, the dairy industry had "earned" a great deal of support in Congress. It had also contributed to the Nixon administration and was willing to contribute much more to get its way. Dairy lawyers and lobbyists began meet-

"I'd vote for the windfall-profits tax on oil companies if I felt I wouldn't miss those windfall contributions they send around campaign time!"

ing with Nixon officials. On March 23 the major lobbyists gained a personal audience with Nixon. During this meeting they pledged $2 million to Nixon's 1972 campaign. Wheels began to turn. On March 25, Hardin announced that further investigation had supported the dairy cooperatives' claim for 85 percent parity and consequently that his earlier decision was being reversed. The decision was worth $2 million to Nixon and between $500 and $700 million to the dairy industry. All the cost, of course, came out of consumers' pockets. William Powell summed the situation up with a letter to his members: "We dairymen cannot afford to overlook this kind of economic benefit. Whether we like it or not this is the way the system works."[28]

Another frequent problem cited by critics is that the need to accumulate large sums of money for campaigns frequently makes candidates desperate enough to accept illegal or unethical contributions or even engage in corrupt actions to obtain the funds. For example, Jim Wright (D., Tex.) the majority leader of the House, is thought by most Washington observers to be a basically honest individual. Yet in 1976 Wright admitted that he used $98,501 in campaign contributions to retire some of his personal debts (an action that was legal at that time). Wright also admitted that he raised an additional $77,000 to pay off campaign debts by allowing special-interest groups such as the road builders to throw a fund raiser for him. Wright said that he recognized "the ethical questions in accepting contributions from people affected by legislation you might help write. But damn it, it takes money to campaign."[29]

The Watergate disclosures revealed that the Nixon administration had engaged in numerous unethical and illegal actions to put together an enormous fund for the 1972 campaign. Maurice Stans, Nixon's secretary of the treasury, and Herbert Kalmbach, Nixon's personal attorney, put intense pressure on corporate executives for personal and corporate campaign donations (corporate donations are illegal). Many corporations yielded to the pressure. Two dozen corporations, including Gulf, American Airlines, Ashland Oil, Associated Milk Producers, Goodyear Tire, Minnesota Mining and Manufacturing, Northrup Corporation, Phillips Petroleum, Sanitas Service Corporation, Lockheed, Occidental, United Brands, ITT, and numerous others were later charged with making illegal contributions. Some of the corporations, such as Gulf, were old hands at giving and laundering illegal funds for donations and bribes in the United States and other countries. Gulf eventually admitted that between 1960 and 1972, $10,300,000 in illegal contributions was made in the United States and other countries.[30] Some $5 million was spent in America. Numerous other corporations admitted making use of slush funds to bribe officials or influence elections in other countries.

Some of the corporate executives testified before Congress that they feared that they would be discriminated against by the Nixon administration if they did not concede to demands for funds.[31] One of the letters sent to corporate executives at the direction of Stans reveals both the heavy handedness of the requests for funds and the unethical spirit of the campaign drive:

> The simplest and most painless way to (avoid gift and capital gain taxes) is by giving appreciated low cost securities to several committees (whose names I can supply) in amounts of $3,000 to each committee. In this way neither gift nor capital gains tax liability is incurred, and I can easily explain to you the way of doing it.
>
> The standard of giving is $1/2$ percent, more or less, of net worth. This makes for a very substantial campaign contribution which will actually have a minimal effect on your lifestyle and personal estate, but will have tremendous effect on your family's stake in the future of our economy and our country.
>
> We have a deadline of April 7th to meet for this important major gift phase of the drive, because this is the effective date of the new Federal Campaign Financing Act which will require reporting and public disclosure of all subsequent campaign contributions in excess of $100, which we all naturally want to avoid.[32]

Another method of fund-raising used by Nixon's men was the sale of ambassadorships. In actuality, individuals in many administrations who wanted to be ambassadors were expected to make sizable campaign donations. Under Nixon the tradition was simply exaggerated. Herbert Kalmbach eventually pleaded guilty to a federal charge of promising government employment in return for a campaign contribution. The size of the campaign contributions associated with the "sale" of some ambassadorships is listed below (figures are from the General Accounting Office):[33]

Country	Ambassador	Contribution
Great Britain	Walter H. Annenberg	$ 250,000
Switzerland	Shelby Davis	100,000
Luxembourg	Ruth L. Farkas	300,000
Belgium	Leonard K. Firestone	112,600
Netherlands	Kingdom Gould	100,900
Austria	John F. Humer	100,000
France	John N. Irwin, II	50,500
France	Arthur K. Watson	300,000
Ireland	John D. Moore	10,442
		$1,324,442

Other tainted funds for the Nixon campaign included a $200,000 cash donation from financier Robert L. Vesco, who was under indictment for stock fraud. International Telephone and Telegraph (ITT) also pledged a $400,000 contribution while it was in the midst of an antitrust suit with the Justice Department. The suit was settled in favor of ITT. Illicit campaign funds to Nixon were eventually used to finance the "White House plumbers' " burglary of the office of Dr. Lewis Fielding, Daniel Ellsberg's psychiatrist, as well as the Watergate break-in and cover-up.

One last ethical problem frequently noted by critics is that organized crime gains some insulation from active investigation and prosecution by providing large donations to candidates. Prominent mafia figures frequently gave money to both state and federal candidates. One investigation concluded:

> If a strict definition of the underworld is used—that it is composed of individuals engaged in illegal activities such as selling narcotics, bootlegging, loan sharking, labor racketeering, running prostitution rings and illegal gambling games, and the like—then the amount of money spent as "campaign contributions" would no doubt run into the millions each year. However, if a broader definition is used, to include individuals who occasionally or even frequently, but with knowledge aforethought, seek the goods and services offered by the underworld, then the yearly amount of "campaign contribtutions" would run into the tens of millions.[34]

Public financing of elections: One solution for political corruption?

The post-Watergate atmosphere stimulated support for some type of reform to control the most obvious problems caused by rapid increases in campaign donations. Many members of Congress believed that some form of public financing of elections was the most viable solution. Public financing, supporters argued, would allow candidates to run for office without accepting large donations from individuals or interests that hoped to influence the candidate. Proponents also believed that public financing would make it easier for people without great personal wealth or wealthy backers to run for office. Many believe that lack of money is generally a larger factor in discouraging would-be candidates than in determining who wins among actual candidates. Thus supporters thought that if elections were publicly financed, more people would have an opportunity to run for office.

The Federal Election Campaign Act of 1974   The spirit of reform produced by Watergate led to the passage of the most significant campaign legislation in American history. In 1925 Congress had passed the Corrupt Practices Act, establishing limits for campaign expenditures, but the provisions were simply ignored by one and all. Congress never made any attempt to enforce the law. In 1972 the Federal Election Campaign Act was passed. This act placed limits on media expenditures (repealed in 1976) and required disclosure of campaign contributions over $100. The reasoning behind the bill was that candidates would be more circumspect about accepting contributions if they had to report them. The records required by the law were eventually quite important in unraveling the Watergate events.

The Federal Election Campaign Act of 1974 was quite comprehensive. It provided:[35]

1. Campaign expenditure limits on congressional and presidential primaries and elections;
2. Matching federal funds for presidential primary candidates. To qualify for matching funds a candidate had to raise $100,000 in amounts of at least $5,000 in each of 20 states or more. Only donations of $250 or less could be matched;
3. That the two major parties could receive optional funding of their presidential conventions. Minor parties could receive lesser amounts depending upon their voter support in past and current elections;
4. Voluntary public financing of general presidential elections. The major parties automatically qualify for full funding. Minor parties and independent candidates could receive some funding, depending upon voter support. If the major party candidate opted for federal funding, no private contributions could be accepted;
5. A $1,000 limit on individual contributions for each primary, runoff, and general election, and a $25,000 ceiling on all contributions to federal candidates annually;
6. A $5,000 limit on campaign contributions by organizations and political committees;
7. For candidates and their families, a limit on personal expenditures of $50,000 in a presidential election, $35,000 in a Senatorial election, and $25,000 in a House election;
8. For the creation of a permanent eight-person Federal Election Commission to administer election laws and the public finance program;
9. That candidates must report all contributions and expenditures to the Federal Election Commission. Reports were required each quarter, and ten days before and thirty days after each election.

While this very comprehensive legislation was passed by Congress, the House and Senate could not agree on a public financing bill for congressional elections. During 1974 the Senate twice passed legislation establishing public funding for congressional races, but both bills were rejected by the House.

Two prominent opponents of the 1974 act, Senator James Buckley (R., N.Y.) and former Senator Eugene McCarthy (D., Minn.), challenged it in federal court. In January 1976, the Supreme Court handed down its decision in the case of *Buckley* v. *Valeo*.[36] The Court ruled that the general concept of public financing was constitutional, but it voided certain provisions of the bill. The Court ruled that limitations on campaign contributions by individuals and groups were legal but unless candidates accepted federal subsidies, limitations on their campaign expenditures were unconstitutional. Since House and Senate candidates received no public subsidies under the 1974 law, spending limits on them were voided.

The Court also ruled that unless a candidate accepted public funding, limitations on expenditures of personal funds in a campaign were unconstitutional. This, of course, opened the door for massive expenditures of personal funds by a few wealthy candidates in the 1976 election. The Court also ruled that the Federal Election Commission exercises functions that are in part judicial and that only the President can appoint members to such an agency. Under the 1974 act, however, appointments to the Federal Election Commission were divided between the President and the leaders of the House and Senate.

Congress passed the Federal Election Campaign Act of 1976 primarily to correct the defects noted by the Supreme Court. Under the new law, appointments to the Federal Election Commission were vested in the President. Limitations on spending and uses of personal funds by candidates not receiving federal subsidies were repealed. Limits on campaign contributions were amended to apply to political parties and other political groups as well as candidates. To cover another point noted by the Court, Congress specified that spending ceilings on presidential candidates receiving public funds could not include funds spent by individuals and groups that acted without cooperation or consultation with the candidate.[37]

The impact of the 1974 act Public financing received its first trial in the 1976 election. Almost everyone agreed that it was a success. During the primaries, fifteen candidates qualified for some matching funds. The top five recipients were Ronald Reagan, Gerald Ford, Jimmy Carter, George Wallace, and Henry Jackson.[38] Ellen McCormack, running on an anti-abortion plank, also received funds, proving that an independent, one-issue candidate could qualify for a federal subsidy. Jimmy Carter and Gerald Ford both opted for federal funding in the general election, and each received $21.8 million to run his campaign.*

---

*The expenditure limits are adjusted for inflation. In 1980 the candidates will be able to spend about $13.2 million (half from matching funds) in the preconvention campaigns and about $29.4 million in the general election.

Federal funding of the general election had a number of impacts. It drastically reduced the amount of money spent in the campaign. In 1972 Richard Nixon spent $63 million in the general election, and George McGovern spent $30 million. The smaller sums for Carter and Ford in the 1976 election meant that they had to spend their funds carefully. For the first time in decades, the Democratic party did not purchase bumper stickers and campaign buttons. Party workers shared rooms on the road, accepted modest salaries, and paid many of their own expenses. While most believed that campaign costs needed to be substantially reduced, there was considerable agreement that the funds in this election were insufficient. Because the funds were so short, the candidates tended to save as much of their money as possible for media expense. The candidates did, however, try to give more press conferences as a method of obtaining free publicity, and the presidential debates were revived as a means of communicating with the public.

Other changes brought about by public financing were fairly obvious. Neither party was overwhelmingly outspent by the other, as was the case in 1968 and 1972. The goal of reducing candidates' obligations to big campaign donors was certainly achieved. The kind of "megabuck" contributions that had been characteristic of other presidential elections were no longer legal. Because of the tight campaign money, however, incumbency provided Ford with a considerable advantage. As President, he received more free publicity than Carter did. He also had many resources at his disposal that helped his campaign effort, even if they were not specifically used for that purpose.

However, public financing for presidential campaigns but not for House and Senate elections caused a problem. Those groups and individuals who could not give their usual sums to presidential candidates tried to retain their influence by making large contributions to congressional candidates. As noted above, in 1978 congressional candidates spent $35.1 million, up from $22.6 million in 1976, $12.5 million in 1974 and $8 million in 1972.[39] These massive increases provoked Common Cause's John Gardner to charge that "a lot of congressmen were bought and sold . . ., just like the good old days except that the going rates were higher . . . the money-heavy special interests couldn't buy themselves a President so they tried to buy as many members of Congress as they could."[40]

The infusion of larger sums by interest groups also increased the cost of running for the House and Senate, making it even more difficult for anyone but established incumbents and candidates with big purses to seek office. In both Senate and House races in 1976, wealthy candidates were able to gain an advantage over opponents by using personal funds to finance their campaigns. In House races, ten candidates gave $100,000 or more to their own campaigns, with three candidates spending over $400,000 of their own money.[41] In Senate races, fifteen candidates gave over $50,000, nine of whom donated over $100,000. H. John Heinz III (R., Pa.) contributed $2,466,910 of his own money to his campaign.[42] Thus, the House and Senate races still suffer all the problems reformers have long been concerned about.

In the 1976 presidential election, public financing eliminated most of the inequities of the old, privately funded system, but the incumbent, Gerald Ford (above), still had an advantage. He was able to use the high visibility of the presidential office to gain more free media coverage than his opponent, Jimmy Carter.

Congressional financing legislation, 1977 To deal with these continuing problems, legislation was introduced again in 1977 to provide public financing of congressional races. Many were optimistic that the legislation would pass, but it did not. Below we will describe the House and Senate legislation proposed to establish public financing, examine the arguments of proponents and opponents, and discuss the prospects for future action.

The House and Senate bills provided optional public financing, but only for general elections. The Senate bill provided matching funds for contributions of $100 or less. Candidates who opted for public financing could spend no more than $250,000, plus a sum equal to $.10 for every eligible voter in the state. Using this formula, limits would have ranged from $273,000 in Alaska to $1,688,000 in California.[43] Candidates accepting public funds would have been limited to spending no more than $35,000 of their personal funds in their campaign.

To help nominees launch their campaigns, major-party candidates would have received an initial grant equal to 25 percent of their spending limits. Independents and minor-party candidates would have been eligible for matching funds for contributions of less than $100, with a maximum public subsidy of $50,000. House candidates accepting public funds would have been limited to total expenditures of $150,000. To qualify for any public funds, candidates would have had to raise $10,000 from small contributions, and then they would have been eligible for matching funds for contributions of $100 or less. Candidates who accepted public funds would not have been allowed to spend more than $25,000 of their own funds.

> *Public financing for presidential campaigns but not for House and Senate elections caused a problem. Those groups and individuals who could not give their usual sums to presidential candidates tried to retain their influence by making large contributions to congressional candidates.*

The most negative feature about these bills is that they would not have covered primaries. Thus, only candidates who made it to the general election could have received a subsidy. This legislation also would not have dealt with the serious problem of citizens being discouraged from seeking office because they could not hope to collect the large sums necessary for a serious contest.

Lack of public funding for primaries would have undoubtedly created an equally serious problem. If big contributors were unable to provide large sums to candidates during the general election, the funds would simply be shifted to the primaries. Thus, dozens of organizations and political action committees could be counted upon to provide primary candidates, especially incumbents, with the maximum donation (it would have been reduced to $2,500 under these bills). This would have had the cumulative effect of pouring large sums into the campaigns of certain candidates. It would be similar to the situation created when presidential races were publicly financed, causing special interests and large donors to shift their funds to congressional races. The only way to end the influence of large contributors is to plug all holes.

On the positive side, the bills would have reduced candidate dependence on funds from interest groups and large donors during the general election. The legislation also would have provided funds for candidates without cutting off private contributions, which are an important form of public participation. The spending limits provided by the legislation also seemed reasonable. They were high enough to allow a strong challenge to an incumbent, and they would have provided challengers with more funds than they generally have to spend. Finally, the bills would have limited the use of personal funds, substantially reducing the advantage of rich over poor candidates.

The defeat of public financing in 1977 Attempts to institute public financing of congressional elections met defeat in the Senate in 1977, leading the House to drop its consideration of the bill. The legislation was defeated in the Senate by a combination of Republicans and Southern Democrats. The late Senator James Allen (D., Ala.), a long-time foe of public financing, led a filibuster against the legislation. A *filibuster* occurs when a senator or senators obtain permission to speak on a bill and continue to speak—sometimes for days—until the Senate's business is so disrupted that members vote to table the issue so that normal business can be resumed. Under Senate rules, the vote of sixty members can end a filibuster. A vote to invoke *cloture* (end debate) has traditionally been hard to obtain, allowing the filibuster to be used primarily in the last thirty years by Southern members to defeat civil-rights bills and other progressive legislation.

The Democratic leadership of the Senate obtained three votes to invoke cloture, but all failed (by narrow margins), and the legislation was tabled. Ironically, four Republican senators who had cosponsored the legislation refused to vote for cloture, which would have allowed the bill to be considered by the full Senate. It is clear that the bill had majority support in the Senate, but the majority never had a chance to vote on the bill.[44] The four Republican cosponsors who refused to vote to end the debate—Clifford P. Case (N.J.), H. John Heinz III (Pa.), Jacob K. Javits (N.Y.) and Richard S. Schweiker (Pa.)—did so after Senate Minority Leader Howard Baker (R., Tenn.) asked them to follow party opposition to the legislation. Thus, these senators and several others—John Danforth (R., R.I.) and Charles Percy (R., Ill.)—who promised to support public financing voted not to end debate.

The Republican leader fought the bill for the stated reason that it would protect incumbents. Baker argued that even though the incumbent and challenger would have had about the same amount of money to spend, the incumbent would have had the advantage because of name recognition and office resources such as the franking privilege, a home office, and more media cov-

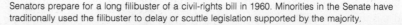

Senators prepare for a long filibuster of a civil-rights bill in 1960. Minorities in the Senate have traditionally used the filibuster to delay or scuttle legislation supported by the majority.

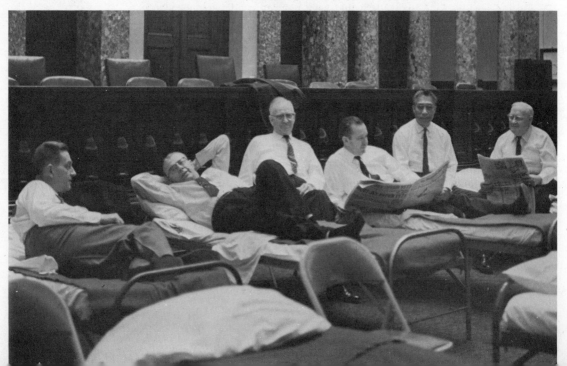

erage. Baker claimed that the bill would have locked the Democratic majority in the Senate and the House, thus threatening the Republican party.

The Southern Democratic opposition led by Senator Allen and backed by Senator Russell B. Long (La.), the powerful chairperson of the Senate Finance Committee, centered around philosophical objection to public financing, but this did not seem to be the real reason for their opposition. As the *Congressional Quarterly* said: "Beneath the surface was the unspoken fear that the bill would encourage Republican opposition in states which had known one-party Democratic dominance."[45] The attitude seemed to be: "Why should I fund my opponents?" It was clear, in other words, that the southern Democrats did not buy the Republican argument that the legislation would protect incumbents. In fact, one non-Southern Democrat, Senator Wm. Hathaway (D., Maine), openly admitted that he decided not to vote for cloture because he concluded that public financing would help his Republican opponent in 1978.[46]

Did the Republicans really believe that the bill would have protected incumbents? As noted above, this argument has some merit because the legislation did not cover primaries. However, it is difficult to conclude that the Republican leadership took this problem seriously because they did not favor extending fundings to the primaries. It is doubtful that the bill would have significantly favored incumbents in the general election. If incumbent and challenger expenditures in the 1976 election are contrasted with the expenditures that would have been allowed under the legislation, the data indicate that public funds would usually have reduced the expenditures of incumbents and raised the expenditures of challengers.[47] Of course, if the Republicans had been serious about incumbent advantage they could have supported legislation providing more funds for the challenger than the incumbent. The Republican leadership, however, found this option unacceptable.

When all the rhetoric is swept aside, it is obvious that the legislation failed because Republicans and Southern Democrats did not want to make it easier for citizens to run for office or for incumbents to be challenged. Why, they were asking, should they pass legislation that might lead to their defeat? The Democratic majority, however, was not without fault, either. They did not want a really effective bill—one that helped expand the opportunities for citizens to run for office—and they also would not have supported a bill that provided more funds for a challenger so that the natural advantages of an incumbent could be overcome. They basically wanted a halfway measure that looked good and did not really threaten them too much.

Such behavior is the norm for Congress. The members of Congress have never liked to limit their own prerogatives, regulate themselves, or take actions which increase public knowledge of their activities. Without Watergate and pressure from public-interest groups, they would not have passed the new ethics codes, and public financing could not have attracted serious attention. But even Watergate did not create enough pressure to get Congress to pass an effective public finance law. The question now is whether the pressures created by Watergate have declined enough to allow Congress to set this matter aside altogether.

Limits on PAC contributions Unable to win congressional endorsement of public financing, Common Cause launched a campaign to convince Congress to limit the amounts that political action committees (PACs) may contribute to campaigns. As the figures below show, PACs increased in number quite rapidly after being authorized in 1974.

PAC	1974	1975	1976	1977	1978
Corporate	89	139	433	570	808
(Oil and Gas)	(12)	(19)	(70)	(93)	(128)
Labor	201	226	224	234	217
Trade Membership, Health	318	357	489	438	451
Non-Affiliated	—	—	—	110	165
Cooperative	—	—	—	8	12
Total PACs	608	722	1,146	1,360	1,653

Thus, the most rapid growth has been in corporate PACs, with oil and gas PACs contributing substantially to this growth.

As orginally authorized in 1974, a PAC could give a candidate $5,000 in any election, with a total contribution to any candidate of $10,000 in both the primary and general election. To deal with the rapid increase in PACs and their contributions to escalating campaign costs, Common Cause proposed limiting candidates to accepting a total of $70,000 from all PACs in any two-year election cycle. In addition, they suggested limiting each PAC to contributions of $6,000 to any one candidate in the primary and general election combined.

In October 1979, this proposal passed the House, over the opposition of a coalition composed mostly of southern Democrats and Republicans. To become law, the proposal must still pass the Senate.

CONFLICT OF INTEREST

The other systematic source of corruption is conflict of interest, which occurs when members have a vested interest in the policy decisions they have jurisdiction over. For example, such a conflict would occur if a member of the House committee that deals with banking owned a significant amount of stock in a bank. The member would have an incentive to make decisions which aided his investments.

Of course, any time a member of Congress owns investments in any sector of the economy affected by federal legislation, there is potential for conflict of interest. Suppose a member owned a significant amount of bank stock but did not sit on the banking committee. There would still be numerous opportunities for the member to aid banks, if he or she were so disposed. This type of conflict of interest occurs regularly.

For example, in 1977, 163 representatives reported earning more than $1,000 from companies doing substantial business with the federal government or subject to federal regulatory agencies.[48] This included 81 representatives who owned stock in banks, savings and loan associations, or bank holding corporations; 41 with oil and gas holdings; 44 who owned stock in top defense contracting firms; 22 who owned stock in power and light companies; 48 with significant real estate investments; 25 with ranch or farm interests; 16 with stock in radio and television stations; 10 with pharmaceutical stock; 15 with stock in air, highway, or rail companies; and 27 with significant holdings in insurance.

Eleven representatives with bank, savings and loan, or bank holding stock sit on either the Banking, Finance and Urban Affairs Committee, or the Ways and Means Committee, which initiates laws controlling the taxes paid by banks. Thirteen representatives with oil or gas holdings sit on subcommittees with legislative responsibility for national energy policy. Six representatives with farm or ranch holdings are members of the Agricultural Committee. Two members with stock in air, highway, or rail transports sit on committees which have jurisdiction over these industries. In addition, 222 members of the House reported receiving honoraria (generally for speeches) in 1977. This money often came from organizations that have an interest in the legislation considered by the committees that the members serve on.

Disclosure reports for senators showed that at least 30 had financial interests that could be affected by the work of the committee on which they serve. Eighty-one senators reported accepting honoraria totaling $1,087,638 in 1977, money that often came from interests they support in Congress. In 1979 the *Congressional Quarterly* reported that 54 senators and 105 House members had financial holdings which appeared to constitute a conflict of interest with their congressional obligations.[49]

One goal of the new ethics codes was to encourage members of Congress to divest themselves of financial holdings that might cause a conflict of interest. Unfortunately, the early evidence indicates that members may be reluctant to sever either their outside relationships or their role in legislation that provides them with financial benefits. So far, few members have been convinced to put their assets into a blind trust as a result of the disclosure requirements.

In fact, many continue to openly pursue their financial interests. For example, in 1977 Representative Heftel (D., Hawaii), who owns all or part of one radio and two television stations, sponsored four bills designed to impose additional regulations on pay and cable television companies that are competing with broadcast television stations.[50] Senator Russell Long (D., La.) reported owning oil and gas leases worth more than one million dollars. Using his position as chairperson of the Senate Finance Committee, Long has persistently fought to end federal controls on natural gas prices. In 1977 Long's committee cast aside Carter's energy tax proposals and substituted generous financial incentives for oil and gas production.[51] Four other members of the Senate Finance Committee also have oil and gas holdings.

There are numerous other examples. Senator Talmadge (D., Ga.), chairperson of the Senate Agriculture Committee, owns two farms. The second-ranking member of the Senate Banking Committee, John Sparkman (D., Ala.) owns considerable bank stock. Another member of the Senate Banking Committee, Robert Morgan (D., N.C.), is a director of Home Savings and Loan in Dunn, North Carolina, and owns stock in two banks.[52] These types of conflict of interest can probably only be eliminated by a requirement that members place all assets in a blind trust during their term of office. Members of Congress, of course, can be expected to resist this reform.

The new ethics code for the executive and judicial branches will also reveal conflicts of interest but will probably not end them. Prior studies have shown many conflicts of interest in these branches. For example, in 1976 Common Cause found 518 employees in 11 federal agencies who had financial interests that conflicted or appeared to conflict with their official duties.[53] There were also 619 employees in these agencies who had failed to file required financial statements.

In 1976 the General Accounting Office (GAO) also reported that there were substantial conflicts of interest in federal departments. In a study of the Commerce Department, GAO investigators found potential conflicts of interest in every major agency. An audit of 300 employees revealed 139 cases of potential conflict of interest involving 86 officials. The GAO reported similar problems in such departments as Interior, Transportation, and Health, Education, and Welfare. The more systematic disclosures required under the new ethics code should reveal many conflicts of interest.

CONCLUSIONS

While American politics has a long history of political corruption, the most overt forms have diminished greatly in the last thirty years. Today, the most pervasive forms of corruption at the national level are subtle rather than overt. But, as we have attempted to show, subtle corruption can be just as destructive to democracy as overt corruption. The effects of either type are the bartering of political influence, the compromising of public officials, the creation of low ethical standards both for those who would purchase political influence and for those who would barter it, and a stigma of dishonesty which tarnishes the political process. This causes many citizens to reject the political system as being unworthy of citizen support and too disreputable to be influenced by honest citizens.

The most systematic source of corruption in the American political system today is the link between money and political power. The corrupting links primarily involve campaign contributions and conflicts of interest. Watergate is perhaps the best example of the corrupting impacts of these subtle links. Many Watergate observers simply tried to explain it in terms of the evil character of President Nixon and his aides. But the problem involves something more serious than a few flawed people. Watergate was possible because of laws which allowed huge sums of money to be given by a small number of people who wanted to buy political influence. Watergate was also possible because many corporations and rich citizens were unscrupulous enough to be willing to buy influence and even aid in laundering contributions to keep them from being traced. Thus, Watergate revealed the corrupting influence of contributions on both citizens and officeholders.[54]

The most systematic source corruption in the American political system today is the link between money and political power.

Some of the laws passed to correct the Watergate abuses, including the new ethics codes and the Federal Election Campaign Acts of 1972, 1974, and 1976, are positive steps toward eliminating corruption in the political system. Unfortunately, however, they are clearly not enough. The link between money and Congress is still intact and is made even worse by public financing of presidential elections but not congressional elections. Now even more money is being poured into congressional races by special interests and wealthy groups, further compromising the members of Congress. Public financing of congressional elections would eliminate the need for candidates to compromise themselves to obtain the increasingly large sums necessary to run for office. Public financing would also make it easier for citizens to run for office. Finally, it would reduce the advantage of incumbents, since they could not outspend challengers by a two-to-one margin as they now generally do.

Conflict of interest, the other subtle link between money and political power, may not have been adequately dealt with by the new ethics codes. More viable methods like divestiture or blind trusts may be required. Any reform, however, is not likely to come easily, no matter how desirable it might be. Congress has long resisted high standards of ethics for itself and effective enforcement of those standards. But a healthy political system must clearly be above the suspicion of corruption. Such a system would have better citizen support, would attract a higher caliber of public servants, and would provide more dignity for honest public servants.

Footnotes

1. George Thayer, *Who Shakes the Money Tree?* (New York: Simon and Schuster, 1973), p. 37.
2. *Ibid.*, p. 37.
3. *Ibid.*, p. 44.
4. *Ibid.*, p. 38.
5. *Ibid.*, p. 38.
6. *Ibid.*, p. 43.

7. See Victor Lasky, *It Didn't Start with Watergate* (New York: Dell Press, 1977), pp. 132–36.

8. See *Congressional Quarterly,* October 30, 1976, pp. 3105–10. See also Jack Anderson, "A Citizen's Committee is Needed to Crack Down on Congressmen Who Cheat," *Parade Magazine,* November 21, 1976.

9. "Senate Adopts New Code of Ethics," *Congressional Quarterly,* April 2, 1972, p. 591.

10. Robert N. Winter-Berger, *The Washington Pay-Off* (New York: Dell Books, 1972), p. 11.

11. *Ibid.,* p. 12.

12. "Candidates' Campaign Costs for Congressional Contests Have Gone Up at a Fast Pace," *Congressional Quarterly,* September 29, 1979, p. 2151.

13. *Ibid.,* p. 2151.

14. *Ibid.,* p. 2153.

15. *Ibid.,* p. 2152.

16. See David Adamany, "Money, Politics, and Democracy: A Review Essay," *The American Political Science Review* March 1977, p. 291.

17. *Ibid.,* p. 291.

18. "Prospects Improve For Public Financing of Congressional Races," *Congressional Quarterly,* April 16, 1977, p. 710.

19. "Money, Incumbency Failed to Guarantee Success in 1976 Senate Races," *Congressional Quarterly,* June 25, 1977, p. 1292.

20. Adamany, "Money, Politics and Democracy," p. 292.

21. "Prospects Improve for Public Financing of Congressional Races," *Congressional Quarterly,* April 16, 1977, p. 708.

22. Cited in Max McCarthy, *Elections For Sale* (Boston: Houghton Mifflin, 1972), p. 46.

23. Cited in Larry L. Berg, Harlan Hahn, and John R. Schmidhauser, *Corruption in the American Political System* (Morristown, N. J.: General Learning Press, 1976), p. 103.

24. Gary Orfield, *Congressional Power: Congress and Social Change* (New York: Harcourt Brace Jovanovich, 1975), p. 306.

25. See "How to Buy a Bill," *The Washington Post,* September 1, 1977, p. A22.

26. *Ibid.,* p. A22.

27. *Dollar Politics,* Vol. 2 (New York: Congressional Quarterly, 1974), p. 13.

28. Mark J. Green, James M. Fallows, and David R.Zwick, *Who Runs Congress?* (New York: Bantam, 1972), p. 28; and Frank Wright, "The Dairy Lobby Buys the Cream of Congress," *Washington Monthly,* May 1971, p. 11.

29. "Wright Admits Campaign Aid," *The Houston Post,* December 20, 1976, p. 12A.

30. *Dollar Politics,* Vol. 2, p. 11.

31. Cited in Thayer, *Who Shakes the Money Tree?,* p. 113.

32. *Dollar Politics,* Vol. 2, p. 15.

33. Thayer, *Who Shakes the Money Tree?,* p. 241.

34. See "Congress Clears Campaign Finance Reform," *Congressional Quarterly,* October 12, 1974, pp. 2865–70.

35. 96 S. Ct. 612 (1976).

36. Adamany, "Money, Politics, and Democracy," pp. 303–4.

37. See "Reagan and Ford Lead in Primary Spending," *Congressional Quarterly,* September 25, 1976, p. 2606.

38. *Frontline,* 3, no. 4, August-September 1977.

39. "Prospects Improve for Public Financing of Congressional Races," *Congressional Quarterly,* April 16, 1977, p. 707.

40. "House Races: More Money to Incumbents," *Congressional Quarterly,* October 29, 1977, p. 2305.

41. "Money, Incumbency Failed to Guarantee Success in 1976 Senate Races," *Congressional Quarterly,* June 25, 1977, p. 1292.

42. For limits of individual states see *Ibid.,* p. 1294.

43. Over half the members voted to end cloture and over half had pledged support for the bill.

44. "Filibuster Kills Carter Campaign Bill," *Congressional Quarterly,* August 6, 1977, p. 1634.

45. *Frontline,* 3, No. 4, August-September 1977, p. 3.

46. See "Money, Incumbency Failed to Guarantee Success in 1976 Senate Races," *Congressional Quarterly,* June 25, 1977, pp. 1293–94. Contrast the limits listed on p. 1294 with incumbent and challenger expenditures on p. 1293.

47. "Financial Disclosure: New Rules Will Have Impact," *Congressional Quarterly,* July 23, 1977, p. 1507.

48. "The Wealth of Congress," *Congressional Quarterly,* September 2, 1978, p. 2726; "Outside Earnings Swell Wealth of Congress," *Congressional Quarterly,* September 1, 1979, p. 1824.

49. *Ibid.,* p. 2316.

50. *Ibid.,* p. 2314.

51. *Ibid.,* p. 2314.

52. "Executive Branch Conflicts of Interest," *In Common,* Summer 1976, p. 15.

53. "Above Suspicion" (editorial), *The Houston Post,* September 6, 1976.

54. Each of these points is noted in Berg et al., *Corruption in The American Political System,* pp. 72–73.

7

Liberty before property; the man before the dollar.

Abraham Lincoln

Most Americans seem to hold two contradictory attitudes toward the economic system within which they live. That complicates the analysis of the relationship between politics and economics in the United States.

On the one hand, most people in this country are firm believers in an economic ideology, though that would come as a shock to them. After all, Americans have always thought of themselves as no-nonsense pragmatists. Ideologies—all of those "isms"—were foreign products, and dangerous foreign products at that. And yet that deep, anti-ideological consciousness was itself an important element in an ideology. Since there was, and is, no mass communist or socialist movement in the United States providing a counter-ideology, capitalism appears not as an ideology but as the expression of common-sense truths about human nature. Yet, as George Cabot Lodge of the Harvard Business School has pointed out, that capitalist faith is anchored in values and attitudes which go back to John Locke in the seventeenth century; values and attitudes which Lodge, a sophisticated defender of the private business sector, does not hesitate to label as outmoded.[1]

The Economic System: Does It Limit Public Influence?

This "American ideology," as Lodge defines it, believes in individual striving in a market economy with minimal intervention from the state. Vigorous, natural competition and the free choices of consumers will produce the common good. No one—and certainly not the government—should be concerned with the whole of the society, which will be adequately taken care of through the interaction of individuals.[2]

In fact, the American economy is more and more dominated by huge uncompetitive corporations which resemble Adam Smith's entrepreneur about as much as a nuclear plant resembles James Watt's steam engine. In addition, in every advanced capitalist country, the state plays a major role in directing the economy, and individuals are more and more dependent upon huge and powerful bureaucracies, private as well as public, for their well-being. But

Trading on the New York Stock Exchange, one of the barometers of economic activity in America. The American economy—and those who wield economic power—profoundly affect the political system.

even though reality contradicts the American ideology at almost every point, that ideology plays a role in our politics because it is still deeply believed. So it is that John Locke's defense of private property as a necessary base for personal freedom in a society dominated by the absolute power of monarchs is used to justify the immunity of multinational corporations from oversight by a democratic government.

On the other hand, the popular consciousness is not so simpleminded as to totally ignore all the tremendous changes which have occurred since the seventeenth century. Side by side with that naive trust in the capitalist ideology, there is a contrary strain which derives from the egalitarianism of the early years of the Republic, from the populism of the late nineteenth century, and from the labor and civil-rights movements of the twentieth century. Corporations and wealth are suspect, and politicians are seen as the agents of the rich. In this view—which intensified in the 1970s, as the surveys cited in Chapter 1 show—the outcomes of the American economic and political system are not the result of an interaction of equals but are rigged by the people at the top.

Clearly, these attitudes are contradictory and confused. So we must ask: What is the reality of the American economy and its relationship to our political system? That, as we will see in a moment, is a question over which sincere and informed scholars can honestly differ. Yet there are some facts which are undisputed. And even if there are many unresolved controversies in this area, just stating and sorting out some of these principal theories should help us in understanding a critical dimension of the nation's life.

CAPITALISM

Most—but as we shall see at the end of this section, not all—analysts describe the American economic system as capitalistic. One of the problems of defining this system has to do with one of its unique characteristics: it is the most dynamic mode of production the world has ever known. In precapitalist societies, the most powerful individuals and groups prized stability and wanted next year to resemble last year, for that would guarantee their continuing rule. But capitalism is a system of almost uninterrupted technological revolution. If one year is only as good as the previous year but if the workers, due to inventions, have become more productive, then people must be laid off (the same last year's output can now be produced by fewer workers). Demand will fall (the laid-off workers will have no money to spend on good and services), and a crisis will ensue. For capitalism, unlike any previous social formation, constant change is a prerequisite for the on-going power of the establishment.

This is why there must be two distinct, but obviously related, elements in a definition of capitalism: the identification of those structures which persist despite all of the changes, and the description of the various stages of the system brought about by those changes.

The enduring elements of capitalism

First, let us examine the characteristics which set off capitalism in all of its phases from previous systems. In order to avoid going into needless detail and opening up complicated controversies which are not relevant to this text, we will define this underlying capitalist structure in terms on which two great intellectual opponents, Karl Marx and Max Weber, would agree. Weber was one of the most penetrating critics of Marx and Marxism. If, then, we develop a definition out of elements which *both* Marx and Weber would see as essential, we will mark out a meaning of the word *capitalism* which can hardly be faulted as one-sided.[3] Five characteristics of capitalism would be found in this Marx-Weber definition.

Industrial   Capitalism in its modern form is the basis of the industrial revolution. In precapitalist times, there had been early "capitalisms" (Weber) or various capitalist elements (Marx). For instance, merchants who tried to buy cheap and sell dear were found very early on in economic history. But it has only been during the last four hundred years that society's entire production system has been organized for the purpose of profit. This development was caused and facilitated by the growth of industry. However, it should be noted that both Marx and Weber agree that the social and intellectual revolution of capitalism preceded the technological take-off.

The market economy   Under capitalism, goods and services are produced to be sold on a market at a profit. In precapitalist times—and in parts of the Third World which have not been thoroughly penetrated by capitalist methods up to this very moment—most people produced for their own (family or village) consumption. They ate what they or their immediate neighbors grew; they wore what they or their immediate neighbors made. Only under capitalism do most people—roughly 85 percent of the American labor force in 1978—work for an employer who sells their output on a market.

Wage labor   Related to this last characteristic, labor under capitalism is a commodity like almost everything else. Most people do not work for themselves, their family, or their neighbors but rather for a company. As we will see later on in this chapter, more and more people work for very large corporations. In the economic history of the world, this is a relatively recent, and quite unique, development.

Profit orientation   The aim of this capitalist production system is profit. Those goods and services which do not yield a sufficient profit will not be produced—or else will be produced at a loss by the government itself or through government subsidies. There have been scholarly debates in recent years as to whether capitalists strive for a maximum profit in a given year or whether they are more concerned with steady profits over a long period of

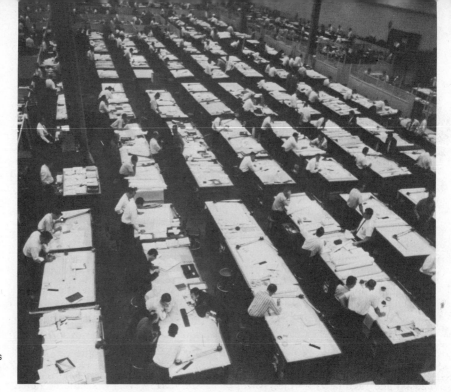

Large corporations have long since replaced entrepreneurs as the basis of the American economic system.

time. The economist John Kenneth Galbraith, who is one of the analysts who deny that corporations set prices to ''maximize'' profits in the short run, nevertheless concedes that in the long run this remains industry's aim.[4]

Periodic crisis All precapitalist systems were subject to crises. These took the form of an *insufficiency* of goods brought about by a bad harvest, a plague, a war, or some other cause which was external to the system. But capitalism suffers from periodic crises which break out at the height of prosperity and take the form of an *excess* of goods and services on the market. The cause of this phenomenon has been—and still is—debated by economists. Joseph Schumpeter, one of the greatest conservative thinkers of the twentieth century, devoted two volumes to analyzing this one issue in the late 1930s.[5] But no matter how scholars account for the fact, the existence of ''overproduction,'' ''underconsumption,'' and monetary inflation is recognized by practically all of them.

For one hundred years capitalism was industrial, characterized by a market economy, wage labor and a profit orientation, and subject to periodic internal crises. But capitalism today is enormously changed from the system of a century ago. And these transformations of the economic structures are particularly important to the student of political science since all of them were the cause or the effect of related changes in the political system. So we turn now to an economic *and* political outline of some of the most important changes in capitalist society.

The periods of capitalism

The laissez-faire economy and the nightwatchman state From the origins of capitalism until roughly the 1890s, the economy was relatively uncontrolled, business was dominated by entrepreneurs who headed small-scale organizations, and the free market operated in something like the way Adam Smith had described. In the first capitalist nation, Great Britain, there was even belief in the doctrine of "free trade." According to this idea, if all countries refrained from putting up tariff walls and each specialized in what it did best, then each would have a "comparative advantage" and all would benefit from the low prices that would result. Of course, as the first capitalist nation, it was to Great Britain's advantage to follow such a policy since it could outcompete and out-sell all the other economies then in the world market. In the United States and Germany, which were trying to catch up with Great Britain during the nineteenth century, "infant industries" were protected by the government from the excessive rigors of international competition.

There were, as we will see in a moment, other contradictions of the free-market doctrine. Still, this was the period in which *laissez faire*—a phrase meaning "let alone" and coined by French economists in the late eighteenth century to describe a policy of non-intervention in the economy by the government—more or less prevailed. The political corollary of this theory was the "nightwatchman state"—a government which guaranteed the right of private property, personal safety and civil order, and left everything else up to the individual.

However, it must be emphasized that even in this first, relatively uncontrolled, period of capitalist history, the state did not stay out of the economy as laissez-faire theory suggested. From the very beginning, business elites always expected government to protect industry from strong competition, provide businesses with services, subsidies, and tax breaks (or even freedom from taxes). As Prewitt and Stone note:

> The growth of modern capitalism, contrary to the laissez-faire myths, has required intimate relationships between the corporate and the political elite. Most of the corporate elite have rejected objectionable government interference while at the same time enthusiastically accepting certain close government-economy relationships.[6]

Even the development of the law of contracts, sales, and negotiable instruments was designed to aid business development and prosperity.

One of the most tangible forms of government assistance has always been outright subsidies. Throughout American history the federal government has provided business with subsidies in the form of cash, property, free facilities, services, and credit (generally below the market rate). An early example was government subsidies to the railroads. During the 1850s and 1860s, the federal government gave "the Union Pacific, Central Pacific, Northern Pacific, and other western railroads 158,000,000 acres of land, an area almost as large as

New England, New York, and Pennsylvania combined, while the states turned over 167,000,000 acres, a domain nearly the size of Texas."[7] Not only were the railroads given these vast acreages, they were granted total ownership of all mineral rights on these lands forever. The federal government also gave the railroads vast sums of money, conservatively estimated at some $707,000,000.[8] By the 1870s, the federal and state governments had paid for 60 percent of the cost of railroad expansion.

Later congressional investigations revealed that the railroads wanted more than just a subsidy and actually defrauded the government out of much of the money provided to aid with construction. The construction companies employed by the railroads (and usually owned by them) simply charged the government about twice the price of actual construction. As Senator George Hoar said at the completion of the transcontinental railroad:

> When the greatest railroad of the world, binding together the continent and uniting the two great seas which wash our shores, was finished, I have seen our national triumph and exaltation turned to bitterness and shame by the unanimous reports of three committees of Congress that every step of that mighty enterprise has been taken in fraud.[9]

This cartoon from the Gilded Age pits the labor movement(right) against the much more powerful monopolies in a one-sided duel.

Many observers saw the government giveaways and the defrauding of the public treasury by the railroads as a part of the times. Young men like Philip Armour, James Hill, Andrew Carnegie, Jay Gould, Jim Fisk, John D. Rockefeller, and J.P. Morgan decided not to serve in the Civil War but instead to stay home and profit from it.[10] And profit they did. Fortunes were amassed which continue in some cases to influence the American political system to this day. These individuals and others became known as the "robber barons," men who exhibited particularly low moral standards and who feasted off less predatory and more honorable people and the public treasury for private profit. Vernon Louis Parrington in his *Main Currents in American Thought* described the Civil War and postwar pillage as a "Great Barbecue" in which government officials were rewarded in kind for allowing the robber barons to raid the public treasury.

> Congress had rich gifts to bestow—in lands, tariffs, subsidies, favors of all sorts; and when influential citizens made their wishes known to the reigning statesmen, the sympathetic politicians were quick to turn the government into the fairy godmother the voters wanted it to be. A huge barbecue was spread to which all were presumably invited. Not quite all, to be sure; inconspicuous persons who were at home on the farm or at work in the mills and offices, were overlooked; a good many indeed out of the total number of the American people. But all the important persons, leading bankers and promoters and businessmen, received invitations. There wasn't room for everybody and these were presumed to represent the whole. It was a splendid feast.[11]

Monopoly and the welfare state   The last quarter of the nineteenth century was a tumultuous period for the capitalist system. As Figure 7.1 shows, there was a panic in 1873, general depression from 1874 to 1878, mild recessions between 1883 and 1885 and in 1891, a collapse of the stock market in 1893, and mainly depressed years between 1894 and 1897. In such a crisis-ridden situation, industrial concentration—monopolies, trusts, cartels—was a defensive measure. A giant company—or a league of companies—could dominate the market, dictate prices to it and, within limits, smooth out the fluctuations which continued to follow the rhythm of boom and bust in the competitive sector. So it was that the difficult and tumultuous years from 1873 to 1897 witnessed the rise of monopoly capitalism.

Charles and Mary Beard described this process as follows:

> At the end of the century three-fourths of the manufactured products came from factories owned by associations of stockholders; in each great industry was a network of federated plants under corporate direction; by 1890 combination was the supreme concept of the industrial magnate. Oil products, iron, steel, copper, lead, sugar, coal and other staples were then in the hands of huge organizations that constituted, if not monopolies, efficient masters of their respective fields. During the following decade (after 1890), the work of affiliation went forward with feverish haste, culminating in the billion-dollar United States Steel Corporation of 1901.[12]

FIGURE: 7.1
Periods of Economic Instability

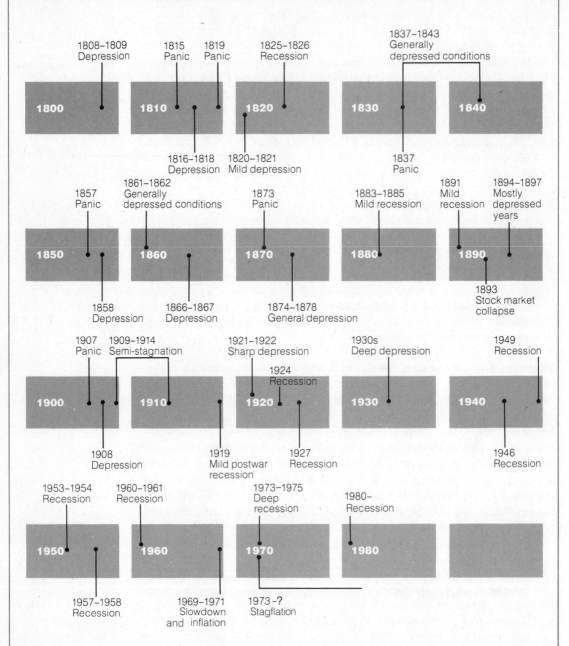

Source: Douglas F. Dowd, *Modern Economic Problems in Historical Perspective* (Lexington, Mass.: D.C. Heath, 1965), p. 143.

For capitalism, unlike any previous social formation, constant change is a prerequisite for the on-going power of the establishment.

In the same period, competition between the capitalist countries became truly global. Indeed, one of the most influential political theories of the twentieth century—V.I. Lenin's analysis of imperialism—holds that this internationalization of capital was the necessary result of the monopoly structures at home. But one does not have to agree with Lenin—whose analysis will be criticized in Chapter 19—to recognize the tremendous worldwide expansion of capitalism in the period when monopoly came to dominate the domestic system. Here is Henry Kissinger's account of this phenomenon:

> In the nineteenth century the Industrial Revolution gave birth to improved communications, technological innovations and new forms of business organization which immeasurably expanded man's capacity to exploit the frontiers and territories of the entire globe. In less than one generation (1880–1900) one-fifth of the land area of the planet and one-tenth of its inhabitants were gathered into the domain of imperial powers in an unrestrained scramble for colonies. The costs—in affront to human dignity, in material waste and deprivation, and in military conflict and political turbulence—haunt us still.[13]

This tremendous internal and external change in capitalism provoked a political response in both the United States and Europe. But there was a significant difference between the politics of the New World and those of the Old.

In Europe, the new capitalism gave rise to movements which used government power to improve the often cruel conditions produced by the private economy. Ironically, the innovator in this area was a conservative German, Otto von Bismarck, who led the kaiser's Germany. Frightened by the growth of the labor and socialist movements on the one hand, and acting on the basis of paternalistic values inherited from German feudalism on the other, Bismarck created the beginnings of the welfare state: between 1883 and 1889 he introduced compulsory insurance to protect workers against sickness, accidents, old age, and the like. In the first decade of the twentieth century, the British Liberals under Lloyd George consciously imitated Bismarck. With an intellectual assist from the Fabians and pressure from the nascent Labour party, they introduced similar measures into their country.

In the United States, the progressives, liberals, and socialists had a considerable influence in the period leading up to World War I, in part because the middle class was becoming as fearful of monopolies and trusts as were the workers, the farmers, and the urban poor. At times, the rhetoric became fairly radical, even in the mainstream of politics. In 1912, for instance, candidate Woodrow Wilson attacked Theodore Roosevelt's proposals:

> I find, then, the proposition to be this: That there shall be two masters, the great corporation, and over it the government of the United States; and I ask who is going to be master of the government of the United States? It has a master now—

those who in combination control the monopolies. And if the government controlled by the monopolies in its turn controls the monopolies, the partnership is finally consummated.[14]

When Wilson became President (and, indeed, under Teddy Roosevelt's earlier Presidency) the emphasis was upon controlling monopoly power and relieving some of the injustices of the economy, though not at all on the scale of Bismarck and Lloyd George. In those years before World War I, there was antitrust legislation, the establishment of the Federal Reserve Bank, the institution of the Federal Trade Commission, the federal income tax, and like measures. In the period right after the end of the war, there was a renewed burst of radicalism—a general strike in Seattle, a great struggle for union organization by the steel workers, the appearance of strong support for a labor party within the American Federation of Labor. On the other side, there was anticommunist hysteria: many sober citizens believed that the Bolshevik Revolution that occurred in Russia in 1917 was now imminent in the United States. Foreign-born people suspected of communist sympathies were deported; the "American Plan," a program to smash unionism, was widely accepted in business circles. There were some stirrings in the 1920s—LaFollette ran for president on a third-party ticket in 1924 with support from both the American Federation of Labor and the Socialist party—but the decade was perhaps best symbolized by the taciturn President Calvin Coolidge, the man who coined the famous phrase that "the business of America is business."

Even in the first, relatively uncontrolled period of capitalist history, the state did not stay out of the economy as laissez-faire theory suggested.

Still, the economic shift within capitalism from entrepreneurs to great monopolies had given rise to significant political movements which sought to limit and regulate concentrated economic power. And during World War I the American government, like every other power at war, had taken over the direction of much of the economy and had even temporarily nationalized the railroads. Small wonder that, even in the 1920s, John Maynard Keynes wrote of "the end of laissez faire."

The Depression and the New Deal   In October 1929—historians usually pinpoint the moment on Thursday morning, October 24, 1929—the Great Crash took place on the New York Stock Exchange. Millions of shares were traded, "many of them at prices which shattered the dreams and the hopes of those who owned them."[15] This event is popularly regarded as the cause of the Great Depression, which followed. It should be seen, rather, as a symptom of the greatest economic crisis American capitalism had ever known, an event which would change our politics as well as the way in which we produce goods and services.

On the worst day of the stock-market crash—October 29, 1929—brokers and investors jammed Wall Street and the New York Stock Exchange building(right), where millions of shares were traded. By early November, stocks had lost 40 percent of their September value.

Paul Samuelson, the Nobel laureate in economics, sums up the Depression in this way:

> If you asked an economic historian just what the Great Depression really meant, his best answer would be: "From a 1929 Net National Product (NNP) of 95.8 billion dollars there was a drop to a 1933 NNP of 48.8 billion dollars. This halving of the money value of the flow of goods and services in the American economy caused hardship, bank failures, riots and political turmoil."[16]

There is widespread and complicated debate among scholars as to exactly why the Great Depression occurred. Most of that discussion is not relevant to this book, but two points should be noted. First, there is agreement between a conservative like Milton Friedman and a liberal like John Kenneth Galbraith that the breakdown of the system was, in some measure, a "self-inflicted wound." Specifically, both Friedman and Galbraith argue that the Federal Reserve in the 1920s followed policies which helped bring on the Crash. With the politicization of the economy, even to the limited degree of the 1920s, the laws and policies adopted in Washington were beginning to become as important as the law of supply and demand.

Second, during the twenties wages and salaries did not go up, but productivity and profits did. Therefore, in order to keep up the momentum of the system, those profits had to be reinvested. With expanding output and restricted consumption, any breakdown could start a downward spiral. Since the mass of the people did not have the money to buy the totality of output, workers were laid off. The layoffs further decreased the buying power of the population, which required further layoffs, and so on until, as Samuelson documents, one half of the production in the United States ground to a halt. Galbraith emphasizes this trend in his study of the Crash; but then so did *Business Week,* a resolutely procorporate publication, in its fiftieth-anniversary retrospective on the economy in 1979.[17]

It would seem that a catastrophe of the dimensions of 1929 would immediately give rise to a political movement demanding immediate and far-reaching change. In fact, the relationship between politics and economics is never as simple as that. At the outset of the Depression, there were people who silently accepted their fate, who were demoralized by the experience rather than radicalized by it. Then there were individual or sporadic group protests: lootings, rent riots, marches. In that second phase, small groups of committed radicals—in the early thirties, socialists and communists—often played a key, catalytic role. But the major responses to the Crash—Franklin Roosevelt's New Deal and the organization of mass production workers into the unions of the Committee (later Congress) of Industrial Organizations (the CIO)—only began four or five years *after* the bottom fell out of the stock market and then out of the economy.[18]

Indeed, in the campaign of 1932, Franklin Roosevelt on occasion attacked President Hoover, his Republican opponent, for spending too much money and thereby creating too big a Federal deficit.[19] And even though Roosevelt moved vigorously once he was elected, he did not immediately create what history calls the New Deal: the Social Security Act, the Wagner Act (making collective bargaining between unions and employers a matter of public policy), the Securities and Exchange Commission, the Soil Conservation Act (which paid farmers for taking land out of production), and so on. These institutional changes which fundamentally transformed the political structure of American capitalism date from 1935; thus, they came seven to eight years after the economic collapse.

The "first New Deal" of 1933–1935 was centered on emergency measures like initiating public employment projects and stopping bank closings. Its main positive measure, the National Industrial Recovery Act, had tried to get each industry to plan full employment on its own. This was done by exempting it from the antitrust laws and allowing, in violation of the free enterprise myth it stood for, "production rather than competition." Indeed, it saw competition as the problem, not the solution.

By 1935, that first New Deal was in a shambles. The Recovery Act had been declared unconstitutional, and Roosevelt was beset by radical critics on his right, like Huey Long and Father Charles Coughlin, demanding much more dramatic change. It was then, and only then, that he improvised the "second

New Deal'' (which is what history calls the New Deal) and, in effect, changed the very organization of American economics and politics. At the time, the New Deal appeared to be bold, even revolutionary, and Roosevelt was denounced by many of the rich as a "traitor to his class." In retrospect, however, it is clear that the New Deal was relatively moderate. Not only was America the last capitalist country to develop a welfare state; it instituted the most minimal of the welfare states. As we have seen, a national health system began in the kaiser's Germany in the 1880s and in Britain in the first decade of the twentieth century. At this writing, such a program exists in every capitalist country except the United States, and welfare programs are much more extensive in other industrialized nations.

The New Deal had two basic thrusts. On the one hand, the government was to use fiscal and monetary policy to assure that there was enough consumer demand to buy the products of the private sector. The fiscal component in this strategy was based on deficit financing during the Depression; that is, Washington would, in effect, "print money." Under conditions of full employment, increasing buying power in this way without simultaneously increasing production would be inflationary since more and more dollars would bid for fewer and fewer goods. But, the Keynesian theory underlying the New Deal economics held that when there were unused resources, both human and

Franklin D. Roosevelt, shown shaking hands with a coal miner during the 1932 campaign, applied Keynesian theory to the American economy in the 1930s, using both fiscal and monetary policy to stimulate economic recovery.

material, a flood of money would motivate industry to put people back to work and to expand the supply of goods and services. Indeed, there would be a *multiplier effect:* the federal dollar would go to someone who would spend it; the company that made the sale would have a profit, which it would reinvest in order to take advantage of the newly enlarged market; and that would mean more jobs and more buying power, and so on. Washington, it was said, would merely have to "prime the pump"; once prosperity was thus set in motion, the private sector would do the rest, and there would be a decreasing need for such programs as relief payments and public jobs.*

"Pump priming," deficit financing, and all the rest would help the employable people suffering from the Depression. But what about those who could not work—the very young, the old, the disabled? One law, the Social Security Act of 1935, was the focus of the American response to that question. In many ways, it was the most important single statute passed under Roosevelt. The priorities it established still profoundly influence American life. The main purpose of the act was to provide support for aging people who were out of the labor market and thus would not be helped by the economic management policies just described. And, indeed, to this day roughly two-thirds of Washington's domestic social spending for individuals goes to people over sixty-five years of age.[20]

In retrospect, it is clear that the New Deal was relatively moderate. Not only was America the last capitalist country to develop a welfare state; it instituted the most minimal of the welfare states.

But other "safety nets" for people who had fallen out of the economy were also established under Social Security. One of them was unemployment compensation. Another, which has become extremely controversial over the years, is Aid to Families with Dependent Children (AFDC), the main federal contribution to what is popularly called "welfare." This program, Daniel Patrick Moynihan has noted, "began almost as an afterthought."[21]

So the New Deal was not a carefully crafted and planned response to the Depression but rather an improvisation. Later on in the text, particularly when we deal with poverty in Chapter 15, we will take up the successes and failures of the welfare provisions of the Social Security Act. For now, let us focus on the efforts to deal with economic collapse and mass unemployment. How well did the Roosevelt programs work in this area?

In 1940, John Maynard Keynes, whose economic theories did much to inspire people around Roosevelt (but who thought that Roosevelt himself did not know "anything about economics"), took a rather gloomy view of the

* In an almost totally urbanized America, the "pump-priming" metaphor is not as obvious as it once was. When you had trouble with an old-fashioned water pump on the farm, you poured a cup of water down into the system and it would often start working. In New Deal theory, Washington simply provided that first cup of water; the private sector continued to operate the pump.

policies he advocated. Perhaps, he mused, it was impossible for a peacetime capitalist government to intervene in the economy to the degree required.[22] There was reason for pessimism. In 1939, after six years of the New Deal, the unemployment rate in the United States was 17 percent, almost twice as high as the worst jobless rate from 1945 to the present. It was World War II, as Keynes predicted in 1940, which brought an end to the mass unemployment of the Depression. The New Deal economics, then, worked quite imperfectly during the worst of the crisis.

Others give Roosevelt higher marks. Leon Keyersling, a participant in the New Deal who became the chairman of the Council of Economic Advisors under President Truman, wrote in 1979:

> Foremost among the misstatements during recent years and today is the claim that the New Deal failed in its primary purpose of reducing unemployment and restoring a healthy economy prior to the advent of World War II. This involves failure to appreciate the task of reviving an economy with an unemployment rate of 25 percent at the start, and with some basic industries running at 11 percent of capacity, at a time when nowhere in the private sector were the resources and confidence available to commence the recuperative process, and when the concept of the positive economic role of government was in its infancy . . . . Yet even in 1939, the about 17 percent rate of unemployment was 32 percent below the 25 percent rate in 1933, an absolute reduction of 3.35 million. These achievements as a whole were far greater in view of all the circumstances than what we have done in recent years . . . .[23]

But even these different evaluations make it clear that the more positive view of the New Deal (Keyserling's) recognizes that many, many problems were not solved in the thirties. Still, those years do show an important, if somewhat complex, relationship between economic and political events. On the one hand, we have seen that even the most dramatic collapse of the capitalist system in its history did not *automatically* produce an adequate political response. From the stock market crash of 1929 to the "second" (or real) New Deal of 1935 there were six years of confusion. And even the heyday of the New Deal proper, from 1935 to 1939 (when the "War Deal" took over), was an ambiguous time with a new recession in 1937 and more than a few problems unsolved as the decade ended. Yet the Depression did have a profound impact on political structures in the United States. From Roosevelt to the present moment, it has been the underlying consensus of the country that the government has a responsibility for the overall management of the economy. That duty was recognized by Gerald Ford, perhaps the most conservative President since Calvin Coolidge, as well as by Lyndon Johnson, who had been a Roosevelt loyalist during the New Deal.

Thus, as we have noted before, the New Deal did not simply pass a series of laws; it created a policy framework within which all political debates took place. There were differences over the proper degree of government intervention into the economy and exactly how it should be carried out, but no practical politician doubted the basic premise itself. In many respects that "public philosophy," as we have also said earlier, began to unravel in the 1970s. But before turning to that momentous event, let us look briefly at the postwar years 1945–1970, when the New Deal consolidated itself and ultimately seemed totally triumphant.

From the Roosevelt coalition to the new economics   Roosevelt's New Deal did not simply alter the structure and responsibility of the American government; it also created a new political movement. From 1932 to 1968 (or perhaps to 1976) the New Deal coalition dominated the Presidency and generally controlled the Congress. It was composed of big-city voters (led by big-city machines) in the earlier years. Later it was based on urban electorates supporting the welfare state bureaucracies which replaced the machines, organized labor, minorities, middle-class liberals, and by the Democratic South (though that element became ambiguous when the civil-rights surge split the Democrats as early as 1948). In 1952 and 1956, Eisenhower was elected President, but he was a charismatic general who probably could have won the office on the Democratic as well as the Republican ticket—there were Democrats who wanted to give him their nomination in 1948—and, in any case, he did not transfer his personal popularity to his party.

So the New Deal political era certainly lasted until the election of 1968 when Richard Nixon won election to the White House. But even that event can be seen as exceptional. It was produced by an unpopular war which split the Democratic party into conflicting camps. In 1972, Nixon won a landslide over George McGovern, but that was precisely because McGovern failed to mobilize the traditional Rooseveltian coalition, most notably a significant section of the labor movement. Nixon's victory was also one more consequence of the Democratic split over the war in Vietnam. In 1976, Jimmy Carter did reassemble the coalition and, as the first President from below the Mason-Dixon line since the Civil War, even brought the South back into the Democratic presidential majority. That Carter coalition, however, only won by a hair. As Chapter 8 will detail, there are many signs that the traditional party alignments, as well as the New Deal public philosophy, are now disintegrating.

That disintegration will be considered later on in the book. For now, the fact to stress is that the Roosevelt political coalition gave a certain political coherence to American society, just as the Roosevelt policy legacy constituted the "public philosophy" of the nation from 1945 to roughly 1970. It was in the period 1961–1968—during the Presidencies of John F. Kennedy and Lyndon B. Johnson—that this process came to a climax. For a brief moment it seemed as if the heirs of Franklin Roosevelt had actually solved the basic problems and contradictions of capitalist society, something Roosevelt himself had failed to do.

In the middle of that Kennedy-Johnson decade, Walter Heller, who served as chairman of the Council of Economic Advisors from 1961 to 1964 and thus counseled both Kennedy and Johnson, summarized this presumed accomplishment:

Economics has come of age in the 1960s. Two Presidents have recognized and drawn on modern economics as a source of national strength and presidential power. Their willingness to use, for the first time, the full range of modern economic tools underlies the unbroken U.S. expansion since early 1961—an expansion that in its first five years created over seven million new jobs, doubled profits, increased the nation's real output by a third. . . . Together with the gradual closing of that huge production gap has come—part as cause, part as consequence—a gradual, then rapid, narrowing of the intellectual gap between professional economists and men of affairs, between economic advisors and decision-makers. . . . These are profound changes. What they have wrought is not the creation of a "new economics," but the completion of the Keynesian Revolution—thirty years after John Maynard Keynes fired the opening salvo. And they have put the political economist at the President's elbow.[24]

Those Kennedy-Johnson years saw the unemployment rate cut in half, reaching a low point only achieved once before in the postwar period. Moreover, prices were stable. Between 1960 and 1964, the Consumer Price Index went up at the incredibly slow rate of 1.2 percent a year. Even in the second half of the decade, when the expenditures for the Vietnam War triggered some inflation, the 1964–1969 annual rate of increase averaged only 3.8 percent. Small wonder that official thinkers concerned themselves with an unprecedented problem: if the economy continued to grow rapidly with stable prices, then the federal government's revenues would sharply increase even if it didn't raise the tax rate, since its constant share would be a portion of a larger and larger economic pie. Therefore, if the policy-makers did not find a way to recycle those revenues back into the economy, they might inadvertently start a recession by siphoning off too much buying power.

All this, Daniel Patrick Moynihan wrote in 1969, pointed to "the beginning of a situation utterly without parallel in modern government: administrations that must be constantly on the lookout for new ways to expend public funds in the public interest."[25] In all previous societies, governments had complained of having too little money; now the success of Keynesian economics was making some highly placed people—Moynihan served in the Kennedy, Johnson, and Nixon administrations before becoming a United States senator—worry that Washington had too much money. Within only a few years Moynihan's fears would appear almost preposterous, but that development will be discussed in the next section.

All this success did not simply unite the Roosevelt coalition and the professional economists; it also acted to bring businessmen into the New Deal consensus. In 1964, for instance, Henry Ford headed up a prestigious committee of corporate leaders who supported the New Dealer, Johnson, against the advocate of free-enterprise economics, Barry Goldwater. Actually, that was the culmination of a process which had begun during World War II. Patriotic businessmen, most of whom had fought Roosevelt, came to Washington or cooperated with the federal government as part of the war effort. They learned that New Deal agencies staffed or influenced by business were far from being antibusiness. When Dwight Eisenhower brought the Republican party into the White House in 1952, the first time it had held presidential power since Roosevelt's election in 1932, that discovery was reinforced. It turned out that it was impossible to repeal the welfare state, as some Republican ideologues had advocated. Indeed, the Department of Health, Education and Welfare (HEW), that quintessential welfare-state bureaucracy, was created by the Republican, Eisenhower.

As we saw earlier, the New Deal never was as radical as its Republican critics charged in the 1930s. The political forces and struggles which brought it into being were more often radical—workers were killed in some of the bitter battles of the '30s and industrialists like Henry Ford had their own private armies—but the institutions which resulted were not. The "pump priming" philosophy of the Roosevelt years tended to expand buying power by increasing the incomes of those at the bottom of the society. But even then there was a considerable element of "trickle down" in the strategy. Then, as the tumultuous '30s ended and businessmen came to recognize the value of once-hated institutions, "trickle down" more and more became the norm. So, the corporate executives were discovering their self-interest when they backed Johnson in 1964. And the patterns and priorities they perceived then still operate today. Consider some of the recent data.

The amount of direct and indirect aid which goes to business in any one year is probably incalculable, but certainly it is vast. For example, one analysis showed that in 1975 corporations received $3.2 billion in cash aid and another $2 billion in services and credit savings.[26] Shipbuilders, farmers, and airlines, as usual, received most of this aid. Another $21.2 billion in direct and indirect tax subsidies went to corporations, the bulk of it to the very largest corporations. Seventy-five billion dollars of the 1975 budget went to companies in the form of procurement, research and development, and consulting contracts.[27]

In 1975, as in most years, many corporations along with the wealthy who own and run them received aid by being allowed to pay little or no federal taxes. Between 1972 and 1975, a total of 590 citizens who had earned incomes in excess of $200,000 paid no federal taxes. Thousands of other citizens had very high incomes but paid very little in taxes. During this same period 29 major corporations reported total profits of almost $3 billion but paid no federal taxes. Sixty-four other corporations paid at rates of 10 percent or less despite profits of almost $11 billion.[28]

In 1976 this type of aid accelerated substantially. Seventeen major corporations paid no federal income taxes despite total worldwide net incomes of more than $2,594,060,000.[29] Among those corporations which paid no taxes were United States Steel, Bethlehem Steel, LTV, Armco Steel, National Steel, General Dynamics, Republic Steel, Singer, Phelps Dodge, Texas Gulf, American Airlines, Eastern Airlines, Pan American World Airlines, The Southern Co., and the Chase Manhattan Corporation. Forty-one other major corporations paid an effective tax rate of 10 percent or less.

Among those firms paying 10 percent or less in taxes were Lockheed

Aircraft (1 percent), Standard Oil of Ohio (2.1 percent), Occidental Petroleum (4.2 percent), Mobil Oil (4.5 percent), Gulf Oil (7.0 percent), Marathon Oil (7.0 percent), International Telephone and Telegraph (7.4 percent), Chrysler Corp. (7.5 percent), the richest corporation in America—Exxon (8.0 percent), Texaco (8.6 percent), Union Carbide (9.1 percent), and AT&T (9.5 percent).[30] These twelve corporations paid extremely low taxes despite combined worldwide earnings of $24,702,468,000.

Corporations and the rich frequently escape most or all taxes because Congress has passed special exemptions for them. Many of those exemptions are summarized in a "tax expenditure" budget. This was mandated by Congress in 1974 on the grounds that deductions for corporations or individuals, which lower the amount of tax they are required to pay, effectively increase their incomes by the same amount. The federal government suffers a loss, the individual or corporation a gain. In general, deductions are justified on the grounds that they encourage business and citizens to behave in ways which help the entire society. That is, deducting the interest portion of a mortgage payment promotes home ownership, community development, and work for the building trades. In the 1979 estimates of the 1980 budget, tax expenditures total $178.1 billion, $41.8 billion for corporations and $126.3 billion for individuals.[31]

"Are you sure you've examined all the loopholes? Mineral depletion? Municipal Bonds? Capital gains?"

The aid given by this program is, of course, primarily camouflaged. Corporations and individuals can be given very considerable aid with little public notice or criticism. This allows them to accept substantial public aid without having to suffer any of the normal stigmas associated with assistance. Aid can be accepted by recipients who simultaneously criticize welfare for the poor and social welfare programs such as Social Security and Medicare.

Actually, a far larger proportion of the population receives aid from the government than is generally appreciated. All citizens who earn enough to itemize deductions are allowed deductions for such items as home-interest expenses and taxes, large medical bills, common interest payments, a proportion of health insurance premiums, work-related expenses such as tools, education courses to help one on the job, and business expenses. Average citizens receive aid from the federal government in dozens of other forms. Examples would include low-cost Federal Housing Administration (FHA) or GI-bill home loans, small-business loans and services, publicly supported educational systems (including colleges and universities), low-cost student loans, government insurance of bank and savings accounts, and, in some parts of the country, low-cost utilities (e.g., the Tennessee Valley Authority). Thus, average citizens receive much more aid from the federal government than they commonly believe.

Still, when the tax system is thought of as an aid program, two points should be emphasized. First, deductions are worth much more to higher-income than middle- or lower-income workers. For example, in 1977, 31 percent of all tax breaks went to the 1.2 million citizens who earned $50,000 or more, even though this group composed only 1.4 percent of the taxpayers. The 45.6 million taxpayers earning less than $10,000 received only 12 percent of all tax breaks. Almost half of all tax breaks went to taxpayers earning $30,000 and up, a group composing only about 5 percent of all taxpayers.[32]

The "pump priming" philosophy of the Roosevelt years tended to expand buying power by increasing the incomes of those at the bottom of the society. Then, as the tumultuous '30s ended and businessmen came to recognize the value of once-hated institutions, "trickle down" more and more became the norm.

Thus, as income increases, a larger percentage of the taxpayer's income can be protected through deductions. Stern has calculated that at the lowest income level ($2,000-$3,000), a taxpayer realizes a savings of 1.4 percent of the official tax rate, whereas taxpayers who earn over $1 million a year reduce their tax obligation from 63.1 percent to only 32.1 percent.[33] Table 7.1 shows the actual dollar savings by income group provided by tax deductions. The figures show that the dollar savings to those below the $15,000–$20,000 income level are rather modest. However, at the highest income levels the savings are astronomical. A millionaire can save over $720,000, whereas a family that earns under $3,000 can save only $16.

TABLE 7.1
The Value of Tax Deductions to Various Income Groups

Income Group		Average Yearly Family Income	Tax Savings
Under	$3,000	$ 1,345	$ 16
3,000 –	5,000	4,016	148
5,000 –	10,000	7,484	339
10,000 –	15,000	12,342	651
15,000 –	20,000	17,202	1,181
20,000 –	25,000	22,188	1,931
25,000 –	50,000	32,015	3,897
50,000 –	100,000	65,687	11,912
100,000 –	500,000	156,998	41,840
500,000 –	1,000,000	673,040	202,751
over	1,000,000	2,316,872	720,490

Source: Adapted from Philip M. Stern, *The Rape of the Taxpayer* (New York: Vintage Books, 1974), p. 11.

The two examples below illuminate the biased impact of tax deductions:

Imagine that during 1977 a taxpayer who earned $10,000 incurred medical expenses of $4,000. This $4,000 expense would represent 40 percent of this taxpayer's income. Quite clearly it is a catastrophic expense to this taxpayer. However, since the value of tax expenditures is determined by one's income bracket (here $10,000), this taxpayer would receive a tax savings of only $703. If, however, during the same year a taxpayer earned $40,000 and had the same $4,000 in medical expenses, his/her tax savings would be $1,176.[34]

The tax break, therefore, was worth more to the higher-income taxpayer, although the need was obviously less. For the second taxpayer the medical expense was only 10 percent of his or her income, whereas it was 40 percent of the first taxpayer's. The deduction system in this case, then, is not only inequitable but ineffective. The taxpayer who had sustained the greatest economic setback and actually needed the most assistance received the least help.

Imagine a second example. The allowance for mortgage interest and taxes is a tax expenditure. The deduction is designed to provide federal aid to citizens to help them purchase homes. But again, this deduction aids the wealthy much more than it aids middle-income citizens, and it does not help those too poor to own a home at all. For example:

If in 1977 a taxpayer earned in excess of $200,000 his or her deduction would result in a tax savings of $.70 for every dollar spent for mortgage interest and taxes. If in the same year a taxpayer earned $10,000 his or her deduction would result in a tax savings of $.19 for each dollar spent for mortgage interest and taxes.[35]

The tax expenditure program, then, would pay 70 percent of the mortgage interest and taxes for the rich, 19 percent for the lower middle-income taxpayer, and nothing for the poor.

Because tax breaks favor higher-income groups and because state taxes are often extremely *regressive* (those at the lowest income levels pay proportionately the highest rate of tax), there is essentially little difference in the overall tax rate paid by citizens of vastly different wealth. Lampman calculated that families in the lowest income quintile pay about 22 percent of their income in various types of taxes, those in the middle quintile pay 25 percent, and those in the highest quintile pay 33 percent.[36]

A second point about tax expenditures is that many of them seem to have little justification other than to provide the wealthy with windfalls. The deductions allow millionaires to deduct most of the cost of their mansions, allow oil companies (and other corporations) to make huge profits while paying little in taxes, and, of course, allow individuals and corporations to earn large incomes and pay little or no taxes. Ostensibly the deductions are designed to achieve such goals as promoting energy exploration, expanding business plants, training new employees, and increasing home ownership. There is, however, little supervision of these "expenditures." The evidence indicates that much of the money does not promote the intended goals. For example, after extensive study the Joint Economic Committee of Congress in 1974 concluded:

> On the whole these studies showed that many subsidies do not work well economically, they are often directed at outmoded or non-existent objectives. They redistribute income to the affluent, and in too many cases, their costs far exceed their benefits to society as a whole.[37]

For instance, in 1978 Congress drastically lowered taxes on capital gains. This measure was designed to motivate investors to put money into creating new jobs, productivity, and other outlays which would combat simultaneous inflation and high unemployment. According to the bill's sponsors, its passage would spark a tremendous surge in the stock market. But six months after the bill became law, the *New York Times* reported "The cut appears to have had little, if any, impact on the American economy." And it added, "The only clear winners from the tax cut appear to be the people who are actively taking capital gains."[38] That latter group would, of course, be disproportionately composed of the rich. But where, then, did all those tax expenditures go? *Business Week* supplied the answer in a decade-end review of the money market in 1979. The last ten years, it said, had been characterized by "feverish speculation" in, among other things, precious gems and works of art.[39]

This development actually anticipates the central point of the next section—that however well or badly Keynesian measures performed between 1933 and 1970, they no longer apply. But before turning to that critical point, it would be well to summarize the stage of capitalist development initiated by Roosevelt and the New Deal.

During the last half-century, America became a welfare state society officially committed to—but rarely achieving—full employment. In political terms this development was a response to the catastrophe of the Great Depression. It was the background for the emergence of a New Deal coalition which has dominated the nation's life, with some exceptions, from Roosevelt to Nixon.

Ostensibly, tax deductions are designed to achieve such goals as promoting energy exploration, expanding business plants, training new employees, and increasing home ownership. There is, however, little supervision of these "expenditures." The evidence indicates that much of the money does not promote the intended goals.

The origins of the welfare state were marked by intense battles, including the most bitter class struggles the society had ever known. As a result, it seemed that the New Deal was a radical, even socialistic (some would say communistic) movement. As time went on, however, it became the consensus ideology of American society, most notably in the heyday of the Johnson administration, when leading capitalists supported the heir of a Roosevelt whom they had once called a "traitor to his class" against an exponent of Herbert Hoover economics, Barry Goldwater.

All of these changes took place *within* capitalism. The point made in Chapter 4 when the "structural" paradigm was described—that the welfare state in the main follows business priorities—has now been documented at greater length. By the late '60s, when this era came to an end, American corporations were much wealthier than they had been when it began and, as we shall see shortly, there had been no radical redistribution of either income or wealth.

At the outset of this section, we quoted Walter Heller writing in 1966 on the triumph of Keynesian economics. A mere ten years later, Heller reviewed recent developments—double-digit inflation, the deepest *recession* since the Great Depression, the highest interest rates and biggest budget deficit in history, and more—and commented wryly: "In short, what couldn't happen, did."[40] What Heller meant, of course, was that what couldn't happen under the old New Deal theories did happen because there was a new reality.

THE NEW PHASE: 1970–?

When Richard Nixon became President in 1969, he embarked on a classic Keynesian strategy, albeit for a conservative purpose. The inflation rate in 1968 had increased at almost a 5 percent rate, which was a very high figure for those times. In 1969, the trend intensified and prices jumped by more than 6 percent. As a Republican with few political ties to the labor movement,

Nixon was much less worried by an increase in unemployment (which would hit the unions) than by the problem of inflation (which struck at some of his constituents). So he reduced government spending in order to slow down the economy. Lyndon Johnson had run a $14.2 billion deficit in 1967—mainly, as we shall see shortly, because of the war in Vietnam—and a $5.5 billion deficit in 1968. During Nixon's first year in office, the federal budget actually went into surplus and Washington collected $10.7 billion more than it spent. The theory behind this tactic was that it would reduce the excessive buying power, which was the cause of inflation. A certain price would be paid by the workers who were laid off, but Nixon was willing to require them to bear that burden.

On the unemployment side, Nixon's plan worked. There were 3.5 percent jobless in 1969, 4.9 percent in 1970 and 5.9 percent in 1971. Just as the theory held, federal austerity had cut down demand and increased the unemployment rate. But the other intended effect, the drastic reduction in inflation, did not occur. As joblessness rose in 1970, prices went up at a 5.5 percent rate. Almost one and a half million people had lost their jobs; yet that shaved a mere one half of 1 percent from the rate of increase in the Consumer Price Index. In 1971, prices did come down to a 3.4 percent rate, which was still higher than in any year between the end of the Korean War and the escalation of the Vietnam War. But by then the social cost of that reduction was two and a half million unemployed Americans. At that point, a new truth became apparent: *the level of unemployment required to bring inflation under control was now so high as to be politically intolerable, even for a conservative President.*

So it was that in 1971, President Nixon dramatically reversed his course, calling for lower interest rates, increasing government spending and, in August of that year, introducing wage and price controls for the first time in two decades. He did so because he was the first President to face the problem of stagflation.

TABLE 7.2
Federal Budget Receipts by Major Source

Major Source	1967	1969	1970	1972	1973	1975	1977	1980
Individual income taxes	41.1%	46.5%	46.7%	45.4%	44.4%	43.6%	43.9%	43.0%
Corporate income taxes	22.7	19.5	16.9	15.4	15.7	14.5	15.4	13.0
Social insurance taxes and contributions	22.3	21.3	23.4	25.8	30.5	30.8	30.5	30.0
Excise taxes	9.2	8.1	8.1	7.4	4.2	5.9	4.9	4.0
Customs, estate, and gift taxes	3.3	3.1	3.1	4.2	3.5	2.9	3.5	5.0
Miscellaneous	1.4	1.5	1.8	1.7	1.7	2.3	1.8	5.0

Source: Charles A. Vanik (D., Ohio), "Annual Corporate Tax Study, Tax Year 1976," *Congressional Record*, Vol. 124 (1978):168; and the United States Budget in Brief, 1980.

Unemployment lines lengthened in the 1970s as Presidents Nixon, Ford, and Carter tried unsuccessfully to control stagflation—simultaneous high inflation and unemployment.

In the New Economics of the 1960s, a theory called the "Phillips Curve," developed by an Australian economist, A. W. Phillips, played a key role. In an analysis of the English economy over a long period of time, Phillips noted a relationship between unemployment and prices: as unemployment went up, prices went down; as unemployment went down, prices went up.[41] This seemingly abstruse and historical survey was central to American politics in the Kennedy-Johnson years. The outgoing Johnson Council of Economic Advisors, for instance, put a discussion of it at the very head of their chapter on prices in their 1969 *Report*.[42] This was not for scholarly reasons but for policy purposes, since it indicated that unemployment and prices could be "traded off" against one another. In the case of excessive unemployment, a little inflation was all that was needed; and when there was too much inflation, a little unemployment would bring prices down.

Between 1969 and 1971, Richard Nixon, who had relied on a theory and strategy developed by liberal Democrats, discovered, as we have seen, that it no longer worked. Why?

Clearly, the problem first surfaced because of Vietnam. That raises the question of the military component in the American economy. As the Council of Economic Advisors described the reasons for inflation in the late 1960s in the 1978 *Report*:

The major factor initiating inflation was the traditional one of excess demand. The economic stimulus from expenditures for the Vietnam war was added to an economy already approaching high employment. . . .If the Vietnam war had been financed out of increased taxes, the economic consequences of the added war expenditures would have been less serious.[43]

There was obviously a political dimension to the problem. If in 1967 Lyndon Johnson had asked the nation for higher taxes in order to finance what was already becoming an unpopular war, he might well have been rebuffed. Moreover, he and his advisers wrongly thought that the war was going to end in the near future, that there was a "light at the end of the tunnel." Those political decisions and errors led the President to finance the war by federal deficits and to set off the inflation that has bedeviled the nation ever since.

The level of unemployment required to bring inflation under control was now so high as to be politically intolerable, even for a conservative President.

At this point, it might be well to look at the issue of military spending in general, for it is an important element in the politics of contemporary economics. Defense spending pumps enormous sums into the economy but does not produce consumer goods, increase the industrial plant, or move into areas of the economy dominated by private industry. In addition, massive amounts of military spending consist of contracts to corporations for planes, tanks, weapons, electronics, and dozens of other goods. If necessary, these weapons can also be used to protect American investments abroad, which increases their attractiveness to the business community. Defense contracts are particularly attractive to business because they guarantee generous profit margins. As Greenwald says, defense contractors

are protected from the normal capitalist marketplace by a self-contained system in which sweetheart contracts, negotiated between friends, have built-in profit margins, long-term schedules, and other amenities. . . .The contractor becomes closely affiliated with the military position since he becomes a quasi-government agent distributing subcontracts on the basis of any criteria his company desires. The result has been a system of cost overruns, late delivery, and poor performance that has bedeviled every major contract in the 1960s and early 1970s.[44]

The attractiveness of military spending for big business largely explains why this part of the budget is so big (see Chapter 13). Between 1945 and 1970 the United States spent $1100 billion on military defense.[45] By 1978 the figure had reached the $1700 billion range. In fiscal 1978 the military budget alone was $107 billion. The staggering nature of these sums is suggested when one considers that World War II cost a total of $285 billion. Former Senator J. William Fulbright (D., Ark.) calculated that between 1946 and 1967 the federal government spent 57 percent of its budget for military power, and only 6 percent for social functions such as education, health, labor, and welfare programs and housing and community development.[46] Melman estimated that in 1970 about 14 million Americans worked directly or indirectly for the military (e.g., military service, defense contractors) and that 22,000 corporations were involved in defense contract work.[47] While defense spending may be good for business, it does have its drawbacks for society: it uses public money for non-social functions. The funds, in other words, might be better spent to rebuild America's central cities, to rebuild the nation's railroads, to vastly expand public transit, to clean up the environment, to redesign and reorient the public schools for improved teaching, and to expand health care services. Most of these functions, of course, would compete with private industry, and business would be even less willing to be taxed to support such expenditures.

Another major problem is that defense expenditures create fewer jobs per $1 billion spent than almost any other type of spending. The reason is that defense spending is capital- rather than labor-intensive. Much of the money simply goes for expensive equipment and materials rather than worker salaries. One recent study shows that for every $1 billion in defense spending, 11,600 American jobs are lost.[48] The 1978 military budget of $107 billion, therefore, cost American society a total of 1,240,000 jobs. The 1979 budget of $117 billion meant a total loss of 1,360,000 jobs. Because of military spending, New York alone lost an average of 392,000 jobs a year between 1970 and 1974. During this same period, Illinois lost an average of 165,000 jobs; Michigan, 115,000; Ohio, 136,000; and Pennsylvania, 121,000.[49] So the military sector of the American economy played a critical role in triggering inflation in 1967–1968. Because of the special characteristics of defense outlays, it reinforces the trend to this day. But one cannot possibly say that military spending is *the* cause of inflation. In 1970, Vietnam, defense, and foreign affairs expenditures totaled 8.7 percent of the Gross National Product (GNP) and the Consumer Price Index rose by 5.5 percent; in 1975, those same outlays had declined to 5.9 percent of GNP and the Index still went up by 9.1 percent.[50] Obviously, then, other factors must be at work to create a stagflation which so utterly disproves the conventional economic wisdom of the past generation. What are they?

According to the old theory, which worked more or less until 1970, the market mechanism was supposed to spread the trade-off through the economy. But what if corporations had achieved such monopoly power that they could dictate to, rather than obey, the market? According to the assumptions of the past, a company was supposed to lower prices when demand fell because of a recession. At the same time, it would increase its volume to offset the shrinking market. But in an administered price industry, where a few giants in effect determine prices, a recession could motivate business to raise prices in order to maintain targeted profits, even though demand had declined. So one possible answer to the riddle of stagflation is this: the American economy has been structurally transformed because of the increasing concentration of corporate power in fewer and fewer board rooms and the resulting ability to raise prices even in bad times. Best and Connally, for example, note that in the face of sluggish growth and slack demand prices rose by 50 percent in the 1967–1975 period. Every year of the 1970s has meant umemployment for at least 4 million workers by official count and excess productive capacity levels of greater than 20 percent (except briefly in 1973). The coexistence of rising prices and excess supply is impossible in a competitive market setting, for, by definition, excess supply signifies falling prices.[51]

The critical question is: How many areas of the economy are dominated by firms that are unharried by competition? The evidence indicates widespread market isolation in the American economy. In the early 1970s, the 100 largest corporations controlled 52 percent of all industrial assets in the nation.[52] The five largest corporations (Exxon, General Motors, Mobil Corporation, Texaco, and IBM) alone control 10 percent of the nation's industrial assets. The top 100 corporations constitute only a small portion of the 200,000 manufacturing corporations in America, but they receive almost 60 percent of all after-tax profits. The largest manufacturing corporations in 1974 controlled 66 percent of the sales of all U.S. industrial firms, received 72 percent of all profits, and employed 75 percent of the industrial work force.[53] The ten largest corporations in 1974 employed 16 percent of the work force, received 20 percent of all industrial profits, and owned 23 percent of all industrial assets.[54]

The size and wealth of some of the major corporations is staggering. In 1974 Exxon's sales were larger than the GNP of Austria, Denmark, South Africa, Belgium, or Switzerland.[55] General Motors employed more people in 1974 (734,000) than the states of California, New York, Pennsylvania, and Michigan combined.[56] The largest corporations even overwhelm their rivals among the top 1000 corporations. For 1972, Dowd reports that "the assets of the top 500 industrial corporations . . . were $486 billion; of the second 500, about $46 billion. The assets of the top ten companies were $109 billion, more than twice that of the second 500."[57]

Concentration in the economy increased rapidly between 1950 and 1970, and this trend shows every sign of continuing. Between 1950 and 1970 the assets of the 100 largest corporations as a percentage of the assets of all corporations increased as follows:[58]

1950	1955	1960	1965	1970
39.8%	44.3%	46.4%	46.5%	52.3%

Greenberg points out one implication: "The 100 largest firms in 1968 held a larger share of manufacturing assets than the 200 largest in 1950; the 200 largest in 1968 controlled as large a share as the 1,000 largest in 1941."[59] In just nineteen years (1955–1974) the percentage of the industrial work force employed by the top 500 corporations increased from 44.5 percent to 75 percent.[60]

Surprisingly, perhaps, these figures actually underestimate the extent of economic concentration quite seriously. The reason is that the figures do not give insight into interlocking directorates. An *interlocking directorate* occurs when the directors of one company sit on the board of other companies. The Clayton Antitrust Act prohibits directors from sitting on the board of direct competitors, but the law is frequently circumvented when directors from competing firms serve on the board of a third institution, such as a bank. In 1965 economist Peter Dooley's research revealed that of the 250 largest industrial, manufacturing, utility, and financial corporations, only 17 were not interlocked with other corporations in the group.[61] Dooley found 4,007 directorships held by directors of the 250 corporations, involving 297 interlocks between companies that were competitors. In 1974 the Center for Science in the Public Interest reported 460 interlocks between the 18 largest American oil companies. One hundred and thirty-two of the interlocks were with banks, 31 with insurance companies, 12 with utilities, 15 with transportation corporations, and 224 with manufacturing and distribution corporations.[62]

> *While defense spending may be good for business, it does have its drawbacks for society: it uses public money for nonsocial functions. The funds, in other words, might be better spent to rebuild America's central cities, to rebuild the nation's railroads, to vastly expand public transit, to clean up the environment, to redesign and reorient the public schools for improved teaching, and to expand health care services.*

The government, of course, has played a key role in promoting economic concentration. The government has encouraged concentration by approving mergers among the largest corporations, and by failing to enforce antitrust laws. Greenberg reports that "of the 14,000 mergers between 1953 and 1968 the top 100 firms accounted for 35 percent of all merged assets."[63] Between 1948 and 1968 the government approved the merger of some 1,200 manufacturing companies, each with assets of $10 million or more, with other firms. As head of the Federal Trade Commission, Casper W. Weinberger testified about the impact of these mergers:

> Overwhelmingly these original companies have been well-established, healthy firms making good profits. These are precisely the kinds of companies—the viable middle tier—which we would expect to grow in the normal way and therefore present a real competitive challenge to the top corporations. The disappearance of healthy, medium, middle-sized firms is a matter of concern not only for competition but for social and political institutions.[64]

The government's antitrust efforts have hardly constituted a major problem for monopolies. In 1976 the Antitrust Division of the Department of Justice had a total of 427 professional employees. The $40 million budget of the Antitrust Division in 1976 was one-seventh the budget of the Fish and Wildlife Service.[65] When Antitrust has filed suit for restraint of trade, the impact has hardly been noticeable. For example, between 1935 and 1970 General Motors (GM) lost all but three antitrust suits filed by the Department of Justice. However, the worst sanction GM suffered was a fine of $56,000, less than 10 percent of GM Chairman Richard Gerstenberg's 1973 salary of $923,000.[66]

The Politics of Economics: A Spectrum

The two central economic problems of the 1980s are high unemployment and high prices, often occurring simultaneously. The main tools for affecting these problems are: fiscal policy (whether the federal budget is balanced, in surplus, or in deficit); monetary policy (the volume of money provided for the economy by the Federal Reserve); and government controls (legislated prices, wages, etc.). The major policy positions in the early 1980s are presented below.

Full Employment Policy

The liberal-labor position. The government should combat high unemployment by stimulating the economy through budget deficits achieved through public spending (schools, housing, solar energy) or through individual tax cuts that favor those at the bottom and middle of the income structure. At full employment, the budget should be balanced or even in surplus. Proponents include the AFL-CIO, the UAW, John Kenneth Galbraith, and Leon Keyserling.

The moderate liberal position. Washington should seek full employment by stimulating demand through both individual and corporate tax cuts. But the government should not try, in a major way, to do this through social spending. Consumers and corporations determine the uses to which the funds thus introduced into the economy should be put. This was the general approach of the Kennedy and Johnson Presidencies. Its theorists include Walter Heller and Paul Samuelson.

The corporate liberal position. The need for planning and restructuring in the American economy should be carried out by the government and business. Washington provides infusions of capital to facilitate these changes. It plays a guiding role in the crisis period but retires from the economy once the changes are made.

The Reconstruction Finance Corporation was a model of these tactics. An innovation designed by Democrats under Herbert Hoover and continued by Franklin Roosevelt, it provided equity capital to business. Felix Rohatyn, an investment banker who played a major political role during the New York City fiscal crisis of the 1970s, is the best known champion of this view.

"Supply side" economics. Developed by scholars like Arthur Laffer and politicians like Representative Kemp (R., N.Y.), it combines elements of John Kennedy liberalism (tax cuts) and traditional conservatism (handsome incentives for corporations and the corporate rich). Excessively high taxes, it is said, act as "disincentives" to reduce the willingness of capital to invest and to hold down the productivity of labor. (Why work hard when the government takes so much from your pay?)

Proponents of this theory argue that an "across-the-board" tax cut of 30 percent over three years would so stimulate both workers and investors that the resultant increase in Gross National Product would compensate for lost tax revenues. A smaller slice of a much larger pie, they say, would yield an absolute increase in Washington's income.

Monetarist policies. Fiscal policy is the wrong instrument for Washington to use: it distorts the free-market allocation of goods and services by imposing political preferences upon the economy. The budget should be balanced; the government should allow the private sector to do its own job. The monetary authorities should provide a steady volume of money and avoid inflating the currency to fight recession or deflating it to counter inflation. Milton Friedman is one fo the main exponents of this view.

Anti-Inflation Policy

Controls. Senator Edward Kennedy was the only exponent of government controls on prices, wages, dividends, and executive compensation during the 1980 primary season. He was supported by part of the labor movement, which favors controls administered by liberals like Kennedy but which has bitter memories of Richard Nixon's controls during 1971–1973.

In addition, the partisans of this view often call for attacks on the "sectoral" sources of inflation: they advocate a national health program to deal with medical costs; federal support for family farmers and family farm corporations but no more subsidies for agribusiness; a strong governmental commitment to shaping a more efficient and environmentally benign energy system, particularly through developing renewable forms of energy (solar, biomass, etc.); and a housing program which will insulate that industry from the roller-coaster effect of monetary policy (which raises the prices of homes when it increases the interest rate to fight inflation).

Keynesian fiscal policy. This was the tack taken by President Carter between 1977 and 1979. It seeks to "trade off" unemployment and high prices by running deficits and incurring the risk of inflation when joblessness is high and by cutting federal spending and inducing unemployment when inflation is considered to be the central problem. The 1980 recession was deliberately sought for these reasons.

Balanced budget policies. Government spending is the chief source of inflation. The cure for that problem is fiscal discipline in Washington. Mr. Carter adopted this tactic in 1980, and there is a movement to amend the Constitution to require a balanced budget. Ronald Reagan is an advocate of this view, which some observers see as in conflict with his support for the "supply side" economics—and tax cutting—proposed by Laffer and Kemp.

In actuality, the major corporations are probably too big to be sued for antitrust violations. Just to audit the books of GM, Exxon, or IBM would probably take several years. Court proceedings against the major corporations sometimes take five to twenty years. Probably the most viable way to deal with restraint of trade would be through legislation. Congress could draw up guidelines specifying how much of a market any one corporation could have, and the vertical and horizontal businesses they could own. This would make enforcement much easier and would restore competition to the market. Congress, however, has shown little interest.

The result of unimpeded economic concentration in America is a phenomenon that economists have labeled *oligopoly,* which occurs when four or fewer firms control 50 percent or more of all sales in an area of the economy. Many economists believe that such a condition creates a shared *monopoly.* Because of recent rapid economic concentration, oligopoly is present in much of the market. In 1972 the Census Bureau divided all products into 422 categories; 110 were found to be oligopolistic by margins of 50 to 97 percent. The 110 products accounted for 64 percent of all manufacturing sales.[67] Areas of the economy that are controlled by four or fewer firms include motor vehicles, telephone equipment, soaps and detergents, glass, gypsum products, tires, computers, cigarettes, typewriters, photographic equipment, industrial chemicals, and numerous areas of the food industry.

Oligopolistic industries are much less subject to market forces than other industries. Two recent studies provide insight into their powers in the market. Economist John Blair analyzed thirty-two products over a number of years, half of which were produced by oligopolistic industries and half from competitive industries. He found that as recessions reduced demand for the products,

those produced by competitive industries declined in price. However, thirteen of the sixteen products produced by oligopolistic industries actually increased in price when demand decreased, showing complete defiance of the laws of supply and demand.[68] Economist Gardiner Means studied product prices between September 1973 and September 1974, a period of rising prices and decreasing demand. He found that both competitive and oligopolistic industries increased their prices, but prices in the competitive sector increased only 5 percent, while those in the oligopolistic sector increased a whopping 27 percent.[69]

The government has played a key role in promoting economic concentration by approving mergers among the largest corporations and by failing to enforce antitrust laws.

Typical of concentrated industries is the practice of *target pricing*. The corporation sets a goal of 15 to 20 percent profit on its investment in a line of production and achieves it by keeping the price high enough to meet the goal, regardless of fluctuations in supply and demand. Economist Howard Sherman's research reveals that the rate of industrial profit is proportional to the rate of oligopoly in the industrial area. Oligopolistic industries have average profits of 20 percent, while competitive industries have an average profit rate of only 12.8 percent.[70]

So, corporate concentration and administered prices may well explain at least part of the inflation component of the crisis of the '70s and '80s. But what about the stagnation? One cause could be the maldistribution of income and wealth. It can, of course, be argued that a lopsided allocation of money, which gives a very few people an enormously disproportionate share, is bad in and of itself. That can be asserted on grounds of social justice. However one views that controversy, it is also possible that maldistribution reinforces stagflation. In a study in 1977, the Congressional Budget Office asked why the recovery from the recession of 1973 had been so slow and disappointing. The rate of revival at that point lagged by about 5 percent behind the normal pattern of previous recoveries. "The gap," the Budget Office reported, "is most marked in spending on durables. . . but it is also apparent in spending on non-durables. The gap reflects stagnation of real income in recent years rather than decisions by consumers to spend a lower portion of their incomes."[71]

If we view income and wealth distribution as a factor in stagflation, it is necessary to separate two trends: the long-range resistance of the American system to redistribution, a situation that long predated stagflation but which may reinforce it; and more recent developments in this area that are both a cause and an effect of stagflation.

Capitalism inevitably leads to an acute maldistribution of wealth. The reasons are several. First, capitalism assumes that some must be allowed to accumulate great wealth so that the capital for business entry, expansion, and innovation will be available. Second, since accumulation of wealth is considered a virtue and since those with wealth tend to be more influential in the political system, laws are generally designed to help large-income earners and the wealthy maintain their wealth. Thus tax laws are generally biased in favor of wealthy citizens, and inheritance laws are riddled with loopholes to allow the wealthy to pass their worldly goods on to their children. Most of America's wealthy class, in fact, inherited their fortunes. As Lundberg says:

> Nearly all the current large incomes, those exceeding $1 million, $500,000 or even $100,000 or $50,000 a year, are derived in fact from old property accumulations, by inheritors—that is, by people who never did whatever one is required to do, approved or disapproved, creative or noncreative, in order to assemble a fortune. And, it would appear, no amount of dedicated entrepreneurial effort by newcomers can place them in the financial class of the inheritors.[72]

The third reason why capitalism leads to maldistribution of wealth is that money begets money. Those with money can go into business more easily, can take advantage of investment opportunities, and can direct their funds to tax shelters (such as tax-free municipal bonds) and live off the interest.

These factors have combined to create severe maldistribution of wealth in America. As Table 7.3 shows, 1 percent of all families owns 33 percent of all wealth, and the top 5 percent owns the majority of all wealth (53 percent). The richest 20 percent owns 77 percent of all wealth, leaving the other 80 percent with 23 percent.

Wealth is even poorly distributed among the bottom 80 percent. Twenty-five percent of these families have virtually no wealth or even negative wealth (more debts than assets), and 61 percent control only 7 percent of all wealth.[73] As economist Paul Samuelson has said: "If we made an income pyramid out of a child's blocks, with each layer portraying $1,000 of income, the peak would be far higher than the Eiffel Tower, but almost all of us would be within a yard of the ground."[74] In 1977 there were only about 240,000 millionaires in the United States, considerably below 1 percent of the total population.

TABLE 7.3
Distribution of Wealth in America

Population Group	Percent of Total Wealth	Percent of all Corporate Stock
Top 1%	33	62
Top 5%	53	86
Top 20%	77	97
Remaining 80%	23	3

Source: Edward C. Budd, ed., *Inequality and Poverty* (New York: Norton, 1967), p. xxi.

Corporate stock is almost entirely owned by the wealthy. One percent of all families controls 62 percent of corporate wealth, the top 5 percent owns 86 percent, and the top 20 percent owns 97 percent of all corporate stock. Studies of public savings show a similar pattern. Thirty percent of Americans have less than $500 in liquid assets, while another 22 percent have less than $2,000. The top 10 percent, however, own about 75 percent of all savings.[75] Assessing these figures, Best and Connally conclude:

> If the idea of class is to refer primarily to ownership of the means of production, then in America today the capitalist class, that is, the class with the capital, consists basically of 2 percent of the population. Perhaps another 15 to 20 percent can be viewed as junior partners in that class.[76]

Like wealth, income is also distributed very unevenly, and as Table 7.4 shows, it always has been in America. Since 1947 the poorest 20 percent of American families have received 5 percent of before-tax income yearly, while the richest 20 percent have consistently received over 40 percent of all before-tax income. If the fourth and fifth richest groups are combined, this top 40 percent have consistently received an average of almost 66 percent of all before-tax income. Indeed, the richest 20 percent have consistently received more income than the combined bottom 60 percent.

Actually, income maldistribution is considerably more severe than the figures in Table 7.4 indicate. The figures are based on data which include welfare payments for the poor but do not encompass such items as realized and unrealized capital gains, which go primarily to wealthy individuals. In a recent study, Peckman and Okner adjusted the data for wage supplements, capital gains, the value of the services of owner-occupied homes, and indirect business taxes. These adjustments reduced the income of the poorest 20 percent 0.6 percentage points and increased that of the wealthiest fifth by 5.3 percentage points.[77]

In recent years, cash-assistance payments to the poor have increased, but the poor have not received a larger share of before-tax income. As Peckman notes, it would seem that "increases in government transfer payments (are) needed to prevent a gradual erosion of (the poor's) income shares."[78] Additionally, during the last fifteen years the effective rate of taxation for the top 15 percent of income groups has declined.[79] This means that in recent years after-tax income has been even more heavily skewed in favor of top income earners.

At this point, we are moving from the perennial maldistribution of income and wealth in all stages of capitalism to the events of the last decade. During the 1970s, wages did not keep pace with price increases. Thus, if one measured weekly earnings in constant dollars, a worker in 1977 had more than five dollars *less* buying power than in 1972.[80]

On the other hand, the people at the top of the society were able to "hedge" against inflation by investing in such things as gold, real estate, rare

TABLE 7.4
Distribution of Income Before Taxes

Year	Lowest Fifth	Second Fifth	Middle Fifth	Fourth Fifth	Highest Fifth	Highest 5 Percent
1947	5.1%	11.8%	16.7%	23.2%	43.4%	17.5%
1948	5.0	12.1	17.2	23.2	42.5	17.1
1949	4.5	11.9	17.3	23.5	42.8	16.9
1950	4.5	11.9	17.4	23.6	42.7	17.3
1951	4.9	12.5	17.6	23.3	41.8	16.9
1952	4.9	12.2	17.1	23.5	42.2	17.7
1953	4.7	12.4	17.8	24.0	41.0	15.8
1954	4.5	12.0	17.6	24.0	41.9	16.4
1955	4.8	12.2	17.7	23.4	41.8	16.8
1956	4.9	12.4	17.9	23.6	41.1	16.4
1957	5.0	12.6	18.1	23.7	40.5	15.8
1958	5.0	12.5	18.0	23.9	40.6	15.4
1959	4.9	12.3	17.9	23.8	41.1	15.9
1960	4.8	12.2	17.8	24.0	41.3	15.9
1961	4.7	11.9	17.5	23.8	42.2	16.6
1962	5.0	12.1	17.6	24.0	41.3	15.7
1963	5.0	12.1	17.7	24.0	41.2	15.8
1964	5.1	12.0	17.7	24.0	41.2	15.9
1965	5.2	12.2	17.8	23.9	40.9	15.5
1966	5.6	12.4	17.8	23.8	40.5	15.6
1967	5.5	12.4	17.9	23.9	40.4	15.2
1968	5.6	12.4	17.7	23.7	40.5	15.6
1969	5.6	12.4	17.7	23.7	40.6	15.6
1970	5.4	12.2	17.6	23.8	40.9	15.6
1971	5.5	12.0	17.6	23.8	41.1	15.7
1972	5.4	11.9	17.5	23.9	41.4	15.9
1973	5.5	11.9	17.5	24.0	41.1	15.5
1974	5.4	12.0	17.6	24.1	41.0	15.3
1975	5.4	11.8	17.6	24.1	41.0	15.5

Source: U.S. Bureau of the Census, "Money Income in 1974 of Families and Persons in the United States" (GPO, 1976), *Current Population Reports,* Series P-60, No. 101, table 22, p. 37.

art, and fine wines, commodities which more than compensated for the rise in the Consumer Price Index. So it was that Martin Feldstein, a Harvard economist, calculated that people with incomes over $100,000 a year were not adversely affected by inflation. But this means that the new economic situation reinforces the trend described by the Congressional Budget Office: now, even with a government officially committed to maintaining buying power, it periodically becomes very difficult for the great mass of people to purchase what they need, and that acts as a stagnating factor in the economy.

In another area, there is a similar meshing of the perennial and the new within the framework of stagflation. It has always been true that capitalism, a highly innovative and dynamic system motivated by profit maximization, imposed "social costs"—sometimes called "diseconomies"—in the process of production. As one of the first theorists of this phenomenon, A. C. Pigou, noted:

> The industrial revolution, when it led the cottager from his home into the factory had an effect on other things beside production. In like manner, increased efficiency in output was not the only result which the agricultural revolution, with its enclosures and large-scale farming, brought about. There was also a social change in the destruction of the old yeoman class.[81]

People in the United States are obviously familiar with this problem. The tobacco industry, manufacturers of children's toys, and American automobile manufacturers are particularly good examples of industries that have often shown a callous disregard for the human consequences of their products. In 1929 General Motors refused to install shatterproof glass in its cars because it would cost a few dollars more.[82] The American automobile industry has always fought safety and fuel economy designs, including recently seat belts, airbags, and emission-control equipment.

In June 1978 the popular television show *60 Minutes* presented a particularly gruesome example of an auto company placing profits above human lives. The evidence presented showed that Ford Motor Company's own tests proved that the gas tank on the Ford Pinto tended to explode when the car was struck from the rear. The explosions, of course, were a serious risk to human life. Ford's experts calculated the cost of correcting the condition, and then compared this cost to the estimated cost of law suits involving traffic deaths which could be expected to result from the car's deficiencies. The experts calculated the legal cost by assuming that the loss of each human life would result in a legal settlement of $200,000 (a serious but nonfatal burn case would cost $67,000). Correcting the gas tank flaw would cost $11 per car. Using these figures, the officials determined that it would cost Ford almost three times as much to correct the car's flaws as it would to sell the defective cars and compensate crash victims and their families. Consequently, Ford placed the cars on the market without correcting the flaw.

Resulting deaths and injuries to Pinto owners brought the sad tale to light. In September 1979 an Indiana grand jury indicted Ford Motor Company on criminal charges stemming from a Pinto crash in which three teenaged girls burned to death. The panel concluded that the tanks were "recklessly designed and manufactured . . . and that Ford had a legal duty to warn the general public." In the trial that followed, a jury decided that there was insufficient evidence to convict Ford.

In 1979 Ford Motor Company was hit with another series of law suits stemming from an automatic transmission that could accidentally shift from park into reverse, causing the car to bolt backwards. The problem was linked to 23 deaths, 259 injuries, and 777 accidents. Ford's own records showed that it had been aware of the problem for six and a half years.

By early 1979, over 1,000 lawsuits had been filed nationally by workers long exposed to asbestos. The suits maintained that the manufacturers had known about the health hazards of asbestos since 1938 but had concealed the information so that they could continue to reap large profits.

In a sense, the problem of social costs has been with capitalism from the very beginning. One of Pigou's examples had to do with the damage caused by the sparks from an old-fashioned train as it crossed a valley. But as capitalism grew and grew in scale after World War II, and as the terrible consequences of these costs—in terms of premature death, loss of limbs, or even the damage done to paint jobs on houses and cars by acid rains—came to be known, the public was moved to demand that at least some limits be placed upon private technology. The Evironmental Protection Agency (EPA) thus mandated standards of pollution, automobile emissions, and the like.

For the first time, the private sector was required to pay for the costs that it had previously imposed upon the public. This came at a time when those costs were becoming more and more expensive because of the huge scale of enterprises. Of course, these expenses increase the costs of doing business and are passed on to the consumer, further fueling inflation. As a result, a portion of American ingenuity—and capital—has had to be employed to undo the harm done by—American ingenuity and capital. This was another structural element in the new economic situation.

So was the organization of some American industries. The health system, in which third-party insurers pay for fee-for-service medicine, is not only unjust—it is also the most expensive health system in the advanced world. The subsidies paid to corporate farmers to remove land from production bid up prices at the supermarket. The policy of fighting inflation by raising the interest rate to discourage borrowing (and spending)—the centerpiece of the Carter administration effort as the '80s began—creates inflation in the housing market, where the cost of finance is the critical element in the price of a house.

CONCLUSIONS

For these and other reasons, the American economy entered a new stage in the 1970s. It is not the "free-enterprise" or "free-market" system of the national ideology. It is a state-managed, state-subsidized economy dominated by gigantic corporations with power over the market. It is undergoing structural transformations which have made the policies and politics of earlier periods inoperative. But just as the political response of the New Deal did not really come up with answers to the problems of the Depression until six, seven, and even eight years after the Crash, so in this case the new economic stage of capitalism has not yet been accompanied by a new political and policy stage. At this writing, then, much of the future is undetermined.

Before trying to sketch just a few of the political possibilities in that future, an objection to the analysis of this chapter should be met. There are thoughtful, serious analysts like Daniel Bell who hold that the very concept of capitalism is outmoded. Capitalism (and feudalism and socialism) are definitions based on "property relations," on who owns the means of production. But, Bell says, now the kind of knowledge used is at least as important as that property relation. The sequence of pre-industrial, industrial, and post-industrial society is more useful, he claims, than terms like feudalism, capitalism and socialism.[83] To the degree that Bell is criticizing a rather simple-minded economic (or technological) determinism, he is obviously quite right. As the data in this chapter have made quite clear, there is no political "super-structure" which is merely a faithful reflection of an economic "base." More and more, politics intervenes and shapes, or tries to shape, economic "laws." However, one might add that theoretical knowledge looks somewhat less secure in the '80s than it did when Bell wrote his book in the early '70s.

> *The American economy entered a new stage in the 1970s. It is not the "free-enterprise" or "free-market" system of the national ideology. It is a state-managed, state-subsidized economy dominated by gigantic corporations with power over the market.*

But if one avoids that simplistic determinism, this chapter has demonstrated that the concept of capitalism helps explain much about the American past and present. And now the unique characteristics of this system, as we defined them at the outset, have clearly come to a historic moment when a new stage is in the process of emerging. It would be foolish to try to specify what the politics of this new economic stage will be, but we can certainly set out some possibilities:

a. America in the '80s will not dismantle the welfare state, which is politically impossible, and will continue along a path of government intervention in the economy, even if that intervention is directed by conservatives. A national economy on the scale and complexity of the United States, located in an uncertain and turbulent world, cannot be run by the "invisible hand of the market."

b. It is possible, as one influential conservative program suggests, that welfare-state spending will be scaled down and subsidies to private producers will be increased.

c. It is also possible that there will be an even more aggressive federal intervention into the economy, with Washington providing subsidies to the private sector to pay for a massive restructuring of entire areas of the economy. One such example is the Carter administration's 1979 proposal to put tens of billions of dollars into the private development of "synthetic fuels."

d. There could very well be wage and price controls.

e. There could be a considerable increase in government planning and even in direct government ownership and production, such as a nationally owned oil and gas corporation. But this will almost certainly take place within the system; that is, it will not change the fundamental relationship between the public and the private economies.

We cannot tell which of these possibilities will prevail—or what unanticipated movement and program might arise. We can say that the 1980s are likely to be a turbulent political decade precisely because of the profound economic changes in capitalism described in this chapter. And we have most certainly demonstrated a critically important methodological truth: if political structures are not mirror reflections of economic power, they are profoundly affected by that power. Thus, a serious political scientist must also be an economist.

Footnotes

1. George Cabot Lodge, *The New American Ideology* (New York: Knopf, 1976).
2. *Ibid.,* pp. 10–11.
3. On Weber, see H. H. Gerth and C. Wright Mills, "Preface," in Gerth and Mills, eds., *From Max Weber: Essays in Sociology* (London: Routledge and Kegan Paul, 1952), p. 65; and H. H. Gerth and Don Martindale, eds., *Ancient Judaism* (Glencoe, Illinois: The Free Press, 1952), p. 345; on Marx, see Karl Marx, *Capital* (Moscow: Progress Publishers, 1971), Volume 3, Chapter 51.
4. John Kenneth Galbraith, *Economics and the Public Purpose* (Boston: Houghton, Mifflin, 1973), pp. 115–116.
5. Joseph Schumpeter, *Business Cycles* (New York: McGraw-Hill, 1939).
6. Kenneth Prewitt and Alan Stone, *The Ruling Class: Elite Theory, Power, and American Democracy* (New York: Harper and Row, 1973).
7. Richard O. Boyer and Herbert M. Morais, *Labor's Untold Story* (New York: United Electrical, Radio and Machine Workers of America, 1976), p. 22.
8. *Ibid.*, p. 22.
9. *Ibid.*, p. 22.
10. *Ibid.*, p. 20.
11. Cited in *Ibid.*, p. 38.
12. Charles and Mary Beard, *The Rise of American Civilization* (New York: Macmillan, 1933), p. 177.
13. Henry Kissinger, *The Law of the Sea* (Washington, D.C.: State Department, 1976).
14. Quoted by Richard Hofstadter, *The American Political Tradition* (New York: Vintage Books, 1954), p. 257.
15. John Kenneth Galbraith, *The Great Crash* (Boston: Houghton, Mifflin, 1961), p. 104.
16. Paul Samuelson, *Economics* (New York: McGraw-Hill, 1967), p. 170.
17. Galbraith, *The Great Crash,* p. 180; *Business Week,* September 3, 1979, p. 9.
18. Francis Fox Piven and Richard A. Cloward, *Poor Peoples' Movements* (New York: Pantheon Books, 1977), Chapter 2.

19. Arthur Schlesinger, Jr., *The Crisis of the OLD ORDER* (Boston: Houghton, Mifflin, 1956), p. 420.
20. Michael Harrington, *Decade of Decision* (New York: Simon and Schuster, 1980), Chapter 7.
21. Daniel Patrick Moynihan, *The Politics of a Guaranteed Annual Income* (New York: Random House, 1973), p. 42.
22. Arthur Schlesinger, Jr., *Keynes and Roosevelt: The Politics of Upheaval* (Boston: Houghton, Mifflin, 1960), p. 206; Ronald Moggridge, ed., *The Collected Writings of J. M. Keynes* (Cambridge, England: Cambridge University Press, 1978), Vol. 22, p. 149.
23. Leon Keyersling, *"Liberal" and "Conservative" National Economic Policies and Their Consequences, 1919–1979* (Washington: Conference on Economic Progress, 1979), p. 36.
24. Walter Heller, *New Dimensions of Political Economy* (Cambridge: Harvard University Press, 1966), pp. 1–2.
25. Daniel Patrick Moynihan, *Maximum Feasible Misunderstanding* (New York: The Free Press, 1969), p. 29.
26. See Ralph Nader, Mark Green, and Joel Seligmon, *Taming the Giant Corporation: How the Largest Corporations Control Our Lives* (New York: Norton, 1976), p. 22.
27. *Ibid.*, p. 22.
28. See Harrell Rodgers, "Welfare Policies For the Rich," *Dissent* (Spring, 1978).
29. These figures are gathered annually by Representative Charles A. Vanik (D., Ohio). See "Annual Corporate Tax Study, Tax Year 1976," *The Congressional Record*, Vol. 124, No. 6, pp. E 168–76.
30. *Ibid.*, p. E 171.
31. *Special Analysis: Budget of the United States Government, Fiscal Year 1980* (Washington: Government Printing Office, 1979), pp. 183ff.
32. These figures were collected by the Treasury Department and made public by Sen. Edmund S. Muskie (D., Maine). See "Muskie News," February 13, 1978.
33. Phillip M. Stern, *The Rape of the Taxpayer* (New York: Vintage Books, 1974), p. 11.
34. Edward Fried et al., *Setting National Priorities: The 1974 Budget* (Washington, D.C.: The Brookings Institute, 1973), p. 115.
35. Stanley S. Surrey, *Pathways to Tax Reform* (Cambridge, Mass.: Harvard University Press, 1973), p. 37.
36. Quoted in Lee Rainwater, ed., *Social Problems and Public Policy: Inequality and Justice* (Chicago: Aldine, 1974), p. 201.
37. U.S. Congress, *Joint Economic Report,* 92nd Cong., 2d sess. March 23, 1972, pp. 37–38.
38. Karen A. Arenson, "Minimal Impact Seen in Capital Gains Tax Cut," *New York Times,* April 30, 1979.
39. "Last Chance for Investment Versus Speculation," *Business Week,* December 31, 1979.
40. Walter Heller, *The Economy: Old Myths and New Realities* (New York: Norton, 1976), p. 7.
41. Robert Lekachman, *Economists at Bay* (New York: McGraw-Hill, 1976), pp. 44ff.
42. *Economic Report of the President, Together with the Annual Report of the Council of Economic Advisors* (Washington, D.C.: Government Printing Office, 1969), pp. 94–95.
43. *Report of the Council of Economic Advisors, 1978* (Washington: Government Printing Office, 1978), p. 139.
44. Carol S. Greenwald, *Group Power: Lobbying and Public Policy* (New York: Praeger, 1977), p. 303.

45. See Edward S. Greenberg, *Serving the Few: Corporate Capitalism and the Bias of Government Policy* (New York: Wiley, 1974), p. 186.

46. Quoted in Sidney Lens, "The Military-Industrial Complex," in Philip L. Beardsley, ed., *Whose Country America?* (Encino, Ca.: Dickenson, 1973), p. 92.

47. Seymour Melman, "From Private to Pentagon Capitalism," in S. Melman, ed., *The War Economy of the United States* (New York: St. Martin's, 1971).

48. "The Empty Pork Barrel: Unemployment and the Pentagon Budget," Michigan's Public Interest Research Group. This research was based on Bruce Russett's book showing similar findings. See Russett, *What Price Vigilance: The Burdens of National Defense* (New Haven: Yale University Press, 1970).

49. See also Seymour Melman, *The Permanent War Economy: American Capitalism in Decline* (New York: Simon and Schuster, 1974), pp. 74–128.

50. Henry Owen and Charles L. Schultze, eds. *Setting National Priorities: The Next Ten Years* (Washington, D.C.: The Brookings Institute, 1976), Table 8–2, p. 328.

51. Michael H. Best and William E. Connolly, *The Politicized Economy* (Lexington, Mass.: D.C. Heath, 1976), p. 47.

52. Nader et al., *Taming the Giant Corporation*, p. 16.

53. Dowd, *The Twisted Dream*, p. 70.

54. Nader et al., *Taming the Giant Corporation*, p. 16.

55. Robert Heilbroner et al., *In the Name of Profit* (New York: Warner, 1973), p. 201.

56. Nader et al., *Taming the Giant Corporation*, p. 16.

57. Dowd, *The Twisted Dream*, p. 71.

58. Thomas R. Dye, *Who's Running America?* (Englewood Cliffs, N.J.: Prentice-Hall, 1976), p. 20.

59. Greenberg, *Serving the Few*, pp. 38–39.

60. Dowd, *The Twisted Dream*, p. 71.

61. Peter Dooley, "The Interlocking Directorate," *American Economic Review* 59, no. 3 (June 1969): 314–23.

62. Cited in Nader et al., *Taming the Giant Corporation*, p. 111.

63. Edward S. Greenberg, *The American Political System: A Radical Approach* (Cambridge, Mass.: Winthrop, 1977), p. 181.

64. U.S. Senate Subcommittee on Antitrust and Monopoly, *Economic Concentration, Part 8: The Conglomerate Merger Problem*, 91st Cong., 2d sess., 1970, p. 4815.

65. Nader et al., *Taming the Giant Corporation*, p. 203.

66. David Hapgood, *The Screwing of the Average Man* (New York: Bantam Books, 1975), p. 220.

67. See Ovid Demaris, *Dirty Business: The Corporate-Political Money-Power Game* (New York: Harper and Row, 1974), pp. 30–36.

68. John M. Blair, *Economic Concentration* (New York: Harcourt Brace Jovanovich, 1972), pp. 322–23.

69. See "The New Monopolies: How They Affect Consumer Prices," *Consumer Reports* (June 1975), p. 378.

70. Sherman, *Radical Political Economy* (New York: Basic Books, 1972), p. 108.

71. "The Disappointing Recovery," Congressional Budget Office (Washington, D.C.: Government Printing Office, 1977), p. 5.

72. Ferdinand Lundberg, *The Rich and the Super-Rich* (New York: Bantam Books, 1973), p. 155.

73. See Michael Harrington, *Socialism* (New York: Bantam Books, 1973), p. 373.

74. Paul Samuelson, *Economics,* 6th ed. (New York: McGraw-Hill, 1964), p. 113.

75. *Statistical Abstract of the United States* (Washington, D.C.: Government Printing Office, 1973), p. 315.

76. Best and Connally, *The Politicized Economy,* p. 76.
77. Joseph A. Peckman and Benjamin Okner, *Who Bears the Tax Burden?* (Washington, D.C.: The Brookings Institute, 1974), p. 46.
78. Joseph A. Peckman, ''The Rich, the Poor, and the Taxes They Pay,'' *Public Interest* (Fall 1969), p. 25.
79. Harrington, *Socialism,* p. 373.
80. *Economic Report of the President, Fiscal 1979* (Washington, D.C.: Government Printing Office, 1979), Table B-36, p. 225.
81. A. C. Pigou, *The Economics of Welfare* (London: Macmillan, 1962), p. 15.
82. Nader et al., *Taming the Giant Corporation,* p. 16.
83. Daniel Bell, *The Coming of Post-Industrial Society* (New York: Basic Books, 1973).

2

AMERICAN POLITICAL INSTITUTIONS AND POLITICS

I'm not a member of any organized party; I'm a Democrat.
Will Rogers

American political parties and elections are among the most unusual ones in the world. In most Western nations, political parties represent rather distinct homogeneous groups within the population and have an *ideology* that they attempt to advance. In addition, they have the power to force those officeholders or candidates who belong to the party to follow the party line, to control the nomination of and electoral procedures for party candidates, and to have a permanent leadership with a supporting bureaucracy. Most Western nations also have more than two major parties.

8

Political Parties and the Electoral Process

American parties bear little resemblance to such organizations. Because America has only two major parties, they are diverse in group membership, rather broad in appeal, and non-ideological. Neither party has any form of developed, centralized leadership or permanent bureaucracy, and neither exercises disciplinary powers to force members to follow the party line. Lacking hierarchical control, the parties cannot set national priorities, establish party strategy, or often even agree on policy stands. Within each state, parties pick their own leaders, nominate candidates, raise and spend their own funds, and develop their own stand on policy issues. Decentralization, then, is the chief characteristic of American parties, just as it is with the United States Congress.[1]

Every four years each party coordinates its efforts in a national convention to formally nominate a presidential candidate, write a party *platform* (which may be ignored by local party officials and candidates), and establish a temporary organization to help the party's candidate in the election. Once the convention is over, this loose confederation dissolves, with each state party going home to run its own affairs. During the four years between elections, the President is the formal spokesperson for his party, while the *out-party* has no official head. Generally the congressional party leaders from the out-party become the chief spokespersons for that party.

Democratic party convention delegates, 1976. American presidential conventions have been characterized as circuses, but they do perform several important functions: they nominate presidential candidates, establish party rules, and put forth a platform.

FUNCTIONS AND CONSEQUENCES
OF THE TWO-PARTY SYSTEM

The functions of American parties are distinct and limited. Essentially, the parties contest elections.[2] The two-party system generally narrows realistic choices, thereby organizing *majorities,* structuring conflicts, and bringing interests together. To some extent the parties also play a role in leadership selection, elevating members through local and state ranks to run for office. With the media and public-relations firms having increased importance, however, many candidates able to raise the money to run an effective campaign can ignore the party structure and run for the party nomination simply by paying a filing fee or obtaining the number of signatures necessary to qualify for inclusion on the ballot. Well-financed candidates are increasingly ignoring the local party and depending upon media expenditures to provide them with the party nomination.

It is often noted that a function of the two-party system is to encourage compromise within the parties because the need to attract a majority forces them to make a wide appeal. It is also frequently pointed out that the two-party system provides an elected President with a broad base of support, thereby increasing the chances of coherence and stability. While compromise on issues has its virtues, it can, of course, so dilute public policies as to make them ineffective. An energy plan or tax reform proposal, for example, may be so watered down by parties trying to please everyone that the issues are simply not dealt with realistically.

In addition, the need to cast a broad appeal may mean that for long periods of time neither party represents some groups in society. For example, between 1880 and 1952 black Americans were not really represented by either of the two major parties, both of which feared the loss of middle-income and working-class support if they did take up the cause of black Americans.

Party identification also serves as a cue to help citizens decide how to vote. Party identification is mostly inherited from one's parents and is fairly enduring. Citizens who have little specific information about candidates can use party identification as an information-saving device, and simply vote for those candidates from their party. Party identification plays its largest role when the office is not highly visible. In presidential elections, the media popularizes the candidates, making them visible to the public and enhancing the chance that the public will vote on the basis of candidate image or issues (see Chapter 2). In elections below the Presidency, including those for members of the House of Representatives, the state legislature, and state and local offices, the public does not perceive the candidates as well, if at all, and is thus more likely to vote on the basis of party identification.

Because the parties are so diverse and undisciplined, voting on the basis of party identification often provides the citizen with little policy control or influence. The reason is that although candidates run under a particular party label, they may not really support the basic positions of that party. Candidates may be considerably more conservative or liberal than the party majority, or they may be mavericks on important issues. Southern Democrats in Congress, for example, have a long history of weakly supporting the national Democratic party. Thus, voting on the basis of party identification is often a poor substitute for knowledge about the candidate.

THE EVOLUTION OF THE TWO-PARTY SYSTEM

From the administration of George Washington to the present, America has had a two-party system.[3] However, third parties have often played an important role in the political process, and the two major parties and their supporters have varied considerably during our history. The primary supporters of George Washington favored a strong central government and generally sided with business interests. They were known as Federalists. The opposing groups—farmers, laborers, and frontiersmen—were led by James Madison and Thomas Jefferson and became known as the Democrat-Republicans. The Democrat-Republicans won the Presidency in 1800 and dominated it until 1828. The Federalist party disappeared and was replaced by the Whigs. The Whigs twice won the Presidency between 1828 and 1860.

The issue of slavery led to the development of a new Republican party consisting primarily of Northern Whigs, Northern Democrat-Republicans, and abolitionists (those who wanted to put an end to slavery). With Abraham Lincoln as their candidate, the Republicans won the Presidency in 1860. With the exceptions of the Cleveland and Wilson administrations, the Republicans dominated the Presidency until 1932. The election of 1860 left the North predominantly Republican, the deep South Democratic, the Southern border states Democratic, and the Northern border states Republican. "One-partyism" in the South would last a hundred years.

Decentralization is the chief characteristic of American parties, just as it is with the United States Congress.

After the Civil War and Reconstruction, the issues that had divided the two parties diminished in importance, and the Democratic and Republican parties became closer in outlook. This left two major groups—western farmers and eastern working people—without a platform in either party. These "outgroups" began to form third parties such as the Grangers (organized by farmers to fight the all-powerful railroads), the Greenbackers (backed by rural and urban groups who wanted currency shortages relieved by the use of silver), the Knights of Labor, the Farmers' Alliance, and finally the Populists. The period from 1870 to the 1890s was one of conflict between the major parties on one side and a series of minor parties on the other. In 1892 the People's party (Populist) called for free silver, a graduated income tax, direct election of senators, and nationalization of railroad, telephone, and telegraph systems. The Populists received a million votes in 1892 (8 percent) and won a *plurality* in five states.

In 1896 William Jennings Bryan briefly consolidated the support of the outgroups and won the Democratic nomination for President. Known as the "Great Commoner," Bryan was the voice of prairie populism. He supported an expansion of the money supply to help working people and small businesses, regulation of the railroads and monopolies that were exploiting the farmers, and improvements in the economic circumstances of city workers. His candidacy constituted a strong attack on the nation's economic power structure. He attempted to forge an alliance of farmers and urban working people (whom he called the toiling masses) into an avowed class party to struggle against those economic forces that had long exploited them.

A Democratic party campaign poster from 1900 showing William Jennings Bryan as the party's presidential candidate. Although unsuccessful in three bids for the Presidency, Bryan advocated many progressive proposals—a graduated federal income tax, stricter regulation of monopolies, and suffrage for women, among others—that became law during the Roosevelt and Wilson administrations.

Bryan lost the election of 1896 to a much better-financed McKinley, but only by a plurality of 600,000 votes out of an extraordinary high turnout of 13.9 million. Still, the Democratic party failed to emerge from the election as the agent of farmers and urban working-class interests. The workers did not trust the established leadership of the Democratic party (Cleveland had been antilabor), and the farmers received little support after Bryan's defeat. Since Cleveland had been more antilabor than McKinley, many workers switched over to the Republican party, leaving the cities of the North mostly Republican and the South still solidly Democratic. The result was a weakened Democratic party, which remained the minority party until 1932.

The turn of the century was the beginning of the Progressive, or Reform, Era. Both major parties were caught up in the movement, and thus party alignments generally remained firm. The progressive movement was stimulated by continued domination of the economic and political structure by big business and an increase in business monopoly. It was also brought on by flagrant political corruption, the continued economic hardship of farmers and urban workers, and by reform groups interested in ending child labor and the sale of alcohol and in promoting women's voting rights. The backbone of the movement were young activists drawn primarily from agrarian groups, liberal Republican groups against local monopoly and for good government, and various groups interested in reform and social legislation to improve the conditions of the urban poor.

Much of the reform campaign took place at the state level, transforming many of the states into active agents of government. This was a role that the federal government would not fully assume until the Great Depression. The victories of the progressive movement at both the state and federal level were considerable. During this period the Constitution was amended to allow a federal income tax (Sixteenth Amendment), to permit popular election of U.S. senators (Seventeenth Amendment), and to extend the franchise to women (Nineteenth Amendment). New federal laws regulated child labor and housing codes, established new food and meat inspection standards, set up the Federal Reserve system, instituted antitrust legislation, and provided for workmen's compensation. Many states established the *initiative, referendum, recall* and city-manager governments.

The election of 1860 left the North predominantly Republican, the deep South Democratic, the Southern border states Democratic, and the Northern border states Republican. "One-partyism" in the South would last a hundred years.

When Theodore Roosevelt tried to lead the Republican party too rapidly into reform, the party split. Roosevelt ran in 1912 as the candidate of the Progressive "Bull Moose" party. He received 27.4 percent of the vote (the Socialist party received another 6 percent), allowing the Democrat, Woodrow Wilson, to win the Presidency by a plurality. Wilson was reform-oriented, and

Teddy Roosevelt (above) left the Republican party in 1912 to form the Progressive ("Bull Moose") party. Roosevelt's support for such measures as workmen's compensation, graduated income and inheritance taxes, and stronger government regulation of big business precipitated his split with the Republican party.

thus the progressives were able to support the two-party system during his administrations. However, in 1924 Republican Robert LaFollette broke away from the party and led a progressive movement that received 16.6 percent of the vote.

In 1928 Republican farm supporters left the Republican party and joined the Democratic party convention. The Democrats adopted the insurgents' farm program but nominated Al Smith as the presidential candidate. He was an Easterner, a Catholic, and a "wet" with Tammany Hall connections. In addition, he knew little about the West, the South, or agriculture. In the Eastern and Northern cities, however, Smith was a working-class hero. He was a poor boy who "made good" and supported social legislation and factory laws. Catholics, immigrants, and minorities threw their support behind him. Smith lost the election, but his campaign stimulated the conversion of Northern and Eastern workers to the Democratic party, a conversion that would be cemented with the Great Depression.

The stock market crash of 1929, signaling the beginning of the Great

Depression, caused a major realignment of public support for the two parties, a pattern of support that basically persists today. As the Depression deepened, President Hoover and the long-dominant Republicans opted for a course of "rugged individualism" and charity. While this was a natural extension of basic Republican conservatism, it served to polarize the country into camps that either favored or opposed federal intervention in the nation's economic life (see Chapter 7).

The nomination of Franklin Delano Roosevelt (FDR) by the Democrats in 1932 proved to be the undoing of Republican domination. Despite a campaign of ambiguity and moderation, FDR captured the progressive imagination while simultaneously capturing the shrinking political center. By doing this, he managed to divert the radical tide of the insurgent left while piecing together a coalition of disaffected Republicans, Independents, and regular Democrats.

The realignment of the 1930s was based upon the fusion of urban, ethnic, and labor blocs within the national Democratic party. Many non-Catholic Northern urbanites broke ties with their Republican past and joined their Catholic brethren. Among the ethnic and racial blocs switching parties were blacks, Jews, and several Eastern European groups. While these three groups were coalescing within the Democratic party, there was a countershift of conservative, usually rural, voters to the Republican party outside the South. However, this movement did not prove significant until after the New Deal had been practically institutionalized.

As the Depression that gave vent to the realignment disappeared, the political polarization between the two parties also declined. The two major parties drew back from the ideological trenches and went about consolidating their gains. Leaders of the Republican or Grand Old Party (GOP) became more moderate in their criticism of the New Deal, while Democratic leaders refrained from calls for radical economic reform.

In the late 1930s and 1940s, many progressive Republicans in the Midwest formally joined the Democratic party, while Southerners sometimes made counter moves into the Republican party. A strong civil-rights plank at the Democratic national convention in 1948 prompted a walkout, climaxing in a Dixiecrat ticket led by Senator Strom Thurmond of South Carolina in four Southern states. Urban and suburban Southern whites who could not support Thurmond or Truman, the Democrat, opted for the Republican candidate, Thomas Dewey. Having once tasted the forbidden fruit of national Republicanism, many of these voters supported Eisenhower in 1952 and 1956. Thus the South had its Eisenhower Democrats just as party attachments in the North had spawned Roosevelt Republicans. These presidential defectors, however, generally maintained their Democratic affiliation at the state and local level.

The 1960s was a turbulent period. The civil-rights movement and the war in Vietnam were both heating up. Within the Republican party rose a group of programmatic conservatives. These activists were adamant in their desire to abolish governmental "excess" stemming from the New Deal and to curtail the extension of federal powers. Barry Goldwater was chosen as the Republican candidate in 1964. He expressed an unabashed right-wing philosophy offering the public an opportunity to vote for a candidate who promised to severely revise the government's role.

The public's fear of noncentrist candidates led to a crushing defeat for Goldwater and the Republican party. Goldwater received only 38.5 percent of the popular vote and carried only six states. Five of the states were in the Deep South, normally Democratic states. Goldwater's appeal in these states resulted primarily from his opposition to civil-rights laws.

The realignment of the 1930s was based upon the fusion of urban, ethnic, and labor blocs within the national Democratic party.

The ghetto riots in 1965, 1967, and 1968 created a white backlash. They paved the way for an avowed racist candidate to launch a national campaign for the Presidency. George Wallace, segregationist governor of Alabama, was unsuccessful in his efforts to win the Democratic party nomination, so he became the candidate of the American Independent party. There was considerable fear that Wallace's campaign would deny an Electoral College majority to one of the major candidates, thus requiring Congress to elect the President. Nixon preempted some of Wallace's support by developing what became known as a "Southern Strategy." Nixon promised the nation that if elected he would slow down the pace of civil-rights progress. Having had some of his thunder stolen, Wallace had to settle for only 13 percent of the popular vote, and five southern states.

In 1972 the Democratic party nominated George McGovern, an unabashed antiwar, liberal candidate, to oppose Nixon's campaign for a second term. McGovern's location in the left wing of the Democratic party offered the voters a clear choice between ideologies, a situation that has traditionally spelled disaster for the noncentrist candidate. McGovern's crushing defeat proved again that the public will not accept a candidate who is too far from the political middle. McGovern received only 37.3 percent of the popular vote, and only 17 Electoral College votes. Nixon carried all of the once-solid Democratic South.

In 1976 native-son Jimmy Carter recaptured the South for the Democratic party, winning a close contest over President Ford. By 1976 it could be said that there was no longer any one-party state in the nation. (However, a couple of midwestern and two New England states are still basically one-party Republican states, and most elected state and local officials throughout the South are still Democrats.) Traditional party ties and the frequent inability of the Republican party to win statewide office in the South causes many citizens and officials to remain in the Democratic party, despite their lack of support for most of the principles of the national Democratic party. This phenomenon often blurs class differences in Democratic party support in the South, making party labels an imprecise indicator of ideology.

While recent presidential elections have moderated one-partyism, the Democratic domination that began with the 1932 election was not reversed by either Eisenhower's or Nixon's tenure. Between 1932 and 1976, the Democratic party won the Presidency eight times, the Republicans only four times. Both houses of Congress have been consistently dominated by the Democratic party since 1952. Since 1964, 46 percent of the public have identified themselves as Democrats (see Table 2.1), while an average of only 26 percent of the public have identified with the Republican party. About 28 percent of the public identified themselves as Independents during this period.

> *McGovern's crushing defeat proved again that the public will not accept a candidate who is too far from the political middle.*

The social-class party divisions that occurred with the New Deal realignment have also basically persisted. The Democratic party remains the party of the working class and lower-income citizens, labor union members, minorities, intellectuals, Catholics, and Jews. The Republican party draws most of its support from the white middle and upper class, business, and rural areas outside the South. Table 8.1 shows the social characteristics of party identifiers in 1976.

Policy differences between Democrats and Republicans

While the two major parties clearly agree on many issues, the frequently made argument that the parties are as similar as Tweedledum and Tweedledee is simply wrong. The two parties basically agree on such broad issues as the free-enterprise system, the sanctity of private property, the necessity of government intervention to solve social problems, the need for government aid for the economy, military preparedness, anticommunism, and even war efforts such as Korea and Vietnam.

Neither party supports such left-wing policies as serious alterations in the distribution of wealth, full employment with guaranteed jobs for everyone, nationalization of energy and utilities, economic planning, or disarmament. Similarly, neither party accepts right-wing policies such as elimination of the income tax, dismantling of social welfare programs, racial and sexual discrimination, property ownership requirements for voting, an end to all or most regulation of business ethics, safety standards, or product quality, or an end to government aid for the economy. Individual members of the parties may support one or more of these policies, but collectively neither party supports them.

There are still very basic differences between the two parties. Since the New Deal, the Democratic party has been the architect and main supporter of domestic policies such as aid to the poor and middle class, the rehabilitation

TABLE 8.1
Social Characteristics of Party Identifiers: 1976

	Strong Democrat	Weak Democrat	Independent	Weak Republican	Strong Republican	Others	Total
Race							
White	12.9%	22.6%	36.8%	16.2%	10.4%	1.2%	100.1
Black	35.1	36.0	23.0	2.7	1.8	1.4	100.0
Other	4.8	40.5	35.7	9.5	2.4	7.1	100.0
Occupation							
Professional	10.8	22.8	38.2	17.4	10.4	.4	100.0
Manager, Official	12.5	17.3	41.8	13.9	13.9	.5	99.9
Clerical, sales	13.2	22.7	38.4	14.6	10.9	.3	100.1
Skilled, semiskilled	19.6	25.4	37.6	12.1	3.9	1.4	100.0
Unskilled, service	18.4	29.8	31.1	12.7	7.0	1.0	100.0
Farmer	20.3	23.2	20.3	21.7	13.0	1.4	99.9
Other (retired, etc.)	12.8	25.3	31.9	15.9	11.4	2.7	100.0
Religion							
Protestant	14.6	22.3	33.5	17.8	11.0	.9	100.1
Catholic	18.1	31.4	33.8	9.1	6.7	.9	100.0
Jewish	26.9	28.8	34.6	5.8	3.8	—	99.9
Education							
None through grade 8	23.4	29.7	22.6	13.9	6.8	3.4	99.8
Grades 9 through 12	15.6	25.2	36.7	13.8	7.5	1.2	100.0
Some college	9.9	19.9	43.4	16.0	10.8	—	100.0
Baccalaureate degree	5.9	19.6	37.3	16.7	20.1	.5	100.1
Advanced degree	13.7	22.2	37.3	15.0	11.1	.7	100.0
Income							
$0–$2,999	23.8	26.5	28.1	11.9	7.6	2.1	100.0
$3,000–$5,999	19.9	30.6	27.3	10.8	10.4	1.0	100.0
$6,000–$8,999	19.8	27.3	30.9	14.4	5.8	1.8	100.0
$9,000–$11,999	14.1	28.1	35.6	15.2	6.3	.7	100.0
$12,000–$19,999	12.0	23.0	43.6	12.5	7.1	1.8	100.0
$20,000 and over	10.4	18.2	37.0	19.6	14.8	—	100.0

Source: American National Election Study, 1976, Center for Political Research, University of Michigan.

of American cities and housing, civil rights, aid to education, mass transit, Medicare and Medicaid, progressive taxation, and the right of workers to organize and engage in collective bargaining. The Republican party has a business orientation and generally supports aid and subsidies to business, while opposing business regulation and taxes. The Republican party also generally supports a large military budget and is less concerned than the Democrats with increasing the public's role in the political process.

Orfield provides some specific examples of differences between the two parties:

> During the 1965–69 period most Democrats were consistent supporters of programs for mass transit, housing subsidies, the poverty program, school aid for poor children, model cities, fair housing, and general domestic program appropriations. Among Republican House members only one in twenty made a similar record. Rural Democrats were more pro-city than urban Republicans. While Southern Democrats cast a significant number of votes for urban programs, Southern Republicans cast virtually none.[4]

The coalitions break up?

There are analysts who think that the old coalitions are breaking up, the New Deal coalition included. And perhaps, some of them say, there is no new coalition on the horizon. Perhaps the United States is entering a period in which political parties will be less important. According to the standard recent theories of American political behavior, voting tended to conform to fairly stable patterns. As V. O. Key described the phenomenon:

> The apparent stability of the popular support of the political party dominant at the moment excites the curiosity of students of American politics. For relatively long periods one party or the other commands so consistently the votes of the majority that the country is said to be either normally Republican or normally Democratic. From 1932 to 1952 elections appeared to be only reassertions by the standing majority of its continued faith in Democratic leadership.[5]

Key was critical of some of the simplifications sometimes associated with that view. He noted, for instance, that "no sooner has a popular majority been constructed than it begins to crumble . . . to govern is to antagonize not only opponents but also at least some supporters. . . ."[6] But the division of elections into realigning (or critical) elections, which establish a new majority, maintaining elections, which repeat the majority, and deviating elections, in which there is a new outcome but the underlying loyalties are only temporarily broken, was a staple of American political analysis until quite recently. The emphasis, as Key noted, was on stability.

In a classic and carefully documented study of the fifties, *The American Voter,* Angus Campbell et al. concluded that there were no "coherent patterns of belief" in the electorate. "Very few of our respondents," they continued, "have shown a sensitive understanding of the positions of the parties on current issues. . . . We have then, the portrait of an electorate almost wholly without detailed information about decision-making in government."[7]

That lack of information, it was sometimes argued, was one source of the stability of voting patterns. People identified with, and voted for, the party of their parents more often than not. In American history, it was said, there

"The old labels just don't seem to mean much anymore."

had been only five turning points: the triumph of Jeffersonian Republicanism in 1800; Jackson's election in 1828; Lincoln bringing the new Republican party to power in 1860; the Republican victory in 1896; and Roosevelt's election in 1932.[8] The Roosevelt case seemed to have been almost staged to prove this analysis. A noncompromisable issue—the Great Depression—shattered the conventional wisdom and the old consensus. New social strata, urbanites and industrial workers in particular, entered politics in massive numbers. A majority coalition of reformers, trade unionists, Southern Democrats, urban machines, and minorities was assembled, and a framework was thus constituted which defined American politics for a generation.

There were, and are, critiques of this thesis as it is applied to the American past. Garry Wills, for instance, holds that the critical elections merely endorse changes made by elites.[9] But there is almost a consensus now that the theory has to be basically revised in the light of recent events. In 1964 Lyndon Johnson won in a landslide against Goldwater and then was effectively forced out of office four short years later. In 1968, Richard Nixon won a very close plurality victory over Hubert Humphrey, then achieved a landslide in 1972 against McGovern, and was literally driven from office in 1974. If politics are stable, how do we explain two landslides in ten years, one for each major party, and two deposed Presidents?

Jean J. Kirkpatrick wrote of these developments:

The wide electoral swings from Johnson's landslide in 1964 to Nixon's in 1972 dramatized the 'abnormal' behavior of large portions of the electorate, whose votes were quite unexpectedly less influenced by party identification than by candidates and issues. These 'abnormal landslides,' as Ladd has called them, suggested how volatile political competition could become, and this in turn cast doubt on everyone's 'normal' expectations.[10]

A careful survey of the seventies, *The Changing American Voter,* went over the same ground as *The American Voter* had and discovered that the findings of the 1950s no longer held.[11] There was a decline in party identification, a rise in issue voting and consistency, and a crumbling of the traditional coalitions.

Since *The Changing American Voter* appeared, a number of developments have reinforced its picture of political volatility in the United States. In particular, single-issue groups—those against legal abortion or gun control, for example—have emerged, judging a candidate on the basis of a single question, which is taken to be of utmost importance. These groups helped to defeat Senator Richard Clark in Iowa in 1978 and to deny the senatorial nomination to then Representative Donald Frazer in Minnesota in the same year. This introduced a "wild card" into American politics, since partisans of the single issue may agree with the candidate they help defeat on most other points. Similarly, the low voter turnout in the presidential election of 1976 and in the congressional ballot in 1978 could well be signs of a new restlessness and uncertainty in the electorate.

In the traditional theory, the breakdown of one coalition is the prelude to an emergence of a new coalition. But there are now analysts who suggest that perhaps America has entered a period in which there will be no stable coalition. Anthony King, who edited a study of American politics for the conservative American Enterprise Institute in 1979, summed up his colleagues' findings:

> If any one message emerges from the pages of this book, it is that fewer and fewer cohesive blocs are to be found in the American polity. Certain words have appeared again and again in the preceeding pages: 'fragmentation,' 'proliferation,' 'decentralization,' 'disintegration,' 'breaking up.' The ideas of the New Deal are no longer the ideas around which American politics is organized; but no new public philosophy has emerged to take their place. Power in Congress is even more widely dispersed than it used to be; the conservative coalition is much less prominent than it was.

And then he adds:

> American politicians continue to try to create *majorities;* they have no option. But they are no longer, or at least not very often, in the business of building *coalitions.* The materials out of which coalitions might be built simply do not exist. Building coalitions in the United States today is like trying to build coalitions out of sand. It can't be done.[12]

In 1973 Arthur Schlesinger, Jr., had already come to that conclusion, or at least had identified it as a distinct possibility. Americans may be, he said, coming to a period of "politics without parties," an era in which political leaders, like Chinese warlords, roam the countryside, organizing personal armies. . . . Without parties, our politics would grow angrier, wilder, and more irresponsible.[13]

If, as we argue throughout this book, the 1980s challenge American democracy with both domestic and international structural crises, and if that momentous development takes place under the conditions described by King and Schlesinger, then our traditional political mechanisms will have failed us at a time of the greatest need. Under these circumstances, it is not at all clear that this nation will be able to respond progressively to its problems. The decade, in short, is going to be both interesting and dangerous.

THIRD PARTIES

Despite the fact that for considerable periods throughout American history some sizeable groups have not had much influence in either major party, third parties have played a limited role in the American party system. On only three occasions during the twentieth century have third-party presidential candidates been able to attract more than 10 percent of the popular vote (see Table 8.2). Still, votes alone do not provide an accurate impression of the role of third parties in American politics.

Throughout American history, third parties have occasionally gained enough popular support to force one or both major parties to respond to the issues upon which the third party was based. Certainly this was true of the Populists, the Progressives, the American Independent party, and even to some extent the Socialist party. Some 140 parties have elected members to Congress in the last 180 years, but since the Civil War no third party has been able to replace one of the two major parties even temporarily. At the state level, third parties sometimes have supplemented the major parties, as the Non-Partisan League in North Dakota and the Progressives in Wisconsin did in the early part of this century. Since 1832, however, only nine third parties have carried more than one state.[14]

Third parties traditionally do poorly in the American political system because elections for members of Congress are held in single-member districts in which the candidate who receives a plurality wins. Third parties are encouraged in many European nations by multimember districts in which seats are allocated to the parties on the basis of the proportion of the total vote they receive. Similarly, in America the Presidency and state governorships can be won only by parties that can win a plurality. In parliamentary systems, such as those in Europe, the prime minister is chosen by the party or coalition of parties that forms the government.

TABLE 8.2
Major Third Parties

Year	Party	Percent of Total Votes Cast
1832	Anti-Mason	8.0
1848	Free Soil	10.1
1856	American	21.4
1860	Breckinridge Democratic Constitutional Union	12.6
1892	Populist	8.5
1912	Theodore Roosevelt Progressives	27.4
	Socialist	6.0
1924	LaFollette Progressives	16.6
1968	American Independent	13.5

Source: *Historical Statistics of the United States.*

The mechanics of the American party system, which hinder the development of third parties, also discourage insurgency. Groups that are quite unhappy within one of the two major parties may feel that leaving the two-party system would be a futile gesture. Lack of alternatives encourages compromise within the two-party system but often discourages policy innovations and can even deny any real alternatives to voters who must choose between the two parties. The lack of third parties also reduces the excitement of campaigns, since both major-party candidates may basically approach policy issues in the same way.

Third parties can increase public interest in elections by forcing a wider range of party dialogue and a more direct discussion of issues. The more issues debated and the more diverse the approaches to the issues, the better the chance that the public will be educated on issues. Thus, the positive features of the two-party system are at least counterbalanced by the negative features; some feel that they are overshadowed.[15]

Despite the almost certain futility of third-party efforts, every presidential election witnesses third-party campaigns (see Table 8.3). The various socialist groups, the Communist party, and the Prohibition party have fielded candidates for most of the twentieth century. In more recent elections, the American Independent and the American party (essentially the same group) have campaigned on racial issues, and the Libertarians have articulated a limited, almost no-government position. The Independent party in 1976 was headed by former Senator Eugene J. McCarthy who argued that both of the two major parties are decadent.

TABLE 8.3
Minor Parties in 1968, 1972, and 1976

1968 Party	Vote	1972 Party	Vote	1976 Party	Vote
American Independent	9,906,141	American	1,080,541	Independent	751,728
New	74,435	People's	78,801	Libertarian	172,750
Socialist Labor	52,588	Socialist Worker	65,290	American Independent	170,780
Socialist Worker	41,300	Socialist Labor	53,614	American	160,600
Peace and Freedom	36,385	Communist	25,222	Socialist Worker	91,226
Prohibition	14,519	Prohibition	13,444	Communist	59,114
Communist	1,075	Libertarian	2,691	People's	49,024
Scattered	19,606	America First	1,743	U.S. Labor	40,045
	10,146,049	Universal	199	Prohibition	15,898
		Scattered	23,959	Socialist Labor	9,590
			1,345,504	Socialist	6,022
				Scattered	48,682
					1,575,459

Source: *Congressional Quarterly*, December 18, 1976, pp. 3335–3336.

NOMINATIONS AND ELECTIONS

Historically, the major functions of our undisciplined and decentralized parties have been to nominate candidates for office and to conduct election campaigns. However, both the nomination and election campaign processes are uniquely American inventions that reveal the limited role American parties play in the political process.

The direct primary: State and federal candidates

The selection of candidates to represent the major parties in elections is determined by the direct primary. The *direct primary* is simply an election in which candidates can run for a party's nomination by either paying a filing fee (usually modest) or obtaining a specified number of signatures from registered voters. In 1978, forty-one states had *closed primaries* in which individuals could vote only in the primary of the party they identified with. In nine states the public could vote in either. The candidate who wins a majority of votes cast in the primary becomes the party's nominee. If there are a large number of candidates or a close race which keeps one candidate from winning a majority, a runoff election is held between the top two candidates.

Ironically, the parties themselves may have little control over who the candidates are or even over who eventually wins the party's nomination. This nomination process is uniquely American; clearly, it severely reduces the importance of political parties. At the local or state level, the party organization may endorse party regulars for the primary, but this does not mean that the party's candidate will win or even that the endorsed candidate will have an advantage. In most states and most urban areas, there are factions within the parties that also endorse candidates. The factions may, and often do, endorse different candidates. For example, the liberal wing of the Democratic party in Houston (the Harris County Democrats) may endorse candidates for local and state contests that are quite different from those endorsed by the local Democratic party regulars. During the primary contest, then, one clique of Democrats may support a different group of candidates than another clique of Democrats from the same state or city.

While endorsements by civics groups, unions, minority groups, distinctly political organizations, newspapers, and the parties are important to any candidate, a well-financed candidate may find it possible to launch a campaign for a party's nomination regardless of that party's attitude toward the candidate. With the mounting cost of elections and growing reliance on public-relations firms to run campaigns, well-heeled candidates are increasingly paying little or no attention to the party organization. The candidates raise large sums to seek nomination and run their campaigns in whatever manner they choose. If they win the nomination, they may feel little loyalty to the local party and little inclination to adopt the policy stands of the local or national party. The party itself has little choice but to endorse the winning candidate and attempt to rally party support behind the nominee in the general election. If the candidate wins the election, the party and elected officials may establish a working relationship, assuring some party support during future elections.

Popular election of the President would encourage third parties and would also probably increase popular participation.

Increasingly, presidential candidates are also chosen in direct primaries, giving the major parties little control over a nomination as important as their candidate. In theory, both major parties nominate their candidates for President at a mid-year convention during election years. In reality, however, the party's nominee is generally selected in the presidential primaries, and the conventions only ratify the winner of the state primaries.

The critical importance of the presidential primaries is a recent phenomenon. In 1968, for example, only about a third of all states held presidential primaries, leaving most delegates to be chosen by state party conventions. In addition, in 1968 most convention delegates were not pledged to support any particular presidential candidate. In 1976 the thirty presidential primaries included the nation's ten most populous states. Nearly three-fourths of the delegates to the Republican and Democratic conventions were selected in these primaries and were obligated to support specific candidates. Those states not conducting presidential primaries in 1976 selected delegates at state or district conventions or combinations of the two. In 1980, thirty-five states held presidential primaries, as did the District of Columbia and Puerto Rico.

Candidates for the nomination of either party, then, must enter the primaries and attempt to win the most delegate votes or at least enough votes to assure the party nomination at the convention. Those states with primaries schedule them during the first six months of the election year. The first state primary is traditionally in New Hampshire in late February; the last in 1976 was in California in early June. In 1980 eight states, including California, concluded the presidential primaries with elections on June 3. Although New Hampshire is a very small state and certainly is not representative of the nation, its primary is extremely important simply because it is first. Candidates

Jane Byrne defeated the Democratic party machine candidate in the primary and easily won the general election to become mayor of Chicago in 1979. Byrne's victory in the primary demonstrates the lack of party control over the nomination process in state and local elections.

generally must enter this primary and as many of the others as they can. The primaries in all the large states are a must because they control a large percentage of all the party delegates.

The primary process is the most democratic means of selecting presidential candidates. For that reason it is unlikely that the parties will attempt to return to the old process of selecting candidates by party convention or *caucus*. Still, the primaries do decrease the importance of our already weak parties, and they also cause a number of other problems.

Running in the primaries is expensive and tiring. Candidates must try to set up an organization and campaign in each state with a primary, while not neglecting those states which still use conventions. This means that the candidates can spend no more than a few days in each state and must stay on the road for months on end. The physical and financial resources necessary to maintain such a regimen are considerable. Senator Robert Packwood aptly refers to this process as ''shuttle candidacy—a condition in which contenders race from state to state, stepping off planes with a jet-lag grin.''

Another serious problem is that a candidate can gain the party's nomination even though he or she receives only a small proportion of the votes cast by members of the party. In 1976, for example, Carter entered all but one of

The major Republican presidential candidates in 1980:(from left) Ronald Reagan, John Anderson, Howard Baker, Robert Dole, Philip Crane, and George Bush. (Missing from the group was John Connally.) Since most states now hold direct presidential primaries, the electorate has more control over presidential nominations than the parties do.

the thirty state primaries. While he won eighteen primaries (more than any other candidate), he received only about 39 percent of the votes cast by Democrats in the primaries. Thus, a majority of the 16 million Democrats who voted in the primaries (out of 60 million Democrats) would have preferred another candidate.

The Republican primaries can distort public opinion even more because they may be winner-take-all events. The Democratic party has outlawed such contests, but the Republicans allow state parties to award all the state's delegate votes to the candidate who receives the most votes, even if the candidate only wins by a plurality. The Democrats use a proportional system, dividing delegates among the candidates in relation to the percentage of the party vote they receive.

With the mounting cost of elections and growing reliance on public-relations firms to run campaigns, well-heeled candidates are increasingly paying little or no attention to the party organization.

The primaries also put a premium on candidates with name recognition. A candidate who is not a known figure or at least a prominent politician must start building up support long before the primaries. Jimmy Carter started his campaign a year before the primaries, traveled tens of thousands of miles, and invested almost two years in obtaining the Democratic nomination. Few candidates would have the time, money, energy, or confidence to engage in such an effort. Even well-known candidates must spend at least a year running for the Presidency. By November 15, 1979, there were six announced major candidates for the 1980 Republican nomination, and four announced dark-horse candidates. Several of these candidates had been raising funds and laying the groundwork for their campaign for a year.

The primary process is the most democratic means of selecting presidential candidates. For that reason it is unlikely that the parties will attempt to return to the old process of selecting candidates by party convention or caucus. Still, the primaries do decrease the importance of our already weak parties.

Reforming the primary system would probably be quite difficult. Some have argued for one national primary, but unless a runoff were held, the winner would undoubtedly have only plurality support. Such events would also give an advantage to well-known candidates, whereas the present system does allow lesser known candidates to build up momentum. A somewhat easier reform, and one that might not be as difficult to obtain, would be to have all the primaries grouped a few weeks apart, with six or eight in a region held on the same day. This system would lessen the killing pace of the campaign, though it would not increase party control over candidates.

The presidential conventions

America's unique political event, the presidential convention, has been described in a variety of ways. It has been called a circus, an old-time revival meeting (or a combination of the two), a rain dance, even a premeditated riot. All descriptions suggest the teeming size, the seeming lack of organization and discipline, the energy, even the gaudiness of the events. Theoretically at least, presidential conventions are held once every four years to select the party's candidate for President and Vice-President, to choose a party chairperson, to write a party platform, and to organize a strategy for winning the presidential election.

During much of the nineteenth and twentieth centuries, these were the basic functions of the conventions. In the last thirty years, the functions and even the operation of the conventions have changed considerably. Increasingly, presidential candidates launch their campaigns long before the convention, hoping to win enough delegate votes in primaries or state conventions to wrap up the nomination before the convention gets under way. The increasing number of presidential primaries contributes to the possibility that a candidate will have enough committed delegates to insure the convention nomination. Since 1952 the outcome of most presidential conventions has been a foregone conclusion; indeed, no more than one ballot has been necessary in any presidential convention since then.

If the presidential candidate is selected before the convention, two other issues are also essentially settled. The vice-presidential candidate is chosen by the presidential nominee, and the convention only ratifies the choice. The presidential nominee also selects the party chairperson, who generally aids in conducting the presidential candidate's campaign. Candidates for the nomination also generally have developed a campaign staff and a strategy to win votes and delegates in the primaries and state conventions. The winning candidate will simply enlarge that organization, in part by accepting workers and supporters from the camps of unsuccessful party candidates.

Even if the outcome of the convention is obvious, it still serves a number of important functions. The convention provides a method of bringing party representatives from across the nation together, with the hope of generating enthusiasm for the party ticket and creating a working (if temporary) unity. The publicity surrounding the convention generates intense media coverage and stimulates public interest. The convention also provides a forum for the discussion of party issues and their conversion into a party platform. To some extent the convention also gives shape and unity to the party by developing certain party rules and determining how many delegates to forthcoming conventions each state will receive.

Preparations for the convention begin at least a year in advance. The national committee of each party handles the convention organization, starting with the selection of the city in which the convention will be held. These committees consist of party representatives from each state and, with the Democrats, from other party groups. In 1976 the Republican National Committee consisted of the national party chairperson (selected by the presidential candidate in 1972), and the national committeeman and committeewoman from each state, Washington, D.C., Guam, Puerto Rico, and the Virgin Islands, and a few other party dignitaries. This formula yielded a Republican National Committee composed of 162 members.

The Democratic National Committee was composed of the chairperson and next highest ranking officer of the opposite sex from each state and territory, 200 members apportioned among the states, the chairperson of the Democratic Governors' Conference and two additional Democratic governors, the Democratic leader and one other top party official from each house of Congress, the chairperson of the Democratic Mayors' Conference and two other Democratic mayors, the President and two other representatives of the Young Democrats, and 25 additional members. This produced a committee of 342. [16]

After selecting the convention site, the national committee establishes a temporary organization and committee system to run the convention. Typically the committee establishes four major committees:

1. *Credentials:* Certifies delegates and alternates to the convention and resolves disputes between groups or individuals about the legitimate slate of delegates from a state.
2. *Permanent Organization:* Selects those officials who will run the convention, including a permanent chairman, a secretary, and a sergeant-at-arms.
3. *Rules:* Revises the rules by which the convention is conducted in order to make the nomination process run as smoothly as possible.
4. *Platform:* Writes the party platform after holding hearings at which delegates, party officials, representatives of the presidential candidates, and private citizens testify.

By the time the party delegates arrive, the convention has a basic coherence. The number of delegates to the convention and the division of delegates among the states are determined at the previous convention. Each party uses a formula to divide the delegates among the states, based essentially on the size of each state's population and the strength of the party in that state. In 1976 there were 3,008 delegates to the Democratic Convention, plus 1,896 alternates, making a total of 4,904. There were 2,259 delegates to the Republican convention, along with an equal number of alternates, making a total of 4,508. Party notables who are not delegates are also generally allowed to attend the convention in a nonvoting capacity. The media adds substantially to the crush by sending about as many representatives as there are delegates. The result is an absolute mob on the convention floor at most hours, much noise, and endless confusion.

After opening speeches, the nominations begin by a roll call of the states. The state delegation can nominate a candidate, defer to another state, or pass. As the roll is called, the candidates are nominated, and seconding speeches are made. Each nomination sets off a "spontaneous" demonstration among delegate supporters, complete with music, banners, stomping, shouting, dancing and parades. The completion of the roll call establishes the list of nominees.

Delegate voting for the presidential candidate proceeds in the same manner. The roll of states is called and each state delegation casts its votes. As noted, most of the delegates are pledged to vote for specific candidates, at least on the first few ballots. One ballot is all that has been necessary since the early 1950s. However, the contest between Ford and Reagan for the Republican nomination in 1976 was a genuine cliffhanger. Each had roughly equal numbers of committed delegates, and the final decision came down to the uncommitted delegates.

When the party nominee is chosen, he or she appears with family before the convention and delivers an acceptance speech. The presidential candidate then decides on a vice-presidential candidate, whom the convention ratifies. With the approval of the party platform the convention adjourns.

The national committees have little continuing jurisdiction over the party, but in recent years the Democratic party has attempted to develop some national unity. In 1956 the Democrats established a loyalty oath requiring delegates to pledge their support for party candidates. This provision was aimed at Southern Democrats, who tended to abandon the party for more economically or racially conservative candidates. In 1964 the party prohibited racial discrimination in the selection of delegates. In 1968, 1972, and 1976, the party established new delegate selection rules designed to insure minority, female, and lower-income representation among the delegates. In 1974, a constitution was adopted (The Democratic Party Charter) which gave the national committee some continuing authority.[17] In 1978 the Democratic party held a mid-term convention to discuss campaign issues and strategies for 1980.

The Electoral College: A constitutional flaw

The winner of the presidential contest is determined by the Electoral College. As originally designed, the Electoral College allowed a small group of eminent citizens in each state to select a President. The rise of political parties democratized this institution but has had no impact on its inherent flaws.

Under the Electoral College system, each state receives a number of electoral votes equal to its congressional representation from that state. In the election, the party that receives the largest number of votes in a state gets to cast all the state's electoral votes for its candidate. Until the rise of political parties, opposing cliques of elite leaders in each state vied for the state's votes. As political parties developed, the electors from each party were selected by party members with the understanding that if the party were victorious in the election, the electors would cast the state's vote for the winning party's candidate.

An example might make the process clearer. In 1976 Texas had two senators and twenty-four representatives in Congress, giving it a total of twenty-six votes in the Electoral College. Each party in Texas chose twenty-six individuals to serve as the party's presidential electors. In the election, Jimmy Carter carried the state of Texas, winning 51.1 percent of the total vote (see Table 8.4). Thus, the Democratic electors got to cast all the state's twenty-six votes for Carter. Carter did not have to receive a majority of all votes cast to win the state; he only had to receive more votes than any other candidate. Since the Electoral College is a winner-take-all system, the Democrats got to cast all the state's votes, not just a proportion of them.

The total number of votes in the Electoral College is 538. This figure reflects the 100 senators and 435 representatives allocated among the states, plus three electoral votes for the District of Columbia. To win the Presidency, one candidate must win a majority of the electoral vote—270 out of the total of 538. If no candidate receives a majority, the House of Representatives selects the President from the top three candidates, with each state delegation casting one vote. The Senate chooses the vice-president from the top two candidates, with each senator having one vote.

When citizens vote for a presidential choice, they generally have the impression that they are voting directly for the candidate. In reality they are voting for a slate of electors who will in turn vote for the candidate. Some states list the names of the electors for each candidate on the ballot; others use the short ballot, which simply lists the names of candidates. The popular vote for the Presidency takes place in early November, and as the vote is counted one candidate is determined to be the winner.

In reality, however, the vote is not yet official. In early December, the winning electors in each state meet at the state capitol and cast their votes, which are signed and sealed by the governor and forwarded to Congress. In early January, the Congress meets in joint session, counts the votes, and announces the official winner.

The announcement of the winner in early January is generally an anticlimax which warrants only a few paragraphs in the newspaper. The official count could, however, be quite important in a close contest. The reason is that on occasion electors refuse to cast their ballot for the candidate they are pledged to, and vote for someone else. For example, in the 1968 election, a North Carolina elector who had pledged to support Richard Nixon voted instead for George Wallace, causing Nixon to receive 301 electoral votes rather than the 302 votes he should have received.

The vulnerability of the system to the whim of electors is only one problem. Critics have long pointed out these additional flaws:

1. If no candidate wins a majority of the electoral vote, causing the election to be thrown into the House and Senate, numerous problems can occur. In the House election of the President, each state gets one vote, thus grossly violating the "one man, one vote" rule.* Representatives

---

*The House has had to elect the President twice. In 1800 Thomas Jefferson was elected after 36 ballots, and in 1824 John Quincy Adams was elected on the first ballot.

TABLE 8.4
Votes in the 1976 Presidential Election

Total Popular Votes: 81,551,659
Carter's Plurality: 1,680,974

State	JIMMY CARTER (Democrat) Votes	%	GERALD R. FORD (Republican) Votes	%	OTHER Votes	%		Plurality	Electoral Votes C	F
Alabama	659,170	55.7	504,070	42.6	19,610	1.7	C	155,100	9	
Alaska	44,055	35.7	71,555	57.9	7,935	6.4	F	27,500		3
Arizona	295,602	39.8	418,642	56.4	28,475	3.8	F	123,040		6
Arkansas	498,604	65.0	267,903	34.9	1,028	0.1	C	230,701	6	
California	3,742,284	47.6	3,882,244	49.3	242,515	3.1	F	139,960		45
Colorado	460,801	42.5	584,456	54.0	37,709	3.5	F	123,655		7
Connecticut	647,895	46.9	719,261	52.1	14,370	1.0	F	71,366		8
Delaware	122,559	52.0	109,780	46.6	3,403	1.4	C	12,779	3	
Dist. of Col.	137,818	81.6	27,873	16.5	3,139	1.9	C	109,945	3	
Florida	1,636,000	51.9	1,469,531	46.6	45,100	1.4	C	166,469	17	
Georgia	979,409	66.7	483,743	33.0	4,306	0.3	C	495,666	12	
Hawaii	147,375	50.6	140,003	48.1	3,923	1.3	C	7,372	4	
Idaho	126,549	36.8	204,151	59.3	13,387	3.9	F	77,602		4
Illinois	2,271,295	48.1	2,364,269	50.1	83,269	1.8	F	92,974		26
Indiana	1,014,714	45.7	1,185,958	53.4	21,690	1.0	F	171,244		13
Iowa	619,931	48.5	632,863	49.5	26,512	2.1	F	12,932		8
Kansas	430,421	44.9	502,752	52.5	24,672	2.6	F	72,331		7
Kentucky	615,717	52.8	531,852	45.6	19,573	1.7	C	83,865	9	
Louisiana	661,365	51.7	587,446	46.0	29,628	2.3	C	73,919	10	
Maine	232,279	48.1	236,320	48.9	14,610	3.0	F	4,041		4
Maryland	759,612	52.8	672,661	46.7	7,624	0.5	C	86,951	10	
Massachusetts	1,429,475	56.1	1,030,276	40.4	87,807	3.4	C	399,199	14	
Michigan	1,696,714	46.4	1,893,742	51.8	63,294	1.7	F	197,028		21
Minnesota	1,070,440	54.9	819,395	42.0	59,754	3.1	C	251,045	10	
Mississippi	381,329	49.6	366,846	47.7	21,205	2.8	C	14,483	7	
Missouri	998,387	51.1	927,443	47.5	27,770	1.4	C	70,944	12	
Montana	149,259	45.4	173,703	52.8	5,772	1.8	F	24,444		4
Nebraska	233,293	38.4	359,219	59.2	14,237	2.3	F	125,926		5
Nevada	92,479	45.8	101,273	50.2	8,124	4.0	F	8,794		3
New Hampshire	147,645	43.5	185,935	54.7	6,047	1.8	F	38,290		4
New Jersey	1,444,653	47.9	1,509,688	50.1	60,131	2.0	F	65,035		17
New Mexico	201,148	48.3	211,419	50.7	4,023	1.0	F	10,271		4
New York	3,389,558	51.9	3,100,791	47.5	43,851	0.7	C	288,767	41	
North Carolina	927,365	55.2	741,960	44.2	9,589	0.6	C	185,405	13	
North Dakota	136,078	45.8	153,470	51.7	7,545	2.5	F	17,392		3
Ohio	2,011,621	48.9	2,000,502	48.7	99,747	2.4	C	11,116	25	
Oklahoma	532,442	48.7	545,708	50.0	14,101	1.3	F	13,266		8
Oregon	490,407	47.6	492,120	47.8	47,306	4.6	F	1,713		6
Pennsylvania	2,328,677	50.4	2,205,604	47.7	86,506	1.9	C	123,073	27	
Rhode Island	227,636	55.4	181,249	44.1	2,285	0.6	C	46,387	4	
South Carolina	450,807	56.2	346,149	43.1	5,627	0.7	C	104,658	8	
South Dakota	147,068	48.9	151,505	50.4	2,105	0.7	F	4,437		4
Tennessee	825,879	55.9	633,969	42.9	16,498	1.1	C	191,910	10	
Texas	2,082,319	51.1	1,953,300	48.0	36,265	0.9	C	129,019	26	
Utah	182,110	33.6	337,908	62.4	21,200	3.9	F	155,798		4
Vermont	78,789	42.8	100,387	54.6	4,726	2.6	F	21,598		3
Virginia	813,896	48.0	836,554	49.3	46,644	2.7	F	22,658		12
Washington	717,323	46.1	777,732	50.0	60,479	3.9	F	60,409		9
West Virginia	435,864	58.1	314,726	41.9			C	121,138	6	
Wisconsin	1,040,232	49.4	1,004,987	47.8	58,956	2.8	C	35,245	11	
Wyoming	62,239	39.8	92,717	59.3	1,387	0.9	F	30,478		3
Totals	40,828,587	50.1	39,147,613	48.0	1,575,459	1.9	C	1,680,974	297	241

Source: *Congressional Quarterly*, December 18, 1976, p. 3334.

from twenty-six states can decide the contest, even if those states do not represent a majority of the nation's population. As an extreme example, Congress in 1968 determined that if the Wallace candidacy denied either Humphrey or Nixon a majority of the electoral vote, seventy-six members of the House from twenty-six states, with a total population of 32 million, could outvote the other 359 members from twenty-four states with a combined population of 150 million.[18] Additionally, the Senate could choose a Vice-President from a different party than the House-selected President, creating an extremely awkward situation.

2. The Electoral College only basically reflects population size in each state since each state has two senators and since representatives are reallocated among the states only every ten years. Nor does it reflect voter turnout in each state. For example, in 1968 Connecticut voters cast 6,000 more votes than Tennessee voters, but Connecticut had only eight electoral votes to Tennessee's eleven. The system can, then, award the Presidency to a candidate who ran second in the popular vote. On three occasions the Electoral College has awarded the presidency to a candidate who lost the popular vote (in 1824, 1876, and 1888). In 1976 Carter received 1.7 million more popular votes than Ford. However, a shift of 9,245 votes in Ohio and Hawaii would have swung the electoral vote to Ford while hardly affecting the popular vote totals.

3. The Electoral College is biased in favor of the small states since it gives them at least three votes, often far more representation in the total vote than their population deserves. For example, in 1968 each electoral vote in Alaska represented 75,000 persons, while in California each represented 393,000.

4. The winner-take-all provision orients candidates toward the large states. If a candidate can obtain the electoral votes of the eleven largest states and the District of Columbia, he wins. This means that candidates concentrate on the larger states and often pay little attention to the smaller states.

The cumulative problems led the American Bar Association in a 1967 study to label the Electoral College as "archaic, undemocratic, complex, ambiguous, indirect, and dangerous."[19] While almost everyone agrees that the Electoral College is seriously flawed, Congress has not been able to remedy the problem. The main obstacle has been the small states, who want to retain the system because it increases their influence in the selection process.

There are numerous proposals for amending or replacing the Electoral College, but only one has received much support in Congress. A proposal to amend the Constitution to allow popular election of the President has received the most support, but not enough to allow it to pass Congress. Under this proposal, election would be by straight popular vote, and the winner would be required to receive at least 40 percent of the total vote. If no candidate

"Whew! Can't we find some other route?"

received 40 percent, a runoff between the top two candidates would take place.

Popular election of the President would encourage third parties and would also probably increase popular participation. With popular election, the parties would work to turn out every voter possible, even voters who live in states that would clearly be carried by the opposition party. Under the present system, parties do not generally worry about turning out the vote in states that will clearly be won by another party. Recent polls have shown that 80 percent or more of the public favors popular election, but opponents continue to prevent reform.[20]

CONCLUSIONS

The difficulty of accomplishing policy goals in the American political system is caused in part by America's peculiar party structure. The collective lack of party unity, ideological or policy firmness, control over nominations, and discipline of party members seriously reduces the parties' ability to promote and accomplish policy goals. When this problem is combined with the decentralization of power in Congress and the separation of power between the various branches of government, the obstacles to policy formulation and enactment are formidable. The combined problems substantially explain why the federal government has been incapable of responding to such problems as unemployment, underemployment, inflation, energy shortages, urban blight, and poverty.

More unified parties that were firmer on policy goals and capable of maintaining some discipline on party issues would help to alleviate some of the problems caused by the decentralization of power in Congress, the nation's major policy-making branch. In fact, in a political system with power divided between three branches, disciplined parties are quite essential. A more responsible party system would also provide voters with clearer choices in elections. It would help to educate the public since the major parties would more clearly express and support specific issues and approaches to policy problems.

A first step toward a more responsible system would be the development of a genuine two-party system in each state. The major area of the nation without a viable two-party system is the South, where progress toward a two-party system is slow but distinct. It may, however, take another twenty years to establish a two-party system there. Public financing of congressional elections and popular election of the President would speed up this progress, but even with these reforms the transition will probably be quite slow. As long as basic one-partyism persists in the South, party labels, especially the Democratic label, will provide only weak cues to the policy positions of candidates and officeholders.

The parties could encourage the development of a genuine two-party system by establishing some rules of party discipline for party candidates or officeholders. In a two-party system there will always be substantial differences on policy among members. But some policy unity could be established by rewarding party supporters with increased chances of congressional committee leadership roles and with party financing and membership support during election campaigns. For example, the Democratic members of Congress could agree to give leadership preference and campaign aid to members who support the party's basic programs. This would reduce the independence of members but would enhance cooperation and cohesion between the President and the party, which would in turn contribute to better policy formulation and implementation. If one major party became more united and disciplined, the other major party could also better play the role of loyal opposition. If one party's policy goals were more obvious, the other party could formulate a response and try to educate the public on party differences.

The encouragement of third parties would also improve the party system. It would force the major parties to be clearer on issues, encourage the major parties to deal with issues raised by third parties, and increase the stimulation and educational role of campaigns. Popular election of the President would foster third parties. Public financing of congressional elections could be designed to encourage third parties, and media rules could be revised to allow third parties with significant public support to have air time. The candidates of the two major parties now receive a certain amount of free air time, and this could be extended to third parties that attract significant popular votes or petition signatures. The media could also be required to allow third-party participation in future presidential debates, even if only the most popular two third parties were included.

As we noted in our discussion of political coalitions, however, these are extremely volatile times. We can only be reasonably certain that politics in 1990 will be very different from anything we have seen in recent years. We are clearly at a moment of transition, but we don't really know where the transition will lead.

Footnotes

1. See Frank J. Sorauf, *Party Politics in America* (Boston: Little, Brown, 1976), pp. 1–28.
2. See the discussion in Jeff Fishel, ed., *Parties and Elections in an Anti-Party Age* (Bloomington, Indiana: Indiana University Press, 1978), pp. xi–xxviii.
3. Most of this discussion is taken from James L. Sundequist, *Dynamics of the Party System: Alignment and Realignment of Political Parties in the United States* (Washington, D.C.: The Brookings Institution, 1973), and Sorauf, *Party Politics in America,* pp. 28–58.
4. Gary Orfield, *Congressional Power: Congress and Social Change* (New York: Harcourt Brace Jovanovich, 1975), p. 53.
5. V. O. Key, *The Responsible Electorate* (New York: Vintage Books, 1968), p. 29.
6. *Ibid.,* p. 30.
7. Angus Campbell et al., *The American Voter* (New York: Wiley, 1960), pp. 10–11.
8. Walter Dean Burnham, *Critical Elections and the Mainspring of American Politics* (New York: Norton, 1970).
9. Garry Wills, *Confessions of a Conservative* (Garden City, New York: Doubleday, 1979), Chapter 9.
10. Jean J. Kirkpatrick, "Changing Patterns of Electoral Competition," in Anthony King, ed., *The New American Political System* (Washington: American Enterprise Institute, 1979), p. 269.
11. Norman H. Nie, Sidney Verba, and John R. Petrocik, *The Changing American Voter* (Cambridge: Harvard University Press, 1976).
12. King, ed., *The New American Political System,* pp. 390–92.
13. Arthur Schlesinger, Jr., ed., *History of U.S. Political Parties* (New York: Chelsea House, 1973), Vol. 1, p. iii.
14. "Third Parties: A Struggle for Attention," *The Congressional Quarterly,* Oct. 16, 1976, p. 2971.
15. See Lawrence C. Dodd, *Congress and Public Policy* (Morristown, New Jersey: General Learning Press, 1975).
16. See Sorauf, *Party Politics in America,* p. 117.
17. See Gerald Pomper (with colleagues), *The Election of 1976: Reports and Interpretations* (New York: David McKay, 1977), p. 7.
18. See Felix Belair, Jr., "Fight in House Rages for Rule on Presidency," *The Atlanta Constitution,* Oct. 21, 1968, p. 44.
19. See "Archaic and Dangerous," *Newsweek,* Dec. 30, 1968, p. 23.
20. *Ibid.,* p. 24.

> Government is not simply a matter of putting a bill in the hopper and letting the legislative process run its course, as taught in the civics texts. It is a matter of personalities regularly relating to each other—not just what you have, but who you know.
>
> Jim Hightower

9

Political power in Washington and at the state and local levels of government is a matter of influence: who has the most on any given issue wins. Lobbying is one of the primary means by which groups exert influence in the policy-making process. *Lobbying* is a collective term used to describe the variety of strategies that groups employ to influence governmental actions. If automobile makers, unions, drug manufacturers, consumers, or other groups organize in an attempt to affect the outcome of legislation, or its administration, they are referred to as an *interest group*.

Lobbying and the Public Interest

Since governmental decisions have a vast impact on everything from business profits, union power, public health, and crime to the quality of air we breath and the water we drink, thousands of interests have organized to influence the policy process. In this chapter we will analyze the types of interest groups, the strategies they employ, and the factors that determine their success. This analysis will provide insights into political influence in America and will show the systemic biases that determine who has power in the political system.

THE WASHINGTON LOBBIES

Washington, D.C., is the center of the policy-making process in America and therefore the site of the most critical struggles between interest groups. Literally thousands of groups and group representatives are based in the nation's capital for the purpose of promoting or protecting particular interests. While no reliable data exist, it is estimated that there are between 5,000 and 10,000 lobbyists in Washington who work full- or part-time to influence domestic

An anti-abortion rally in Washington, D. C. Some interest groups are organized around political or social issues like abortion; others, like the AFL-CIO and the American Petroleum Institute, are formed to promote a group's economic interests.

policy. In addition, there are thousands of lobbyists located in Washington who represent foreign governments. In 1974, 11,432 foreign government lobbyists registered with the Department of Justice.[1] The executive branch of the federal government also has 1,000 or so persons on the public payroll whose primary job is to lobby Congress. Also located in Washington are hundreds of trade associations, foundations, social, ideological, civic, religious and humanitarian groups that attempt at one time or another to influence public policies.

Of the thousands of groups and individuals who attempt to influence federal policies, there are great disparities in the money they have to spend, in the expertise they can apply to an issue, in the group membership they can draw upon or mobilize behind an issue, and in their access to and influence with legislators and administrators. Thus there are big differences in their ability to successfully promote or defend their interests. Some of the most powerful interests have impressive office buildings in the capital, employ hundreds of people, and spend millions of dollars per year.

Big businesses are particularly well represented in Washington. The Chamber of Commerce and the National Association of Manufacturers are two of the best-known business lobbies. Recently these two organizations merged to form the Association of Commerce and Industry. In 1972 the chief executives of the top 160 corporations in America formed a new business lobby, which they named the Business Roundtable. The wealth, position, access, and expertise of the members of the Business Roundtable gave this group instantaneous clout. Since its formation, the Roundtable has primarily been involved in lobbying against full employment legislation, minimum-wage increases, antitrust legislation, consumer protection laws, and controls on toxic chemicals and industrial pollution. Friends and foes alike are quick to admit that the Roundtable has scored impressive victories in these areas.

Other powerful business lobbies include the Pharmaceutical Manufacturers Association (PMA), the Tobacco Institute (TI), the Grocery Manufacturers of America (GMA), the American Petroleum Institute (API), and the National Rifle Association (NRA). The American Petroleum Institute is one of the major oil lobbies. It is supported by membership dues paid by its oil clients. Dues to the API, which is a nonprofit, tax-exempt organization, are tax deductible. In 1975 eight of the largest oil companies paid dues of $1 million or more. Dues were also paid by 260 to 350 other corporate members and 7,000 independent members.[2] The API has a permanent headquarters in Washington, D.C., a large professional staff, and an estimated $20 to $25 million a year to spend on influencing legislation. When the API combines its efforts with those of other oil and gas lobbies, an enormous amount of money and personnel can be mobilized to influence public policies.

The NRA represents the multimillion-dollar hunting and handgun lobby. Located in a nine-story glass and marble building with a staff of 292 and financed by a membership of one million, the gun lobby is readily conceded to be the most effective of all lobbies. Despite the fact that since the 1930s over two-thirds of the American public have favored stricter gun laws,[3] the NRA has regularly been able to intimidate Congress.

The gun lobby's success can be traced to two factors. First, its membership tends to be almost hysterical in its opposition to any laws designed to control guns. Because of the intensity of members' feelings, they are easily mobilized against any member of Congress who favors more restrictive laws. Such one-issue voters are fairly rare among the electorate. Second, the passion of NRA members discourages congressional members from subjecting themselves to the abuse they will receive if they support gun-control laws. NRA letters to members of Congress sometimes contain death threats or other forms of extreme hostility. More often, however, the letters are simply nasty. Sherrill provides an example of a letter from an NRA member sent to a representative with an Italian name:

> You dirty wop. You should go back to your Italy and mafia. How did you get in this country anyway? I bet you are the type who has no gun in his house to protect himself and would let any housebreaker come in and help himself to anything, even your wife, and then you would pray for a humble spirit to bear it. God help America with such as you in office. Were your parents ever married?[4]

The major labor unions, conservationist groups, and *public-interest groups* such as Common Cause are other examples of powerful interest groups based in Washington. The major labor unions, working through Political Action Committees (PACs), provide large sums in campaign funds to friendly candidates and members of Congress, maintain staffs in Washington to do research on topics of interest to them, and lobby members of Congress and the executive branch to support those issues. Conservationist groups and public-interest groups such as Common Cause have grown in importance in recent years. In the wake of Watergate, Common Cause was credited with pressuring Congress into passing new ethics codes for its members and adopting legislation providing optional public financing of presidential primary contests and elections. Conservationists have won passage of numerous environmental protection acts and have mobilized to defeat some members of Congress who have opposed environmental causes.

Political power in Washington and at the state and local levels of government is a matter of influence: who has the most on any given issue wins.

Some of the most effective lobbying in Washington is conducted by major law firms there. Creatures of their environment, the major Washington law firms that represent clients before Congress, the executive branch, and the courts are well staffed with highly paid and well-connected lawyers. Some of the most powerful firms are Covington and Burling, Hogan and Hartson, Ar-

John Gardner, chairman of Common Cause from its founding in 1970 until 1977. Common Cause, a prominent public-interest group, has lobbied for such measures as public financing of presidential and congressional elections and stricter ethics codes for public officials.

nold and Porter, and Wilmer, Cutler and Pickering. These firms often have more than 100 attorneys, many of whom have served in government and know powerful public officials on a first-name basis. As Sherrill says:

> The most certain way to success in Washington pressure politics is surely not in knowing how to bribe a crooked politician—probably not, so many are so crooked that they can be bribed—but in knowing the right lawyer with the right contacts and in having the money to afford him or her.[5]

The major lobbying law firms hold millions of dollars worth of retainers with major corporations. As Green notes, the primary function of these law firms is to "advocate positions that make the wealthy more so, consumers weaker, and corporations less accountable."[6] When major industries such as drug manufacturers, the auto makers, or tobacco growers feel threatened by pending bills or want to obtain helpful legislation from Congress, they inevitably turn to these giant law firms. The firms are masters at representing their client's views through personal interactions with policy-makers, research, bill writing or amendment, and testimony before agencies and committees. If delay is necessary, the firms may inundate committees or agencies with requests for information or answers to interrogatories, and drag out proceedings until they can force concessions or win outright victories. If all else fails, the issue can be taken to court, using all appellate processes.

In addition to the considerable talent, expertise, and financial resources these law firms can draw upon, the value of law-partner friendships with high government officials can hardly be overstated. The late Drew Pearson once provided an example of how such friendships can be utilized by the powerful:

> The smartest thing Detroit motor moguls did in the auto safety hearings was to hire Lloyd Cutler (of Wilmer, Cutler, and Pickering) as their attorney. Cutler is a close friend of Secretary of Commerce John T. Connor (formerly a president of the Merck drug house, and on the board of directors of General Motors) who will be entrusted with enforcing the safety standards if and when Congress writes them. Connor thought so highly of Cutler that he wanted to appoint him Undersecretary of Commerce.[7]

THE IMBALANCE OF INFLUENCE

As noted above, interest groups vary considerably in their power in the political system. Those interests that can afford a representative in Washington, a staffed headquarters in the capital, and/or a law firm to represent their interests in Washington clearly have a decided advantage over interests that cannot afford to engage in such activities. Hightower provides one example of advantages of being there:

> Food firms get what they want from government because they are there to get it. The dominant processors, distributors and retailers of food maintain a constant and powerful presence in the Capitol, and there is no food-related legislation, federal regulation or bureaucratic action that escapes their imprint.[8]

In 1975 there were seventeen food corporations and food trade associations with offices within eight blocks of the White House.[9]

The wealth necessary to be in Washington also allows an interest to make itself heard in a variety of ways. Large groups such as the auto industry, drug companies, and the American Medical Association (AMA) spend vast sums of money each year in an effort to shape and mobilize public opinion in support of their activities. When the auto manufacturers were faced with tougher auto emission standards in the early 1970s, they spent considerable sums to run ads in daily newspapers. They argued in those ads that tougher emission standards were unnecessary and would cause layoffs and increases in the cost of automobiles. The Tobacco Institute attempts to counter government bans of television advertising for cigarettes and health warnings by the American Cancer Society through newspaper and magazine ad campaigns. The AMA has long used its extensive treasury to fight alterations in traditional fee-for-service medical practices. Greenwald reports that in 1962 alone the AMA spent between $7 and $12 million dollars to defeat Medicare by stigmatizing it as a form of socialism.[10]

"There's getting to be a lot of dangerous talk about the public interest."

Another advantage of wealth is that it provides the interest with a mantle of legitimacy. Wealth alone denotes prestige in our society. Wealth allows interest-group officials to frequent exclusive restaurants and social clubs, which provide an urbane setting for interactions between group representatives and high government officials. Exclusive private clubs such as the Chevy Chase, Burning Tree, and the Metropolitan Club are often the setting for such interactions. As Hightower says, lobbyists can use these occasions to quietly articulate "a viewpoint from a position of economic and political strength. It is sophisticated, and it is effective."[11]

An interest group that can afford to organize can enhance its clout by developing expertise in an issue area. An adequately financed interest group can carefully research issues and draw up and disseminate evidence to support its positions. Lobbyists frequently supply friendly members of Congress with research supporting their position; they even engage in bill writing and editing. If a politician is firmly in the camp of labor or a particular business interest, lobbying groups that represent that interest may supply the official with speeches, statements for release to the press, arguments to calm constituents back home, and even "off the cuff" comments and suggested amendments to make the legislation more attractive to the interest group.[12]

The federal tax code is designed to make it easier for some groups to be able to afford the cost of lobbying. Internal Revenue Service (IRS) regulations specify that businesses and unions may deduct as a normal business expense all costs involved in lobbying on issues that are of "direct interest" to them. However, tax-exempt public charities that solicit tax-deductible contributions are not allowed to devote "substantial" efforts to lobbying. This means that while corporate and union advertising, dues to trade associations, salaries for lobbyists, and other expenditures associated with lobbying are tax deductible, charities which seek to promote health, education, and environmental causes may lose their tax-exempt status if they do too much lobbying. In 1968 the Sierra Club was stripped of its tax-deductible status because of its lobbying efforts against dams in the Grand Canyon.

Some interests also have another advantage in the policy process. They often have a monopoly over the information needed to make a policy decision. For example, Congress has no independent source of information on oil reserves. It must base its decisions on data supplied by the oil industry. The same is true of information on natural gas reserves and on profit margins for a variety of industries.

Interest groups also have one last advantage in obtaining their policy goals. Quite often the policy concessions an interest seeks would cost each individual taxpayer only a small amount of money. For example, an additional tax break for the oil industry might cost each taxpayer no more than $10 or $20 a year. The cost to each citizen is so low that individuals may consider it too trivial to merit the organization and mobilization necessary for successful opposition. Of course, if dozens of interest groups gain concessions that even modestly benefit them at the expense of consumers and taxpayers, the cumulative impact can be quite considerable.

INTEREST-GROUP STRATEGIES

The power and sophistication of many organized interest groups in Washington is further indicated by the strategies they employ in their efforts to influence legislation. The first rule of lobbyists is to personally interact with as many public officials and staff members who have control over the legislation at issue as possible. In meeting with these officials, a certain set of rules is generally followed. Greenwald lists them as follows:[13]

1. be pleasant and inoffensive;
2. be well prepared and informed;
3. be personally convinced of your arguments;
4. use the soft sell;
5. convince the official of the issue's importance to him in his constituency or in terms of the public interest; and
6. leave a written summary behind.

Cultivating friendships

Whatever approach the lobbyist uses, the primary prerequisite to influence is access. The lobbyist must be able to establish contact with key public officials or staff members. The cultivation of contacts or friendships among policy-makers is thus a primary goal of interest groups. The lobbyist's effectiveness is greatly increased if he or she is a personal friend of the policy-makers who have to be convinced to support the interest. As Sherrill notes:

> The most successful kind of personal lobbying is that which requires no pressure, except the pressure of a handshake or a chummy arm around the shoulder. A lobbyist is, naturally, most potent when dealing with old pals.[14]

Friendship may only insure access. In extreme cases, though, it may even guarantee the support of some officials for particular interest groups. Some members of Congress, for example, are closely aligned with particular interests and can always be counted on to support that interest. If the friendships are really enduring, the interest group may be able to exert its influence almost completely outside the public view. Hightower provides an excellent example of how large food manufacturers and retailers can often exert influence without public activities or participation in forums which would allow questioning by opponents.

Some interests have a monopoly over the information needed to make a policy decision. For example, Congress has no independent source of information on oil reserves. It must base its decisions on data supplied by the oil industry.

During 1973 and 1974, two congressional committees held public hearings to investigate the role of monopoly in rising food prices. Although specifically invited to appear before the committee, the food giants such as Ralston Purina, Del Monte, and Safeway refused to appear. Del Monte did, however, draw up a list of questions the members of the committee could ask of witnesses critical of the food industry. Although the food industry refused to appear in public, that does not mean that they were unable to communicate their views to the committee. During the hearings, the chair-person of the committee inadvertently admitted that he had breakfasted with executives of some of the major food industries that very morning. As Hightower says:

> There is nothing illegal about this, nor is it heavyhanded. There would be no request at breakfast to lay off the food industry, nor any hundred dollar bills slipped under the chairman's toast. It simply would be an opportunity for big business to make its position known directly, personally, comfortably, and off the public record.[15]

There are many ways in which representatives of interest groups can cultivate friendships with policy-makers. The most frequent method is through campaign contributions. Interest groups generally provide their supporters with contributions and attempt to gain access to policy-makers who might be persuaded to support their position by providing them with financial aid. Even policy-makers who are downright hostile to the interest may receive a contribution in the hope that the gesture will at least provide an opportunity for an exchange of views.

The effect of a campaign contribution may not alter policy-makers' views, but often this is unnecessary. Policy-makers may have supported the interest even before running for office, or their support may have been carefully cultivated over the years. Most members of Congress, for example, would have probably found it impossible to run for office if they did not have the support of some interest groups. Without interest-group money, most politicians could not afford the cost of a campaign.

The campaign contribution route to friendship is supplemented in many other ways. Interest-group representation may cement friendships through social interactions, favors such as research assistance and bill writing, luncheons, dinners, fees for speeches before the group, free plane rides, small gifts, and discounts on goods and services. Some industries assign each of their top executives a politician whom they are charged with getting to know. The executive befriends the politician and regularly reports back to the company on his charge's activities and disposition on certain issues. Large corporations like ITT can cultivate and monitor large numbers of politicians by this approach.[16]

On occasion, interest-group methods involve corrupt or unethical acts. For example, party girl Elizabeth Ray, who publicly admitted that Congressman Wayne Hays kept her on his congressional payroll in return for sexual favors, also revealed that she had been hired by lobbyists and members of Congress to swap sex for political favors.[17]

Until 1970, Ford Motor Company provided key members of Congress with fully equipped cars for very small fees. Those eligible to receive the cars were those members of Congress with power over decisions that most directly affected Ford Motor Company. General Motors, a major defense contractor, curries favor with the Pentagon by leasing Cadillacs to high Pentagon officials for $100 a year.[18]

Corporations also sometimes establish large, illegal slush funds to dole out to congressional supporters. In recent years it was revealed that the 3M Company hid a $634,000 fund by keeping it on the books as insurance premiums; Northrop Corporation laundered over $1.2 million through a Paris consulting firm; Gulf Oil laundered money through its Bahamas subsidiaries; Ashland Oil, Phillips Petroleum, and Goodyear all hid funds in Swiss banks; American Airlines recorded $275,000 in illegal campaign contributions as entertainment expenses; and Braniff Airways hid a $1 million fund by failing to

register the sale of 3,626 airline tickets.[19] Defense contractors have also frequently been caught manipulating the cost of defense equipment to cover contributions and entertainment expenses for members of Congress.

Interest groups often cultivate friendships in the executive branch, especially with federal agencies that have regulatory powers over the industry. For example, drug industries, through their lobbying associations such as the Pharmaceutical Manufacturers' Association (PMA), interact closely with the Food and Drug Administration (FDA). The drug lobbies provide the FDA with studies on drugs, attempt to counter arguments that drugs or chemicals are ineffective or harmful, and work to obtain FDA certification of new products they wish to place on the market.

Interest groups generally provide their supporters with campaign contributions and attempt to gain access to policy-makers who might be persuaded to support their position by giving them financial aid.

Critics have for years charged that the FDA is industry-dominated.[20] Critics point out that many FDA employees are former employees of drug industries, that FDA employees often resign to go to work for drug companies, and that the drug industry can generally convince the FDA to allow dangerous and ineffective drugs to stay on the market for long periods of time. Even FDA employees often charge that their agency supervisors are industry representatives. In 1974 FDA employees, in testimony before Congress, claimed that every time they made a decision to keep a drug off the market, they were called on the carpet, had their decisions overridden, their objections were removed from the files, and in many cases they were transferred out of their fields of expertise.[21]

Similar charges are frequently leveled against such agencies as the Interstate Commerce Commission (ICC), the Federal Maritime Commission (FMC), the Federal Communications Commission (FCC), the Nuclear Regulatory Commission (NRC), and the Civil Aeronautics Board (CAB). In 1975 a Senate committee concluded: "CAB has for the last five years regularly violated its own rules . . . while acting to protect the interest of the airlines at the expense of the traveler."[22] Lee Loevinger, former chief of the Justice Department's Antitrust Division, once discussed how the agencies became industry captives:

All of these agencies were fine when they were first set up, but before long they became infiltrated by the regulatees and are now more or less run by and for them. It's not a question of venality, either. More, the agency people consort with this or that representative of some special-interest group, and finally they all come to think alike. Every company that's concerned about government control and is big enough to manage it hires a man—or maybe four or five men—at anywhere from thirty to seventy thousand dollars a year to find out what we're up to. And, by God, they find out! They wine and dine the agency people and get to be great friends with them. Like a lot of people without much money some bureaucrats are impressed by being around big shots and by the big life. Sooner or later, all of these agencies end up with constituents. And they represent them damned well, too.[23]

Getting an early start

Washington-based lobbyists are uniquely situated to gain an advantage over other interests: they are in a position to know if new policies are being considered which might affect them. Even before a bill is introduced into Congress, they can start trying to influence the content of that bill. Joseph Califano, former Secretary of Health, Education and Welfare (HEW) under President Carter and a former Washington lawyer, explains the process:

Long before an issue is unveiled for public debate, Washington lawyers and lobbyists begin their work. As the issue percolates through the staffs of executive departments and regulatory agencies, the shrewd and able Washington lawyer is working away, providing facts, arguing his case to young staffers before they have even prepared the first draft of regulations to be published in the Federal Register.[24]

Thus, one strategy of lobbyists is to win some concessions for their side and influence the ground rules long before the public and even the media are aware that the issue will be coming before Congress.

Research and bill drafting

Two of the primary activities of interest groups are research and drafting legislation. Interest groups conduct research and write reports designed to substantiate their positions and to refute positions taken by their opponents. Lobbyists frequently supply friendly members of Congress or the executive branch with research their interest group has conducted, which can be used to support the interest group's position. Lobbyists also frequently draft legislation which can be introduced by congressional or executive supporters. It has been estimated that as much as 50 percent of all the legislation introduced into Congress is wholly or partially written by lobbyists.[25]

If an interest group cannot participate in drafting legislation, their lobbyists may suggest alterations that supporters can offer. These take the form of amendments which will make the legislation more palatable. Sometimes even a small alteration in a bill can completely change its impact. Oppenheimer reports that a one-word amendment to a 1966 federal water pollution bill designed to regulate oil spills completely negated the bill's intent:

> A one-word amendment to the bill offered by an oil district Congressman at the request of industry officials led the Justice Department to comment several months later that the legislation was unenforceable because of the amendment.[26]

While it is unusual for such a small alteration to have such a substantial impact on legislation, lobbyist-inspired alterations often considerably change, and sometimes effectively cripple, legislation.

Sometimes lobbyists find it politically expedient to offer a substitution for a bill rather than come out against it. For example, rather than take the risky position of being against consumer interests by opposing a proposed Consumer Protection Agency, a number of business groups suggested the establishment of a substitute agency which would have had no real power to regulate industry activities or protect consumers.[27]

Some interest groups have begun to use computers to aid their efforts. Computers can be programmed to provide answers to questions or even responses to opposing arguments. For example, the Washington law firm of Covington and Burling, which represents the tobacco industry, has a computer programmed to provide a rapid response to any of a large number of criticisms of that industry.[28] The Chamber of Commerce programs its computer to provide information on issues, plus the names of all Chamber members in particular districts. This allows the Chamber to alert its members that an issue of concern to them is at hand and to advise them to get in touch with their representative.

Sometimes interest groups set up research groups or committees, which give the public the impression they are engaged in some type of public-spirited activity. In fact, the intent is just the opposite. For example, the Keep America Beautiful (KAB) organization is a front for the beverage and packaging industry. It hopes to fend off legislation requiring returnable bottles and reusable packages by convincing the public to clean up after itself. Similarly, the Consumer Research Institute (CRI) is an arm of the Grocery Manufacturers Association. The CRI does not conduct research on how food issues affect consumers; it does research on consumers with the intent of helping food manufacturers enhance their profits. The Nutrition Foundation is also an arm of the food industry. The foundation does research designed to prove that industry products are nutritionally sound but that the public causes itself some problems by eating poorly.[29]

Advertising and promotion

Well-financed interest groups can increase their influence through advertising and promotional campaigns designed to convince the public that their policies merit public support. The major labor unions, business groups, conservationist organizations, and others spend money on media commercials, magazine and newspaper ads, and letter campaigns to influence public opinion. The wealthier interest groups can often spend very large sums, giving them a decided advantage over interests that are less well organized and financed.

Many interest groups spend large sums of money to persuade the public to support their positions on the issues. For example, the gun lobby, led by the National Rifle Association, uses promotions like the one below to publicize its opposition to gun control.

Some interest-group promotion campaigns are designed to maintain or strengthen public support for an industry or for a broad principle such as free enterprise, the right to collective bargaining, or the need for better quality air. Others are designed to mobilize public support for an interest-group position on an issue under consideration in Congress or the executive branch. The American Medical Association, for example, is renowned for the money it has spent in the last thirty years in an attempt to maintain the status quo in the medical field.

During the oil crisis of 1973, when many Americans had to wait in long lines for scarce gasoline, the American Petroleum Institute and the American Gas Association spent $12 million on various campaigns designed to convince the public that the scarcity was not the result of industry hoarding. They tried to show that in fact the problem resulted from government intervention and regulation of the energy industry.[30] Since 1973, the energy industries have continued to advertise heavily, both through company campaigns and their major trade associations. They have sought primarily to convince the public that industry profits are small and that the energy crisis can be solved if the industry is freed from price regulations.

The auto industry has used promotional campaigns to mobilize public support for, and to counter attacks on, the industry for its pollution-control and car-safety stands and performances. Pending emission-control and auto-safety bills have regularly prompted heavy advertising by General Motors, Ford, Chrysler, and American Motors in daily newspapers.

Other interests regularly budget rather large sums for promotional campaigns to spread their point of view. In 1975 the National Association of Manufacturers put together a multimedia entertainment package designed to promote free enterprise and dramatize the problems that government intervention causes business. The package rented for $3,500 with live performers, and $500 without them.[31] In the same year, the Business Roundtable spent $1.2 million on a *Reader's Digest* advertising campaign to promote the concept of free enterprise.[32]

Logrolling

A pragmatic strategy used by some interests is to form a mutual-support alliance with other interests, thereby strengthening their position through a collective effort. This strategy is known as *logrolling* and is effectively used by a variety of interests. One of the most powerful and enduring interest alliances in Washington is known as the highway lobby (or the "highway men" by critics). This group is composed of those major business interests which profit from the dominance of the private automobile and truck as the major forms of public and industrial transportation.

The alliance brings together the construction, asphalt, rubber, oil, automobile, bus, and truck industries. These interests have traditionally combined their efforts to promote spending federal funds for highways, especially the interstate highway system. (The federal government currently funds 90 percent of this system.) The alliance has also struggled mightily to keep the federal government from promoting alternate forms of transportation, such as public transit.

Both critics and supporters consider this alliance to be one of the most powerful and successful in Washington. In 1956 the group convinced Congress to specifically use federal taxes collected on gasoline, tires, and other transportation-related sources to develop the interstate highway system. With allocations of about $6 billion a year, this special fund has long been one of the biggest pork-barrel and public-works projects in the nation. It has also provided an annual guaranteed subsidy to the highway lobby.

By 1973, a number of groups, including conservationists, Common Cause, and the Conference of Mayors combined to create the Highway Action Coalition. This group argued that the guaranteed expenditures were illogical and that they stood in the way of a sane transportation policy. After a three-year struggle beginning in 1973, the coalition was able to convince Congress to allocate some of the transportation tax funds for the development of rapid transit. In 1977 and 1978, the coalition continued to make inroads against the highway lobby.

Logrolling strategies can create some peculiar alliances. For example, the AMA accepted a $10 million contribution for cancer research from the tobacco interest in return for the AMA's silence on the issue of whether tobacco advertising and products should carry a health warning.[33]

Delay

One last strategy used by interest groups is to delay any federal policies considered to be adverse. The groups hope that if delay will not defeat the policy, it will lead to its weakening through amendment or will at least postpone its consequences. The major Washington lobbying law firms are often hired by businesses to employ delaying strategies to give industries time to alter their production practices, liquidate inventories, or continue to reap profits from a lucrative product or activity that federal policy may prohibit.

The auto industry, for example, has typically used law firms to fight safety and emission standards. It has been said that when the Clean Air Act of 1970 was passed, the Japanese hired engineers and Detroit hired lawyers.[34] Japanese cars could meet the standards long before American cars, even though the American auto industry convinced Congress to delay the standards for them on several occasions.

Corporations have also used the law firms to delay the day when more strict pollution and safety standards would have to be complied with. The drug industry also frequently hires law firms to delay suspending from the market profitable drugs that research has found to be dangerous or ineffective. As the case studies below will show, a good lawyer can delay or even frustrate the implementation of a policy for a very long period of time.

CASE STUDIES

The following case studies provide insight into interest-group power in Washington. Basically, the studies show how well-heeled interest groups can use their resources and skills to increase their influence, sometimes winning government concessions that protect their practices and profits, sometimes defeating policies designed to protect unorganized consumer interests. While the struggles are waged with skill and intensity, they rarely attract much public attention.

The drug industry and Panalba: A profitable but ineffective drug

The drug industry is the most profitable of all American manufacturing enterprises. The high markups allowed by brand-name rather than generic-name sales largely explain why the drug industry has long enjoyed the highest manufacturing profits in the nation. Doctors are often agents for high drug profits because they receive most of their information about drugs from the drug industry.

In the 1970s, the drug industry was spending over $1 billion annually to advertise its products—about $3,000 per doctor and four times the cost of all industry expenditures for drug research.[35] Since doctors receive their information about drugs from the firms, and since they do not have to personally bear the cost of the drugs they prescribe, there is little incentive for cost control. Consumers who do pay the cost generally have few alternatives except to take the prescription to the local pharmacy and pay the cost of the prescribed drug.

This arrangement is not only lucrative for the drug industry and expensive for consumers, but it can also be hazardous. Drug industries may fail to inform doctors of dangers, and may be opposed to the removal of a profitable but certifiably ineffective or unsafe drug, such an Panalba, from the market.

Since 1962 the Food and Drug Administration (FDA) has had the power to order drugs that research has shown to be ineffective or dangerous removed from the market. When profits are high, the drug industry has an obvious motive for attempting to prevent such bans. To keep its profitable products on the market, the major drug companies generally have their own lobbying staffs, and each contributes to its major lobbying association—the Pharmaceutical Manufacturing Association (PMA).

PMA represents 135 drug industries and has an annual budget in excess of $5 million. In negotiations with Congress over laws affecting the drug industry or in conflicts with the FDA over a specific drug, PMA or a particular drug firm may hire one of the major Washington law firms to assist it. The firm of Covington and Burling has attorneys who specialize in aiding the drug industry, and they are most often retained.

Like most powerful lobbying groups, the PMA tries to influence the congressional laws which affect its operations. Then it uses agency, Cabinet, and executive lobbying—supplemented by court actions—to influence the im-

Like most special-interest groups, the drug industry has a well-financed lobbying organization designed to influence government policy-making. In fact, critics claim that the drug industry dominates the agency that is supposed to regulate it—the Food and Drug Administration (FDA).

plementation of the laws. The PMA and the Covington and Burling attorneys hired to assist it worked closely with the congressional committees that were investigating and writing legislation to provide more effective regulation of the drug industry in the early 1960s. By congressional testimony, bill substitution and rewriting, and by winning support from sympathetic members of Congress and the executive branch, the PMA was able to influence the 1962 Drug Amendments. The industry failed in its attempts to set the standards and procedures for testing drugs, but it did manage to convince Congress not to prohibit drug patents which allow an industry to monopolize a drug for long periods, thereby reaping huge profits.

The Panalba case shows how a powerful lobby shifts its emphasis from the legislative to the administrative stage in an attempt to win a battle at one level that it could not win at another level. Panalba is an antibiotic consisting of a mixture of tetracycline and novobiocin. Manufactured by Upjohn, the drug grossed $18 million in sales in 1968, and was Upjohn's fifth largest seller. Combination antibiotics had been under attack since the 1950s because, according to the Council on Drugs of the American Medical Association, they represented an irrational (shotgun) therapy based on the assumption that if one drug did not work, the other might.

With the 1962 Drug Amendments, the FDA could order research on such drugs to determine if they were safe and effective. In 1968, after six years of research, the National Academy of Sciences-National Research Council issued its report on Panalba. Their verdict was that Panalba was "ineffective as a fixed combination." There was also substantial evidence that a significant percentage of Panalba users suffered serious side effects, resulting even in death in some cases.

On the basis of this information, the FDA informed Upjohn on December 24, 1968, that it intended to order the removal of Panalba from the market. Upjohn protested that the research findings were not conclusive enough to warrant the removal of Panalba and requested a full hearing on the issue. Upjohn also enlisted the PMA to assist it and hired a staff of attorneys from Covington and Burling to help press its case.

Well-heeled interest groups can use their resources and skills to increase their influence, sometimes winning government concessions that protect their practices and profits, sometimes defeating policies designed to protect unorganized consumer interests.

The company representatives, lobbyists, and attorneys immediately won a 120-day delay from the FDA. During this period, the FDA ordered Upjohn to turn over its own research records on Panalba to its inspectors. Upjohn's files contained eight reports on Panalba, all revealing that Panalba was ineffective and sometimes hazardous. By law, Upjohn should have turned these reports over to the FDA by 1964. Upjohn's own research also showed that Panalba was less effective than tetracycline taken alone.

Undaunted even by its own research, Upjohn continued to argue that the evidence did not merit the decertification of Panalba. Unable to convince the FDA not to go ahead with its ban, Upjohn representatives and attorneys asked the Secretary of Health, Education, and Welfare, Robert Finch, to intervene in its behalf. On the day of the meeting, Finch agreed to allow Upjohn a hearing before the recall, but he reversed himself the same day after FDA officials showed him the research on Panalba.

Still determined to either escape the ban or delay its implementation, Upjohn's attorneys filed suit, seeking a full hearing in district court. Upjohn filed the case before a district judge who had a history of being sympathetic to the drug industry, and subsequent evidence showed him to be a drug industry stockholder. The district judge ruled on July 10, 1969, that although the 1962 Drug Amendments did not entitle drug companies to hearings under these circumstances, in the interest of fair play they had to be given one.

Under court order, the FDA allowed Upjohn to make an oral presentation, but again concluded that the evidence required the decertification of Panalba. Now Upjohn appealed to the court of appeals for an injunction against the FDA. On February 27, 1970, however, the court of appeals overruled the District Court's decision, ruling that Upjohn had not been entitled to a hearing and that the FDA could ban Panalba. Upjohn appealed to the Supreme Court, but the Court refused to hear the case. On March 19, 1970, the FDA finally ordered the removal of Panalba from the market.

   Although Upjohn had lost, it had managed to keep Panalba on the market for fifteen months after the FDA first threatened to decertify it. This delay allowed Upjohn a second chance to use personal negotiations and the courts to influence the procedures for testing drugs. It also gave Upjohn time to liquidate its inventory of Panalba and allowed it to continue for many months to reap huge profits on an ineffective and dangerous drug. Since Panalba sold for three times the cost of tetracycline alone, Upjohn grossed approximately an extra $1.5 million per month while Panalba was still on the market. One authority estimated the total cost to the public to be $12 million.[36]

Peanut butter: A sticky business

The FDA struggle with the makers of peanut butter provides a good example of how much money and energy an interest often devotes to a policy issue, even when most of the public would consider the disputed issue to be trivial.[37] In 1958 the FDA discovered that some brands of peanut butter contained ingredients other than peanuts, often in substantial proportions. For example, Jif, made by Proctor and Gamble (P&G) contained only 75 percent peanuts and 20 percent of a Crisco-type base (or lard), a product also manufactured by P & G. Since the FDA had received some public complaints about the use of lard in peanut butter, and since it was charged by Congress with "promoting honesty and fair dealings in the interest of consumers," it decided to establish some standards. Because even small changes in the formula for peanut butter can substantially affect industry profits, the industry launched a vigorous, well-financed campaign against any new standards. The industry turned the issue into such a battle that it took 12 years before new standards could be established and put into effect.

   FDA first proposed that peanut butter be 95 percent peanuts and 5 percent stabilizer. The industry claimed that this would make the product too sticky. Testing and negotiations between the FDA and the industry lasted until 1965, when the FDA proposed that peanut butter should contain at least 90 percent peanuts, with 10 percent optional ingredients. No more than 3 percent of the optional ingredients could be lard. Because it manufactured lard, Proctor and Gamble was upset by the 3 percent standard. The Peanut Butter Manufacturers' Association (yes, there is one!) wanted a peanut minimum no higher than 87 percent.

   To resolve the continuing dispute, the FDA held hearings on the topic. Proctor and Gamble's counsel, a Covington and Burling attorney, adopted a strategy of drawing the hearings out as long as possible. The strategy seemed to be to wear the government down. The attorney insisted on debating every term, on seeing individual letters from consumers, and on questioning every witness for hours, even days, on end. The hearing lasted four months. The final hearing transcript was 24,000 pages long and was supplemented by 75,000 pages of documents.

In the end, the FDA agreed to a standard of 90 percent peanuts, with 10 percent optional ingredients. The 3 percent limit on lard was dropped. The hearing had begun seven years after the FDA launched its original investigation, and it would take another five years before the new standard would take effect. The additional delay was caused by industry court challenges that took years to complete.

The Office of Consumer Representation: A business victory

Since the late 1960s, consumer groups have been trying to obtain an agency in Washington that would represent consumer interests. In the early and mid-1970s, both houses of Congress passed legislation establishing such an agency, but lack of coordination and a threatened veto kept the agency from becoming a reality. The Senate passed legislation to set up an Agency for Consumer Protection in 1970. The House followed suit in 1971 and 1974. Both houses agreed upon and passed the bill in 1975. However, the bill was never sent to the White House because President Ford announced that he would veto it. Not having the votes to override a veto, the House decided it would be futile to send the bill to the President.

The proposed consumer agency received a boost when Carter announced that he supported the legislation. The Carter administration revised the proposal to make it more appealing to business, and suggested that the new agency be named the Office of Consumer Representation (OCR). OCR would have been responsible for a broad range of consumer matters. It would have served as a clearinghouse for consumer complaints, encouraged and contracted for consumer research, sponsored conferences and investigations on consumer issues, published consumer materials, proposed consumer legislation to Congress, and worked with state and local governments to protect consumer interests. In other words, it would have been a joy to consumers and a pain to business.

With a supportive President, conditions seemed perfect for passage of the bill. But surprisingly, perhaps, the Carter-backed proposal met its doom in early 1978 when the House, which had passed the bill three times, voted it down. What happened? Supporters of the bill blamed its defeat on a massive lobbying and campaign-contribution effort by big business. Proponents claimed that business interests, which could not provide funds to the presidential candidates in the general election of 1976, had invested those funds in congressional campaigns, thereby buying a lot of influence (see Chapter 6).

Business did significantly increase its campaign contributions in 1976 and 1978, and it waged an intense campaign against the proposed agency. The

Speaker of the House, Thomas P. O'Neill, claimed that in his twenty-five years in the House he had "never seen such extensive lobbying."[38] The campaign against the proposal was directed by the U.S. Chamber of Commerce, the National Association of Manufacturers, the Business Roundtable, and other business groups, and its defeat was clearly their victory.

Consumer groups took the defeat hard and with some bitterness. Charges of vote buying, corruption, and consumer heavy-handedness filled the air as charges and counter-charges were flung by opposing sides. Ralph Nader and his consumer group, Public Citizen, were in the thick of the fray, and some members of Congress expressed annoyance at Nader's charges that Congress was in the hip pocket of big business. After the House defeat, Nader was interviewed by the *National Journal* about the controversy and about his charge that the legislation was defeated by members of Congress who sold their vote for campaign contributions from big business.

The excerpts below, from the Nader interview, provide insight into the strategy and the perceptions of the most prominent consumer leader in America. They reveal his views on the impact of lobbying, campaign contributions, and recent House reforms on the defeat of the consumer agency in particular, and on the policy-making process in general.[39]

Q: (Linda E. Demkovich, *National Journal*) Was it impossible to believe that any of the members may have legitimately changed their minds, or may have read their constituents differently than perhaps the consumer lobby was reading them?

A: (Ralph Nader) Not their consumer constituents, because the support, according to the Harris polls, has been increasing among consumers. What they did read was the business letters that were coming in. People like John Anderson (R., Ill.) know that his reelection and position out there in Rockford rests on how the Rotary Club types look at him, and because he doesn't have any real roots among the people, he interprets the Rotary Club types as being equivalent to "the people." You see, if there was a shift in the popular mood, if there was a shift in the polls, then you could take your question and say maybe some of them read it that way, but it was just the opposite.

Q: The objection that I heard most frequently was the sort of heavy-handedness of the tactics, going in and saying he's being bought or she's being bought.

A: That's really amazing, because the people who buy them are not considered heavy-handed. The people who lease them are not considered heavy-handed. The people who wine and dine them and serve them at their spas are not considered heavy-handed.

Q: But they're less visible than you are.

A: Well, we're looking at it from the point of view of the legislature, who's playing a game with the media. That's the heavy-handedness. And it's often illegal, what the business lobbyists are doing. What they consider heavy-handed, though, is not their tactics, but the use of the first amendment by

Ralph Nader, consumer advocate and founder of a
citizens' lobby group, Public Citizen.

people who disagree with their voting inclinations, namely the consumer advocates. And it's just absurd to say that campaign contributions don't have any influence. First of all, any school boy knows that. Second of all, the record of campaign contributions having an influence in corrupting Congress has been overwhelmingly made in the press in the last 10 years. And third, the members themselves tell you, and the staffs tell you, that if they vote for this bill, they'll lose x thousands of dollars in the next campaign, and the first rule of politics is survival. They admit it. But these Congressmen expect us to be forever naive and give them the benefit of the doubt that the money they're taking for their campaigns doesn't affect their attitudes on Capitol Hill. There are very few members of Congress where that's true, very few. They do admit this to us because we press them, we work through their staffs, and they just blurt it out. We know how to cross-examine these people. One member from California said in exactly the following words, "If you can get me $100,000 for my next campaign, I'll tell my business community to go to hell on this bill."

Q: When the Carter administration came in, consumer groups were optimistic that this would make a big difference. Obviously, at least on this bill, it hasn't. Does that just say that this administration doesn't have as much clout as it should on the Hill?

A: First of all, as far as the consumer bill was concerned, you had a situation where you had a clean President trying to deal with a dirty House. I'm talking about the majority now, not the minority who voted for it. That is, the majority was wheeling and dealing in the terms of campaign finance politics. And Carter had nothing to counteract that. All he had was the merits of the bill. The second change over the years has been the breakdown of discipline, or policy cohesiveness, in the House of Representatives. The Speaker of the House and the chairmen of the various committees used to have tremendous influence. If the chairman of a major committee like Government Operations came to the floor with a bill with the blessings of the Speaker of the House and the Majority Leader, the chances were very good that it would go through. But now that the congressional reforms have weakened the power of the Speaker and the power of the chairmen, there's a vacuum, and that vacuum has been filled by Business Roundtable-type efforts. It's a vacuum that in effect lets every member of the House say, "I'm going to vote according to my own political opportunism, and I can rely on my own ability to raise campaign funds from all these new political action committees, and I don't need the Speaker, I don't need my committee chairmen because they can't deny me things the way they used to be able to before the reforms." So there's no party discipline in the House and there's no cohesive policy direction in the House and that's made it very vulnerable to the temptations of money. Everywhere, there's campaign money. Take that out, and the final votes would be completely different.

Q: I would think, though, that you would have been in favor of those committee reforms, that you would have supported decentralizing the power structure of the House.

A: Coupled with public financing. You see, they got one half of the reform and not the other. Therefore, they've got a worse situation. When there's no discipline in the House on a party basis, and there's no penetration from the electorate on a voting basis, then you've got a kind of anarchy operating that is only given direction by the flow of campaign money and other temptations that special interest groups put before members.

THE PRESIDENT AND THE EXECUTIVE BRANCH AS LOBBYIST

Since the President is the chief policy architect at the federal level, both he and his representatives throughout the executive branch must work to influence members of Congress to support his programs. While Presidents vary in style, most modern chief executives have spent much of their time attempting to convince members of Congress to support their policies. All recent Presidents have had staffs for lobbying Congress. All executive Cabinet departments and agencies also have staffs for this purpose.

Some Presidents have been exceptionally good at reading the pulse of Congress, at convincing key members to support their programs, and even at trading favors with individual members of Congress for support on a particular bill. Presidents Woodrow Wilson, Franklin Roosevelt, and Lyndon Johnson were particularly effective lobbyists for their own programs. A President who knows how Congress works, has long-time friends in Congress, and knows how to bargain with individual members is most likely to be effective. Generally speaking, Presidents who have served in Congress, especially for long periods or in an important capacity (which generally requires seniority), are most likely to know how to work with Congress.

Johnson's long tenure and leadership role in Congress had taught him to be a masterful manipulator of his colleagues. He knew the members of Congress, knew what they needed, and what he could do for them. He also knew how to massage the egos of members of Congress and provided them with the type of assistance that indebted them to him. His personal approach in dealing with members of Congress is explained by one of his past aides:

> He would say to us, "I want you to go up there today and find out what the members need. What do they need in the district? Do they need the little wife invited down to the White House or can we help with a constituent?" Then we would go up to the Hill and say, "The President asked me to come see you and ask if you need anything." That was impressive.[40]

While not all Presidents have Johnson's powers of persuasion, all must try to influence Congress. In recent administrations, this role has become more automated and somewhat scientific. Carter's White House Congressional Liaison Office, for example, has programmed a computer to help identify members of Congress who might be persuaded to back the President on a particular bill. The computer has been fed information on each member of Congress, including party, seniority, committee assignments, margin of victory in his or her last election, rating by various interest groups, and votes on key bills.

On a particular bill, the staff can use the computer to select those members who might be expected to support a certain type of legislation, but who have not yet made a commitment on that particular bill. This provides a list of potential supporters who can be singled out and lobbied for support.

Most modern-day chief executives have spent much of their time attempting to convince members of Congress to support their policies. All recent Presidents have had staffs for lobbying Congress. All executive Cabinet departments and agencies also have staffs for this purpose.

The various executive departments all have their own staffs, which provide aid to members of Congress and work with Congress in an attempt to gain support for administration programs. In 1978 the Office of Management and Budget (OMB) estimated that at least 675 persons in the thirty-two Cabinet and major non-Cabinet agencies were employed in congressional relations work. OMB conservatively estimated that the cost of this executive lobbying was $12 to $15 million per year.[41]

To be effective at influencing Congress, these congressional relations staffs must provide aid to members of Congress who request information or help with a constituency issue. The work load associated with congressional inquiries and requests for aid is enormous. For example, the State Department's congressional liaison office received more than 1,600 letters per month from Congress in 1977. The Department of Defense's liaison staff received 112,136 written inquiries from Congress and 229,089 telephone queries in 1977. The Agriculture Department averaged 325 letters a day from Congress in 1977. If an administration does a good job of aiding Congress, it can trade on the good will generated to gain support for key programs.

PUBLIC DISCLOSURE OF LOBBYING

The ability to organize as a group and finance lobbying activities can clearly enhance the influence of an interest in the policy-making and administrative processes. In fact, in many cases those interests which are the best organized and have the most money to spend on lobbying, attorneys, and campaign contributions can win policy victories over interests that have more members but are less well organized, financed, and skilled at lobbying. Money, in other words, can be a powerful substitute for public representation and backing.

While everyone agrees that the ability to organize to influence public policy is an important constitutional right, critics of the current lobbying situation point to two problems. First, interest-group expenditures to influence legislation are often very substantial, but there is no way to determine if wealthy interests prejudice the decision-making process by spending huge sums to lobby Congress or the executive branch. Critics argue that if interest groups had to report their expenditures, the public would have some insight into the relationship between interest-group expenditures and policy decisions. If expenditures were greatly lopsided, the public would be alerted that money might have played a bigger role than reason in the outcome of the decision, and could therefore take actions to equalize the influence situation.

In the past, Congress has made some efforts to pass legislation which would provide a public record of lobbying expenditures by major interest groups. The Federal Regulation of Lobbying Act of 1946 was designed to require interest groups to report expenditures intended to directly or indirectly influence the passage or defeat of legislation. The Supreme Court, however, ruled that the legislation was overly broad. It limited the registration requirement to those who use another's money for the principal purpose of communicating directly with a member of Congress in order to influence legislation.

Many of the most powerful and active interest groups seized upon the Supreme Court's narrow definition as a rationale for not registering as lobbyists or reporting any of their expenditures. In recent years only 1,000 organizations

and individuals have registered as lobbyists each year, with total reported expenditures in the $10 million range. No one pretends that the registration figures provide even a modestly accurate representation of reality. Some groups who are clearly covered by the law simply violate it with impunity. For example, the Chamber of Commerce, the National Association of Manufacturers, ITT, and numerous other big spenders simply refuse to comply.

There have been many efforts to amend the 1946 law or to substitute a more effective law for it. All such efforts have long been vigorously and successfully opposed by the major business lobbies. Watergate stimulated new efforts to pass an effective lobbying bill. Opposition between 1975 and 1979 was substantial, but a proposal stayed before Congress. After several years of debate, the House passed the Public Disclosure of Lobbying Act in April 1978. The House bill attempted to accurately reflect interest-group expenditures without discouraging groups from making their views on legislation known to public officials.

The Public Disclosure of Lobbying Act would have required annual registration and quarterly reporting by major paid lobbying groups that make oral or written lobbying communications to members of Congress and public officials in the executive branch. Individuals who communicated with public officials for redress of grievances or to express a personal opinion would not have had to register, nor would small lobbying groups. The bill would have required reporting expenses for direct and indirect lobbying such as computerized mass mailings designed to prompt grass-roots pressures on members of Congress. The bill also would have compelled lobbying organizations that spend more than 1 percent of their budgets on lobbying to report the names or organizations from which they received more than $3,000 a year in dues and contributions. This latter provision was designed to keep interest groups from secretly financing front groups to do their lobbying for them. President Carter praised the House bill and urged the Senate to also quickly pass it. In late 1978 the bill died when the Senate failed to consider it. Supporters reintroduced it in 1979.

The second criticism frequently raised about lobbying practices is that the consuming public often has little ability to organize and spend sums even remotely equal to those routinely spent by wealthy business and labor groups. Thus, critics argue, the policy-making process is generally biased against the public interest. The alterations that could be utilized to balance this situation include a limitation on group expenditures, public financing of citizen lobbies, or mobilization of the public interest through private contributions to public-interest lobbies such as Common Cause and Public Citizen.

The first alternative would almost certainly constitute an unconstitutional abridgment of the First Amendment. The second alternative is more practical but unlikely to win congressional approval. Private interests would vigorously oppose public fundings of citizen interest groups as they opposed and defeated the Office of Consumer Representation. Nevertheless, some continue to advocate public financing of citizen lobbies. Oppenheimer explains the role such groups might play:

> Such organizations would first develop independence, and at times, competing sources of information on major issues; second, publicize important issues for public attention; and, third, provide access for independent experts into the political process. The last point is vital. It is not in the public interest that the most qualified experts on policy issues are attracted solely to private interests. Public interest organizations could attract experts to work for the public and not for vested interests.[42]

The third alternative is the most likely option for increasing citizen influence. In recent years, public-interest lobbies have gained power and have won some notable victories. The evidence indicates that these groups will continue to grow in the immediate future and will at least increase the public influence at both the federal and state level. If the lobby disclosure bill eventually passes, the impact of public-interest lobbies is likely to improve since they will be able to better educate the public about the role of money in shaping public policies.

CONCLUSIONS

Lobbying is one of the most important methods by which some groups achieve their policy goals from government. Groups that can afford to engage in well-financed lobbying activities clearly have an advantage over groups that cannot. The most powerful interest groups have raised lobbying to an art form, involving sophisticated strategies, the employment of prestigious law firms, extensive advertising, and even computer technology. Critics claim that wealthy groups have such a substantial advantage over unorganized and poorly financed groups that some reforms are required to help equalize the balance of power between private and public interests. The reforms most often mentioned are effective lobby disclosure laws, public financing of congressional campaigns, and public expenditures to promote policy-maker consideration of consumer views.

Money can be a powerful substitute for public representation and backing.

Groups that cannot effectively organize to promote their interests—the poor, migrant workers, housewives, battered spouses, the emotionally and mentally disturbed—do have severely reduced chances of wielding any real power in Washington. Other groups that represent positions or views that are not considered legitimate may not be able to exert much influence over the policymaking process. These groups, though large and sometimes even fairly well financed, may have to resort to demonstrations and even violence to make themselves heard (see Chapter 5). Recent examples of such groups would include black Americans seeking economic and political equality and antiwar groups that sought to end the American presence in Vietnam. As Greenwald points out:

> Between 1967 and 1971, the anti–Vietnam War movement engaged in a wide range of mass involvement techniques: the 1967 nationwide local demonstrations, October 1967 March on the Pentagon, January 1968 counter-inaugural, 1969 nation-wide day of moratorium in honor of war dead, and the seventeen days of spring protests in 1971 beginning with Vietnam Veterans reenactment of the war as they saw it, followed by a middle-class, middle-aged demonstration by 200,000, followed by the "people's lobby" that sat in at key decision-making centers, and climaxed by the Mayday Tribe who tied up Washington traffic and offices to implement their motto—"if the Government won't stop the war, the People will stop the Government."[43]

These actions against the war were, of course, only the tip of the iceberg: opposition occurred in hundreds of other events and ways. The necessity for such large-scale, often violent methods to exert some influence suggests how seriously groups are disadvantaged if they pursue policies that are not supported by elites, if they lack standing with business, labor, and public officials, or if they don't have enough money.

Footnotes

1. All figures are from Carol S. Greenwald, *Group Power: Lobbying & Public Policy* (New York: Praeger, 1977), p. 334.
2. *Ibid.*, p. 109.
3. See Harrell R. Rodgers, Jr., *Crisis In Democracy: A Policy Analysis of American Government* (Reading, Mass.: Addison-Wesley, 1978). pp. 217–18.
4. Robert Sherrill, *Governing America* (New York: Harcourt Brace Jovanovich, 1978), p. 190.

5. *Ibid.,* p. 202.
6. Mark J. Green, *The Other Government: The Unseen Power of Washington Lawyers* (New York: Norton, 1978), p. 11.
7. *Washington Post,* May 5, 1966, p. F16.
8. Jim Hightower, *Eat Your Heart Out: How Food Profiters Victimize the Consumer* (New York: Vintage Books, 1975), p. 269.
9. *Ibid.,* p. 256.
10. Greenwald, *Group Power,* p. 77.
11. Hightower, *Eat Your Heart Out,* p. 258.
12. Greenwald, *Group Power,* p. 69.
13. *Ibid.,* p. 70.
14. Sherrill, *Governing America,* p. 194.
15. Hightower, *Eat Your Heart Out,* p. 259.
16. See Greenwald, *Group Power,* p. 74.
17. Elizabeth Ray, *The Washington Fringe Benefit* (New York: Dell, 1976), pp. 17, 21.
18. Greenwald, *Group Power,* p. 82.
19. See Greenwald, *Group Power,* p. 151.
20. See Theodore Lowi, *The End of Liberalism* (New York: Norton, 1969); and Grant McConnell, *Private Power and American Democracy* (New York: Vintage Books, 1966).
21. Greenwald, *Group Power,* p. 258.
22. *Ibid.,* p. 259.
23. Quoted in G. William Domhoff, *Who Rules America?* (Englewood Cliffs, N.J.: Prentice-Hall, 1967), p. 108.
24. Green, *The Other Government,* p. 174.
25. Sherrill, *Governing America,* p. 196.
26. Bruce Ian Oppenheimer, "Interest Groups In The Political Process," *Current History,* August 1974, p. 77.
27. See Hightower, *Eat Your Heart Out,* p. 264.
28. Green, *The Other Government,* p. 166.
29. See Hightower, *Eat Your Heart Out,* p. 270.
30. Greenwald, *Group Power,* p. 76.
31. *Ibid.,* p. 97.
32. *Ibid.,* p. 102.
33. *Ibid.,* p. 207.
34. Green, *The Other Government,* p. 168.
35. This case study is drawn from Green, *The Other Government,* pp. 106–35.
36. *Ibid.,* p. 134.
37. Based on Green, *The Other Government,* pp. 136–45.
38. "Carter Dealt Major Defeat on Consumer Bill," *Congressional Quarterly,* February 11, 1978, p. 323.
39. Excerpts from "Ralph Nader Takes On Congress As Well As Big Business," *National Journal,* March 11, 1978, pp. 388–90.
40. "Carter Seeks More Effective Use of Departmental Lobbyists' Skill," *Congressional Quarterly,* March 4, 1978, p. 586.
41. *Ibid.,* p. 579.
42. Oppenheimer, "Interest Groups In the Political Process," p. 78.
43. Greenwald, *Group Power,* p. 79.

It might be helpful if we simply acknowledge that Congress is, and always will be—for better or worse—our slow institution.

Richard Fenno

By constitutional design, Congress is the most critical link in the federal policy-making process. Yet for many years critics have charged that Congress is incapable of playing its intended role. Members of Congress are frequently among its most severe critics. For example, Richard Bolling (D., Mo.) writes:

> In the many years I have been a member of Congress, the House has revealed itself to me as ineffective in its role as a coordinate branch of the Federal Government, negative in its approach to national tasks, generally unresponsive to any but parochial economic interests. Its procedures, time-consuming and unwielding, mask anonymous centers of irresponsible powers. Its legislation is often a travesty of what the national welfare requires.[1]

10

Congress and the Policy Process

Another member of Congress is even more blunt:

> It's an outrageous and outmoded institution. All Congress has ever done since I've been in Congress is pass the buck to the President and then blame him for what goes wrong . . . Congress is gutless beyond my power to describe to you. Most members of Congress think that most people are clods . . . most of the guys down there are out of touch with their districts . . . we aren't living in the 1930s anymore. Of course some members of Congress are . . . I could never understand the lack of congressional sensitivity to the problems of the elderly. There are so many of them there.[2]

Scholars and media representatives often agree that Congress is fundamentally flawed. Sherrill, for example, makes the following charge:

> Few lofty and shining moments have ever broken through the career of Congress as a body. In the face of the most pressing social demands, it almost always acts sluggishly, grudgingly, suspiciously, if it acts at all. The periods of congressional

Leaders of the House of Representatives in the Ninety-sixth Congress: (left) Speaker Thomas P. "Tip" O'Neill (D., Mass.), and (right) Minority Leader John J. Rhodes (R., Ariz.).

dominance in federal life, Stewart Alsop has remarked, "as after the Civil War, or in the Nineteen-twenties, or in the early McCarthy period, have not been proud chapters in American political history."[3]

What is the basis for such harsh evaluations? The core issues revolve around both the institutional characteristics of Congress and the collective personal characteristics of its members. These factors often keep it from playing a decisive role in shaping and overseeing the administration of public policies. Most major policy problems that come before Congress are simply not dealt with forthrightly. Policy issues are often permanently stymied in Congress, seriously delayed, or addressed through legislation that is incapable of really coping with the problem.

For example, Congress has had great difficulty dealing with issues such as discrimination against blacks, other minorities, and women; pollution and auto safety standards; energy policy and urban decay; and most other serious problems that affect the country. Most legislation introduced into Congress, in fact, simply fails to emerge. For example, in the Ninety-fourth Congress (1975–76), 24,283 bills were introduced. Only 3,156 came out of a committee in one or both houses, and only 588 bills became public laws. While many of the bills introduced are duplicates and some are trivial, it is significant that only about 2 percent of all bills introduced actually survived the congressional process, and many of these were mere shadows of the original proposals.

A critic might ask: "Do we *want* to make Congress more efficient, just so that it could pass more laws?" But the issue is not one of more laws but the ability of Congress to respond to national needs and to pass high-quality legislation when it does act. Perhaps the greatest cause of law proliferation is flawed and inadequate legislation. When Congress passes legislation of poor quality, it fails to accomplish needed goals and often even causes serious problems. Both conditions create increased demands for additional legislation. It is not uncommon for Congress to pass a dozen laws over a ten-to-twenty-year period to deal with an issue that could have been handled with one good bill.

Inadequate legislation also contributes substantially to the growth of government bureaucracy. Rather than comprehensively deal with a policy issue and vest responsibility for its administration in one agency, Congress often can only respond in piecemeal fashion, passing dozens of laws and vesting their administration in a dozen or so agencies. Welfare legislation is an excellent example. There are dozens of welfare programs administered by dozens of agencies. Quite naturally, the jurisdiction of the agencies often overlaps, and their actions duplicate and even contradict one another. One comprehensive poverty program and one agency to direct it would be much more efficient. Welfare, of course, is not an isolated example. The federal budget shows over 200 federal health programs, 150 or so income security and social service programs, and 80-plus housing programs.

DECENTRALIZATION

Why does Congress have so much trouble responding to social problems and playing a decisive role in shaping public policies? The key problem reflects the constitutional design of the federal system. Basically, the federal government

Policy issues are often permanently stymied in Congress, seriously delayed, or addressed through legislation that is incapable of really coping with the problem.

was designed to limit government activity, making the policy process complex and ponderous and giving each branch of the federal government some checks over the other branches.

Thus, successful policy-making generally requires coordination and basic agreement between the executive and congressional branch. The Supreme Court may nullify any legislation brought before it in a case if it determines that the law is inconsistent with the Constitution. Power in the federal system, then, is highly decentralized.

Power in Congress is also highly decentralized, so decentralized in fact that it is very difficult to achieve a majority consensus on a bill. The most obvious form of decentralization in Congress is its division into two branches. Congress consists of the House of Representatives and the Senate. Members of the House are elected to two-year terms and represent much smaller constituencies than do senators. There are 435 members of the House. Each state receives a number of representatives equal to its proportion of the nation's total population. Thus, New York currently has thirty-nine representatives in the House, Texas twenty-four, Iowa six, and North Dakota only one. The Senate is composed of 100 members, two from each state. Senators are elected to six-year terms; one-third are up for election every two years. No bill can emerge from Congress unless it is passed in the same form by both houses in the same congressional term.

THE COMMITTEE SYSTEM

Within each house of Congress, power is also decentralized. Power in Congress is located primarily in the standing committees, and in the heads of these committees and the subcommittees they are divided into. During the Ninety-sixth Congress (1979–80), the House had twenty-two standing committees and the Senate twenty. The committees were as follows:

Senate Committees	House Committees
Agriculture, Nutrition, and Forestry	Agriculture
Appropriations	Appropriations
Armed Services	Armed Services
Banking, Housing, and Urban Affairs	Banking, Finance, and Urban Affairs
Budget	Budget
Commerce, Science, and Transportation	District of Columbia
Energy and Natural Resources	Education and Labor
Environment and Public Works	Government Operations
Finance	House Administration
Foreign Relations	Interior and Insular Affairs
Governmental Affairs	International Relations
Human Resources	Interstate and Foreign Commerce
Judiciary	Judiciary
Rules and Administration	Merchant Marine and Fisheries
Veterans' Affairs	Post Office and Civil Service
Aging	Public Works and Transportation
Indian Affairs	Rules
Intelligence	Science and Technology
Small Business	Small Business
Ethics	Standards of Official Conduct
	Veterans' Affairs
	Ways and Means

Each standing committee is broken down into numerous subcommittees. In the Ninety-sixth Congress there were 163 subcommittees in the House and 140 in the Senate. Each member of the Senate served on an average of 3.9 committees and 11.9 subcommittees. House members averaged 6.1 committee and subcommittee assignments.[4]

Among the most powerful members of Congress are the committee and subcommittee chairpersons. To chair a committee, one must belong to the party that is in the majority in the chamber and have an established tenure on the committee. In the recent past, both the Republicans and the Democrats used a strict *seniority system* to determine committee chairs. The chairperson was always the individual from the majority party who had the longest continuous service on the committee. Typically, this placed committee chairs in the hands of southern Democrats who were assured long tenure in Congress by the South's one-party system. Under the old strict seniority system, the chairperson also had enormous power. Dodd and Oppenheimer describe the result:

In the years from 1946 to 1970 Democrats organized the House for twenty of twenty-four years. Power in the House rested in committee chairs, who maintained the authority to choose committee staffs, create subcommittees and select their chairs, control committee agendas and parliamentary procedure, schedule committee proceedings, report committee legislation to the full House, and serve as floor managers for committee bills. The committee meetings themselves, particularly important meetings, often were held in closed session. The individuals who chaired the meetings were conservative, southern, and elderly. Throughout much of this time, the House was precisely what the public perceived it to be: an insulated, closed, and largely unresponsive institution.[5]

The effect was little different in the Senate.

Since the early 1970s, there have been many reforms in Congress. One of them has been a slight reduction in the role of seniority in determining committee chairs. In 1971 both the Democrats and the Republicans adopted new rules permitting party votes on committee chairmanships. In the Ninety-third Congress (1973–74), the Democratic party in the House agreed to require an automatic, separate vote on each committee chairperson by secret ballot. In 1975, in an unprecedented action, the Democrats in the House voted to replace three veteran committee chairpersons—Wright Patman (D., Tex., Banking Committee), F. Edward Hebert (D., La., Armed Services Committee), and W. R. Poage (D., Tex., Agriculture Committee). In 1978, three junior Democrats were awarded House subcommittee chairs, bypassing more senior colleagues.

While seniority remains the key to committee chairmanship, the power of chairpersons has been reduced substantially. Subcommittee chairs are now awarded by a vote of the majority-party members on the committee. The subcommittees can control their staffs and set their own agenda. A committee chairperson can still be influential in setting the agenda of the standing committee and controlling its staff, as long as he or she is not abusive. The reduction in the power of the committee chairs was an important move in democratizing Congress, but it further decentralized power since each member of Congress is now free to make decisions without concern for the wishes or programs of the chairperson or, to some extent, even of the party.

"He considers just getting to and from Congress a productive day."

CONGRESSIONAL LEADERSHIP

While recent reforms have reduced the power of the chairs, they have increased to some extent the power of the congressional leadership. In the House, the leadership consists of the *Speaker of the House;* a *majority leader, majority whips* and their aides and assistants; and the *minority leader* and a number of *minority whips*. Whips are party leaders who work to convince other members to support party legislation and round up members for important votes. The Speaker is elected by the members of the majority party in the House, as is the majority leader. The Speaker and majority leader appoint the whips. The minority party in the House elects a minority leader.

In the Senate, the majority party elects a *president pro tempore* to preside over the Senate in the absence of its constitutionally designated chair, the Vice-President. The pro tempore position is mostly honorary and goes to the member of the majority party with the longest continuous service in the Senate. The majority party also elects a majority leader, who chooses a majority whip and consults with him on the reelection of deputy whips. The minority party elects a minority leader and a number of whips.

Under recent Democratic party reforms, the Speaker of the House chairs a Steering and Policy Committee which sets party policy, appoints the Democratic members to the Rules Committee, and has increased authority to determine which standing committee will consider new bills introduced into Congress. The Speaker and the House majority leader work with the Rules Committee to schedule debate on bills, and they negotiate with the committee chairpersons on policy and procedural matters. The House majority leader is the party's floor leader and, together with the Speaker, is the codirector of policy strategy.

The congressional leaders also play an important role in assigning members to the various standing committees. In both the House and Senate, the parties have committees which make committee assignments; the congressional leaders serve on or chair these committees. Committee assignments are extremely important to members of Congress because assignment determines the nature of the legislation they will be most directly involved with.

Members want to be on the most important committees and on those which deal with policy matters of importance to their constituency. A member from a farm state, for example, might not want to serve on the Banking, Housing and Urban Affairs Committee. In addition, some standing committees are much more important than others because they control authorization and funding of programs or deal with important policy issues. The most prestigious committees in the House are Appropriations, Rules, and Ways and Means. In the Senate, Appropriations, Finance, Foreign Relations, and Armed Services are the most coveted.

The congressional leaders also participate in or control the assignment of members to four other types of committees. Special and select committees conduct special investigations and deal with topics that cut across standing committee jurisdictions. Joint committees are composed of members of both chambers and deal with issues such as atomic energy and the economy. If both houses pass a bill but in somewhat different form, a conference committee composed of members from both houses is appointed to work out the differences. The congressional leaders and the chairpersons of the standing committees with jurisdiction over the legislation determine who the members of the conference committee will be. Those selected usually include members of the committees that originally considered the bill.

LACK OF PARTY DISCIPLINE

Despite the powers of the congressional leaders, they have limited ability to bargain with or to coerce members of their party to support party positions. Party discipline in fact is very low, and leaders have no means of improving it. For example, in 1976 only 37 percent of all recorded votes in Congress reflected divisions along party lines.[6] In both the House and the Senate, the average member voted with his or her party only about 60 percent of the time.[7] These voting rates are rather typical. They reveal why Congress cannot plan party or policy strategy, or agree upon an agenda. This inability to plan and execute substantially reduces the ability of Congress to act decisively.

The lack of party discipline in Congress reflects in part the diversity of political beliefs among its members. For example, Dodd and Oppenheimer classified the members of the House during the Ninety-fourth Congress by party and ideology. As Table 10.1 shows, both the Republican and Democratic members are divided by ideology. While the Democrats tend to be liberal and the Republicans conservative, there are some differences within the parties (especially among the Democrats), and substantial division among the total membership. Thirty-seven percent of the members were liberal, 23 percent moderate, and 40 percent conservative. Quite naturally, members may find their ideological inclinations more important than their party affiliation when voting.

TABLE 10.1
Ideological Divisions in the House of Representatives: 1975

	Northern Democrats	Southern Democrats	All Democrats	Republicans	All Members
Liberal	74% (148)	11% (10)	55% (158)	1% (2)	37% (160)
Moderate	24% (47)	30% (27)	26% (74)	19% (28)	23% (102)
Conservative	2% (4)	59% (53)	20% (57)	79% (115)	40% (172)
	(N = 199)	(N = 90)	(N = 289)	(N = 145)	(N = 434)

Source: Lawrence C. Dodd and Bruce I. Oppenheimer, "The House in Transition," in Dodd and Oppenheimer, eds., *Congress Reconsidered* (New York: Praeger, 1977), p. 24.

PAROCHIALISM

The tendency of members of Congress to think of policy issues in terms of parochial (local) rather than national interests also limits the ability of Congress to reach a consensus on legislation. The standard wisdom is that to be re-elected, members of Congress must consider constituent interests first, and national interests second. Certainly it is true that members of Congress must try to represent their constituents, or at least the most organized interests in their *constituency*. This causes members to often emphasize parochial over national interests. The President and, to some extent, party leaders in Congress must, however, try to represent the national interest, thereby leading to conflict over policies in which members of Congress have a local stake.

Parochialism is not entirely bad, since it provides a forum for local interests which might not exist at the executive level. Still, the frequent inability of members of Congress to think in terms of the national good stymies many policy initiatives and often allows wasteful or unnecessary programs to be passed in Congress or to remain in effect. Members of Congress tend to adopt the view that challenging unnecessary dams, military bases, federal facilities, and grants in someone else's district only enhances the chance that similar pork-barrel projects in their constituency will be challenged. This mutual support for unnecessary ego and constituency-stroking expenditures costs the na-

Representative Jack Kemp (R., N. Y.) meets with constituents. Members of Congress must try to balance two responsibilities—representing the local concerns of their constituents and framing national policy goals—which often conflict with each other.

tion dearly. Also, policies that affect many constituencies and that may require some compromise of individual constituency interests, such as national energy legislation, may be almost impossible to get through Congress. Thus Sunquist notes:

> Congress can skirmish for limited objectives but it cannot think strategically. It can, for instance, devise policies affecting energy but not a national energy policy. It can enact measures affecting the nation's growth but not a national growth policy—even though in 1970 it committed itself by statute to do so.[8]

AMATEURISM

It is frequently charged that Congress cannot play a sophisticated role in policy formation because it does not have policy expertise or policy experts. While this criticism is exaggerated, Congress does not have the policy formulation and evaluation resources of the executive branch, or of special-interest groups in many cases. Orfield argues that this not only limits the policy-making abilities of the Congress, but that it also distorts the representational process:

> Probably the most serious representational problem in Congress is that most members and most committee staffs must basically rely on policy analysis materials produced by agencies or interest groups. . . . This system usually produces reasonable information about the impact of proposed policies on major economic and governmental institutions, but seldom generates good information on the impact of policies on less affluent and less organized groups in the society. This is a severe problem, not only for Congress but also for administrative policy-making.[9]

Congress does have research and information-gathering organizations, as well as committee staffs which provide considerable policy expertise. The General Accounting Office, the Congressional Research Service of the Library of Congress, the new Office of Technology Assessment, and the new Congressional Budget Office (CBO), all provide Congress with needed expertise. In recent years, Congress has increased personal and congressional committee staffs considerably. In 1960 Congress employed 6,382 staff personnel. By 1978 Congress employed a staff of 17,374.

Part of this growth has resulted from increases in the staff allowance for representatives and senators in recent years, allowing them to deal more completely with legislative issues and constituency needs. In 1978 the average House member received an office allowance of $346,000. Senators were allowed expenditures ranging from $708,000 to $1.2 million, depending on the size of the state population represented. By 1977 members of Congress employed a total of 6,939 personal aides. The average member of the House employed about sixteen aides; the average senator about thirty-five. One senator in 1977 had 75 aides.[10]

Members of the House and Senate, assembled in the House Chamber (above), listen to President Carter's 1980 State of the Union Address. Because of the rule complexity, decentralized power, and lack of party unity in Congress, it is difficult for legislators to pass laws or reach a consensus on national priorities.

Despite increases in staff size and new research and oversight organizations within Congress, other changes have made it increasingly difficult for a member of Congress to deal effectively with policy issues. The most obvious problem is the increasing complexity of public issues, which has led to an increase in the number of subcommittees and special, select, and joint committees. More committees and subcommittees require more meetings for members, placing increasing demands on members' time. In the Ninety-fourth Congress there were 6,975 committee and subcommittee meetings, making it difficult for members of Congress or other groups to grasp and deal with the complexity of issues under consideration.

With an increase in the complexity of issues, the already harried job of members of Congress has gotten worse. In 1977 a study found that the average member of Congress worked eleven hours a day. Members spent so much time on meetings and routine matters that they had little time to study policy issues:

> The average House member's work day runs from 8:30 A.M. to 7:30 P.M. Of that time the member spends four hours and 25 minutes on the floor or in committee, three hours and 19 minutes in the office, two hours and two minutes in other locations in Washington, and one hour and 40 minutes in other places, including travel to and from appointments . . . of the time in the office . . . 53 minutes was spent with staff members, 46 minutes answering mail, 26 minutes on the telephone, 17 minutes with constituents and 12 minutes preparing speeches and legislation.[11]

This same study estimated that the typical member of Congress has only eleven minutes to himself each day. With schedules this frantic, most members of Congress cannot afford to invest adequate time in studying issues. Most depend upon aides, party leaders, representatives from the executive branch, or interest groups for voting cues.

The impact of this pace is reflected in the fact that in 1978 a record fifty-nine members of Congress decided to retire. Eighteen decided to run for other offices, and some were aged veterans. But the number of nonveteran members resigning was unusually high. Many of those who decided to retire cited the pressures on members of Congress, their inability to invest the necessary time in studying issues, and the high cost of campaigning. Representative James Mann (D., S.C.) expressed the general sentiment: "It's no longer the power, fun and glory job our fathers once knew. It's a tough, political, nitty-gritty service job." Representative Shirley Pettis (R., Cal.), who served on five committees and subcommittees, also cited the complexity of the job. "I've been in meetings where I don't feel prepared. I often have to run back and forth between simultaneous committee sessions, not hearing all the testimony before voting. I feel fragmented."

Rep. John Moss (D., Cal.) said: "Our laws are being written by tired people. Quitting just seemed sort of attractive." Rep. Michael Harrington (D., Mass.)—no relation to the author of this book—claimed no disillusionment but said:

> I had a low threshold of expectation about the institution, and I think the American public has been right all along in their bemusement, indifference and downright animus. We haven't done our job in educating people. The country has no goal, no sense of direction, no vision. Congress is a bureaucracy. We have government by managers and engineers.[12]

The complexity of the job can be expected to get worse, and it will become one of Congress' most serious problems.

RULE COMPLEXITY AND RIGIDITY

A major criticism of Congress is that its rules, procedures, and norms are excessively complex, cumbersome, and undemocratic. As a result, it is extremely difficult to successfully maneuver a piece of legislation through the multiple stages of the congressional process. A small number of members (sometimes even one) can prevent a floor vote on legislation favored by a simple majority of Congress. There is no doubt that the procedure for passing legislation is extremely arduous, burdened by very complex rules, and full of veto points that allow small groups to alter or even kill any bill.

The bias of such a system is toward immobility, the often chronic condition of Congress. Congressional leaders must carefully orchestrate an individual strategy for each piece of major legislation they hope to guide through

Congress. Having little formal power, they must rely primarily upon appeals to party loyalty or the national interest. The energy, talent, and power of persuasion of the legislative leadership, especially the Speaker of the House and the Senate majority leader, are thus extremely important in determining whether important legislation will make it through Congress.

A brief review of the process a bill must go through to become a law shows why so little legislation ever surmounts all the obstacles.

1. Introduction

Most legislation is simultaneously introduced into the House and the Senate by members who support the legislation and who have agreed to coordinate their efforts to get it through Congress. Introduction is simple. A member of the House simply gives the bill to the clerk of the House; senators deposit the bill with the secretary of the Senate. The bill is numbered and printed. The chamber parliamentarian acting on behalf of, or in coordination with, the Speaker and the majority leader, refers the bill to a standing committee. House and Senate rules specify which committee will consider a bill. If there is any doubt about committee jurisdiction, the leadership makes the decision.

2. Committee consideration

Upon receipt of a bill, the committee usually assigns one of its subcommittees to consider it. The subcommittee, the full committee, or both, will study the bill and hold hearings at which members of Congress, representatives of the executive branch, and public representives (lobbyists, "experts," etc.) will testify. At a mark-up session, the committee will consider the bill section by section, voting on alterations or deletions. As a result of a recent reform, these votes are now recorded. In 1972 the House also voted to open most mark-up sessions to public and media scrutiny. In 1975 the Senate passed a similar "sunshine law."

If a bill survives the committee review process, and only about 10 percent do, it is reported out for floor consideration. The committee provides a report which summarizes the bill and analyzes the arguments for and against it.

3. The Rules Committee

Most House bills that survive the committee process must then be sent to the House Committee on Rules. This committee serves as the "traffic cop" of the House, deciding which bills will be considered on the floor and the circumstances under which they will be considered. The Rules Committee determines how much time will be allowed for debate on the bill and decides whether amendments to the bill can be offered.

from Article 1, Section 8: "The Congress shall have the power to lay and collect Taxes, Duties, Imposts, and Excises to pay the Debts and provide for the common Defence and general welfare of the United States . . .

To borrow money . . .

To regulate commerce with foreign Nations, and among the several States, and with the Indian Tribes;

To establish a uniform rule of Naturalization, and uniform Laws on the subject of Bankruptcies . . .

To coin Money, regulate the Value thereof . . .

To provide for the punishment of counterfeiting . . .

To establish Post Offices and Post Roads;

To . . . secure for limited Times to Authors and Inventors the exclusive Right to their respective Writings and Discoveries;

To constitute tribunals [courts] inferior to the supreme Court;

To define and punish Piracies and Felonies committed on the high Seas, and Offences against the Law of Nations;

To declare War . . .

To raise and support Armies . . .

To provide and maintain a Navy;

To make Rules for the Government and Regulation of the land and naval Forces;

To provide for calling forth the Militia to execute the Laws of the Union, to suppress Insurrections and repel Invasions;

To provide for organizing, arming, and disciplining, the Militia . . .

To exercise exclusive Legislation in all Cases whatsoever, over such District [the District of Columbia] as may . . . become the Seat of the United States . . . ;—And

To make all Laws which shall be necessary and proper for carrying into Execution the foregoing Powers, and all other Powers vested by this Constitution in the Government of the United States, or in any Department or Officer thereof.

Congressional Powers

During the 1940s, '50s, and much of the '60s, the Rules Committee was chaired by Southern members who used their position to delay, dilute, or kill most progressive legislation, especially civil-rights bills. Retirements and recent reforms have altered considerably the power of the Rules chairperson and the committee's role in the House. All chairpersons now have less power, and the Speaker selects the Democratic members of the committee.

A major criticism of Congress is that its rules, procedures, and norms are excessively complex, cumbersome, and undemocratic. As a result, it is extremely difficult to successfully maneuver a piece of legislation through the multiple stages of the congressional process.

These reforms have converted the Rules Committee to an agency of the Democratic leadership. The committee works with the leadership to get the legislation it wants passed sent to the floor for a vote, and sets agreeable rules for debate and amendment. The committee also helps the leadership dislodge legislation delayed elsewhere. Thus, Rules still plays the critical role of traffic cop, but its actions are designed to aid legislation that the leadership supports and to discourage or kill legislation it does not support. In 1979 the new chairperson of the Rules Committee was Richard Bolling(D., Mo.), a liberal and a longtime critic of the House.

4. Floor consideration

Bills that survive the committee process are placed on a calendar, which is simply an agenda for business. The Senate has only one calendar (unanimous consent), and all bills are placed on it in the order reported out of committee. Normally, bills are considered in order, but by unanimous consent or motion, the leadership may call a bill out of order.

The House has five calendars:

1. *Consent:* Noncontroversial bills are placed on this calendar and can normally be called on the 1st and 3rd Monday of each month. The first time a bill is called, the objection of any one member can delay consideration. On the second call, three members must object.
2. *Discharge:* If 218 members sign a discharge petition, a motion is placed on this calendar to hold a vote on whether a committee should be forced to report a bill.
3. *House:* Bills that do not require an appropriation or review are placed on this calendar.
4. *Private:* Bills affecting individual matters, such as immigration problems, are placed on this calendar and can be called on the 1st and 3rd Tuesdays of each month.
5. *Union:* Bills that require revenue or appropriations are placed on this calendar.

The calendars separate and order the bills so that less controversial legislation can be more easily considered. On designated days, bills on the Consent and Private Calendars can be called. And any bill can be brought to the floor if two-thirds of the members present vote to "suspend the rules."

In both the House and the Senate, the parliamentary rules governing debate and voting are extremely complex. They can be used "as weapons of delay, obstruction, obfuscation, and manipulation" by those members who understand them and are skilled at employing them for their own ends.[13] The rules are so complex, in fact, that few members of Congress understand them even modestly well. One study concluded that "few members of Congress have learned the rules well enough to be able to use them—indeed, estimates of the number of knowledgeable representatives range from only ten members to ten percent of the House."[14]

In the House, a majority of the membership is normally required for general debate. When the House considers legislation that has reached the floor through the Rules Committee, however, it sits as a Committee of the Whole, requiring a *quorum* of only 100 members.

There are four methods of voting in the House. Members may vote by voice, by standing, by teller, or by roll-call vote. In a teller vote, members march past a clerk of the House who records their "yea" or "nay" vote. If one-fifth of a quorum demands it, teller votes are recorded and published. Roll-call votes, required when one-fifth of those present demand it, are also recorded and published. Senators vote by voice, standing, or roll call. As in the House, most votes are by voice.

The leadership plays its most critical role in trying to obtain votes for or against bills that reach the floor. In both the House and the Senate, the party leaders use personal persuasion and appointed whips to round up votes. The whip system is quite elaborate. For example, in the Ninety-fifth Congress the majority whip in the House was John Brademas (D., Ind.). Brademas was chosen by Speaker Thomas P. O'Neill (D., Mass.), and he helped O'Neill and Majority Leader Jim Wright (D., Tex.) choose a chief deputy whip, three deputy whips and ten whips at-large. Twenty-two zone whips were elected by Democratic representatives from nineteen zones. As part of the party leadership, the whips round up votes and take head counts. The more organized the whips and the harder they work, the more likely they are to be successful in obtaining voting commitments. As one whip notes: "Taking a whip count is like fishing. The more you do, the more you catch."[15]

Despite its greater size, the House of Representatives generally is able to deal more efficiently with policy issues than the Senate. The Senate is smaller and less formal but operates under extremely complex and archaic rules that make it easy for small numbers of senators—sometimes even one—to paralyze the decision-making process. The filibuster is the major technique used by senators who wish to prevent Senate consideration of legislation.

Under Senate rules, senators who wish to speak on an issue before the chamber may speak for as long as they wish. This rule of unlimited debate allows one or more senators to hold the floor for long periods, bringing all

Senate business to a complete standstill. The senators' intention is to force the Senate to table the legislation they object to so that the normal business of the chamber may be resumed.

When one or more senators employ this technique, a *filibuster* is said to be in progress. During the twentieth century, most filibusters have been conducted by southern senators, who have used the technique to force the Senate to table civil-rights or other progressive legislation. Senate rules do provide a method by which an extraordinary majority of members can end debate and allow a vote on the contested legislation. Since 1975, the rule has been that debate can be ended (*cloture* invoked) if sixty senators vote to end it. Since 1917, when the cloture rule was first adopted, only about one-fourth of all attempts to end debate have been successful.

At least thirteen of the successful cloture votes occurred during the 1960s and 1970s, when official and public determination to end the basic denial of rights to black Americans peaked. The struggle to overcome southern resistance, however, was intense. As Orfield notes:

> Until 1964 all twentieth-century attempts to enact significant civil rights legislation had been killed by filibuster. Decades of struggle to forbid even so intensely condemned an outrage as Southern lynchings proved futile, when Southerners repeatedly showed their willingness to bring the legislative process to a standstill. Eleven times the Senate had voted on ending filibuster against measures to curb lynchings, poll taxes, job discrimination, and unfair literacy tests for voter registration. Eleven times the two-thirds rule for ending debate had given the Senate a veto. Almost half of all filibusters had concerned racial issues, and Southerners were the leading defenders of the unlimited debate rule.[16]

The southern filibuster against the 1964 Civil Rights Act lasted seventy-four days before cloture was invoked. Cloture also had to be invoked to end southern filibusters against the 1965, 1968, and 1975 civil-rights bills.

During the 1940s, '50s, and much of the '60s, the Rules Committee was chaired by Southern members who used their position to delay, dilute, or kill most progressive legislation, especially civil-rights bills.

In recent years, a small number of Southern senators have continued to use the filibuster to defeat other legislation they disagree with. One senator, James Allen (D., Ala.), who died in early 1978, used the filibuster and a sophisticated knowledge of Senate rules to stymie any legislation he personally did not support. Allen even introduced what he called the postcloture filibuster in which he used Senate rules to prevent a floor vote on legislation, even after cloture had been voted for. Allen's frequent successes were further proof that the Senate often cannot act as a majority body when even a small number of senators want to prevent it from doing so. In February 1978 the Senate voted

Senators (left to right) John Stennis (D., Miss.), Herman Talmadge (D., Ga.), and Russell Long (D., La.) pause after helping to lead a filibuster of a 1960 civil-rights bill. Senate rules, permitting unlimited debate, allow a few senators to block legislation unless cloture is invoked. Today, each of these senators is chairman of an important Senate committee: John Stennis chairs the Armed Services Committee; Herman Talmadge, the Agriculture Committee; and Russell Long, the Finance Committee.

to limit postcloture debate to 100 hours. This will not end filibusters, of course, but if cloture is voted for, further delays will be limited. While the new rule is an improvement, any legislation which involves major issues or touches the important power bases of the country will still have to have extraordinary support in the Senate, often two-thirds or more, to pass.

5. The conference committee

Before a bill can become law, it must be passed by both houses of Congress in the same form. If the two chambers cannot resolve any differences in the versions of the bill passed, a conference between representatives of the two houses may be called. The leadership chooses the representatives from each house, generally from the committee that handled the legislation. These members meet and attempt to work out the differences in the bill.

When their deliberations are completed, they prepare a conference report, listing the alterations agreed to. If the conferees agree on changes, the bill goes back to each house, where it must then be accepted or rejected in that form. No further amendments may be offered. If the bill is then accepted by both houses, it is signed by the Speaker of the House and the Vice-President, and sent to the President for his consideration.

6. Presidential consideration

When Congress is in session, the President has ten working days to either accept or reject a bill. If he takes no action during that period, the bill automatically becomes a law. If he decides to *veto* the bill, it can become law only by two-thirds vote of both branches of Congress. If Congress sends a bill to the President as it adjourns, the bill is considered vetoed if he takes no action within ten working days. This is known as a *pocket veto*.

7. Authorization and appropriation

If a bill passes all the hurdles necessary to become a law, it may still be relatively meaningless. The reason is that each program established by Congress requires two bills. The first bill authorizes the program; the second appropriates the funds necessary to operate the program. A set of comittees different from those which handled *authorization* decides an *appropriations*. Thus, a bill establishing a $3 billion program to provide medical care for the aged has only authorized the program and established a bargaining point for appropriation.

A second bill must be passed to actually appropriate money for the program, and it may not allow the $3 billion that the authorizing legislation provided. It is not uncommon for members of Congress to vote to authorize a program and then vote for a very low appropriation for the program. This allows legislators to establish a record of supporting certain programs while actually giving them little support.

INSULATION AND UPPER-CLASS BIAS

In addition to all these institutional problems, which keep Congress from responding to the nation's policy needs, critics frequently charge that the members of Congress poorly represent the diverse national population. They argue that the membership reflects a bias toward the needs of wealthier citizens and interests. As both elite and pluralist theory predict (see Chapter 4), the people who serve in Congress are predominantly white males, drawn primarily from upper-middle-income occupations.

There are few representatives of minority groups in Congress, and few women. By 1978, 1,715 men but only 12 women had served in the Senate. Almost 10,000 men had served in the House, but only 87 women had served there.* In 1979 there was only one woman in the Senate, but she was elected outright; the other women who served in the Senate were appointed to fill the

---

*No woman has ever served on the Supreme Court, and only nine women have served in the Cabinet. In 1978 women constituted 51 percent of the population but held only 8 percent of all public offices.

unexpired terms of their husbands, who died in office. In 1979 there were only 14 women and 16 black members in the House. As of 1979, 65 senators and 205 representatives were attorneys. Persons from occupations such as primary education, art, factory workers, and small businesses infrequently serve in Congress.

Most members of Congress are also considerably wealthier than the general public. In 1978 over half of the 535 members of Congress declared a net worth in excess of $100,000.[17] At least 30 senators and 30 representatives were clearly millionaires, and another 21 may be millionaires. Perhaps most importantly, very few members of Congress share the economic status of most Americans—assets of less than $50,000. A study by Ralph Nader's Public Citizen group showed a distinct correlation between members' wealth and their voting record. Wealthier members tended to vote to support policies which aid the wealthy. Average citizens are disadvantaged, therefore, because few members of Congress represent their financial situation.

Senator Nancy Kassebaum (R., Kan.), the only woman in the Senate in 1980.

Average citizens may also be disadvantaged because many members of Congress may use their position to protect or enhance their financial interests. For example, in 1979 the *Congressional Quarterly* counted 159 members of Congress who, through stock or bond ownership or employment position, had interests that they could affect through their positions in Congress (see Chapter 6.)[18] This conflict of interest may, of course, distort the representational process by predisposing members to vote for certain interests and against others.

Each program established by Congress requires two bills. The first bill authorizes the program; the second appropriates the funds necessary to operate the program.

The wealth and the salary—$60,662.50 in 1980—of members of Congress may also restrict their circle of friends and acquaintances, often in a way that removes them from contact with average citizens and normal public problems. Washington, D.C., and the mores of that community, can contribute significantly to that problem. Washington and its suburbs are filled with expensive restaurants, prestigious clubs, and wealthy neighborhoods where the in-crowd in Congress and the executive branch live and play. There are also wealthy groups and interests in Washington who cater to and pamper members of Congress and other high officials. The overall impact can create a rather unreal world for senators and representatives. Former Representative Abner Mikva (D., Ill.) makes this point:

It's my impression that you can live your whole life in Congress being only nominally exposed to the real outside world. Even the real world in Washington. You park in the underground garage of the House office building, you walk from your office to the Capitol in the underground walkway. You drive back to your better-than-average apartment or house without having to pass through the areas that reflect the real Washington. I think there are guys who have been here 15 or 20 years who have forgotten what the real world looks like.[19]

Perhaps even more revealing are the actions and statements of members of Congress. Policies designed to aid the general public are almost always more controversial than public policies designed to aid upper-class interests. For example, during his first year in office, President Carter attempted to convince Congress to pass a tax-cut bill which would have given a $50 rebate to taxpayers making less than $30,000 a year. The bill created little enthusiasm in Congress and finally had to be withdrawn by Carter. One senator (a senior Democrat) pointed to one of the drawbacks of the bill: "You have to remember that most senators don't see or talk to anybody eligible for the rebate."[20]

CONCLUSIONS

Congress is an institution besieged with problems. Decentralization of power, lack of party unity, and limited leadership powers make it difficult for Congress to reach a consensus on policy issues, to plan, or to set an agenda. Parochialism, amateurism, rule complexity, and increasingly heavy work loads also limit congressional responsibility and decisiveness, making it difficult for Congress to play a sophisticated role in national policy-making.

Recent reforms have served to democratize Congress. They have made it easier for outsiders to scrutinize congressional activities. But some of the reforms have further decentralized power in Congress. The decrease in the power of committee chairs, for example, has increased member independence considerably, but has further reduced the ability of parties to establish a consensus.

At the same time that freedom from party leadership has increased, the cost of running for and staying in office has increased drastically. This has often caused members of Congress to be less concerned with leadership, party, and national interests and needs than with pleasing those interests that provide the considerable sums necessary to conduct campaigns. Public financing of elections would, of course, easily deal with this problem (see Chapter

6) and would also make it possible for a broader sector of the population to run for Congress.

Making Congress a more viable institution, however, would not be easy. Congressional rules could be modernized and designed to ensure the orderly administration of business by a majority, rather than allowing them to continue to be the vehicle for frustrating majority will. Staffs and research programs could also be improved. The central problem, however, is how to increase party discipline so that party members could formulate a program and then work together to achieve it. Party discipline would require each member of Congress to give up a certain amount of independence and support policies agreed upon by the party. This, of course, is precisely what most members do not want to do. But it should be obvious that the price for unlimited member independence is congressional impotence—the continuing malady of Congress.

Footnotes

1. Richard Bolling, *House Out of Order* (New York: Dutton, 1965), p. 17.
2. Richard F. Fenno, Jr., "U.S. House Members in Their Constituencies: An Exploration," *The American Political Science Review,* (September 1977): 905.
3. Robert Sherrill, *That's Why They Call It Politics* (New York: Harcourt Brace Jovanovich, 1974), p. 110.
4. Lawrence C. Dodd and Bruce I. Oppenheimer, eds. *Congress Reconsidered* (New York: Praeger, 1977), p. 15.
5. *Ibid.,* p. 23.
6. "Partisan Voting Shows Election-Year Drop," *The Congressional Quarterly,* November 13, 1976, p. 3173.
7. *Ibid.,* p. 3173.
8. James L. Sundquist, "Congress and the President: Enemies or Partners," in Dodd and Oppenheimer, eds., *Congress Reconsidered,* p. 240.
9. Gary Orfield, *Congressional Power: Congress and Social Change* (New York: Harcourt Brace Jovanovich, 1975), p. 50.
10. Richard E. Cohen, "Congressional Allowances Are Really Perking Up," *National Journal,* February 4, 1978, pp. 180–183.
11. "Study Gives Committee Reform A Push," *The Congressional Quarterly,* September 3, 1977, p. 1855.
12. All quotes from Marguerite Michaels, "Why Congressmen Want Out," *Parade,* November 5, 1978, pp. 11–14.
13. Ted Siff and Alan Weil, *Ruling Congress: How the House and Senate Rules Govern the Legislative Process* (New York: Penguin Books, 1975), p. 19.
14. *Ibid.,* p. 20.
15. "House Democratic Whips: Counting, Coaxing, Cajoling," *The Congressional Quarterly,* May 27, 1978, p. 1304.
16. Orfield, *Congressional Power,* p. 39.
17. "The Wealth of Congress," *The Congressional Quarterly,* September 2, 1978, p. 2312.
18. "Outside Earnings Swell Wealth of Congress," *The Congressional Quarterly,* September 1, 1979, p. 1823.
19. Quoted in Sherrill, *That's Why They Call It Politics,* p. 113.
20. Quoted in Rowland Evans and Robert Novak, "Tax Rebate Boosters Slimming," *The House Post,* March 30, 1977, p. 3C.

> The Presidency is not merely an administrative office. That is the least of it. . . . It is preeminently a place of moral leadership. All our great Presidents were leaders of thought at times when certain historic ideas in the life of the nation had to be clarified.
>
> **Franklin D. Roosevelt**

11

The framers of the American Constitution intended to make Congress the primary policy-making branch of the federal government. The inherent problems of Congress, however, made it poorly suited for such a role, and by the mid-twentieth century the function of the Presidency in the policy-making process had expanded drastically. While the President's role has increased, the formal powers of the office often have not. Thus, Presidents frequently find themselves powerless to accomplish policy goals, even though they are held responsible by the public for their resolution.

The Presidency and Public Policy

The result is that the Presidency may be the most impossible job on earth. The President is expected to serve as the symbol of the nation's strength, ideals, and accomplishments; to be an honest, hardworking, almost error-free leader; and to be the solver of all national ills. If unemployment is high, it is, to a large extent, considered to be the President's fault. If inflation rages, the President is blamed. If energy is in short supply, the President has let the country down. Indeed, Presidents are not only expected to prevent all problems, but also to quickly solve those they have failed to prevent.

In past years, the public granted new Presidents a honeymoon of about one year in which to get their feet on the ground. In recent years, however, perhaps because of Watergate, the public has been impatient, even cynical about the system, and the honeymoon period seems to have been reduced to about six months. President Carter's approval rating by the public dropped below 50 percent during his tenth month in office, when he was trying hard to get major legislation through Congress. Carter's handling of the investigation of his director of the Office of Management and Budget, Bert Lance, seemed to contribute to his problems, as did his hesitant leadership. But loss of public support by a President seems to be a foregone conclusion. As Cronin says: "No matter what Presidents do, their popularity declines. It hardly seems to matter what they attempt or even who is President. When news is good, a President's popularity goes down; when news is terrible, it merely goes down faster and further."[1]

President Gerald Ford speaks at a 1976 press conference in front of the White House.

THE PRESIDENT'S POWERS

Traditionally, we think of Presidents as being extremely powerful. Most citizens seem to believe that if Presidents really work at it they can accomplish almost any national goal. It is not surprising that Americans tend to hold this belief because it is precisely the image projected by most elementary, high-school, and even some college texts on the Presidency.[2] For example, Clinton Rossiter's *The American Presidency* says: "There is virtually no limit to what the President can do if he does it for democratic ends and by democratic means."[3] In describing the Presidency, Rossiter says: "He is, rather, a kind of magnificent lion who can roam widely and do great deeds so long as he does not try to break loose from his broad reservation."[4]

Contributing perhaps to this omnipotent image of the President have been revelations of misuse of power by some chief executives, especially Lyndon Johnson and Richard Nixon in recent years. Lyndon Johnson escalated the war in Vietnam into a major disaster while withholding much information from Congress and distorting much of the data he did provide. Nixon, as James Barber says, "very nearly got away with establishing a Presidential tyranny in the United States."[5] The case study presented later in this chapter reviews Nixon's role in Watergate and attendant misdeeds.

The Presidency may be the most impossible job on earth. The President is expected to serve as the symbol of the nation's strength, ideals, and accomplishments; to be an honest, hardworking, almost error-free leader; and to be the solver of all national ills.

Clearly, the Presidency can be abused by incumbents and their aides who are so disposed. But does this mean that the President is really very powerful, even too powerful? Most Presidents do not think so.[6] In response to a question about his power, Lyndon Johnson once responded: "Power? The only power I've got is nuclear and I can't use that."[7] Truman insisted that the power of the Presidency consisted of the power to persuade people to do things they should have done without persuasion.[8] Kennedy suffered great frustration in trying to get his programs through Congress. He was led to quip that such minor projects as the White House Rose Garden and his remodeling of Lafayette Square across from the White House might be his only accomplishments while in office. Even some students of the Presidency believe the office is essentially rather weak. Cronin, for example, concludes: "Despite all the experts and resources Presidents supposedly command, they are unable to accomplish a reasonable proportion of what they promise or even what they try hard to do."[9]

The contradiction—Presidents wielding extensive, even abusive powers while failing to achieve many of their goals—results in part because they have great authority over some matters but rather limited powers over many other matters within their jurisdiction. Presidential powers are most substantial in the area of international relations. By constitutional provision and by tradition, the President represents America in world affairs, develops and administers the broad outlines of the nation's foreign policy, and makes the basic decisions about the conduct of wars. Congress is not organized to participate very directly in world affairs. It usually must depend upon the President and the State Department for information about many aspects of international relation.

Greater authority over foreign policy is one reason that some Presidents stress international rather than domestic policy. Nixon particularly emphasized foreign policy, even professing to see little reason why a President should be concerned with domestic problems: "I've always thought this country could run itself domestically—without a President, all you need is a competent Cabinet to run the country at home. You need a President for foreign policy; no Secretary of State is really important; the President makes foreign policy."[10] To a large degree, this attitude simply reflected Nixon's personal political priorities—especially his lack of concern about such issues as unemployment, pollution, and urban blight. It also reflected his disdain for waging the political struggles and developing the alliances necessary to deal with domestic policies.

In domestic politics, the President is considerably weaker, but the problems are no less complex. When Presidents have to deal with issues like crime, health care, hunger, business subsidies, and agricultural policy, they are only one link in a decision network which includes Congress, special interests, the federal bureaucracy, and often the courts. At any point in the decision process, the President's policies may be substantially amended or even defeated. The public, however, tends to hold the President, not members of Congress or anyone else, responsible for the continuation of domestic problems, especially unemployment, inflation, and energy needs. Thus, Presidents are ultimately held accountable, even though they are not responsible, for the performance of the total system. Because power is so decentralized, they may not be able to deal with some problems, no matter how hard they try.

Below we will consider both the strengths and weaknesses of the Presidency to assess the ability of Presidents to perform up to public expectations.

Specific presidential powers

The Constitution gives the President little formal power. The President is commander in chief of the armed forces, has the power to issue pardons and reprieves, can negotiate treaties (which must be approved by a two-thirds vote of the Senate), has the power to make appointments to the executive departments and federal courts, and may veto legislation passed by Congress. Except for the President's personal staff—the White House Office—all presidential appointments must be approved by the Senate. Congress may also vest the appointment of lower officials in the executive branch with someone other than the President. Many of these employees are now covered by civil service laws and are hired on the basis of merit. The presidential veto can be overturned by a two-thirds vote of both houses of Congress.

The President was given little formal authority for two basic reasons. First, the framers expected and wanted Congress to be the dominant branch of government. Congress, representing the whole nation and responsible to the public, was considered the most democratic branch of government. Second, the framers felt that the first President, George Washington, could be trusted to give the office some of its shape and focus. Washington did, in fact, leave a substantial imprint on the office. Because of changes imposed by particular Presidents and innovations required by national emergency or new federal functions, the Presidency has expanded greatly in prestige, form, and function.

President George Washington (below, left) and the four menbers of his Cabinet. The size of the Cabinet today—thirteen people—reflects the tremendous expansion of government since Washington's time.

TABLE 11.1
President Carter's Cabinet*

Position	Name
Secretary of State	Edmund S. Muskie
Secretary of the Treasury	William Miller
Secretary of Defense	Harold Brown
Attorney General	Benjamin Civiletti
Secretary of the Interior	Cecil D. Andrus
Secretary of Agriculture	Robert S. Bergland
Secretary of Commerce	Philip M. Klutznick
Secretary of Labor	R. Ray Marshall
Secretary of Health and Human Services	Patricia R. Harris
Secretary of Housing and Urban Development	Moon Landrieu
Secretary of Transportation	Neil Goldschmidt
Secretary of Education	Shirley M. Hufstedler
Secretary of Energy	Charles W. Duncan

*As of May 1980.

Although it is not specifically mentioned in the Constitution, the Cabinet is an excellent example of presidential innovations. Washington used his department heads to provide advice, meeting with them individually and collectively. Washington's Cabinet consisted of his three full-time department heads—the secretaries of state, treasury, and war—and his part-time attorney general. Other Presidents continued the practice of using the executive department heads as an advisory body, and the *Cabinet* became an established institution. Over the years, the executive departments and thus the Cabinet have expanded considerably.

Currently there are thirteen executive departments, with jurisdiction over thousands of policy matters. They employ the bulk of the federal government's 2.8 million civilian employees. Table 11.1 shows the current executive departments and their heads as of May 1980. This vast bureaucracy is theoretically under the President's direction, but most employees of the departments are under civil service jurisdiction and cannot be replaced by new administrations for partisan purposes. The President can appoint only the top officials in each department (with Senate approval) and hope that these appointees will be able to organize and lead the department in achieving the President's goals. As we shall see, in practice the employees of the executive department may have a commitment to a line of policy quite different from the President's and they may resist initiatives for change quite vigorously.

The President's authority over most executive agencies is limited. The Presidents can direct the executive departments to conduct studies and can

FIGURE 11.1
Carter's Executive Office

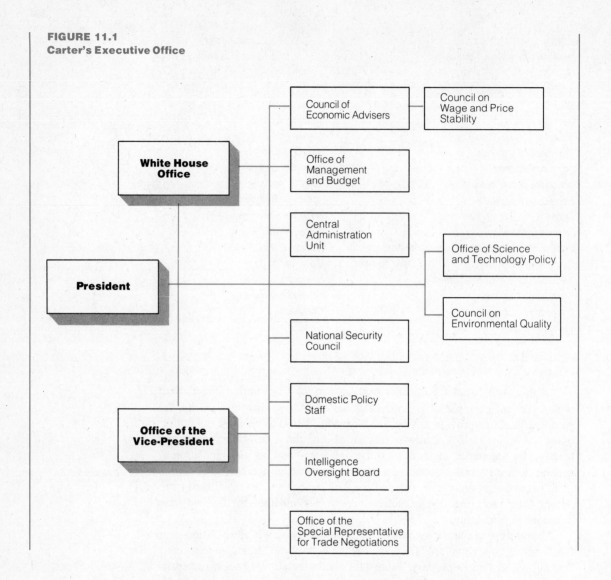

order some of their personnel to draw up legislation. They can even borrow employees of departments to work temporarily within the Executive Office of the President to help with the activities of the President's staff. But their major power over the executive departments has to result from leadership, personal persuasion, and the ability to sell their programs.

While Presidents have only tenuous control over the executive department, they can exercise firm control over the Executive Office of the President (EOP). The EOP was created in 1939 and has expanded greatly since then. It houses the personal and administrative staffs of the President. Each President puts his particular stamp on the EOP. President Carter gained congressional authority to reduce the number of EOP units from 21 to 12, and to reduce the number of full-time staff positions from 1,712 to 1,459. Carter's streamlined staff emphasizes foreign, economic, and domestic policy. The most important units are the National Security Council, the Domestic Policy Staff, the Council of Economic Advisers, the Office of Management and Budget, and the Central Administrative Unit. Figure 11.1 shows the organization of the EOP under President Carter.

The White House Office, located within EOP, consists of the President's personal advisers and assistants. Carter's White House staff includes about 350 persons. Members of the White House Office are the only presidential appointments that do not have to clear the Senate. The tradition of giving Presidents total discretion over their personal staff allows them to emphasize those policy areas that interest them most, and to appoint those persons in whom they have complete confidence. Carter broke his staff down in the following way:

Office

Assistant for National Security
Assistant for Public Liaison
Assistant for Domestic Affairs and Policy
Assistant to the President, Political
    Counsel to the President
Assistant for Congressional Liaison
Assistant for Reorganization
Press Secretary to the President
Assistant for Cabinet and Intergovernmental Relations
Special Assistant, Ombudsman
Special Assistant, Health Matters
Special Assistant, Administration
Director, Intelligence Oversight Board
Rosalynn Carter's Staff
Staff Secretary
Special Assistant, Personnel
Special Assistant, Appointments and Scheduling
Special Assistant, Special Projects
Director, White House Projects

If a President can galvanize his staff and department heads into a working team oriented toward achieving his major policy goals, his power is enhanced considerably. Achieving this, however, depends on many factors, including the President's personality and leadership ability.

The President's staff allows him to formulate foreign policy, develop domestic and economic policy proposals, generate publicity for his proposals, and develop a liaison with key members of Congress, the bureaucracy, and outside interests concerned about a particular policy. The President also wields considerable authority through budget formulation. The Office of Management and Budget helps him prepare a yearly budget. The budget is always amended by Congress, but the President's proposal sets the broad limits of funding for most projects and gives him some influence over the thrust of the final budget.

A last formal source of presidential power is the veto. Table 11.2 shows the number of times each President used the veto. Notice that all Presidents found some occasion to use it. However, Monroe employed it only once, and several other Presidents used it only a few times. Only a few invoked it extensively. Notice also that vetoes are usually not overriden by Congress. Grover Cleveland and Franklin Roosevelt were the champion vetoers, with over 1200 vetoes between them (their vetoes were rarely overriden by Congress). Kennedy, Johnson, and Nixon used the veto rather sparingly; only Ford among recent Presidents employed it somewhat regularly.

Presidents are ultimately held accountable, even though they are not responsible, for the performance of the total system. Because power is so decentralized, they may not be able to deal with some problems, no matter how hard they try.

While the veto power can be a powerful presidential tool, it has substantial limitations. First, Presidents generally find it difficult to veto major bills, such as appropriations or defense legislation, because the effort is too disruptive. Such bills take months to go through Congress and involve hundreds of decisions and compromises. To veto them would generally bring the wheels of government to a halt until Congress could override the veto or reconsider the bill. For this reason, most vetoed bills are rather trivial.

Second, the veto (or the threat of one) is a rather stark power. Used crudely, it can cause considerable animosity in Congress, leading to the erosion of congressional support. Gerald Ford, for example, used the veto primarily to kill welfare, education, and pollution-control bills. His vetoes were overriden twelve times, only three short of the record fifteen defeats suffered by President Andrew Johnson. But Ford served in office for only two and a half years, and several other vetoes were reversed when Congress took up the bills in a new session and successfully passed them. Thus, Ford's relationship with Congress was particularly poor, and he was unusually ineffective in getting his programs through Congress.

Some presidential powers are informal. For example, the President's unique position as head of the government gives him the opportunity to turn to the public for support in his efforts to obtain his goals. But this is a more limited power than might be expected. Except in times of genuine crisis (generally wars), the public is difficult to stir, and Presidents normally find it

TABLE 11.2
Presidential Vetoes

	Regular Vetoes	Pocket Vetoes	Total Vetoes	Vetoes Overridden
Washington	2	-	2	-
Madison	5	2	7	-
Monroe	1	-	1	-
Jackson	5	7	12	-
Van Buren	1	-	1	-
Tyler	6	4	10	1
Polk	2	1	3	-
Pierce	9	-	9	5
Buchanan	4	3	7	-
Lincoln	2	4	6	-
A. Johnson	21	8	29	15
Grant	45	49	94	4
Hayes	12	1	13	1
Arthur	4	8	12	1
Cleveland	304	109	413	2
Harrison	19	25	44	1
Cleveland	43	127	170	5
McKinley	6	36	42	-
T. Roosevelt	42	40	82	1
Taft	30	9	39	1
Wilson	33	11	44	6
Harding	5	1	6	-
Coolidge	20	30	50	4
Hoover	21	16	37	3
F. Roosevelt	372	263	635	9
Truman	180	70	250	12
Eisenhower	73	108	181	2
Kennedy	12	9	21	-
L. Johnson	16	14	30	-
Nixon	24	19	43	5
Ford	44	22	66	12
Carter (as of Nov. 1978)	6	13	19	0
Total	1369	1008	2378	90

Source: *Historical Statistics of the United States.*
Note: Presidents John Adams, Thomas Jefferson, John Quincy Adams, William Henry Harrison, Zachary Taylor, Millard Fillmore, and James Garfield did not veto any legislation.

difficult to mobilize the public behind their programs. If Presidents appeal to the public—over the head of Congress—too many times, their credibility quickly becomes used up. Especially in recent years, Presidents have found it particularly difficult to get the public to voluntarily conserve energy, to back their party during mid-term elections, or to communicate their support for presidential programs to their representative in Congress.

Presidential Powers

from Article 2, Section 2: "The President shall be Commander in Chief of the Army and Navy of the United States . . . ;

he may require the Opinion, in writing, of the principal Officer in each of the executive Departments, upon any Subject relating to the Duties of their respective Offices, and

he shall have Power to grant Reprieves and Pardons for Offences against the United States, except in Cases of Impeachment.

He shall have Power, by and with the Advice and Consent of the Senate, to make Treaties, provided two thirds of the Senators present concur; and

he shall nominate, and by and with the Advice and Consent of the Senate, shall appoint Ambassadors, other public Ministers and Consuls, Judges of the supreme Court, and all other Officers of the United States, whose Appointments are not otherwise herein provided for . . . ."

from Article 2, Section 3: "He shall from time to time . . . recommend to their [Congress'] Consideration such Measures as he shall judge necessary and expedient;

he may, on extraordinary Occasions, convene both Houses, or either of them . . . ;

he shall receive Ambassadors and other public Ministers;

he shall take Care that Laws be faithfully executed, and

[he] shall Commission all the Officers of the United States."

from Article 1, Section 7: "Every Bill which shall have passed the House of Representatives and the Senate, shall, before it become a Law, be presented to the President of the United States; if he approve, he shall sign it, but if not he shall return it, with his Objections to that House in which it shall have originated . . . ."

Constraints on the President

There are all kinds of constraints on Presidents, but on legislative matters three are paramount: Congress, special interests, and the bureaucracy. By constitutional design, Congress has more power over legislation than does the President. Recall some of the points raised about Congress in Chapter 10. Congress is better adapted to delay or defeat legislation than to formulate and enact new laws. At dozens of stages in the congressional process, legislation can be amended, pigeonholed, or killed. Bills being considered by Congress can often be defeated by only a handful of persons (sometimes even one), especially if the chairperson of the committee that has jurisdiction over the legislation does not approve it, or if it is subjected to a filibuster in the Senate.

The power of special interests often determines how Congress will deal with a particular bill. As noted in Chapters 9 and 10, special interests are highly organized in Washington, D.C., and exert enormous influence within the government. The influence of the special interests arises from several basic factors. First, the special interests can afford to hire staffs to function full-time as lobbyists. Their staffs, who are generally well paid and skillful, are on hand to make their case daily, if necessary. But representatives of opposing interests, including the public's, may not have anyone to lobby for their point of view. Second, members of Congress may be particularly amenable to certain special interests because they have investments in the area of the economy the special interest represents, because they are ex-employees of that interest (bankers, farmers, manufacturers), because the interest represents an important economic group within their constituency, and/or because the interest group may contribute heavily to their campaigns.

The bureaucracy—the executive departments—can also frustrate the President's policy initiatives because particular agencies or key individuals within them may have a commitment to a different line of policy. Nixon, for example, had great difficulty in slowing down the thrust of school desegregation because the Civil-Rights Division of the Department of Justice and the Office for Civil Rights in HEW were committed to civil-rights goals.

The bureaucracy is also frequently more amenable to special interests than to the President. Numerous studies have shown that particular agencies in the bureaucracy tend to think of themselves as representatives of constituent industry.[11] The charge is often made—and frequently documented—that particular agencies have become the captives of the very groups they were designed to regulate.[12] Whether the agency has been captured by a special interest or is just on friendly terms with its representatives often makes little difference in terms of its willingness to work with the special interest in protecting or advancing its cause. For many years, it has been common practice for bureaucrats and representatives of special interests to move back and forth between jobs in the "regulated agency" and the target industry. This, of course, will be substantially curtailed by the new government-wide federal ethics code adopted in 1978 (see Chapter 6).

The bureaucracy also frequently develops ties with Congress. These generally take the form of alliances between a particular agency and the committee which has jurisdiction over the policy area that the agency deals with. These alliances may result from a shared interest between the agency and a congressional committee member (or key members of the committee) in promoting a certain policy or protecting a particular interest. Or they may stem from a pragmatic need on the agency's part to get along with those members of Congress who have authority over its funding. Johnson's secretary of health, education and welfare (HEW), Wilbur Cohen, described the latter pressures:

If you're the secretary of HEW, you're responsible really in the end, to the Ways and Means Committee, and to the Interstate and Foreign Commerce Committee and the House Education and Labor Committee. And, boy, they can tell you in the White House, they can tell you in the Office of Management and Budget, and they can tell you everywhere, do this, that and the other thing. But if you come back next time to Capitol Hill, and you've violated what is their standard for their delivery system, you're not going to get what you're asking for.[13]

To complicate matters even further, members of Congress, special interests, and agencies in the bureaucracy often form an alliance to promote and protect a particular interest. The President and even the secretaries of executive departments may have great difficulty in altering a policy when it is protected by this triple alliance. John W. Gardner, secretary of HEW under John Kennedy, discussed this problem before the Senate Government Operations Committee:

As everyone in this room knows but few people outside of Washington understand, questions of public policy normally lodged with the Secretary are often decided far beyond the Secretary's reach by a trinity consisting of (1) representatives of an outside body, (2) middle level bureaucrats, and (3) selected members of Congress, particularly those concerned with appropriations. In a given field these people may have collaborated for years. They have a durable alliance that cranks out legislation and appropriations in behalf of their special interest. Participants in such durable alliances do not want the Department Secretaries strengthened. The outside special interests are particularly resistant to such change. It took them years to dig their particular tunnel into the public vault, and they don't want the vault moved.[14]

The obstacles that Presidents face in getting their legislative programs through Congress or even in getting the bureaucracy to follow their policy directives, then, are considerable. Most Presidents complain at one time or another about their frustration in dealing with the bureaucracy. Truman once said: "I though I was the President, but when it comes to these bureaucracies, I can't make 'em do a damn thing."[15]

Some students of the Presidency believe that a chief executive can increase his successes with the bureaucracy if certain conditions are met. Neustadt, for example, studied the conditions that prevailed when Presidents were able to issue orders to the bureaucracy and have them executed without problems. Studying such decisions as Truman's seizure of the steel mills, Truman's firing of General MacArthur, and Eisenhower's decision to send federal troops to Little Rock, Arkansas, to insure implementation of a school desegregation order, Neustadt isolated five conditions that must exist before a President's directives to the bureaucracy are self-executing:[16]

1. the President's involvement must be unambiguous;
2. the presidential order must also be unambiguous;
3. the order must be widely publicized;
4. those who receive the order must have control of everything needed to carry it out; and
5. there must be no doubt about the President's authority to issue the order.

from Article 2, Section 1: "No Person except a natural born Citizen, or a Citizen of the United States, at the time of the adoption of this Constitution, shall be eligible to the Office of President; neither shall any Person be eligible to that Office who shall not have attained to the Age of thirty five Years, and been fourteen Years a Resident within the United States."

Qualifications for President

The problem with Neustadt's observations is that the situations he studied involved high drama, not a President's legislative program or basic policy initiatives. While Cronin believes the bureaucracy will always serve as in important check on Presidents (for most of the reasons noted above), he believes that they can strengthen their relationship with the bureaucracy considerably by:

1. knowing what he wants to do and what he can do, and displaying a serious commitment to the intended goals;
2. communicating his views effectively and thereby strengthening the hand of those in and out of government who share them;
3. devoting considerable time to both the formulation and implementation stages of his priorities; and
4. transforming both the departments and his own executive office into far more sophisticated educational institutions, which would learn from mistakes and experiment carefully, and which could establish machinery capable of producing the feedback needed to alter, amend, and redirect on-going programs.[17]

Presidents also complain vigorously about how difficult it is to get legislation through Congress and how hard they must work just to win some successes. Lyndon Johnson, a master of legislative strategy, was one of the most successful Presidents in getting his programs enacted, but he worked at it very hard. Johnson had his staff keep a blackboard-size chart showing exactly where all his legislative programs were in Congress. Meetings were held daily to discuss how each bill was progressing. If a piece of legislation was stalled, Johnson would put his people to work to get it moving again.

If necessary, Johnson would summon the member or members of Congress responsible for holding up his bill to the White House for a private talk. Johnson's powers of persuasion in one-to-one relationships were legendary. To get a favorable decision from a member of Congress, Johnson would sweet-talk, beg, bargain, stroke, and even threaten the member until he got his way. Johnson was persuasive enough to convince many legislators that he supported a bill only because he knew they wanted him to. When dealing with powerful members of Congress, Johnson frequently cleared decisions ahead of time so they would not be surprised by his moves.[18]

Part of Johnson's strategy was a conscious effort to understand the individual members of Congress and the bureaucracy. He learned their strengths, weaknesses, and vanities, and manipulated them to his own ends. He once explained:

> When you're dealing with all those senators—the good ones and the crazies, the hard workers and the lazies, the smart ones and the mediocres—you've got to know two things right away. You've got to understand the beliefs and values common to all of them as politicians, the desire for fame and the thirst for honor, and then you've got to understand the emotion most controlling that particular senator when he thinks about this particular issue.[19]

Most Presidents are far less persuasive and far less sophisticated about the inner workings of the governmental process and personal psychology than Johnson was. They are also generally much less successful in achieving their goals. As noted in Chapter 10, President Carter was particularly clumsy at working with Congress during the first year of his administration. Only by trial and error did he and his staff learn how to deal with Congress in an even modestly sophisticated way. While Carter's approach has improved, he probably will never excel at working with Congress.

But even powerful Presidents who do excel do not obtain all their goals. Most Presidents, in fact, decide against trying to get legislation passed on many topics because they feel it would be futile. They also avoid some policy problems because they believe it would be too difficult to overcome all the vested interests determined to maintain the status quo. Presidents also tend to believe they can get Congress to deal with only so many problems at a time and that to throw too much at them would only bog down the deliberative process.

Ironically perhaps, the congressional process does basically bog down without presidential leadership. Given the fact that there are two houses of Congress, with a total of 535 members, Congress has great difficulty in establishing the type of unified leadership necessary to develop and consider policy needs—unless the leadership comes from the White House. Presidents who develop a legislative program, forge a working relationship with the leaders of both houses of Congress, and organize the executive branch to work as a part of a team effort to achieve political goals can direct the attention and work of Congress and have a much greater chance of achieving their programs.

Johnson's powers of persuasion in one-to-one relationships were legendary. To get a favorable decision from a member of Congress, he would sweet-talk, beg, bargain, stroke, and even threaten the member until he got his way.

But one point should be emphasized. Few Presidents have had great success in getting their legislation through Congress. In the twentieth century, only three—Woodrow Wilson, Franklin Roosevelt, and Lyndon Johnson—have had major success in this regard. In fact, most of the important legislation passed in the twentieth century has come from these administrations. The

Most modern-day Presidents have had difficulty getting their legislative programs through Congress. President Carter, a Democrat, had more trouble than most, even though he had a solidly Democratic Congress to work with.

existence of wars, civil strife, and severe social problems set the stage for very strong Presidents to accomplish many of their goals. Outside of these rare periods, the national government is normally deadlocked, or nearly dead-locked.

There are three other fundamental constraints on presidential powers: the courts, the media, and the public. The federal courts can constrain Presidents by overruling their programs or activities. Throughout American history, Pres-idents have frequently run afoul of the courts, and have lost most such con-frontations. Franklin Roosevelt saw many of his early legislative victories go down to defeat before the Supreme Court. After Roosevelt attempted unsuc-cessfully to increase the numbers of Supreme Court justices so that he could appoint judges sympathetic to his views, the Court was more amenable to his program. Roosevelt won a victory of sorts, but Presidents in recent years have generally not been able to reverse federal court decisions that go against them. For example, the Supreme Court ruled that Truman's seizure of the steel mills during the Korean War—to avoid a shutdown over a collective bargaining disagreement—was unconstitutional. He was ordered to relinquish federal con-trol, and he did.

Eisenhower and Nixon had a different set of problems with the courts. Eisenhower did not want the government to pursue civil-rights objectives, but the courts kept the issue alive and forced him on several occasions to act in favor of civil rights. Nixon wanted to drastically reduce the pace of civil rights, but the courts ruled against his actions numerous times. They forced his administration to continue to pursue busing and other forms of school desegregation.[20] The federal courts also declared that Nixon's *impoundment* of funds approved by Congress for various programs was unconstitutional. They refused to allow him to abolish a number of federal programs without congressional authority.[21] In the end, of course, the federal courts played a major role in causing Nixon and his aides to pay the price for Watergate and its cover-up. The courts, then, can be a powerful check on the Presidency.

The *media* represent another powerful check on both Congress and the Presidency. The media can center attention on public issues, analyze the President's approaches toward resolving these problems, point out inconsistencies in programs and public statements, illuminate alliances (some of which may be embarrassing), and publicly probe the President about unresolved issues. The media can also probe misbehavior by Presidents or their aides, perhaps forcing congressional investigations. Most Presidents feel a great deal of pressure from the press. They are therefore undoubtedly encouraged to avoid situations which might embarrass them if widely publicized and to try to resolve problems that make them look bad.

On the other hand, strong Presidents can use the press to publicize their goals and to put pressures on others to go along with their policies. For example, a President who publicly points out that Congress is not making progress on a particular program because of excessive sensitivity to special interests puts pressure on those involved. Presidents vary greatly in their use of and attitude toward the media. Franklin Roosevelt and Lyndon Johnson were rather

Unlike some other recent Presidents, John F. Kennedy handled his relations with the media well, using press conferences to his advantage.

astute at dealing with the media, while Richard Nixon hated and distrusted the media. In twelve years in office, Roosevelt averaged eighty press conferences a year. Eisenhower, Kennedy, and Johnson averaged twenty-one to twenty-five a year, while Nixon held only thirty-seven in five and a half years, for an average of seven per year.[22]

Few Presidents have had great success in getting their legislation through Congress. In the twentieth century, only three—Woodrow Wilson, Franklin Roosevelt, and Lyndon Johnson—have had major success in this regard.

As noted earlier, the public constrains Presidents primarily by failing to support them. Presidents have generally found it extremely difficult to mobilize the public on their behalf. The American public is simply too apathetic and too uninformed to be used by the President to put pressure on members of Congress in support of his programs. The public is most inclined to feel that whatever the problem, correcting it is the President's job. Not wanting to be bothered with supporting Presidents, the public is still willing to hold them responsible for the continuation of public problems. Except in rare cases, then, Presidents receive little assistance from the public.

WATERGATE: A CASE STUDY

Even critics of the Presidency tend to believe that our political system requires a strong chief executive. Certainly Congress is not capable of leading the nation, and thus a strong, unifying leader in the White House does seem necessary. Watergate, however, raised frightening questions: Is the Presidency too powerful? Can the nation protect itself against an abusive President? The ultimate resolution of Watergate answered, at least in part, these questions.

Below we will analyze the Watergate crisis, with an emphasis on defining its dimensions and answering two questions:

1. How well did the existing system of checks within and outside the government work? Were they effective in uncovering political irregularities, bringing them to public and institutional attention, and resolving them?
2. Did Watergate and its ultimate resolution suggest constitutional and institutional weaknesses that require reform? If so, have the reforms been instituted?

The crisis

On the night of June 17, 1972, five men were arrested in the Democratic party's headquarters at the Watergate Towers in Washington, D.C. The subsequent investigation of this burglary set off one of the worst constitutional crises in American history and led to the resignation of President Richard Nixon. As with most of the individual events that together made up the Watergate scandal, there are various interpretations of the type and extent of the crisis.

The evidence, however, makes two facts indisputable. First, in an attempt to insulate himself and his aides from congressional investigation, judicial control, and public scrutiny, a democratically elected President attempted to vastly expand his constitutional powers. In the process, Nixon and some of his appointees were guilty of many serious violations of specific laws. They were also guilty of many unethical acts that, while not specifically illegal, were not in the nation's best interest and reflected badly on the government. Second, as Watergate climaxed, Nixon increasingly became incapable of performing his duties, leaving the nation for some period without a functioning President.

The Watergate tapes and other evidence revealed that Nixon participated in and directed the Watergate cover-up. He engaged in various acts which constituted obstruction of justice, perjury, bribery, obstruction of a congressional committee, and obstruction of a criminal investigation.* As part of the cover-up, Nixon specifically approved payment of "hush money" for participants in the Watergate and Ellsberg burglaries;** authorized offers of clemency to them; coached his aides on how to commit perjury; suggested to one of his attorneys (Buzhardt) that phony, favorable evidence be created and submitted to the courts; and ordered his aides to use the CIA to block the Watergate investigation by the FBI.

While in office, Nixon also ordered his aides to use the IRS to punish his enemies. He ordered wiretaps and surveillance of reporters and administrative officials. In addition, he cheated on his income taxes, used campaign money to buy his wife gifts, used public funds to improve his private residences, approved the maintenance of a secret cash fund, authorized the Huston plan (which involved serious violations of constitutional rights), and approved the use of dirty campaign tricks.

Nixon may have ordered both the Watergate break-in and the burglary of Daniel Ellsberg's psychiatrist's office. He may also have accepted political contributions in return for favors—the ITT, Vesco, and milk parity cases—may have approved the laundering of campaign contributions, may have allowed the sale of government offices in return for campaign contributions, and may have destroyed evidence under subpoena in a criminal case (the eighteen-and-one-half-minute gap in the tapes). The evidence, in fact, is strong enough to believe that he was guilty of many of these offenses.

Nixon clearly lied to the public and many of his aides (including his lawyers) about his role in Watergate. He directed the preparation of a purposefully

---

*A federal grand jury concluded that sufficient evidence existed to indict Nixon on each of these charges, although he was named only as an "unindicted co-conspirator."

**On the nights of September 3 and 4, 1971, White House aides E. Howard Hunt and G. Gordon Liddy supervised the burglary of the office of Daniel Ellsberg's psychiatrist.

The law-and-order administration team players.

distorted transcript of the subpoenaed tapes, temporarily defied a court order to turn over the tapes, and fired a Watergate special prosecuter who had not violated the terms of his employment. He threatened to defy any Supreme Court decision that was not unanimous. Nixon also attempted to use the doctrine of *executive privilege* and the cloak of national security to conceal his and his aides' illegal acts rather than to protect the Presidency and the nation's interest. Further, he directed a secret war in Asia, encouraged the violent overthrow of a constitutionally elected government (Chile), and illegally impounded funds authorized by Congress.

The Watergate tapes and the books written about Watergate by Nixon's aides place Nixon squarely in control of the cover-up. Two of Nixon's closest aides maintain that the President not only directed the cover-up but also ordered the Watergate burglary.[23] Post-Watergate accounts by presidential aides place the responsibility for Watergate on Nixon's shoulders because, in his determination to ''get the goods on'' and punish his political enemies, assure his reelection, and stop leaks, he sanctioned a climate of lawlessness within the executive branch.

Some of the abuses and crimes that Nixon and his appointees were guilty of had certainly been committed by other administrations. Illegal campaign contributions, wiretapping, political surveillance, ''dirty tricks,'' and the use of the IRS to harass opponents had all certainly occurred before. But for three reasons the abuses and crimes of the Nixon administration reached crisis proportions: they were much more extensive than in previous administrations; Nixon and his aides got caught; and Nixon and his aides attempted to obstruct and defy those institutions required by law and the Constitution to deal with such crimes and abuses.

The other dimension of the crisis was Nixon's inability during the final months of Watergate to perform his presidential duties. As White says: "What the men in the White House were involved in, without ever admitting it to themselves, was the management of an unstable personality."[24] Woodward and Bernstein concur, reporting that near the end Nixon began to drink to excess, was unable to sleep at night and thus often slept late into the work day, and could not concentrate on his work.[25] White believes, and the evidence seems to support him, that for a short period General Alexander Haig* was acting President of the United States.

Most of those closest to Nixon believed that he had always suffered from personality defects, problems severe enough to require his aides to ignore or conceal his often intemperate, unethical, and even illegal behavior and orders.[27] Haldeman describes Nixon as "the weirdest man ever to live in the White House."[28] Ehrlichman apparently was in the habit of referring to Nixon as "the mad monk."[29] Buchanan, Ehrlichman, and Safire** all discuss, reluctantly, the negative side of Nixon's personality. Buchanan: "There's a mean side to his nature you've never seen—I can't talk about it."[30] Ehrlichman: "There was another side of him, like the flat, dark side of the moon."[31] Safire: Nixon "was the first paranoid with a majority."[32]

The collective portrait of Nixon, then, contributed even by those who still admire him, was that for a period of six months or so he was unfit to hold office and that he was probably always temperamentally unsuited for the Presidency.

Why did the illegal acts and cover-up take place?

Watergate and the other Nixon crimes and abuses might be explained in terms of four factors. First, Nixon had character and personality defects. Everyone close to Nixon admits that he tended to paranoia, being especially sensitive and vindictive about criticism. Anyone who criticized Nixon's policies and actions was considered an enemy, at least for a short period of time. John Dean, counsel to the President, relates a number of instances in which Nixon, in childish vindictive pique, ordered him to use the IRS and other forms of harassment to punish authors of satirical articles and plays, and others whose

---

*White House chief of staff after the resignation of Nixon's orginal Chief of Staff, H. R. Haldeman.

**Haldeman, along with John Ehrlichman, assistant to the President for Domestic Affairs, resigned on April 30, 1973. Patrick J. Buchanan was a White House speech writer. William Safire was a White House speech writer who resigned to accept a position with the *New York Times*.

Maurice Stans (left), the main fundraiser for President Nixon's 1972 re-election campaign, and John Mitchell (right), who managed the campaign, meet the press after their trial. Stans was convicted of accepting illegal campaign contributions and failing to report other contributions made to Nixon's re-election campaign. Mitchell was convicted of conspiracy to obstruct justice in the Watergate case.

criticism was hardly threatening.[33] Of course, the record revealed that Nixon had offending reporters wiretapped and that he ordered an FBI check of newsman Daniel Schorr. Haldeman admits that he often had to ignore Nixon's odd, illegal, and unethical orders. He states that Nixon even tried to get his aides to wiretap and place under surveillance members of Congress who criticized his policies.[34]

Combined with Nixon's mean side was a fear of failure. Past failures, such as the loss of the 1960 presidential campaign and the California governorship, seemed to haunt him. Determined to accomplish his foreign policy goals and end his administration in triumph, he was adamant about winning the 1972 election. Nixon sent his aides out to raise the largest campaign fund of any President in history. This was accomplished, but only by many illegal and unethical acts on the part of Nixon's aides and members of the corporate world. Though his reelection campaign was never in trouble, to insure success Nixon and his people used some of the money they had raised to harass Democratic candidates, infiltrate their campaigns, and burglarize the Democratic National Committee (DNC) headquarters. Nixon simply wanted to win so badly that he would do almost anything.

Second, Nixon's character weaknesses could be countered or encouraged by his aides. Unfortunately, some of his aides played to his mean side. Haldeman, Ehrlichman, Colson, Mitchell,* and Dean must share the major responsibility for failing to curb and, even on occasion, for encouraging the base side of Nixon. Had people of more integrity served in place of these aides, Nixon's negative side might have been held in check, and his positive side emphasized.

Third, until the passage of the Federal Election Campaign Act of 1974 (see Chapter 6), the way campaigns were financed contributed significantly to Watergate and other crimes during the Nixon administration. Many of the crimes of the Nixon administration were either related to fund-raising or expenditures. In an effort to raise huge amounts of money, unethical and illegal contributions were accepted, and unethical and illegal tactics were used to encourage, even coerce, contributions. A Texas lawyer explained to Bernstein and Woodward how Stans** managed to raise a large sum of money in Texas—money that eventually was laundered through Mexican banks:

> Maury came through here like a goddamned train . . . he was really ballin' the jack. He'd say to the Democrats, the big money men who'd never gone for a Republican before, "You know we got this crazy man Ruckelshaus† back East who'd just as soon close your factory as let the smokestack belch. He's a hard man to control and he's not the only one like that in Washington. People need a place to go, to cut through the red tape when you've got a guy like that on the loose. Now don't misunderstand; we're not making any promises, all we can do is make ourselves accessible. . . ."[35]

Stans and his aides were so successful that Nixon's people ended up with more money than they knew what to do with. And the money was frequently untraceable. Even Haldeman is moved to say, "I agree with all Nixon's critics: we had too much cash floating around for our own good."[36] If the Nixon people had not had excess, often unaccountable money to finance Watergate, it simply could not have happened.

Fourth, Nixon and his aides committed illegal and unethical acts in part because those acts were common practice in Washington. Acceptance of illegal campaign contributions, wiretapping, abuse of the IRS, and dirty campaign tricks had all happened before. In fact, sixteen of the thirty-eight members of the House Judiciary Committee, which eventually brought impeachment charges against Nixon, had accepted contributions from the same milk producers with whom Nixon was accused of doing illegal business. This is not to say that all politicians were as corrupt as Nixon or that Nixon did not carry practices to extremes. The point, however, is that the overall ethics of political life in America were then, and perhaps still are, a bit on the expedient, shabby side. Thus, it was easy for Nixon and his aides to rationalize that they were only doing what everyone else had, and was, doing.

---

*Charles W. Colson was special counsel to the President. John Mitchell was Nixon's first attorney general and the manager of his 1972 presidential campaign.

**Former secretary of commerce and Nixon's chief fund-raiser for the 1972 campaign.

†William D. Ruckelshaus, then head of the Environmental Protection Agency.

Internal and external checks on political abuse and corruption

The Constitution and federal law provide methods of dealing with errant federal officials. The Twenty-fifth Amendment establishes a procedure for removing an incapacitated President from office, temporarily or permanently. Like all federal officials, those involved in the Watergate scandal could have been indicted and tried in a federal or state court for criminal acts. Or they could have been impeached by the House and tried by the Senate for criminal acts or for abuse of power that reached criminal proportions. Thus, depending on the actions involved, the courts or Congress or both can play a role in bringing errant federal officials to justice.

In practice, a sitting President could probably only be indicted for a very serious crime. But he probably would not be, if the House were engaged in *impeachment* proceedings involving the President or if the Senate were trying the President, wholly or partially because of that criminal act. With sitting Presidents, the constitutional process works best if substantial evidence of criminal acts or criminal abuse of power stimulates congressional investigation, allowing the House to determine if impeachment, followed by a Senate trial, is necessary. Once the congressional process has run its course, a President, like any federal official, can be indicted and tried for any crimes revealed by the congressional review. In the case of the President, indictment and trial after congressional review would be most likely to occur if he had been removed from office, if his term had expired, or if the crimes uncovered were serious.

Even critics of the Presidency tend to believe that our political system requires a strong chief executive. Watergate, however, raised frightening questions: Is the Presidency too powerful? Can the nation protect itself against an abusive President?

If a federal crime were involved, the federal prosecutor could launch an investigation and present evidence to the grand jury. The grand jury could vote to indict, except possibly as noted above, and the grand jury evidence could be used to bring the accused to trial. Or it could be turned over to any congressional body engaged in an investigation of the acts.[37] Also, if a federal crime were involved, the FBI would be obligated to launch an investigation, turning evidence over to federal prosecutors.

The procedure for removal of an incapacitated President from office is provided for in the Twenty-fifth Amendment. The procedure requires the Vice-President and a majority of the Cabinet heads (or a majority of any other body specified by Congress) to transmit to Congress a written declaration that the President is unable to discharge his duties. A President reassumes his office by notifying Congress of his recovery. If the Vice-President and a majority of the Cabinet officers disagree with the President's assessment of his fitness, Congress must decide the issue.

The primary external check on political abuse and crime is probably the media. The media can uncover and bring errant official acts to public attention. This disclosure creates and shapes public opinion in the form of public support or even demands for official action to end the abuse or bring errant officials to justice.

How well did the checks work?

Before Watergate ran its course, the FBI, the Justice Department, a federal grand jury, the federal courts, Congress, and, of course, the media became deeply involved. It is instructive to review the evidence on how well each institution performed. We will discuss each one in the approximate order in which it entered the fray.

The media The media have been given much credit for the eventual resolution of Watergate. Characteristically, Haldeman claims: "When the press did move massively into Watergate, all other power blocs were seen as frail in comparison. And in the end, it was the press, more than the other power blocs combined, that did the most to bring Nixon down."[38] The collective evidence, however, suggests that while the media were important, they were not as important as generally assumed. Bernstein and Woodward's untiring efforts in tracing the authorization and financing of the Watergate burglary represented perhaps the most critical phase of the media's role. They kept the issue alive, uncovered facts that certainly cast suspicion on the early contention of the Watergate burglars that they acted on their own, and probably caused or at least reinforced Judge John Sirica's belief that the burglars were hiding the truth. Further, they raised suspicions among some members of Congress and created insecurity and even some panic among the White House guard. Later, as the Watergate story began to unravel, the media kept the scandal before the public, definitely created panic on the part of some of the Watergate principals, shaped public opinion, and kept government officials under pressure.

The Justice Department and the FBI The role of the Justice Department, the special prosecutor, and the FBI in the Watergate events revealed serious problems with the institutional procedures for dealing with crime or criminal abuse of power by the President or his aides. An obvious problem is that the attorney general, other top Justice Department officials, and the director of the FBI are presidential appointees who must try to serve both the law and the chief executive, even when the two are in conflict. Watergate revealed that this situation can become untenable.

While the FBI director does not necessarily have to be an appointee of the sitting President, the acting director during Watergate was a Nixon appointee. L. Patrick Gray's performance in that position became a source of serious embarrassment to the administration, casting suspicion on the agency and the integrity of its investigation of Watergate. The FBI problems centered primarily around the fact that Gray saw himself as an agent of the President and willfully attempted to help Nixon and his aides in the Watergate cover-up.

At his confirmation hearings, Gray admitted three startling facts: that while he was acting director he had allowed John Dean, the White House counsel, to sit in on the FBI's interrogation of Watergate witnesses; that he had given Dean all the FBI files on Watergate (eighty-two documents); and that he had personally destroyed Watergate evidence. Gray also revealed that Dean had been allowed to clean out the White House office of E. Howard Hunt, one of the Watergate conspirators. Bernstein and Woodward's investigation suggested that the FBI never conducted anything other than a half-hearted investigation of the Watergate break-in. They discovered that the FBI did not even check out the names of persons (including Howard Hunt) found in the address book of one of the burglars.[39]

> *The primary external check on political abuse and crime is probably the media. The media can uncover and bring errant official acts to public attention.*

The Justice Department's role in Watergate varied over time, but because of its need to serve two masters it was strained, even when it was directed by Elliott Richardson.* Richard Kleindienst, attorney general during the first nine months of Watergate, immediately found himself in a distressing situation. To investigate the break-in thoroughly might have jeopardized some of Nixon's top aides, including Kleindienst's good friend John Mitchell. Kleindienst told Dean that he would resign his post before he would prosecute Mitchell.[40] Kleindienst basically soft-peddled the investigation, passed FBI information to Dean, and held private meetings with Dean, Haldeman, and Ehrlichman to keep them informed.

The criminal investigation of Watergate was the responsibility of Henry Peterson, assistant attorney general in the Criminal Division. Peterson agreed at the outset to limit the Justice Department investigation to the break-in. He also kept Nixon informed about the investigation, even providing the President with information about criminal investigations involving Haldeman and Ehrlichman, which Nixon passed on to these two aides to help them prepare their defense.[41]

Kleindienst's unwillingness to prosecute his friend Mitchell led to a fateful decision: the appointment of a special prosecutor. Before his resignation on April 30, 1973, Kleindienst told Nixon that the Justice Department had sufficient evidence to prosecute Haldeman, Ehrlichman, and Mitchell. Not wanting the burden of prosecuting Mitchell, Kleindienst suggested that a special

---

*attorney general, former secretary of defense.

prosecutor be appointed. Nixon agreed in principle, persuaded in part by Kleindienst's assurance that he had discussed the issue with Chief Justice Warren Burger, who also felt that a special prosecutor should be appointed. A bipartisan group of senators, led by Charles Percy (R., Ill.), also spearheaded a resolution through the Senate calling for the appointment of a special prosecutor.

When Richardson became attorney general, he chose Archibald Cox* to be special prosecutor. He gave Cox full authority to take over the Justice Department's discredited investigation and authorized him to investigate the White House's role in the Watergate cover-up. Cox lasted just over five months. In what became known as the "Saturday Night Massacre," Nixon fired Cox despite the fact that both a federal district and appellate court had upheld Cox's subpoenas of Nixon's tapes of Oval Office conversations. Richardson and Deputy Attorney General Ruckelshaus refused to fire Cox, resigning instead. Haldeman claims that Nixon was so frightened by the special prosecutor's attempt to subpoena tapes of his private conversations that he intended to completely abolish the position: "Nixon intended [to] . . . abolish the special prosecutor's office completely, firing every one of its hungry young attorneys, and not reinstate the office, no matter what the howls of outrage."[42]

But the "howls of outrage" were greater than Nixon expected. Within days of the firing, forty-four Watergate-related bills were introduced into Congress, half calling for an impeachment investigation. Only three days after the firing, Nixon reversed himself and announced that the tapes would be released. White is probably correct when he says that any special prosecutor appointed by Richardson would have met Cox's fate.[43]

On November 7, 1973, Leon Jaworski became the new special prosecutor. Jaworski had originally been approached about the job but had declined because he did not feel the office would have enough independence. Haig now assured Jaworski that he would have complete control, telling him that he could take the President to court if necessary.[44]

The tapes were destined to be the center of the continuing conflict between Nixon and those investigating Watergate. Only seven of nine originally subpoenaed tapes were released; two were either nonexistent or missing. One of the seven tapes, including a conversation about Watergate three days after the break-in, had an eighteen-and-a-half-minute gap. Haig told Judge Sirica that the gap was the result of some "sinister force."

In April 1974, the Judiciary Committee and Jaworski subpoenaed additional tapes (42 and 62, respectively). In late April, James D. St.Clair, special counsel to the President, announced that Nixon would not release the subpoenaed tapes. Instead, he said that the White House would release typed transcripts of the tapes. The transcripts proved to be severely distorted and self-serving. Jaworski refused to accept the transcripts as a substitute for the tapes and tried to negotiate with the White House for a reduced number of tapes. Upon being rebuffed, Jaworski turned to the courts.

---

*Cox, a Harvard law professor, became the first special prosecutor on May 18, 1973.

Leon Jaworski (left) replaced Archibald Cox (center) as Special Prosecutor in the Watergate case after Nixon fired Cox in October 1973. Judge John Sirica (right) presided over the Watergate trials.

In Judge Sirica's chamber, St.Clair argued that Jaworski was an employee of the executive branch, and thus was not entitled to take any actions contrary to the President's wishes. Jaworski protested that this violated the terms under which he had accepted the job and would make a farce of the special prosecutor's investigation. Sirica agreed, refusing to quash the special prosecutor's subpoena. When the White House still refused to release the tapes, Jaworski appealed directly to the Supreme Court.

On July 24, 1974, the Supreme Court in *United States* v. *Nixon* unanimously ruled in favor of Jaworski. The Court ruled on three key points. First, it declared that the dispute between Jaworski and Nixon did not simply involve a controversy within the executive branch, outside the reach of judicial review. The Court ruled that the attorney general has the independent power to conduct the criminal litigation of the United States, that the special prosecutor was a duly appointed and proper agent of the attorney general, and that the President could not unreasonably limit the Justice Department's scope of review in a criminal case. Second, the Court held that Jaworski had shown a compelling need for the subpoenaed tapes. Third, it said that while the President could protect some of his communications from outside scrutiny, in a criminal investigation he did not have the power to protect the tapes on a general assertion that all his communications were confidential.

The Court's unanimity may well have stemmed a very serious constitutional confrontation. Haldeman claims that before the Court announced its decision, Nixon had told him that if the Court leaves "any 'air' we can handle it."[45] Haldeman writes: "What Nixon was threatening was potentially one of the greatest constitutional crises of this century. By 'air,' he meant anything other than a unanimous decision would not be obeyed. If the U.S. Supreme Court had handed down a majority decision, Nixon would have defied the Court and refused its order to turn over the tapes."[46] The Court's unanimous decision forced Nixon to release (among others) the June 23, 1972 tape (the "smoking gun"), which proved that he had been involved in the cover-up from the beginning. His lawyers, who had been lied to, scrambled for the exits, his remaining Republican supporters in Congress abandoned and even denounced him, and Nixon resigned.

The attorney general, other top Justice Department officials, and the director of the FBI are presidential appointees who must try to serve both the law and the chief executive, even when the two are in conflict. Watergate revealed that this situation can become untenable.

The court system With one almost minor exception, it is difficult to fault the role of the courts in the resolution of Watergate.* The district judge before whom the Watergate burglars, and eventually most of the other Watergate figures, found themselves proved to be a key figure in the drama. Judge John Sirica, renowned for his sternness and candor, was openly insulted by the burglary defendants' claims of ignorance. To bring out the truth, he gave the defendants long preliminary sentences (thirty-five years for Hunt and forty years for the other defendants). He also told them that he would not promise leniency, that he expected them to cooperate with the Senate inquiry, and that he would take their behavior before the Senate into consideration upon final sentencing. Sirica's sternness and long sentences not only frightened some of the break-in defendants, but the thought of ending up in his court frightened some of those persons involved in the cover-up.

Sirica's threat to give stiff sentences seems to have played an important role in Hunt's decision to demand cash payments from the President. Hunt and the other defendants began to fear that they would be without their families for a long time. Because of this, they expected the White House to cover their attorney fees and provide funds for their families. Hunt sent a message to Dean saying that if funds were not provided, he would turn evidence against Ehrlichman—reveal his role in the Ellsberg break-in—and Charles Colson, special counsel to the President. Hunt's demands frightened Dean, who realized that he was being drawn deeper and deeper into a criminal conspiracy, and led to the approval of hush funds by Nixon.[47]

*Larry O'Brien's civil suit for the Democratic party against Maurice Stans and the Reelection Committee ended up before Judge Charles Richy, a Nixon appointee. Richy proved to be partisan and engaged in a number of unprofessional acts. See John Dean, *Blind Ambition* (New York: Pocket Books, 1977), pp. 132–33.

James McCord's fear of Sirica also caused him to break his silence. McCord, chief of security for the Committee to Reelect the President (CREEP), an ex-CIA employee, and one of the Watergate and Ellsberg burglars, had originally pleaded innocent to the charges against him but was found guilty. Before sentencing by Sirica, he sought leniency by sending a letter to the judge stating that perjury had been committed at the trial, that hush money had been paid, and that Nixon officials had approved the break-in.

Sirica played a role in two other fateful decisions. He twice upheld the power of the special prosecutor to subpoena presidential conversations needed as evidence in a criminal investigation, and he approved the release of the grand jury report to the House Judiciary Committee.

The other federal courts involved also played important roles. The court of appeals concurred without delay in both of Sirica's decisions. The Supreme Court allowed Jaworski to bring the tape question—the second dispute—directly before it (bypassing the appellate court). With a minimum of delay, it ruled unanimously on the key issues raised by the conflict between the special prosecutor and the President. Had the Supreme Court not ruled quickly on the issues, it would have left the government strained and divided. Had the House Judicary Committee not had the grand jury report, the impeachment investigation would have been delayed by many months. The courts, then, in a fair, impartial, and timely manner, performed their constitutional role and were indispensable in administering justice and making the constitutional process work.

Congress By constitutional design, the House should have been the first branch of Congress to investigate Watergate. The Senate, however, took the first initiative. Partly because of a campaign pledge, and partly in anger over the dirty tricks played on Humphrey and Muskie during the 1972 campaign, Mike Mansfield, the Senate majority leader, announced that he would appoint a committee to investigate the DNC break-in and the financing and conduct of American elections. With Senate approval, he established a Senate Select Committee to be headed by Sam Ervin (D., N.C.).

The Select Committee had instant successes. Sirica's admonishment to the Watergate defendants convinced McCord to give evidence to the committee, causing Magruder to break the conspiracy and turn evidence. Dean quickly followed suit, as did Kalmbach* and numerous other employees of Nixon's reelection committee. The Senate Select Committee was a sieve. Testimony given "in confidence" was leaked by the committee staff, often by committee members, and by defendant attorneys, provoking counterleaks and even new confessions.

By the time the committee began its public hearings (May 17, 1973), the investigation had become a circus. Those who had confessed to the committee were brought before the television cameras to tell their stories; those who con-

---

*Herbert Kalmbach was personal counsel to the President.

Sam Ervin (center) was the chairman of the Senate select committee that investigated the Watergate affair. Howard Baker (left) was the ranking Republican senator on the committee.

tinued to stonewall—Haldeman, Ehrlichman, and Mitchell—were brought before the cameras to be probed, taunted, and recorded in perjury. High drama prevailed. Magruder testified that Mitchell had approved the Watergate break-in. Dean, reading from a prepared statement, laid out the break-in and subsequent cover-up in elaborate detail, fixing Nixon himself as the chief architect of the cover-up. Butterfield* told the world that Nixon taped his conversations. Kalmbach confessed to directing the payoffs. Ehrlichman angered and frightened the committee by arguing that the Ellsberg break-in was justifiable because a President had the power to commit illegal acts in the name of national security. The committee ended by voting to pursue the President through legal means and bring him to court.

The "Saturday Night Massacre" (October 20, 1973) stimulated twenty-two impeachment bills in the House, finally forcing the House to take some action on the events that began sixteen months earlier with the DNC break-in. All through the summer of 1973, with the events of Watergate on daily national television, Carl Albert, then Speaker of the House, had refused to authorize a House investigation. Then the impeachment bills were sent to the House Judiciary Committee. Peter Rodino, Judiciary Committee chairperson, ap-

*Assistant to H. R. Haldeman.

pointed John Doar as chief counsel to the committee in late December, 1973. Doar assembled a staff and began to develop a carefully documented and detailed report on Nixon's transgressions. Rodino wanted to make certain that the circus atmosphere which prevailed during the Senate investigations did not characterize the House's investigation. He wanted a careful, well-documented, fair, nonpartisan record upon which to base the committee's work.

Doar and his team had a wealth of information to build upon. Both the Senate's and the special prosecutor's records were available, and new witnesses and leads produced additional evidence. When the Judiciary Committee's report—3,888 pages—was released on July 12, 1974, it was a model of exhaustive and judicious research. It was also a devastating indictment of Nixon and his administration.

Part of Rodino's strategy was to document a case against Nixon based on criminal abuse of power, not simply on evidence of a statutory crime. Rodino concluded that such a strategy would establish a precedent upon which needed legislation defining and prohibiting criminal abuse of power could eventually be passed. The Supreme Court's decision on July 24, requiring Nixon to turn over subpoenaed tapes, negated that strategy because the "smoking gun" tape was made public. That tape revealed beyond a shadow of a doubt that Nixon had been involved in the criminal act of obstruction of justice.

Using the "smoking gun" tape and the report as a base, the committee—including six Republicans—voted the first article of impeachment on July 27, 1974. Within the next three days, two more articles of impeachment were voted. Only eight days after the third article of impeachment was voted, Nixon resigned.

Peter Rodino (D., N.J.), chairman of the House Judiciary Committee. The committee recommended that the House impeach Nixon, but Nixon resigned before the proceedings could begin.

Why did the Watergate cover-up fail?

It is important to note that only one of the five major reasons for the failure of the Watergate conspiracy had anything directly to do with the constitutional and institutional procedures and protections against official misconduct. First, the cover-up failed because of a lack of mutual trust, unity, courage, and selflessness among those involved in the conspiracy. Within weeks of the DNC break-in, a large number of people in the Nixon administration knew about it and were involved in the attempt to cover it up. Success required that everyone stick together, trust one another, and be confident that the cover-up could be carried off without fear of detection or punishment. It also demanded that, if necessary, one or more of Nixon's aides take the rap for everyone else. Given the personalities involved and their interrelationships, these conditions simply did not exist.

The principals involved did not trust one another, some did not like one another, some were basically weak, easily frightened people, and none was willing to take the fall for the greater cause. As Dean told Haldeman, "Everybody's going to have to trust everybody else to commit perjury. If even one person cracks and starts looking for a deal, we're in an obstruction-of-justice situation."[48] This knowledge particularly worried Dean, who was squeamish about breaking the law, rather easily panicked, fearful of going to jail, and distrustful (with good cause) of Haldeman, Ehrlichman, and Colson. Magruder was simply a weak man, incapable of holding up under pressure. Media pressure, Hunt's demands for a payoff, awkward and obvious attempts by Nixon, Haldeman, Ehrlichman, and Colson to set Dean up, and fear of the weakness of others panicked Dean and Magruder, causing them to abandon the conspiracy.

Early on, one top official probably could have saved Nixon and his major aides by taking the fall for Watergate. The most obvious candidate would have been Mitchell. If Mitchell had taken the heat for the others, and if Hunt had been paid off, the investigation would have probably ended there. But while Mitchell was given many hints that his sacrifice would be noble, he was determined not to go to jail or to testify about his role in the break-in. Dean could not have taken the rap without taking Mitchell with him, and he had much less reason, and no less inclination, to do so.

Second, the cover-up failed because many of Nixon's aides were honorable people who would not participate in the conspiracy, or allow him to break or defy the law. After the departures of Colson, Haldeman, Ehrlichman, and Dean from the White House, there was no one among Nixon's top policy or legal aides who would deliberately lie for him or permit him to defy the law. While some of his aides counseled him to burn the tapes, fire Cox, and refuse court orders that could be appealed, all did so believing that Nixon was innocent and that he was acting within his rights and powers. When the tapes revealed that he had lied to them and to the country, his aides and attorneys conspired to force his resignation.

August 9, 1974: President Richard Nixon (right) leaves the White House after resigning from office the night before. Gerald Ford (left), who succeeded Nixon as President, pardoned Nixon of any wrongdoing in the Watergate case.

At first blush, Nixon probably considered defying the Supreme Court's July 24th decision, despite the fact that it was unanimous.[49] He quickly learned, however, that Haig, Garment,* and Buzhardt would not stand for it. The honorable people among Nixon's aides included conservatives and liberals, Democrats and Republicans. Some seemed to be particularly ill-cast for their role. Haig had originally attracted Nixon's attention because the President liked his "tough talk about 'pinkos' and 'peaceniks' and those queer, soft, left-leaning eggheads who went to Harvard and couldn't be counted on to storm the trenches in Asia."[50]

Third, the cover-up did not succeed because Nixon lacked decisiveness. Had Nixon simply burned the tapes, refused to appoint a special prosecutor,

*Leonard Garment, special counsel to the President.

and refused to allow his aides to testify before the Senate, he could have probably saved his top aides. Everyone, including Jaworski,[51] agrees that Nixon could have saved himself. The House Judiciary Committee's impeachment resolutions were based in part on the original seven subpoenaed tapes. Without the tapes, the House probably would not have had the evidence to build a case against Nixon and might not have launched an investigation. Without the tapes, the committee would certainly have been so slow to act that Nixon would have probably served out his term. Nixon's desire to posture as a law-abider, while he was breaking the law, was his downfall.

The cover-up failed because of a lack of mutual trust, unity, courage, and selflessness among those involved in the conspiracy.

Fourth, the conspiracy failed because it involved a specific crime. The national judicial system is well prepared to investigate criminal acts and to punish those involved. A tough judge could bring out the truth, the grand jury could call witnesses who could not invoke presidential privilege or attorney-client relationships, bargains could be struck, and immunity given. The crime involved was also well defined, and the consequences for conviction clear, especially to lawyers. Had the controversy involved only criminal abuse of power, it would have been more of a political than a legal problem and much more difficult to resolve.

Fifth, the conspiracy failed because it involved not just a crime but a particularly clumsy crime. Not only was the Watergate burglary botched (as was the Ellsberg burglary), but one of the arrested burglars, McCord, was an employee of the Nixon reelection committee who had known connections to two other administration employees, Hunt and Liddy. The burglars had $2,300 in cash on them, most in sequential $100 bills. The money was eventually traced to the reelection committee. One of the burglars had an address book with Hunt's name on it.

SHOULD THE PRESIDENCY BE CHANGED?

Proposals to alter the American Presidency have centered around attempts to strengthen its powers in relationship to Congress and efforts to restrict its general powers. Because of Watergate and the Vietnam War, proposals to limit the President's powers in recent years have been more widely debated than attempts to strengthen them.

Watergate, in fact, stimulated three major reforms: the Federal Election Campaign Act of 1974, providing optional public financing of presidential primaries and general elections; new, more stringent ethics codes in both the House and the Senate; and, late in 1978, an ethics bill requiring financial disclosure by top officials in all three branches of government. The latter act also places some restrictions on ex-government officials, establishes an Office of Government Ethics, and allows the attorney general to request the appointment of a special prosecutor (see Chapter 6).

All of these reforms are significant and impressive. The government is now much better prepared to limit, uncover, and prosecute corruption and conflict of interest. The Supreme Court's decision in *U.S.* v. *Nixon* also establishes an important precedent. The decision clearly places presidential actions within the criminal jurisdiction of the attorney general and limits the President's ability to withhold evidence in a criminal investigation.

On the negative side, the failure of Congress to define criminal abuse of power decreases its ability to control future Presidents who exceed their authority. This is particularly troublesome since Congress works so slowly. Congress was slow to get involved in Watergate, and once involved, its pace was laborious. If the Senate had been forced to try Nixon, Watergate would have dragged on for at least another six to twelve months. During this period, the nation would have been basically leaderless. Only Nixon's decision to resign saved the nation from an ordeal that may one day become a reality.

The reforms also failed to address Congress' refusal to pass legislation providing for public financing of congressional elections. Public financing of presidential but not congressional elections has simply stimulated influence-seekers to invest the funds in congressional candidates that they can no longer give to presidential contenders. This has significantly raised the cost of running for or staying in Congress, and has further compromised congressional members and candidates, who must raise large sums of money to direct their campaigns.[52] The extraordinary expenditures of many congressional races in 1978 attracted considerable media attention and will undoubtedly prompt new efforts to pass a campaign finance bill for Congress.

Watergate revealed a basic problem with the Twenty-fifth Amendment that has not been resolved or even considered. Those persons who worked for Nixon claim that for a period perhaps as long as five to seven months he was incapable of fully performing his duties as President of the United States. To remove the President from office even temporarily, however, would have undermined his defense strategy. It would have created the specter of a coup by the Vice-President and would have probably met resistance from Nixon, bringing Congress into the fray. Thus, while Nixon was incapacitated, his duties were either neglected or performed by unelected aides (such as Haig), who often were able to make important decisions with great discretion. Although it should not be easy to remove a President from office for political reasons, the Twenty-fifth Amendment provides far too little defense against rule by an emotionally or mentally disabled chief executive. The requirement that the Vice-President initiate the removal action is the most serious flaw because it may appear to be a self-serving act. An independent board, staffed perhaps in part by persons professionally qualified to judge the physical, mental, or emotional health of the President and restricted by statute, might be better.

The post-Watergate era revealed one last problem that simple reform could not remedy. The public's political apathy results in short memories. Four years after Nixon's resignation from the Presidency, an Associated Press-NBC news poll revealed that, in retrospect, 36 percent of the American public rated his presidential performance as either good or excellent.

Although it should not be easy to remove a President from office for political reasons, the Twenty-fifth Amendment provides far too little defense against rule by an emotionally or mentally disabled chief executive.

Congress' frustration with Johnson and Nixon over their handling of the Vietnam War and its disputes with Nixon over the budget and his impoundment of federal funds resulted in two measures restricting the President's powers. The first was the War Powers Act of 1973. Congress was displeased with Johnson and Nixon for being excluded from many decisions involving the Vietnam War, and it was afraid that Nixon was expanding the war. These sentiments finally led to a congressional decision in 1970 stipulating that no funds could be used to send ground troops into Cambodia or Laos. This unprecedented action was followed by the passage—over a veto by Nixon—of the War Powers Act in 1973.

Under the act, a President can commit troops only under three conditions:

1. if Congress officially declares war;
2. by specific authorization of Congress;
3. in a national emergency created by an attack on the United States or its armed forces.

If condition three exists, the President is required to submit a written report to Congress, explaining his actions. If Congress does not declare war within sixty days or authorize troop use, the President is required to withdraw the troops. If the President certifies to Congress that the safety of U.S. troops requires it, he can continue the troop commitment for an additional thirty days. At the end of the sixty-to-ninety-day period, Congress may, by concurrent resolution, direct the President to withdraw American troops. The act remains untested, and it does not keep Presidents from engaging in short-term interventions. It should, however, restrain Presidents from committing troops to major engagements unless they believe they can obtain the approval of Congress and the support of the nation.

The Budget Control and Impoundment Act of 1974 was the second congressional constraint on presidential power. It resulted from Congress' determination to have more control over the federal budget and from its anger over Nixon's abusive *impoundment* of funds appropriated by Congress. The act required Congress to establish a procedure for developing a budget, and then to see that individual committees responsible for appropriating and authorizing federal spending stay within this budget. Previously, Congress had received the President's budget, prepared under his direction by the Office of Management and Budget, in January, and had reacted to each section without having a proposed congressional budget to define its overall priorities or by which to evaluate the President's budget. The new act created a budget committee in each house to formulate a congressional budget. The budget committees work with individual committees to keep spending consistent with the comprehensive design. The new Congressional Budget Office (CBO) also makes economic assessments to give Congress a second opinion on anticipated economic growth, unemployment, inflation, income receipts, spending, and deficits (see Chapters 8 and 12).[53]

This act has given Congress much more authority over the budgetary process and has reduced the President's powers substantially. While the President's budget sets priorities and establishes a framework that Congress may largely operate within, Congress is now more capable of obtaining an overview of the total budget and of making the President's budget fit within its design. The act's impoundment provisions were a direct response to Nixon's abuse of a time-honored practice. Under a 1950 act, Presidents were allowed to *impound,* or withhold, some appropriated funds to save money and improve management. Truman, Eisenhower, Kennedy, and Johnson all impounded some funds, but the amounts were generally not large enough to cause a serious flap with Congress. Nixon not only impounded very large sums—some $18 billion—but also tried to convert these expenditures to his own priorities. Several court suits resulted. The Supreme Court eventually ruled that Nixon had exceeded his authority by trying to reorder spending priorities rather than save money or promote efficiency.[54]

The public's political apathy results in short memories. Four years after Nixon's resignation from the Presidency, an Associated Press-NBC news poll revealed that, in retrospect, 36 percent of the American public rated his presidential performance as either good or excellent.

Under the new act, if a President wants to rescind a spending decision, he must send a message to Congress requesting a rescission. Unless Congress passes a bill supporting the rescission within forty-five days, the President's request is officially denied. Clearly, this procedure makes it very hard for a President to rescind part of the budget. If a President wants only to defer part of the budget (temporarily delay spending), he must also submit a request to Congress. However, unlike rescission, a deferral goes into effect automatically unless either house passes a resolution disapproving it. Presidents are much more likely to have success in obtaining deferrals. The War Powers Act and the Budget Control and Impoundment Act were the only formal restraints placed on presidential powers as a result of the long struggle over Vietnam and the Watergate scandal.

CONCLUSIONS

The American Presidency is a paradoxical institution. It is at once a very powerful office and an office with many weaknesses. Presidents are expected to lead the nation, develop policy to deal with major social problems and guide it through Congress, represent the country in world affairs, and symbolize the strengths and values of the American political system. But there are many constraints within the political system which make it difficult for a President to play all these roles unless highly unusual conditions prevail. The major limitations on the President, however, probably result more from problems with Congress, the bureaucracy, and the public than from the office of the Presidency and its powers.

Footnotes

1. Thomas E. Cronin, *The State of the Presidency* (Boston: Little, Brown, 1975), p. 106.
2. See Cronin's discussion, *Ibid.*, pp. 23–51.
3. Clinton Rossiter, *The American Presidency* (New York: New American Library, 1960), p. 84.
4. *Ibid.*, pp. 68–69.
5. James David Barber, *The Presidential Character: Predicting Performance in the White House* (Englewood Cliffs, N.J.: Prentice-Hall, 1977), p. 458.
6. *Ibid.*, p. 458.
7. Cronin, *The State of the Presidency*, p. 5.
8. *Ibid.*, p. 9.
9. *Ibid.*, p. 4.
10. Theodore White, *The Making of the President 1968* (New York: Atheneum, 1969), p. 147.
11. See, for example, Grant McConnell, *Private Power and American Democracy* (New York: Vintage Books, 1966); and Theodore Lowi, *The End of Liberalism* (New York: Norton, 1969).
12. See "Executive Branch Conflicts of Interest," in *Common Cause* (Summer 1976), p. 21.
13. Cronin, *The State of the Presidency*, p. 198.
14. John W. Gardner, testimony before the Senate Government Operations Committee, reprinted in the *Congressional Record*, 92nd Cong., 1st sess. (June 3, 1971), p. 8140. Cited in Cronin, *The State of the Presidency*, p. 69.
15. Cronin, *The State of the Presidency*, p. 19.
16. Richard E. Neustadt, *Presidential Power: The Politics of Leadership* (New York: The New American Library, 1960), pp. 29–39.
17. Cronin, *The State of the Presidency*, p. 98.
18. See Doris Kearns, *Lyndon Johnson and the Great American Dream* (New York: The New American Library, 1976), pp. 244–62.
19. *Ibid.*, p. 130.
20. See Harrell R. Rodgers, Jr., "The Supreme Court and School Desegregation: Twenty Years Later," *Political Science Quarterly* (Winter 1974–75), pp. 751–76.

21. See Louis Fisher, *The Constitution Between Friends: Congress, the President and the Law* (New York: St. Martin's, 1958), pp. 42–43, 180–81.

22. Cronin, *The State of the Presidency*, pp. 71–73.

23. H. R. Haldeman, *The Ends of Power* (New York: Times Books, 1978), p. 155; John Dean, *Blind Ambition: The White House Years* (New York: Pocket Books, 1977), p. 198.

24. Theodore H. White, *Breach of Faith: The Fall of Richard Nixon* (New York: Dell, 1975), p. 24.

25. Bob Woodward and Carl Bernstein, *The Final Days* (New York: Avon, 1976).

26. White, *Breach of Faith*, p. 60.

27. Haldeman, *The Ends of Power*, pp. 51–63; Dean, *Blind Ambition*, pp. 22–55.

28. Haldeman, *The Ends of Power*, p. 65.

29. *Ibid.*, p. 112.

30. White, *Breach of Faith*, p. 211.

31. *Ibid.*, p. 211.

32. *Ibid.*, p. 23.

33. Dean, *Blind Ambition*, pp. 22–55.

34. Haldeman, *The Ends of Power*, p. 31.

35. Carl Bernstein and Bob Woodward, *All the President's Men* (New York: Warner, 1975), pp. 57–58.

36. Haldeman, *The Ends of Power*, p. 222.

37. This procedure was upheld by the district and appellate courts, both of which ruled that grand jury evidence could be turned over to Congress.

38. Haldeman, *The Ends of Power*, p. 182.

39. Bernstein and Woodward, *All the President's Men*, p. 209.

40. Dean, *Blind Ambition*, p. 14.

41. *Ibid.*, p. 107.

42. Haldeman, *The Ends of Power*, p. 307.

43. White, *Breach of Faith*, p. 320.

44. *Ibid.*, p. 14.

45. Haldeman, *The Ends of Power*, p. 310.

46. Richard Nixon, *RN: The Memoirs of Richard Nixon* (New York: Grosset and Dunlap, 1978), pp. 1051–52.

47. Dean, *Blind Ambition*, p. 194.

48. *Ibid.*, p. 165.

49. White, *Breach of Faith*, p. 17; Nixon, *RN*, p. 1052.

50. Woodward and Bernstein, *The Final Days*, p. 21.

51. Leon Jaworski, *The Right and the Power: The Prosecution of Watergate* (New York: Pocket Books, 1977), p. 164.

52. "House Races: More Money to Incumbents," *Congressional Quarterly*, October 29, 1979, p. 2299.

53. See Lance T. LeLoup, *Budgetary Politics: Dollars, Deficits, Decisions* (Brunswick, Ohio: King's Court Communications, 1977), pp. 126–51.

54. *Train* v. *City of New York*, 420 U.S. 35 (1975); *Train* v. *Campaign Clean Water*, 420 U.S. 136 (1975).

> Bureaucracy is like sin: we all know something about it, but only those who practice it enjoy it. . . . If you hold that all sex is sin, you simply mean you wish you never had been born; if you believe that all bureaucracies are degenerate, you are simply registering a protest against modern society.
>
> Brian Chapman

12

When the federal bureaucracy is discussed, it is usually talked about with concern and alarm. The specter of a strangling octopus is evoked, a sea of suffocating red tape is imagined, and a geometrically increasing army of tax-burdening, paper-shuffling, rule-expounding, nit-picking public menaces is described as one of life's major plagues. How did modern government spawn this malignancy?

The Federal Bureaucracy: A Government Within the Government

In truth, the bureaucracy has become an extremely costly, important, and powerful segment of our government. It has grown for mostly good reasons, and it provides thousands of necessary and important services. But it is often too powerful—subject to too little oversight by other levels of government, like Congress, to which it is supposedly subordinate—and it is often impervious to public influence.

The modern bureaucracy is the child of the *positive state,* a government that provides vast services to its citizenry and plays a major role in shaping the economic, social, and political structures. Modern government plays this expansive role in our lives because we demand that it do so. The public now expects the government to regulate and moderate economic cycles; to play a major role in cleaning up and protecting our water and air; to insure that food will be sanitary and nutritious; to protect against consumer fraud, common crime, threats by foreign armies, and hundreds of other evils and inconveniences.

The government did not simply assume authority over increasing aspects of our lives; it did so in response to demands from big business, farmers, consumers, environmentalists, the poor, minorities, and hundreds of other

Kaiser Aluminum Company employees stand next to the records and forms that the firm needs to meet the requirements of the federal bureaucracy for conducting one year's business.

groups. As Meier says: "Powerful bureaus do not develop because bureaucrats conspire to bureaucratize American life. Rather powerful bureaucracies develop in response to environmental demand."[1]

The functions of the modern *bureaucracy* can be divided into five categories:

1. the provision of basic national services such as the development, maintenance, and supervision of the nation's defense, supervision and subsidization of interstate highways, postal services, and diplomatic relations with foreign nations;
2. protection and services to powerful interest groups such as business, labor, and farmers;
3. aid and regulation of the economic and monetary systems;
4. regulation of products and services to protect the public interest; and
5. protection and services to groups deprived by poverty, illness, unemployment, discrimination, and other misfortunes.[2]

Services and activities of this magnitude require an extremely large, skilled, costly, and complex bureaucracy. However, as noted below, if the federal government abandoned all functions except maintaining the nation's defense and providing absolutely essential services, it would still be huge.

STRUCTURE AND SIZE
OF THE FEDERAL BUREAUCRACY

The size of the federal bureaucracy has increased with the population of the nation and the functions of the federal government. In 1816 the federal government had 4,479 employees. By 1871 it employed 50,155 persons; by 1931, 596,745. The government expanded enormously during World War II, dropped considerably after the war, and has not changed very much in size since. In 1979 the federal government employed 2.8 million persons, 10 percent less than it employed in 1967 and 25 percent less than at the end of World War II.[3] Only about 12 percent of all federal employees are located in Washington; the rest are spread across the nation. The federal bureaucracy is dwarfed by state and local government bureaucracies, which employ about 12 million persons.

The federal government's employees are spread among thirteen cabinet-level departments; some 150 independent agencies, independent regulatory commissions, government corporations, and bureaus; and about 1400 temporary advisory commissions. Figure 12.1 shows the major branches of government, the Cabinet-level departments, and some of the major permanent agencies, bureaus, commissions, and corporations.

FIGURE 12.1
The United States Government

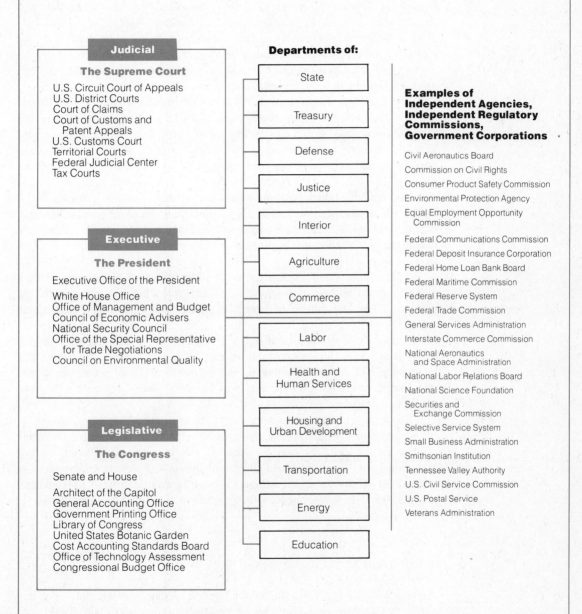

Judicial

The Supreme Court

U.S. Circuit Court of Appeals
U.S. District Courts
Court of Claims
Court of Customs and
  Patent Appeals
U.S. Customs Court
Territorial Courts
Federal Judicial Center
Tax Courts

Executive

The President

Executive Office of the President

White House Office
Office of Management and Budget
Council of Economic Advisers
National Security Council
Office of the Special Representative
  for Trade Negotiations
Council on Environmental Quality

Legislative

The Congress

Senate and House

Architect of the Capitol
General Accounting Office
Government Printing Office
Library of Congress
United States Botanic Garden
Cost Accounting Standards Board
Office of Technology Assessment
Congressional Budget Office

Departments of:

State

Treasury

Defense

Justice

Interior

Agriculture

Commerce

Labor

Health and
Human Services

Housing and
Urban Development

Transportation

Energy

Education

**Examples of
Independent Agencies,
Independent Regulatory
Commissions,
Government Corporations**

Civil Aeronautics Board

Commission on Civil Rights

Consumer Product Safety Commission

Environmental Protection Agency

Equal Employment Opportunity
  Commission

Federal Communications Commission

Federal Deposit Insurance Corporation

Federal Home Loan Bank Board

Federal Maritime Commission

Federal Reserve System

Federal Trade Commission

General Services Administration

Interstate Commerce Commission

National Aeronautics
  and Space Administration

National Labor Relations Board

National Science Foundation

Securities and
  Exchange Commission

Selective Service System

Small Business Administration

Smithsonian Institution

Tennessee Valley Authority

U.S. Civil Service Commission

U.S. Postal Service

Veterans Administration

Source: *U.S. Government Manual*, 1977, p. 280.

The Cabinet departments

As noted in Chapters 11 and 13 (see Table 11.1 and Figure 13.1), the bulk of federal employees are employed by the thirteen Cabinet-level departments and two of the largest independent agencies—the Postal Service and the Veterans Administration. In fact, the Department of Defense—with one million employees—the Postal Service, and the Veterans Administration combined employ almost 70 percent of all federal employees.[4] Contrary to popular belief, only a very small percentage of all federal employees work for social welfare agencies—probably no more than 10 percent.

The thirteen Cabinet-level departments are organized around major international and domestic policy needs (see Figure 12.1). For example, the Treasury Department collects taxes, prints money, and finances the public debt. The Department of Transportation was created in 1967 to coordinate the nation's transportation programs and promote a comprehensive transportation strategy. In 1979 the Department of Education was created, and the Department of Health, Education, and Welfare was renamed the Department of Health and Human Services. The Department of Health and Human Services oversees the major health-care programs (Medicare and Medicaid), administers health research funds, and administers social security and a number of major welfare programs.

At the request of President Carter, the Department of Energy was created in 1977 in the hope of developing a unified approach to the nation's energy problems. The Department of Justice comprises the legal arm of the federal government, representing it in tax cases, federal criminal cases, federal civil cases, antitrust suits, and civil-rights matters. Three of the departments are clientele agencies, representing the interests of specific groups. These are the Departments of Labor, Commerce, and Agriculture. Labor represents workers, Commerce looks after the needs of business, and Agriculture represents the nation's farmers.

The Cabinet departments vary greatly in size, but all are large enough to be very complex organizations that can be supervised only with substantial efforts. Figure 12.2, for example, shows the organizational structure for the Department of Agriculture. As the chart shows, the department provides a wide range of services and is complex enough to make it difficult for Congress and the President to oversee its vast spectrum of activities, large and small.

Independent executive agencies

There are approximately sixty federal agencies located outside the major departments. They report directly to the President, who appoints and can remove the agency heads. The *independent agencies* exercise numerous important functions. Included among these agencies are the Central Intelligence Agency,

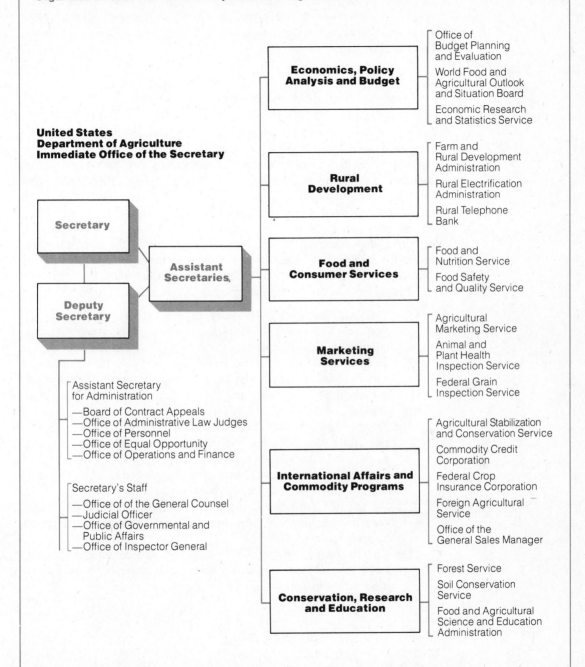

FIGURE 12.2
Organization Chart for the U.S. Department of Agriculture

United States
Department of Agriculture
Immediate Office of the Secretary

Secretary

Deputy Secretary

Assistant Secretaries,

Assistant Secretary
for Administration

—Board of Contract Appeals
—Office of Administrative Law Judges
—Office of Personnel
—Office of Equal Opportunity
—Office of Operations and Finance

Secretary's Staff

—Office of of the General Counsel
—Judicial Officer
—Office of Governmental and
Public Affairs
—Office of Inspector General

Economics, Policy Analysis and Budget

Office of
Budget Planning
and Evaluation

World Food and
Agricultural Outlook
and Situation Board

Economic Research
and Statistics Service

Rural Development

Farm and
Rural Development
Administration

Rural Electrification
Administration

Rural Telephone
Bank

Food and Consumer Services

Food and
Nutrition Service

Food Safety
and Quality Service

Marketing Services

Agricultural
Marketing Service

Animal and
Plant Health
Inspection Service

Federal Grain
Inspection Service

International Affairs and Commodity Programs

Agricultural Stabilization
and Conservation Service

Commodity Credit
Corporation

Federal Crop
Insurance Corporation

Foreign Agricultural
Service

Office of the
General Sales Manager

Conservation, Research and Education

Forest Service

Soil Conservation
Service

Food and Agricultural
Science and Education
Administration

Source: *U.S. Government Manual*, 1977.

the National Aeronautics and Space Administration, the Office of Personnel Management, the Environmental Protection Agency, the General Services Administration, the Small Business Administration, the National Labor Relations Board, the National Science Foundation, and the National Foundation for the Arts and Humanities.

Independent regulatory commissions

The *independent regulatory commissions* are hybrid institutions created by Congress to deal with complex issues affecting the public interest. They were designed to regulate areas of the public sector and often have been granted extensive rule-making and licensing power by Congress. They decide such issues as who will receive licenses to operate a television station, open an airline route, or build a pipeline. They also make decisions about airline and railroad rates. To carry out their duties, Congress has given them judicial, legislative, and executive powers, making them some of the most interesting institutions in the government. The members of these commissions are appointed by the President, but they report directly to Congress.

The major independent regulatory commissions are listed below:[5]

The Interstate Commerce Commission. Established in 1887, this commission sets and supervises rates for railroads, truck companies, bus companies, and oil pipelines.

The Federal Trade Commission. Established in 1914, this commission was designed to protect consumers from price-fixing, deceptive advertising, false packaging, mislabeling, unfair competition, and other abuses.

The Federal Power Commission. Created in 1930, this commission sets rates for electric utilities, hydroelectric projects, national gas companies, and interstate gas pipelines.

The Federal Communications Commission. Established in 1934, this commission issues licenses for television and radio stations and regulates the use of air frequencies by air transportation, police, and citizen operators. It also sets rates for interstate telephone and telegraph communications.

The Civil Aeronautics Board. Created in 1938, this commission sets airline rates and fares, and passes upon airline requests for merger and stock acquisitions.

Government corporations

Some federal agencies are actually government-owned economic enterprises. These agencies are under presidential control. Examples include the U.S. Postal Service; the Federal Deposit Insurance Corporation, which protects bank deposits; the Federal Crop Insurance Corporation, protecting farmers against crop losses; and the Tennessee Valley Authority, which builds and administers hydroelectric dams and power plants serving an eight-state area.

Appointment of civil servants

Until 1883 all employees of the federal government were appointed by the President and members of his party (with Senate approval). This system of *political patronage* rewarded the winning presidential party, providing it with jobs to be passed out to the party faithful. This tradition became known as the *spoils system* and attracted much criticism. Critics pointed out that competent employees were often replaced with incompetent supporters of the winning party.

In 1883 the U.S. Civil Service was created to establish a merit system by which federal employees could be hired, promoted, and rewarded. Currently, almost 70 percent of all federal employees are hired under the *merit system*. These employees qualify for their positions by competitive exams and are generally paid according to their ranking on a job classification scale that ranges

An aerial view of the Pentagon, headquarters for the U.S. Defense Department. The Defense Department employs about 1 million people, more than six times as many as the next biggest executive department.

from GS-1 to GS-18. When a federal position covered by the merit system becomes available, the agency in which the job is located receives a list of the three most eligible applicants, from which one may be chosen.

The modern bureaucracy is the child of the positive state, a government that provides vast services to its citizenry and plays a major role in shaping the economic, social, and political structures.

To further protect federal employees from partisan forces, the *Hatch Act* prohibits them from actively participating in a political campaign or running for public office. Federal employees may, however, contribute money to a campaign, vote, wear a campaign button, and participate in other normal political activities.

Federal employees are also protected from job loss for partisan reasons and cannot be fired except for incompetence, neglect of their duties, or other serious reasons. A civil service appointment is not, however, a guarantee of lifetime employment by the federal government. In any given year, almost one-fourth of all merit employees voluntarily or involuntarily leave the government.

The President's appointment powers are currently limited to the Cabinet heads, his major assistants in the White House Office and the Executive Office of the President, sub-Cabinet officials, agency and commission heads, and ambassadorships. These appointments number only about 2,500, but include the most important positions in the bureaucracy. In addition, many of the President's appointees will be able to appoint their aides and the chief policy-makers in the departments and agencies. The President hopes that his appointees will be able to provide the organization and leadership necessary to rally the bureaucracy behind his programs. As noted in Chapter 13, however, there are many reasons why this strategy often does not work.

THE ROLE AND INDEPENDENCE OF THE BUREAUCRACY

Bureaucracies are important in part because they engage in a wide spectrum of activities that affect all aspects of modern life. Bureaucracies provide a very diverse range of public services, regulate many areas of business and individual behavior, and collect and redistribute public wealth. Bureaucratic authority comes from Congress and from executive powers specified in the Constitution. Congress provides most of the authority by creating agencies and departments, and then passing laws for them to administer.

When considering legislation that empowers the bureaucracy to administer, implement, and evaluate policies, Congress normally frames a rather broad law, giving the bureaucracy considerable discretion to develop guidelines and rules to enforce the policy. This discretion generally gives the bureaucracy great power. In developing the rules and procedures to implement a policy, the bureaucracy engages in policy-making. The policy-making powers are often on a small scale, but the cumulative impact of bureaucratic rule-making can be quite significant. In any given year, Congress will enact about 600 public laws. The federal bureaucracy will adopt around 6,000 administrative rules—rules that affect millions of people.[6]

There are four reasons why Congress gives the bureaucracy such extensive powers. First, no matter how hard it tried, Congress could never pass laws that were specific enough to deal with all aspects of the vast range of policy areas over which the federal government currently has jurisdiction. In addition, laws can never be written in enough detail to cover every possibility that might arise. Thus, Congress passes fairly broad laws, leaving their conversion to operating form, their implementation, and, in some cases, even their interpretation to the bureaucracy.

Second, the vast range of topics over which the federal government now exercises jurisdiction prohibits Congress from carefully monitoring every aspect of public policy. Thus, Congress purposely vests the responsibility for many actions in agencies to free itself of the burden.

Bureaucracies provide a very diverse range of public services, regulate many areas of business and individual behavior, and collect and redistribute public wealth.

Third, the magnitude of some tasks is so large that only the bureaucracy could carry them out. For example, only the bureaucracy could organize and implement tasks such as keeping Social Security records on 150 million current and retired workers and providing benefit checks to 34 million retired or disabled persons per month.

Fourth, Congress recognizes that many public policies involve extremely complex topics that require expert guidance and administration. For example, only experts can establish the procedures for testing the safety of drugs, the toxicity of pesticides, the long-range hazards of radiation, or the adequacy of defense weapons. Each of these four factors causes Congress to give discretion and authority to the bureaucracy, and the cumulative impact makes it quite powerful.

The power of the bureaucracy is enhanced by the fact that in administering programs, making rules, granting contracts and licenses, and providing services, the various agencies develop alliances with, and supporters among,

"I'm sorry, dear, but you knew I was a bureaucrat when you married me."

Drawing by Weber © 1980; The New Yorker Magazine.

powerful members of Congress and private interest groups. For example, the Department of Agriculture may acquire powerful supporters among farm or agribusiness groups and among those members of Congress who have the most power over agricultural matters and appropriations. The Department of Defense may develop alliances with defense contractors and influential members of Congress. These alliances can operate to the mutual benefit of all three groups, giving the bureaucracy a chance to increase resources, autonomy, and power. Meier discusses how this alliance works:

> Together Congress, interest groups, and bureaus have all the necessary resources to satisfy each other's needs. Bureaus supply services or goods to organized groups but need resources to do so. Congressional committees supply the bureau with resources but need electoral political support to remain in office and political support to win policy disputes in Congress. The interest group provides the political support that the member of Congress needs, but the interest group needs government goods and services to satisfy members' demands. The result is a triparte relationship that has all the resources necessary to operate in isolation from politics if no great crises occur.[7]

These relationships enhance the power of the bureaucracy and the interests of the other members of the alliance, but the consequences for executive, congressional, or public control of the bureaucracy may be quite negative. Obviously, if bureaus develop independent resources and power, accountability may be difficult or impossible to achieve. Many experts believe that lack of accountability is growing:

There is no government today that can still claim control of its bureaucracy and of its various agencies. Government agencies are all becoming autonomous, ends in themselves, and directed by their own desire for power, their own rationale, their own narrow vision rather than by national policy.[8]

The alliances that give bureaus independence also frequently pervert their purpose. Rather than operating in the public or national interest, a bureau may promote only the interests of its clientele group. Thus, the Food and Drug Administration may become the advocate of the drug manufacturing companies. The Civil Aeronautics Board may become the captive of the major airlines. The Department of Agriculture may become the tool of agri-business, making rules that discriminate against family farms and the consumer. The evidence is overwhelming, in fact, that bureaus are often the captive representative of special interests.[9] Rourke charges that "in its most developed form the relationship between an interest group and an administrative agency is so close that it is difficult to know where the group leaves off and the agency begins."[10]

Presidents Ford and Carter both argued that the Civil Aeronautics Board, the Interstate Commerce Commission, and the Federal Communications Commission had all developed relationships with clientele groups that restricted competition and artificially inflated prices, needlessly costing the public millions of dollars a year. Efforts by both of these Presidents to deregulate the trucking and airline industries were vigorously resisted by those industries because regulation had actually become a form of protection with agreed-upon high profits, government subsidies, and guarantees of freedom from competition.

CONTROLLING THE BUREAUCRACY

Can bureaucracies as powerful and large as those at the federal level be held publicly accountable and be efficiently and effectively administered? Probably the best way to answer this question would be to say that they can be made more accountable and effective than they currently are.[11] It can be assumed that a bureau subjected to effective oversight will do its job better. This is not to say, however, that all bureaus are ineffective and wasteful.

The evidence indicates that government bureaucracies are no more inefficient than bureaus found in the private sector. In fact, they often work very well. Government bureaucracies often carry out massive activities in a highly efficient manner. For example, in a relatively short time period the National Aeronautics and Space Administration was able to put the American space program on the map and a man on the moon. The Department of Defense and other agencies effectively house, clothe, and feed two million men and women in the armed services. The Internal Revenue Service in the Treasury

Department processes millions of tax returns a year. The Federal Aviation Administration has greatly improved the safety record of airlines and has almost ended skyjacking.

Even bureaucratic *red tape* is not as villainous as it is made out to be. Some of the red tape that businesses and the public complain about is designed, often effectively, to protect the public from fraud, unsafe products, unfair competition, or arbitrary actions by officials.[12] Much of the so-called red tape, therefore, is sensible and functional.

In administering programs, making rules, granting contracts and licenses, and providing services, the various agencies develop alliances with, and supporters among, powerful members of Congress and private interest groups.

For anyone who believes that government bureaucracy is inferior to private bureaucracy, a few reminders might be in order. Big business rarely carries out activities that are as massive and complex as those handled by federal bureaucracies. Also, businesses make many serious errors in terms of products (e.g., the Edsel), the quality of products (e.g., automobile performance records), and investment and management. In recent years, businesses such as Lockheed, Chrysler, and Penn Central have been managed so poorly that only government aid could save them from financial collapse. A recent study by Professor Robert Lehrer raised serious questions about the soundness of much business management. Lehrer found that the productivity rate of white-collar workers is only 40 to 60 percent of their potential. He found that because of poor management many white-collar workers are engaged in jobs that do not contribute to company goals. Often they do not even know the goals. Lehrer estimated that "50 percent of the productivity shortfall of white-collar workers comes from failure to relate the activities of the worker to the company's mission. Only 20 percent of the fault related to how efficiently the worker does his job."[13]

There are many ways that the federal bureaucracy can be made more efficient and accountable. For example, in Chapter 11 we surveyed the President's ability to control the bureaucracy. As noted there, Presidents have more control if they appoint effective administrators with leadership skills to the top policy-making positions in the bureaus, make their program goals clear, devote considerable time to the formulation and implementation of their goals, and monitor the impact of programs to iron out problems that are limiting progress.

Presidents vary considerably in their ability to manage the bureaucracy. They are often inhibited by a lack of adequate program information, too little time to deal with all programs, and the power of bureaucracies to go their own way because of their interest group and congressional support. To deal with these problems, Presidents should be allowed to appoint more administrative heads—up to 5,000, rather than the current 2,500—and should be given broader reorganization powers. Since reorganization often helps a President make bureaus responsible to him, it greatly increases his control.

Many critics feel that Congress is far too lax about its responsibility to oversee the bureaucracy. Congress, of course, shares this responsibility—called *oversight*—with the executive branch and has its best opportunity to do this during its annual review of each agency's programs and budget requests. Congress probably is too lax, but as the activities and budget of the bureaucracy expand, the task becomes more awesome. In addition, the value of Congress' annual evaluation of agency activities is diluted because the committees often have working relationships with the agencies under their jurisdiction. They also have a vested interest in seeing that the agency continues, and even expands, its current activities.

Since Congress could never hope to conduct a comprehensive evaluation of more than selected agencies each year, and since political and interest-group alliances often make a sham of congressional oversight, alternative oversight techniques are necessary. One alternative is to create agencies to conduct evaluation studies that would be publicly reported to Congress. The General Accounting Office (GAO) was created for this purpose. The GAO is quite active,

A congressional budget committee meets to review federal programs and budget requests.

completing up to one hundred audits a month. Many of its audits report performance failures or deficiencies and lead to program or organization revisions. The high quality of the GAO's work and its expertise make it one of the most respected of all federal agencies. Students of bureaucracy generally believe that oversight could be improved by expanding the GAO so that more performance audits could be conducted.

An oversight alternative frequently suggested by consumer groups is adoption of sunset legislation. *Sunset laws* limit the life of agencies. In its classic form, a sunset law would authorize agencies for a number of years; at the end of that time period, they would cease to exist unless they received a new authorization. The intent is to force Congress to periodically evaluate agencies to determine if they are still performing necessary services. Advocates argue that programs and agencies (not whole departments) should be subjected to sunset laws. They believe that authorization should be designed to allow Congress to conduct a comprehensive evaluation of most programs every five to ten years. Despite the obvious merits of the proposal, many members of Congress have resisted adoption because they fear that their own pet agencies and programs might be allowed to die.

To overcome resistance to sunset legislation, proponents introduced a new version in 1979. The new proposal would require a committee in each house to annually draw up a list of bureaus, agencies, and programs and decide which of them needed review. Those chosen would be reviewed, and recommendations would be made as to whether the programs should be retained, modified, or terminated. A program could be terminated only by majority vote of both houses of Congress. This proposal, which is somewhat less threatening than a traditional sunset law, gained considerable support in the House in 1979.

Another alternative developed in Europe is the concept of a public or consumer representative, known as an *ombudsman*.[14] This program simply establishes an agency to which the public can turn for aid in dealing with the bureaucracy. As developed in Europe, the ombudsman deals with fairly minor problems, but several states have adopted the program and considerably expanded the services and scope of aid provided.[15] While members of Congress often provide constituents with aid in dealing with the bureaucracy, an ombudsman program does hold the potential of providing the public with additional needed services that would make the bureaucracy more responsive.

One last method by which the bureau can be checked is by citizen groups. There are literally thousands of groups that scrutinize the activities of one or more government agencies. They may be consumer groups such as Common Cause, one of the Nader organizations, an environmental group, or a specialized organization representing a specific interest such as neglected children, tobacco growers, or unwed mothers. These groups often release reports on specific agencies, and lobby and testify before Congress. Such activities tend to bring attention to agency actions. In so doing, they provide an oversight function.

CONCLUSIONS

Because of the extremely diverse functions it performs and because of its extensive rule-making authority, the federal bureaucracy is an extremely important part of the federal government. While the bureaucracy undoubtedly deserves more praise than it receives, it is often poorly supervised by other federal officials. Frequently it does not represent the public interest as well as it represents the needs of special interests. Because the powers of the bureaucracy will continue to expand in response to public pressures for more services, a clear challenge in the future will be to devise methods to better supervise and hold accountable the vast bureaucracy.

Footnotes

1. Kenneth J. Meier, *Politics and The Bureaucracy: Policymaking in the Fourth Branch of Government* (North Scituate, Mass.: Duxbury, 1979), p. 67.
2. See Francis Rourke, *Bureaucracy, Politics, and Public Policy* (Boston: Little, Brown, 1976).
3. Meier, *Politics and the Bureaucracy*, p. 31.
4. See *The United States Budget in Brief, Fiscal Year 1980,* Office of Management and Budget, p. 84.
5. See Marver Bernstein, *Regulating Business Through Independent Commission* (Princeton: Princeton University Press, 1955); Louis Kohlmeier, *The Regulators* (New York: Harper & Row, 1970); Robert Burkhardt, *The Federal Aviation Administration* (New York: Praeger, 1967); Robert Fellmeth, *The Interstate Commerce Commission* (New York: Grossman, 1970).
6. M. W. Kirst, *Government Without Passing Laws* (Chapel Hill: University of North Carolina Press, 1969).
7. Meier, *Politics and Bureaucracy,* p. 51.
8. Peter F. Drucker, *The Age of Discontinuity* (New York: Harper & Row, 1969), p. 220.
9. See Theodore Lowi, *The End of Liberalism* (New York: Norton, 1969); Grant McConnell, *Private Power and American Democracy* (New York: Vintage Books, 1966); and Lester M. Solomon and Gary L. Walmsley, "The Federal Bureaucracy—Responsive to Whom?" (Paper presented at the annual meeting of the Midwest Political Science Association, Chicago, May 1–3, 1975.)
10. Rourke, *Bureaucracy, Politics and Public Policy,* p. 15.
11. See Herman Finer, "Administrative Responsibility in Democratic Government," *Public Administration Review* 1 (Summer 1941): 335–50.
12. Peter M. Blau and Marshall W. Meyer, *Bureaucracy in Modern Society* (New York: Random House, 1971).
13. "White Collar Output Shows Room to Grow," *The Houston Post,* October 10, 1979, p. 3A.
14. Stanley V. Anderson, ed., *Ombudsman for American Government* (Englewood Cliffs: Prentice-Hall, 1968).
15. See William Angus and Milton Kaplan, "The Ombudsman and Local Government," in Stanley V. Anderson, ed., *Ombudsman for American Government* (Englewood Cliffs: Prentice-Hall, 1968).

Financing government and its vast activities is a complex political process that reflects entrenched political power, partisan politics, priorities, and goals.[1] It is also the single most expensive item in most of our lives. The size of American government and the extensive range of services it provides explain this. In 1979 there were 82,000 federal, state, and local governing bodies in America, and over 500,000 elected public officials. The federal government employed 2.8 million civilian employees in eighty departments and agencies, not counting more than 2 million military personnel. State and local governments employed 12.3 million persons. Another 30 to 50 million persons received all or part of their income from government contracts. In 1979 governments at all levels directly employed about 18 percent of the total American work force.

13

Dollars, Deficits, and Governmental Finance

Table 13.1 shows the basic distribution of federal civilian employees throughout the government in recent years. The figures show the relative size of the three branches of the federal government, which in turn gives some idea of its commitment to various activities. The Department of Defense, for example, employs over a million nonmilitary employees. That is twenty-five times the number working in the legislative branch, more than six times as many as the next biggest executive department, and more than all the other executive departments put together. More people plan and execute defense strategy, in fact, than the combined total of people who deliver our mail, formulate our laws, administer justice, and plan transportation, energy, and labor policy.

The vast size of the military sector is only the most obvious example of the priorities reflected in government spending. As presidential administrations come and go, the priorities of government change to some extent, reflecting differences in political philosophy about the type and size of the role the federal government should play in all our lives. A Democratic administration, for example, can generally be counted on in peacetime to spend more on social-welfare goals, while a Republican administration can be expected to cut back

Social Security programs are one example of the vast range of expensive services provided by the federal government. In 1980, Social Security payroll deductions contributed about 30 percent of every tax dollar.

on social-welfare expenditures and increase military spending. Although the parties shift priorities somewhat, neither has had much success at reducing the size or cost of government.

Just as administrations attempt to make the kinds of expenditures in the *federal budget* reflect their political philosophies, the President and Congress try to make monetary and tax policies reflect to some extent their priorities and philosophy.[2] As noted in Chapter 7, monetary and tax policies are the key to Keynesian economics. Within the framework of Keynesian economics, a presidential decision to pursue a balanced, deficit, or surplus budget reveals the administration's priorities and goals for unemployment, inflation, and economic growth. The budget and the tax policies it is based on, in other words, are major strategies of administrations—strategies which are critical to most other policy goals.

TABLE 13.1

The Federal Civilian Bureaucracy: June 1977

Branch	Number of Employees
Executive	2,840,149
Legislative	40,715
Judicial	12,471
Total	**2,893,335**

Executive Departments	Number of Employees	Largest Independent Agencies	Number of Employees
Defense	1,008,690	Postal Service	658,390
Health, Education and Welfare	159,469	Veterans Administration	224,178
Agriculture	131,756	General Services Administration	37,786
Treasury	127,321	Tennessee Valley Authority	35,736
Interior	87,437	National Aeronautics and Space Administration	25,613
Transportation	76,177		
Justice	53,259		
Commerce	39,661		
State	30,578		
Housing and Urban Development	17,948		
Labor	17,096		

Source: U.S. Civil Service Commission. The Department of Energy was created in 1978 and employed 19,000 persons in 1979. In 1979, the Department of Education was established and the Department of Health, Education and Welfare was renamed the Department of Health and Human Services.

THE BUDGET PROCESS

The federal budget cycle consists of a series of complex stages spread over a number of years. The budget must be formulated, submitted to Congress for authorization and fund appropriation, executed, and finally audited. From start to finish, the process takes three years for any one fiscal year. The President and his assistants are responsible for the formulation of the budget. The President's agent in this process is the Office of Management and Budget (OMB). OMB has existed since 1921, but until 1970 it was known as the Bureau of the Budget. In addition to preparing the federal budget, this powerful bureau monitors agency budgeting, engages in management and planning activities, and serves as a clearinghouse for all legislative proposals.

Working with the President and the executive agencies, OMB completes its preparation of the budget in about nine months.[3] The budget it puts together consists of the approved budget for each agency, which reflects presidential priorities. These priorities include decisions on total spending, tax changes, *deficits* or *surpluses,* and new program and spending initiatives. OMB often has to slash requests to make agency goals balance with presidential priorities. Once formulated, the budget is presented to Congress in January each year.

In formulating the budget, the President and OMB must make certain assumptions about the cost of maintaining current levels of spending and about the state of the economy in forthcoming years. These estimates are made for the next five years and constitute the current service budget, which is also submitted to Congress by November 10 each year.

Table 13.2 shows some of the economic estimates made by OMB in 1978 for fiscal years 1979–1983. Notice that OMB attempts to estimate yearly Gross National Product (GNP), personal income, wages and salaries, corporate profits, the consumer price index, unemployment rates, and interest rates on treasury bills. The President and OMB use the data to inform their budget decisions, while Congress uses them to evaluate the President's budget. The Congressional Budget Office (CBO), a research agency in the legislative branch, formulates a current policy budget which provides Congress with an assessment of current expenditures and with economic estimates based on congressional rather than presidential assumptions.

Until 1974 Congress' role in the budget process was limited because it did not have an independent source of data. Therefore, it had to depend upon presidential recommendations, OMB data, and agency testimony. Congressional overview was also highly fragmented. The standing committees and their subcommittees (see Chapter 12) made budget decisions without inter-committee or house coordination. To deal with these problems and President Nixon's impoundment of funds, Congress in 1974 passed the Budget Control and Impoundment Act. With this act, Congress reasserted its influence over the budget, placed restraints on presidential impoundment of appropriated funds (see Chapter 11), and established a procedure to coordinate congressional budget decisions.

TABLE 13.2
OMB Estimates for the Federal Budget: 1979–1983*

Item	1979	1980	1981	1982	1983
Gross National Product (current dollars):	$2,335	$2,587	$2,858	$3,133	$3,400
Constant (1972) dollars:	$1,467	1,537	1,614	1,690	1,761
Incomes (Current dollars):					
Personal income	$1,892	2,095	2,315	2,538	2,754
Wages and salaries	1,219	1,363	1,521	1,670	1,812
Corporate profits	217	245	274	301	326
Consumer Price Index	6.1	5.7	5.2	4.7	4.2
Unemployment rates (%)	5.9	5.4	5.0	4.5	4.1
Interest rate, 91-day Treasury bills (%)	6.1	6.1	6.1	5.8	5.3

Source: Fiscal 1979 Budget
*Dollar amounts are in billions.

The act established a budget committee in each house to coordinate congressional authorization and appropriations. After the President delivers the State of the Union message, the budget committees hold hearings on the budget and analyze information on anticipated economic conditions and national needs. The standing committees—both authorization and appropriation—submit reviews and estimates of acceptable expenditures to the budget committees. By April 15, the budget committees coordinate all the data and produce a proposed budget that recommends spending ceilings and priorities, estimates anticipated revenues, and predicts deficits or surpluses. The budget is submitted to each house; once accepted by vote, it is known as the First Concurrent Resolution. This first resolution, however, is only a goal. In July the President sends Congress a revised budget that takes into consideration any alterations in the economy or anticipated spending needs.

Throughout the summer, federal agencies appear before the appropriation and authorization committees to defend their budget requests, justify their programs, and discuss anticipated future activities. By mid-September, the budget committees hopefully have again coordinated all data on spending into a second budget. This one reaffirms or revises the estimates contained in the first resolution. The second resolution is voted on by each house. Then, differences between the houses are worked out by a conference committee. Once the differences are worked out, each house votes to accept the second resolution, which is binding.

After the binding resolution is passed, the budget committees issue instructions to the standing committees on how they can make their budget decisions consistent with the second resolution. This may include lowering appropriations or raising or lowering revenues. This process is called reconciliation. On October 1 the new fiscal year begins.

In its first year of operation, the new budget process worked well. Congress missed a few deadlines but managed to coordinate budget actions much better and exercised a larger role in the budgetary process than in the past.[4] In subsequent years, Congress has had additional problems meeting deadlines, but has still managed to maintain more coordination and control over the budget as a result of the new process. The figures below show the various decisions made by Congress in 1978 on the fiscal 1979 budget, which went into effect October 1, 1978 (the figures are in billions of dollars).[5]

	Budget Authority	Outlays	Revenues	Deficit
First budget resolution	$568.85	$498.8	$447.9	$50.9
Administration re-estimates (July)	571.4	496.6	448.2	48.5
House	561.0	489.8	450.0	39.8
Senate	557.7	489.5	447.2	42.3
Conference agreement	555.65	487.5	448.7	38.8
Second budget resolution	555.65	487.5	448.7	38.8

Notice that over the course of the congressional review, outlays were reduced by some $11 billion, and the anticipated deficit declined by some $12 billion. The decline began with the President's July re-estimates but resulted primarily from congressional slashes in spending. Both houses approved about $7 billion less in outlays, and the conference committee reduced the total by another $4 billion. One result of the review process, then, was to tighten federal expenditures.

At the beginning of the fiscal year, OMB apportions funds to agencies and departments for expenditures. The agencies must align their operations and spending with the budget approved for them. After the fiscal year, the General Accounting Office (GAO) selectively audits agency and department activities to make certain that expenditures are consistent with budget guidelines and that funds have not been wasted. GAO reports its findings to OMB, Congress, and the audited agency.

Financing government and its vast activities is a complex political process that reflects entrenched political power, partisan politics, priorities, and goals.

RECEIPTS AND EXPENDITURES

As the figures above show, the size of the federal budget is very large. In fiscal 1980, outlays exceeded a half trillion dollars. Decisions about where the budget revenues will come from have a very significant impact on individual prosperity and on the distribution of wealth in society. The sources of federal receipts have changed over the last twenty years; a larger share of the budget burden is now placed on individuals, especially middle-income citizens.

Table 7.2 (Chapter 7) shows the sources of budget receipts for fiscal years 1967–1980. Some 75 percent of all revenues come from individual income taxes and Social Security deductions. Corporate contributions are quite small by comparison and are generally declining. During the 1950s, corporate taxes contributed about one-third of all revenues. By 1964 corporate contributions had dropped to about 20 percent of all receipts, and by 1980 they had dropped to about 13 percent. The individual income tax has consistently contributed about 40 percent of each tax dollar over the last fifteen years, but Social Security contributions have almost doubled during the same period. In 1964 Social Security deductions contributed about 18 percent of each tax dollar, but by 1980 they contributed about 30 percent.[6] Social Security deductions are particularly burdensome to middle-income citizens because the tax is not propor-

BOB ENGLEHART
Courtesy Dayton Journal Herald

tional to income. For example, in 1979 Social Security receipts were collected on the first $22,900 in earnings. This meant that a taxpayer who earned $22,900 paid as much in Social Security as a taxpayer who earned $1 million.

While the burden of taxation has increasingly been shifted to individuals, public expenditures have also been shifted toward human services. For a considerable period after World War II, about half of all federal expenditures were for military defense. As late as 1964, almost 45 percent of all federal expenditures were still for defense. While defense expenditures have remained quite high, expenditures for public services have increased enough to dominate budget outlays.

The figures below show a rough comparison of expenditures in fiscal 1964 and fiscal 1980 (expressed as a percent of total spending).[7]

	National Defense	*Direct Benefit Payments to Individual*	*Grants to States and Localities*	*Other Federal Operations*	*Net Interest*
1964	44%	22%	8%	19%	7%
1980	24%	39%	16%	12%	9%

National defense expenditures dropped from 44 percent of the total in 1964 to 24 percent in 1980. Direct benefits to individuals increased significantly, from 22 to 39 percent, as did grants to the states, which often finance public services. Grants and direct benefits constituted 55 percent of the total in 1980.

Table 13.3 shows a breakdown of the fiscal 1977–1980 budgets by expenditure item. The largest expenditures are for defense, health care, income security, and interest on the debt. In 1980 these four categories of expenditures constituted 75 percent of the total budget.

BUDGETS AND DEBTS: THE POLITICAL CONTROVERSY

The size of the federal budget and the national debt are often partisan issues. The Republican party and conservatives generally argue that spending is too high. They maintain that the size of the federal debt threatens economic stability and will burden future generations, who will have to pay it off. The Democratic party and liberals generally favor higher expenditures to support social welfare goals and to stimulate the economy. They consider the size of the debt quite reasonable, given the nation's wealth and yearly productive output.

The budget and the national debt can be conceptualized in a number of ways. Examined only in terms of current dollars, which is the usual method of presenting the budget, the size of the budget and its growth does look awesome. As Table 13.4 shows, in 1958 the federal budget was only $82.6 billion. By 1980 it had increased sixfold to $531.6 billion. However, compar-

TABLE 13.3
Federal Government Spending by Function: Fiscal 1977–1980*

	1977	1978	1979 (est.)	1980 (est.)
National defense	$ 97.5	$105.2	$114.5	$125.8
International affairs	4.8	5.9	7.3	8.2
General science, space and technology	4.7	4.7	5.2	5.5
Energy	4.2	5.9	8.6	7.9
National resources and environment	10.0	10.9	11.2	11.5
Agriculture	5.5	7.7	6.2	4.3
Commerce and housing credit	—	3.3	3.0	3.4
Transportation	14.6	15.4	17.4	17.6
Community and regional development	6.3	11.0	9.1	7.3
Education, training, employment of social services	21.0	26.5	30.7	30.2
Health	38.8	43.7	49.1	53.4
Income security	137.9	146.2	158.9	179.1
Veterans' benefits and services	18.0	19.0	20.3	20.5
Administration of justice	3.6	3.8	4.4	4.4
General government	3.4	3.8	4.4	4.4
General purpose fiscal assistance	9.5	9.6	8.9	8.8
Interest	38.0	44.0	52.8	57.0
Grand total:	$402.7	$450.8	$493.4	$531.6

Source: Fiscal 1980 Budget.
*Dollar amounts are in billions.

isons of this type are distorted in a couple of ways. First, the population was considerably larger in 1980 than in 1958, requiring the government to provide more services to more people. Second, the purchasing power of the dollar decreased considerably over this twenty-one-year period. Because of inflation, substantial budget increases were necessary just to continue current levels of revenues. For example, between 1965 and 1975 the dollar lost half its purchasing power. Thus, in 1975 it took two dollars for every one required to provide a service in 1965. Considered in terms of inflation, then, the budget has not increased nearly as rapidly as some assume. In 1956 dollars the budget in 1976 was only $170 billion, rather than $365.6 billion—215 percent below current dollars.[8]

The budget can also be conceptualized as a percentage of America's productive output, or yearly Gross National Product (GNP). This measure takes inflation into consideration and provides an indication of federal expenditures in relationship to yearly economic growth and output. Many analysts consider this the best single indicator of budget growth. Table 13.4 provides such a comparison. Notice that federal outlays have been a rather steady proportion of GNP during the last twenty-one years, averaging about 19 percent between 1958 and 1966, and about 21 percent between 1967 and 1980. Thus, consistent with the constant dollar comparison above, in relationship to GNP the budget has increased very little in recent years.

The size of the federal debt can also be conceptualized in constant dollar terms and as a proportion of GNP. In 1980 the *national debt* reached $830.0 billion. Conservatives labeled this a frightening amount, claiming that it showed serious weaknesses in the federal fiscal structure. Liberals argued that the debt in 1980 was only about 35 percent of GNP, while as recently as 1958 the debt equaled 63 percent of GNP, and in 1950 it was 80 percent of GNP.[9] In addition, liberals note that yearly deficits are a small proportion of GNP, averaging about 2.5 percent between 1975 and 1980.

A small, seemingly technical issue has substantial bearing upon how one calculates federal spending. The goods and services bought or financed by Washington, Charles Schultze pointed out shortly before he became chairperson of the Council of Economic Advisers, are more subject to inflation than the average of items in the Consumer Price Index. Therefore, for the government to maintain the same share of the nation's *real* output, its income has to increase by 1 to 1.3 percent. In short, a slight rise in the government's share of the national income is required if the welfare state is to maintain a constant level of goods and services.

Thus, the stability of the federal expenditure share in national income between 1955 and 1965 actually masked a falling share in real output, from 18 to 16 percent. And from 1965 to 1977, Washington's portion of that real output was constant, which meant that it had to spend more. "Paradoxically," Schultze writes, "in an affluent nation where productivity in the manufacture of goods rises rapidly, the relative cost of providing public services tends to increase sharply. The wealthier the nation grows, the more likely are its people to complain about the 'outrageous' cost of government."[10]

Some 75 percent of all revenues come from individual income taxes and Social Security deductions. Corporate contributions are quite small by comparison and are generally declining.

Liberals also often point out that the debt is caused in large part by high unemployment rather than excessive spending. High unemployment rates mean that millions of potential taxpayers are out of the job market and frequently on welfare. This reduces tax revenues and increases welfare outlays. Economists estimate that each percentage of unemployment reduces GNP by 3 percent, decreases tax revenues by about $14 billion, and raises welfare and unemployment compensation spending by $3 billion, resulting in a total deficit of $17

TABLE 13.4
The Federal Budget and the GNP*

Fiscal Year	Gross National Product	Budget Receipts		Outlays		Surplus/Deficit		High Employment Surplus/ Deficit**
		Amount	% of GNP	Amount	% of GNP	Amount	% of GNP	
1958	$ 442.1	$ 79.6	18.0%	$ 82.6	18.7%	$ − 2.9	0.6%	$+ 3.3
1959	473.3	79.2	16.7	92.1	19.5	−12.9	2.7	+ 0.2
1960	497.3	92.5	18.6	92.2	18.5	+ 0.3	—	+ 8.1
1961	508.3	94.4	18.6	97.8	19.2	− 3.4	0.6	+ 8.4
1962	546.9	99.7	18.2	106.8	19.5	− 7.1	1.3	+ 3.4
1963	576.3	106.6	18.5	111.3	19.3	− 4.8	0.8	+ 4.7
1964	616.2	112.7	18.3	118.6	19.2	− 5.9	0.9	+ 2.1
1965	657.1	116.8	17.8	118.4	18.0	− 1.6	0.2	+ 3.1
1966	721.1	130.9	18.1	134.-	18.7	− 3.8	0.5	− 4.6
1967	774.4	149.6	19.3	158.3	20.4	− 8.7	1.1	−11.7
1968	829.9	153.7	18.5	178.8	21.5	−25.2	3.0	−14.9
1969	903.7	187.8	20.8	184.5	20.4	+ 3.2	0.3	+ 1.1
1970	959.0	193.7	20.2	196.6	20.5	− 2.8	0.2	+ 2.6
1971	1,109.3	188.4	18.5	211.4	20.7	−23.0	2.3	− 7.5
1972	1,110.5	208.6	18.8	232.0	20.9	−23.4	2.1	− 9.3
1973	1,237.5	232.2	18.8	247.1	20.0	−14.8	1.2	−13.1
1974	1,359.2	264.9	19.5	269.6	19.8	− 4.7	0.3	− 0.9
1975	1,454.6	281.0	19.3	326.1	22.4	−45.1	3.1	− 6.2
1976	1,625.4	299.2	18.4	365.6	22.5	−66.4	4.0	−21.0
1977	1,887.0	356.9	19.4	501.9	21.9	−45.0	2.4	−14.1
1978 (est.)	2,106.0	402.0	19.6	451.0	22.6	−49.0	2.7	−24.8
1979 (est.)	2,343.0	456.0	19.7	495.0	21.4	−37.0	1.7	−27.6
1980 (est.)	2,565.0	503.0	19.6	532.0	20.7	−29.0	1.1	—

Source: Office of Management and Budget; Council of Economic Advisers.
*Dollar amounts are in billions.
**On a national incomes account basis.

billion.[11] For example, the 1976 fiscal year deficit was $66.4 billion. If, however, unemployment in 1976 had been 4 percent rather than 8.5 percent there would have been no deficit. Full employment—which actually means 1 to 2 percent unemployment—would, of course, have yielded a substantial surplus.

Liberals also note that the national debt is in reality owed to the American public. Most of the debt consists of savings bonds and treasury bills held by the public and businesses. In 1978, for example, $617.8 billion of the $785.6

billion in debt was held by the public. The remainder of the debt was held by federal agencies and trust funds, meaning that the government owed money to itself. Many argue that there is little danger that the government will go bankrupt because, as the debt is repaid, it goes back into the economy and can be borrowed again.

Indeed, the financing of the federal debt has very regressive tendencies, favoring the rich people who so often denounce Washington's spending. If average citizens invest in government bonds, it is usually in small-denomination notes with very low rates of interest. If they put money into a savings account, it is at a rate of return which in recent years has been set by the Federal Reserve at well below the rate of inflation. But wealthy people can buy large-denomination Treasury certificates with extremely high rates of interest. This tendency has increased since the Federal Reserve in 1979 adopted an aggressive policy of increasing the price of money in order to control inflation. For the man or woman in the street, this meant a shrinking living standard; for the affluent investor it meant an opportunity to ''hedge'' against inflation by purchasing riskless federal paper.[12]

Thus, liberals tend to reject conservative arguments that the debt is too large and that it imperils the nation, especially future generations. Liberals feel that the debt is reasonable in relationship to GNP, pointing out that it has declined relative to GNP. Further, they argue that it is caused by a weak

Al Ullman (left), chairman of the House Ways and Means Committee and Russell Long (right), chairman of the Senate Finance Committee. Most general revenue measures in Congress are handled by these two committees.

economy, not excess spending, and that indebtedness is a necessary part of Keynesian economics. LeLoup sums up these arguments in a direct response:

> Impassioned arguments that increasing the national debt will lead to a national financial collapse are nonsense. Proposals to require an annual balanced budget would be to render the government virtually impotent to affect the course of the economy. A constitutional amendment requiring a balanced budget would take away the ability of the federal budget to compensate for deficiencies in the private sector and head us back to 19th century economics.[13]

There is another irony. The overwhelming bulk of federal expenditures go for programs which, at least until now, have been extremely popular, particularly Social Security and Medicare. In 1977, for instance, the amount spent on retirement, disability, and unemployment was four times the outlays for low-income assistance.[14] Indeed, Henry Aaron has convincingly demonstrated that "in dollar terms, most of the War on Poverty was a by-product of programs intended primarily for the middle class."[15] So it was often true that those who protested against excessive federal largesse for "them"—the nonwhite, the poor, the slum dwellers—were in fact the people who benefited most from the welfare state.

One last point often made by liberals is that the ratio of U.S. spending to GNP—about 21 percent—is a much smaller one than in most other industrialized nations. For example, government spending constitutes a much higher

The budget debate: William Simon (below, left), a spokesman for the conservative position, argues that high government spending is inflationary and that the size of the federal debt threatens the financial security of the United States; John Kenneth Galbraith (right), a prominent liberal economist, sees high government spending as a means of stimulating the economy and addressing social problems.

proportion of GNP in Canada, France, Germany, the United Kingdom, Italy, Sweden, Norway, and the Netherlands.[16] Thus, the private sector remains a much larger and viable sector of the economy in America than in most modern Western nations.

CONCLUSIONS

Decisions about the size and nature of federal expenditures and who will bear its costs (see Chapter 7) are political issues that reflect partisan conflicts and political power. The budget, therefore, not only reveals policy priorities but also provides insight into economic philosophies and strategies. Decisions to pursue a balanced, surplus, or deficit budget reflect partisan values about the relative importance of inflation, unemployment, and economic growth.

The size of the federal budget and the national debt can be conceptualized in a variety of ways. In current dollar terms, both have increased considerably. But as a proportion of economic growth and prosperity, the budget has been rather consistent over the years, and the debt has declined considerably.

Footnotes

1. See Aaron Wildavsky, *The Politics of the Budgetary Process* (Boston: Little, Brown, 1974).
2. See Lance T. LeLoup, *Budgetary Politics: Dollars, Deficits, Decisions* (Brunswick, Ohio: King's Court, 1977).
3. For a detailed discussion, see LeLoup, *Budgetary Politics,* pp. 126–51.
4 "487.5 Billion Budget Compromise Approved," *Congressional Quarterly,* September 23, 1978, pp. 2584–86.
5. *Ibid.,* p. 2584.
6. "Carter Asks $500.2 Billion in Spending," *Congressional Quarterly,* January 28, 1979, p. 155.
7. *The United States Budget In Brief: Fiscal Year 1980,* Office of Management and Budget, 1979.
8. LeLoup, *Budgetary Politics,* p. 34.
9. "Carter Asks $500.2 Billion in Spending," p. 110.
10. Henry Owen and Charles L. Schultze, eds., *Setting National Priorities: The Next Ten Years* (Washington: The Brookings Institute, 1976), pp. 330–32.
12 See Leon Keyserling, "'Liberal' and 'Conservative' National Economic Policies," Washington Conference on Economic Progress (1979), Chapter 14.
13. LeLoup, *Budgetary Politics,* p. 43.
14. Owen and Schultze, eds., *Setting National Priorities,* Table 8-6, p. 334.
15. Henry Aaron, *Politics and Professors: The Great Society in Perspective* (Washington: The Brookings Institute, 1978), p. 28 and Tables A1 to A4, pp. 11–14.
16. United Nations, Yearbook of National Accounts Statistics (1974), Volume 2.

> The problem is not whether the judges make the law,
> but when and how much.
>
> **Felix Frankfurter**

The federal courts are an extremely important part of the policy-making process of the federal government. The courts often share in policy-making, and even formulate, supervise, and enforce many important public policies. Indeed, many of the most important government policy decisions throughout our history have been made by the courts rather than by Congress or the executive branch. For example, in recent years the courts have been the most important branch of the government in formulating school desegregation policy (see Chapter 17), in defining the relationship between church and state, in articulating the rights of those accused of crime, in defining and regulating censorship, in setting standards for abortions, and in apportioning legislative and congressional seats.

14

The Courts and Civil Liberties: Filling in the Gap

American courts play a larger policy role in the political process than do the courts of any other modern nation. There are a number of reasons why American federal courts play this unusual role. First, early in American history the Supreme Court ruled that the Constitution implicitly, if not explicitly, gave the federal courts the power of judicial review. This power, Chief Justice Marshall concluded in 1803, was necessary if the courts were to be the final arbiter of the Constitution.[1] *Judicial review* is the authority to accept cases in which the decisions of Congress and the executive are questioned to determine if they are consistent with the Constitution. If the court decides that they are not, they are rendered null and void. This is an extraordinary power, one which allows a nonelected branch to overrule the actions of the popularly elected Congress and executive.

Many feel, however, that the independence of the judiciary is a positive, not a negative, factor, since it allows the courts to make judgments without fear of transitory public or official passions. Still, the potential for abuse of the

Outside the Capitol Building looms this statue of John Marshall, the Supreme Court chief justice who established the Court's important power of judicial review.

democratic process is obvious, even though the courts have generally used the power of judicial review over federal legislation and executive acts sparingly. When the power has been used, however, its impact has often been quite significant. Simply having the power has elevated the role of the courts and has probably increased their willingness to make bold decisions in their normal cases involving judicial interpretation.

Throughout American history, the Supreme Court, which explicitly or implicitly makes the final decision in such cases, has overruled or upheld the actions of lower federal courts in voiding only a little more than one hundred congressional acts or parts of acts. Some of the acts were revised to pass judicial challenge. In other cases the Supreme Court changed its mind on the issue, and others involved relatively trivial matters. One of the most active periods of judicial review was between 1920 and 1936. During this period, the Supreme Court invalidated thirty-two federal laws, including legislation regulating child labor,[2] a minimum wage for women and children in the District of Columbia,[3] and many of the early legislative programs of Roosevelt's New Deal.

Roosevelt's proposal to allow him to appoint more judges to the Supreme Court so that his legislation would have a better chance of survival persuaded the Court to deal more leniently with New Deal legislation.[4] Many of his programs were revised and were then upheld by the Court. Until the New Deal, the Court generally played a distinctly conservative role in the political process, generally emphasizing property rights over individual rights. The preeminence of property rights was particularly pronounced during the tenure of Chief Justice William Taft (1921–30), who felt that most legislation designed to protect individual liberties intruded on the free enterprise system.[5] Individual rights were increasingly protected by the courts after the New Deal, reaching preeminence during the tenure of Chief Justice Earl Warren (1953–69).

Many of the most important government policy decisions throughout our history have been made by the courts rather than by Congress or the executive branch.

In addition to the extraordinary power of judicial review, a second major reason why American federal courts play such an important policy-making role is that the Constitution is short and ambiguous (see Appendix), leaving a great deal of discretion to those officials who must function under, and interpret, it. For example, the First Amendment to the Constitution says, "Congress shall make no law respecting an establishment of religion, or prohibiting the free exercise thereof; or abridging the freedom of speech, or of the press; or the right of the people peaceably to assemble, and to petition the Government for a redress of grievances." What does the amendment mean? Does it really mean that Congress can place no restraints on the exercise of religion or speech, or does it allow "reasonable" restraints to protect life and public order? What is reasonable? The Constitution leaves these types of decisions to the political and judicial branches, with the ultimate arbiter being the courts. This degree of ambiguity naturally gives the courts considerable latitude and often brings them into conflict with the other branches of government.

Third, the power of the federal courts has often been expanded because the other branches of government have failed to deal with problems that normally would be under their jurisdiction. This is often true of state governments, too. The Constitution also gives the federal courts the power of judicial review over state political and judicial decisions; Article VI of the Constitution declares that federal law and the Constitution are superior to state laws and constitutions. The federal courts often find issues before them because the U.S. Congress or one of the states has failed to deal with problems that ultimately deny citizens their rights guaranteed under the Constitution. The Court also receives a substantial number of cases from the states in which state actions or laws are in obvious violation of the Constitution. Sometimes state officials pass clearly unconstitutional legislation to pander to public prejudices, knowing that the Supreme Court or a federal court will nullify the legislation. The nullification powers of the courts greatly expand their power.

Policy failure at the federal level is also frequent. The Supreme Court's early decisions on school desegregation, for example, involved issues that should have been handled by Congress (see Chapter 17). But since Congress refused to deal with public school segregation, the Court was ultimately faced with the issue in a suit maintaining that segregation denied black children the equal protection of the law. The Supreme Court agreed.[6]

Similarly, the federal courts have had to confront issues involving sex discrimination, malapportionment of state legislative and congressional districts, voting rights of minorities, prison conditions, and many other problems that should have been resolved by Congress or the state legislatures. U.S. District Judge Frank M. Johnson, who was dubbed the unofficial governor of Alabama during George Wallace's long tenure in that position, was blunt in discussing the problem:

> I didn't ask for any of these cases. In an ideal society, these judgments and decisions should be made by those to whom we have entrusted these responsibilities. But when government institutions fail to make these judgments and decisions in a manner which comports with the Constitution, the federal courts have a duty to remedy the violation.[7]

While the courts are often thrust into a legislative role, they are poorly suited to do this job. The problem is that most issues are too complex to be comprehensively dealt with through adjudication, or judicial decision. Courts generally attempt to decide only specific issues raised by a given case. They do not formulate technical and broad guidelines except in unusual instances. This generally leaves a policy issue, such as school desegregation, in limbo, requiring case after case to be brought before the court to establish a piecemeal policy that almost always still leaves many critical questions unanswered. This imperfect process causes many problems, but in the face of legislative or executive inaction it is often the only way that important policy issues are dealt with.

STRUCTURE OF THE FEDERAL COURT SYSTEM

The Constitution stipulates that there will be one Supreme Court and such inferior courts as Congress deems necessary. Congress has established six additional types of courts at the federal level, but four are specialty courts that handle a narrow range of issues (see Figure 14.1). The three most important federal courts are the district courts, the courts of appeal, and the Supreme Court.

The district courts are the workhorses of the federal judicial system. They are courts of *original jurisdiction;* that is, most federal cases begin here. And they are the only federal courts that use juries. There are currently ninety-four district courts located throughout the United States and its territories, with 515 judges in all. In 1979 the district courts handled 143,000 cases, most of which went no further. Cases at this level are normally heard by one judge, and the parties to the case have the option of a jury trial.

The courts of appeal hear cases that are appealed from the district courts and the U.S. tax court. There are eleven courts of appeal (called circuits) distributed throughout the United States, with a total of 132 judges. Cases at this level are normally heard by a three-judge panel. In 1979 the courts of appeal dealt with 18,000 cases, only about 12.5 percent of all the cases heard by the district courts.

The Supreme Court sits at the top of the judicial hierarchy. It has both original and appellate jurisdiction. The Court has original jurisdiction over cases involving disputes between the states, and in cases involving ambassadors, consuls, or representatives of foreign governments. The Court has *appellate jurisdiction* over federal cases and state cases involving constitutional interpretation or a substantial federal question.

To bring a state case before the Supreme Court, a *plaintiff*—the person who initiates the action—must exhaust all state remedies. That is, the case must be taken as far as possible in the state courts. Even if the case does involve constitutional interpretation or a substantial federal question, the Supreme Court is not actually required to hear it. In fact, in most cases brought before the Court from the state or federal level, the Supreme Court simply declines to hear the case or dismisses it for lack of a substantial issue. Thus, in 1979 the Supreme Court handled about 5,500 cases, but actually heard arguments in 168 cases and wrote full opinions in only about 130 of them.

Congress decides how many judges will serve on each court, sets the salary of judges, and can determine the jurisdiction of the courts. Congress

FIGURE 14.1
The Federal Court System

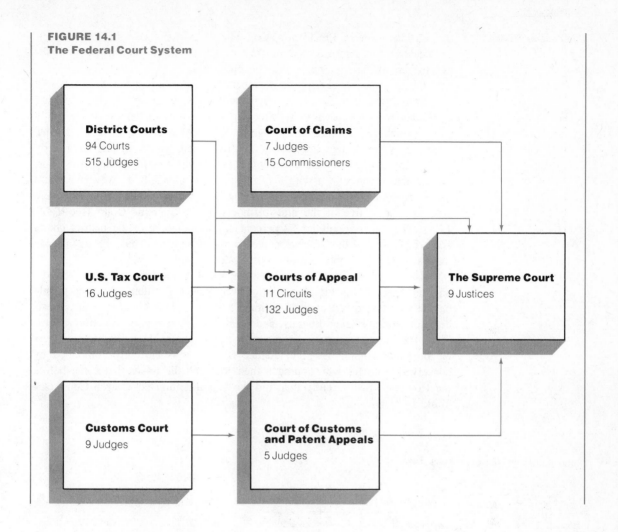

District Courts
94 Courts
515 Judges

Court of Claims
7 Judges
15 Commissioners

U.S. Tax Court
16 Judges

Courts of Appeal
11 Circuits
132 Judges

The Supreme Court
9 Justices

Customs Court
9 Judges

Court of Customs
and Patent Appeals
5 Judges

cannot abolish a judicial position that has an occupant, but it can abolish vacant positions or expand the size of the courts. There have been nine Supreme Court positions since 1869. But during American history there have been as few as five and as many as ten. Congress cannot lower the salary of a sitting judge, but can establish the salary for new judgeships and determine the rate of salary increase for all judges. Congress' control over jurisdiction is substantial, but Congress could not strip the Supreme Court of its original jurisdiction (this jurisdiction could, however, be shared with some other court).

The President makes all appointments to federal courts, but the Senate must ratify these selections. Traditionally, the President selects Supreme Court justices, while district and appeals court selections are made by the senators and/or representatives from the President's party. If a President fails to accept the recommendations of the senator(s) from the state or region, by tradition the senators from the President's party will refuse to approve the appointment. This custom gives senators patronage power but often results in poorly qualified persons being appointed to the bench.

Presidents generally appoint members of their own party to the courts. All Presidents since Franklin Roosevelt have chosen 90 percent or more of their candidates from their own party. Since appointment to a federal court generally qualifies one for extraordinarily high-paying jobs in private firms, and since most judges are in their late forties or fifties when appointed, there is a fairly high turnover of district and appeals judges. The prestige of the Supreme Court is sufficient to provide it with a fairly stable membership. However, because of retirements prompted primarily by age, Presidents Nixon and Ford were able to appoint five of the nine members of the Supreme Court (see Table 14.1). They also appointed 59 percent of the members of the district courts and 55 percent of the judges on the courts of appeal.[8] Thus, Presidents can have a substantial impact on the court system in only a few years.

The Supreme Court is the most important of the federal courts, and the one the President has the most control over. Presidents attempt to place people on the Court who reflect their political and judicial philosophy. Thus, President Johnson appointed liberals, and President Nixon appointed conservatives. Since Presidents Ford and Nixon were able to appoint a total of five members of the Court, including Chief Justice Burger, it is currently dominated by conservative judges who approach their jobs and the issues that come before the Court much differently than did the liberal-dominated Warren Court (see Table 14.1).

TABLE 14.1
Supreme Court Members: 1969–1978

Member	Appointed by	Replaced	Date Appointed	Date Resigned
Hugo L. Black	Roosevelt	Van Devanter	8/12/37	9/17/71
William O. Douglas	Roosevelt	Brandeis	3/20/39	11/12/75
Earl Warren	Eisenhower	Vinson	9/30/53	6/23/69
John M. Harlan	Eisenhower	Jackson	1/10/55	9/23/71
William J. Brennan, Jr.	Eisenhower	Minton	10/16/56	
Potter Stewart	Eisenhower	Burdon	1/17/59	
Byron R. White	Kennedy	Whittaker	3/30/62	
Abe Fortas	Johnson	Goldberg	7/28/65	5/14/69
Thurgood Marshall	Johnson	Clark	6/13/67	
Warren E. Burger	Nixon	Warren	5/21/69	
Harry A. Blackmun	Nixon	Fortas	4/14/70	
Lewis F. Powell, Jr.	Nixon	Black	10/21/71	
William H. Rehnquist	Nixon	Harlan	10/21/71	
John Paul Stevens	Ford	Douglas	11/28/75	

The Supreme Court, 1980: (left to right) John Paul Stevens, Lewis F. Powell, Jr., Harry A. Blackmun, William H. Rehnquist, Thurgood Marshall, William Brennan, Chief Justice Warren E. Burger, Potter Stewart, and Byron R. White.

Below we will analyze the Court's role in a number of policy areas. The review provides insight into the complexity of the issues that the federal courts must face, the very important, even extraordinary, role the courts play in the policy process, and the impact of judicial personality on court decisions.

FREEDOM OF SPEECH

Freedom of speech is probably the core liberty in a democracy. By its very nature, democracy assumes that citizens will be free to criticize their government, openly debate the qualifications and performance of public officials, and discuss the pros and cons of various political positions and policies. Without these rights, no society can truly be democratic, nor can error in policy decisions or official actions be corrected.

While the necessity of freedom of speech in a democracy is generally accepted in theory, in practice the protection, extension, and definition of free speech has often been complex and controversial. The reasons are several:

1. There is a natural tendency for the public and officials to support freedom of speech for those whom they like and support but not for those whom they disagree with or even fear.
2. During some periods of American history, the courts have been as reluctant as the majority to provide genuine protection for free speech.

3. Speech can take complex forms, such as subversive organizations that are not interested in open communication, or be combined with some type of action, like picketing or demonstrations. In such cases, the courts must decide if actions can ever be defined as a form of speech, or whether speech which advocates the replacement of the democratic process can be defended.

During most of American history, speech was often not well protected, despite the Constitution's seemingly ironclad guarantees. Courts have always agreed that speech cannot be absolute because an absolute right would allow some to severely abuse the rights of others. The Court's first attempt to formulate a standard for determining when speech was protected, however, came in a 1919 case. Speaking for the Court, Justice Holmes concluded: "The question in every case is whether the words are used in circumstances and are of such a nature as to create a clear and present danger that they will bring about substantive evils that Congress has a right to prevent."[9]

The *clear and present danger doctrine* is a very liberal standard. Basically, it says that while freedom of speech is not absolute, it is so important that government can regulate or suppress it only if the connection between speech and action is so direct that the speech itself can be considered to be action. The action can be regulated only if it is imminent and constitutes the type of major substantive evil—such as a riot—that government has a right to prevent.

A much more conservative standard has also been applied by the Court. The *bad tendency doctrine* articulated by the Court in a 1925 case[10] held that speech could be suppressed if it had a tendency to lead to a substantive evil. Thus, the government did not have to prove a clear and present danger; all that was necessary was a conclusion that the speech might lead to a substantive evil.

While the courts are often thrust into a legislative role, they are poorly suited to do this job. Courts generally attempt to decide only the specific issues raised by a given case. They do not formulate technical and broad guidelines except in unusual instances.

A short example reveals how drastically these two standards differ. Suppose an individual gave a speech in which he argued that a crowd of listeners should join him in burning down a pornographic store. Under the bad tendency standard, the speaker could be convicted because he might have been successful in convincing the audience to undertake the act. Under the clear and present danger standard, the Court would uphold conviction only if the evidence showed that the speaker was serious, the audience took the speaker seriously, the audience was convinced or on the very verge of being convinced to act on the speaker's prompting, and that the audience had the potential to successfully commit the substantive evil. (For example, did the speaker bring gasoline and matches with him?) The speaker's impact on his audience, then, and the complex of circumstances would be the critical factors.

One other standard used by some members of the Court in recent years is the *preferred-position doctrine*. This standard is an extension of the clear and present danger doctrine, and is built on the assumption that First Amendment rights are the most important liberties in a free society. Thus, any law seeking to restrict a First Amendment right carries a heavy burden: the presumption of unconstitutionality. The presumption can be lifted only if the government can show some compelling necessity for the restraints, such as an imminent and serious substantive evil that will result in their absence.

The theories applied reflect the personalities on the Court and the complexity of the times and the issues that end up before it. Rarely are applications simple in execution, and this can cause highly divergent, even seemingly contradictory standards. Consider, for example, two cases that came before the Court only two years apart.

In a 1949 case, a priest had been convicted of breach of peace after he had given a speech in which he referred to particular politicians and racial groups as "slimy scum," "snobs," and "bedbugs," and called Eleanor Roosevelt the "Queen of the world's Communists." A crowd gathered outside the auditorium reacted with hostility, breaking windows and throwing stink bombs inside. Father Terminiello was arrested and convicted of breach of the peace. The trial court defined breach of peace to include speech which "stirs the public to anger, invites dispute, (or) brings about a condition of unrest."

Justice William Douglas, speaking for the Court, applied a clear and present danger doctrine in striking down the breach of peace ordinance. Douglas noted that it was not Terminiello's audience that created the breach, but outsiders who disagreed with his positions. Those who disagreed with the speech, Douglas said, were under no compulsion to listen to it. In addition, he noted:

> A function of free speech under our system of government is to invite dispute. It may indeed best serve its high purpose when it induces a condition of unrest, creates dissatisfaction with conditions as they are, or even stirs people to anger.[11]

Terminiello would lead one to believe that the Court's position on free speech was quite liberal. However, in 1951 the Court struck an entirely different posture. In *Feiner* v. *New York*[12] the Court dealt with another case in which a speaker stirred some of his listeners to anger. Feiner had given a speech on a street corner in a predominantly black neighborhood in Syracuse, New York. A crowd of seventy-five to eighty persons gathered. Feiner gave an impassioned speech in which he called the President a bum and the American Legion "a Nazi Gestapo." At one point he exclaimed: "The Negroes don't have equal rights; they should rise up in arms and fight for them."

Two police officers witnessed the speech. During the speech, some whites in the racially mixed audience told the police that if they (the officers) did not "get that s.o.b. off the stand" they would do it. The police testified that there was additional "angry muttering and pushing." The police warned

Feiner to end his speech, and when he would not, he was arrested and convicted of disorderly conduct. Justice Vinson, speaking for the Court, upheld the conviction:

> When clear and present danger of riot, disorder, interference with traffic upon the public street or other immediate threat to public safety, peace, or order, appears, the power of the state to prevent or punish is obvious.

Even though it was cloaked in terms of clear and present danger, this was a much more conservative standard. The speaker was held accountable for the actions of those in the audience who did not agree with him, even though there was no real evidence of an imminent disorder.

Justice Douglas dissented from the Court's position, saying in part:

> As to the existence of a dangerous situation on the street corner, it seems far-fetched to suggest that the 'facts' show any imminent threat of riot or uncontrollable disorder. . . . Moreover, assuming that the 'facts' did indicate a critical situation, I regret the implication of the Court's opinion that the police had no obligation to protect petitioner's constitutional right to talk. The police of course, have power to prevent breaches of the peace. But if, in the name of preserving order, they ever can interfere with a lawful public speaker, they first must make all reasonable efforts to protect him. Here the policemen did not even pretend to try to protect petitioner.

The Court's fluidity on free speech, caused by judicial personality and the nuance of particular cases, continued throughout the turbulent '60s and up to the present. In the 1960s the Supreme Court rendered a number of decisions that seemingly contradicted Feiner. Most of the cases that reached the Court involved speech plus action—demonstrations, picketing—of some sort. In *Gregory* v. *Chicago,* a group accompanied by Chicago police peacefully marched to the mayor's residence to protest the continuation of school segregation in the city. Along the route bystanders became increasingly hostile, causing the police to fear that the crowd might become too unruly to control. Acting on this fear the police asked the marchers to disband. When the marchers refused, they were arrested and convicted of disorderly conduct. Chief Justice Warren reversed the conviction, saying that "there is no evidence in this record that petitioners' conduct was disorderly. Therefore, convictions so totally devoid of evidentiary support violate due process."[13]

In *Edwards* v. *South Carolina* the Supreme Court reversed the conviction of blacks who had walked to the South Carolina State House grounds to protest

In the *Gregory* case, demonstrators who had been marching peacefully to protest school segregation were arrested and convicted for refusing to disperse. The Warren Court, which generally expanded free-speech protection during the 1950s and 1960s, reversed the conviction.

racial discrimination. The evidence showed that the demonstrators were nonviolent, that they did not disrupt traffic, and that police protection was adequate.[14] In *Cox* v. *Louisiana,* the Supreme Court overturned the breach of peace convictions of another group of nonviolent, black demonstrators who had been convicted under an extremely broad statute.[15]

In another Louisiana case, the Court reversed the breach of peace convictions of blacks who had visited and refused to leave a local public library that did not permit use by nonwhite citizens. Justice Fortas, speaking for the Court, said:

> We are here dealing with an aspect of a basic constitutional right. . . . As this Court has repeatedly stated, these rights are not confined to verbal expression. They embrace appropriate types of action which certainly include the right in a peaceable and orderly manner to protest by silent and reproachful presence, in a place where the protestant has every right to be, the unconstitutional segregation of public facilities.[16]

There is a natural tendency for the public and officials to support freedom of speech for those whom they like and support but not for those whom they disagree with or even fear.

In 1966 and 1972 cases, the Court upheld restraints on speech. In one case, the Court supported the right of a state to prohibit peaceful demonstrations on jailhouse or courthouse grounds.[17] In the other, the Court let stand the breach of peace convictions of protesters who had conducted a peaceful, orderly, and quiet demonstration 100 feet from a public school. Justice Marshall, speaking for the Court, said: "The nature of a place, the pattern of its normal activities, dictates the kinds of regulations of time, place, and manner that are reasonable."[18]

Symbolic speech

Another area of speech the Court has had to deal with in recent years is symbolic speech: actions of some type which are designed to communicate a thought. The struggle over civil rights and the turmoil of the Vietnam War brought a number of important symbolic speech cases before the Court in the 1960s and '70s. In 1968 the Supreme Court was faced with a case involving protest against the war in Vietnam. To protest the war, draft-age males frequently burned their draft cards. In 1965 Congress amended the federal law to make it illegal to "knowingly destroy or knowingly mutilate" a registration certificate. O'Brien and three companions were convicted by a district court of publicly burning their cards. O'Brien appealed, arguing that his actions constituted symbolic speech protected by the First Amendment, and that the freedom of expression which the First Amendment guarantees included "all modes of communication of ideas by conduct."

The Supreme Court disagreed. The Court concluded that when speech and action are combined, a "sufficiently important governmental interest in regulating the nonspeech element can justify incidental limitations on First Amendment freedoms."[19]

In *Tinker* v. *Des Moines School District* the Court ruled on whether students could wear armbands to school to protest the Vietnam War. The school system had dismissed the students for disruptive conduct. The Supreme Court ruled that the students' actions involved protected speech. In the absence of actual or potentially disruptive conduct, the Court said, it could not be prohibited or punished.[20] In 1971, the Court heard a case from California in which a man who wore a jacket bearing the words "Fuck the Draft" was convicted of disturbing the peace.[21] The Court ruled that the message was not obscene, that it did not constitute fighting words, and that it was a form of protected speech.

In another case, the Court dealt with a New York malicious mischief statute under which a man protesting the shooting of civil rights activist James Meredith had burned an American flag on a public street. In a closely divided opinion, the Court overruled the conviction, stating that the New York statute was overbroad because it allowed a person to be found guilty who only spoke defiantly or contemptuously about the flag.[22] Under a more tightly drawn statute, the Court would probably uphold a conviction for burning a flag, especially if it were burned in a public place.

Subversive speech

One of the most volatile free speech issues facing the Supreme Court in recent years is the extent to which groups that advocate violence or the violent overthrow of the government can be regulated. The first case to reach the Court on this issue was *Dennis* v. *U.S.* in 1951, a period of Cold-War hysteria in America. In *Dennis,* the leaders of the American Communist party were charged under the Smith Act with knowingly advocating and teaching the necessity of overthrowing and destroying the government by force and violence.

The Court upheld the convictions, concluding that teaching and advocating the necessity of the violent overthrow of the government created a clear and present danger. The Court said that the government did not have to wait until a putsch was about to be executed before it could act. Since there was no evidence that the Communist party actually had plans to use violence against the government, the Court's decision reflected a bad tendency rather than a clear and present danger standard.

Justices Black and Douglas dissented from the Court's opinion. Neither felt that mere advocacy created any real danger to the Republic, since only speech, not action, was involved. Both judges felt that the Court had watered down the First Amendment to pander to a hostile public mood. Black spoke prophetically:

> Public opinion being what it now is, few will protest the conviction of these Communist petitioners. There is hope, however, that in calmer times, when present pressures, passions and fears subside, this or some later Court will restore the First Amendment liberties to the high preferred place where they belong in a free society.[23]

In 1957 the Court sought to rectify the error made in *Dennis*. In *Yates* v. *U.S.*,[24] the Supreme Court ruled that a distinction had to be made between speech advocating abstract belief and speech designed to prompt action. Anyone, the Court said, could attempt to convince others to believe anything they wished, but restraint could only be imposed if they tried to convince others to engage in violent actions designed to overthrow the government.

During the 1940s and 1950s, writers and actors were blacklisted in Hollywood for allegedly belonging to or supporting communist or socialist organizations. The actors and actresses above protested the blacklisting of their colleagues in their testimony before the House Un-American Activities Committee. Left to right: Jane Wyatt, June Havoc, Geraldine Brooks, Paul Henreid, Lauren Bacall, Humphrey Bogart, Evelyn Keyes, Danny Kaye, Betty Veihl, and John Conte.

In 1969 the Court upheld a conviction under the membership clause of the Smith Act, but ruled that a conviction could be upheld only if it could be proven that

> the Communist party advocated the violent overthrow of the Government, in the sense of present advocacy of action to accomplish that end as soon as circumstances were propitious; and . . . petitioner was an active member of the party, and not merely a nominal, passive member, with knowledge of the Party's illegal advocacy and a specific intent to bring about violent overthrow as speedily as circumstances would permit.[25]

Also in 1969 the Court dealt with an Ohio statute which prohibited "advocating the duty, necessity, or propriety of crime, sabotage, violence, or unlawful methods of terrorism as a means of accomplishing industrial or political reform." A member of the Ku Klux Klan had been convicted under the statute. The Court overruled the conviction, specifying carefully the conditions that must exist before speech could be prohibited:

> The constitutional guarantees of free speech and free press do not permit a state to forbid or proscribe advocacy of the use of force or law violation except where such advocacy is directed to inciting or producing imminent lawless action and is likely to incite or produce such action.[26]

Prior restraint

The Court has long held that any efforts to suppress speech prior to its utterance or publication—prior restraint—bears a particularly heavy burden. The Court did rule that states could establish movie review boards and forbid the showing of movies until they were reviewed, but this was an exception to its normal posture.[27] In the early 1970s, the Supreme Court restated its position on this point in a case of particular importance.

In 1971 a government employee turned over to the media materials disclosing the government's behind-the-scenes foreign policy-making during much of the Vietnam War. Several major newspapers began publishing the documents—the so-called Pentagon Papers—many of which showed that Presidents Kennedy, Johnson, and Nixon had often lied to the American people and Congress about the government's role in Vietnam and the situation within that country. President Nixon sought injunctions against the *New York Times* and the *Washington Post* to end their publication of the documents. The Court refused to uphold the injunctions, the majority stating that a free press was essential in a democracy and that government claims of national security could not be used to suppress embarrassing information.[28] If the newspapers broke any laws in publishing the materials, the majority said, they could be prosecuted, but only publication could prove whether the newspapers had acted illegally.

In the spring of 1979, a highly emotional free speech issue was raised when *Progressive* magazine made known its intentions to publish an article which explained how to make an H-bomb. An MIT professor who was responsible for a prepublication review of the article turned it over to government officials. Government scientists claimed that the article contained top-secret information and would help Third-World nations develop the bomb. Free speech, the scientists and government lawyers claimed, did not give anyone the right to help irresponsible persons blow up the world. The editors of *Progressive* argued in response that all the information in the article had been obtained from public sources, and that the method of H-bomb construction was known by scientists all over the world. They said that the public needed to know how easily this information could be obtained, and thus, how dangerous such technology is.

In March 1979, the government sought an injunction prohibiting the publication of the article until it could be determined if secret information would be jeopardized. In an unprecedented move, the district court issued the injunction. The controversy continued through the summer of 1979, ending basically when a small newspaper published a fugitive copy of the article. In late September 1979, the U.S. Seventh Circuit Court of Appeals ruled that the publication of the article made the injunction moot, and gave *Progressive* permission to publish it. The article, entitled "The H-bomb Secret," appeared in the November 1979 issue of the magazine.

Censorship

The incessant efforts of groups to regulate the content and type of books, magazines, movies, and plays available in their community thrust the Warren and Burger Courts into a particularly sensitive area of free speech. Throughout much of American history, the basic standard used to determine what was "obscene," in both state and federal courts, was the definition expounded in the English case of *Queen* v. *Hicklin* in 1868:

> . . . whether the tendency of the matter charged as obscenity is to deprave and corrupt those whose minds are open to such immoral influences, and into whose hands a publication of this sort may fall.

The Hicklin test was expansive by nature and thus vulnerable to interpretations which covered a broad range of materials. Increasingly, the test was criticized and disregarded by courts on the grounds that it did not take into account changing community standards, or the reputation, social purpose, or artistic or scientific value of a work. In addition, the Hicklin formula allowed a work to be judged by isolated parts, instead of as a whole, and by its effect on the most susceptible persons—children and disturbed adults. Also, under the test a work could be suppressed because of presumed thoughts evoked rather than any illegal or antisocial actions spawned by the material.

It was not until 1957 that the Supreme Court rejected Hicklin and adopted a new standard for judging obscenity.[29] The Court ruled that "obscenity" was not protected speech, but that obscenity had to be determined by the following standard: "whether to the average person, applying contemporary community standards, the dominant theme of the material taken as a whole appeals to prurient interests." This new formula corrected three of the most objectionable aspects of the Hicklin test. The material would have to be judged as a whole, by its dominant theme, and by its effect on the average person. Still, the new standard failed to explain how the "average person" or contemporary community standards were to be determined. Nor did the Court indicate whether the community standard was to be a national or local one. Prurient material was defined only as that "having a tendency to excite lustful thoughts."

Some of these questions were clarified as the Court applied the standard. The Court's applications revealed the standard to be quite liberal, one under which little could be considered obscene. In a 1964 case, the Court tightened the standard further, ruling that to be obscene "an item had to shock" or be "patently offensive," and it had to be "utterly without redeeming social importance."[30] The Court did, however, rule that prurient interest could be judged in terms of specific groups (nudists, homosexuals, fetishists) if the material was directed to these groups and that states could restrict the sale or exposure of certain material to preadults.[31] In a controversial decision, the Court held that if a distributor claimed in advertising that his publications were obscene and if they lent themselves to such an interpretation, the claim could be accepted at face value and result in conviction.[32] In 1964 the Court also suggested that national community standards should be used in judging obscenity.[33]

In 1969 the Court ruled that a private individual could legally possess obscene materials, as long as the materials were for personal use.[34] This led some lower courts to conclude that if adults had a right to own obscene materials, someone must have a right to sell them. The Court said no, ruling that the federal government could ban obscene materials from the mails and from importation. The Court also upheld a federal act allowing persons to obtain a post office order requiring their name to be removed from a company's mailing list.

While the Court's decisions protected a broad range of sexual speech, the standards were still vague enough to require the Court to make the final determination in most cases. Some of the confusion resulted from the differences inherently involved in any effort to define obscenity, which caused the members of the Court to frequently disagree about interpretations and applications. Still, the Burger Court decided that it could do better.

In 1973 the Burger Court announced a revision of the basic test, one that dropped the "utterly without redeeming social importance" test. The new guideline was:

a.   whether the average person, applying contemporary community standards would find that the work, taken as a whole, appeals to the prurient interest;

Although the Supreme Court has agreed that obscenity is not protected by the First Amendment, it has had difficulty defining what "obscenity" is.

b. whether the work depicts or describes, in a patently offensive way, sexual conduct specifically defined by the applicable state law; and

c. whether the work, taken as a whole, lacks serious literary, artistic, political, or scientific value.[35]

All three parts of the standard would have to be applied, and the Court now said that community standards could be local rather than national.

The Court's new standard was certainly no easier to understand or apply than the Warren Court's standard, but basically it seemed to limit censorship to "hard-core" materials. And it allowed local communities to decide whether they wanted to permit such materials or not. The Court said: "Under the holding announced today, no one will be subject to prosecution for the sale or exposure of obscene materials unless these materials depict or describe patently offensive 'hard-core' sexual conduct specifically defined by the regulating state law, as written or construed." Thus, only "hard-core" materials could be banned, and they had to be specifically defined by state law.

To prove its point, the Court allowed states to close down adult book and movie houses that showed or sold hard-core materials, even though the establishments limited their clientele to adults.[36] However, in a 1974 case the Court ruled that a community could not ban the movie "Carnal Knowledge." Justice Rehnquist said the movie could not be banned because it did not portray "hardcore sexual conduct for its own sake. . . . Cameras did not focus on genitalia or concentrate on 'ultimate sexual acts.' "[37] In 1975 the Court also said that a drive-in movie theater could not be fined for showing movies containing nudity, even though the movies were visible to passersby.[38]

In 1976 the Court ruled that in criminal suits against alleged pornographers, the question of the obscenity of the materials involved had to be submitted to the jurors. The state of Alabama had tried to bypass the issue in criminal cases where there had been a civil finding that a certain publication or material was obscene. The Court held that this procedure was unconstitutional, since community standards might be changing.[39]

In summary, the Court's present stand is that obscenity is not protected speech. Communities may prohibit its communication or sale as long as obscenity is understood to be hard-core pornography.

RELIGION

Another very important First Amendment right that the courts have played a large role in defining and defending involves the relationship between church and state and the free exercise of religion. The First Amendment says that "Congress shall make no law respecting an establishment of religion, or prohibiting the free exercise thereof." The reference to an "establishment of religion" clearly meant that the government could not establish a state religion like the Church of England. What else, if anything, the framers meant has long been disputed. Some members of the Court have believed that the framers meant to establish a wall of separation between church and state; others have thought that the government is only required to show no preference between religions. The Court's role in interpreting the establishment clause has thrust it into the policy process, often leading the Court to overrule the policy decisions of state and local governments and even Congress.

Two of the most controversial decisions rendered by the Supreme Court since World War II involved school prayers and Bible reading. Both, the Court said, constituted religious exercises required and conducted by government and thus violated the establishment clause of the First Amendment. In the prayer case, Justice Black concluded:

> The establishment clause must at least mean that in this country it is no part of the business of government to compose official prayers for any group of the American people to recite as part of a religious program carried on by government.[40]

Bible reading requirements ran into the same objections. The Court held that the impact of the regulation was to advance religion and that government could neither legally advance nor inhibit religion.[41]

The Warren Court did uphold Sunday closing laws (or blue laws). It said that their intent was secular, not religious, since they were designed to provide a day of peace and quiet.[42] In 1968 the Court struck down an Arkansas statute which forbade the teaching of evolution in a public school. Justice Fortas concluded that the establishment clause "does not permit the state to require that teaching and learning must be tailored to the principle of prohibition of any religious sect or dogma."[43] In 1971 the Court ruled that the property-tax exemption for church property used only for religious purposes did not violate the First Amendment. The Court felt that taxing church property would require more government-church entanglements than exemptions.[44]

State attempts to provide aid to financially pinched nonpublic (mostly parochial) schools have frequently run into trouble with the Court. In 1947 the Court upheld state provision of bus transportation for parochial students on the ground that such aid was no different than fire protection.[45] Also, the Warren Court allowed a state to provide textbooks to parochial students, even allowing the parochial schools to choose the books the state would buy.[46] However, a state law designed to pay part of the salary of parochial teachers who taught some secular subjects and the costs of educational materials was struck down because state supervision of the expenditure of the funds produced an "entanglement" of church and state.[47]

A New York law allowing the state to repay parochial schools for state-required tests and record-keeping was ruled unconstitutional.[48] Another New York law providing funds for maintenance and repair of parochial schools, tuition grants, and tax breaks for parents of children attending schools was also held unconstitutional. In striking down the law, the Court established the following test that aid programs would have to pass to be found constitutional:

> The law in question, first, must reflect a clearly secular legislative purpose, . . . second, must have a primary effect that neither advances nor inhibits religion . . . and, third, must avoid excessive government entanglement with religion.[49]

In 1973 and 1975, two Pennsylvania laws failed to pass the Court's standard. The 1973 case involved state reimbursement of tuition to all parents who sent their children to private schools.[50] The 1975 case involved the direct loan of instructional equipment and auxiliary staff and services to private schools, 75 percent of which were religiously affiliated.[51] In both cases, the Court ruled that the laws were designed to advance religion, and that in the latter, excessive entanglements were also created.

While the Court's decisions often seem far from consistent, they do provide an excellent example of the Court's ability to establish strict judicial guidelines that policy-makers must follow.

The Court's authority to interpret the free exercise clause is undisputed, but its decisions often involve complex topics and consequently are frequently controversial. One topic the Court had to face was whether people could be compelled to profess religious beliefs. The Court said no. In 1961 the Court struck down a Maryland statute which required all officeholders to profess a

"Today's agenda is a tough one, dealing primarily with religion in the public schools. But first, let us pray."

belief in God.[52] Another question is whether the right to free exercise of religion is absolute. Again, the Court said no. "Religious liberty," the Court said, "includes absolute freedom to believe, but only limited power to act." Unrestricted religious practice could clearly infringe upon the rights of others.

In its attempts to balance the right of citizens to practice their religious beliefs against the right of other citizens not to have their rights abused, the Court has often had to uphold outright state prohibitions of certain religious practices. For example, the Court has upheld the right of states to prohibit religious practices which constitute fraud or the unlicensed practice of medicine, involve serious risk of harm to followers (such as snake handling), or create a level of noise which disturbs the peace.

In other instances, the Court has allowed states to place an indirect burden on certain religions by requiring them to conform to general laws. For example, the Court has upheld the right of states to require vaccinations for all school children and blood tests for marriage licences, even if such requirements conflict with religious beliefs. In a few extreme cases, states have been allowed to order medical care for children or the aged despite religious objections from parents or the sick.

In upholding prohibitions or indirect burdens on religions, the Court has generally applied the secular regulation rule. This rule states that a religion has no right to an exemption from a general law designed for all members of society. In the 1960s, the Court began to alter the rule, requiring the states to be more sensitive to religious beliefs and practices. In general, the Court began to compel the states to write laws in a manner which placed the smallest possible burden on religion.

The Court's new standard became apparent in a 1963 case in which a woman had been fired from her job because her religion did not allow her to work on Saturdays. Once fired, the woman was also denied unemployment benefits because state law required that anyone receiving benefits be available for work Monday through Saturday. The Court ruled the state law unconstitutional, saying that it was unnecessarily rigid.[53] Also in 1963, the Court held that a woman could not be punished because her religious principles forbade her to serve on a jury. In 1972 the Court exempted Amish children from a state's compulsory education laws.[54]

The Vietnam War served as the catalyst for a number of important cases. In 1965 the Court held that a person did not have to specifically believe in God to qualify as a conscientious objector under the Universal Military Training and Service Act. In this case the petitioner based his objection to service on religious principles which included belief in a "Supreme Being" rather than a God.[55] In 1970 the Court ruled that conscientious objection could be based on ethical and moral beliefs which required nonparticipation in all wars. The petitioner had defined his philosophy as being religious in an ethical sense.[56] In 1971 two individuals, one basing his objection on humanitarian grounds and the other on religious beliefs, sought exemption only from the war in Vietnam, which they considered to be illegal and immoral. The Court denied both requests, concluding that only those who objected to all wars could obtain exemption.[57]

In summary, the overall thrust of the Court's decisions in recent years has been to provide more protection to religious beliefs and the exercise of those beliefs.

RIGHTS OF THOSE ACCUSED OF CRIME

The courts have played a major role in defining the rights of those accused of, tried, and imprisoned for, criminal acts. Unlike some of the other policy areas discussed here, control over police, court, and prison procedures involves interpretation of statutes and the *Bill of Rights* (the first ten Amendments). Thus, it is often more suitable for judicial than legislative consideration. While these policy areas are generally considered to be the primary preserve of the courts, the decisions of the Supreme Court in the 1960s and 1970s have often been the focus of considerable controversy.

Until the early 1960s, the Supreme Court generally enforced Bill of Rights protections in federal cases, but judged the fairness of state procedures on a case-by-case basis without assuming that the states were obligated by the Bill of Rights. The Bill of Rights was originally added to the Constitution to encourage the states to ratify it and was designed to restrict the *federal* rather than state governments. With the adoption of the Fourteenth Amendment, however, the Court was increasingly asked to determine if the states were now restricted by the Bill of Rights. Until 1925, the Court ruled that they were not.

In that year, however, the Court ruled that the Fourteenth Amendment, which said in part that *states* could not "deprive any person of life, liberty or property, without due process of law," incorporated the First Amendment's protections of freedom of speech and press.[58] The Court's reasoning was that freedom of speech and press "are among the fundamental personal rights and liberties protected by the *due process clause* of the Fourteenth Amendment from impairment by the states." The doctrine of *incorporation* means that some of the Bill of Rights protections are implicitly included in the Fourteenth Amendment. Thus, they apply to the states, too.

Still, the Court refused to simply rule that all the Bill of Rights applied to the states. In 1937 the Court ruled that it would examine issues brought before it to determine if particular provisions of the Bill of Rights should be made obligatory upon the states. The Court said the states could be obligated by the Fourteenth Amendment to abide by rights "implicit in the concept of ordered liberty."[59]

This selective incorporation principle primarily lay dormant until the Warren Court between 1961 and 1969 ruled that ten of the specific guarantees of the Bill of Rights applied to the states. The incorporation decisions of the Warren Court included the Fourth Amendment's protection against illegal search and seizure; the Fifth Amendment's protection against double jeopardy and self-incrimination; the Sixth's provisions for a speedy trial, assistance of counsel, confrontation of hostile witnesses, and right to obtain witnesses; the Seventh's right to trial by jury; and the Eighth's protections against cruel and unusual punishment.

The Warren Court's rulings were labeled a revolution, and they stirred up a great deal of controversy. Charges were made that the Warren Court was tying the hands of police and courts, making it impossible for persons to be tried for criminal acts. The evidence proved such charges to be false, but the police and courts were obligated to do their jobs in a more professional manner, to show more respect for individual liberties.

President Nixon was quite annoyed by the Warren Court's opinions. He purposefully chose people for the Court who would be more oriented toward the concerns of the police and prosecution. The Burger Court has generally moderated the prodefendant rules adopted by the Warren Court. While the major rulings of the Warren Court have not been overruled by the Burger Court, the Burger Court has used the harmless error rule—originally developed by the Warren Court—and the "totality of circumstances rule" to reduce the strictness of the procedural rules formulated by the Warren Court. The Warren Court worked on the assumption that an error—the violation of a suspect's rights—was not harmless if it could reasonably have contributed to a finding of guilt. Under Burger, a violation of a constitutional right is permissible if other evidence against the *defendant,* or the accused, is overwhelming. The differences between the two Courts show to some extent the importance of Court personality.[60]

Interrogation, counsel, and speedy trial

Some of the most important decisions in the Bill of Rights revolution led by the Warren Court extended protections to those suspected or accused of crime in the pretrial stage. In 1963 the Court ruled that through the Fourteenth Amendment the states were obligated to observe the Sixth Amendment's guarantee of counsel to those accused of crime. If the defendant could not afford counsel, the Court would have to appoint one and bear the cost.[61] Justice, the Court said, could not be made dependent upon the wealth of the person accused of crime.

Over the next few years, the Warren Court extended the right-to-counsel rule to some pre- and posttrial proceedings and ruled that juveniles had to be appointed counsel in adversary proceedings.[62] In 1967 the Court held that right to counsel extended to police lineups. Counsel, the Court said, could protect the defendant against suggestive lineups and contaminated identification that could prejudice the accused's defense.[63]

The Burger Court both extended and narrowed the right-to-counsel rule. It extended the rule by throwing out the Warren Court's major-minor standard for appointment of counsel and broadly ruling that the right extended to any criminal proceeding in which the defendant faced a jail term. The Court also held that states were required to make law libraries and trained legal personnel available to prisoners to provide them with realistic access to the courts. The

Clarence Gideon (below), who was convicted of breaking and entering and theft, appealed his case to the U.S. Supreme Court, asking the Court to overturn his conviction because he had not been represented by a lawyer during his trial. Gideon won his case. The *Gideon* ruling established that all defendants in criminal cases have a right to counsel.

Court restricted the right, however, in two ways. First, the Court ruled that the right to counsel extended only to lineups after a defendant had been indicted. Prior to indictment the state did not have to appoint counsel.[64] Second, the Court declined to extend the appointment obligation to discretionary state appeals or petitions to the U.S. Supreme Court.[65]

Building on its right-to-counsel decision, the Warren Court in 1964 ruled that when the police interrogated a person accused of a crime, they could not deny that person's request for his counsel to be present.[66] The Court's interest was in making certain that any confession given police was not given in ignorance of one's constitutional rights, or the result of physical or mental coercion. As early as 1957, the Court had said that in federal cases a confession was invalid if there was any unnecessary delay in bringing the suspect before a judge for arraignment.[67] The decision was designed to keep the police from holding suspects incommunicado and interrogating them over extended periods (a common practice at the time) in which there was no judicial determination that sufficient grounds existed for holding them.

In 1966 the Warren Court consolidated its rules for pretrial interrogation in one of its most celebrated and controversial decisions. In *Miranda* v. *Arizona,* the Court ruled that anyone arrested for a criminal act or on suspicion of a criminal act has to be informed of his or her constitutional rights. According to the decision, suspects had to be informed that they do not have to answer any questions, that any statement they make can and will be used against them in court, that they can have a lawyer present during questioning, that if they cannot afford counsel, one will be appointed, and that if they submit to questioning, they can end the conversation anytime they wish. If these warning are not given, no confession by the defendant will be considered valid.[68]

Miranda caused a storm of protest. Right-wing groups often predicted the wholesale emptying of American prisons and demanded the impeachment of Chief Justice Warren. The dire predictions failed to materialize. The police found that many suspects would provide a confession despite the warnings, and the police developed the habit of gathering evidence to present against defendants who refused interrogation. Still, the *Miranda* decision remains a source of annoyance to right-wing law-and-order advocates. Many people expected Nixon's appointees to the Court to reverse the decision.

The Burger Court has disappointed many of its supporters by failing to nullify Miranda, but it has diluted the standard considerably. The Court upheld the right of police to use inadmissible confessions as leads for locating witnesses. The Court also ruled that if a defendant made an inadmissible confession and then took the stand at trial and gave testimony contrary to statements in the confession, the prosecutor could use the illegal confession to impeach the defendant's testimony. In another case, the Court held that the *Miranda* warning did not have to be given to grand jury witnesses.[69] Finally, the Court concluded that *Miranda* warnings did not have to be given to a suspect prior to arrest. These decisions substantially narrowed the importance of *Miranda;* they constitute some of the most substantial revisions of Warren Court standards.

The Burger Court did rule, however, that the states had to abide by the Sixth Amendment's guarantee of a speedy trial. If the state did not provide a speedy trial, the Court ruled, the defendant had to be released.[70]

Search and seizure

The Burger Court has launched its most direct assault on the Warren Court's rules governing searches and seizures. In 1961 the Warren Court ruled that the Fourth Amendment's protections against unreasonable searches and seizures were binding on the states through the Fourteenth Amendment.[71] To enforce the safeguards the Court used the standard applied at the federal level since 1921: illegally seized evidence could not be used as evidence. This is known as the *exclusionary rule*. The principle behind the rule is that the police will not illegally seize evidence if it cannot be used to prosecute a defendant. The Court also ruled that evidence derivatively obtained by an illegal search is also inadmissible. For example, leads to evidence of crime produced by an illegal search could not be used. This was known as the ''fruit of the poisonous tree'' doctrine. If the tree is tainted, so is its fruit.

The Warren Court's general standard was that a search could not be conducted without a warrant, which had to be issued by a judge. The judge could legally issue the warrant only if the officer had ''probable cause'' to believe that necessary evidence or contraband was in a certain place. The warrant had to specify who and/or what was to be searched and what items could be seized. Exceptions included the search of a person arrested for a crime, and often an automobile if the driver had been arrested for a crime. In the case of an arrest, the Court held that the police could search the immediate area under the defendant's control, such as the room he or she was in. If the police wanted to search any other area of the house, they would have to obtain a warrant.

Chief Justice Burger particularly dislikes the exclusionary rule because he feels that it punishes prosecutors rather than the police. Since he has not been able to offer an alternative deterrent to illegal police behavior, however, he and the other Nixon appointees have upheld a broader range of legal police searches rather than simply casting out the general rule.

In 1968 the Court expanded police power by ruling that an officer could stop and frisk citizens on a public street if the officer believed that the person was acting illegally or was intent upon committing a crime.[72] This decision allowed the police a larger grant of discretion than the Warren Court would have upheld. In two cases in 1973, the Burger Court continued to expand police authority by holding that even when a driver was arrested only for a traffic offense the police could search the driver and his or her vehicle. If any *the Fourth Amendment:* "The right of the people to be secure in their persons, houses, papers, and effects, against unreasonable searches and seizures, shall not be violated, and no Warrants shall issue, but upon probable cause, supported by Oath or affirmation, and particularly describing the place to be searched, and the persons or things to be seized."

from the Fifth Amendment: "No person shall be held to answer for a capital, or otherwise infamous crime, unless on a presentment or indictment of a grand jury . . . ; nor shall any person be subject for the same offense to be twice put in jeopardy of life or limb; nor shall be compelled in any criminal case to be a witness against himself, nor be deprived of life, liberty, or property, without due process of law . . . ."

from the Sixth Amendment: "In all criminal prosecutions, the accused shall enjoy the right to a speedy and public trial, by an impartial jury of the State and district wherein the crime shall have been committed . . . and to be informed of the nature and cause of the accusation; to be confronted with the witnesses against him; to have compulsory process for obtaining witnesses in his favor, and to have the assistance of Counsel for his defence."

from the Seventh Amendment: "In Suits at common law, where the value in controversy shall exceed twenty dollars, the right of trial by jury shall be preserved . . . ."

the Eighth Amendment: "Excessive bail shall not be required, nor excessive fines imposed, nor cruel and unusual punishments inflicted."

Bill of Rights Safeguards for Those Accused of a Crime

illegal evidence was found, the driver could be charged, even if the seized evidence had nothing to do with the initial arrest.[73] This decision gave the police substantial freedom to abuse public rights. In 1973 the Court also ruled that a search and seizure was legal if the defendant consented to the search, even if the defendant had not been told that he could refuse the search.[74]

In 1974 the Court partially overruled the "fruit of the poisonous tree" doctrine. It said that a grand jury could question a witness about loan-sharking activities even though the evidence of his involvement had been obtained during an illegal search.[75] In 1976 the Court ruled that evidence seized illegally but in good faith by state law-enforcement officers could be introduced as evidence in a federal civil proceeding.[76] In the same year, in an unprecedented decision, the Court effectively denied federal court review of many search challenges. The Court said that "where a state had provided an opportunity for full and fair litigation of a Fourth Amendment claim," a state prisoner could not be granted federal *habeas corpus* relief on the ground that illegal evidence was used at his trial. The Court was saying that the states' decisions in this area would generally be final.[77] Thus, the Burger Court has seriously diluted the constitutional protection against illegal search and seizure without actually overruling the exclusionary doctrine.

OTHER FUNDAMENTAL RIGHTS

Between 1964 and 1969 the Warren Court ruled that four other provisions of the Bill of Rights were "necessary to a concept of ordered liberty." Thus, they were made obligations of the states by the Fourteenth Amendment. In 1964 the Court held that the Fifth Amendment's prohibition against compelling anyone in a criminal case to be a witness against oneself—the right against self-incrimination—applied to the states.[78] In 1965 the Court ruled that defendants did not have to give testimony that might be used to convict them of a crime, but the prosecutor could not comment on their failure to testify.[79] In the same year the Court held that the Sixth Amendment's guarantee that individuals accused of a crime must be confronted by witnesses used against them in open court was binding on the states.[80]

In 1968 the Court ruled that the Sixth Amendment's provision for trial by jury applied to the states. In any case in which a person could be sentenced to jail for six or more months, the defendant had to be offered a jury trial.[81] The Burger Court later upheld six-person juries in non-capital, state cases, and non-unanimous (10–2 and 9–3) verdicts in twelve-person state criminal juries. (Prior to this ruling, non-unanimous verdicts would have resulted in hung juries, with no conviction.) The Warren Court's criminal procedure revolution ended in 1969 when it ruled that the Fifth Amendment's ban on double jeopardy—being tried twice for the same offense—applied to the states.[82] Neither the state nor the federal government could try a person for the same crime more than once. The Court's rule has long been that incomplete trials or hung juries do not count as a trial, and thus defendants can be tried again. Also, if defendants break both a state and a federal law in the commission of a crime, both jurisdictions may legally try them. The Burger Court did hold, however, that trial by both the state and local government was unconstitutional, because a local government is an agent of a state.

The Bill of Rights was originally added to the Constitution to encourage the states to ratify it and was designed to restrict the federal rather than state governments. With the adoption of the Fourteenth Amendment, however, the Court was increasingly asked to determine if the states were now restricted by the Bill of Rights.

The Burger Court found itself enmeshed in a controversy that showed the Court's policy-making powers even when it was extremely unclear about the basis of its decisions. In 1972 the Court ruled that state death penalties which allowed too much discretion in the imposition of this punishment were cruel and unusual. Thus, they were unconstitutional since they violated the Eighth Amendment.[83] The Court's decision was extremely murky because none of the five judges in the majority concurred with any other judge on the exact basis for the decision. In general, the Court seemed to have said that states could impose the death penalty for murder, but that juries and judges could not be given so much discretion in imposing the penalty as to make its administration arbitrary.

The decision effectively nullified all state statutes prescribing the death penalty. Thirty-five states wrote new laws, trying as best they could to obtain some guidance from the Court's intensely divided opinion. Insight into the type of statute the Court would accept came in 1976 when it heard five cases on the subject. It overruled a Louisiana statute making death the mandatory sentence for anyone convicted of killing a police officer.[84] The Court said the state could impose the death penalty in such cases, but the judge or jury would have to take into consideration the circumstances of the murder and the psychological and behavioral background of the murderer. In a Georgia case, the Court held that a state could not impose the death penalty for rape.[85]

The Warren Court's criminal procedure revolution ended in 1969 when it ruled that the Fifth Amendment's ban on double jeopardy—being tried twice for the same offense—applied to the states.

The Court upheld the death penalty statutes of three states. In these cases, the state law gave specific circumstances under which the death penalty could be imposed for deliberate murder, required that the circumstances of the killing and the background of the defendant be taken into consideration, and established a quicker appeals procedure when the penalty was imposed.[86] Thus, the Court's original decision in 1972 had stimulated all the states that wanted to provide a death penalty option to write their statutes in keeping with its standards—standards which were far from clear.

In summary, the Warren Court's Bill of Rights revolution greatly expanded the constitutional protections of those accused and subjected to trial for criminal acts. It forced the states and often the federal government to alter their approach and frequently change their laws on this subject. The more conservative Burger Court undermined the Warren Court's standards in a couple of areas, but extended it in others. Under both Warren and Burger, the Supreme Court became the most important branch of government in determining what the rules and procedures must be when the government seeks to put citizens in prison.

IMPORTANT POLICY AREAS

The range of topics dealt with by the Supreme Court is as broad as the policy decisions that face the nation. Few policy topics fail to receive some judicial consideration, whether they involve regulation of ethical drugs, food additives, industrial safety standards, pollution controls, or business mergers. In some important policy areas not covered above, the Supreme Court has over

the last twenty-five years played the dominant role. Below we will provide a sampling of some of the Supreme Court's more important policy decisions to provide insights into the often expansive and critical role the Court plays in a wide range of areas.

Abortion

In one of the Supreme Court's most controversial decisions, the abortion laws of most states were nullified in early 1973. The Court ruled that the right to privacy, implicit in the Fourteenth Amendment's "due process" guarantee of personal liberty, encompassed a woman's decision whether to bear a child or not.[87] State laws which made it a crime for a woman to have an abortion except when necessary to save her life were thus unconstitutional. During the first trimester (three-month period) of pregnancy, the Court held that a woman, in consultation with her physician, could decide whether to terminate the pregnancy. During the second trimester, the state could reasonably regulate abortion procedures to protect the health of the mother. During the last trimester, the state could, if it wished, prohibit all abortions except those necessary to save the life of the mother.

The Court's decision was vigorously protested by some citizens, primarily Catholics. Small but vocal, sometimes fanatical groups at the state and federal level lobbied for a constitutional amendment to overturn the decision. Anti-abortion groups staged rallies and parades, picketed and even attacked abortion clinics, and pressured state legislators to pass legislation that circumvented the decision. The anti-abortionists have been unable to stimulate a serious movement for a constitutional amendment, but they have won some victories. The Right-to-Life movement was credited with convincing Congress to prohibit the use of Medicaid funds to finance abortions for poor women. In 1978 the Right-to-Life chapter in Iowa played a significant role in the defeat of incumbent Senator Dick Clark.

The movement has also suffered some defeats at the hands of the Supreme Court. In 1976 the Court ruled that during the first trimester a woman did not have to have her spouse's consent before she could have an abortion. Also, during the first trimester an unmarried female under eighteen did not have to obtain parental consent to obtain an abortion. In addition, states could not prohibit the use of saline amniocentisis as a method of performing an abortion after the first trimester. The procedure, the Court ruled, was widely considered to be medically safe and had been prohibited only to harass abortion clinics. Finally, the Court said that doctors could not be required to take as much care to preserve the life of an aborted as a nonaborted fetus.[88]

In one of the Supreme Court's most controversial decisions, the abortion laws of most states were nullified in early 1973. The Court ruled that the right to privacy, implicit in the Fourteenth Amendment's "due process" guaranteee of personal liberty, encompassed a woman's decision whether to bear a child or not.

Reapportionment

A series of Warren Court decisions fundamentally altered the representation process at both the federal and state levels. In 1946 the Supreme Court received a case asking the Court to hold that the failure of a state to base the division of representation upon population rather than geography violated the Fourteenth Amendment. The Court refused to address the issue, saying that decisions about how seats in the state legislature and in Congress were apportioned within a state represented a political, rather than a judicial, question.[89]

In 1962 the Warren Court reversed this decision. The Court declined to consider the merits of the case before it but did rule that the issue raised was a legitimate judicial question which could be decided in federal courts.[90] One year later the Court heard a case involving apportionment of congressional districts within a state and issued its famous *one person, one vote rule*. Congressional districts had to be based as equitably as possible on population; and to keep pace with population movements, they had to be reapportioned at least once every ten years.[91] In 1964 the Court extended this rule to state legislatures, saying that both houses of state legislatures had to be based on population. Chief Justice Warren said:

> Legislators represent people, not trees or acres. Legislators are elected by voters, not farms or cities or economic interests. . . . The right to elect legislators in a free and unimpaired fashion is a bedrock of our political system.

In 1968 the rule was extended to local governments.[92]

The implications of the Court's decisions can hardly be overemphasized. Before the decisions, rural areas with a small proportion of the population most often had the majority of seats in the state legislatures. Even congressional seats were biased toward rural representation. This meant that a rural legislator might represent 5,000 citizens while an urban representative might represent several times that many persons. In reality, therefore, rural citizens had voting power that was considerably in excess of their numbers. With the shift of representation to the metropolitan areas, where the population is, the urban/suburban viewpoint began to receive its proportionate voting strength on issues. Ironically, perhaps, suburban representatives often join with rural legislators to deny cities financial or statutory aid.

The Burger Court diluted the Warren Court standards to some extent but did not attempt to overturn the basic doctrine. The Burger Court made a distinction between congressional and state legislative seats. Congressional seats, the Court ruled, have to be apportioned with as much mathematical precision as possible. Thus, deviations as small as 3 percent between districts are unjustified unless the state can prove that it took every measure possible to make the district as equitable as possible.[93] The Court was willing to allow much more latitude in the distribution of state legislative seats. In a 1973 case the Court altered the basic rule by stating that congressional districts would be judged strictly on a ''one person, one vote'' standard, while state districts would be required to be ''as nearly of equal population as is practicable.''[94] In the same year the Court upheld a Texas state legislature reapportionment plan despite a 9.9 percent difference in population between the largest and smallest districts.[95]

Sex discrimination

Just as the Court has played a very significant role in eliminating racial discrimination (see Chapter 17), it has also played a very significant role in ending discrimination based on sex. In a job discrimination case, the Court ruled that a company could not refuse to hire women with preschool children when it did not prohibit the hiring of males with preschool children.[96] In a very significant decision, the Court held that men and women doing the same job had to be paid the same wage. Women could not be paid a lower wage simply because they were not men.[97] Neither, the Court said, could women be forced to terminate their employment at an excessively early period simply because they are pregnant. A state law establishing a mandatory maternity leave policy requiring teachers to resign five months before the expected birth of the child violated due process.[98] In another case, the Court did uphold a state disability insurance program which excluded benefits for women employees disabled because of pregnancy-related problems.[99]

Men benefited from two rulings. The Court said that a state law which presumed that an unwed father was an unfit parent was unconstitutional.[100] A provision of the Social Security Act which allowed payment to widows with small children but not widowers with small children was also ruled unconstitutional. Under the law, the Court said, men received fewer benefits from

In a very significant decision, the Court held that men and women doing the same job had to be paid the same wage. Women could not be paid a lower wage simply because they were not men.

"Well I'm just as qualified as you are, and I got this job fair and square."

their social security contributions than did women. Justice Brennan said in part, "It is no less important for a child to be cared for by its sole surviving parent, when that parent is male rather than female."[101]

A Louisiana law generally exempting women from jury duty was ruled unconstitutional as an unnecessary distinction between the sexes and as a burden on the constitutional guarantee that juries be drawn from a cross-section of the community.[102] A Utah law establishing the age of eighteen as adulthood for women and twenty-one for men was held unconstitutional. The rationale of the state law was that men needed parental support longer than women so that they could obtain a higher education. Speaking for the Court, Justice Blackmun said: "No longer is the female destined solely for the house and the rearing of family and only the male for the marketplace and the world of ideas."[103]

CONCLUSIONS

The federal court system is a major policy-making branch of the federal government. The ambiguity of the American Constitution and the complexity of the issues brought before the courts give federal judges much discretion in the decisions they make. Rarely is the courts' job one of only interpreting clearly worded and easily understandable provisions of the Constitution or laws. Rarely is the outcome of their deliberations a foregone conclusion. The cases that reach the Supreme Court are generally very complex, raising unique questions, which have not been decided before. The power of judicial review and the frequent failure of the legislative branches to deal with issues also give the federal courts unique powers.

The personalities and the judicial and legal philosophies of the majority of the judges on the courts at any given time determine how the law will be interpreted and how expansive the courts will be in making decisions. The courts, especially the Supreme Court, which are much less accountable to public opinion than the other branches of government, take up some of the slack in the policy-making process by deciding important issues. Some of these are issues that should have been decided by the political branches or by prodding the political branches to act. Since Presidents generally understand the Supreme Court's important policy-making role and the impact of judicial personality on this role, they try to appoint judges to the Court who share their political views. Thus, it is ironic that in democratic America many of the most important policy decisions are made by a branch of government which is distinctly undemocratic.

Footnotes

1. *Marbury* v. *Madison,* 1 Cranch 137, 2 L. Ed. 60 (1803).
2. *Bailey* v. *Drexel Furniture Co.,* 259 U.S. 20 (1922).
3. *Adkins* v. *Children's Hospital,* 261 U.S. 525 (1923).
4. See C. Herman Pritchett, *The Roosevelt Court: A Study in Judicial Politics and Values* (New York: Macmillan, 1948).
5. See *The Supreme Court: Law and Justice* (Washington, D.C.: Congressional Quarterly, 1977), p. 7.
6. *Brown* v. *Board of Education,* 347 U.S. 483 (1954).
7. *The Supreme Court: Law and Justice,* p. 4.
8. *Ibid.,* p. 4.
9. *Schenck* v. *U.S.,* 249 U.S. 47 (1919).
10. *Gitlow* v. *New York,* 268 U.S. 652 (1925).
11. *Terminiello* v. *Chicago,* 337 U.S. 1 (1949).
12. *Feiner* v. *New York,* 340 U.S. 315 (1951).
13. *Gregory* v. *Chicago,* 394 U.S. 111 (1969).
14. *Edwards* v. *South Carolina,* 372 U.S. 229 (1963).
15. *Cox* v. *Louisiana,* 379 U.S. 536 (1965).
16. *Brown* v. *Louisiana,* 383 U.S. 131 (1966).
17. *Adderley* v. *Florida,* 385 U.S. 39 (1966).
18. *Grayned* v. *Rockford,* 408 U.S. 104 (1972).
19. *United States* v. *O'Brien,* 391 U.S. 367 (1968).
20. *Tinker* v. *Des Moines School District,* 393 U.S. 503 (1969).
21. *Cohen* v. *California,* 403 U.S. 15 (1971).
22. *Street* v. *New York,* 394 U.S. 576 (1969).

Footnotes

23. *Dennis v. United States*, 341 U.S. 494 (1951).
24. *Yates v. United States*, 354 U.S. 398 (1957).
25. *Scales v. United States*, 367 U.S. 203 (1961).
26. *Brandenburg v. Ohio*, 395 U.S. 444 (1969).
27. *Freeman v. Maryland*, 380 U.S. 51 (1965).
28. *New York Times Co. v. United States*, 403 U.S. 713 (1971).
29. *Roth v. United States*, 354 U.S. 476 (1957).
30. *Jacobellis v. Ohio*, 378 U.S. 184 (1964).
31. *Mishkin v. New York*, 383 U.S. 502 (1966).
32. *Ginsberg v. New York*, 390 U.S. 629 (1968).
33. *Jacobellis v. Ohio*, 378 U.S. 184 (1964).
34. *Stanley v. Georgia*, 394 U.S. 557 (1969).
35. *Miller v. California*, 413 U.S. 15 (1973).
36. *Paris Adult Theatre v. Slaton*, 413 U.S. 49 (1973).
37. *Jenkins v. Georgia*, 418 U.S. 153 (1974).
38. *Erznoznik v. City of Jacksonville*, 422 U.S. 205 (1975).
39. *McKinney v. Alabama*, 424 U.S. 669 (1976).
40. *Engle v. Vitale*, 370 U.S. 421 (1962).
41. *School District v. Schempp*, 374 U.S. 203 (1963).
42. *Braunfield v. Brown*, 366 U.S. 599 (1961).
43. *Epperson v. Arkansas*, 393 U.S. 97 (1968).
44. *Waltz v. Tax Commission of the City of New York*, 397 U.S. 664 (1970).
45. *McCollum v. Board of Education*, 333 U.S. 203 (1948).
46. *Board of Education v. Allen*, 392 U.S. 236 (1968).
47. *Lemon v. Kurtzman*, 403 U.S. 602 (1971).
48. *Levitt v. Committee for Public Education and Religious Liberty*, 413 U.S. 472 (1973).
49. *Committee for Public Education and Religious Liberty v. Nyquist*, 413 U.S. 756 (1973).
50. *Sloan v. Lemon*, 413 U.S. 825 (1973).
51. *Meek v. Pittinger*, 421 U.S. 349 (1975).
52. *Torcaso v. Watkins*, 367 U.S. 488 (1961).
53. *Sherbert v. Verner*, 374 U.S. 398 (1963).
54. *Wisconsin v. Yoder*, 406 U.S. 205 (1972).
55. *United States v. Seeger*, 380 U.S. 163 (1965).
56. *Welsh v. United States*, 398 U.S. 333 (1970).
57. *Gillette v. United States*, 401 U.S. 437 (1971).
58. *Gitlow v. New York*, 268 U.S. 652 (1925).
59. *Palko v. Connecticut*, 302 U.S. 319 (1937).
60. On these points see Stephen L. Wasby, *Continuity and Change: From the Warren Court to the Burger Court* (Pacific Palisades, Ca.: Goodyear, 1976), pp. 168–69.
61. *Gideon v. Wainwright*, 372 U.S. 335 (1963).
62. *In re Gault*, 387 U.S. 1 (1967).
63. *U.S. v. Wade*, 388 U.S. 218 (1967).
64. *Kirby v. Illinois*, 406 U.S. 682 (1972).
65. *Ross v. Moffitt*, 417 U.S. 600 (1978).
66. *Escobedo v. Illinois*, 378 U.S. 478 (1964).
67. *Mallory v. United States*, 354 U.S. 449 (1957).
68. *Miranda v. Arizona*, 384 U.S. 436 (1966).
69. *U.S. v. Mandujano*, 96 S.Ct. 1768 (1976).
70. *Klopfer v. North Carolina*, 408 U.S. 238 (1967).
71. *Mapp v. Ohio*, 367 U.S. 643 (1961).
72. *Terry v. Ohio*, 392 U.S. 1 (1968).

73. *U.S.* v. *Robinson*, 414 U.S. 318 (1973); *Gustafson* v. *Florida*, 414 U.S. 260 (1973).
74. *Schneckloth* v. *Bustamonte*, 412 U.S. 218 (1973).
75. *U.S.* v. *Calandra*, 414 U.S. 338 (1974).
76. *U.S.* v. *Janis*, 428 U.S. 433 (1976).
77. *Stone* v. *Powell; Wolff* v. *Rice*, 428 U.S. 465 (1976).
78. *Malloy* v. *Hogan*, 378 U.S. 1 (1964).
79. *Griffin* v. *California*, 380 U.S. 609 (1965).
80. *Pointer* v. *Texas*, 380 U.S. 400 (1965).
81. *Duncan* v. *Louisiana*, 391 U.S. 146 (1968).
82. *Benton* v. *Maryland*, 395 U.S. 784 (1969).
83. *Furman* v. *Georgia*, 408 U.S. 238 (1972).
84. *Roberts* v. *Louisiana*, 428 U.S. 325 (1976).
85. *Gregg* v. *Georgia*, 428 U.S. 153 (1976).
86. *Proffitt* v. *Florida*, 428 U.S. 242; *Jurek* v. *Texas*, 428 U.S. 262; *Gregg* v. *Georgia*, 428 U.S. 153 (1976).
87. *Roe* v. *Wade*, 401 U.S. 113 (1973).
88. *Planned Parenthood of Central Missouri* v. *Danforth*, 428 U.S. 152 (1976).
89. *Colegrove* v. *Green*, 328 U.S. 549 (1946).
90. *Baker* v. *Carr*, 369 U.S. 186 (1962).
91. *Westbury* v. *Sanders*, 376 U.S. 1 (1963).
92. *Reynolds* v. *Sims*, 377 U.S. 533 (1964).
93. *White* v. *Weiser*, 412 U.S. 783 (1973).
94. *Gaffney* v. *Cummings*, 412 U.S. 755 (1973).
95. *White* v. *Regester*, 412 U.S. 755 (1973).
96. *Reed* v. *Reed*, 404 U.S. 71 (1971).
97. *Corning Glass Works* v. *Brennan*, 417 U.S. 188 (1974).
98. *Cleveland Board of Education* v. *La Fleur*, 414 U.S. 632 (1974).
99. *Geduldig* v. *Aiello*, 417 U.S. 484 (1974).
100. *Stanley* v. *Illinois*, 405 U.S. 645 (1972).
101. *Weinberger* v. *Wiesenfeld*, 420 U.S. 636 (1975).
102. *Taylor* v. *Louisiana*, 419 U.S. 522 (1975).
103. *Stanton* v. *Stanton*, 421 U.S. 7 (1975).

3

SOCIAL PROBLEMS, POLITICS, AND ECONOMICS

> The strong do what they can and the weak suffer what they must.
>
> Thucydides

Although America is rich and prosperous, a large percentage of the American public has never shared in that prosperity. Throughout our history, a small segment of the public has been extremely rich; another small percentage has been prosperous; the majority has lived at moderate levels with few liquid assets; and a significant proportion of the population has lived in acute poverty. As recently as 1961, the government estimated that 40 million Americans lived in poverty, about 22 percent of the total population. Millions of other Americans have always lived just above the poverty level, most of them in constant jeopardy of slipping into poverty.

15

Poverty in America

During most of American history, poverty was an accepted fact of life. The government took no actions to alleviate it. Piven and Cloward describe the standard approach to poverty during the first several decades of the twentieth century:

> At the time of the Great Depression the main legal arrangement for the care of the destitute was incarceration in almshouses or workhouses. In some places the care of paupers was still contracted to the lowest bidder, and destitute orphans were indentured to those who would feed them in exchange for whatever labor they could perform. The constitutions of fourteen states denied the franchise to paupers. . . . By such practices the relief system created a clearly demarcated and degraded class, a class of pariahs whose numbers were small but whose fate loomed large in the lives of those who lived close to indigence, warning them always of a life even worse than hard work and severe poverty.[1]

The U.S. government did not even attempt to determine how many people lived in poverty until 1964. In that year, the Council of Economic Advisers (CEA) rather arbitrarily set the poverty threshold at $3,000 for a family of four. Half this amount was to serve as the standard for a single individual. This highly unscientific process yielded a poverty count of 35 million people for 1962, about 20 percent of the population.[2]

In 1965 the Social Security Administration (SSA) developed a more scientific measure of poverty. An Economy-Food budget was formulated as a

The United States is usually thought of as a wealthy nation, but many Americans—about 25 million, by government estimates—live in poverty. And contrary to popular belief, most of America's poor people—about 57 percent—are white.

TABLE 15.1
Poverty Standard: 1977

Size of Family Unit	Average	Non-Farm			Farm		
		Total	Male Head	Female Head	Total	Male Head	Female Head
1 person	$3,067	$3,075	$3,214	$2,969	$2,588	$2,672	$2,498
14 to 64	3,147	3,152	3,267	3,023	2,709	2,776	2,569
65 yrs. and over	2,895	2,906	2,936	2,898	2,475	2,495	2,563
2 persons	3,928	3,951	3,961	3,907	3,318	3,325	3,176
Head 14 to 64 yrs.	4,054	4,072	4,095	3,981	3,466	3,474	3,278
Head 65 yrs. and over	3,637	3,666	3,670	3,646	3,128	3,131	3,097
3 persons	4,806	4,833	4,860	4,708	4,093	4,110	3,893
4 persons	6,157	6,191	6,195	6,162	5,273	5,274	5,213
5 persons	7,279	7,320	7,329	7,238	6,247	6,247	6,237
6 persons	8,208	8,261	8,268	8,197	7,026	7,026	7,040
7 persons and more	10,137	10,216	10,249	9,995	8,708	8,706	8,738

Source: U.S. Bureau of the Census, "Money Income and Poverty Status of Families and Persons in the United States: 1977 (Advance Report)," *Current Population Reports,* Series P–60, No. 116, 1979, p. 20.

base, theoretically representing the cost of a nutritionally adequate diet.* Since a 1955 Department of Agriculture study had shown that poor people spend about one-third of their income on food, the Economy-Food budget was multiplied by three to obtain the necessary total income for one person. The SSA then multiplied the budget for one person by the number of people in a family. This standard has since served as the government's official measure of poverty.

Table 15.1 shows the standard for families of various sizes in 1977. Notice that the standard varies by family size, the sex of the family head, and whether the family lives in an urban or rural area. Farm families are presumed to need only 85 percent of the cash income required by nonfarm families. (Until 1969 they were presumed to need only 70 percent as much.) The rate for single persons and couples is adjusted upwards to compensate for the higher cost of living alone. Female-headed families receive slightly less than male-headed families, and two-person elderly families are presumed to need 8 percent less than nonelderly two-person families.

Table 15.2 shows the SSA standard for a nonfarm family of four backdated (by SSA) to 1959, with the SSA's total poverty count by year. Until

---

*The limitations of this diet were severe. A four-member family could spend only $.95 per meal. Meat had to be limited to one pound per day for all four members, and less than two dozen eggs could be purchased per month for all purposes.

TABLE 15.2
Poverty Schedule for a Non-Farm Family of Four: 1959–1978

Year	Standard	Millions of Poor	Percent of Total Population
1959	$2,973	39.5	22%
1960	3,022	39.9	22
1961	3,054	39.9	22
1962	3,089	38.6	21
1963	3,128	36.4	19
1964	3,169	36.1	19
1965	3,223	33.2	17
1966	3,317	30.4	16
1966*	3,317	28.5	15
1967	3,410	27.8	14
1968	3,553	25.4	13
1969	3,743	24.1	12
1970	3,968	25.4	13
1971	4,137	25.6	12.5
1972	4,275	24.5	12
1973	4,540	23.0	11
1974	5,038	24.3	12
1974*	5,038	23.4	11.5
1975	5,500	25.9	12
1976	5,815	25.0	12
1977	6,200	24.7	12
1978	6,662	24.5	11.4

Source: Derived from U.S. Bureau of the Census, "Characteristics of the Low-Income Population," *Current Population Reports,* Series P-60, various years.
*Revision in Census calculations.

1969, the yearly changes in the poverty standard reflected changes in the cost of the Economy-Food Budget. Since 1969 the standard has been adjusted yearly according to changes in the Consumer Price Index. The figures show that considerable progress was made in reducing poverty between 1959 and 1977. In 1959, 1960, and 1961, 40 million Americans were counted among the poor. By 1966 the poverty count had dropped to 28.5 million, about 16 percent of the total population. Since 1966 the poverty count has varied by only a few million, despite considerable increases in welfare expenditures. In fact, in 1975 and 1976 there were even some reversals, with poverty running higher than in earlier years. In 1968 there were about 25 million poor, and in 1977 and 1978 there were *still* 25 million poor—about 12 percent of the total population.

A critical question is: How realistic is the government's measure of poverty? An examination of the measure suggests serious shortcomings. One problem is that the standard assumes that the poor can live on very small sums. For example, Tables 15.1 and 15.2 show that in 1977 the poverty threshold for a nonfarm family of four was $6,191. This standard allowed $1,548 per person per year, or $4.24 a day, one-third of which was the allotment for food ($1.41). The family could spend a total of $1.88 per meal for all four persons, or $39.48 per week on food. An annual budget for a four-person family would look like this:

$2,063.66 for food: $1.41 a day ($.47 per meal) per person; $9.87 per week per person.

$2,063.66 for shelter: $171.97 a month for rent or mortgage for four persons.

$2,063.66 for necessities: $42.99 a month per person for clothing, furniture, transportation, health care, utilities, taxes, entertainment, etc.

This breakdown shows the obvious shortcomings of the standard. No matter how carefully a family of four shopped, $39.48 ($1.88 per meal) would be an inadequate food budget. The budget for shelter and other necessities is also extremely inadequate. Despite these shortcomings, any family or individual whose before-tax and before-payroll deductions income exceeds the threshold for their family size by even one cent is not counted among the poor.

Of those who are counted by the government, many do not have as much income as the threshold for their family size. For example, in 1977 the average poor family's income was $1,775 less ($1,626 for white families, $2,023 for black families) than the threshold for their family size.[3]

Although America is rich and prosperous, a large percentage of the American public has never shared in this prosperity.

Interestingly, a federal government agency that is not responsible for defining poverty attempts to determine how much families need to live adequately in our society and reaches vastly different conclusions than SSA. The Bureau of Labor Statistics (BLS) annually calculates budgets which reflect the income needed by families to enjoy a moderate, austere, or modestly luxurious lifestyle. In 1978 the BLS calculated that a nonfarm family of four would require $19,000 for a moderate lifestyle. This standard is far out of reach of the poor. An austere lifestyle could have been sustained on $11,546, 86 percent more than the SSA poverty standard.[4] If $11,546 were used as the poverty threshold for a nonfarm family of four in 1978, 65 million Americans would have been judged poor. This would overestimate destitution, but it would probably not seriously exaggerate economic hardship.

The general public's estimate of the financial needs of a family of four are much closer to the BLS's calculations than SSA's official standard. Each year since the 1930s, the Gallup Poll has asked citizens to estimate the minimum budget they believe a nonfarm family of four needs to make ends meet. The figures below show the public's estimate for related years:[5]

Year	Per Week	Per Year
1978	$201	$10,452
1977	199	10,348
1976	177	9,204
1967	101	5,252
1957	72	3,744
1947	43	2,236
1937	30	1,560

The SSA's poverty standard of $6,191 for a nonfarm family of four in 1977 is only 60 percent of the minimum budget suggested by the public for that year.

The problems with the SSA's measure of poverty go far beyond the unrealistically low threshold. The standard does not consider regional variations in the cost of living; the 15 percent reduction for farm families is frequently not justified; the percentage of the poor population's budget spent for food has changed in recent years but has not been reflected in the standard; and it does not consider assets or in-kind benefits such as food stamps. Studies show that if in-kind benefits were taken into consideration, the poverty count would be reduced by some 10 to 15 million persons.[6] However, if the food budget were made more realistic and multiplied by 3.4 rather than 3, to reflect changes in the poor's food expenditures, the number of poor would be increased by 15 million, to 31 million. For example, the Department of Health, Education and Welfare calculated that if the food budget were multiplied by 3.4 rather than 3, 39.9 million persons would have been counted among the poor in 1974. If a more realistic food budget were used along with a multiplication factor of 3.4, the poverty count in 1974 would have been a staggering 55.4 million.[7] Thus, if the poverty standard were made more realistic, when the corrections were balanced out they would show an increase in the poverty population of 5 to 20 million persons.

The federal bureaucracy, however, is more interested in minimizing the extent of poverty than in correctly measuring its dimensions, and some scholars have contributed to this effort. In the 1970s, some influential scholars tried to prove that poverty had been systematically *over*estimated. One full-length book argued that poverty had been essentially eliminated in the United States. Of even greater impact, a study by the Congressional Budget Office (CBO) held that the nation might be exaggerating the number of the poor by a factor of two.[8] These revisions of the poverty measure all focused on the fact that the government's definitions are based on *money* income and do not include the cash value of *in-kind* transfers. There is no question that the poverty measure

"How could the government possibly afford a guaranteed annual income? As I see it, the average family needs at least $65,000 per year."

would be made more realistic if such computations were included. But there were extremely serious flaws in the way these critics made their point.

First, they assumed that the value of in-kind services received by the poor was equal to the amount paid for them by the federal government. This ignored the existence of "Medicaid mills," where unnecessary and even dangerous therapies were provided and it was assumed that all of the bureaucratic costs were completely justified. Second, they equated a dependent form of income, subject to the will of the government and liable to be withdrawn, with cash in the pocket. Yet economically and psychologically, the two forms of "buying power" are obviously very different, the one a means of independence, the other a form of dependence. Third, a significant portion of the federal outlays for health are not spread uniformly among the poor but are concentrated in the care of the terminally ill. It would, therefore, be possible for a person with an expensive, interminable death agony to rise into the middle class because of federal payments.

Moreover, the Congressional Budget Office and those who agreed with its assessment only examined this one possibility of an overcount, but they scrupulously ignored all of the evidence of an undercount. For example, it is well known that millions of "undocumented workers," mainly from Latin America and the Caribbean, reside in the U.S., mainly in California, New York, Florida, and Texas. Indeed, in the period prior to the 1980 census, various governors demanded that Washington find some way to count these officially nonexistent human beings, who have an extremely high incidence of poverty. They do not, however, show up in the government statistics. In short, even if one adopted what is valid in the CBO critique, but made the other revisions that had been indicated here, the poverty population would increase, not decrease.

MYTHS ABOUT POOR AMERICANS

Americans have many strong beliefs about poor people, most of which are wrong. Incorrect beliefs, or myths, are quite functional, however. They allow citizens and public officials to dismiss poverty as a serious problem by blaming the condition on those who are poor. If people are poor because of personal deficiencies, then the political and economic systems are not at fault. If anything needs correcting, according to this view, it is the poor themselves. Clearly, some persons are poor because of personal deficiencies, but individual inadequacies cannot begin to explain why 30 to 40 million Americans live in poverty. The following analysis of the most prominent myths reveals how unrealistic most public perceptions are.

"The poor are black"

Because of racial prejudice, many Americans take comfort in the belief that most poor people are black. This belief gives comfort to many people because they believe blacks are particularly prone to shiftlessness. Most of the poor, however, are white, and this has always been true. The figures below show the racial breakdown of the poor in 1977.[9]

	Number (in millions)	Percent of All Poor	Percent of All Persons of that Race Who Are Poor
White	13,716	56.8%	8.9%
Black	7,726	32.0	31.3
Spanish origin	2,700	11.1	22.4

As the figures show, about 57 percent of all the poor in 1977 were white, 32 percent were black, and 11 percent were of Spanish origin. Another 3 percent were Asians or American Indians.

Minorities do have a much greater chance of being poor, however. While only 8.9 percent of all whites were poor, 31.3 percent of all blacks and 22.4 percent of all citizens of Spanish origin were poor. Clearly, there are social and economic conditions which make poverty a greater hazard for minorities.

"The poor refuse to work"

The public believes that the poor are not willing to work for a living. Employment problems definitely lie at the core of much poverty in America, but the problem is more complex than simply shiftlessness. Many of the poor are either unemployed, underemployed, or unemployable. The heads of many poor families, especially women and minority males, have great difficulty obtaining a job, or in obtaining a job which pays a decent wage.

If the poverty standards were made more realistic, there would be an increase in the poverty population of 5 to 20 million persons.

Two points, however, should be noted. First, many of the poor cannot support themselves because of age or incapacity. In 1977 53.3 percent of all the poor were either sixty-five or older or under eighteen years old. Poor children alone numbered 10 million and constituted 40.5 percent of all poor Americans. One American child in six was poor. The aged poor numbered 3.2 million, 12.8 percent of all poor Americans.[10] Another 5 percent of all poor adults in 1977 were non-aged, handicapped persons.

Second, most heads of poor families *are* employed in some manner. In 1977, 48.5 percent of all heads of poor families were employed, and 20 percent were employed full-time. Fifty-one percent of all heads of poor families were not in the job market.[11] Most of those outside the job market were women with dependent children, disabled persons, and the elderly.

"Welfare recipients are mostly ablebodied men"

The prevailing myth about welfare recipients is that most of them are healthy males who prefer to live off the dole rather than work. This myth is completely wrong. Males generally have great difficulty in qualifying for assistance. For example, only twenty-eight states allow an unemployed father to receive benefits from the Aid to Families with Dependent Children (AFDC) program, regardless of the reason for their unemployment and poverty. But even in those states that allow some fathers to receive AFDC benefits, the restrictions are so severe that only a modest number of families ever manage to qualify.

Recent program figures are revealing. In 1975, 3.5 million families (with 11.3 million recipients) received AFDC benefits. The monthly average for families headed by a male was only 120,000 in 1975 and 147,000 in 1976. Because of discrimination against men, 80.1 percent of all AFDC families in 1975 were headed by women.[12] Single males, or couples without children, cannot qualify for AFDC in any of the states.

For most of America's
urban poor people,
crowded living conditions,
deteriorating
neighborhoods with high
crime rates, and
substandard schools are
the norm.

"The poor squander their money"

The prevailing belief is that poor people waste the small sums they do have. The evidence, however, indicates that the poor spend most of their money on essentials such as food, housing, and medical care. In 1975 HEW's studies showed that an average poor family spent 29 percent of its income on food, 34 percent on housing, and 9 percent on medical care.[13] The figures below compare spending of poor families to those of affluent families:

Spending Category	Poor	Affluent
Food	29%	20%
Housing	34	29
Transportation	9	6
Medical Care	9	12
Clothing	7	5
Recreation	2	5
Tobacco	2	1
Alcohol	1	2
Other	7	10

These comparative figures show that poor people spend considerably more of their income on essentials than do the affluent. In addition, the poor have little left over to spend for luxuries or to squander on tobacco and alcohol. Studies of poor people's food shopping habits also show them to be more conscientious than other citizens in their buying habits. In other words, they are not as inclined as other economic groups to buy junk or luxury foods.

"The poor get rich off welfare"

Many people believe that poor people get wealthy from welfare. They imagine the poor using welfare payments to buy color T.V.s, Cadillacs, liquor, and luxury foods. In truth, most welfare families barely survive. Under current laws, welfare benefits vary greatly by state: In the most generous states, welfare benefits barely allow recipients to get by; in the least generous states, welfare benefits keep families in a state of desperation. The figures below show the variations in average family AFDC benefits, by state, in August 1977.[14]

State	Benefit	State	Benefit
Alabama	$112.42	Missouri	$155.16
Alaska	301.64	Montana	181.39
Arizona	141.57	Nebraska	203.22
Arkansas	134.09	Nevada	168.24
California	305.37	New Hampshire	201.07
Colorado	194.90	New Jersey	270.70
Connecticut	293.16	New Mexico	149.78
Delaware	206.68	New York	378.51
District of		North Carolina	153.55
Columbia	235.19	North Dakota	223.00
Florida	144.16	Ohio	202.72
Georgia	104.05	Oklahoma	206.86
Hawaii	373.13	Oregon	263.33
Idaho	252.40	Pennsylvania	276.52
Illinois	274.97	Rhode Island	254.55
Indiana	177.54	South Carolina	83.57
Iowa	260.76	South Dakota	206.07
Kansas	228.38	Tennessee	103.35
Kentucky	164.49	Texas	104.69
Louisiana	121.75	Utah	256.59
Maine	187.77	Vermont	261.24
Maryland	183.11	Virginia	190.88
Massachusetts	304.30	Washington	284.17
Michigan	287.41	West Virginia	248.32
Minnesota	280.04	Wisconsin	308.01
Mississippi	47.30	Wyoming	195.02

The average AFDC family in August, 1977, received $241.98 per month, or $78.73 per recipient. The variations in benefits, however, were extreme. In Mississippi an average family received only $47.30, or $14.57 per person per month. In New York the average family received $378.51, or $116.92 per recipient. As the figures show, even in the most generous states recipients have little cash income. A family receiving $378.51, or $116.92 per person, could buy few if any luxuries.

In addition to cash aid, many citizens receive in-kind benefits. Some welfare recipients also receive aid under more than one program. For example, in 1978, 99 percent of all AFDC families received some services under Medicaid. Seventy-five percent of AFDC families also participated in the food-stamp program. Even among those families who can qualify for AFDC (mostly female-headed families) and other programs, such as food stamps or Medicaid, the cash income of the families ranges from extremely low to very modest. Even multiple benefits can leave recipients in acute poverty. For example, in 1975, the ''combined benefits of AFDC and food stamps in twenty-six states totaled less than three-fourths of the official poverty income level in America.''[15] Thus, even multiple welfare benefits are generally low, leaving little cash for luxuries.

''It is easy to get on welfare''

Many believe that anyone can get on welfare and that all one has to do to start receiving a monthly check is go down to the local welfare office and fill out a form or two. As noted above, welfare programs are categorical, permitting benefits only to restricted groups of the poor. Non-aged males, single adults, and couples have great difficulty obtaining assistance, regardless of their need or the reason for their destitution. Most welfare goes to female-headed families, the aged, the disabled, and blind.

Second, getting on welfare and staying on welfare is complex even for those who qualify for aid. An applicant must fill out numerous forms and provide complete records on income (if any), bills, assets, and expenditures. These forms are usually long and complex. Former HEW Secretary Joseph Califano provides some examples:

> The complexity of the rules and regulations is legendary. The forms used by the Los Angeles welfare department, for example, measure 70 feet long when laid end to end—the manuals stack 6 feet high. In Atlanta, 29 separate forms are used in the AFDC application process. Welfare offices and poor Americans are buried in a demoralizing blizzard of paper all over the country. And each assistance program has separate and different forms, eligibility requirements, benefit schedules, regulations, and administrative policies and procedures. No system should be so complicated.[16]

Furthermore, an applicant who makes it through the paper blizzard must submit to an initial home visit and periodic home visits while on welfare. During the period of benefit, all welfare recipients must submit to an ongoing audit of their income and expenditures.

"He's at that awkward age . . . too young for Old Age Security, too old for Opportunity for Youth Grants, too late for family allowances, too conventional for Culture Council grants, too poor for tax loopholes, too rich for subsidized housing . . ."

An analysis of who obtains welfare assistance also reveals something about the difficulty of obtaining aid. Welfare recipients represent the poorest of the poor, but certainly not all the poor (even among the most destitute) receive aid. For example, unlike AFDC or Medicaid, poor non-aged males, single adults, and childless couples can receive food stamps if they meet the income and asset criteria. Still, the evidence shows that food-stamp recipients are very poor. In September 1975, the average monthly gross income of food-stamp households was only $298; that comes to $3,576 annually, or 23 percent of the mean family income of all American families in 1975.[17] The gross income of 78 percent of all food-stamp households in 1975 fell below the Social Security Administration's poverty threshold, and 90 percent earned less than 125 percent of the poverty threshold.[18] Eighty-six percent of all food stamp bonuses went to families below the poverty level.[19]

Recipients of food stamps are overwhelmingly the elderly, blind, disabled, welfare mothers and their children, unemployed workers, and low-income working families. Still, many of the poorest families do not receive food stamps. In 1975, of all the four-person families that earned $3,000 or less, only 58 percent received food stamps. In fact, only about 55 percent of all families (or 5.9 million out of 10.4 million potentially eligible families) who could have qualified for food stamps in 1975 actually utilized them.[20] In 1977, Congress passed a new law specifying that only those families and individuals with net incomes below the poverty line may receive food stamps.

"The poor are cheats"

The public generally believes that much welfare goes to people who are ineligible to receive it. The facts indicate that such charges are highly exaggerated. Many studies have been conducted to try to determine how many poor people are welfare cheaters. None of the studies has ever reported finding that a significant percentage of all recipients were involved in fraud.[21] For example, in 1975 a United States Department of Agriculture (USDA) study reported that food-stamp fraud equalled twenty-four thousandths of 1 percent of all participating households.[22] Other studies have found as much as 1 to 3 percent of program funds going to ineligible persons because of fraud or computational error.

Three points about incorrect expenditure of welfare funds should be noted. First, welfare recipients sometimes receive the wrong amount of aid because the welfare laws are so complex that even case workers cannot always keep the rules straight or learn all the various rules that might apply to a particular case. In general, computational error is a bigger problem than fraud. Computational error is caused, of course, by strict laws designed to reduce fraud.

The food stamp program allows poor families to buy low-priced coupons that can be redeemed for food. Financed by federal government tax revenues, the program cost about $7 billion in 1979 and served about 17 million people per month.

Incorrect beliefs, or myths, allow citizens and public officials to dismiss poverty as a serious problem by blaming the condition on those who are poor. If people are poor because of personal deficiencies, then the political and economic systems are not at fault; but individual inadequacies cannot begin to explain why 30 to 40 million Americans live in poverty.

Second, it is extremely difficult to uncover many types of welfare cheating. If a recipient or applicant wants to cover up some small source of income, such as a few hours overtime or an extra half-day of work, it is not very hard to do. Studies of fraud, therefore, are unlikely to ever be very accurate. What the studies can do is detect serious fraud, such an ineligible people on the rolls.

Third, the cumulative evidence indicates that, on the average, the poor are neither particularly virtuous or particularly corrupt. Morally, they are much like the rest of the population. Some are very honest, some are very dishonest, and others can be tempted by a chance to increase their income by a little deception. This is similar to public cheating on tax reports, business cheating on government contracts, or dozens of other forms of dishonesty that a significant proportion of the population engages in (see Chapter 17).

"Once on welfare, always on welfare"

The public tends to imagine a career dependence class that draws welfare all their lives. But both the poor and welfare recipients are actually a rather fluid group. In a 1973 study, female-headed families were found to have averaged twenty months on AFDC, while male-headed families averaged only nine months.[23] Generally, about 25 percent of all families leave AFDC rolls within six months, half leave within two years, and three-fifths are terminated within three years. However, because of severe economic conditions in 1974 and 1975, the average AFDC recipient stayed on the rolls for a record thirty-one months.[24]

Some AFDC families, however, are repeaters. One study found that in both 1961 and 1971, one-third of all AFDC families had received assistance before.[25] Many AFDC recipients were also raised in families that received assistance. Another study showed that more than 40 percent of mothers and/or fathers on welfare in 1961 had been raised in homes where assistance had been received.[26]

In addition, an HEW study showed that between 1967 and 1972, 21 percent of all Americans were poor in at least one of those years.[27] Each year, 30 to 40 percent of the poor "escape" poverty: they earn enough or receive enough supplemental aid to push them over SSA's artificially low poverty standard. Only about 6 to 8 percent of the population is permanently poor (always below SSA's standard). However, in any given year about 25 percent of the population is at risk—either below the poverty standard or in danger of falling below it.[28]

"Welfare families are large"

The public imagines welfare families as being large because additional children mean increased benefits. In fact, the size of welfare families is average. In 1977 the average AFDC family had 2.2 children.[29] The increased benefits an AFDC family would receive by having an additional child would hardly make it a lucrative investment. In most states, benefits do increase modestly up to four to five children, but the increase would average no more than $30 to $40 per month and would be much lower in the South, where 41 percent of the poor lives.

MAJOR WELFARE PROGRAMS AND THEIR IMPACT ON POVERTY

Table 15.3 shows the major social welfare programs in operation between 1977 and 1979, the basic eligibility qualifications for assistance, the source of funds, the form of aid, the number of persons served by each program, and the yearly cost. Some of the programs are not strictly welfare programs: Social Security and Medicare are financed by employer and employee payroll taxes, and unemployment compensation is financed by a tax on employers. Social Security is the largest program, costing $102.3 billion in 1979 and serving an average of 34.5 million persons per month. Medicare is the second largest program, costing $29.1 billion in 1979 and serving a monthly average of 26.7 million persons.

> *The public generally believes that much welfare goes to people who are ineligible to receive it. The facts indicate that such charges are highly exaggerated.*

Only two of the welfare programs provide cash assistance. AFDC provides cash aid and services, such as job training programs and some child care. As noted above, most AFDC benefits go to female-headed families with dependent children. In 1979 AFDC cost approximately $11.2 billion and served an average of 10.4 million persons per month in some 3.5 million families. Supplemental Security Income (SSI), a program that began in 1974, is a guaranteed income for the aged, disabled, and blind. Benefits from SSI are quite modest. In 1979 the average recipient received $133.58 per month. To

TABLE 15.3
Social Welfare Programs

Programs	Basis of Eligibility	Source of Funding	Form of Aid
Social Insurance Programs			
Social Security [Old Age Survivors & Dependent Insurance (OASDI)]	Age, disability, or death of parent or spouse; individual earnings	Federal payroll taxes on employers and employees	Cash
Unemployment compensation	Unemployment	State and federal payroll tax on employers	Cash
Medicare	Age or disability	Federal payroll tax on employers and employees	Subsidized health insurance
Cash assistance			
Aid to Families with Dependent Children (AFDC)	Certain families with children; income	Federal, state, and local revenues	Cash and services
Supplemental Security Income (SSI)	Age or disability; income	Federal, state revenue	Cash
In-kind programs			
Medicaid	Persons eligible for AFDC or SSI and medically needy	Federal state, and local revenues	Subsidized health service
Food stamps	Income	Federal revenues	Vouchers

Source: Social Security Bulletin, September 1979, pp. 35–104.
*All figures for 1978 and 1979 are preliminary.

be eligible for SSI, a single person cannot have liquid assets worth more than $1,500, and a couple cannot have liquid assets in excess of $2,250. SSI was designed to supplement low Social Security payments and to replace many inadequate state and local programs for the aged, blind, and disabled. SSI cost $6.3 billion in 1979 and served a monthly average of 4.2 million persons.

The Medicaid and food-stamps programs provide in-kind (noncash) benefits to recipients. Medicaid is an assistance program for the medically needy. In twenty-one states, only AFDC and SSI recipients may receive medical assistance under Medicaid. In twenty-eight states, AFDC, SSI, and some specifically defined needy persons can obtain some care. Arizona is the only state

Fiscal 1977		Fiscal 1978*		Fiscal 1979	
Expenditures (billions)	Beneficiaries (monthly average in millions)	Expenditures (billions)	Beneficiaries (monthly average in millions)	Expenditures (billions)	Beneficiaries (monthly average in millions)
81.9	33.3	89.3	34.0	102.3	34.5
14.8	11.0	12.3	11.1	10.3	9.5
21.2	25.2	26.0	25.3	29.1	26.7
11.4	10.3	11.0	10.7	11.4	10.4
6.3	4.4	6.3	4.3	6.3	4.2
17.2	10.4	20.0	10.7	22.7	11.0
5.0	17.7	6.3	17.1	7.0	17.4

that does not participate in the Medicaid program, which is quite expensive. In 1979 it cost $22.7 billion and served a monthly average of 11 million persons.

The foot-stamp program is designed to help needy persons obtain enough food for a nutritious diet. It provides families with net incomes below the poverty level with stamps that can be redeemed at food markets for groceries. The stamps can be used only for food items, not for tobacco, liquor, toilet articles, household cleaners, wax paper, toilet paper, soap, and other items.

The number of stamps a family can receive depends upon income and family size. For example, as of early 1979 a four-person family with no income could receive $191.00 worth of stamps free. If the family had net earnings of $100 per month, they could receive $161.00 in stamps. If the family earned $389, they could receive $75.00 worth of stamps. If the family earned $544 or more they would no longer be eligible for assistance. In addition, families with liquid assets of $1,750 or more are ineligible for food stamps. (For example, recreational homes and campers, boats, and expensive cars are considered liquid assets, as are cash, stocks, and bonds.) Food-stamp recipients are required to register for employment or employment training, with exemptions like those for AFDC (mothers of preschool children, for instance). Beginning in 1979, some recipients were required to accept public service jobs to pay for their stamps. The food-stamp program is the least expensive of the major welfare programs. In 1979 it cost $7 billion and served about 17 million persons per month.

Welfare programs serve a large number of people. Social Security, SSI, and Medicare primarily serve the aged, with a large proportion of the aged receiving benefits from more than one of these programs. SSI, Medicaid, AFDC, and the food-stamp program serve the needy, with AFDC recipients making up a significant proportion of all food-stamp and Medicaid recipients. All the major social welfare programs cost $189.1 billion in 1979. Social Security and Medicare accounted for 69 percent of the total costs. AFDC, SSI, food stamps, and Medicaid had a combined cost of $47.4 billion in 1979, or some 25 percent of the total cost of major social welfare programs.

With expenditures this large, why has poverty persisted and even increased in recent years? There are many reasons, but two major ones can be noted. First, most welfare programs are not designed to end poverty. Most of them are so modest in benefits that all they can do is supplement poverty incomes enough to push some of the poor over the poverty line and provide some minimal help to the most destitute among the poor. Thus, while welfare programs do reduce the incidence of poverty, they are too modest to end it. For example, Plotnick and Skidmore estimated that in 1974, 17.6 million households, including 39.5 million persons, were poor before receiving cash welfare or Social Security benefits. Cash welfare and Social Security benefits reduced the number of poor to about 23 million persons, a 44 percent reduction in the pre-aid poor.[30] SSA's poverty count of 25 million for 1977 was after cash welfare and Social Security had been taken into account. Without this aid, some 41.5 million persons would have fallen below the poverty level. Of the 25 million left in poverty in 1977, some received no assistance. Others received aid but too little to help them surpass the poverty level.

Ironically perhaps, welfare programs even *cause* a considerable amount of poverty. A good example is the anti-family impact of AFDC. Because male-headed families have great difficulty receiving assistance under AFDC even in the 28 states with an AFDC-UF program, many destitute fathers conclude that the only way to obtain aid for their family is to abandon it. Even some employed, low-income male heads of families desert their families because often AFDC, Medicaid, and food-stamp benefits exceed the value of their income.[31]

Second, welfare programs rarely have an impact on the root causes of poverty.[32] Poverty is caused by systemic economic, social, and political problems in the system, as will be discussed below. Programs such as food stamps, AFDC, and SSI are not designed to deal with these problems; they are designed only to provide limited aid to some of the impoverished. Even job training programs have little impact on poverty because frequently jobs are not available to those who receive the training.

CAUSES OF POVERTY

There are many causes of poverty and many ways to analyze these causes. Below we will center attention on five of the most important.

Lack of political power

As noted in Chapter 4 and expanded upon in Chapters 8–14, national and state political power is difficult to obtain. To be influential, a group must be fairly well organized, well financed, and on the scene. The poor simply do not meet these conditions. Basically, they are politically apathetic, unorganized, and only modestly represented in the power structure. Hence, their needs are generally not taken into consideration. This often allows the government to ignore or inadequately deal with conditions such as unemployment, subemployment, and discrimination, which cause poverty.

Economic problems

Because America has so much prosperity and such a large GNP ($2.3 trillion in 1979), most Americans tend to think of our economy as being extremely viable. But while our economy has provided great prosperity, it has not been dispersed across the total population. The economy has always provided unequal opportunities and benefits. As a result, some have always prospered, while many others have not been able to earn enough income to enjoy a comfortable lifestyle and still others have always been relegated to abject poverty.

America's long history of recessions, panics, and depressions has always taken a terrible toll on the public (see Chapter 7). Generally speaking, during both boom and bust many Americans have always had great difficulty finding employment that pays a decent wage. In fact, throughout our history, America has been in an almost constant job crisis. Millions of Americans have always found themselves outside the job market, employed part-time when they wanted full-time work, or employed full-time at a job which paid only poverty wages. In 1977, 18.1 million persons worked full-time, year-round and earned below $9,000; 21.5 million earned below $10,000.[33]

TABLE 15.4
Total Money Income in 1977

Total Money Income	Families*	Single Adults**
Under $2,000	2.0	9.8
2,000 to 2,999	1.6	12.5
3,000 to 3,999	2.7	12.6
4,000 to 4,999	3.1	8.3
5,000 to 5,999	3.5	7.6
6,000 to 6,999	3.7	6.2
7,000 to 7,999	3.7	5.5
8,000 to 8,999	3.7	4.9
9,000 to 9,999	3.5	4.4
10,000 to 10,999	3.7	4.4
11,000 to 11,999	3.4	3.1
12,000 to 12,999	4.0	3.2
13,000 to 13,999	3.6	2.6
14,000 to 14,999	3.7	2.5
15,000 to 15,999	4.0	2.1
16,000 to 16,999	3.6	1.8
17,000 to 17,999	3.4	1.5
18,000 to 19,999	6.7	2.0
20,000 to 24,999	13.9	2.5
25,000 to 49,000	19.8	2.3
50,000 and over	2.6	0.4
Percent	100.0	100.0
Median Income	$16,009	$5,907
Mean Income	$18,264	$7,981

Source: Bureau of the Census, "Money Income and Poverty Status of Families and Persons in the United States: 1977 (Advance Report)," *Current Population Reports,* Series P–60, No. 18, March 1979, p. 2.
*The total number of families was 57,215,000.
**The total number of single adults was 23,110,000.

Table 15.4 shows the division of money income in 1977. The data show that a large percentage of American families have very low earnings. Almost 17 percent of all families had earnings of less than $7,000. Over 27 percent of all families had incomes of less than $10,000. Around 30 percent had incomes in the $10,000 to $17,999 range. Only 22.4 percent of all families had incomes which exceeded $25,000. Among single adults, 50.8 percent earned less than $7,000, and 72 percent earned less than $10,000.

Two factors account for the large number of families with low yearly incomes—unemployment and subemployment. America has not had full employment—an actual rate of 1 to 2 percent unemployment—since 1944, when the official unemployment rate was 1.2 percent (see Table 15.5). Between 1950 and 1978, official unemployment averaged about 5 percent. In 1975 unemployment mushroomed to a yearly average of 8.5 percent, the highest un-

TABLE 15.5
Average Unemployment: 1929, 1933, 1944, 1947–1977

Year	Number	Percent of Labor Force
1929	1,550,000	3.1
1933	12,830,000	24.9
1944	670,000	1.2
1947	2,311,000	3.9
1948	2,276,000	3.8
1949	3,637,000	5.9
1950	3,288,000	5.3
1951	2,055,000	3.3
1952	1,883,000	3.0
1953	1,834,000	2.9
1954	3,532,000	5.5
1955	2,852,000	4.4
1956	2,750,000	4.1
1957	2,859,000	4.3
1958	4,602,000	6.8
1959	3,740,000	5.5
1960	3,852,000	5.5
1961	4,714,000	6.7
1962	3,911,000	5.5
1963	4,070,000	5.7
1964	3,786,000	5.2
1965	3,366,000	4.5
1966	2,875,000	3.8
1967	2,975,000	3.8
1968	2,817,000	3.6
1969	2,832,000	3.5
1970	4,088,000	4.9
1971	4,993,000	5.9
1972	4,840,000	5.6
1973	4,304,000	4.9
1974	5,076,000	5.6
1975	7,830,000	8.7
1976	7,830,000	7.7
1977(April)	6,855,000	7.0
1978	6,047,000	6.0

Source: *Employment and Earnings* (January 1974), p. 24. Data includes 14-and 15-year-olds prior to 1947. *Social Security Bulletin*, April 1977, p. 212.

employment since the Great Depression. By official figures, in each month of 1975 some 7.9 million Americans sought jobs unsuccessfully. In 1976 the job situation improved little, averaging 7.7 percent with an 8.1 percent unemployment rate in December 1976. Estimates are that some 18 million persons were unemployed at some time during 1974, and this figure rose to 20.4 million in 1976. In 1977 unemployment still hovered in the 7 percent range, dropping into the 6 percent range in 1978 and 1979.

An alternative way of examining the viability of the job market is the subemployment rate. Subemployment includes those who are unemployed, those who have given up looking for a job, those working part-time who want full-time work, and those working full-time who cannot earn enough to escape poverty. Subemployment handicaps a staggering number of Americans. Economists Vietorisz, Mier, and Harrison constructed an index for 1972. The index showed that some 18 million Americans were subemployed if only the unemployed, discouraged, involuntary part-time, and full-time workers earning less than $2.00 an hour were considered. When full-time workers earning $2.00 to $3.85 were added, subemployment affected 36.8 million workers.[34] Since 1972, the employment situation has gotten worse, not better.

These figures make terribly obvious, then, one reason for poverty and economic hardship: millions of Americans have never been able to earn a decent living in the job market. Ironically, despite these obvious flaws in the economy and their impact on the population, many Americans strongly believe that poverty is almost entirely a self-inflicted condition. It is widely believed that anyone who wants a job can find one, including a well-paying job. Because of this, poverty is considered to be an illegitimate condition. Because it is considered to be a self-inflicted condition, no systemic approach to the problem has been adopted, and any aid given has been less than generous.

Racism

The long history of racism in America has taken a considerable toll on minorities. Long denied opportunities for education and job advancement, many minorities currently bear the handicaps caused by two hundred years of discrimination. Black schools, for example, failed for decades to really educate many of their graduates. Poor schools are not limited to black neighborhoods, of course, but the situation was exaggerated for many blacks. Black schools were traditionally underfinanced, often surviving on used texts and supplies passed down from white schools.[35] Until the 1950s and 1960s, many universities did not admit black students, especially in the South and Southwest. Thus, blacks were long denied opportunities for a college education. As noted above, blacks, even well-educated ones, also faced discrimination in the job market. Blacks were excluded from most professions, and well-paying jobs were mostly reserved for white males. Conditions and opportunities, therefore, were never really equal for blacks in white, prejudiced America.

While civil-rights laws in the 1950s and 1960s outlawed the most overt forms of officially sanctioned racism and provided methods for attacking private discrimination, racism and its legacy have not been completely overcome (see Chapter 17). Millions of blacks currently in the work place were denied a decent education in their youth and suffered job discrimination as young adults. Long relegated to low-skill jobs paying poverty- or subsistence-level wages, they have had difficulty moving into good jobs. Younger blacks who faced fewer barriers have made gains in the job market, but on the whole, blacks still have far less opportunity in the job market than whites.

Sexism

Like racial discrimination, sexual discrimination has long been a part of the American experience. Women were long taught that their place was in the home, that attempts to develop a career were unwomanly and antifamily, and that politics was male business. A male-dominated society enforced this philosophy by denying women entry into graduate schools, by refusing to allow women to move into executive- and management-level jobs, and by refusing generally to take women political candidates seriously or treat them equally if they did win public office.

While the women's movement, backed up in part by numerous recent laws and court decisions, has made some progress against these forms of dis-

About one-half of all poor families are headed by women. Families headed by a female have a greater chance of being poor than those headed by a male, in part because of discrimination against women in the job market.

crimination, this struggle is far from over. In addition, the legacy of sexual discrimination handicaps its victims, often placing them at a lifetime of market disadvantage. Data on women's earning power and job placement are illuminating. In 1977 the median income for women working year-round and full-time was $8,620; the median income for men was $14,630.[36] In 1975, women college graduates had average incomes which were lower than those of men with only a high-school education.[37] The job placement of women reveals in part why women have such low incomes. In 1974 women held 63 percent of all jobs which paid between $3,000–$4,999, 58 percent of all jobs that paid between $5,000–$6,999, but only 5 percent of all jobs which paid in excess of $15,000.[38]

Discrimination against women has a substantial impact on poverty because single women are increasingly becoming the heads of households. Between 1960 and 1977, the number of female-headed families increased 73 percent. In 1977 female-headed families numbered over 8.2 million and constituted 14 percent of all families. The number of children in female-headed families grew from 4.2 million in 1960 to 6.9 million in 1970 and to 10.5 million in 1975.[39] Simultaneously, of course, the proportion of all poor families headed by a female has increased substantially. In 1959 only 23 percent of all poor families were headed by a female; by 1977, the figure had risen to 49 percent.

The market disadvantage of women is made clear by figures for 1976, which show that while only 5.5 percent of all male-headed families are poor, 31.7 percent of all female-headed families are poor. Although poverty among female-headed families is severe for all races, it is even more severe for minority females. In 1977, 39 percent of all poor white families were headed by a female; 71 percent of all poor black families were headed by a woman.[40] With increases in divorce, separation, and single parenting, the number of female-headed families can be expected to increase, thus escalating the impact of past and present sexual discrimination as a cause of poverty.

Geographic isolation

Millions of Americans live in rural areas where job opportunities are very limited and unlikely to improve in the immediate future. Considerable areas of the rural South, Appalachia, and the West have little chance of being economically viable. These same regions tend to have poor educational systems, limited health-care facilities, and inadequate funds to help their poor.[41]

These areas not only contain millions of America's most hopeless poor people, but have also contributed considerably to America's urban poor. Most of the urban poor fled to the cities to escape rural poverty, frequently only to find that conditions were little better, even sometimes worse, in urban areas.

ENDING POVERTY

Overcoming the interrelated set of problems that cause poverty will never be easy. Nor is it likely to be accomplished over a short period of time. Considerable reform, however, is possible. A viable approach to ending American poverty would include:

a. creating economic conditions that allow as many persons as possible to earn their own living in the job market;

b. simplifying and streamlining welfare programs, and designing them to prevent and break the cycle of poverty rather than just administer to the poor; and

c. adequately caring for those who, because of age, disability, motherhood, or economic deficiencies, cannot care for themselves.

Interestingly, experts on welfare reform are in fundamental agreement about how these goals could be achieved. Most of them believe that reform would require a series of programs designed to create full employment; child care, preschool education, and health-care programs for the children of the poor; and one cash-aid program to take the place of all existing cash-aid programs and most in-kind programs.

Achieving full employment

While experts tend to agree that full employment is necessary to deal with poverty, the two major parties are not as strongly committed to this goal. Traditionally, the Republican party has been more concerned with inflation than unemployment, and has allowed unemployment to be rather high. The Democratic party is more concerned about unemployment. But faced with recalcitrant unemployment in the 1970s, it was not able to reach a consensus about how to deal with it. President Carter has shown much more concern for inflation than unemployment. Both parties seem to realize that achieving full employment would require some serious alterations in the role of the government in the economic system.

Regardless of how hard it would be to achieve full employment, the evidence indicates that joblessness causes severe problems—problems that are aggravated in some ways by modern welfare programs. Some of the most serious problems include the following:

a. Unemployment reduces GNP, slowing economic growth and shrinking tax revenues. Estimates are that each 1 percent of unemployment causes a loss of $12 to $15 billion in tax revenues. While tax revenues decrease, social welfare expenditures increase. For example, in 1976 the government's financial deficit was $75 billion. If full employment had existed in 1976, tax revenues would have increased $50 to $55 billion, unemployment compensation would have cost $15 billion less, and welfare expenditures would have decreased $5 billion. With full employment, then, there would have been no deficit.[42]

b. In a scarce job market, some people may find crime their best economic alternative. This increases crime, societal violence, and the cost of dealing with social deviance.

c. Unemployment also undermines government programs. The government's efforts to provide decent housing for the poor are often frustrated by the fact that tenants frequently earn too little to contribute significantly to housing costs. Some tenants may turn to crime, terrorizing more peaceful and elderly residents. And social tensions detract from the quality of life. Government job-training programs are also frequently undermined by high unemployment: job training does little good if there are no jobs for those who have been trained.

d. High unemployment causes industrial resistance to civil-rights goals. When jobs are scarce, women and minorities frequently cannot be hired or promoted without bypassing men (most often white men). This creates tensions and serves as one reason not to press for rapid minority or female advancement. In addition, when jobs are scarce, employees, knowing they can be replaced, make fewer demands on their employers. When jobs are scarce, even unions moderate their demands and concentrate more on salaries than working conditions.

e. Unemployment has severe physical and psychological impacts on the jobless. For example, recent research conducted by M. Harvey Brenner showed that the strain of joblessness caused by a 1.4 percent rise in unemployment in 1970 led to a substantial number of physical and mental breakdowns, murders, and suicides between 1970 and 1975. The study concluded that at least 26,440 deaths from stress-related diseases, 1,540 suicides, and 1,740 homicides resulted from the strain of involuntary unemployment.[43]

While the problems caused by unemployment are severe, the government has never committed itself to achieving and maintaining full employment. In the past, the only time full employment has been achieved has been during periods of war, with munition booms, wage and price controls, and rationing. Short of war, full employment could be achieved only by government regulation of the market to increase production and consumption. This could be done through government financing of projects that create jobs or by having the government underwrite and stimulate such projects by private industry.

To be influential, a group must be fairly well organized, well financed, and on the scene. The poor simply do not meet these conditions.

Most experts agree that an economy with full employment is the primary requirement for reducing both poverty and welfare programs.

The government might decide to revitalize and rebuild American cities in the Midwest and North that have suffered severe decay, such as constructing mass transit or numerous other projects. The government could encourage industry to undertake the projects by providing tax breaks, low-cost loans, or outright subsidies. If enough projects were not undertaken to provide full employment, the government could become the employer of last resort. Since the Great Depression, all these strategies have been used by the government in some form. They have not, however, been used extensively enough to maintain full employment.

The extent of unemployment in the 1970s has made joblessness a continuing political issue. One response was the Full Employment and Balanced Growth bill (or Humphrey-Hawkins, after its sponsors). The bill went through numerous revisions but was basically designed to make full employment a goal of all administrations, to coordinate government economic policies to promote employment and control inflation, and to specify economic approaches and programs that might be used in response to unemployment or inflation.

In its original form, the Humphrey-Hawkins bill was a genuine full-employment plan involving comprehensive federal planning to produce and upgrade millions of jobs. The bill would have required in-depth analysis and fiscal planning to achieve economic growth and full employment. Gainful employment at fair compensation for all adults seeking work would have been guaranteed. If government programs could not produce sufficient jobs to lower unemployment to the 3-percent level within four years, the government would have established enough public-service jobs to meet that goal.

The original version of the Humphrey-Hawkins bill could not win support from President Carter or a majority of the members of Congress. Most business lobbies, such as the National Association of Manufacturers and the Business Roundtable, opposed the bill. In the fall of 1978, a Carter-backed compromise version of Humphrey-Hawkins was passed by Congress. This version is more ambiguous and does not require the government to act as the employer of last resort if unemployment cannot be reduced by other means. The basic provisions are as follows:[44]

Commitments

a. The federal government will accept an obligation to achieve full employment, balanced growth, and price stability.
b. It will be recognized that all persons able, willing, and seeking work have a right to useful paid employment at fair rates of compensation.
c. The government recognizes inflation as a major national problem, probably requiring new methods of control. New methods might include stronger antitrust laws, stockpiling of critical materials, a reexamination of regulatory policies, and productivity and supply incentives.

Economic Planning

a. Requires the President, as part of his annual economic report, to develop a five-year plan, which on a yearly basis establishes numerical targets for employment, production, real income, and productivity;
b. Establishes an interim goal of 4 percent unemployment among workers sixteen or older, with 3 percent for adults twenty and over. Achievement of these goals would be expected within five years of passage of the bill;
c. Requires the President to submit a budget compatible with achieving the goals stated in his five-year plan;
d. Allows the President to modify the unemployment goals and timetable if, at least three years after enactment, they seem unreasonable;
e. Requires the Federal Reserve Board to specify how its monetary policies would help achieve the goals specified in the President's plan.

Programs

a. Requires the President to spell out the policies needed to achieve his goals;
b. Lists a number of program options that the government might want to consider as a means of improving employment. Included are public-works programs, public-service employment, special programs for depressed areas and special youth programs;

c. Requires the government to create some jobs directly (such as public-service employment) if other types of programs do not create enough new jobs.

In the form passed by Congress, the Humphrey-Hawkins act is primarily symbolic. It could lead to a more careful analysis of economic conditions and may improve the government's economic strategies, but it can probably do little else. Congress' refusal to pass a better law reveals much about government priorities and about who has power and influence in Congress. The failure also probably means that unemployment and poverty will remain high for the foreseeable future.

Full employment and inflation

One of the strongest and most persistent arguments against efforts to achieve full employment is that the result would be runaway inflation. As more workers were brought into the market, the argument goes, demands on products would increase, resulting in scarce supply and a rapid increase in prices—inflation. Of course, as the job market increased, production should also, so inflation would result only if production did not increase as fast as demand. This would be especially true if the job market were gradually improved over a number of years.

Some economists believe that any inflation caused by the transition to full employment would be temporary. Economist Bradley Schiller, for example, argues:

> Expansion of demand will, indeed, lead to higher prices but . . . the stepped up rate of inflation is only a temporary phenomenon. As new workers are absorbed into the production process, the pressure on prices is abated. Hence what the Phillips Curve may portray on an aggregate level is the rate of inflation necessary to evoke the required labor force adjustment. It should not necessarily be understood to mean that the same high rate of inflation will continue once the adjustment is made. Not only may the price rise be temporary, but it is an integral feature of the adjustment mechanism. Hence, we might be able to say that a 5 percent rate of inflation is necessary to reduce the unemployment rate from 4.5 to 3.5 percent, but we have no firm reason for anticipating continued high rates of inflation once the lower level of unemployment is reached.[45]

Many economists do not believe that there is an immutable relationship between employment and inflation. Schiller says:

> A fixed rate of inflation is not associated with any given level of unemployment or with efforts to reduce unemployment by any given amount. Policymakers have a variety of options available at all times to effectuate an improved tradeoff between inflation and unemployment. By changing the pattern of demand or improv-

ing the function of the labor market, policymakers can achieve lower rates of unemployment with little pressure on prices. To formulate the goal of price stability as an alternative to fuller employment is to ignore other options and rob the poor.[46]

Some of the techniques a government can use to deal with inflation were specified in the original versions of the Humphrey-Hawkins bill: restoration of competition to much of the market by an attack on oligopoly; wage and price controls: stockpiling; and development of an energy policy to drastically reduce the need for expensive imported oil.

A negative income tax

In recent years both Democratic and Republican administrations have proposed *Negative Income Tax* (NIT) plans as a method of streamlining welfare programs. NITs have been proposed in many forms, but the idea is basically a simple one.[47] All NIT proposals recommend a guaranteed income that varies with family size, a cutoff point for aid, and a scheme called a tax rate, which is designed to encourage family heads to work and achieve earnings above the guaranteed floor.

For example, a proposal might guarantee any family of four a basic income of, say, $6,000, with a cutoff point of $8,500, and a tax rate of 50 percent. Under such a plan, a family of four with projected yearly earnings of less than $6,000 would receive a monthly subsidy large enough to bring it up to that level. If the family had earnings above $6,000, but below the $8,500 cutoff point, the tax rate would be used to determine a subsidy. If the tax rate were 50 percent, a family would receive half the difference between earnings above the floor ($6,000 in this case) and the cutoff point ($8,500). Thus, a family that earned $7,000 would receive another $750 from the government ($8,500 − $7,000 = $1,500 ÷ .50 = $750). Families of four earning $8,500 or more would not receive any aid.

Both parties seem to realize that achieving full employment would require some serious alterations in the role of the government in the economic system.

The NIT is attractive for several reasons. A NIT could eliminate all other cash-aid programs. It would provide a national floor of income for all families, thereby eliminating the acute disparities that currently exist. It would also assist all the poor, including male-headed families and single individuals. In addition, it would not penalize marriage or work, and it would be much simpler than current programs.

In 1969 Richard Nixon proposed a NIT plan to Congress which was twice passed by the House but was defeated in the Senate. Congress formulated its own NIT plan in 1974. Gerald Ford also forwarded a NIT plan to Congress but dropped the project when both unemployment and inflation became serious problems during his administration. President Carter introduced a reform plan in the fall of 1977 involving a NIT proposal entitled "The Better Jobs and Income Program."

Carter's proposed welfare reforms would have a very modest impact, would not help to alleviate the causes of poverty, but would increase welfare costs. This, of course, is the traditional approach to poverty and explains in large part why poverty continues.

Carter's plan was to provide a job for most poor citizens who could work; the job would be supplemented if wages fell below levels established for varying family size. Those unable to work would have been eligible for a Negative Income Tax program which would have provided a guaranteed income based on family size.

Carter's welfare reform proposal failed to attract much support from Congress. Many members of Congress were afraid the proposal would substantially increase welfare costs; many are afraid of any NIT proposal; and most members of Congress found the bill too complex to understand. Given the hectic schedules of members of Congress, any bill that requires a large investment of time to evaluate has difficulty attracting support. Of course, the power structure in Washington is such that there were few powerful groups there to work on behalf of reform and many powerful groups to work against it.

In 1979 Carter announced that he would not reintroduce his proposal. Instead, he asked for a national minimum for AFDC payments, which would reduce state variations and raise payments in low-paying states, and extension of eligibility for AFDC to male-headed families to all states. These changes would have a very modest impact, would not help to alleviate the causes of poverty, but would increase welfare costs. This, of course, is the traditional approach to poverty and explains in large part why poverty continues.

Child care and preschool education

Any viable reform to eradicate poverty must include an expanded child-care program as part of a full employment strategy, but none of the plans proposed in the last decade has done so. Without expanded child care, heads of poor families will often not be able to enter the job market or educational or training programs.

Well-designed child care could also play a very important role in breaking

Children at a Head Start school in San Francisco. Head Start has been a successful preschool education program for children from poor families.

the cycle of poverty. Child-care centers could provide poor children with educational training, needed nutrition, and medical care. Recent studies have shown that preschool education programs such as Head Start have greatly improved their ability to enhance the educational foundation of children.[48] The studies always showed that children in such programs received needed nutritional and medical care. Unfortunately, only about 2.2 million students receive any type of preschool or elementary education service, with Head Start currently serving only about 350,000 students per year. Such programs would have to be greatly expanded if poverty is to be alleviated.

CONCLUSIONS

There is now, and always has been, much poverty in America. While the personal characteristics of some of the poor are primarily responsible for their poverty, most poverty results from other causes. The main causes of poverty are lack of political power, an economic system that does not provide enough jobs that pay decent incomes, past and even some present discrimination against minorities and women, and geographic isolation. Thus, a lack of opportunity—not sloth— lies at the heart of American poverty.

To avoid facing up to the economic deficiencies and the discrimination that have always characterized our society, those most interested in preserving the status quo have developed an elaborate set of myths about who the poor are and why they are poor. These myths have been widely, even enthusiastically, accepted by the public and provide a rationale for dismissing poverty and the poor as a legitimate problem.

American welfare programs reflect the biases and myths about poverty in our society. The programs are designed to serve only those whose suffering is most difficult to rationalize—mothers, children, the aged, blind, and disabled. Those who benefit are served by a patchwork of poorly related, frequently overlapping programs that don't even serve the beneficiaries well. Sometimes they even produce detrimental impacts on the poor. The thrust of the programs is to administer modest, inadequate aid to the poor, not to eliminate poverty.

Efforts to eradicate poverty would require some serious changes in the American economy. Most importantly, the job market would have to be greatly improved. Improving the economy would not be easy. It would require the government to play a much more systematic role in the management of the economy. There is considerable resistance to expanding the government's role, especially since the poor have little power in the system and since those who do have power primarily want to maintain the status quo.

Footnotes

1. Francis Fox Piven and Richard A. Cloward, *Poor People's Movements: Why They Succeed, How They Fail* (New York: Pantheon Books, 1977), p. 42.
2. Mollie Orshansky, "Children of the Poor," *Social Security Bulletin,* 25 (1963): 2–21; Clair Wilcox, *Toward Social Welfare* (Homewood, Illinois: Irvin-Dorsey, 1969), p. 27.
3. Bureau of the Census, "Money Income and Poverty Status of Families and Persons in the United States: 1977 (Advance Report)," *Current Population Reports,* Series P-60, No. 116, 1978, p. 28.
4. "Cost of Moderate Living Standard Up 9%," *The Houston Post,* April 29, 1979, p. 22A.
5. "Family of 4 Needs $201 a Week to Live," *The Houston Post,* April 21, 1978, p. 3C.
6. U.S. Department of Health, Education and Welfare, *The Measure of Poverty* (Washington, D.C.: Government Printing Office, 1976), p. 109; Timothy M. Smeeding, "Measuring the Economic Welfare of Low-Income Households and the Anti-Poverty Effectiveness of Cash and Non-Cash Transfer Programs," (Ph.D. Dissertation, University of Wisconsin, Madison, 1975).
7. HEW, *The Measure of Poverty,* p. 77.
8. See Congressional Budget Office, "Poverty Status of Families under Alternative Definitions of Income" (Background Paper No. 17), February 1977. In response, see Michael Harrington, "Hiding the Other America," *The New Republic,* February 26, 1977, pp. 15–17; and Harrell R. Rodgers, Jr., "Hiding versus Ending Poverty," *Politics and Society,* 8, No. 2 (1978): 253–66. See also Michael Harrington, *Decade of Decision* (New York: Simon and Schuster, 1980), pp. 222–25.

9. Bureau of the Census, "Money Income and Poverty Status of Families and Persons in the United States: 1977 (Advance Report)," *Current Population Reports,* Series P-60, No. 116, 1978, p. 3.

10. *Ibid.,* p. 3.

11. *Ibid.,* p. 26.

12. Social Security Administration, *Public Assistance Statistics: January 1977,* p. 9.

13. Hearings Before the House Subcommittee on Public Assistance and Unemployment Compensation, 95th Cong., May 4, 1977, pp. 8 and 25.

14. Social Security Administration, *Public Assistance Statistics: August 1977,* Publication No. (SSA), 78-11917, February 1978, p. 8.

15. Hearings Before the House Subcommittee on Public Assistance and Unemployment Compensation, 95th Cong., May 4, 1977, p. 8.

16. *Ibid.,* p. 8.

17. Joint Economic Committee, Subcommittee on Fiscal Policy, "Income Security for Americans: Recommendations of the Public Welfare Study" (Washington, D.C.: Government Printing Office, 1974), p. xv.

18. *Ibid.,* p. xv.

19. *Ibid.,* p. xv.

20. *Ibid.,* p. xv.

21. See "Income Security for Americans: Recommendations of the Public Welfare Study," p. 75.

22. "Food Stamp Mythtake," editorial in the *Houston Post,* October 10, 1975.

23. Social Security Administration, *Aid to Families with Dependent Children: 1973 Recipient Characteristics Study,* Publication No. (SSA), 77-11777, June 1975, p. 11.

24. Social Security Administration, *Aid to Families with Dependent Children: 1975 Recipient Characteristics Study,* Publication No. (SSA), 77-11777, September 1977, p. 5.

25. Sar Levitan, Martin Rein, and David Marwick, *Work and Welfare Go Together* (Baltimore: Johns Hopkins University Press, 1972), p. 50.

26. Hanna H. Meissner, ed., *Poverty in the Affluent Society* (New York, Harper and Row, 1973), p. 61.

27. Hearings Before the House Subcommittee on Public Assistance and Unemployment Compensation, 95th Cong., May 4, 1977, p. 7.

28. *Ibid.,* p. 27.

29. *Aid to Families with Dependent Children: A Chartbook,* Publication No. (SSA) 79-11721, 1979, p. 4.

30. Robert D. Plotnick and Felicity Skidmore, *Progress Against Poverty: A Review of the 1964–74 Decade* (New York: Academic Press, 1975), p. 51.

31. "Income Security for Americans: Recommendations of the Public Welfare Study," p. 3.

32. Joint Economic Committee, Subcommittee on Fiscal Policy, "Public Welfare and Work Incentives in Theory and Practice," (Washington, D.C.: Government Printing Office, 1974), p. 13.

33. See Bradley R. Schiller, *The Economics of Poverty and Discrimination* (Englewood Cliffs, New Jersey: Prentice Hall, 1976), p. 70; Bureau of the Census, "Money Income and Poverty Status of Families and Persons in the United States: 1977 (Advance Report)," p. 17.

34. See Thomas Vietorisz, Robert Mier, and Bennett Harrison, "Full Employment at Living Wages," in Stanley Moses, ed., *Planning for Full Employment: The Annals of the American Academy of Political and Social Sciences,* March 1975, p. 104.

35. See Harrell R. Rodgers, Jr., and Charles S. Bullock, III, *Coercion to Compliance* (Lexington, Mass.: Heath, 1976), pp. 13–31.

36. Bureau of the Census, ''Money Income and Poverty Status of Families and Persons in the United States: 1977 (Advance Report),'' p. 2.

37. Bureau of the Census, ''A Statistical Portrait of Women in the U.S.,'' *Current Population Report,* Series P-23, No. 58, p. 45.

38. *Ibid.,* p. 7.

39. Bureau of the Census, ''Money Income and Poverty Status of Families and Persons in the United States: 1977 (Advance Report),'' p. 6.

40. *Ibid.,* p. 20.

41. See Dale Tussing, *Poverty in a Dual Economy* (New York: St. Martin's, 1975), p. 80.

42. See testimony of Leon Keyserling, Hearings Before the Subcommittee on Equal Opportunities of the Committee on Education and Labor, Part 1, 1975, p. 14.

43. See Joint Economic Committee, ''Estimating the Social Costs of National Economic Policy: Implication for Mental and Physical Health and Criminal Aggression,'' Washington, D.C.: Government Printing Office, 1976; see also Arthur M. Okum, *The Battle Against Unemployment* (New York: Norton, 1972), p. viii; and William Kapp, ''Socio-Economic Effects of Low and High Employment,'' in Moses, ed., *Planning for Full Employment,* pp. 60–71.

44. See Mary Eisner Eccles, ''Backers Defend Revised Humphrey-Hawkins Bill,'' *Congressional Quarterly,* Nov. 26, 1977, pp. 2475–76.

45. Schiller, *The Economics of Poverty and Discrimination,* p. 62.

46. *Ibid.,* p. 65.

47. See Christopher Green, *Negative Taxes and the Poverty Problem* (Washington, D. C.: The Brookings Institution, 1967); Robert J. Lampman, *Ends and Means of Reducing Income Poverty* (New York: Academic Press, 1971); and Michael C. Barth, George J. Carcagno, and John L. Palmer, *Toward an Effective Income Support System: Problems, Prospects, and Choices* (Madison, Wisconsin: Institute for Research on Poverty, 1974).

48. See Bernard Brown, ''Long Term Gains from Early Intervention: An Overview of Current Research'' (Paper presented at the 1977 Annual Meeting of the American Association for the Advancement of Science, Denver, Colorado, February 23, 1977).

A society gets the criminals it deserves.
Jean Lacassagne

Crime is the largest growth industry in America. A United States senator referred to the recent crime wave as "a riot in slow motion."[1] Statistics indicating the dimensions and growth of crime tell an ominous tale: between 1960 and 1978, the rate of violent crime in America doubled. Between the early 1960s and the late 1970s, the incidence of robberies increased 255 percent; forcible rape, 143 percent; aggravated assault, 153 percent; murder, 106 percent.[2]

16 Crime as a Social Issue

THE INCIDENCE OF CRIME

The FBI collects data on the yearly incidence of seven major crimes. In 1977 they tabulated almost 11 million major crimes, about 10 million serious property crimes and 1 million crimes of violence. The figures show the breakdown.[3]

Murder—19,120
Forcible rape—63,020
Robbery—404,850
Aggravated assault—522,510
Burglary—3,052,200
Larceny-theft—5,905,700
Motor-vehicle theft—968,400

In 1977, these impersonal figures reflected one violent crime every thirty-one seconds, one property crime every three seconds. A murder occurred every twenty-seven minutes, a forcible rape every eight minutes, a robbery every seventy-eight seconds, a burglary every ten seconds, a larceny-theft every five seconds, and a motor-vehicle theft every thirty-three seconds.[4] Crime was most severe in the South and in large cities. While crime in the suburbs has increased dramatically in recent years, suburbs, small cities, and rural areas still suffer significantly less crime than big cities (see Table 16.1).

Why is America's crime rate higher than that of any other major industrialized nation? Experts have cited poverty, ineffective gun-control laws, and America's fascination with violence, among other reasons, to help explain the high incidence of crime.

TABLE 16.1
Crime Rate by Area: 1977

	United States: Total	United States: Rate per 100,000 Inhabitants	Standard Metropolitan Areas: Rate per 100,000 Inhabitants	Other Cities: Rate per 100,000 Inhabitants	Rural Areas: Rate per 100,000 Inhabitants
Crime index total	**10,935,777**	**5,055.1**	**5,813.6**	**4,198.0**	**2,012.5**
Murder and non-negligent manslaughter	19,121	8.8	9.7	5.0	7.8
Forcible rape	63,022	29.1	34.6	14.2	14.1
Robbery	404,847	187.1	243.7	47.9	20.9
Aggravated assault	522,509	241.5	271.0	200.2	130.0
Burglary	3,052,189	1,410.9	1609.3	997.0	767.2
Larceny/theft	5,905,731	2,729.9	3,092.9	2,718.3	954.4
Motor vehicle theft	968,358	447.6	552.5	215.4	118.1

Source: FBI Uniform Crime Reports, *Crime in the United States, 1977* (Washington, D.C.: Government Printing Office, 1978), p. 37.

Some crimes, such as rape and robbery, have a much lower rate of occurrence in suburbs and rural areas than in major cities.

The incidence of reported crime makes America the most violent of all major industrialized nations. Even though crime has been increasing in many nations,[5] none has a crime rate equal to ours. While FBI statistics portray an ominous crime problem in America, there is considerable evidence that the figures are highly inaccurate. Numerous studies indicate that crime is much worse than the official figures indicate;[6] actual crime is from two to four times greater than FBI figures suggest. A Law Enforcement Assistance Administration (LEAA) study released in 1977 reported that the actual rate of crime is four times the official rate.[7] Some crimes—such as robberies, rape, and aggravated assault—are severely underreported. For any given city, the study showed that the actual crime rate was from two to five times the reported rate.

Why don't citizens report crime? Crimes like rape go unreported because of the embarrassment and stigma involved. Others are not reported because the victim does not believe that the police will care or that the culprit will be caught. Some victims are frightened to report a crime because they fear that the offender will return to harm them. The attitudes suggested by the extent of unreported crimes are contempt for the police and a lack of confidence in the judicial and correctional systems.

The most accurately reported of all crimes, and the one which reflects most dramatically the violence afflicting our society, is murder. During the 1970s, America averaged about twenty thousand murders per year. The murder rate is worst in large cities, especially in poverty pockets, and in the South. Rather typically, 41 percent of all murders in 1977 occurred in the South.[8] Murder is most often an act of passion; about 60 percent of all murder victims are related to, or acquainted with, their killers.[9]

The magnitude of the problem is indicated by the sobering thought that, in any three-year period in the 1970s, more Americans were murdered than were killed during the war in Vietnam. In fact, firearm murders alone in the twentieth century have exceeded 800,000, considerably more casualties than have resulted from all American wars. In 1976, Atlanta, with a large poverty population, a high unemployment and subemployment rate, and an arsenal of privately owned guns, was the murder capital of America. A study by an MIT mathematician revealed that at the current rate, one of every eleven children born in Atlanta in 1974 would eventually be murdered. The same study showed that an urban male born in 1974 had a greater chance of being murdered than the typical American soldier in World War II had of dying in combat.[10]

None of the major industrial nations had a homicide rate that remotely approaches that of America. In fact, more firearm deaths occur in America each year than in all other free nations combined. Nations which carefully control or prohibit private ownership of handguns have almost eliminated gun deaths. The lax gun regulations in America produce 10 times the gun death rate in Canada, 18 times the rate in France, 19 times the German, 68 times the Dutch, 136 times the rate in England and Wales, and 275 times the Japanese rate.[11] In 1973 three persons were killed with handguns in Tokyo, while Detroit—with an eighth of Tokyo's population—had 500 handgun deaths. St. Louis, with about 500,000 residents, recorded 173 gun deaths in 1974; England and Wales, with 54 million residents, had 27 murders.[12]

High rates of crime and personal violence clearly have a substantial impact on society. Citizens feel less safe on the streets and even in their homes, feel less security about their personal property, and have less trust in strangers and often in their neighbors. In some big-city neighborhoods, citizens, especially the elderly, are afraid to go out on the streets even in broad daylight, and almost completely avoid some areas of the city after dark. Citizens and merchants invest heavily in alarms, locks, burglary bars, watch dogs, private security services—and guns. Such fear and costs greatly reduce the quality of life for everyone.

America is the most violent of all the major industrialized nations. Even though crime has been increasing in many nations, none has a crime rate equal to ours.

CHARACTERISTICS OF CRIMINALS

The chief characteristic of those who commit violent and property crimes is that they are young males. More crimes are committed by youths under fifteen than by adults over twenty-five.[13] Fifteen is the peak age for violent crimes. Those arrested for the FBI's seven major crimes in 1977 were predominantly young. Sixteen percent were under fifteen, 41 percent were under eighteen, 59 percent were under twenty-one, and 73 percent were under twenty-five.[14] About 75 percent of those who commit street crimes are under twenty-five, and this age group is also responsible for about 80 percent of all property crimes.

An analysis of specific crime categories shows a high incidence of crimes committed by juveniles. Of those processed for motor-vehicle theft in 1977, 64 percent were juveniles. Juveniles made up 57 percent of those processed for burglary, 38 percent for larceny-theft, 33 percent for robbery, 23 percent for forcible rape, 17 percent for aggravated assault, and 9 percent for murder. A large percentage of those arrested for arson and vandalism were also juveniles.[15]

Black citizens are arrested for a large percentage of all violent and property crimes. In 1977 blacks were arrested for 46 percent of all violent crimes and 31 percent of all property crimes. They were arrested for 51 percent of all murders, 47 percent of all forcible rapes, 57 percent of robberies, 39 percent of aggravated assaults, 29 percent of burglaries, 32 percent of larceny-thefts, and 26 percent of all motor-vehicle thefts.[16]

Clearly, blacks commit a disproportionate percentage of all crimes, but arrest figures may distort the racial factor to some extent. There are more police assigned to black neighborhoods, so naturally more arrests are made. Blacks are also more likely to be arrested and convicted for offenses than are white offenders.[17] The median age of blacks is also lower than the median for whites, thereby increasing the prime crime group among blacks.

APPREHENDING, CONVICTING, AND SENTENCING CRIMINALS

Most crimes are not solved. Typically, only 21 percent of those in the FBI's seven major crime categories in 1977 were cleared.[18] Violent crimes are cleared more often than property crimes. In 1977, 75 percent of all murders, 51 percent of all forcible rapes, 62 percent of aggravated assaults, and 27 percent of robberies were cleared. Only 16 percent of burglaries were cleared, as were 20 percent of larceny-thefts, and 15 percent of the motor-vehicle thefts.[19]

Despite the fact that there are probably 40 million serious crimes committed in the nation each year (including both reported and unreported crimes), only about 9 million arrests are made.[20] About 40 percent of all arrests are for "victimless crimes"—prostitution, gambling, drunkenness, vagrancy, and curfew and loitering law violations. These arrests occupy a great deal of the police's time, and clog city jails and courts.

Of those arrested for serious crimes, most will never be tried, convicted, or imprisoned. For example, of the average one hundred arrests, prosecutors will immediately decide not to press charges in twenty-four cases. Prosecutors will later drop, or judges will dismiss, charges against another forty defendants. Twenty-six of the original one hundred will bargain (plea bargain) with the prosecutors and plead guilty to a lesser offense. Only ten of the original one hundred will be tried in court, and three of these will be acquitted. Of the seven convicted, three will be fined and/or placed on probation and released. Among those released on probation will be many defendants with prior criminal records.[21] Only about 400,000 persons are sentenced to prison each year. Most of those committed to prison will be released when they first become eligible for parole. The average prison stay is about two-and-a-half years, with an eight-year average for those sentenced to a life term.

For every one hundred people arrested for serious crimes, only ten cases will go to trial, and only seven people will be convicted. Most cases are either dismissed for lack of evidence or settled out of court through plea bargaining.

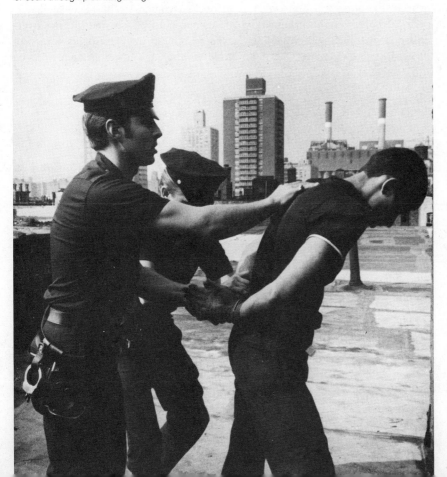

The criminal justice system is criticized because so few criminals are caught, sentenced to prison, and kept there. There are, however, many reasons for this situation. The police are too few in number to carefully investigate all crimes, and they often cannot solve them because the public will not cooperate. Without a cooperative public the police cannot obtain leads, witnesses, and plaintiffs. Of those arrests made, some cannot be prosecuted because the police do not have the evidence needed to support a conviction. Some arrests are aborted by victims who refuse to provide evidence or cooperate in other ways. Prosecutors, especially in big cities, often have more cases than they can handle, so they sometimes dismiss cases that cannot be easily won. Judges dismiss some cases because their dockets, city jails, and prisons are grossly overcrowded and only the surest cases seem worthy of final resolution. Some judges such as those in New York City, often preside over as many as 200 criminal cases per day.[22] Even among those convicted, justice is often not done. Many of those convicted are allowed to plead guilty to a lesser offense in return for a guilty plea, a process called *plea bargaining*. Often the sentence does not begin to match the crime. Defendants are allowed to plea bargain, however, because the courts are too crowded to try more than a small percentage of all cases. About 90 percent of all convictions for serious crimes result from plea bargaining. If only 10 percent more cases were taken to trial, the already overcrowded court docket would literally be swamped. If only 10 percent more criminals were sentenced to prison, the already overcrowded prison system would be forced to release more prisoners to accept them. Ironically perhaps, the more crime there is, the fewer criminals can be tried and sent to jail.

WHITE-COLLAR CRIME

When we think of crime, we tend to think of acts of violence. But in terms of its incidence, impact, and costs, white-collar crime is at least as serious as violent crime. *White-collar crime* includes everything from shoplifting, employee thefts, Medicaid fraud by doctors, and deceptive advertising, to illegal campaign contributions, embezzlement, restraint of trade, and other forms of business fraud.

The evidence on white-collar crime is rather unsystematic, but available data indicate that it is both frequent and expensive. Estimates of the cost of white-collar crime range from $100 to $300 billion per year.[23] Even the conservative estimate of $100 billion dwarfs the costs of violent crimes such as larceny, robbery, burglary, and auto theft. These crimes impose a cost on society of about $4 billion a year, a fraction of the cost of white-collar crime. One study estimates that fraudulent car repairs alone cost consumers $9 billion a year, deceptive grocery billing $14 billion, and lack of competition in the auto industry $16 billion.[24] Banks lose about five times as much to fraud (mostly by their own employees) as to robbers. Organized crime costs society about $20 billion a year and causes a great deal of violent crime.[25]

Shoplifting alone imposes a staggering cost on society. In 1977 its estimated cost, including employee thefts, was $26 billion.[26] Surveillance studies of customers show that about one in ten is a shoplifter, a depressing ratio.[27] Still, employees commit about 75 percent of business thefts. In one recent year, Montgomery Ward fired 3 percent of its workforce (about 4,000 employees) for theft.[28] Of course, this was the tip of the iceberg, since most thieves were surely not caught. Between 15 and 30 percent of all business failures are caused by financial losses due to employee and customer thefts.[29]

> *Defendants are allowed to plea bargain because the courts are too crowded to try more than a small percentage of all cases. About 90 percent of all convictions for serious crimes result from plea bargaining.*

The impact of white-collar crime is very severe. Violent crime threatens our peace and security, but white-collar crime undermines the moral base of society. Societal ethics are lowered when the prevailing philosophy is the accumulation of wealth and material objects and whatever one does that results in wealth is acceptable. In a society which venerates wealth and the wealthy, the temptation to make heroes of the wealthy but morally flawed among us is strong. Business elites who pollute the air, produce shoddy, unsafe products, and engage in restraint of trade rarely suffer public censure. Even gangsters, such as Al Capone, sometimes become celebrities and are paid homage to by politicians and sports figures.[30] The old joke that anyone who steals $50 is a crook while anyone who steals a million is a financier often has a tragic ring of truth in our society. Political corruption also undermines society by disrupting the representational process, giving political advantage to those with money and stunted morals.

Despite the extent, cost, and impact of white-collar crime, society does not take it very seriously. Unlike street crime, no systematic attempts are made to even determine how extensive white-collar crime is on a yearly basis. A yearly report on the extent and cost of antitrust violations, Medicaid fraud, and shoplifting might have a considerable impact on public attitudes.

In the permissive atmosphere which surrounds white-collar crime, arrests and prosecution are rare, and punishment of those convicted is lenient. Criminal acts by upper-income citizens rarely result in conviction, but prosecution of other citizens engaged in white-collar crime is also infrequent. One study showed that only 17 percent of those persons who were arrested for stealing from three different employers were prosecuted.[31] Business crime, including fraud and restraint of trade, infrequently results in prosecution. Between 1940 and 1961 only twenty businessmen actually received jail sentences for antitrust violations.[32] Even elaborate antitrust conspiracies generally result only in modest fines—penalties generally far below the profits from the illegal acts.[33]

There are a number of reasons why white-collar crime, particularly business crime, is rarely prosecuted. First, juries, judges, and prosecutors may feel that theft from a big company or by a big company really does not hurt anyone very badly. Second, they often feel that the disgrace resulting from criminal charges is alone sufficient punishment for businessmen. Third, judges are particularly prone to empathize with a businessman accused of crime, seeing him not as a criminal but as an important citizen who simply made a mistake. Fourth, businessmen with money are often able to hire law firms that can frustrate the legal process, drawing the proceedings out, bombarding the courts with motions and appeals, and generally disrupting court procedures. Recently, a Texas millionaire even bragged to the press that his personal fortune, which allowed him to spend $1 million to hire attorneys and investigators, enabled him to avoid conviction on a wiretapping charge.[34] Some businessmen have always shown contempt for the law. Daniel Drew, the legendary robber baron, once said:

> Law is like a cobweb; it's made for flies and smaller kinds of insects, so to speak, but lets the big bumblebees through. When technicalities of the law stood in my way, I have always been able to brush them aside easy as anything.[35]

CAUSES OF CRIME

Social scientists are not in complete accord about the causes of crime, but some factors are rather consistently identified as significant contributors. Below we will discuss four of the most frequently identified causes.

Poverty and unemployment

The evidence indicates that violent crimes and street crimes result largely from the brutalizing and dehumanizing conditions millions of Americans live in and from the lack of legitimate opportunities for many citizens. As Ramsey Clark has said: "Most crime in America is born in environments saturated in poverty and its consequences: illness, ignorance, idleness, ugly surroundings, hopelessness."[36]

The data clearly show that most violent crime is committed by people of lower socio-economic status, people who are products of poverty and discrimination. This has always been true. Crime in the ghetto has always been severe, regardless of the race or ethnicity of the residents. "Crime rates," for example, "in tawdry sections of Chicago have remained high over the decades, though inhabited at different times by Swedes, Poles, Germans, Italians, Syrians and blacks."[37]

Ghettos not only breed violence, but also restrict opportunities for economic achievement. The poor are isolated from the job market, often handicapped by ghetto schools, poor health, and lack of transportation. Generally,

A gang in the South Bronx. Studies have shown that crime increases with the unemployment rate, and the unemployment rate for teenage minority males is much higher than it is for any other group in the population.

life conditions there deny ghetto residents the skills needed to compete in a highly technological society, and many still suffer from racial discrimination. Of course, those who accumulate in the ghettos are those excluded from the viable job market, people who are unemployed or who are employed at jobs which pay a particularly poor wage. While the nation's unemployment rate has been at the 6 to 8 percent rate during most of the 1970s, the unemployment rate for males in poverty pockets is two to four times the national rate, and unemployment among black teenagers has typically been in the 30 to 40 percent range. Large numbers of idle, unemployed teenagers are an almost perfect prescription for violence and crime.

The consensus among criminologists and big-city police chiefs is that the unemployment rate is directly related to the incidence of crime.[38] This conclusion is supported by a number of empirical studies. Delinquency, property crimes, violent crimes including homicide, and admissions to prisons have all been shown to vary with unemployment. Cross-national studies of the United States, Canada, England and Wales, and Scotland between the years

1920–1940 and 1947–1973 have substantiated trends between unemployment and the incidence of crime.[39]

One of the main reasons that ex-convicts have such a high rate of return to prison is that most cannot find employment. About 50 percent of all ex-cons are unemployed.[40] Even a study by the Bureau of Prisons verified the relationship between unemployment and crime. The study reported that "when unemployment of males twenty and over goes up or down, the population of the Federal Prison System usually follows the same pattern, allowing for a time lag of fifteen months."[41]

Violent crimes and street crimes result largely from the brutalizing and dehumanizing conditions that millions of Americans live in and from the lack of legitimate economic opportunities for many citizens.

Some criminologists have theorized that the brutalization and lack of opportunities imposed by ghetto life breed resentment, hostility, and acts of violence against the larger society. Certainly, the ghetto riots were an outburst against an oppressive majority. Some criminals undoubtedly commit violence against participants and businesses in the prosperous sector of society, at least in part out of frustration and revenge. Still, the data show that most of the victims of crime are as poor as their assailants, and are usually of the same race. In fact, a large percentage of crime victims are the most defenseless of the American poor—old people, children, and women.

Violence

H. Rap Brown, the militant civil-rights leader, once told an audience that "violence is as American as cherry pie." America does have a violent past and present, in terms of both the incidence of crime and its extensive involvement in wars, civil strife, modes of entertainment, and heroes. Violence is so much a part of the American fabric that it dominates some popular American sports, and is a common theme of movies, television, the stage, literature, and art. Both sports and entertainment figures, such as Clint Eastwood, the late John Wayne, and Charles Bronson, are venerated for their portrayal of heroes who excel at violence.

Studies show that the average 18-year-old American high-school student has spent 11,000 hours in classrooms, but 15,000 hours watching television. The television fare in these studies included, on the average, 18,000 murders and countless other forms of violence such as rapes, beatings, torture, and robberies.[42] Ironically, children's shows have four times the violent content of adult shows. Some authorities believe that exposure to so much violence desensitizes Americans, facilitating acceptance of violence as a normal condition. Some experts believe that so much exposure to, and even glorification of, violence causes people not just to accept it but to commit it. Particularly harmful, some researchers believe, are presentations of violence that do not result in punishment and that help one obtain a goal.[43] In recent years there has been increasing sensitivity to the impact of entertainment violence on society and some modest efforts to control it.

The gun is a symbol and frequent instrument of American violence. No major industrialized nation on earth has gun laws that are as lax as ours. Americans may own as many as 200 million guns, the largest private arsenal in the world. The ready availability of guns frequently causes personal quarrels to end with shootings; it encourages suicides and emboldens robbers, burglars, and other criminals. The temptation to settle personal quarrels with a gun is so strong that privately owned guns are six times more likely to kill a family member or friend than an intruder.[44] The South, which has the most lax gun laws and the largest supply of weapons, has the most crime and the highest rate of murder by gun. In the Northeastern states, where gun ownership laws are strict, 46 percent of all murders are committed with guns. In the South, 73 percent of all murders result from guns.[45]

"We can't let anything spoil the sacred dealer-patient relationship."

Since 1938, polls have shown that Americans want more restrictive gun ownership laws, but Congress has long been intimidated by the National Rifle Association (see Chapter 10). In 1975 only 15 percent of those interviewed by the Harris Poll opposed a law requiring registration of all handguns, and 77 percent favored a law requiring people carrying a gun outside their home to have a license. Still, the billion-dollar-a-year profit from gun and ammunition sales stimulates powerful and successful resistance to regulation.

Greed

White-collar crime cannot be explained by the same factors which cause street crimes and crimes of passion. A large proportion of white-collar crime is quite simply caused by greed. Businessmen in search of wealth or more profits commit a great deal of crime. Trusted middle-management employees, and even some top-management executives, steal from their own companies to support a more elaborate life-style. Wage employees steal from employers out of greed, because of hostility toward the employer, because they believe the company is too rich to be hurt by the theft, to supplement low wages, or even to relieve some of the boredom their jobs cause them.

Greed is a normal consequence of an economic philosophy that puts pressures on people to consume and defines personal success in terms of material consumption and wealth. Such a philosophy can serve as a strong competitor to other values, such as Christianity. The poor are as vulnerable to the social pressures to accumulate wealth as other citizens are, and thus are led toward crime by multiple factors. In a society which condemns the poor and provides modestly for them, some will also steal because of a sense of insecurity. In America, one's life-style and well-being are much more dependent upon personal wealth than in most other industrialized nations.

Problems with courts and prisons

Overworked police and overcrowded and unenlightened courts and prisons contribute significantly to the incidence of crime. The evidence indicates that the single best deterrent to crime is certainty of punishment.[46] The degree of certainty that an act will result in punishment is generally more important than the severity of the punishment. A mandatory life sentence for burglary is not much of a threat if burglars know that in our society they have only 1 out of 412 chances of going to jail for any single offense.[47] However, an almost certain two-year term for any burglary provides a very strong deterrent. The inability of the police to solve most crimes and the inability of prosecutors and courts to effectively bring most criminals to justice encourages rather than discourages crime.

An effective criminal justice system would not only provide a high certainty of conviction for crimes, but would systematically evaluate those con-

"Hey, Joe—says here our chances of becoming a crime victim are increasing . . . Joe. . ."

victed, with the goal of making the punishment fit the criminal and the crime. Criminologists refer to this as prescriptive penology, the administration of confinement, discomfort, and aid in the combination most likely to reform each defendant.[48] Such a strategy would remove the most dangerous criminals from society and would provide the best chance of reforming those prisoners capable of reform. There is some evidence to indicate that a significant percentage of all crime is committed by relatively small numbers of hard-core repeaters.[49] Simply removing these people from society for specific periods would reduce crime. Some argue that such a strategy would reduce the crime rate significantly.[50]

Even a rational sentencing policy would be frustrated considerably by conditions in American prisons, however. An almost universal problem with American prisons is that they are overcrowded. In 1976 federal prisons had 21 percent more inmates than they were designed to hold.[51] Most state prisons are severely overcrowded. In 1976 Florida had more than 200 prisoners living in tents. Two states purchased old ships to convert into prisons, a throwback to nineteenth-century England.[52] Overcrowding makes it much more difficult to properly supervise prisoners, increasing the chances that the institution will be brutal, dangerous, and dehumanizing. Unless a prison is well run, there is always the chance that prisoners will be hardened by incarceration, educated in crime, and introduced to a wide range of criminal associates to draw upon once they leave prison.

For the most part, prisons put minimal effort into rehabilitation. The efforts that are made are not guided by systematic research. One authority maintains:

> The primary deficiency of contemporary corrections, from the standpoint of social policy, is the fact that it is not systematically and adequately guided by research. Failure to invest even 1 percent of correctional expenditure in research and failure to focus much research on measuring effectiveness means that correctional policy is determined more by expediency, custom, or unsystematic impressions of new procedures than by the demonstrated long-run effectiveness of correctional practices.[53]

The limited studies that are available indicate that rehabilitation success depends primarily upon the characteristics of the offenders. Prisoners with little prior criminal experience who seek rehabilitation tend to benefit greatly from aid. Offenders with extensive criminal experience are likely to use rehabilitation and counseling situations

> primarily to manipulate staff, rationalize their criminality, and avoid the humiliations of traditional prison life, rather than to prepare realistically for the problems they would encounter in pursuing a noncriminal life outside of prison.[54]

The available evidence shows not only a shortage of rehabilitation programs and efforts, but also a lack of sophistication in the selection of prisoners for the programs. The result is that most prisoners reenter society as poorly (or more poorly) prepared for success than when they entered. Poorly trained for the job market and uncounseled in societal success, they often encounter obstacles which would hamper anyone. Many states deny driver's licenses to ex-convicts; some jobs cannot be held by anyone convicted of a felony. This generally includes jobs handling money, liquor, and tobacco. Restricted in job opportunities in an already tight market and discriminated against by employers, ex-convicts suffer unemployment at about three times the national average.

An effective criminal justice system would not only provide a high certainty of conviction for crimes, but would systematically evaluate those convicted, with the goal of making the punishment fit the criminal and the crime.

Since most felonies involve property thefts, crime often serves as an alternative to legitimate employment. In fact, some citizens find crime their best economic alternative. This point is so well-documented that any rational approach to crime reduction should include a full-employment economy, job training for prisoners, and available jobs for ex-convicts—subsidized, if necessary, by the state.[55] The evidence indicates that if ex-convicts could be guaranteed a chance to make an honest living, crime would be reduced significantly.

CONCLUSIONS

Ramsey Clark once wrote that "crime reflects the character of a people. . . . Crime reflects more than the character of the pitiful few who commit it. It reflects the character of the entire society."[56] Clark is undoubtedly correct. The high incidence of crime in America reveals that millions of Americans live in environments that brutalize them and socialize them to view society as an enemy to be battled for survival. People who are suppressed, dehumanized, and denied opportunities can hardly be expected to docilely accept poverty and neglect, especially not in a wealthy society whose prevailing philosophy includes material accumulation as a critical function of a successful life.

In addition to poverty and restricted opportunities, our society accepts and is fascinated with violence. While on one hand violence is feared and abhorred, in other ways it is accepted as a legitimate trait (especially among men) and an important form and subject of entertainment. Until poverty is eradicated, opportunities significantly expanded, and the exposure to and acceptance of violence greatly diminished, crime in America will continue at a very high rate.

Crime is also caused by the conflict between the philosophy of capitalism and the human values of society. Capitalism's overemphasis on material consumption and accumulation of wealth as a measure of a successful life often overwhelms civilized values such as honesty, sharing, sacrifice, and development of the human spirit. The pressures of capitalist philosophy are so strong that they often lead both the poor and the non-poor to commit crimes.

Footnotes

1 See John E. Conklin, *The Impact of Crime* (New York: Macmillan, 1975), p. 1.

2 *Readings in Criminal Justice* (Guilford, Connecticut: Dushkin Publishing, 1977), p. 5.

3 FBI Uniform Crime Reports, *Crime In The United States 1977* (Washington, D.C.: Government Printing Office, 1978), p. 35.

4 *Crime In The United States 1977*, p. 6

5 Virginia Adams, *Crime* (New York: Time-Life Books, 1976), pp. 7–41.

6 Philip H. Ennis, "Crime, Victims, and the Police," *Transaction*, 4, no. 7 (June 1967): 36–44; Washington, D.C.: U.S. Department of Justice, Law Enforcement Assistance Administration, National Criminal Justice Information and Statistics Service, 1975, "Criminal Victimization in 13 American Cities"; "Survey of Five Biggest Cities Shows Crime Double the Rate Reported," The Houston *Post*, April 15, 1976, p. A5.

7 "Tracking Crime," The Houston *Post*, September 8, 1977, p. 2C.

8 *Crime In The United States 1977*, p. 8.

9 *Ibid.*, p. 9.

10 *Readings In Criminal Justice*, p. 5.

11 Harry Wilensky, "U.S.: Most Guns, Most Lawless," The Houston *Post*, April 28, 1975, p. 3C.

12 Firearms Legislation Hearings before Subcommittee on Crime, Vol. 4, 94th Cong., 1975, pp. 1629–31.

13 *Readings In Criminal Justice,* p. 174; Keith D. Harris, *The Geography of Crime and Justice* (New York: McGraw-Hill, 1974), p. 43.

14 *Crime In The United States 1977,* p. 171.

15 *Ibid.,* p. 214.

16 *Ibid.,* p. 172.

17 Alphonso Pinkney, "Crime and Justice In America," The Houston *Post,* Oct. 6, 1977, p. 14B.

18 *Crime In The United States 1977,* p. 160.

19 *Ibid.,* p. 161.

20 *Ibid.,* p. 172.

21 *Readings In Criminal Justice,* p. 21.

22 Gary F. Glenn, "Crime Does Pay," *Readings In Criminal Justice,* p. 106.

23 John E. Conklin, *Illegal But Not Criminal: Business Crime In America* (Englewood Cliffs, N.J.: Prentice-Hall, 1977), p. 4.

24 *Ibid.,* p. 4.

25 Glenn, "Crime Does Pay," p. 107.

26 "Shoplifting Costly 'Gift' on Holidays," The Houston *Post,* Dec. 7, 1978, p. 5A.

27 *Ibid.,* p. 5A.

28 Conklin, *Illegal But Not Criminal,* p. 6.

29 *Ibid.,* p. 7.

30 Adams, *Crime,* p. 108–111.

31 Conklin, *Illegal But Not Criminal,* p. 109.

32 *Ibid.,* p. 104.

33 *Ibid.,* pp. 102–9.

34 *Ibid.,* p. 115.

35 *Ibid.,* p. 115.

36 Ramsey Clark, *Crime In America* (New York: Pocket Books, 1971), p. 41.

37 *Readings In Criminal Justice,* p. 8.

38 Carl T. Rowan, "Chiefs Note Bad Times Spur Crime," The Houston *Post,* August 1, 1976, p. 12A.

39 Daniel Glaser and Kent Rice, "Crime, Age and Unemployment," *American Sociological Review,* October 1959, pp. 679–86; Belton M. Fleisher, "The Effects of Unemployment in Delinquent Behavior," *Journal of Political Economy,* 81(1963): 545–55; U.S. Bureau of Prisons, "Correlation of Unemployment and Federal Prison Population," *U.S. Bureau of Prisons Report,* March, 1975; M. Harvey Brenner, "Effects of the Economy on Criminal Behavior and the Administration of Criminal Justice in the United States, Canada, England and Wales, and Scotland," in *Economic Crises and Crime: Correlations Between the State of the Economy, Deviance and the Control of Deviance* (Rome, Italy: United Nations Social Defense Research Institute, 1976); and Daniel Glaser, *The Effectiveness of a Prison and Parole System* (New York: Bobbs-Merrill, 1964), pp. 232–59.

40 Daniel Glaser, *Adult Crime and Social Policy* (Englewood Cliffs, New Jersey: Prentice-Hall, 1972), p. 104.

41 *Readings In Criminal Justice,* p. 113.

42 *Television and Growing Up: The Impact of Televised Violence,* Report to the Surgeon General (Rockville, Maryland: National Institute of Mental Health, 1971), p. 5.

43 *Ibid.,* p. 9.

44 S. Oberbeck, "Safe with a Gun? Don't Believe It," *Readers' Digest,* February, 1975, p. 135.

45 Glaser, *Adult Crime and Social Policy,* p. 36.

46 The literature here is extensive. For a review see Harrell R. Rodgers, Jr., and Charles S. Bullock, III, *Coercion to Compliance* (Lexington, Mass.: Lexington Books, 1976), pp. 1–10, 123–31.

47 Glenn, "Crime Does Pay," p. 107.

48 Glaser, *Adult Crime and Social Policy,* p. 105.

49 Adams, *Crime,* p. 169.

50 *Ibid.,* p. 169.

51 *Readings In Criminal Justice,* p. 92.

52 *Ibid.,* p. 92.

53 Glaser, *Adult Crime and Social Policy,* p. 109.

54 *Ibid.,* p. 105.

55 *Ibid.,* p. 104.

56 Clark, *Crime In America,* pp. 3, 5.

> God knows how little we've really moved on this issue, despite all the fanfare. As I see it, I've moved (blacks) from D+ to C−.
>
> Lyndon Johnson

17

In earlier chapters we examined the public's role in the political system, discussed and evaluated theories of power in American government, and looked at violence as a form of public influence and elite power. Each of these topics provides insight into power and influence in the American political system. In Part 2 we showed how the public's limited role is reflected in the operation of the political process and its policies. Additional insight into the political process can be gained by examining one group's attempts to substantially alter and improve its position in the American political system. Such a case study reveals much about the biases, priorities, institutional flaws, and dynamics of the political process and the cumulative impact on American citizens and democracy.

The Civil-Rights Movement: Did It Fail?

In recent history, three major groups have engaged in such a struggle— blacks, labor, and women. This chapter will evaluate the success of black Americans' attempts to substantially improve their condition. We will emphasize the techniques and conditions that produced changes in civil rights; the quantity and quality of progress achieved; and the insights suggested by incomplete progress in black liberation.

THE CIVIL-RIGHTS MOVEMENT

The black struggle for freedom and equality in America is a tapestry that runs the length of American history. The Civil War and attendant events theoretically freed blacks from suppression. Only months after the end of the Civil War the Thirteenth Amendment was ratified, abolishing slavery. In 1868 the Fourteenth Amendment gave citizenship to black citizens, reversing the Supreme Court's infamous *Dred Scott* decision of 1857.[1] In 1870 the Fifteenth Amendment, guaranteeing blacks the right to vote, became law.

During the Reconstruction era (1863–77), Congress also passed a number of civil-rights laws, but they were effectively nullified by the Supreme Court. In 1883 the Supreme Court ruled that the Fourteenth Amendment protected

Led by Martin Luther King, Jr., two hundred thousand people staged a demonstration in Washington, D.C., in 1963 to promote civil rights and jobs for blacks.

The Civil War Amendments

from the Thirteenth Amendment: "Neither slavery nor involuntary servitude, except as a punishment for crime whereof the party shall have been duly convicted, shall exist within the United States, or any place subject to their jurisdiction."

from the Fourteenth Amendment: "All persons born or naturalized in the United States and subject to the jurisdiction thereof, are citizens of the United States and the State wherein they reside. No State shall make or enforce any law which shall abridge the privileges or immunities of citizens of the United States; nor shall any State deprive any person of life, liberty, or property without due process of law; nor deny to any person within its jurisdiction the equal protection of the laws."

from the Fifteenth Amendment: "The right of citizens of the United States to vote shall not be denied or abridged by the United States or by any State on account of race, color, or previous condition of servitude."

blacks from discrimination by states, but not from discrimination by private citizens. This left blacks vulnerable and unprotected against individual acts of discrimination and even violence. In practice, it also stripped them of defenses against discrimination by public officials.

In 1896 the Supreme Court ruled that blacks could be barred from the use of public facilities as long as they were provided with "separate but equal" accommodations.[2] The "equal" part of the standard was ignored, and segregation in transportation, housing, schools, restaurants, jobs and other phases of life was legitimized by law. The doctrine of "separate but equal" survived for fifty-eight years.

The period from 1883 to the 1950s came to be known as the era of "Jim Crow": legal segregation and suppression of blacks supplemented by white terror against blacks who tried to resist. The NAACP recorded some 5,000 cases of known lynchings during this period.[3] Beatings and other acts of terror were too numerous for accurate estimate. It was not the wealthy white landowners—who profited from black suppression—who personally inflicted injury on blacks. This role was rather cheerfully assumed by poor whites—people who ironically were as much victims of the land-holding white elites as the blacks were.

The "separate but equal" doctrine was finally overturned in 1954 in the famous case of *Brown* v. *Board of Education of Topeka, Kansas*. The Supreme Court was asked to decide if separate educational facilities for blacks were by definition unequal and thus a violation of the *equal protection clause* of the Fourteenth Amendment. Chief Justice Earl Warren, speaking for a unanimous court, posed the basic question raised by the case and answered it decisively:

Does segregation of children in public schools solely on the basis of race, even though the physical facilities and other 'tangible' factors may be equal, deprive the children of the minority group of equal educational opportunities? We believe that it does. . .we conclude that in the field of public education the doctrine 'separate but equal' has no place. Separate educational facilities are inherently unequal. Therefore, we hold that the plaintiffs. . .are, by reason of the segregation complained of, deprived of the equal protection of the laws guaranteed by the Fourteenth Amendment.[4]

In 1955 the Supreme Court ruled that the *Brown* decision was to be implemented "with all deliberate speed," a standard so meaningless that compliance with *Brown* long was the exception rather than the rule.[5] Still, *Brown* was the catalyst for the modern civil-rights movement. Blacks and their supporters were encouraged by the decision, and struggles to gain compliance with *Brown* increasingly brought public attention and federal support for black citizens.

In 1957 President Eisenhower sent federal troops to Little Rock, Arkansas, to quell the violence associated with efforts to integrate Central High School. Under the protection of federal paratroopers, the school was integrated, despite mobs of screaming whites, racist public officials, and National Guard troops that had been mobilized by the governor to block integration. Conflicts on a less dramatic scale occurred in hundreds of communities during the next fifteen years.

The civil-rights movement received a considerable boost from one woman's simple act of courage. In late 1955, Rosa Parks, a quiet and dignified resident of Montgomery, Alabama, refused to give her seat in the front of a bus to a white rider. She was arrested and fined $10. Her stand stimulated a year-long boycott of the Montgomery bus line. The boycott was led by Dr. Martin Luther King, Jr., a Baptist minister from Atlanta.

Dr. Martin Luther King, Jr.

The remarkable solidarity of Montgomery's black citizens in supporting the boycott, the eloquence of Dr. King, and the ultimate victory for black citizens in November 1956—when a federal court issued an injunction against the segregation of buses—brought national publicity for the black cause and thrust King into the forefront of the civil-rights struggle. King, a devotee of Gandhi, preached nonviolent confrontation and *civil disobedience* as the methods of producing change. King formed the Southern Christian Leadership Conference (SCLC) to promote civil-rights change by challenging discrimination at the state and local level.

SCLC was, of course, only one of many organizations involved in the struggle for racial equality. The National Association for the Advancement of Colored People (NAACP) sought to promote change primarily by filing court actions against discriminatory statutes or acts. The Congress of Racial Equality (CORE), formed during World War II, was active during the 1960s under the leadership of James Farmer. The Student Nonviolent Coordinating Committee (SNCC), formed in 1960, was led by two of the most militant black leaders, Stokley Carmichael and H. Rap Brown.

In 1960 another phase of the civil-rights movement began: four black students in Greensboro, North Carolina, started the sit-in movement. The students sat down at Woolworth's lunch counter and ordered coffee. When they were refused service, they continued to sit quietly. Day after day they repeated this strategy, along with other students who began to join them. Whites splattered them with mustard and ketchup, but they remained seated. The strategy caught on quickly and spread to communities throughout the South. Within a few months, hundreds of lunch counters started serving blacks.

Dr. Martin Luther King was in the forefront of the civil-rights struggle. King, a devotee of Gandhi, preached nonviolent confrontation and civil disobedience as the methods of producing change.

In 1961 the technique was applied to interstate buses and terminals. Civil-rights activists launched "Freedom Rides" into Alabama, where they were savagely beaten by hostile whites, and one of the buses was burned. The riders and the violence they evoked dramatized the segregation in interstate transportation, even though the Supreme Court had outlawed it in 1946.[6] In 1979 the ACLU released documents revealing that the FBI kept a Birmingham, Alabama, police sergeant who was a known member of the Ku Klux Klan informed of the buses' progress, allowing the Klan to organize its attacks. Further, the ACLU charged that the FBI provoked the Klan to carry out terrorist acts against civil-rights workers.

Integration of universities also produced conflict. Riots resulting in two deaths occurred at Oxford, Mississippi, in 1962, when James Meredith, a black student, enrolled in the University of Mississippi. President Kennedy sent federal troops in to restore peace and assigned federal marshals to protect Meredith. In 1963 Governor George Wallace of Alabama dramatically tried to block the enrollment of two black students at the University of Alabama. Wallace's grandstand ploy failed when Kennedy federalized the Alabama National Guard and ordered it to protect the black students.

In 1963 Dr. King led massive demonstrations against segregation in Birmingham, Alabama. The behavior of Birmingham's police, under the direction of Police Commissioner Eugene "Bull" Connor, did much to turn public sympathy in favor of black citizens. The police broke up demonstrations with fire hoses and brutalized demonstrators with cattle prods and police dogs. From a local cell Dr. King wrote his famous "Letter from a Birmingham Jail," a defense of nonviolent civil disobedience as a method of forcing change in unjust laws.

While the violence in Birmingham continued, Dr. King led a massive demonstration to Washington, D.C., in quest of jobs and freedom. The sight of 200,000 people, black and white, peacefully marching in the nation's capital carried a powerful message to the country, a message exceeded only by Dr. King's visionary words:

> I have a dream that one day this nation will rise up and live out the true meaning of its creed. . . . I have a dream . . . that my four little children will one day live in a nation where they will not be judged by the color of their skin but by the content of their character . . . So let freedom ring. . . . From every mountainside let freedom ring . . . to speed up that day when all of God's children, black and white men, Jew and Gentiles, Protestants and Catholics, will be able to join hands and sing in the words of that old Negro spiritual, ''Free at Last! Free at Last! Thank God Almighty, we are free at last!''

Two weeks later, while King's words still rang across the nation, a black church in Birmingham was rocked by a dynamite blast which killed four little girls attending Sunday school.

In 1965 Dr. King organized a march from Selma, Alabama, to Montgomery, the state capital, to dramatize racial barriers to black voting in that state. The fifty-mile march was first marred by state troopers who, acting under orders from Governor Wallace, beat and gassed the marchers. This prompted President Johnson to federalize the Alabama National Guard and order it to protect the marchers. As the marchers neared Montgomery, the ranks swelled until a large crowd reached the steps of the Alabama capitol.

Civil-rights activists marched from Selma to Montgomery, Alabama, in 1965 to protest the restrictions on black voting in that state.

Just as the sit-ins and demonstrations in the South began to dwindle, the ghetto riots flared up (see Chapter 5). Watts exploded in 1965, followed by disturbances in Chicago and Cleveland in 1966. In 1967 riots swept the nation. In July, forty cities from Buffalo to San Francisco were hit by burning and looting. The assassination of Dr. King in 1968 set off an even larger wave of riots, including a riot in Washington, D.C., that spread to within a few blocks of the White House. For nearly two weeks, the capital had to be occupied by federal troops.

THE POLICY RESPONSE

The civil-rights movement—and white reactions to it—produced a steady stream of legislation from Congress. The first civil-rights bill since 1875 was passed in 1957. The 1957 act sought to protect the right of blacks to vote. It provided that persons denied the right to vote could seek injunctive relief from the federal district courts. The act also created the U.S. Commission on Civil Rights and established a Civil Rights Division in the Department of Justice. The law proved far too modest to end barriers to black enfranchisement.

The Civil Rights Act of 1960 also sought to expedite black registration and voting. The law specified that federal judges or federal referees could be authorized to register qualified blacks who had been discriminated against by local officials. Local officials were required to keep all voting records for at least twenty-two months, and to make them available to the U.S. attorney general upon request. The act also contained provisions making certain acts of bombing and obstruction of federal court orders a crime.

LADIES   MEN   COLORED

When President Kennedy was assassinated, he left behind a major civil-rights bill he had recommended to Congress in 1963. President Johnson asked Congress to pass the bill as a memorial to the slain President. The House of Representatives quickly passed the bill, but it was stymied in the Senate by a fifty-seven-day filibuster by Southern senators. In June 1964, the Senate voted to invoke cloture (end debate), and the bill was approved. The 1964 act was the most comprehensive passed thus far. Basically, the act:

1. Prohibited discrimination in public accommodations that affect interstate commerce. This included businesses that served people traveling in interstate commerce, or in which a substantial proportion of the products used in the business had moved in interstate commmerce. Thus, almost all hotels, motels, restaurants, cafeterias, service stations, theaters and other businesses were covered.
2. Prohibited the application of different standards to black and white voters by registrars and outlawed the rejection of black voting applications because of immaterial errors or omissions. It required that literacy tests must be in writing and not consist of some arbitrary standard adopted by local registrars. A sixth-grade education in an American school would serve as a presumption of literacy.
3. Prohibited job discrimination because of race, color, sex, religion, or national origin by employers or labor unions.
4. Provided that federal funds to public or private programs that practice discrimination could be terminated.
5. Specified that the attorney general could bring suit to enforce the public accommodation provisions and provided that private citizens could file suit to protect their rights under the statute.
6. Created the Equal Employment Opportunity Commission (EEOC) to enforce the fair employment section of the act.

Continued resistance to black voting, dramatized by the events at Selma and the march to Montgomery, prompted Congress to pass an act designed to overcome both blatant and subtle barriers to black voting. The 1965 Voting Rights Act was predicated on the assumption that a *prima facie* case of voter discrimination existed in states and counties in which less than 50 percent of the potential electorate was registered or had voted in the 1964 election. Six Southern states and some counties in North Carolina were immediately affected by the act. In these states and counties, all qualifications for voting except age, residency, and criminal record had to be eliminated. In counties with a pattern of discrimination, federal registrars could be sent in to register black voters. To insure that black voters could safely go to the polls and have the vote counted, federal poll watchers could also be sent into the county.

In 1966 the Supreme Court ended another barrier to voting—the poll tax. In the mid-1960s, five Southern states were still requiring voters to pay a small tax as a prerequisite to voting. The twenty-fourth Amendment, ratified in 1964, had prohibited any tax on federal voting. In *Harper* v. *Board of Elections,* the Supreme Court ruled that it was unconstitutional to impose any charge for voting or voting registration.

Outlawing the Poll Tax

The Open Housing Act of 1968 was designed to make most housing available to Americans of any race. In three phases, ending in 1970, the act was designed to make all rental and property sales handled by realtors subject to fair housing laws. Estimates were that this would include 80 percent of all housing sales. The act also included criminal penalties for those who injured or interfered with civil-rights workers or people attempting to exercise their civil rights. Ironically, two months after passage of the housing act, the Supreme Court ruled that the Civil Rights Act of 1866 prohibited all discrimination in housing, whether agents or private owners were involved.[7]

In 1970 the Voting Rights Act was extended for another five years. Its coverage was extended to parts of New York, several New England states, Oregon, Idaho, California, Alaska, and Arizona. The use of literacy and "good character" tests were barred for five years. In 1975 the act was again extended (to 1982), and language minorities were covered. Election materials must be made bilingual in areas with significant numbers of Spanish-speaking Americans, Indians, Asians, or Alaskan natives. This provision extended the act to about a dozen more states. The use of literacy and "good character" tests was permanently banned nationwide.

Throughout American history few policy issues have received such sustained and concentrated attention of Congress and the executive branch over such a short period of time. Between 1957 and 1968 five civil-rights bills were passed, three of which could be described as major pieces of legislation. How did blacks and civil-rights supporters manage to obtain so much legislation so quickly?

The answer is that the actions of civil-rights workers and the often violent resistance of southern whites created a national mood favoring relief for blacks. The violence of white racists, much of which was shown on television and documented by picture and word, so repelled much of white America, including many public officials, that the situation simply demanded resolution. Two sympathetic Presidents, Kennedy and Johnson, also provided moral leadership and policy initiatives to spur Congress on.

In addition, the unity of black citizens in support of relief, the intensity of their demands, public sympathy and support, and the obvious moral legitimacy of black demands put pressure on public officials for corrective legislation. Millions of citizens across the nation expected Congress and the executive to deal with the issue, and millions of voters depended upon their actions. The movement also disrupted the political tranquility, placing the spotlight on injustices and congressional and executive reactions. Restoring public peace required the passage of corrective legislation. The riots even threatened elite positions. Supportive legislation, such as improvements in welfare laws, was required to pacify and reestablish black support for the political system.

THE POLICY CONSEQUENCES

How valuable were the civil-rights acts, improvements in welfare programs, and Supreme Court decisions in favor of black freedom and equality? In general, they were extremely important. Between 1950 and 1970 the position of blacks in American society changed drastically. Progress and gains were made in hundreds of ways; white attitudes toward black Americans and their right to equal treatment and opportunities improved markedly; and many blacks were brought into the mainstream of the social, political, and economic systems.[8]

But, specifically, how extensive has progress for black Americans been? Have most black Americans been able to enter the mainstream of society, or have many, even most, blacks been left behind? Have blacks gained real power in the political system? Have blacks captured their fair share of good jobs? Have they been able to obtain good housing and send their children to integrated schools? A policy-by-policy analysis provides insight into these questions. Since the civil-rights movement sought to establish both black political power and economic gains, both types of policies will be analyzed. We begin by examining black gains in political strength.

Voting and black representation

The cumulative impact of the four modern civil-rights acts that dealt wholly or partially with the black franchise drastically increased black registration, voting, and political power in the South. Change did not come easily, and all four acts were necessary to overcome many of the most serious obstacles to black enfranchisement. The 1957 act was valuable primarily for its symbolic impact. It put the federal government's approval on black enfranchisement and designated the Department of Justice as the protector of blacks. Alone, however, it did not serve as the vehicle for substantial increases in black registration and voting.

Table 17.1 shows the increase in black registration in the South between 1940 and 1974. In the 1940s, before the civil-rights movement, black registration was extremely low. Despite the 1957 act, black registration increased very modestly between 1956 and 1960.

Initially, the 1960 act also had little impact on black registration. Between 1960 and 1962 the number of registered blacks in the South increased by only 17,000.[9] Between 1962 and 1964, however, black registration increased significantly, stimulated primarily by voter registration projects and

TABLE 17.1
Black Voter Registration in Southern States

Year	Percent of Eligible Blacks Registered
1940	5
1947	12
1956	25
1958	25
1960	29
1962	29
1964	43
1966	54
1968	62
1970	58
1972	64
1974	55
1976	58

some federal actions under the 1957 and 1960 acts. The 1964 act also removed some barriers to black registration, further increasing black power at the polls.

The real breakthrough against the most virulent racism was the Voting Rights Act of 1965. Unlike most laws, it was designed to take effect immediately upon passage. During the first seven and one-half months after its passage, 300,000 new black voters were registered. Where federal examiners and registrars were sent in under the law, black registration increased 50 percent, while in non-examiner counties it increased by 22.3 percent.[10] Between 1966 and 1974, black registration was slightly more than 50 percent in congressional election years and in excess of 60 percent in presidential election years.

The number of actual voters among both blacks and whites is always less than the number registered. Black registration and voting, even at their highwater marks, in 1964 and 1968, have remained below white registration and

TABLE 17.2
Reported Voter Participation by Race

Race	Percentage of Eligible Voters						
	1964	1966	1968	1970	1972	1974	1976
Black vote (%)	58	42	58	44	52	34	49
White vote (%)	71	57	69	56	64	46	61

Source: U.S. Bureau of the Census, "The Social and Economic Status of the Black Population in the United States," *Current Population Reports,* Series P-23, No. 54, p. 145; and Bureau of the Census, *Current Population Reports,* Series P-20, No. 304.

voting. For example, Table 17.2, which contrasts black and white voting in recent elections, shows that a simple majority of qualified blacks voted in the presidential elections of 1964, 1968, and 1972, but that only 44 percent voted in 1970, dropping to only 34 percent in 1974. In the presidential election of 1976, only 49 percent of eligible blacks voted.

Increased black registration and voting have been converted into increased black political power. For example, Table 17.3 shows the increases in black elected officials across the nation and in the South between 1964 and 1978. In 1964 there were only 103 black elected officials in America, only 16 of which held elective office in the South. By 1971 the number of black elected officials had increased dramatically. Fourteen blacks were serving in Congress, almost 200 were in state legislatures and state executive offices, and 81 were mayors (47 in the South). Progress continued, with 3,503 black elected officials in 1975. Eighteen of them were in Congress, 281 were in state legislatures and executive posts, and 135 were mayors. By 1978 the total number of black elected officials exceeded 4,000.

As impressive as these gains are, black representation in elective offices in 1978 equaled less than 1 percent of all elected offices in America. Still, it is extremely important to note that blacks hold elective office in every state in the Union. Local mayors and sheriffs in the South are now often blacks who frequently replaced the white racist officials who once discriminated against them. With some 6.6 million black voters nationwide, blacks have the potential for real political clout in many local and state elections and often at the national level. Voting as a unit, blacks can often win or swing elections. As

TABLE 17.3
Black Elected Officials

Office	1964	1971	1973	1975	1978
Total	103	1,860	2,621	3,503	4,503
U.S. senators	—	1	1	1	1
U.S. representatives	5	13	15	17	16
State legislators and executives	94	198	240	281	294
Mayors	(NA)	81	82	135	170
Other	(NA)	1,567	2,283	3,069	4,022

Source: U.S. Bureau of the Census, "The Social and Economic Status of the Black Population in the United States 1974," *Current Population Reports,* Series P-23, No. 54, p. 151: News Release, Joint Center for Political Studies, 1978. Figures for 1978 are as of July 1978.

noted in Chapter 2, the unity of black support for Jimmy Carter probably provided his electoral edge in 1976. Ninety-four percent of all black voters supported Carter. In the elections of 1968 and 1972, black voters were also unified behind the Democratic party, voting Democratic by margins of 87 percent and 86 percent, respectively. Blacks also gave Truman his electoral edge in 1948 and Kennedy his margin in 1960.

What changes have black voting and increased black representation in public office brought? Analysts disagree on many points, but a few gains are obvious. First, overt violence by whites against blacks has almost ceased. During the civil-rights movement, white violence against blacks did not generally occur after blacks had won the franchise, integrated restaurants, or desegregated schools; it occurred just as these gains were about to be made. Since the 1970s, overt violence against blacks, especially in organized form, has been relatively rare and decreases yearly. For people who lived so long under the threat of violence, this is no small gain.

Second, black voting power has moderated the rhetoric and racial positions of white Southern politicians. Some white politicians who once flaunted their racism now hide or moderate it. And the most rabid racists are often passed over by the party for more moderate whites. Jimmy Carter is an example of a moderate, even liberal, white politician whose racial stands would have probably prevented his election to the governorship of Georgia before the civil-rights movement.

Black voter registration drives have helped increase voting rates, especially in the South.

Third, while the subject has not been well researched, there is some evidence that public services to black communities have improved somewhat with increased voting strength.[11] This would seem only logical since local black officials could be expected to look after black neighborhoods better, and black voters would be in a better position to bargain with white officials. As black voting strength has increased, more blacks have also been placed in patronage jobs and in local positions such as police and fire departments.

Finally, even a small number of blacks in elective office may serve to discourage legislation prejudicial to blacks. The small number of blacks serving in state legislatures or in the U.S. Congress may not be able to pass legislation by themselves, but they can often defeat or discourage the passage of detrimental legislation that might otherwise have passed in their absence. Black officials can also sometimes win amendments to legislation to make it more beneficial to black constituents.

Housing and school desegregation

As noted, the Supreme Court ruled that legally segregated school systems were unconstitutional in 1954. In 1955 the Court ruled that the standard for desegregation would be "all deliberate speed." Segregationists were so heartened by this standard that they openly predicted that schools would never be desegregated in the South. A decade after *Brown* these predictions looked prophetic. In 1964 seven of the eleven Southern states had not placed even 1 percent of their black students into integrated schools. Five years later (1969) only one of every six black students in the South attended a desegregated school.[12]

With passage of the 1964 Civil Rights Act, the executive branch was given the authority to cut off federal funds to school districts that failed to make good faith efforts to achieve desegregation. The Department of Health, Education and Welfare began to use this power to enforce desegregation guidelines within the states. The Supreme Court also began to show signs of irritation with delays and began to sharpen the legal standard that school districts had to comply with. In 1964 the Supreme Court noted the long history of dilatory and unlawful behavior of Southern officials in avoiding their obligations under *Brown,* concluding that the standard of "all deliberate speed" never contemplated an infinite number of delaying tactics to defeat desegregation.[13]

In 1968 the Supreme Court ruled against the use of nonproductive "freedom of choice" plans; school boards were obligated to "come forward with a plan that promises realistically to work . . . now . . . until it is clear that state imposed segregation has been completely removed."[14]

In an equally important case in 1969, Nixon's HEW tried to provide a one-year delay of a desegregation plan for a district that had already dragged its heels for fifteen years. The Court overruled the delay, and declared that all school districts were "to terminate dual school systems at once."[15]

In 1971, in *Swann* v. *Charlotte-Meklenburg Board of Education et. al.,*[16] the Supreme Court tied up a few loose details concerning its desegregation standard and approved busing as a method of achieving school desegregation. The Court again said that Southern districts were obligated to achieve immediate desegregation and that federal district courts had broad power to formulate desegregation plans for stubborn districts. In addition, the Supreme Court said that racial ratios could be used to guide assignments of students to schools and to judge how much progress toward desegregation had been made. The Court pointed out that busing has traditionally been the primary method of transporting children to school (42 percent by school bus, plus 25 percent by public transportation in 1970[17]) and that it was the only method by which many districts could be desegregated.[18]

Swann basically capped the legal framework needed to end school desegregation in the border states and the South. By 1975 almost all rural and medium-to-small urban areas in the border states and the South had achieved desegregation.[19] In literally several thousand cities, towns, and villages across the South and in the border states, the dual system had ended. Segregation remained only in districts in which all white students withdrew to private segregationist academies, and in large urban areas, such as Houston and Atlanta, where segregation continued because of white flight or because of the reluctance of HEW or the courts to fashion remedies requiring massive busing to achieve desegregation.

By the early 1970s, only two major issues involving school desegregation remained to be resolved. First, what were the obligations of Northern school districts? If school desegregation in the South was unconstitutional, was it also unconstitutional in the North? Until the mid-1960s this question was rarely raised. A legal distinction had long been made between *de jure segregation* (that required by law), and *de facto segregation* (which supposedly resulted from fortuitous events such as neighborhood racial patterns). Since school segregation was never mandated by law in the North, Midwest, or West, the assumption was that school segregation in these parts of the nation was fortuitous and thus not illegal. The distinction between de jure and de facto segregation began to break down, however, when federal district courts started to hear cases from communities outside the South which showed that blacks had become isolated in particular areas of communities because of discrimination in housing, loan distribution, school assignment patterns, and dozens of other discriminatory actions. Increasingly the courts began to rule that segregation outside the South resulted from a history of discriminatory acts and was thus illegal.

The issue reached the Supreme Court in 1973. In *Keyes et. al.* v. *School District No. 1, Denver, Colorado,*[20] the Supreme Court ruled that the distinction between de jure and de facto segregation hinged on whether there had ever been any intent to segregate the races in a community, not on whether segregation had been mandated by law. Further, the Court held that if discriminatory acts (regardless of how long ago they had occurred) caused the segregation of a significant number of children in a district, then the whole district had to be desegregated. In addition, if segregation did exist in a community outside the South, the burden for proving that the segregation did not result from discrimination would rest with the school board.

Keyes transformed school desegregation into a national rather than a regional issue. Courts across the nation began to hold school desegregation illegal, and often mandated busing as the method of overcoming it. Violence broke out in a number of Midwestern and Eastern cities as white parents sought to block busing orders. Public disorders subsided as the inevitability of busing was established. In a number of cases in the mid and late 1970s, the Supreme Court ruled that lower federal courts could not simply assume that de facto segregation resulted from intentional discrimination. Desegregation, the Court said, could be ordered only if specific discriminatory acts could be proven.[21] In the cases involved, documentation of discrimination proved rather easy.

The second issue left undecided was whether the courts could order the consolidation of separate school districts as a method of achieving desegregation. This issue arose because in some communities, especially very large ones, the white population had long avoided desegregation by establishing suburbs with their own school districts on the fringe of the city. This generally left blacks in the central city with segregated schools, surrounded by primarily white suburban districts.

The issue was first raised in 1972 when a federal district court judge ordered the Richmond, Virginia, public schools to be combined with those of two neighboring, mostly white districts as a method of achieving desegregation. The court of appeals overruled the order, and the decision was left unresolved when the Supreme Court divided 4–4 on the issue.[22] The Supreme Court's position was clarified in a case involving Detroit and its suburbs in 1974. In *Milliken vs. Bradley*,[23] the Court ruled that separate districts could be consolidated only if it could be proven that all the districts involved in the plan had engaged in either intradistrict or interdistrict school segregation. In 1975 Louisville, Kentucky, and Wilmington, Delaware, became the first cities in which the Court found that a city and a surrounding county could be merged because of past intradistrict discrimination.[24] Documentation of discrimination will probably occur in other cities, allowing consolidation of districts for desegregation purposes.

> *In 1971, the Supreme Court approved busing as a method of achieving school desegregation. The Court again said that Southern districts were obligated to achieve immediate desegregation and that federal district courts had broad power to formulate desegregation plans for stubborn districts.*

While the legal arsenal for attacking school segregation in the courts is now rather formidable, segregation in metropolitan areas is still the rule. Progress is made yearly, but quite slowly because the problems involved in desegregating large cities are a hundredfold more complex than desegregating medium to small cities and rural areas. Thus, in the mid-1970s, most black children in metropolitan areas were still attending segregated schools. In 1974, for example, two of every three black children living in metropolitan areas attended predominantly minority schools, with two out of five attending 90 to 100 percent minority schools. In the twenty-six largest cities in the United States, three of every five black children attended such schools. In 1976, 4.9 million minority students (46 percent of the total) still attended segregated schools, with 65 percent of all minority pupils in the Northeast and 68 percent of all minority pupils in the North Central region attending segregated schools.[25] Thus, most black and Hispanic children in large cities remain racially isolated)

One reason school desegregation progress has been difficult, of course, is that most blacks still live in segregated neighborhoods. Progress in housing integration has been one of the most elusive of all civil-rights goals. While some blacks have been able to move to white suburbs their proportion of the total black population is relatively small. Only 5.3 percent of those living in the suburbs in 1977 were blacks, and many blacks lived in racially isolated suburbs. Only about 10 percent of all Americans actually live in integrated neighborhoods. About three-fifths of all blacks live in central cities; a majority of them still live in inadequate housing, often lacking proper heat, ventilation, and life space. Much of this housing is located in ghettos with high crime rates, poor neighborhood schools, severe unemployment, and few job opportunities.[26] The evidence indicates that racial discrimination in housing is still the rule rather than the exception. In 1978 the Department of Housing and Urban Development released a nationwide study showing that blacks encountered a 75 percent chance of discrimination in attempting to rent property, and a 62 percent chance on the purchase of a house.

Employment and income equality

The lack of more significant progress in housing indicates a lack of economic progress for millions of black Americans. Indeed, the evidence indicates that despite efforts to remove discrimination from the job market and attempts to improve the skills and education of black citizens, economic gains for black Americans have not come easily.

Between 1964 and 1974, considerable progress was made in upgrading the employment of black Americans. The percentage of blacks and other minorities in white-collar jobs—sales, managerial, and clerical positions—increased from 16 to 24 percent. About 40 percent of all whites hold white-collar jobs. Within the white-collar ranks, blacks still occupy a very small percentage of all high-status, high-paying positions. Blacks also made gains in craft occupations—from 12 to 16 percent.

By 1977 about half of all white men were in relatively high-paying professional, managerial, or skilled craft occupations. Only 30 percent of minority men, 15 percent of minority women, and 25 percent of white women were so employed. Blacks continue to be overrepresented in low-paying, low-skill jobs. Blacks, who represent only about 9 percent of the work force, constitute about 19 percent of all service workers and non-farm laborers. Also, while blacks make up only 6 percent of the workers in wholesale and retail trades, finance, insurance, and real estate, they constitute 21 percent of the workers in personal service industries, 14 percent of hospital and health service workers, and 12 percent of public employees.[27]

Of the most unpleasant, dead-end, dirty, and unrewarding jobs, blacks still hold a disproportionate percentage. Of the progress that blacks have made in employment, most of the gains came between 1964 and 1970. Since 1970, high rates of inflation and unemployment and a slow rate of economic growth have seriously retarded progress, as have continued discrimination in hiring and lack of job seniority.

Progress in housing integration has been one of the most elusive of all civil-rights goals. Only about 10 percent of all Americans actually live in integrated neighborhoods.

An obvious indication of black difficulties in the job market is the continuing high rate of black unemployment. Between 1948 and 1977, black unemployment averaged about 9 percent (see Table 17.4), about twice the rate for whites. Between 1975 and 1977 black unemployment remained above 13 percent, the highest unemployment for blacks since World War II. Black teenage unemployment remained at crisis levels. In 1976 black teenage unemployment was 39.3 percent. In 1977 it rose to 41.4 percent. If discouraged black job seekers, both adult and teenagers, were added to these figures, black unemployment rates would be even worse.

The limited extent of black economic gains since 1964 is made apparent by the marginal income gains blacks have made compared to whites. As Table 17.5 shows, black median family income between 1964 and 1976 averaged about 58 percent of white median family income. Between 1964 and 1968 the income gap decreased significantly, but progress slowed considerably and even suffered reversals in later years. In 1975 black median family income was 61.5 percent of white median family income, but fell to 59 percent in 1976, and 57 percent in 1977. In constant dollar terms, black incomes did not move upward between 1970 and 1976.

Table 17.6 also shows the breakdown of black and white incomes between 1960 and 1976. Black incomes were concentrated toward the lower end of the scale across the years, while white incomes were clustered in the upper end. By 1976, a majority (52.5 percent) of all white families earned more than $15,000. Only 27.6 percent of all black families had incomes over $15,000, and 75 percent of these families earned below $25,000. At the other end of the continuum, 38.6 percent of all black families earned less than $7,000 in 1976, compared to 15.7 percent of all white families.

TABLE 17.4
Unemployment Rate

Year	White (Percent)	Black and Other Races (Percent)	Ratio: Black and Other Races to White
Average	**4.5**	**9.0**	**2.0**
1948	3.5	5.9	1.7
1949	5.6	8.9	1.6
1950	4.9	9.0	1.8
1951	3.1	5.3	1.7
1952	2.8	5.4	1.9
1953	2.7	4.5	1.7
1954	5.0	9.9	2.0
1955	3.9	8.7	2.2
1956	3.6	8.3	2.3
1957	3.8	7.9	2.1
1958	6.1	12.6	2.1
1959	4.8	10.7	2.2
1960	4.9	10.2	2.1
1961	6.0	12.4	2.1
1962	4.9	10.9	2.2
1963	5.0	10.8	2.2
1964	4.6	9.6	2.1
1965	4.1	8.1	2.0
1966	3.3	7.3	2.2
1967	3.4	7.4	2.2
1968	3.2	6.7	2.1
1969	3.1	6.4	2.1
1970	4.5	8.2	1.8
1971	5.4	9.9	1.8
1972	5.0	10.0	2.0
1973	4.3	8.9	2.1
1974	5.0	9.9	2.0
1975	7.8	13.9	1.8
1976	7.0	13.2	1.9
1977	6.2	13.9	2.2
1978	5.2	12.6	2.4

Source: U.S. Bureau of the Census, *Social Indicators 1976,* December 1977, p. 379.

The percentage of black families who earn low incomes compared to whites is quite striking. In 1977, 31.3 percent of all black families had incomes that were below the poverty threshold for their family size (see Chapter 15). Only 8.9 percent of all white families were poor in 1977. A staggering 41 percent of all black families in 1977 were either below the poverty level or had incomes that were less than 25 percent above the poverty level for their family size. Only 13.3 percent of all white families were living in poverty or earning less than 25 percent more than the poverty threshold for their family size.[28] The potential for black families to extricate themselves from poverty is lower than for many white families because 69 percent of all poor black families are headed by a woman. Since these women are often poorly educated, untrained in marketable skills, low in self-confidence, and needed in the home, their chances of escaping poverty are often quite low.

As modest as black economic gains compared to white incomes have been, there is evidence that the gains are in some ways more meager than the national figures indicate. McCrone and Hardy have shown that the decreases between white and black incomes are almost entirely limited to the South.[29] Outside the South, black citizens have made almost no gains relative to white incomes. In the South, however, where about 50 percent of all blacks live, and where the gap between black and white incomes was severe, blacks have made some significant gains. Of course, Southern blacks have not managed to close—or come close to closing—that gap.

McCrone and Hardy raise two important points. First, they show that black gains in the South are significantly related to conditions in the economy. Low rates of unemployment and healthy economic growth characterize those periods in which blacks do make gains relative to whites. However, when the economy is sluggish, blacks do not make gains, regardless of civil-rights laws. Thus, a healthy and growing economy, they suggest, is essential to economic gains for black citizens.

TABLE 17.5
Median Family Income: Black and White

	Black	White	Black Income (As a Percent of White)
1964	$3,724	$6,858	50%
1965	3,886	7,251	50%
1966	4,507	7,792	58%
1967	4,875	8,234	59%
1968	5,360	8,937	60%
1969	5,999	9,794	61%
1970	6,279	10,236	61%
1971	6,440	10,672	60%
1972	6,864	11,549	59%
1973	7,269	12,595	58%
1974	7,800	13,400	58%
1975	8,780	14,270	61.5%
1976	9,240	15,540	59%
1977	9,560	16,740	57%

Source: U.S. Bureau of the Census, "Social and Economic Status of the Black Population in the United States in 1974," *Current Population Reports,* Series P-23, No. 54, p. 25; Bureau of the Census, "Money, Income and Poverty Status of Families and Persons in the United States: 1976 (Advance Report), September, 1977, p. 1; Bureau of the Census, "Money Income and Poverty Status of Families and Persons in the United States: 1977 (Advance Report)," *Current Population Reports,* Series P-60, No. 116, July, 1978, p. 1.

TABLE 17.6
Distribution of Family Income: Black and White

Income	Distribution of White Families (Percent)					Distribution of Black Families (Percent)				
	1960	1970	1974	1976	1977	1960*	1970	1974	1976	1977
Under $4,000	28.3	12.2	7.3	5.5	4.9	60.5	30.4	23.4	18.7	17.1
$4,000 to $6,999	35.0	16.2	12.1	10.2	9.2	25.8	25.2	21.7	19.9	19.8
$7,000 to $9,999	21.3	20.1	13.5	11.5	10.4	8.7	18.1	16.4	14.9	15.2
$10,000 to $14,999	11.2	27.9	25.1	20.4	18.5	4.4	16.9	19.1	18.9	18.0
$15,000 to $24,999	3.1	18.7	29.7	33.4	33.0	0.6	8.5	16.2	20.8	20.9
$25,000 or more	1.0	5.0	12.4	19.1	23.9	—	1.0	3.2	6.8	9.0
Median income	$5,835	$10,236	$13,356	$15,537	$16,740	$3,230	$6,279	$7,808	$9,242	$9,563

Source: U.S. Bureau of the Census, "Money Income and Poverty Status of Families and Persons in the United States: 1976 (Advance Report)," *Current Population Reports,* Series P-60, No. 107, September 1977, p. 9.
*Figures for 1960 are for blacks and other races; U.S. Bureau of the Census, "Money Income and Poverty Status of Families and Persons in the United States: 1977 (Advance Report), *Current Population Reports,* Series P-60, No. 116, July 1978, p.9.

Second, McCrone and Hardy question whether it is possible within our current economic framework to ever close the gap between black and white incomes. Outside the South, black incomes seem to have stabilized at about 75 percent of white incomes. This condition seems highly resistant to improvement, either because of economic conditions or civil-rights laws. The authors speculate that black gains in the South might peak at the 70 to 75 percent level, leaving blacks disproportionately and permanently mired in the lower fifth of the income scale.

AN ANALYSIS OF PROGRESS ACHIEVED

Great strides have been made in black political equality and economic security. The vote has generally been made available to blacks and other minorities, and blacks are much better represented in public office. Public accommodations have been desegregated, as have thousands of school districts and institutions of higher learning in the South. Many blacks have made job gains. The gap between black and white incomes has decreased somewhat, primarily in the South. Equally important, most white Americans have increasingly come to accept the justice of black demands for equal treatment, and there is a substantially different and more positive attitude toward black Americans in general.

Two questions, however, might be raised: First, have the gains been significant enough? Second, will progress continue, with the prospect that blacks will achieve equality with whites in the near future? These are not easy questions to answer, and they involve obvious value judgments. The first question asks whether the degree of progress that might have been achieved by a fair-minded and just nation has been achieved. Most would probably agree that, while change has been significant, it has also been in many respects disappointing. Blacks still have only very modest representation in the political system; urban schools mostly remain segregated; housing gains for blacks have been minimal; and economically, blacks are far behind whites, with no significant gains in the North, and none in the South since 1970.

The evidence shows that the civil-rights movement opened the door to middle-class American prosperity for a small percentage of all blacks—mostly those with the best education and background—who could easily take advantage of such opportunities. Perhaps as many as 30 percent of all black families have found their way into the middle class. But a large percentage of all blacks, perhaps a majority, seems to have been affected very little by the movement.

Large black communities in America's cities, including Harlem, Watts, the South Bronx, and the ghettos of Detroit, Chicago, Washington, D.C., Newark, Cleveland, St. Louis, Gary, Houston, Memphis, and New Orleans, remain relatively untouched by change. Combined, these areas would constitute a metropolis of misery. As John Herbes has said:

> A composite of them would be a land of several thousand square miles, of rubble-strewn streets and vacant blocks, abandoned stores, stripped-down hulks of automobiles, bleak and comparted public and private housing projects, battered school buildings, old men with glazed eyes.[30]

Within these ghettos live millions of black Americans who may have been banished from the Great American Dream. Millions of middle-aged and old people have simply been left behind. In addition, one economist has estimated that as many as one million youths who live in these cities will never have a decent job, a home, or stable family.[31] Given the limits of the American economic system, there may simply be no place for them.

Black Americans in general seem to increasingly feel that they have been left behind and that progress in the future is not very likely. These sentiments showed up in a 1978 survey of urban blacks in the North (printed on the next page), which contained a number of questions that had been submitted previously to blacks in 1968.[32] The figures in parentheses reflect the percentage of those who agreed with each category.

Would you say there has been a lot of progress in getting rid of racial discrimination over the last 10 or 15 years? Or would you say there hasn't been much change for black people?

1968

Lot of progress (63%)
Not much change (34%)

1978

Lot of progress (45%)
Not much change (51%)

Do you think there will always be a lot of racial prejudice and discrimination in the United States, or is there a real hope of ending it in the long run?

1968

Real hope (49%)
Prejudice always (46%)

1978

Real hope (37%)
Prejudice always (53%)

On the whole, do you think most white people in your town want to see blacks get a better break, do they want to keep blacks down, or don't they care?

1968

Keep blacks down (28%)
Whites don't care (33%)
Want a better break
    for blacks (29%)

1978

Keep blacks down (17%)
Whites don't care (44%)
Want a better break
    for blacks (25%)

The questions show that significantly few blacks now believe that a lot of progress has been made in overcoming racial discrimination; a majority in the survey said that not much change has been achieved. In 1978 a majority (58 percent) of blacks believed that there will always be racial prejudice in America—up from 46 percent in 1968. Interestingly, blacks were less inclined in 1978 than in 1968 to believe that whites wanted to keep blacks down. Instead, blacks tend to believe that whites are simply unconcerned about their plight. These feelings reflect not anger but cynicism, resignation, and even futility.

If progress is far from complete, will it continue? Certainly it can be expected that blacks will continue to make gains, but the evidence indicates that progress will be extremely slow. Many of those blacks trapped in the inner city will undoubtedly be left behind. The chance that blacks will obtain income equality with whites in the near future is remote. Only a tremendous upsurge in the economy—the type brought about by a war effort, for example—could measurably improve the economic conditions of significant numbers of blacks over a short period of time. Thus, at the current rate of progress, blacks will lag behind white Americans in jobs, income, quality of housing, and political power, for many years to come, perhaps well into the twenty-first century.

Racial tensions touched off burning, looting, and killing in Miami in May 1980. The riots—the most serious since those in Detroit in 1967—reflected increasing black frustration over the lack of economic and educational opportunities for blacks.

WHY HAS PROGRESS BEEN LIMITED?

Two social scientists have suggested a provocative answer to the question: Why has such limited progress been made? Piven and Cloward argue that black progress has stalled because blacks stopped using violence and disruption to get their message across.[33] They claim that only defiance by poor people can produce concessions from political leaders and that concessions can be won only when disruption is severe enough to undermine the stability and certainty of political power. Disruption can produce this condition only when events change or disturb the economic order, undermining the political status quo.

Piven and Cloward suggest these as general principles, pointing to the civil-rights movement as a specific example. They argue that there were two reasons why blacks were able to mount successful protests against the political system in the 1950s and 1960s. First, after the 1930s the rural economy of the South was transformed, producing a change in Southern economic elites and forcing millions of blacks to leave the rural South for urban areas in the Midwest, North, and South. The new Southern economic elites had less reason to try to keep blacks in their place. Urban blacks were less dependent on whites for survival and much less easy to control and subordinate than when they were dispersed across the rural South. The greater freedom of blacks, brought about by changes in the economic order, freed them to organize against suppression.

The civil-rights movement opened the door to middle-class American prosperity for a small percentage of all blacks—mostly those with the best education and background—who could easily take advantage of such opportunities.

Second, the black protests that resulted had more impact on political leaders when blacks threatened to abandon the Democratic party. As long as Southern whites and blacks had no political alternative but to stay with the Democratic party, Democratic leaders such as Adlai Stevenson tried to avoid taking strong stands on civil-rights issues. When both Southern whites and blacks increasingly decided to support Eisenhower and the Republican party, the Democratic party was forced to be more forthright in its support of blacks.

Once the stage for black protests and support for black demands within the Democratic party had been set, Democratic leaders outside the South, with the support of some liberal Republicans, began to make policy concessions in response to black protests and disruptions. At this stage, Piven and Cloward believe that the leaders of the civil-rights movement made a critical error. Rather than encourage blacks to escalate protests and even violence, movement leaders encouraged peace as a tradeoff for policy gains—civil-rights laws or improvements in welfare laws—and tried to organize blacks for political activities like electioneering and lobbying.

Piven and Cloward consider this a fatal flaw for three reasons. First, it took the momentum out of the protest movement, removing the key element which forced political elites to respond to blacks: threats to the tranquility of the political system and elite control over it. Second, the policy concessions were incapable of substantially altering the life conditions of most black Americans. But they gave the appearance of change, pacifying enraged and mobilized blacks, undermining black support among liberal whites who felt that black grievances had now been addressed, and making the political system look just in the eyes of the world. Third, elite overtures to black leaders allowed them to co-opt many movement leaders into the political system, robbing poor blacks of their organizational leadership. Once inside the system, the black leaders were unable to force the type of fundamental changes that would substantially alter the life prospects of most black Americans. Black leadership was further decimated by ideological disputes and assassinations.

Thus, Piven and Cloward argue that only protests can produce fundamental political change for poor people. But protests can be successful, they say, only when conditions in the political and economic systems force elites to be responsive to protests.

How much of their thesis is correct? Their basic arguments about changes in the economic and political system setting the stage for successful protests, and the resulting importance of protests in forcing concessions, seem to be supported by the whole history of agrarian and labor struggles in America (see Chapter 5). Their argument that the policy concessions granted to blacks produced important gains in voting rights, public accommodations, and relief from violence, but did not fundamentally alter the economic system or blacks' position in it, seems to be supported by the empirical evidence reviewed above. Blacks have made substantial political and social gains, but economic advances have been modest and ephemeral. Those economic gains blacks have made have resulted more from the economic boom caused by the Vietnam War than from civil-rights laws. Without war or a boom economy in the 1970s, blacks have made little or no economic progress, and black unemployment has soared.

Also, as Piven and Cloward predicted, elite concessions to blacks did seem to result in the co-optation of many black leaders and the eventual division of the black population. The concessions produced by the civil-rights movement allowed the most well-educated and well-prepared blacks to move into the middle class. This resulted, in large part, in a severe diminution of black unity; now middle-class blacks, who once spearheaded the civil-rights movement, no longer have the same grievances and political needs as poor blacks. Thus, by the early 1970s, prosperous and poor blacks were out of touch with one another.

Frustrated by the lack of change in their lives, many poor blacks have increasingly come to believe that the ballot is a waste of time. As we noted above, black registration and turnout have actually decreased during the 1970s. Poor blacks are increasingly as alienated from middle-class blacks as they are from middle-income and wealthy whites. In July 1977, when a blackout occurred in New York City, poor blacks looted businesses with little concern for whether they were owned by whites or blacks. To the looters, businessmen were businessmen—whether they were black or white.

Two critical points about Piven and Cloward's thesis can be made. First, they argue that once protest recedes into history, any gains made by poor people will vanish. Protest leaders who were co-opted into the system will not be able to alter this inevitable outcome. This is at least an exaggeration. Black political and social gains have not disappeared. While black officeholders have not been able to gain concessions which fundamentally alter the economic status quo, they can use their position to defend gains that were made and im-

Jesse Jackson, leader of PUSH(People United in Support of Humanity), uses speeches, boycotts, and demonstrations to try to increase job opportunities for blacks.

prove the impact of general legislation on black citizens. Certainly black gains would be more precarious if blacks were not represented in the political process.

Second, Piven and Cloward provide little analysis to techniques of mobilization and disruption, leaving the general impression that one form is as good as another. But the success of various techniques is likely to vary with the times. Riots are likely to have a positive effect only under limited circumstances. More common techniques of demonstration and mobilization that cause some disruption of normal business, traffic, and services are likely to be successful much more often. Dr. Martin Luther King's strategy of nonviolent civil disobedience rallied public support and discredited those who used violence against civil-rights demonstrators. Use of violence by civil-rights workers, however, would have probably invited backlash and repression.

Where from here?

Where does this leave black America? Can we expect blacks to continue to occupy a disproportionately large share of the lower strata of economic society? Or is there a real chance that their economic situation will improve in the years to come? Unfortunately, the evidence does not auger well for black economic progress. Only a full-employment economy and an all-out attack on subemployment and job discrimination could measurably improve the life conditions of millions of black (and white) citizens. But, as we noted in Chapter 7, neither the Republican nor the Democratic party seems to consider this a priority issue. President Carter seems at least as concerned with inflation as unemployment. The political alternatives for black Americans are also not encouraging. The Republican party, which basically supported black demands for the franchise, public accommodations, and protection from white terrorism, is not at all likely to support full-employment policies. This type of policy simply conflicts too severely with the interests of big business, the main constituency of the Republican party.

> *Blacks have made substantial political and social gains, but economic advances have been modest and ephemeral.*

What alternatives does this suggest for poor blacks? Must they resort to protest and disruption to alter their conditions? It would seem that blacks would have to take to the streets again or perhaps withhold support from both parties until concessions are made. But lacking unity and robbed of much of their leadership, blacks do not seem likely to pursue either strategy in the near future.

CONCLUSIONS

The civil-rights movement provides excellent insights into political power and influence at the national level. Our review of the movement has highlighted the factors that provoked the black struggle for equality, the conditions that made protest possible and politically influential, and the policy changes that resulted. Only extraordinary events and pressures were capable of stimulating congressional actions in the form of civil-rights laws.

In a relatively short period of time, five civil-rights bills were passed, numerous supporting decisions by the Supreme Court and lower federal courts were reached, and many supportive executive decisions and actions were made. While the policies and decisions produced very important improvements in race relations and life opportunities for black Americans, the economic circumstances of millions of black Americans have improved very little. The reason is that some of the laws and decisions were primarily symbolic. None of the policies was capable of significantly altering the position of black Americans in the economic system. In the final analysis, the policy responses produced an image of change greater than the change that has actually occurred. This has taken the steam out of the civil-rights movement while leaving much to be done.

Only a full-employment economy and an attack on subemployment and job discrimination could measurably improve the life conditions of millions of black (and white) citizens.

The increased black potency at the polls and in the political system has not been substantial enough to provoke the types of policies that would improve the economic circumstances of the vast majority of black Americans. This has been true of even the Carter administration—an administration that would not have been in power without black support in 1976. Thus, while black leaders have worked for full employment, an increased minimum wage, national health insurance, and other economic and social welfare reforms, success has been elusive. The result is that black progress has slowed considerably, leaving blacks far behind white America, with little hope of immediate improvements.

Thus, demonstrations, riots, and disruption were incapable of fundamentally altering power in the American political system. These activities did, however, produce the changes that blacks achieved. The question is: Can black Americans achieve further significant progress in the immediate future without resorting again to demonstrations and even confrontations?

Footnotes

1. *Dred Scott* v. *Sandford,* 19 Howard 393 (1857).
2. *Plessy* v. *Ferguson,* 1963 U.S. 537 (1896).
3. Cited in Frances Fox Piven and Richard A. Cloward, *Poor People's Movements: Why They Succeed, How They Fail* (New York: Pantheon Books, 1977), p. 186.
4. *Brown* v. *Board of Education of Topeka, Kansas,* 347 U.S. 483 (1954).
5. *Brown* v. *Board of Education of Topeka, Kansas,* 349 U.S. 294 (1955).
6. *Morgan* v. *Commonwealth of Virginia,* 328 U.S. 373 (1946); *Henderson* v. *United States,* 339 U.S. 816 (1950).
7. *Jones* v. *Mayer,* 392 U.S. 409 (1968).
8. See Harrell R. Rodgers, Jr., and Charles S. Bullock, III, *Law and Social Change: Civil Rights Laws and Their Consequences* (New York: McGraw-Hill, 1972); and Charles S. Bullock, III, and Harrell R. Rodgers, Jr., *Racial Equality in America: In Search of an Unfulfilled Goal* (Pacific Palisades, California: Goodyear, 1975).
9. Rodgers and Bullock, *Law and Social Change,* p. 24.
10. *Ibid.,* p. 31.
11. *Ibid.,* pp. 41–49.
12. Harrell R. Rodgers, Jr., "The Supreme Court and School Desegregation: Twenty Years Later," *Political Science Quarterly,* 89, no. 4 (Winter 1974–75): 752.
13. *Watson* v. *City of Memphis,* 373 U.S. 526 (1964); and *Griffin* v. *County Board,* 377 U.S. 218 (1964).
14. *Green* v. *New Kent County School Board,* 391 U.S. 430 (1968).
15. *Alexander* v. *Holmes County Board of Education,* 396 U.S. 19 (1969).
16. 402 U.S. 1 (1971).

17. The Select Committee on Equal Educational Opportunity, United States Senate, *Toward Equal Educational Opportunity,* 1972, p. 188.

18. 402 U.S. 30.

19. See Rodgers, ''The Supreme Court and School Desegregation: Twenty Years Later,'' pp. 763–767.

20. 404 U.S. 407 (1973).

21. See *Austin Independent School District* v. *U.S.;* 429 U.S. 990 (1976); *School District of Omaha* v. *United States,* 433 U.S. 667 (1977); *Brennan* v. *Armstrong,* 433 U.S. 672 (1977). See also *Washington* v. *Davis,* 426 U.S. 229 (1976); and *Village of Arlington Heights* v. *Metropolitan Housing Development Corporation,* 429 U.S. 252 (1977).

22. *Bradley* v. *School Board,* 338 F. Supp. 67 (E.D. Va., 1972).

23. 94 S.Ct. 3112 (1074).

24. *Newberg Area Council, Inc.* v. *Board of Education of Jefferson Co., Ky.,* 510 F.2d 1358 (6th Cir., 1974), cert. denied, 427 U.S. 931 (1975); *Evans* v. *Buchanan,* 423 U.S. 963 (1975). Through legislation, the Louisville district was consolidated with the county before the court order was put into effect.

25. U.S. Commission on Civil Rights, *Statement on Metropolitan School Desegregation,* 1977, p. 6; U.S. Commission on Civil Rights, *Desegregation of the Nation's Public Schools: A Status Report,* 1979, pp. 20–21.

26. U.S. Commission on Civil Rights, *Twenty Years After Brown: Equal Opportunity in Housing,* 1975, p. 10.

27. All figures are from Bureau of the Census, ''The Social and Economic Status of the Black Population in the United States, 1974,'' *Current Population Reports,* Series P–23, No. 54, 1975, p. 57.

28. Bureau of the Census, ''Money Income and Poverty Status of Families and Persons in the United States: 1976 (Advance Report),'' *Current Population Reports,* Series P–60, No. 107, 1977, p. 24.

29. Donald J. McCrone and Richard J. Hardy, ''Civil Rights Policies and the Achievement of Racial Economic Equality, 1948–1975,'' *American Journal of Political Science,* 22, no. 1 (February 1978): 1–17.

30. John Herbes, ''Black–White Split Persists a Decade After Warning,'' New York *Times,* February 26, 1978, p. 28.

31. Joel Dreyfuss, ''Black Progress Myth and Ghetto Reality,'' *The Progressive,* November 1977, p. 22.

32. Robert Reinhold, ''Poll Indicates More Tolerance, Less Hope,'' New York *Times,* February 26, 1978, p. 28.

33. Piven and Cloward, *Poor People's Movements: Why They Succeed, How They Fail.*

> The deterioration of urban life in the United States is one of the most complex and deeply rooted problems of our age.
>
> Jimmy Carter

The South Bronx is one of the most frightening ruins in America.

The Bronx is one of the five boroughs of New York City. Until World War II, its southern section was a teeming home for the white, often Jewish, working class. One of its avenues, the Grand Concourse, was a middle-class goal for the immigrant poor who lived in the slums of Manhattan's Lower East Side. These earlier generations had come to a growing, bustling New York economy with a tremendous need for muscle power. The South Bronx, to be sure, had suffered through the Great Depression like the rest of the nation. But overall, the first half of the twentieth century had provided the economic possibility of personal advancement for most of the people who lived there.

18

The Decline and Fall of Great American Cities

After the war, and particularly in the 1960s, all that began to change. Slowly at first, and then with the speed of a prairie fire, the white working class and middle class left, to be replaced by blacks and Hispanics. Between June 1969 and April 1977, New York City lost 686,200 jobs, many of them in the classic "entry" occupations, like the garment industry, which had been the first step up on the old immigrant ladder. And in the twenty years between 1960 and 1980, New York State lagged behind the nation so much that it would have needed an *additional* 2.7 million jobs to keep pace. Therefore, the new migrants of the postwar period encountered an entirely different situation than their prewar predecessors.

A third of the people of the South Bronx became welfare recipients, and a third of its labor force was unemployed. The resultant problems of family breakdown, alcoholism, and crime began to overwhelm the once stable neighborhoods. An impoverished population could not afford even the controlled rents, and the market price of an apartment fell below the ceiling mandated by city law. As a result, landlords either burned down their own buildings for the insurance or else abandoned them in lieu of paying taxes.

Block after block of the South Bronx was thus deserted or burned. Because the hulking structures became "shooting galleries" for drug addicts and hazards for children, the city began to raze the buildings. In the midst of a

An interior of a burned-out building in the South Bronx.

great metropolitan area, vast stretches of rubble appeared. In 1978, President Carter and then-Secretary of Housing and Urban Development Patricia Harris visited Charolette Street, where the tenements were about to be torn down. There was talk of a bold new program, but later the New York City Council could not even agree on what to propose to the federal government. Two years after the presidential visit and pledge, the situation in the South Bronx had continued to worsen.

The South Bronx is unquestionably the most dramatic example of urban decay in the United States. But something like that process has taken place in most of the great cities of the Northeast and industrial Middle West, in Cleveland and St. Louis and Detroit. Major population trends were obviously a factor in this ominous development. Between 1950 and 1960, almost six million whites fled the central cities for the suburbs, followed by another 6.5 million between 1960 and 1970. Some major cities lost 25 to 40 percent of their white population during this period. In Washington, D.C., and Newark, the white population declined by 40 percent; in Chicago, 24 percent. This loss of the white middle class eroded the cities' tax base; left behind were people too poor to pay for the services they needed and too poor to flee.

Black Americans are particularly likely to be left in the central city because they are disproportionately poor and are excluded by continuing racial barriers from much of the suburban housing. By 1970, 81 percent of all blacks lived in metropolitan areas, with 58 percent living in central cities. In 1971 blacks composed almost 21 percent of all central city population, but less than 5 percent of the suburban population.[1] In 1976, the central cities contained 4.2 million blacks living below the government's poverty standard—about 56 percent of all poor blacks in the nation.[2] Also left behind were large numbers of aged citizens, most living on fixed incomes.

As the middle-income population fled the cities, jobs and industry followed. This left the stranded city poor people with fewer job opportunities, and cities with a decreased industrial and business base to derive tax revenues from. The job loss in the cities and the gains in the suburbs are often quite substantial. In the 1960s Chicago lost 13.9 percent of its jobs while its suburbs gained 64.4 percent. For New York the loss and gains were 9.7 percent and 24.9 percent, and for Los Angeles 10.8 percent and 16.2 percent.[3]

TAXES AND CITY SERVICES

Cities typically pay a large proportion of the cost of essential public services such as health care, housing assistance, education, police and fire protection, mass transit, water and sewage treatment, local parks and recreation, sanitation, and libraries. While they provide this extensive range of critical services, they have a severely limited revenue base. Cities are primarily restricted to the property tax and some percentage of the sales tax. About 80 percent of all city revenues are obtained by the property tax, perhaps the least popular of all taxes. The states and the federal government dominate the other major tax resources, with the federal government receiving about 90 percent of all income taxes.

With rising costs and limited revenues, cities have had to raise property taxes or beg more and more aid from state and federal sources. Increasing the property tax has become extremely unpopular since it burdens home owners, especially those on fixed incomes. The tax revolt in California in 1978 was set off by very high property taxes. Through a state initiative, California citizens overwhelmingly approved a law that, among other things, limited property tax collections by local governments to 1 percent of the full cash value (based on 1975–76 assessments) of their homes. *Proposition 13* effectively lowered property taxes an estimated 57 percent, creating a severe crisis for local jurisdictions. A large state surplus was used to offset most of the initial impact of the new law, but as the surplus is exhausted, California cities will be forced to cut back on services. The notoriety surrounding Proposition 13 stimulated drives to lower or limit tax increases in twenty-one other states in 1978. These events further limited local revenue resources in many states, and made increases in property taxes particularly unpopular.

> *The South Bronx is unquestionably the most dramatic example of urban decay in the United States. But something like that process has taken place in most of the great cities of the Northeast and industrial Middle West.*

The central cities in the East and Midwest that have suffered the worst from white flight and suburbanization are particularly hard-pressed by any further restrictions on revenues. While these cities have lost their tax base, their problems have increased, necessitating a need for more rather than less revenue. And while the problems are in the cities, the wealth is in the suburbs.

The problems facing the cities are enormous. Welfare and social service costs are much higher in the cities because there are more unemployed, poor, and aged citizens. Until the 1960s, such citizens did not impose high costs on cities because they received very few services. With the expansion of welfare programs and social services in the 1960s and 70s, however, a large poor population began to impose very extensive costs on municipalities. In addition to the various income and in-kind support programs for the poor, which the cities often contribute to, cities must also deal with large numbers of educationally handicapped children. Special programs for such children are expensive—but so is the alternate. If the schools fail to adequately deal with the children, the dropout rate becomes very high. Dropouts often join the ranks of the unemployed and/or become welfare recipients. In some inner city schools, the dropout rate for high-school students is exceptional, often in the 25 to 30 percent range.

The central cities also have more slums; in fact, the central cities contain the major slum areas in America. The slums have large numbers of inadequate housing, providing particularly poor environments for residents and limiting life opportunities very severely. Slum children tend to grow up in an environment full of crime, defeated adults, and moral and physical decay. This environment spawns juvenile delinquency and disease, and provides exceptionally poor role models for children and teenagers.

As the middle-income population fled the cities, jobs and industry followed. This left the stranded city poor people with fewer job opportunities, and cities with a decreased industrial and business base for tax revenues.

The slums and other areas of the central city also have large numbers of old buildings which are either more vulnerable to fire or constitute outright fire hazards. As we have seen in the case of the South Bronx, the increased rate of fires requires a larger fire department, imposing additional costs on the city. Cities also generally have some modest programs to repair, clean up, or raze decrepit housing, another costly process even when done in a modest way.

Destruction and abandonment cause the city slums to spread. As housing within the poverty pocket deteriorates to the point of uninhabitability, the residents move to the nearest available housing, which also soon reaches the uninhabitable stage. The city poor, then, essentially wear out neighborhoods, spreading *urban blight*. The spread of the slums is facilitated by the lack of decent housing alternatives for ghetto residents and by flight from neighborhoods which border the slum. As the slums spread, neighboring residents panic, leaving behind only those too poor to flee with them (frequently the aged who are trying to hold on to their homes). The border neighborhoods become known as "gray ghettos," neighborhoods on the verge of conversion to slums.

Cities also have conditions that necessitate a larger police force. The cities have more crime and more traffic than the suburbs. Much of the traffic is caused by suburbanites who work in the city but flee at the end of the work day back to the peace and relative serenity of the suburbs. As the police, firemen, teachers, and other municipal employees have unionized in recent years in response to low city salaries, the cost of employee payrolls has increased considerably.

Cities are also burdened with expensive mass transit and street maintenance costs, often to deal with the transportation needs of suburbanites who work in the city. Water treatment facilities and sewer systems are also often old and in poor repair in the cities, requiring expensive repairs and renovations, often to meet federal standards.

Because the cities' problems are so severe, they must tax their residents at a high rate, often a rate much higher than that prevalent in the suburbs. Lineberry and Sharkansky report that typical suburbanites pay property taxes equal to 5.4 percent of their income, while typical central city residents pay 7

Two views of the cities:
Poverty and slums exist alongside
prosperous business districts
in many urban areas.

percent of income.[4] Thus, suburbanites generally pay at a lower rate, but because their income base is higher, suburbs usually can afford better services and much better schools.

THE CAUSES

What caused the devastation of major areas in once-great cities?

One answer, which a number of serious scholars proposed in the 1960s, has been disproved by events; yet it is so revealing of basic attitudes that it is worthwhile discussing it for a moment. The urban crisis, these thinkers said, does not exist—or, rather, it is a psychological state of mind based upon a misperception of reality. And, most significantly, some of these theorists then went on to argue that to the degree that a problem existed, it could be explained by the personal characteristics of those who suffered from it—mainly the poor and the minorities. The victims were blamed for their misery.

A book by Raymond Vernon *(The Myths and Reality of Our Urban Problems)* articulated part of this thesis; so did a volume edited by James Q. Wilson *(The Metropolitan Enigma: Inquiries into the Nature and Dimensions of America's "Urban Crisis")*.[5] But the most influential study to take this position was unquestionably Edward Banfield's *The Unheavenly City*.[6] Life in the city, Banfield argued, was getting better. He cited a report which predicted that substandard housing would be eliminated by 1980, a projection we now know to be utterly wrong. Then Banfield asked, "If the situation is improving, why . . . is there so much talk of an urban crisis? The answer is that the improvements in performance, great as they have been, have not kept pace with rising expectations."[7] So the sense of foreboding about the future of urban America which gripped many in the sixties and early seventies was simply based on a frightened and very inaccurate reading of the facts.

Given that judgment, America's concern with poverty during the sixties, Banfield said, probably made the problem worse.

> The poor today are not 'objectively' any more deprived relative to the nonpoor than they were a decade ago. Few will doubt, however, that they *feel* more deprived—that they perceive the gap to be wider and that, this being the case, it *is* wider in the sense that matters most. By constantly calling attention to income differences, the war on poverty has probably engendered and strengthened feelings of relative deprivation. This subjective effect may have more than offset whatever objective reduction occurred in income inequality.[8]

The last sentence gets to one of Banfield's most important—and questionable—themes. There is, he held, a culture of poverty—and "poverty is its effect rather than its cause."[9] Indeed, "lower class culture is pathological . . . because of the relatively high incidence of mental illness in the lower class and because human nature seems loath to accept a style of life that is so radically present-oriented."[10]

Since this last thesis raises some fundamental issues of social science methodology, it is worth examining for a moment. The notion of a culture of poverty has been developed by a number of analysts, most of whom disagree very much with Banfield. Writers like Oscar Lewis see that culture as a way in which people adapted to circumstances that have been imposed upon them. One example, the pattern of "serial monogamy"—in which one woman would live with, and bear children by, a series of men without marrying any of them—derived from the lack of steady work for the males and the consequent difficulty in playing the economic role of father and husband.[11] But Banfield turns that proposition upside down: it is not the deteriorating city and job market which force certain personal characteristics upon the residents of the slums and ghettos; it is those characteristics which make them slum and ghetto dwellers. But if this were the case, one might expect the poor to come from all social classes. The slum would then be the assembly point for all those who had "present-oriented pathologies." There are, to be sure, differences among scholars as to the exact nature of *social mobility*—of movement, up and down, between social classes—in the United States, and recent discussions have demonstrated that the issue is far from settled.[12] However, no one would argue that there is the kind of pervasive downward mobility which Banfield's analysis clearly implies.

> *Slum children tend to grow up in an environment full of crime, defeated adults, and moral and physical decay. This environment spawns juvenile delinquency and disease, and provides exceptionally poor role models for children and teenagers.*

Methodologically, we encounter here one more argument within the framework of *social determinism* and psychological explanation. The sophisticated determinist position does not argue that everyone in a slum behaves in the same way. The *majority* of people who live under those extremely difficult and inhuman conditions do *not* become criminals or drug addicts. However, the general incidence of certain kinds of problems is much higher in a slum than in a suburb. In addition, when groups leave the slums, their personal characteristics change. In the mid-nineteenth century, the Irish immigrants in New York had all of the "pathological" conditions which Banfield describes. (The term "paddy wagon," for a vehicle used by the police to haul prisoners, got its name from the "Paddies"—the people named Patrick—who, it was well known at the time, had an innate and ethnic tendency toward crime.) With the achievement of relative prosperity after World War II, the grandchildren of those immigrants became largely middle class and suburban.

As often happens, contradictory theories can be put forward to explain the same data. A Banfield could argue that the Irish—or any other upwardly mobile group which escaped from poverty—had changed their personal ways of behavior and that explained why they moved up the social ladder. However, the determinist view—which the authors of this text hold—can point out that full employment and rising real income seems to be the greatest single cause of those personal conversions. In short, the evidence does indeed demonstrate that pathologies are to be found in the ruined neighborhoods of once-great cities, but those pathologies are cruelly imposed upon people and are not the consequence of their personal inadequacies, as Banfield implies.

A second theory about the urban crisis—which is part of a larger attack upon the social reforms of the past generation—argues that it is the result of foolish government spending. This argument was advanced by Ken Auletta in *The Streets Were Paved With Gold,* a book which tried to account for the spectacular financial collapse and near bankruptcy of New York City in the mid-seventies.[13]

Auletta wrote:

> New York City is the left's Vietnam. Their traditional weapons—more money, more programs, more taxes, more borrowing—didn't work here; just as more troops, more bombs, more interdiction, more pacification programs didn't work there. And as that miserable war should have instructed military adventurists on the limits of American power, New York's fiscal war, unavoidably, *teaches the limits of government intervention.*[14]

In criticizing this view, it is important to recognize the truth that it contains. There is no doubt that a succession of municipal administrations in New York played fiscal games. Mayor Lindsay, for instance, spent capital funds—which are supposed to be used for long-range investments and which are raised through borrowing—for the day-to-day operations of the school system, on the grounds that education was an "investment" in "human capital." However, the established—conservative—powers in New York City collaborated profitably in such games. As the 1977 report of the Securities and Exchange Commission documented, the major banks in the city were deeply involved in the city's financial shuffle and may even have knowingly withheld information about the dubious value of some of the municipal (bonds) they sold. This dimension of the crisis, then, is not liberal or conservative, but the responsibility of the entire political spectrum in New York.

It should also be remembered that American corporations did exactly what New York City did. In the late sixties, as we have seen, it was widely assumed—on the mainstream Right and Left—that an endless prosperity with stable prices stretched into an infinite future. Under such circumstances, why not borrow today, since there would be plenty to pay off the debt tomorrow. In 1972–74, business turned to credit markets in an unprecedented way and in 1974 actually borrowed more short-term funds (for day-to-day operations) than long-term.[15] When the recession came in 1974 the corporations were, like New York City, in precarious conditions. In that year the largest bankruptcy in American banking history—the collapse of the Franklin National—took place. Here again, Auletta's thesis that the New York crisis is the result of specifically liberal tactics does not hold up.

But what about the proposition that this case "teaches the limits of government intervention"? There *are* limits. People and neighborhoods are com-

BOOTH.

"I haven't said anything up to now, but now I'm going to speak my piece. I think New York City had better get back to the good old days of buy-now-pay-as-you-go days, and pretty darn soon or there's going to be trouble. That's what I think!"

plex organisms and cannot be manipulated by planners like building blocks. And that reality was sometimes overlooked by the creators of hygenic, modern, and socially disastrous housing projects. It is, we have learned, foolish to think that one can take a population that has antisocial miseries heaped upon it and change their condition merely by improving the physical quality of their housing. The Pruitt-Igoe project in St. Louis, a gigantic housing complex for the poor which became uninhabitable and which was finally blown up by municipal officials, is the most dramatic (though often misunderstood) case in point. But granting, and even insisting that there are limits, Auletta's indictment does not stand. He unquestionably proves that government intervention without thought of social consequences and on the basis of corporate priorities can help ruin a city. But that is a far cry from the thesis that government intervention *per se* is the problem.

Strangely enough, Auletta refers to an incident which marvelously illuminates this critique of his own theme. "On January 16, 1955," he writes:

> the Triboro Bridge and Tunnel Authority and the Port Authority agreed to a $1.2 billion scheme to construct a second deck on the George Washington Bridge and miles of new bridge approaches and roads that would bulldoze neighborhoods. The architect of this scheme was Robert Moses, who borrowed from the first regional plan. As Robert Caro observes in *The Power Broker* . . . the pact 'sealed perhaps for centuries, the future of New York and its suburbs. . . .' Had that money been spent on mass transit, New York might today be a very different place. Caro calculates that the same $1.2 billion could have completely modernized the city's subway system and the Long Island Railway . . . which would have lessened the city's dependence on the automobile.[16]

That dependence, it should be noted, is extremely costly in terms of pollution, congestion—which reduces the productivity of business and the desirability of New York as an economic center—and the like.

What Auletta's own example proves is that irresponsible government intervention oriented toward the private automobile rather than mass transit can indeed have destructive consequences for a city. But he himself admits that if the same amount of money had been put into the subway system and the Long Island Railroad, "New York might today be a very different place." We have already shown, in Chapter 7, that there is a structural tendency, in an economy in which corporations make major investment decisions, for government to adapt itself to corporate purposes. Thus, it was not an accident or bad luck that Moses' decision prevailed, but an outcome at least partly determined by the system. This point will be explored at greater length in a moment. For now, suffice it to say that Auletta concedes that a socially responsible government intervention might have helped New York, and that subverts his own central thesis.

Finally, Newark, right across the river from New York, was fiscally conservative. Yet it collapsed even before New York, suggesting that the fiscal crisis was the symptom of a problem—the loss of hundreds of thousands of jobs and therefore of economic stability—rather than the cause. So let us now turn to the theories that try to explain the economic decline, which is the underlying basis of New York's troubles.

Careful planning of urban renewal projects may have much to do with their success or failure. The Pruitt-Igoe public housing project (opposite page) in St. Louis was such a failure that it was partially demolished by city officials. The project was massive and impersonal and lacked open spaces, making it difficult for people to meet or children to play. The Marcus Garvey Square Development (left) in San Francisco has been relatively successful. It provides a more humane environment with two-story townhouses and open spaces.

Most of these theories explain the plight of the cities in terms of economic trends rather than political decisions. That makes the outcome somehow tolerable, as if it were a natural event like a storm. George Sternlieb and James W. Hughes put it this way: "The abandonment which characterizes many central cities is, in substantial part, a function of the laws of demand as well as of a deterioration in the physical amenities." Industry had become over-specialized, like the industrial lofts of lower Manhattan. There was a high degree of unionization, bidding up wages; automation and rationalization came with technology; there was competition from international and regional sources; and new regions attained a critical mass.[17]

A Rand Corporation study follows a similar line of analysis:

The relatively rapid growth in areas outside the Northeast and Midwest appears to be the result of underlying social and economic changes, although it has been augmented by a number of federal policies . . . .

Over the years, rising costs, high crime, traffic congestion, increasing tax burdens, and deteriorating services and facilities have made central cities progressively less attractive than suburbs as places to live, work, and conduct business.[18]

And the London *Economist* commented, "The natural outflow of people from the overcrowded, overtaxed, cold, old North cannot be halted; indeed in the United States as a whole it is a rejuvenating and healthy migration."[19]

The *Economist* uses a key concept: these trends are a "natural" outflow of people. In suggesting that this proposition is, if not completely wrong, then dangerously one-sided—that political decisions were an essential aspect of these developments—one is not saying that the United States should have stayed as it was right after World War II, with a dominant Northeast and Midwest, a dependent South, and a lagging Southwest. That obviously makes no economic sense, and in terms of social justice it is an indefensible policy. The South is still poorer than the North. Its industrialization is thus to be welcomed. Change, even basic change, was, and is, inevitable. The question is: How will these urban transformations take place? Who will pay the enormous social cost of "rationalizing" the economy? And the answer thus far given in the United States is that government policy will favor large corporations and the costs will be, and have been, largely borne by those least able to pay them—by working people, the poor, and minorities.

To begin with, for a generation the federal government has been a prime determinant of housing patterns and urbanization. Through a variety of devices—including the Federal National Mortgage Association (known as "Fanny Mae") and the Government National Mortgage Association ("Ginny Mae")—Washington has provided below-market interest rates to home buyers.[20] The federal tax expenditure for people who can afford to buy a house is another case in point. In the 1980 budget, that one provision provided almost $16 billion in subsidies, with the highest support going to the people with the biggest houses and the largest incomes. (Their tax-deductible mortgage interest and property-tax payments are higher than those of the less affluent, and so is their tax rate. This means that every dollar deducted actually reduces their tax by 50 cents.)[21] In that same year, the direct outlays for all community and regional development, which included housing as a subtotal, were less than *half* that $16 billion figure![22]

In short, suburban housing for the middle and upper-middle classes received much more of a subsidy than housing for the poor. The latter, however, took a quite obvious form: high-rise housing projects rather than discrete tax deductions which subsidize the private wealth of the homeowner.

The suburbanites—as well as the fleeing businesses—traveled to the federally subsidized houses and factories on federally subsidized roads. Thus, although a study by the Academy for Contemporary Problems—a study which tended to minimize the federal impact on urban patterns—insisted that the Interstate Highway Program was not the "*cause* of major changes in the distribution of national economic activity," it conceded that the program did indeed *reinforce* "trends induced by the adoption of new technologies and the reorganization of economic activity."[23] The fact of the matter is that highways and air travel received much more federal assistance than the railroads. This was one of the critical factors facilitating the reorganization of the American economy.

Federal tax policy also contributed to this transformation. Senator Daniel Patrick Moynihan has documented how the monies which New York pays into

Congested expressways are a familiar sight in American cities. Government priorities have reinforced this problem by subsidizing highway construction more than mass transit projects.

Washington exceed federal outlays in the state; that is, there is a net loss. He also has shown how defense spending in the Southwest has further aggravated the imbalance—in 1978, California received $16 billion in defense contracts, New York $5 billion.[24] So both the collections and the expenditures discriminate against this northeastern state. Moreover, powerful, indirect consequences of various governmental policies impose enormous costs upon the Northeast and Midwest. During the entire post–World War II period, Washington subsidized the mechanization of the farm, a process leading to the high-technology agriculture described in Chapter 7.

That high-technology agriculture, we have seen, is capital-intensive. Consequently, millions of farm laborers, many of them black, poor, and uneducated, have been driven out of the fields, in some measure as an unintended consequence of federal policies. Those displaced persons then moved to St. Louis, Detroit, New York, and similar cities, where they formed a reservoir of unskilled workers at a time of declining demand for such labor. Ironically, southern California is now suffering from a somewhat analogous problem. The failure of America to help the Third World—indeed, the outflow of funds from Latin America to the United States, which will be documented in Chapter 20—has forced millions of Mexicans, Haitians, and other Latins (not to mention Puerto Ricans, who are American citizens), to come to this country. Los Angeles is thus becoming a major Third World city within the United States.

This last point relates to another very important consideration. It is sometimes argued that the "snow belt" is losing because the "sun belt" is gaining. In fact, 62 percent of the American ghetto population lives in the "sun belt." The number of families with incomes below the "modest but adequate" level defined by the Bureau of Labor Statistics is 5 percent greater in the South than in the North.[25] One could go on but the point is plain: the sun belt is still a major poverty center, and the problems of the North cannot be solved at its expense. But there is a critical difference between the two poverties: Northern poverty tends to be a poverty of unemployment; Southern poverty, a poverty of cheap labor. And that raises an important political and class dimension of the urban issue.

Suburban housing for the middle and upper-middle classes received much more of a subsidy than housing for the poor. The suburbanites—as well as the fleeing businesses—traveled to the federally subsidized houses and factories on federally subsidized roads.

From the very beginning, social class played a role in the very structure of the city. Cities in the nineteenth century were built on rivers. The commercial "downtown" was ringed with factories and rail yards; then came working-class housing; and the further one moved from the center the higher the social class. In many cases, the rich actually lived on the tops of hills looking down upon the rest of the people. At first, there were mill towns, not cities. Then, with the triumph of monopoly in the 1890s, what David Gordon calls "the Corporate City" appeared. It was huge, with great working-class populations concentrated in grim neighborhoods.[26] That was an advantage for big business, but it also created turbulent centers of discontent. So at least part of the outward move began long before the technological inventions—trucking, automatic factories—which usually are cited to explain the trend. The reason, Gordon suggests, was fear of the class struggles in the city center.

As we have already seen, even the "natural trend" theories of Northeastern and Midwestern deterioration sometimes cite the high rate of unionization to account for the movement out of the old industrial centers. But the point needs to be sharpened. As Alfred Watkins puts it:

> The real war is not between regional public officials, chambers of commerce, or corporations. Instead the war pits corporations and their political allies against unions, welfare recipients, the unemployed and publicly financed social service agencies. The corporate arsenal includes such weapons as threats of plant closings, the ability to wreak economic havoc on local economies, and a propaganda campaign suggesting that in some form or other, we are all in the midst of a struggle for regional honor and power. The corporations are fighting for the restoration of a 'good business climate' in the Northeast—a codeword for a lack of union militancy, the ability to pay lower wages, and a political environment that views most taxation, social services and corporate regulation as unwarranted intrusions on the rights of private property.[27]

Thus, Watkins notes, it is not an accident that in recent years there is a correlation between unionization and economic development. In North Carolina only 6.9 percent of the workforce is organized—and business is booming. In some cases, North Carolina authorities have actually tried to keep Northern business from moving in when they would bring a union with them. That, North Carolina officials seem to feel, would offset the advantage of their low union rates. And, as Watkins notes, this situation then motivates Northern politicians and corporate leaders to argue that the states with more humane welfare provisions must lower their standards in order to be competitive with nonunion and backward areas.

When the New York City fiscal crisis became public, this political and class aspect of the urban situation became quite obvious. A new institution, the Municipal Assistance Corporation (MAC), was created. It was composed of prestigious bankers and businessmen. Rather than the city itself, it was going to do the borrowing for New York. In theory, investors around the country would be impressed with the probity and conservatism of the MAC leaders and would lend them money, which they would not make available to the prodigal spenders in City Hall. But, as David Rockefeller and other pillars of the Establishment soon discovered, their reputations and connections were not enough. The potential lenders quickly made it known that there was a social price for their financial aid: dangerous innovations, like free tuition at the City University of New York, had to be done away with in order to demonstrate that the city had truly given up its excessive humanity.

So, the urban crisis of the past generation is not the mere result of spontaneous economic trends working through an impersonal market. There were and are, to be sure, technological developments with unintended impacts. But the crisis is also the result, not of "government," but of government following corporate priorities. This can be seen in a whole range of federal programs: the tax deductions and subsidized credit for suburbia; the massive investment in the highway system undertaken without thought of economic and social consequences; and the funds for the mechanization of agriculture and therefore for the displacement of people who have become a chief source of city social problems. This pattern is also found in local governmental actions like the fateful investment in the second deck on the George Washington Bridge in New York and the competition in social meanness among states and cities eager to lure business away from one another.

SAVING THE CITIES

If, then, government at all levels plays a major role in the creation of this crisis, government must take steps to undo the harm it has already imposed upon millions of city dwellers. There are two dimensions to this effort. The first is not directly targeted for the cities but involves policies, desirable in and of themselves, which would enormously alleviate the urban crisis. The second set of policy departures is directly and specifically designed to deal with the plight of the cities.

"Help!"

Indirect programs

In the case of the Northeast and Midwest, we have seen that a decline in jobs is one of the critical sources of the deterioration of city life. Therefore, the greatest single step Washington could take in order to help the cities would be to bring unemployment down to very low levels and to specifically channel some of the new work into the old, depressed areas.

The problem, as we saw in the discussion of American capitalism, is that the trends in this stagflationist era make that goal extremely difficult to achieve. In President Carter's budget for fiscal 1981, which was submitted in January 1980, there were projections of increasing joblessness in the early 1980s. The industries most likely to be hit are precisely those—auto, steel, and their myriad suppliers—which are the very center of the Northeastern and Midwestern economies. In other countries, there are attempts at regional planning to offset such "natural" economic tendencies. In France, for instance, a desire to avoid overconcentration and congestion in the Paris region led to tax disincentives to industries wanting to locate there and tax incentives for business in other regions.

In any case, without returning to the issue of full employment planning, it can be said that the fate of the deteriorating cities depends in considerable measure upon success in this difficult task. There is, however, a more limited initiative which could offset some of the more socially harmful current trends. The proposed Riegle-Ford bill provides that major corporations which intend to leave an area must give notice some years in advance and must publicly demonstrate that the social costs of their decision are defensible and can be dealt with. If they cannot do this, they will then be deprived of all federal tax privileges usually available to a corporation that moves, such as deducting the cost of the move as a business expense and receiving investment tax credits for new facilities. This approach is something like the effluent tax charged against a polluter. It attempts to force companies to "internalize," or pay for, costs which they have up until now simply imposed upon defenseless communities.

Other federal policies which would indirectly aid the cities and which have already been discussed in other contexts include the federalization of welfare costs, the creation of a national health system, and the passage of reforms in the labor laws facilitating union organization in the unorganized areas of the country. Most of these measures can be grouped under a single heading: they seek to create a truly *United* States with a single standard of human care and rights. That, not so incidentally, would not benefit the Northeast and the Midwest at the expense of the South and Southwest. Rather, it would seek to raise the level of living in the entire country.

There are also a series of specific steps which can be taken at various levels of government.

Direct programs

As we have seen, the problems which plague many of America's largest cities, and burden all major cities at least to some extent, are fairly obvious. A decaying, under-financed, problem-ridden urban core is slowly being strangled by a noose of white, middle-income suburbs, complacent state governments, and inconsistent federal policies. Remedying the problems of the city will require both state and federal efforts.

The states could aid the cities in four ways. First, the states could develop policies designed to encourage land-use planning. The current laissez-faire approach to land use has created a crazy-quilt pattern of municipal development leading to unsightly and wasteful urban spread. In addition to other problems, sprawl makes delivery of standard services such as education and garbage collection more difficult. Property owners are also frequently confronted with drainage or even flooding problems caused by hasty housing construction in underdeveloped areas. Cities usually must bear the cost of water control systems. Coordinated state and federal land-use policies for housing and mass transit would help deal with these problems.

Second, the states are the only level of government that could develop policies to control, limit, and reorganize the proliferation of governing units

More rational land-use planning policies would help to control urban sprawl and urban blight.

at the municipal level. The 1972 Census showed a total of 22,185 local governments inside the nation's major metropolitan areas.[28] This fragmentation weakens the taxing power of the city and dilutes its authority to deal with urban problems which show no respect for arbitrary governmental jurisdictions. The states could eliminate many of these governing bodies and reorganize the remaining units into rational jurisdictions capable of responding to urban needs.

Third, since cities are creations of the state, the state can use its authority to stop the development of suburban tax havens and allow the cities to annex their suburbs. A liberal annexation policy would let the cities expand their boundaries to grow with their populations, and end the free ride of suburbs that live off the central city but refuse to help support it. Since the suburbs contain middle- and upper-middle-income citizens who often have the wealth, expertise, and motivation to work to solve urban problems, their inclusion in the city is very important for fiscal and nonfiscal reasons. While not as attractive, an alternative to liberal annexation policies would be a Municipal Taxing Authority. Such an authority could devise county and metropolitan-wide tax policies and distribute revenues using a formula that considered the needs of recipient cities.

Fourth, the states should accept the responsibility of aiding the financially troubled central cities, with aid to education being a high priority. The states have long aided rural areas through state agricultural experiment stations, county agents, and rural roads. Many central cities cannot adequately finance first-rate educational programs for their students, especially those with educational handicaps. Given the importance of a good education to the student, the state, and society at large, there should be no question as to the importance of adequate state assistance. Failing to help children develop the skills that will enable them to become self-supporting citizens is obviously shortsighted.

> *A decaying, under-financed, problem-ridden urban core is slowly being strangled by a noose of white, middle-income suburbs, complacent state governments, and inconsistent federal policies. Remedying the problems of the city will require both state and federal efforts.*

One form of aid that the cities must have more of is cash assistance. Even with state aid, the cities will need additional financial help and only the federal government can raise the kinds of sums needed to overcome the chronic and long-neglected problems of many cities. In addition to financial aid, the federal government could assist the cities by developing a more coordinated, consistent set of urban policies. The Advisory Commission on Intergovernmental Relations notes this problem:

> The Federal role often has been contradictory; on the one hand, Congress has enacted a number of areawide planning requirements, strengthened representative regional bodies, and adopted a variety of programs to assist in the rehabilitation of central cities. On the other hand, the Federal-state highway program, the activities of the Federal Housing Administration and Veterans Administration, and the varying ways local and national decisions are made by the Defense Department and other federal agencies more often than not have predetermined or affected urban development patterns without regard for regional planning objectives.[29]

GOVERNMENT PROGRAMS FOR THE CITIES

Beginning shortly after World War II, Congress passed a number of programs to aid central cities.[30] The Housing Act of 1949 was designed to clear city slums and stimulate building to alleviate the postwar housing shortage by subsidizing private enterprise. Under the act, cities could purchase slum property and resell it at bargain prices to contractors for development. The act made $500 million in funds available, but by 1954 only $75 million had been spent.

In 1954 the Omnibus Housing Act required cities seeking funds for housing assistance to submit a comprehensive plan for the elimination and prevention of slums.

In 1966 the Model Cities and Metropolitan Development Act was passed. This ambitious plan attempted to coordinate local and federal programs for a concerted attack on urban blight. Under the plan many communities razed and renovated inner-city slums and declining business areas. The program was controversial, however, because much of the funding was used to destroy slum housing without comparable efforts being made to build alternate housing for the poor. Some communities used the funds to remove poor citizens from their boundaries simply by condemning and destroying their homes. Nationwide, a great many more homes were destroyed than built. President Nixon ended the program in 1975, and recommended no alternative to it.

President Ford followed in Nixon's footsteps and did not put forward a program for dealing with urban problems. President Carter promised a forthright attack on city ills in his campaign and during his first year in office. To demonstrate his commitment he made that personal tour of New York's South Bronx. In 1978 he recommended to Congress a package of programs designed to deal with various urban ills.

Kenneth Gibson (left), mayor of Newark, and Tom Bradley, mayor of Los Angeles.

Carter's urban package consisted of eighteen different programs designed to deal with various aspects of big city problems. If passed, the federal agencies with jurisdiction over each program would be responsible for allocating and supervising expenditures in eligible cities. Carter continued the traditional federal policy of not tying fundings to improved state efforts to help their own cities. Critics have long argued that the federal government should coerce the states into an examination of their responsibilities for their cities by making state reform a prerequisite to federal aid. Rather than use coercion, Carter attempted to deal with the problem by recommending a $400 million, two-year program of state incentive grants to encourage the development of urban revitalization programs at the state level. Congress, however, took no action on this proposal in 1978, effectively letting it die.

Employment programs

The largest component of Carter's urban package consisted of eight programs that would have directly or indirectly provided inner-city jobs through employment projects, funding, or subsidies that would have stimulated the job market. Some of these programs had earlier been recommended to Congress by Carter, but since they would have an impact on the inner-city he included them in his urban package. Three of the most important programs failed to win congressional approval, including a welfare reform package and a three-year, $3 billion program of labor-intensive construction projects to renovate public facilities. At least one-half of all employees hired under this program would have had to be from the ranks of the hard-core unemployed. Carter's proposal for a National Development Bank, which would have guaranteed $11 million in loans to businesses locating in distressed areas, also failed.

Congress passed a proposal to give employers who hired the hard-core unemployed a $3,000-per-employee tax credit for the first year of employment, and $1,500 per employee for the second year. Congress also agreed to give business an additional investment tax credit for building rehabilitation if they located in distressed areas. A proposal to increase federal aid to cities for parks and recreation by $150 million was also passed. While not insignificant, these programs could not be expected to have a major impact on inner-city unemployment.

Congress also reauthorized expenditures for the Comprehensive Employment and Training Act (CETA), a package of training and job programs that provides employment for about 700,000 persons each year. Carter initially opposed a proposal for a Consumer Bank, but included it in his urban package after becoming convinced that the proposal had considerable support. The proposal, which was passed by Congress, established a consumer cooperative bank to provide credit and technical assistance to consumer cooperatives.

Housing programs

The Carter package included only a modest increase in federal housing assistance. Carter recommended an increase of $150 million for interest subsidies to city buyers who agree to rehabilitate homes in distressed areas. Congress appropriated $120 million. This brought the total federal expenditure for low-income housing to $3.2 billion in fiscal 1979. The other major programs include rent subsidies to low-income families and interest subsidies for families earning 90 percent or less of the median income in their community. A majority of the $3.2 billion goes directly or indirectly to help lower middle-income citizens rather than the hard-core poor. The poor benefit primarily from the rent subsidy program.

Since cities are creations of the state, the state can use its authority to stop the development of suburban tax havens and allow the cities to annex their suburbs.

The federal approach to urban housing is far too modest to deal with the vast amount of decrepit, crowded, unsanitary housing which persists in central cities. Estimates vary, but it is certain that at least 20 percent of all Americans live in poor-quality, often life-threatening, housing.[31] In 1968 Congress set a goal of assisting in the construction of 6 million housing units for the poor over a ten-year period. The goal was contained in Title XVI of the Housing and Urban Development Act. By 1978 only 2.7 percent of the target 6 million units had been built.[32]

The states should accept the responsibility of aiding the financially troubled central cities, with aid to education being a high priority.

Implicitly, the federal government abandoned the housing goal, especially during Nixon's and Ford's administrations. Carter also seemed to be uninterested in rebuilding inner-city housing or in subsidizing on a large scale suburban housing for the poor or marginally poor. Carter's stated goal was to improve the economic circumstances of the poor through better welfare programs and expanded employment programs, allowing them to obtain better housing in the market. This goal is unlikely to be met because alternative housing for the poor who improve their earnings only marginally is very limited, because Carter's welfare reform bill did not pass, and because Carter has not been able to bring the unemployment rate much below 6 percent nationwide. Under current efforts and conditions, then, the slums will persist and will remain home for millions of the poor.

Miscellaneous programs

Carter recommended eight other programs to Congress. Six of the programs gained congressional approval, one was withdrawn, and one failed congressional scrutiny. Those bills approved included:

1. $200 million annually for fiscal years 1979–83 to aid urban bus transit;
2. $50 million for fiscal 1979 for community health clinics in needy communities;
3. A $600 million increase in Title I funds under the Elementary and Secondary Education Act (ESEA) for communities with large concentrations of poor families;
4. $5 million to stimulate cultural arts programs in urban communities and neighborhoods;
5. A $150 million increase for Title XX social service grants, raising the ceiling to $2.9 billion in fiscal 1979; and
6. Up to $1.7 billion to New York City to help it avoid default.

CONCLUSIONS

The United States is in a period of great transition. It is not simply that the Keynesian liberalism of the past fifty years has become problematic and inadequate in the 1980s, as we suggested in Chapter 7. More to our present point, the economic geography and physical infrastructure of this country are being drastically rearranged, usually with devastating effect upon the human communities involved. Even growth areas like the Southwest experience all the problems of rapid progress: congestion, sprawl, and the social tensions which accompany any sudden transition, even a transition to higher economic levels. And in the areas of deterioration, we are witnessing the death of vast areas of once-great cities.

There is no possibility of stopping change and returning to a simpler, more peaceful time. America cannot begin to meet its problems unless it has an even more productive economy—but that also means a less wasteful and destructive economy. The issue, then, is not *whether* there is going to be a time of reshaping and transition but *who* is going to be in charge of it, *who* is going to pay for it, and *who* is going to suffer. Until now there has been no one person or institution in charge. Some say that that is good, an example of the free market at work. But we have seen that the jumble of governmental policies actually seems to follow a coherent agenda, even if it is not consciously intended to do so. At every point thus far, the costs of change have been borne by the most vulnerable in the society—by uneducated farm workers forced into great cities at a time of high unemployment; by steel workers and auto workers who lose their jobs when their company ''rationalizes'' production; by municipal administrations faced with increasing problems and declining revenues. The beneficiaries have been the corporations, which have thus been able to impose the social cost of their policies upon others.

The urban crisis, then, like so many other crises of this period, requires a much greater democratization of economic and social decisions which are now considered to be in the private sector, even though they are regularly subsidized by public funds. Here again, our democracy is unfinished.

Footnotes

1. Daniel Patrick Moynihan, "The Federal Government and the Economy of New York State," *Congressional Record,* June 27, 1977, p. S10829; Daniel Patrick Moynihan, "What Will They Do for New York," *New York Times* Sunday Magazine, January 27, 1980, p. 30.
2. "Money, Income and Poverty Studies of Families and Persons in the United States: 1976" (Advance Report), *Current Population Reports,* Series P-60, No. 107, September, 1977, p. 7.
3. *Urban America: Policies and Problems* (Washington, D.C.: Congressional Quarterly, 1978), p. 7.
4. Robert L. Lineberry and Ira Sharkansky, *Urban Politics and Public Policy* (New York: Harper & Row, 1974), p. 29.
5. Vernon (Cambridge: Harvard University Press, 1966); Wilson, ed. (Washington: U.S. Chamber of Commerce, 1967).
6. Banfield (Boston: Little Brown, 1970).
7. Banfield, p. 19.
8. Banfield, p. 124.
9. Banfield, p. 125.
10. Banfield, p. 54.
11. Oscar Lewis, *La Vida* (New York: Random House, 1966), p. xlii.
12. See Stephen Threnstrom and Seymour Martin Lipsett in S. M. Lipsett and John Laslett, eds., *Failure of a Dream* (Garden City: Doubleday, 1974), p. 509ff; S. M. Lipsett, "Why No Socialism in the United States," in Sesvern Biales and Sophia Sluzer, eds., *Sources of Contemporary Radicalism* (New York: Westview Press, 1977), p. 110ff; and Richard H. deLone, *Small Futures* (New York: Harcourt Brace Jovanovich, 1979).
13. Auletta (New York: Random House, 1979).
14. Auletta, p. 253. (emphasis added).
15. *Report, Council of Economic Advisers* (1979), Table B-85, p. 282.
16. Auletta, p. 40.
17. George Sternlieb and James W. Hughes, "The Wilting of the Metropolis," in *Toward a National Urban Policy* (Subcommittee on Banking, Finance and Urban Affairs, 1977), p. 1ff.
18. Roger J. Vaughan, *The Urban Impact of Federal Policies,* Vol. 2 (Santa Monica: Rand, 1977), pp. xii and 9.
19. Dudley Fishburn, "Where Next New York," *Economist,* March 25, 1978, p. S-4.
20. Michael J. Stone, "Housing, Mortgage Lending and the Contradictions of Capitalism," in William K. Tabb and Larry Sowers, eds., *Marxism and the Metropolis* (London: Oxford University Press, 1978), p. 184.
21. U.S. Treasury, *Special Analyses, Budget of the U.S. Government, 1980,* p. 208.
22. *The United States Budget in Brief, 1980,* p. 44.

23. Academy for Contemporary Problems, ''Revitalizing the Northeastern Economy'' (1977), p. 74.
24. Moynihan, ''What Will They Do for New York,'' p. 32.
25. David C. Perry and Alfred J. Watkins, ''Saving the Cities, the People and the Land,'' *New York Times,* April 27, 1978.
26. David Gordon, ''Capitalist Development and the History of American Cities,'' in Tabb and Sowers, eds., *Marxism and the Metropolis.*
27. Alfred Watkins, ''Good Business Climates and the Second War Between the States,'' *Dissent* (Fall 1980).
28. Advisory Commission on Intergovernmental Relations, *Improving Urban America: A Challenge to Federalism* (1976), p. 91.
29. *Ibid.,* p. 5.
30. For a review, see *Urban America: Policies and Problems,* pp. 62–63.
31. See U.S. Commission on Civil Rights, *Twenty Years After Brown: Equal Opportunity in Housing,* p. 33.
32. *Urban America: Policies and Problems,* p. 61.

How does America act politically in the world?

Several important complexities arise as soon as one poses that question. There are profound historical reasons why Americans do not view themselves as the citizens of an ordinary power—grasping, greedy, expansionist. On the whole, the American landmass—protected by oceans, bordered on the north by a friendly Canada and on the south by dependent Mexico—was secure without any great show of military strength. With a few exceptions, like the Philippines and Cuba, this country never had colonies.

19

American Foreign Policy: Morality and Realism

To be sure, there was more than a whiff of imperialism in the invasion of Mexico in the 1840s—which Abraham Lincoln opposed—and in the Spanish-American War of 1898. And we have always claimed a paramount role in Latin America, from the *Monroe Doctrine* on. Yet even our assertion of power in the hemisphere did not disturb our image of ourselves. The Latin nations were politically independent, not colonies, and if we exerted enormous influence in them, we rarely ruled them through viceroys.

It was within this historical context that President Harry Truman defined American foreign policy in October 1945:

> We seek no territorial expansion or selfish advantage. We have no plans for aggression against any other state, large or small. We have no objective which need clash with the peaceful aims of any nation. . . . We believe that all peoples who are prepared for self-government should be permitted to choose their own form of government by their own freely expressed choice, without interference from any foreign source . . . .[1]

That statement probably struck most of Truman's listeners as the definition of the obvious. Indeed, most Americans would probably still regard it as an accurate description of America's role in the world.

There are also serious and decent scholars, however, who regard this virtuousness as one of the greatest vices in America's foreign policy. Here, for example, is a thesis developed by George Kennan, one of the architects of

Soviet Premier Nikita Khrushchev (left) and U.S. President John Kennedy held friendly talks at the Vienna summit conference in 1961. A year later, the Cuban missile crisis brought the two Cold War superpowers to the brink of nuclear holocaust.

America's policy of "containing" Soviet power after World War II: "I see the most serious fault of our past policy formulation to lie in something that I might call the legalistic-moralistic approach to international problems. This approach runs like a red skein through our foreign policy of the last fifty years."[2]

Kennan cites as examples the exaggerated hopes which this country placed in the League of Nations, in various disarmanent pacts between World War I and World War II, and in the United Nations itself. This approach also shaped Russian-American relations after World War II: the *Cold War* began around the issue of Eastern Europe. Stalin was determined to establish Russian power in the border areas which, historically, had provided a corridor for attacks on the Soviet Union. The United States, upholding its moral commitment to self-determination, objected to the subjugation of countries like Poland. Some have suggested that if the United States had acquiesced in Russia's insistence on protecting its security by actions which were "overpowering, cruel and ruthless," then perhaps the entire postwar period would have been different.[3] (We will explore this important point later in this chapter.)

One of the issues we will have to deal with, then, is whether America's relative historic innocence and moral decency cause it to make unrealistic and self-defeating choices in an evil and indecent world. Our second complexity, however, points in the opposite direction: Is American foreign policy a high-blown, moralistic cover for American economic interests? In the same book in which George Kennan singled out that legalistic-moralism as the critical defect of American foreign policy in the twentieth century, he also showed how our lofty values sometimes function in a crass way. When the United States became concerned about China around the turn of the century, that hapless nation had already been divided up by the European powers. Our support for an *Open Door* policy, in which all nations would have access to China, might have seemed to be an anticolonialist move aimed at the European occupiers. But in fact it was a way of asserting America's economic right to exploit China along with the other Western powers: our anticolonialism was more than a little colonialist.[4]

This has led some to explain American foreign policy as *merely* a reflex of economic interest. Pacifists in the 1930s, for instance, often argued that World War I had been brought about by the "merchants of death"—the munitions makers. More importantly, an enormously influential book by V. I. Lenin, *Imperialism: The Highest Stage of Capitalism* (1917), has convinced millions of people throughout the world that the United States is an aggressive, warlike power which must subjugate the people of the Third World in order to resolve the contradictions of its capitalist economy at home.[5]

We will discuss this view at some length in the next chapter. But for now we can anticipate some of the conclusions from that analysis: American foreign policy *cannot* be explained by any simple relationship between economic interests and international behavior; Lenin's theory is both outmoded and contradicted by the facts of the postwar period.

At the same time, there is no question that the domestic structure of

American power, including its economic dimensions, exercises an important *but quite complex* influence upon foreign policy. One of the most fateful American strategies of the entire postwar period, the massive intervention into Vietnam, clearly cannot be explained in terms of the profits that could be made in that poor country, or even on the grounds that war spending primed the economy at home. (By setting off the current inflationary spiral, it probably did more economic harm than good.)

Still, an analysis of American foreign policy cannot ignore the fact that America is a ''have'' nation in a world characterized by the revolt of the ''have-nots.'' Nor can it ignore the fact that we have often allied ourselves with authoritarian right-wing dictators, like Chiang in China, Batista in Cuba, Somoza in Nicaragua, and the various cliques in Saigon, against national liberation movements which often, but not always, fall under the control of communists. The subtitle of a book on European politics after the French Revolution, written by Henry Kissinger (secretary of state under Presidents Nixon and Ford), might be considered an apt characterization of many of our policies: ''The Politics of Conservatism in a Revolutionary Age.''[6]

In the analysis that follows, we will discover no single ''factor'' that explains American actions around the globe, but rather a complex interrelationship of the political, the moral, and the economic. This chapter will primarily

President Nixon (right) and the Shah of Iran. Despite its endorsement of human rights, the United States has sometimes supported authoritarian regimes like the Shah's.

deal with the period from the outbreak of the Cold War (1946) to the Cuban missile crisis (1962). It treats the outbreak of the East-West conflict in Europe, its spread to Asia with the Korean War (1950), the relaxation of tensions after 1956, and the most dangerous confrontation of the whole period, the Cuban missile crisis. In the course of discussing these events, a number of interpretative themes will emerge:

> the "moralizing" strand in American foreign policy defined at the outset of this chapter;
>
> the contrary trend in which an elite of "crisis managers" used technical expertise to develop a pragmatic foreign policy in the name of a calculating realism;
>
> the difficulties inherent in "twilight wars," in which neither side could decisively win or lose;
>
> the domestic consequences of global tensions as charges of subversion, and even treason, were made in the early fifties.

The next chapter will concentrate upon the period from the escalation of the American intervention in Vietnam (1965) to the present. It will deal with the North-South dispute—between the rich, mainly Northern, countries of the world and the poor, newly independent, and mainly Southern nations—which became increasingly important during these years. In looking at these developments we will see:

> the rise of an "imperial Presidency" in response to a challenge from outside our borders;
>
> the issue of "American imperialism," defined as an economic or political tendency within the very structure of the society making it aggressive in international affairs;
>
> America's place defined in the North-South conflict.

Finally, we will conclude with some brief comments on America's position in the 1980s. For just as these times pose unprecedented problems within the domestic economy and society, so also do they undercut much of our conventional wisdom with regard to world politics.

THE EAST-WEST STRUGGLE

Even while Allied troops were still struggling in the final phase of the war against the Germans and the Japanese, the soon-to-be victorious powers were involved in the preliminary maneuvers of a confrontation which would pit them against each other and eventually bring the earth to the brink of nuclear holocaust. There are some analysts who argue that World War III followed immediately upon World War II—but that the Third World War was fought with the "cold" weapons of diplomacy, proxy armies, and limited engagements, and without Russians actually meeting Americans in open combat.

Then, in the mid-fifties, a counter-trend emerged. The two camps of the

As the Allied Powers closed in on victory in World War II, Britain's Prime Minister Churchill (left), U.S. President Roosevelt (center), and Soviet Premier Stalin (right) met at the Yalta Conference in 1945 to discuss the postwar status of Germany and Eastern Europe.

East, which included those portions of Central Europe under Soviet control, and the West, which counted Japan among its members, began to talk to one another and even to come to agreements defusing some of the hostilities.

But history and politics are rarely neat and orderly. The most dangerous single moment of the East-West rivalry did not occur in the early phase of the conflict when the antagonists were defining their differences in the most implacable and ideological terms. The Cuban missile crisis of 1962 took place some years after the "thaw" in Cold-War relationships. To further complicate matters, the end of that confrontation opened up a period of improved communications between powers which had marched to the very brink of atomic havoc.

Clearly, this chapter cannot even begin to explore all of the intricacies of postwar American policy in the East-West contest. What we can do is pick out some of the most salient events and utilize them in order to develop some basic themes about the nature of United States power in the world. This will be done by looking at the successive phases of the process which pitted America and its allies against the camp led by Russia. When this survey is completed, the reader should have, not a comprehensive knowledge of complicated happenings (which would require a library of explanations), but some sense of the leading forces and patterns in American foreign policy and the various theories which have been developed to interpret them.

The Cold War: 1946–1949

The first phase of the East-West struggle—dubbed the *Cold War* by the policy analyst Walter Lippman—centered on Europe and started soon after the German surrender in the spring of 1945, lasting until the lifting of the Berlin blockade and the formation of the North Atlantic Treaty Organization (NATO) in 1949.

To set the stage for analysis, consider just a few of the critical events during those turbulent years. In the spring of 1945, the French communist leader, Jacques Duclos, wrote an article in effect telling communists around the world that their wartime policy of collaboration with antifascist capitalist powers was at an end. That same spring, the United States successfully tested, and in the summer used, an atomic bomb, thus permanently changing the nature of war.

In 1946, Winston Churchill told of an "Iron Curtain" which was dividing Europe between East and West. President Harry Truman responded to communist pressures in Greece and Turkey by committing American power to counter the Russians.

In 1947, the Marshall Plan, Washington's massive program for rebuilding Western Europe and thus undercutting communist movements in France and Italy, was announced. The diplomat-scholar, George Kennan, coined a new word—containment—to describe the American response.

In 1948, the Russians left the German Control Commission established by the victorious Allies in 1945. Czechoslovakia was taken over by a communist coup. The Yugoslavs under Tito defected from the Eastern bloc, and Berlin was blockaded.

In 1949, the American airlift in defense of the Berliners succeeded. NATO was formed, and Mao was victorious in China.

In order to reduce this bewildering flow of events to proportions manageable in the framework of this chapter, let us look at the two issues which underlay most, if not all, of these developments: the Soviet takeover in Eastern Europe; and the Western defense of the autonomy of Berlin. In the American response to these problems, many interpreters—including both proponents and critics of Washington's policies in those years—believe that one can see that "legalistic-moralistic" impulse in our country's behavior in the world. Let us examine that thesis in two ways. First, was it in fact true that a peculiarly American kind of moralism was in part responsible for the Cold War? Second, if that is the case, what are the roots and functions of that moralism?

The Cold War began around the issue of Eastern Europe. Stalin was determined to establish Russian power in the border areas which, historically, had provided a corridor for attacks on the Soviet Union. The United States, upholding its moral commitment to self-determination, objected to the subjugation of countries like Poland.

"Is heating up the Cold War like cooling off detente?"

On the first count, here is a summary statement by Arthur Schlesinger, Jr., a historian and an active liberal who supported the American response to the Russian challenge in 1945–48:

> One theme indispensable to an understanding of the Cold War is the contrast between two clashing views of world order: the "universalist" view by which all nations shared a common interest in all the affairs of the world, and the 'sphere-of-influence' view, by which each great power would be assured by the other great powers of an acknowledged predominance in its own area of special interest. The universalist view assumed that national security would be guaranteed by an international organization. The sphere-of-interest view assumed that national security would be guaranteed by the balance of power.[7]

One can go back to the summer of 1941—before Pearl Harbor brought America into World War II—to get a revealing glimpse of the "universalist" strand in American foreign policy. When Franklin Roosevelt met with Winston

Churchill at that time, he asked the British prime minister to publicly affirm that ''no postwar peace commitments as to territories, populations or economics have been given.'' Out of this concern came the Atlantic Charter, a British-American document pledging both nations—and eventually the entire Allied camp in World War II—to just such a selfless set of war aims.

The British accepted, an action which was hailed in the United States, but Churchill told Parliament that these principles did not apply to the internal affairs of the British empire, that is, to *his* sphere of influence. And the Russians similarly agreed, with the very significant qualification that ''the practical application of these principles will necessarily adapt itself to the circumstances, needs and historic peculiarities of particular countries . . . .'' In other words, the Atlantic Charter would not apply in *their* sphere of influence.[8]

Was it in fact true that a peculiarly American kind of moralism was in part responsible for the Cold War?

So, Churchill assumed that the Allied war aims did not require that Britain give up its empire, and Stalin made it very plain that he was going to establish some kind of control over the Eastern European nations on the Soviet border. Roosevelt felt that he could work out these problems with the other two leaders, and he deferred many of them to the end of the war—and then died just as victory was at hand.

The radical contrast between Roosevelt and both Churchill and Stalin can be seen in an exchange between the latter leaders in October 1944. Churchill handed Stalin a sheet of paper on which he had worked out the relative weight the great powers were to have in Eastern Europe: Russia was to have 90 percent sway in Rumania; Britain, 90 percent in Greece; Hungary was to be 50–50; and so on. Stalin agreed, making a pencil mark on the paper. Churchill later wrote:

> After this there was a long silence. The penciled paper lay in the center of the table. At length I said, ''Might it not be thought rather cynical if it seemed we had disposed of these issues, so fateful to millions of people, in such an offhand manner? Let us burn the paper.'' ''No, you keep it,'' said Stalin.[9]

Americans would indeed be shocked by the cynicism of the moment. But there are sincere scholars and political leaders who believe that our idealism, refusing ''balance-of-power'' politics and insisting upon the democratic right of national self-determination for *all* peoples, is self-defeating. For instance, Hans Morgenthau concedes that there were unprecedented elements in the situation after World War II—''Stalin's fusion of the traditional national interests of Russia with the tenets of communism . . .''—but he still sees Roosevelt's universalism as a most unrealistic element in our policy.[10]

Indeed, there are some who think that American intransigence actually contributed to the loss of the very freedom we were trying to defend in Eastern Europe. Many years after the event, Henry Kissinger wrote:

> I am inclined to doubt that Stalin originally expected to lock all of Eastern Europe into his satellite orbit; his first postwar steps—such as permitting free elections in Poland, Czechoslovakia, and Hungary, all of which the communists lost—suggest that he might have been prepared to settle for their having a status similar to Finland's (i.e., freedom in domestic affairs so long as foreign policy did not challenge the Soviet Union).[11]

If Kissinger is right (and it should be noted that his view is shared by many who disagree on most other questions with him) then there were fateful misperceptions on both sides in the early, formative stages of the Cold War. The Soviet Union viewed the American refusal to accommodate realistically to their control of Eastern Europe as a sign of belligerent anticommunism. They therefore may have extended their power in that area more brutally and openly than they had intended.

The United States interpreted these moves, which may have been essentially defensive in character, as the prelude to an invasion of Western Europe, something which was intolerable both from the moralistic point of view *and* from a *Realpolitik* based on spheres of interest. As Arthur Schlesinger, Jr., put it, "Each side felt compelled to adopt policies which the other could not but regard as a threat to the principles of peace."[12]

Let us tentatively assume that American "universalism" did play the role these critics suggest. That leads to our second question, which is particularly relevant to the overall topic of America and the world: Why did the United States make this mistake?

National character is one answer. This is not necessarily a vague psychological category. As indicated at the outset of this chapter, there are unique geographical and political factors at work in American history. Our imperialism was largely internal: the genocidal attack on the native American population and the effective subjugation of the South as a domestic colony, producing (like the European colonies in Asia, Africa and Latin America) raw materials and agricultural products.

We were protected by two oceans from the quarrels of Europe and Asia. So we could look down on the politics and compromises of the Old World politicians who had to deal with intense national and religious rivalries concentrated within the narrow confines of Europe. And that tendency was reinforced by the fact that so many Americans had fled those conflicts and come to this land in search of an ideal. Moreover, the national ethos was heavily influenced by some of the more fundamentalist strains of Protestantism, which tended to see the world as divided into the Good and the Evil. (That theological factor, as we will see shortly, was probably at work in the mind of the statesman-theologian, John Foster Dulles.)

So we can certainly explain the American tendency toward universalism in world politics. But how do we *evaluate* it? In most of the analyses just presented, that idealistic element in the national character is seen negatively, as a source of unrealism which produces the direct opposite of the intended results: to defend freedom and democracy in Poland, we adopted policies which provoked Stalin into a more rigid totalitarian approach than he had initially planned. But that does not exhaust the subject. To act as though such ideals are or can be easily made to be real is indeed foolish, but that does not discredit the ideals themselves.

As Churchill rightly understood, it is a completely cynical act when leaders dispose of the fate of millions of people without consulting them and without concern for their own desires and needs—because it suits great power purposes. It is one thing to say that such accommodations sometimes have to be made in the pursuit of justice; it is another thing to say that they are just. So the universalist approach cannot be seen solely in a negative light; indeed, a dramatic example of its positive nature occurred during the Western defense of the autonomy of Berlin.

The Berlin blockade was one of the critical points in the first phase of the Cold War. Here was an isolated, beleaguered, and democratic city in the midst of a totalitarian, Russian-dominated society. There were some in the West— including Anueran Bevan, the leader of the *left* wing of the British Labor party—who wanted to respond to the Soviet blockade of Berlin by force, sending an armed convoy to the city. Instead, the United States organized an airlift which brought in the tons of food and supplies that the people needed.

Berlin, it should also be noted, was under democratic-socialist rule. (This fact is one of the most dramatic refutations of some Americans' tendency to equate socialism with communism.) In other words, American capitalism was giving aid to a people who had freely chosen anticapitalists as their leaders. This turned out to be a realistic defense of the American ideal of self-determination. The point is that America's moralistic strain is also the source of an internationalism that can be generous and decent. If one must guard against the oversimplifications which sometimes accompany this spirit, it is also wrong to overlook the sense of human solidarity which is a part of it.

The American national ethos was heavily influenced by some of the more fundamentalist strains of Protestantism, which tended to see the world as divided into the Good and the Evil.

A second explanation for America's conduct in those years has to do with its view of the enemy: *communism, it was said, was not a normal political movement which could be accommodated on the basis of balance-of-power politics; it sought to conquer the whole world.* The United States, in this perspective, acted not so much out of a misguided idealism, but because it correctly perceived the character of an unprecedented foe.

The Western Allies flew in food and supplies to the West Berliners during the Soviet blockade of Berlin in 1948 and 1949.

One version of this theory (but not the only one, as will be seen) was part of the official American government position during this period. When Harry Truman announced the *Truman Doctrine* in March 1947—committing the United States to replace British power in Greece and Turkey in order to resist the communists—he said:

> At the present moment in world history nearly every nation must choose between alternative ways of life. The choice is too often not a free one. One way of life is based upon the will of the majority and is distinguished by free institutions, representative government, free elections, guarantees of individual liberty, freedom of speech and religion, and freedom from political oppression. The second way of life is based upon the will of a minority forcibly imposed upon the majority. It relies upon terror and oppression, a controlled press and radio, fixed elections, and the suppression of personal freedoms.[13]

There was considerable truth in that statement, but it was, as we will see, an oversimplification. As time went on, despots like Chiang, Batista, Trujillo, the Shah of Iran, Somoza, and many others were welcomed into the ''Free World.'' For now, however, let us focus on the critical analytic element in the Truman view. The Cold War, the President was saying, was not simply a conflict between counterposed nations but between counterposed systems. This was usually stated as an antagonism between democracy and totalitarianism; it was sometimes described as the hostility of capitalism and communism. Clearly, this very neatly corresponded to the moralistic mood in America, for it pictured the United States as leading the forces of light against the legions of darkness arrayed behind the Soviet Union.

There was, however, a much more sophisticated statement of this theme, and it had enormous influence during the first phase of the Cold War. In 1947, George Kennan published an article in *Foreign Affairs* entitled "The Sources of Soviet Conduct." In part, he accepted the view that two systems were at war. The Russians, Kennan said, believed that there was an

> innate antagonism between capitalism and socialism. We have seen how deeply that concept has become imbedded in foundations of Soviet power. It has profound implications for Russia's conduct as a member of international society. It means that there can never be on Moscow's side any sincere assumption of a community of aims between the Soviet Union and powers which are regarded as capitalist.[14]

That was in keeping with Truman's view and the attitude of the average anticommunist citizen. But, Kennan continued, precisely because the Soviets took a long view of the conflict, they were not in a hurry—they believed that history was on their side. So, since Russia "is under the compulsion of no timetable, it does not get panicky under the necessity for . . . retreat. Its political action is a fluid stream which moves constantly, wherever it is permitted to move toward a given goal."[15]

Therefore, Kennan concluded, "it is clear that the main element of any United States policy toward the Soviet Union must be that of a long-term, patient but firm and vigilant containment of Russian expansive tendencies." If the Soviets were thus "contained"—a key word of the period—then internal forces looking for an accommodation with the West might come to the fore. The Russians were assuming "complete lack of control by the West over its own economic destiny . . . (and) Russian unity, discipline and patience over an infinite period. Let us bring this apocalyptic vision down to earth . . ."[16] Time, Kennan was saying, was actually on the side of the West, for it would corrode both the Soviet will and ideology.

This doctrine more or less provided the basis for American policy until John Foster Dulles returned to a much more moralistic approach in the fifties (a development which will be treated shortly). For now, however, let us examine just one aspect of this very important turning point: the way that the "containment" approach illuminates the tendencies within American foreign policy.

There was, and is, as we have seen, that "legalistic-moralistic" strand in this country's relations with the world. But Kennan's thesis—and the very major political impact it had—are the evidence of an important, recent counter-trend. Intellectuals and policy analysts began to take on a much greater importance than ever before. Eventually this fact became so well known that it was dramatized in an antiwar and antiestablishment movie, "Dr. Strangelove," which portrayed one of the academic specialists in "crisis management."

America's moralistic strain is also the source of an internationalism that can be generous and decent.

How do we reconcile this picture of a cool, calculating foreign policy under the control of realistic technicians with the theme of America's tendency toward moralizing in international politics? One answer to that question raises issues about the relationship between economics and politics. It asserts that the universalist rhetoric is only a cover for self-interested and very materialistic goals. We will treat that notion at greater length in the next chapter but take a first look at it here because it offers an important interpretation of the idea under discussion here: that America's actions in the world in the postwar period were dominated by an elite at the service of corporate priorities.

That theory usually comes from the Left, but one of its chief proponents, Charles de Gaulle, was a fervent nationalist and foe of the Left. Yet De Gaulle wrote of Roosevelt that for him

> . . . international democracy was a panacea. According to him, the nations of the United Nations would examine their differences and, in each case, take those measures which would keep them from going to war. Moreover, they would cooperate in the progress of the human race. "Thanks to this institution," he told me, "American isolationism will come to an end and one will, on the other hand, be able to bring back Russia into the Western World." *Beyond that—though he did not speak of the point—he thought that the mass of small countries would smash the "colonialist" powers and assure the United States a vast political and economic clientele.*[17]

So, like George Kennan in his interpretation of America's Open Door policy in China at the turn of the century, De Gaulle believed that this country's high-flown idealism was a cover for an old-fashioned power drive.

More recently, a number of American scholars, most of them on the political Left, have linked the growing role of experts in foreign policy with what they see as the corporate domination of our decisions in this area. They argue that organizations like the Council on Foreign Relations—which publishes *Foreign Affairs,* the journal which printed Kennan's original, and enormously influential, article on containment—are run by an Eastern upper-class elite from Wall Street law firms and investment banks. Henry Kissinger, who hardly shares this leftist criticism, described the men (for women have been almost completely excluded from any significant role in this area) who crafted American foreign policy in the post–World War II period as an "aristocracy."

In 1977, when Jimmy Carter chose his Cabinet, a remarkable number of its most powerful members had belonged to the "Trilateral Commission." Cyrus Vance, Carter's first secretary of state, had been a member; so had Harold Brown, the secretary of defense. And Zbigniew Brzezinski, the President's national security adviser, had been the organizer of the Commission. And, not so incidentally, the President himself had been a member.[18]

The Trilateral Commission was organized under the aegis of David Rockefeller, head of the Chase Manhattan Bank and a member of one of America's richest families. It therefore was often presented from the Left as evidence that foreign policy was dominated by a corporate elite. However, there were those on the conservative Right who regarded people like Rockefeller as representatives of a decadent and overly liberal Republicanism which lacked the courage to stand up to the communist threat. In the Republican primary in New Hampshire in 1980, George Bush was attacked from the Right because he had been a member of the Trilateral Commission.

The conservative version of this theory is expressive of a tendency to see world politics in the twentieth century as determined by sinister conspiracies. (That view, as the next section will show, had a major impact on American domestic politics during the 1950s.) But the scholarly statement of this theme from the Left, by analysts like G. William Domhoff and Gabriel Kolko, is not at all melodramatic, and it is well documented. So, let us face up to the basic question: Was America's post–World War II foreign policy an instrument of corporate power because it was shaped by the members of the corporate elite? That notion will be examined in greater detail in the next chapter when we consider the assertion that America is imperialist. But the period under discussion offers a perfect test case—the *Marshall Plan,* begun in 1947—and we will look at it now.

Named for then-Secretary of State General George C. Marshall, the Plan was a multibillion dollar proposal for the reconstruction of Europe. Was it, as Marshall himself said, "directed not against any country or doctrine but against hunger, poverty, desperation, and chaos"? Or was it, as Moscow said at the time, "political pressure with the help of dollars, of interference in the internal affairs of other countries"? More broadly, did this development prove there was corporate domination of foreign policy, as asserted by many serious (and noncommunist) scholars?[19]

First, there was a conscious linking of the political and economic in Marshall's proposal. Europe, he said, had economic needs which it could not pay for, and if there was not substantial help there would be "economic, social, and political deterioration of a very grave character" in the Old World.[20] It does not take a trained analyst to understand that this was a reference to the possibility that the mass communist movements of Italy and France might take power "as a result of the desperation of the people concerned . . ." That, it can be cogently argued, is not wrong in and of itself. The American policy did not envision depriving the French and Italians of their right to choose their government, even including a communist government. It clearly did intend to affect the economic environment in which that choice was made.

Second, Marshall was also aware that the U.S. economy would benefit from this program. He specifically noted that the main supplier for the reconstruction of Europe would be America. Many years later, in 1974, a House Foreign Relations Committee report was quite explicit. Under the Marshall Plan, it said, "the infusion of capital goods [to Europe] was to be supplied by

George C. Marshall.

the United States, thereby helping to hold up the postwar demand level of the American economy.''[21]

Some conservatives at the time thought that Washington was lavishly handing money over to foreigners. In fact, since almost all of the Marshall Plan funds were spent in the United States, American business made a profit from the government's grants to the Europeans.

On the basis of such facts, there are scholars who concluded that the Marshall Plan was a conscious and sophisticated scheme to shore up capitalism. Franz Schurmann writes:

> For all the progressive rhetoric that accompanied the Marshall Plan, interests, not ideology, lay at its base. The internationalist segment of the capitalist class was alarmed by the prospects of economic chaos in Western Europe which eventually would threaten big business in America. The internationalists well remembered that although the world depression of the 1930s was symbolized by the stock market crash of 1929 in America, the real cause was the collapse of the European economies. They were convinced that another depression in America would produce something far worse than a New Deal—a socialist dictatorship over the economy.[22]

In Schurmann's view, then, the Marshall Plan was designed to avoid communism in Europe and depression in America. On the other hand, the Soviet expert Adam Ulam argues that the Russians did not really think they could move into Western Europe during these years. Indeed, a Marxist anti-Stalinist, Fernando Claudin, later attacked the Russian leader for having been on the defensive and for *not* having pushed for power in France and Italy.[23] Of course, if the United States thought that communist takeovers were imminent in France and Italy, that would explain part of its reaction. Still, it is a critique of Schurmann's view if one asserts that the ''chaos'' in Europe was exaggerated. Even more to the point, Ulam argues that it was only because of the American fears that the Marshall Plan was legislated into law.[24] It took, he is saying, the Soviet threat to create support for the measure. That would mean that far from being a conscious scheme of the internationlist capitalist, the Marshall Plan was ''imposed'' on the United States by the Russians.

Marshall was also aware that the U.S. economy would benefit from this program. He specifically noted that the main supplier for the reconstruction of Europe would be America.

How does one resolve these conflicting interpretations? The structuralist paradigm, described in Chapter 4, permits one to recognize an element of truth in all of these theories—as well as an exaggeration of the truth that is one-sided. It is true that the American policy-makers wanted to reconstruct capitalism in Europe, that they saw the Western portion of the Old World as an indispensable part of an Atlantic community that was crucial to the American economy as well as to the American political system. Moreover, whenever programs were designed in this period—the Marshall Plan, Truman's "Point Four"—the goals of public policy were to create a "favorable climate" for private American investment.

Finally, there is no question that the Marshall Plan did play a significant role—as a necessary, but not a sufficient, condition—for the remarkable growth of the American economy after World War II. So, the way the United States responded to the Cold War promoted its economic interests. This fact is hardly an accident but is related, among other things, to the views of policy-makers from elite backgrounds

The mere fact that a policy has certain consequences, however, does not mean that it was *consciously designed* to yield them. For example, World War II had the effect of doing what the New Deal could not do: end mass unemployment. But that does not mean that Roosevelt maneuvered America into the War *in order to* end the Depression. Insofar as Schurmann and similar analysts view the procapitalist outcomes as the result of capitalist intentions, they simplify the impact of economic influences upon foreign policy. America's involvement in the Cold War was affected by democratic values; cultural solidarity with the Europeans; religious-based anticommunism on the part of the people; the voting strength of East European ethnic minorities within the American electorate; and many other factors.

In addition, the leaders of American capitalism have often demonstrated an ability to misunderstand their own class interest. Their hostility toward Roosevelt's salvation of capitalism under the New Deal is one example. In a way, Schurmann's view requires one to give the capitalists too much credit, viewing them as remarkably acute global thinkers.

It is true that the American policy-makers wanted to reconstruct capitalism in Europe, that they saw the Western portion of the Old World as an indispensable part of an Atlantic community that was crucial to the American economy as well as to the American political system.

But this does not mean that America's domestic economic structures had nothing to do with the foreign policy decisions, like the Marshall Plan. Without conjuring up a master plan on the part of corporate executives but rather focusing upon the way in which it is always "normal" in the United States to respond to problems by utilizing capitalist means, the *ad hoc* and often improvised response of this country to the Soviet challenge (whether real or imagined) had a consistency that came more from its structures than from the conscious and wily plans of its elites. This, it should be noted, means that America did respond in a status quo way, a fact which will be explored at some length later on.

We have now concluded our examination of the first period of the Cold War, which was centered in Europe in the years 1946–1949. We have seen that two seemingly counterposed interpretations of American conduct at that time—that this country acted out of a moralistic spirit that was sometimes self-defeating; and that its actions were decided by calculating elites dedicated to corporate interests—both contain elements of truth but are one-sided statements. This emphasizes a fact which we have stressed from the very outset: that the interrelationships of the political, moral, and economic in American foreign policy are very complex. No single "factor," no matter how huge, can explain our conduct of international affairs.

Now let us turn to the next phase of the Cold War, the years from 1950, when North Korea invaded South Korea, to 1956, the time of a "thaw" in Soviet-American relations *and* of the brutal Russian repression of the Hungarian Revolution.

The second phase: the Korean War

The Korean War began in June 1950, when North Korea, a Russian (not Chinese) client, invaded South Korea, an American ally under the leadership of an authoritarian and increasingly unpopular ruler, Syngman Rhee. By accident, the Soviet Union was boycotting the UN Security Council at the time. Thus, it was not able to exercise a veto over a resolution putting the UN on record against North Korea's invasion. This eventually led to the commitment of troops from a number of UN member countries in the conflict.

On June 25, Truman decided to send American soldiers to Korea to fight this "breach of the peace"—but he did not consult the Congress until two days later. We thus encounter another aspect of American foreign and military policy, one which would have tremendous consequences later for our intervention into Vietnam: the growth of presidential power on the grounds that the White House has to be able to act almost instantaneously in an unstable and militarized world. Arthur Schlesinger, Jr., refers to the phenomenon as the "imperial presidency."[25]

In defense of Truman's action, the State Department held that "the President, as commander in chief of the Armed Forces of the United States, has full control over the use thereof." Therefore there is "a traditional power of the President to use the armed forces . . . without consulting Congress."[26] Truman soon amplified this thesis. As President, he said, he had the authority to send troops anywhere in the world without asking Congress.

There was a debate over these claims but it was inhibited by another domestic political development brought about be the Cold War. During the first phase of what then seemed to be a Soviet attack on the entire Western world, the Republican opposition in the Senate, led by Arthur Vandenberg of Michigan, pledged itself to a "bipartisan" foreign policy in the name of overriding national security. When Truman asserted his sweeping right to deploy the armed forces at will, a dying Vandenberg was deeply troubled, but the logic of the Cold War—and the popular feeling that the communists had to be stopped in Korea—prevailed.[27] A patriotic bipartisanship stifled criticism.

President Truman (left) and General Douglas MacArthur at Wake Island in 1950. MacArthur was commander in chief of the American (technically the United Nations) forces in Korea until Truman relieved him of his command in 1951.

In the previous section, we talked of the impact of domestic structures upon foreign policy. Now we are in the presence of the opposite causal sequence: international issues shaping domestic structures. The Presidency had grown considerably under Roosevelt and the New Deal because a greatly increased executive department was necessary to counter the Depression.

During the Second World War, which had the support of the overwhelming majority of the population, the President acted as commander in chief, but this was clearly understood to be an exceptional situation. In any case, Congress had declared war. Now the country was in a kind of "nether-nether" world. The Cold War pitted the United States against the Soviet Union, but the major antagonists did not openly fight one another. Rather, the armed confrontations matched America against Soviet allies (North Korea, North Vietnam) or the Russians against national movements in Eastern Europe (Poland, Hungary, Czechoslovakia). So this country was not engaged in a conventional war—but it was certainly not at peace, either. Under these circumstances, the welfare state increasingly became a warfare state and the powers of the Presidency were dramatically expanded.

There was a very important related development, which had to do with civil liberties From the Russian revolution on, the American establishment tended to view communism as a conspiracy rather than a social movement. Much was made of the fact that the Bolshevik party which seized power in Russia had less than 100,000 members. If, many thought, a small and dedicated band of professional revolutionists could thus take over one sixth of the world's surface, then the explanation must be subversion. In the more dramatic and sinister versions of this thesis, all the other determinants of the Russian Revolution in 1917—the war-weariness of the entire people, the land-hunger of the great mass of the peasants, the social weight of a small working class concentrated in very large factories, the indecisiveness of the various bourgeois and socialist governments—were ignored.

Lenin was credited with having invented a tremendously powerful, almost occult, organizational form: the disciplined, monolithic revolutionary party. As it turns out, the Bolshevik party in the days before October 1917 was a heterogeneous, undisciplined, and quarrelsome institution, a fact which is contrary to both the official Soviet and the official American Cold War myths.[28] All these complexities were lost, particularly once American soldiers were being killed by communist bullets in Korea. Communism was subversion, no more and no less.

The Cold War pitted the United States against the Soviet Union, but the major antagonists did not openly fight one another. Rather, the armed confrontations matched America against Soviet allies (North Korea, North Vietnam) or the Russians against national movements in Eastern Europe (Poland, Hungary, Czechoslovakia).

The American law already had two measures which could become the basis of an "antisubversive" campaign: the Smith Act, passed in 1940, and the Attorney General's List of Subversive Organizations, promulgated (without any hearings) in 1947 by the Department of Justice. The Smith Act did not merely make it a crime to overthrow the government by force and violence; that had been a crime of treason from the very beginning of the Republic. Nor did it simply outlaw conspiring to overthrow the government, which also could be covered under traditional legal concepts. It outlawed conspiring to *advocate* the overthrow of the government at some future date.

This law was utterly remote from real internal threats, as can be seen from its first victims. In 1941, the government indicted and convicted the leaders of the Socialist Workers party under the Smith Act. The Communist party approved the act because it was directed against "Trotskyites." The Socialist Workers party was indeed a small Trotskyist group of revolutionary Marxists who were the sworn enemies of Joseph Stalin. At the time its leaders were jailed, it counted less than 2,000 members. There were a few positions of organizational strength, most notably in the Teamsters Union in Minneapolis. But it was utterly impossible to say the this tiny band in any way menaced the security of the United States.

The American Communist party, whose leaders were first indicted under the Smith Act in 1949, was much larger than the Trotskyists and had some significant influence in the mass production unions. But at the time the Communists were brought into court they were rapidly losing ground in the labor movement because of their complete and total submission to the Soviet line. Moreover, the Communist party had been infiltrated by the Federal Bureau of Investigation and its activities were, for the most part, known by Washington.

Nevertheless, under the new political atmosphere generated by the Cold War—and particularly after Korea became a hot war—the Smith Act was used against an entire generation of Communists. Since these men and women were convicted of advocacy, there was a chilling effect on all those who voiced unorthodox opinions, whether pro-Communist or not.

At the same time, the Attorney General's List became the basis of public and private screening programs. There were loyalty investigations in government agencies, in private industries deemed essential to the national security (shipping, longshoreing), and even in Hollywood, where "blacklists" kept real and alleged Communists from working in innocuous capitalist films and television. Vigilante groups emerged around the nation, dedicated to chasing "subversives" out of local school systems and off public platforms.

In February 1950, Senator Joseph McCarthy, a Wisconsin Republican, denounced the State Department as a haven for Communist spies and agents. He began to develop the theme that America's difficulties were the result of plotters from within who had helped the nation "lose" China to the Communists, had delivered the atomic bomb to the Russians, and so on.

If the Korean War had not broken out in June 1950, McCarthy's speech probably would not have had a great impact. But when that conflict erupted and America's sons were once again drafted, this time to fight their former allies of World War II, or at least their North Korean proxies, the McCarthy thesis suddenly took on new life. And this development was related, in turn, to another unique aspect of the Cold War: it was a limited struggle, even though it was sometimes rhetorically described as an Armageddon. That fact became plain in the dispute between General MacArthur and President Truman.

MacArthur had led the American (technically the United Nations) counterattack in Korea. In the fall of 1950, he commanded a brilliant combined land and sea attack which outflanked the North Koreans and turned the military tide of the war.MacArthur's troops pursued the enemy almost to the Chinese border. There were warnings, from India and other neutral powers, that such a tactic would bring the Chinese communists into battle. Washington ignored this problem; so did MacArthur. Then, in November 1950, Chinese "volunteers" surged across the border, cut the American forces in two, and turned the American triumph into a near rout.

MacArthur, an old "Asia Firster" who believed that his country had wrongly given top priority to Europe during World War II, wanted to accept the challenge and attack targets within China. Truman, now under pressure from NATO allies to refuse such a tactic, would not go along. Here is how one scholar—an implacable anticommunist of moderate conservative convictions, it should be noted—described the situation:

> It is true that the massive introduction of the Chinese communist element transformed the character of the Korean War. On the other hand (contrary to the universal chorus of experts who after 1945 proclaimed that from now on there were but two alternatives in political history: Universal Peace or Universal War), the Korean War, no matter how extreme the opposition between the two sides and their ideologies, was a limited war indeed. . . . If Manchuria, as MacArthur said bitterly, was a 'privileged sanctuary' of the Chinese attackers, so was Japan for the American defenders.[29]

In April 1951, Truman fired MacArthur, who was trying to rally support within the United States for his point of view. This was, of course, another stage in the development of the imperial Presidency, for it dramatically illustrated the supremacy of the White House over all military commanders. It

At the Army-McCarthy hearings, Senator Joseph McCarthy tried unsuccessfully to show that Communists had subverted the U.S. Army. Using congressional committees hearings as his forum, McCarthy had earlier charged that communists had infiltrated all levels of the federal government. His accusations, although unsubstantiated, contributed to the strong anticommunist mood in America during the early 1950s. The Senate finally censured him in 1954.

was also a tremendous encouragement to Senator McCarthy. It seemed to many people that the United States was fighting a war with at least one hand tied behind its back. The sophisticated rationales of a Kennan—who, incidentally, welcomed America's military intervention in Korea—were difficult for the average citizen to comprehend. If America was Good and the communists were Evil, why not destroy the satanic enemy totally? McCarthy had a false answer which sounded compelling to many people: domestic traitors, "pinkos," intellectuals soft on communism, were keeping us from winning the fight.

In February 1950, Senator Joseph McCarthy denounced the State Department as a haven for Communist spies and agents. He began to develop the theme that America's difficulties were the result of plotters from within who had helped the nation "lose" China to the Communists, had delivered the atomic bomb to the Russians, and so on.

So it was that the first protest against the crisis managers and their theories came from the Right. Indeed, this led some scholars at the time to conclude that there was a new, and reactionary, "populism" abroad in the land. According to this view, the working people who had supported the New Deal were now turning against the Eastern Establishment and its insistence on fighting a limited war. Dean Acheson, the secretary of state, a Wall Street lawyer and the very incarnation of the foreign policy "aristocrats," was a favored target of McCarthy and his allies.

In retrospect, however, it would seem that the sweeping generalizations about McCarthyism were wrong. The most salient single characteristic of the senator's supporters was that they were Republicans while his foes were Democrats.[30] It is therefore somewhat ironic that McCarthy's downfall was the result of the election of the first Republican President in a quarter of a century.

When Dwight Eisenhower ran for the Presidency, he accepted McCarthy's support, even though the Wisconsin senator had cast doubts on the loyalty of General George C. Marshall, Eisenhower's friend and mentor. Moreover, Eisenhower's secretary of state, John Foster Dulles, returned to the fundamentalist themes of the early Cold War. He was for "liberation," for rolling back communist power, and for relying on the threat of nuclear war to implement American possibility, going to the very brink of holocaust if necessary. Dulles was legalistic, a lay theologian who tended to see the world in terms of Light against Darkness. In 1954, for instance, he refused to shake hands with Chou En-lai at the negotiations of French withdrawal from Indochina, a symbolic act which was to haunt Sino-U.S. relations for years.

In many ways, Eisenhower followed Dulles' lead. If the Republican President—and military hero—was skeptical about involving American military forces as such in anticommunist actions in Asia, he nevertheless turned to the Central Intelligence Agency (CIA) as a weapon in the struggle. Under Eisenhower, the CIA helped to overthrow governments in Iran (1953) and Guatemala (1954), and tried but failed to do so in Indonesia (1958). It helped to install governments in Egypt (1954) and Laos (1959), and organized the ill-fated Bay of Pigs operation (which was actually carried out under John F. Kennedy). Thus, as Arthur Schlesinger, Jr., points out, the "imperial Presidency," with its tendency toward secret executive decisions, was further strengthened.[31] In the areas of loyalty and security, White House control of the military and covert operations of the Cold War had a pronounced—and negative—effect upon American society.

Eisenhower was not merely a follower of Dulles, however. In 1954, the secretary of state was in favor of "Operation Vulture," a major allied military operation to save the deteriorating French position in Indochina. After much discussion within the administration, including talk of using nuclear weapons, Eisenhower came down against such a policy. In 1956—one of the most critical years of the Cold War—Eisenhower and even Dulles realized that the United States could not intervene when Soviet tanks crushed the Hungarian Revolution. Ironically, that awareness of the limits of American power arose precisely when the moment awaited by Kennan and the "containment" strategists had arrived. The communist monolith had developed cracks after Stalin's death. Then, at the Twentieth Congress of the Soviet Communist party in February 1956, Khrushchev had given his famous secret speech, which detailed at least some of the crimes of the dead dictator. Shock waves were felt throughout the communist world.

In the fall of 1956, the communist "thaw" turned to a near boil in Poland and Hungary. Students, workers, and peasants began to demonstrate against the Russians and their local agents, demanding democratic freedoms within a socialist framework. In Hungary, this process went further than in any other country. The Communist party was dissolved, and a new, much broader, coalition Socialist party took over the government. That turned out to be more than the Russians could tolerate. Ironically, during the anniversary season of their own revolution, they moved in to brutally repress the vast popular movement.

It was clear to Eisenhower and Dulles that American military intervention would bring a direct military confrontation with the Soviets—World War III. So, the administration, which had talked of "liberation," gave reluctant, but unmistakable, de facto acknowledgment to Russian domination in Eastern Europe. The issue which had set off the Cold War at least eleven years before had been resolved, albeit in a tragic way with the destruction of a genuine peoples' revolution.

An important aspect of American politics becomes visible in this development. Eisenhower had agreed to a settlement of the Korean War which a Democratic President would not have dared to accept in that period for fear that the Republicans would impeach him. Similarly, in 1956, an anticommunist general took a nonintervention stand with regard to Hungary which would have earned a liberal Democrat charges of "treason." Much later, Richard Nixon, who had been one of the extreme hawks in the debates over American military involvement in Indochina in 1954 and was long known as a bitter anticommunist, was the President who negotiated a rapprochement with the

John Foster Dulles.

Hungarian "freedom fighters," having occupied the Soviet controlled military police building, await renewed attacks by Soviet troops and tanks during the 1956 Hungarian revolt.

Chinese communists. This is not simply a quirk of national politics. It is one further aspect of the development of the strong Presidency during the Cold War period. Indeed, one can even see this process at work during the Kennedy administration when the young President reached his highest popularity in the polls immediately after the disastrous Bay of Pigs invasion.

Presidents, as Lyndon Johnson was to learn, cannot lead the nation in a long, losing war. In the area of foreign policy, however, they are freer than in domestic issues, not least because the people lack any direct knowledge of what is going on overseas but have daily information about wages, prices, employment, and the like. This freedom of maneuver is greater for anticommunist Republicans than for Democrats, yet it is a characteristic of the Cold War Presidency. In 1979 and 1980, for instance, crises in Iran and Afghanistan enormously aided President Carter's failing political fortunes.

From the Cold War to détente

It has been argued—by John Lukacs, for instance, in a 1961 study—that the Cold War ended in 1956 and was replaced by a Cold Peace.[32] That does not mean that the years between 1956 and 1961 were without conflict. During those years, there were two Berlin crises, a shooting war between India and China, the erection of the Berlin Wall, the Bay of Pigs fiasco, confrontations in the Congo, and so on. Yet in those same years, Soviet leader Nikita Khrushchev visited the United States, which would have been unthinkable prior to 1956. And if there were extremely ugly and dangerous moments, particularly over Berlin, the world no longer seemed to teeter on the very brink of nuclear holocaust, as it had at various point between 1945 and 1956.

The Russians still routinely denounced American "imperialism," but they also talked of "coexistence." When, for instance, Khrushchev published an article in *Foreign Affairs* in 1959 (and thereby used an establishment publication for his purposes) he insisted that coexistence was a policy dictated by Soviet strength and confidence in its own success. In that context he wrote, "We say to the leaders of the capitalist states: Let us try out in practice whose system is better, let us compete without war."[33]

Then, in the fall of 1962, six years after what seemed to be the end of the Cold War, there occurred the single most dangerous confrontation between the United States and the Soviet Union. It revealed yet another truth about the impact of foreign policy upon domestic political structures in the United States. But, strangely enough, this truth was almost the opposite of the one which was almost universally deduced immediately after the event (and which persists until today).

When Soviet missile sites were discovered in Cuba in October 1962, the White House was understandably furious. In the previous period, President Kennedy and Khrushchev had been communicating with one another through informal channels. "Behind the obligatory Cold War rhetoric," wrote Arthur Schlesinger, Jr. (a participant-observer in these dramatic happenings), "the two leaders were trying to forestall conflict and to seek accommodation. All this built in the course of 1962 a measure of understanding, even of mutual confidence."[34] Then, when Khrushchev's duplicity was discovered, the crisis managers swung into action. An ExCom—Executive Committee of the National Security Council—was convened, and there were sharp debates over alternatives: invasion, "surgical" air strikes aimed at the missile sites alone, blockade (later to be called a "quarantine"). Then, the legend tells us, the young President made his choice, and the American forces carefully implemented the quarantine.

The two superpowers, in Dean Rusk's famous phrase, stood "eyeball to eyeball"—and then the Russians blinked. At the time—and even now—the Cuban crisis was seen as a model of cool and informed power politics, a triumph of careful planning and strategy.

The reality was considerably less neat. This point has more than academic interest, since it relates to the greatest single American foreign policy failure of the entire postwar era, the massive intervention in Vietnam. How was it that the very same leaders who had acted with such intelligence and restraint in the Cuban confrontation also initiated the Vietnam tragedy? Part of the answer is that the Cuban missile crisis did not conform to the legendary scenario.

There have been no end of theories to explain why the Soviets decided to put intercontinental missiles into Cuba in the first place: to recoup lost prestige due to defeats at Berlin and in Africa; to protect Cuba from American invasion; to get "bargaining chips" in negotiations with the United States; to achieve decisive missile superiority over the United States; and so on. All of these theories hold that the Russians must have acted in some rational manner. Similarly, the accounts of the American response emphasize its rational, instrumental character. But Graham Allison suggested in his brilliant book *Essence of Decision* that this model doesn't really fit the facts.[35]

Take two examples, one from each side of the conflict. At the critical moment, John F. Kennedy decided to move the quarantine line—the point where the American navy would intercept Soviet ships to inspect them for missiles—closer to Cuba, in order to give Khrushchev more time to consider his decision. Since this choice involved nothing less than postponing a moment which might have triggered a nuclear war, it was not unimportant. Yet the evidence is clear that the navy did not follow the President's explict orders but stuck to its own plan. With the world tottering on the brink, Allison argues, organizational routine and attitudes were more significant than the orders of the commander in chief.[36]

The Russian example is even more bizarre. Why did the Soviets observe great secrecy in shipping the missiles to Cuba and then proceed, at a leisurely pace and without attempt at concealment, to construct missile emplacements which were exactly identical to those in Russia itself and thus immediately recognizable to any American analyst? It would seem that they did it this way because the Russian crews followed the book and went about building the sites just as they would have done in the Soviet Union!

More to the point, it is still widely thought that Kennedy forced Khrushchev to back down with no *quid pro quo*. Adlai Stevenson's proposal to trade off American missile sites in Turkey for the Soviet missile cites in Cuba (both would be dismantled) was rejected by the ExCom as being too "dovish." Allison concluded, however, that just such a deal must have been made. When Robert Kennedy published his own account of the crisis, he confirmed Allison's deduction.[37] It was, Arthur Schlesinger was to note many years later, "a singular exercise in secret diplomacy—secret not only in process, as most diplomacy must be, but in result, which is generally inadmissable."[38]

In other words, one important "moral" of the Cuban missile crisis is that it is wise to compromise. But this is exactly what most people thought, and perhaps still think, that the event *disproved*. This most frightening confrontation of the entire Cold War dramatically illustrates how decisions affecting not simply the security of the American people but the fate of the world and perhaps the habitability of the planet are now made, even in a democracy, by small groups within the executive and without any kind of democratic political consultation. Worse, the control of these crisis managers over their own subordinates is tenuous. This development is often viewed as a necessary result of the very nature of military confrontations, hot or cold. That can be—and should be—questioned, but the point to be made here is that those thirteen days of nuclear uncertainty in October 1962 show how foreign policy has transformed domestic power structures in the United States in the post–World War II era.

CONCLUSIONS

It could be argued that the history we have traced, from 1946 to 1962, has a happy ending. Shortly after the Cuban missile crisis, John F. Kennedy drew a moral from the event:

> "Above all, while defending our own vital interests, nuclear powers must avert those confrontations which bring an adversary to the choice of either a humiliating defeat or a nuclear war. To adopt that kind of course in the nuclear age would be evidence only of the bankruptcy of our policy—or a collective death wish for the world."

So, an optimistic reading of the events chronicled and analyzed in this chapter could go something like this: after an excessively moralistic beginning and then an overconfidence in a calculated and realistic policy, the United States learned, through the tragedy of the Hungarian Revolution in 1956 and the near holocaust over Cuba in 1962, that it must accept limits upon its power and be prepared to negotiate an end to the East-West conflict.

There is a certain truth to that version of the period. A treaty banning nuclear tests, signed by the United States and the Soviets in the fall of 1963 in Moscow, opened up what many thought was a new era in world politics. Instead of "Cold War," people now spoke of *détente*—the French word for relaxation, in this case, the relaxation of international tensions between the two superpowers.

At the same time, however, there were tendencies within this country to radically extend the presumed reach of its power. In the spring of 1965, America qualitatively escalated its intervention in Vietnam. That development, the most fateful in the postwar history of the United States, demonstrated that this country had not learned the lessons of 1946–1962 as well as many had thought it had. It also dramatized the relationship of this nation to the vast majority of humankind, the peoples of Asia, Africa, and Latin America.

Footnotes

1. Harry S. Truman, *Vital Speeches of the Day,* September 15, 1945, pp. 707–708.
2. George Kennan, *American Diplomacy: 1900–1950* (Chicago: University of Chicago Press, 1970).
3. Arthur Schlesinger, Jr., in Thomas G. Paterson, ed., *Containment and the Cold War.* (Boston: Addison Wesley, 1973).
4. Kennan, *American Diplomacy.*
5. Lenin, *Collected Works,* Vol. 22 (Moscow: Progress Publishers, 1964).
6. Henry Kissinger, *World Restored: The Politics of Conservatism in a Revolutionary Age* (New York: Grosset & Dunlap, 1964).
7. Lloyd C. Gardner, Arthur Schlesinger, Jr., and Hans J. Morgenthau, *The Origins of the Cold War* (Waltham, Mass.: Ginn and Co., 1970), p. 47.
8. *Ibid.,* pp. 9–10.
9. Quoted in André Fontaine, *History of the Cold War,* Vol. 1 (New York: Pantheon Press, 1968), p. 211.
10. Gardner, Schlesinger, Morgenthau, *Origins of the Cold War,* p. 92.
11. Henry Kissinger, *White House Years* (Boston: Little, Brown, 1979) p. 63.
12. Arthur Schlesinger, Jr., in Thomas G. Paterson, ed., *Containment and the Cold War,* p. 219.
13. H.L. Trefousse, ed., *The Cold War: A Book of Documents* (New York: Putnam, 1965), p. 100.
14. George Kennan, "The Sources of Soviet Conduct," in Norman A. Graebner, ed., *The Cold War* (Lexington, Mass.: D. C. Heath, 1976), p. 32.
15. *Ibid.,* p. 33.
16. *Ibid.,* p. 34
17. Charles de Gaulle, *Memoires de Guerre: Le Salut* (Paris: Plon, 1959), pp. 233–34; emphasis added.
18. Kissinger, *White House Years,* p. 22; G. William Domhoff, *Who Rules America?* (Englewood Cliffs, N.J.: Prentice Hall, 1967), pp. 71ff; Gabriel Kolko, *The Roots of American Foreign Policy* (Boston: Beacon Press, 1969).
19. Marshall in Trefousse, ed., *The Cold War,* p. 105; Moscow in Fontaine, *History of the Cold War,* pp. 327–28.
20. Trefousse, ed., *The Cold War,* p. 104.
21. Committee on Foreign Relations, *Report,* June 24, 1976, p. 12.
22. Franz Schurmann, *The Logic of World Power* (New York: Pantheon, 1974), p. 121.
23. Adam Ulam, *Expansion and Coexistence: Soviet Foreign Policy, 1917-1973* (New York: Praeger, 1974), p. 442; Fernando Claudin, *The Communist Movement* (New York: Monthly Review Press, 1975), Part 2, p. 576.
24. Ulam, *Expansion and Coexistence,* p. 432.
25. Arthur Schlesinger, Jr., *The Imperial Presidency* (New York: Popular Library, 1974).
26. *Ibid.,* p. 136.
27. *Ibid.,* p. 141.
28. Stephen Cohen, "Stalinism and Bolshevism," *Dissent* (Spring 1977).
29. John Lukacs, *A History of the Cold War* (New York: Doubleday, 1961), pp. 93–94.
30. Michael Paul Rogin, *The Intellectuals and McCarthy* (Cambridge: MIT Press, 1967), p. 233.
31. Schlesinger, *Imperial Presidency,* p. 167.
32. Lukacs, *History of the Cold War,* p. 139.

33. Graebner, ed., *The Cold War,* p. 79.
34. Arthur Schlesinger, Jr., *Robert F. Kennedy and His Times* (Boston: Houghton Mifflin, 1978), p. 502.
35. Graham Allison, *Essence of Decision* (Boston: Little, Brown, 1971).
36. *Ibid.,* p. 130ff.
37. *Ibid.,* p. 107ff.
38. Schlesinger, *Robert F. Kennedy,* p. 522.

In the long sweep of history, the future of peace and progress may be most decisively determined by our response to the necessities imposed by our economic interdependence. . . . The urgent need for cooperative solutions to the new global problems of the world economy . . . dominate(s) the agenda of the evolving relationship between North and South, the industrial and the developing countries.

Henry Kissinger

The American intervention in Vietnam was clearly one of the most decisive experiences for this nation in the years since World War II. Tens of thousands were killed, an ancient land was devastated, a sitting President was, in effect, driven from office, and America went through bitter and sometimes violent confrontations between the proponents of our policy and a mass antiwar movement. The events in Vietnam were also part of a larger process which has so affected the political, economic, and social structure of the planet that one might call it a second creation of the world.

20

The Second Creation of the World

With the end of World War II, the people of Asia, Africa, and Latin America began to challenge the system. They had been subordinate and often colonized—parts of an international political and economic system utterly dominated by Western power.

In some cases, "decolonialization" came about as a result of armed struggle—and terrorism—by populations which had passively submitted to foreign rule (Algeria, Kenya). In others, the imperial power retreated in order to avoid that violence (India, the sub-Saharan French colonies). In countries which had been formally independent but subject to economic and political control by a great power, there were movements which challenged that dependent relationship (Cuba, Nicaragua). But the most dramatic single example of this revolutionary process was found in Indochina, which is now divided into the three countries of Laos, Cambodia, and Vietnam.

In analyzing the new shape of the world in the late twentieth century, we will have to deal with a number of interrelated themes:

the thesis, widely believed around the globe, that America's involvement in Vietnam and its relations with poor countries in general are a function of its economic and/or political "imperialist" drives;

546

U.S. soldiers in Vietnam.

the problems arising from this country's position as a "have" power in a time when the "have-nots" are on the march;

the United States' response to the poor countries' demand for a new international economic order.

VIETNAM: AN IMPERIALISTIC WAR?

It was not just the Vietnamese Communists who said that American intervention in their country was imperialist. That idea is probably accepted by a majority of the politically literate people in Asia, Africa, and Latin America, including some who are rightist anticommunists.

To most citizens of this country, however, that notion is preposterous. The United States was not a major *colonial* power, occupying and administering foreign places. In this regard, we have always thought ourselves superior to the French and the British, who were overtly colonialist.

As we have already seen, Franklin Roosevelt fought against the return of European colonialism in the debates among the Allied leaders during World War II. Roosevelt was not simply opposed to Stalin's plans to take control of Eastern Europe; he was specifically against the French coming back to run Indochina. As David Halberstam recounts the moment: "The French, Roosevelt was fond of telling people, had been in Indochina for fifty years and the people were worse off than when they arrived. He had determined that the French would not automatically come back and reassert their control over Indochina; there would be some kind of international trusteeship . . ."[1] President Truman had to face the issue shortly after he succeeded Roosevelt. Truman did not share Roosevelt's views, and he allowed the French to return to Indochina.

Still, don't these facts prove that America cannot be an "imperialist" country? Don't they show that the nation's involvement in Vietnam was a mistake, not a structural necessity? That, we will see, is an oversimplification. If it is true that every American move in Vietnam—or even the strategy of massively intervening there—was not predetermined, and even it if is true (as appears quite possible) that John Kennedy would have reversed this trend in his second term in office, that does not disprove the concept that there was something in American life—in the society, the economy—which predisposed us to the tragic error we made. That some versions of this theme are overly deterministic and even simpleminded should not blind us to the possibility of a complex interrelationship. Moreover, it is particularly important to explore this point since most people in the Third World believe that the United States is imperialist.

To begin with, it is necessary to distinguish between imperialism and colonialism. *Imperialism* is the economic domination of one country by another; *colonialism* is direct political domination. Imperialism can be colonialist—Britain ran the Indian government as well as its economy during the heyday of empire. But it need not be. The United States has rarely occupied Latin American countries but has played a major and often decisive role in their lives for more than a century. The confusion of imperialism and colonialism is one source of the American misunderstanding of the issues. But even with that confusion removed, the question of whether America is imperialist is difficult to answer.

The most influential single statement of the theory of imperialism—but one which, as we will see, does not apply to the United States—was V.I. Lenin's *Imperialism: The Highest Stage of Capitalism*.[2] It was not the only Marxist anaysis of imperialism (Rosa Luxembourg wrote a much more serious study of the issue from a Marxist perspective, which differed with Lenin on a number of crucial points). And there were other, non-Marxist theories (Joseph Schumpeter, the great conservative economist, authored one).

Lenin's little book was entitled "A Popular Outline" and contained nothing new in economic theory. It borrowed most of its analytical material from a British liberal, J.A. Hobson, and an Austrian socialist, Rudolf Hilferding, who was later to be an implacable critic of Soviet totalitarianism. Nevertheless, Lenin's study has become a bible in the Third World and is accepted by noncommunists as well as communists. Let us briefly restate his thesis and then see if it illuminates American foreign policy and particularly the intervention in Vietnam.

There were, Lenin argued, five characteristics of imperialism. First, capitalism must have reached a monopoly, noncompetitive phase. Second, there is a merging of industrial capital (corporations) and finance capital (banks).

President Carter's principal foreign policymakers in 1980: Donald McHenry (left), ambassador to the United Nations; Zbigniew Brzezinski (center), national security adviser; and Edmund S. Muskie (right), secretary of state.

Third, in part because of capitalist success in organizing the domestic market, the opportunities for new investment at home dry up and capital must therefore be invested abroad. Fourth, this leads to capitalist cartels on a world scale and, fifth, to a division of the globe among the various capitalist powers.

Imperialism can be colonialist, but it need not be. The United States has rarely occupied Latin American countries but has played a major and often decisive role in their lives for more than a century.

Lenin argued, however, that the entire system was inherently unstable since it pitted the big powers against one another in a scramble for markets, raw materials and, above all, investment outlets.[3] This point must be emphasized because it relates to a central aspect of the critique of Lenin's theory. In his theory, the export of capital—advanced capitalist investment in what we now call the Third World—plays a central role.

There are considerable elements of truth in Lenin's analysis, particularly with regard to the period before World War I. But it does not apply to the United States in the post–World War II period and does not, therefore, account for the American involvement in Vietnam. Consider a major qualification which Lenin himself made with regard to his own thesis:

> It goes without saying that if capitalism could develop agriculture, which today is everywhere lagging terribly behind industry, if it could raise the living standards of the masses, who in spite of the amazing technical progress are everywhere still half-starved and poverty-stricken, there could be no question of a surplus of capital. . . But if capitalism did these things it would not be capitalism; for both uneven development and a semi-starvation level of existence of the masses are fundamental and inevitable conditions and constitute premises of this mode of production. As long as capitalism remains what it is, surplus capital will be utilized not for the purpose of raising the standard of living of the masses in a given country, for this would mean a decline in the profits for the capitalists, but for the purpose of increasing profits by exporting capital abroad to the backward countries.[4]

Lenin turned out to be wrong on almost every count in the paragraph above. Leaving the issue of agriculture aside for the moment, it is simply not true that Western capitalism since 1945 has maintained the masses at "a semi-starvation level of existence." The welfare state has provided the people with a higher standard of living throughout this period. Even though there has been an undeniable decline in real income in the early eighties, it has hardly led to "semi-starvation."

Yet, as Chapter 7 showed, capitalism remains capitalism. Lenin, in short, based his analysis on a rigid, simplistic, and ultimately nineteenth-century model. There are pages in Marx's *Capital* which might seem to support this theory, but a more careful reading shows that Lenin's mentor did not hold an "immiseration" theory of capitalism. Whatever Marx thought, in the post–World War II period the masses saw the greatest rise in their living standards in all of human history. This affluence, as we have seen, is maldistributed and contains an entire substructure of poverty, yet it contradicts Lenin's analysis.

That relates to a second, critical point in Lenin's theory. Capitalism, he argued, had to export capital to the poor countries because it could not find profitable investment opportunities at home. But the post–World War II boom, which coincided with the institutionalization of the welfare state throughout Western capitalism, made it profitable for rich countries to invest in one another rather than in the poor countries. That is precisely what they did. Moreover, since the advanced powers had favorable terms of trade during almost the entire period—that is, the prices they received for the goods they sold to the Third World rose relative to the prices they paid for goods from the Third World—there was actually a shift of capital from the poor to the rich and not, as in Lenin's theory, an export of capital from the rich to the poor. Finally, the Western investments did not, as Lenin (and Marx and every other analyst of imperialism prior to World War II) thought, develop the Third World. It turned out that the West created enclaves of modernity, high-technology islands in societies which still remained backward.[5]

Many of these facts are recognized by scholars who have tried to adapt Lenin's argument to the contemporary world. Harry Magdoff, for instance, concedes the ''greater involvement by United States capital in Western Europe, as contrasted with investment in the underdeveloped countries,'' but holds that this point is ''untenable if one recognizes that antagonism between unevenly developing industrial centers is the hub of the imperialist wheel.''[6] But that does not compensate for Lenin's error. He argued that it was not a policy but an absolute necessity for capitalism to increase its investments in the poor countries. The fact that the greatest boom in the history of capitalism occurred when the Third World was becoming *less* important to that system robs Lenin's analysis of all of its specificity. To then add that there is still uneven development between the advanced and underdeveloped lands is both true and irrelevant to the argument.

Magdoff also agrees that ''the killing and destruction in Vietnam and the expenditure of vast sums of money are not balanced in the eyes of U. S. policy-makers against profitable business opportunities in Vietnam,'' for if one takes that ''bookkeeping'' view of imperialism it was clearly irrational for America to have become involved in the first place.[7] But when Magdoff then comments that the Vietnamese intervention was necessary ''in order to keep the entire area within the imperialist system in general, and within the United States sphere of influence in particular,'' he assumes what is to be proved— that the United States is imperialist.

Another sphere of American policy which is regularly invoked to show the imperialist nature of our politics, the Middle East, also refutes Lenin's theory. When President Truman recognized the new state of Israel in 1948, he did so against the explicit advice of both the State Department and the Pentagon. (He took a position which coincided with that of the Soviet Union.) One way of describing that event is to say that State and Defense followed the Leninist scenario but Truman and the nation did not. America's *economic* interest in the Middle East does not center upon a tiny Jewish state with limited natural resources, but rather upon oil-rich Arab powers. If foreign policy were the simple pawn of economic interest, Washington would have long ago broken its alliance with Tel Aviv. But in this case American politics put the right of Jewish self-determination ahead of those more crass concerns.

To be sure, this country came to support both Jewish *and* Palestinian self-determination in the area, which is to say, a negotiated settlement of the dispute. Yet that does not change the basic point. Leninist theory would predict that this country would be decisively behind Saudi Arabia and against Israel, but that is not the case at all.

Thus, the Leninist thesis fails in significant instances of American economic and political policy around the globe. But if America is not "imperialist" in Lenin's sense of the word—which is more than half a century old—that does not mean that there are not internal drives toward expansion within the American system. Let us examine this possibility on two levels: first the political, then the economic.

A number of theorists have come up with what are essentially variants on Joseph Schumpeter's political theory of imperialism. Capitalism, Schumpeter argued, is essentially pacifist: the businessman wants peace and quiet in which to make profits. Insofar as there are imperialist tendencies within capitalist countries, Schumpeter continued, they derive from a precapitalist military mentality, vestiges of a feudal ruling class which was essentially composed of warriors. There is, of course, no one who argues that feudal remnants in the United States were the cause of the intervention in Vietnam. But there are a number of analyses that explain that tragedy in terms of the attitudes, and arrogance, of particular classes or strata in the society. That is, they use Schumpeter's method but not his conclusions.

Franz Schurmann, for instance, argues, "If a popular leftist notion of America as a gigantic corporation with the President meekly taking orders from a supreme board of directors were true, the American Empire, world capitalism, and, ironically, the socialist countries as well would be safer and more secure." For, Schurmann asserts, capitalism wants profits; imperialism wants control. It is the state—the militarized, expansionist state—which is the source of the imperial drive.[8]

Noam Chomsky develops a similar theme but focuses on the technocrats and crisis managers:

> It is, I believe, reasonable to attribute the increasing irrationality of United States Indochina policy in the 1960s at least in part to the influx of technical intelligentsia into Washington and the expansion of the state role in the system of militarized state capitalism which has been evolving in the United States since World War II. The primary allegiance of the technical intelligentsia is to the state and its power rather than to the specific interests of private capital, insofar as these interests can be distinguished. Furthermore, the claim of the technical intelligentsia to a share in power rests on their alleged expertise. For this reason, it is difficult for them to concede error or to shape state policy in terms of a pragmatic calculation of interests, once a commitment has been made to a particular policy.[9]

Another sphere of American policy, the Middle East, also refutes Lenin's theory. America's economic interest in the Middle East does not center upon a tiny Jewish state with limited natural resources, but rather upon oil-rich Arab powers. If foreign policy were the simple pawn of economic interest, this country would be decisively behind Saudi Arabia and against Israel, but that is not the case at all.

David Halberstam's *The Best and the Brightest* is not as analytic and abstract as either Chomsky or Schurmann; yet it presents a brilliant reportorial statement of their case. America, as Halberstam presents the history, slipped into Vietnam. It was the *hubris* of the "best and the brightest"—the young, confident, superbly trained cadres around Kennedy and then Johnson—which made the extraordinary error of underestimating the political aspect of the struggle. These people, according to Halberstam, were not sinister and bent on evil. They were sincere and dedicated to the good, *and* they led the nation into the worst military and political tragedy of its entire history.

Two classic political theorists, Karl Marx and Max Weber, developed concepts which might help us understand these accounts of America's role in Vietnam. Marx argued that the state sometimes rose above the various social classes, even above the economically dominant class itself, and became an independent power on its own. He called this phenomenon "Bonapartism." That, Schurmann and Chomsky are saying, is what happened in the case of Vietnam. Weber distinguished between "functional" rationality, which describes whether a task is performed in a way which properly adapts means to end, and "substantive" rationality, which tells us whether the goal made sense in the first place. The American war in Vietnam, Halberstam argued, was incredibly rational in all of its functional aspects: computerized, technological to the nth degree, and so on. Only it was also insane, substantively irrational.

In the late seventies, after these authors had developed their insights, there were new revelations which offered startling confirmation of them. In *Side Show,* William Shawcross told how the bombing of Cambodia—an act of war against a country theoretically at peace with us—was decided in secret and was not even communicated to people high in government.[10] Henry Kissinger defended himself against the charge, essentially by claiming that Cambodia was not really neutral.[11] But Kissinger did not refute Shawcross' devastating account of the way this decision was kept from all but a handful of people in the Executive Office of the President. Not so incidentally, Shawcross also noted that Kissinger was the proponent of the notion that a new class, "separate from the businessmen, lawyers and bureaucrats who traditionally ran American foreign policy," was now at the helm in international affairs.[12] One typical member of that class would, of course, be Henry Kissinger.

So, the "Schumpeter" mode of analysis—deriving American foreign policy trends from the attitudes and character of elites rather than from the structure of the economy—has a certain validity. Yet a basic question remains:

Henry Kissinger served as national security adviser from 1969 to 1973 and as secretary of state from 1973 to 1977.

Why were these elites able to impose their views upon the greatest military-political power in human history? Chomsky's analysis has the merit of suggesting a response. The possibility of crisis managers playing such a decisive role relates to the growth of state capitalism, in general, that is, to the vastly enhanced role of the government in the West during the past fifty or so years.

Limited government was precisely one of the Lockean elements of the capitalist ideology and, to a lesser degreee, practice, and it served to differentiate the system from its feudal predecessor. But now, if the effective management of capitalism required the state to become much more interventionist, then that set up the possibility of technocratic elites having much more power than ever before. Chomsky is, of course, a leftist critic of American society, but something like his insight is shared by John Lukacs, who is much more moderate, and perhaps even conservative, in his outlook.[13]

Indeed, Lukacs even suggests the possibility that the Soviets may become more ''American,'' taking on Western technology, while the United States could become more ''Soviet,'' with the state playing a greater and greater role. (Eventually, in Lukacs' worst case, it might turn into a Russian-style police state.)[14] This concept of a structural convergence of Soviet and American society is also to be found in the ''postindustrial'' school of sociology, which sees capitalism as an outmoded term (as we noted in Chapter 7) and holds that all economies which move beyond mass production and base themselves on theoretical knowledge under the direction of the ''new men'' of the scientific-technical revolution will come to resemble one another.[15] Whatever validity this thesis might have in the long run, clearly the differences between the United States and the Soviet Union predominated in the period under discussion. Still, it is true that the stratification of the American economy and society has increased the potential power of technocrats. This phenomenon had a real bearing—whether in Chomsky's, Halberstam's, or Lukacs' readings—on the American intervention in Vietnam. The decision to move into Southeast Asia was one of the most carefully wrought, scientifically rigorous stupidities in history.

There is another theory of American foreign involvement which is quite un-Leninist yet gives an economic interpretation of American foreign policy. At first glance it might seem to be only a bizarre revision of Lenin's theory of imperialism, substituting agriculture for industry as the moving force behind American behavior. On more serious reading it has the merit of focusing on a surprising fact about American life: the growing importance of agriculture, a classic, preindustrial department of the economy, in a supposedly "post industrial" society.

The notion of an agricultural imperialism has been developed by William Appleman Williams. For Williams, the *frontier thesis*—that Western expansion was what made America uniquely great and created the economic basis for its thriving democracy—taught the nation that it must move outward or decay. In the 1890s, the frontier closed up, and the corporation supplanted the entrepreneur as the main form of capitalist activity. At that point, the expansionism which had derived from the agricultural conquest of the continent became a critical element in an industrial strategy. Indeed, Williams argues that the "containment" theory of anticommunism was based on America's experience of the frontier. We assumed, he holds, that any society which could not expand would necessarily lose its internal cohesion. We projected our fears about a stagnant America and turned them into our hopes for a stagnant Russia. All of this also led to American liberalism being the most private-property oriented reform movement in the world; it was one factor in the absence of a socialist alternative in the United States.[16]

There is no point in exploring Williams' complex theory at length here. It should be merely noted that he seems to overstate the role of agriculture in American politics, a point which has been documented by one of the authors of this book elsewhere.[17] Even with that criticism there is a very contemporary value in Williams' history. He focuses on a dimension of American economic and political life which is extremely important in the 1980s. Here, for instance, is the London *Economist's* summary of its survey of American agriculture: "'Farming is America's biggest business; with a workforce as large as that of the steel, car, and transport industries put together. . . . Agriculture exports are double imports. Farm labor productivity has increased ten fold in the past 50 years.'"[18]

In 1979, the *Economist* points out, one out of every three acres in the United States was planted for export crops. In that year, those exports brought in $32 billion. Thus, the farm is no longer the bucolic place of the nostalgic imagination. "Agriculture as practiced in the United States has become a high-technology industry with a huge ratio of capital to labor, rapid changes in methods of production, a great willingness to adopt new ideas and a large flow of reserves into research.'' This development, like everything else in the United States, was subsidized by the government—through the land-grant university system and its socialized research, as well as the work of the extension service of the U. S. Department of Agriculture—to the primary benefit of the affluent farmer and the agribusiness corporation.

In 1980, President Carter used this tremendous power over food as a weapon in countering the Soviet invasion of Afghanistan. Americans, who had been shocked by the use of oil as a political weapon when the Organization of Petroleum Exporting Countries (OPEC) declared an embargo to fight American support of Israel in the 1973 Yom Kippur War, did not notice that their country was engaging in the same tactic, although for a different purpose. Indeed, it would not be unfair to describe America as the Saudi Arabia of the ''Organization of Wheat Exporting Countries.'' Our ''OWEC'' dominates food almost to the degree that OPEC dominates energy. To complicate matters, a considerable number of American farmers were against the Carter move and reminded the President that, as a candidate, he had declared that he would never embargo the export of crops. So, America's high-technology, high-productivity agricultural system is a factor in its international politics.

We have now dealt with a number of theories about the relationship between American domestic structure—political, economic, and social—and foreign policy. How do these considerations help us to understand the intervention in Vietnam? The Leninist analysis, and even the up-dated neo-Leninist revisions, do not, we have seen, apply. The various discussions of the role of the technocratic elite in Vietnam have an obvious relevance and were, for the most part, developed in response to that war. But one must still explain the structural factors which made it possible for the crisis managers to have the impact they had. And even if William Appleman Williams' thesis about the role of the frontier and expansionism in American history provides some general background information, it has nothing particular to say about the Vietnam case.

Is it, then, possible that Vietnam was simply a policy error and not a structurally determined event? Certainly Halberstam's account stresses the way that some of the crucial decisions—above all, Truman's reversal of Roosevelt's position in acquiescing to the French return to Indochina—were taken casually and without any careful consideration of long-range consequences. That initial choice was then reinforced by Washington's concern to recruit France into what became the North Atlantic Treaty Organization (NATO) and then by North Korean aggression against South Korea. When the French were defeated at Dienbienphu in 1954, Eisenhower put the weight of the American government behind the South Vietnamese regime of Diem. Diem had credentials as a nationalist, but demonstrated from the very first moment the authoritarian tendencies which were to lead to his downfall.[19] The United States chose to ignore the fact that their chief ally was progressively narrowing his base and ultimately provoking the Viet Cong into an armed uprising.

So far, one can argue persuasively that America's Vietnam involvement was the result of a chain of accidents. But then, as one imagines the position

Snow White and the Seven Experiments.

that this country found itself in that situation—identified with an authoritarian status quo defended by officers who had been in the pay of French colonialism, counterposed to a genuine national movement which was controlled by a Communist cadre—it bears a striking resemblance to a whole series of events. Something like that happened on mainland China in the late forties, in Cuba in the late fifties, and in a number of African countries in the sixties and seventies. The "Free World" has included authoritarians like Diem (South Vietnam) and Rhee (South Korea), outright dictators like Franco (Spain), Batista (Cuba), Trujillo (Dominican Republic), and Jiminez (Venezuela), and friendly relations with racist South Africa. Communist totalitarians have often successfully appealed to democratic movements. Does this pattern represent a remarkable convergence of accidents—or does it express some deeper, more coherent, tendency in American life?

In a 1977 speech at Notre Dame University, President Carter recognized the phenomenon and offered an explanation for it. There had been, Carter said, "an inordinate fear of communism which once led us to embrace any dictator who joined us in that fear." His corollary was that, since the fear had now dissipated, it was no longer necessary to make such concessions. Not too long after that declaration, Carter visited the Shah of Iran and warmly toasted him as a beloved leader of his people. Within less than two years, the Shah was overthrown by those people, despite the fact that he led the most modern army in the region. Mr. Carter, in short, had followed the very pattern he had denounced. The anti-Shah opposition was not led by Communists, but by Islamic revolutionaries. Still, the United States was identified with the repressive past and opposed to a popular movement. But even ignoring the contradictions in Carter's conduct, does his explanation account for the pattern we have identified?

Fear is a psychological category. If Americans were afraid, was that emotion based upon a realistic view of what was happening, or did it have elements of the irrational in it? And if the latter is the case—which the thrust of this chapter would suggest—why did America succumb to a kind of national paranoia? There is a way of answering that question which uses insights from thinkers who are otherwise counterposed to one another.

"Marxist theory," Henry Kissinger writes, "combines with Russian national advantage to place the Soviet Union on the side of all radical anti-Western movements in the Third World, regardless of what practical accommodations are made between East and West on nuclear matters."[20] Stanley Hoffman of Harvard is often quite critical of Kissinger, yet on this point he says much the same thing as the former secretary of state: "Geopolitically, as the main status quo power in a world of change, the United States is on a kind of universal defensive, while its rival can pick and choose the points for attack among the many ferments of trouble."[21] If Kissinger and Hoffman are right, as would seem to be the case, that offers some insight into the American pattern in the Cold War, which culminated so tragically in Vietnam.

In this framework, America's stance toward the world is not determined by some single cause, like the need to export capital or to cope with the closing of the frontier. More broadly, the United States at the end of World War II found itself as a status quo power in a revolutionary world of decolonialization and insurgent social movements. It sincerely wanted to ally with the anticolonialists. But in almost every case, the anticolonialists were not fighting for a "bourgeois" revolution—for national independence within a capitalist framework. They saw themselves as involved in an anti-imperialist, and even socialist, struggle. There was a brief moment under John F. Kennedy when the White House thought it could come to grips with this problem. In Latin America, it was said, the United States would ally itself with a democratic Left which sought to change social structures and improve the life of the masses. Thus, we would no longer be outflanked by the Communists and watch as they captured the leadership of revolutions which they then turned into totalitarian channels.[22]

But, as Arthur Schlesinger, one of the theorists of this new tactic, was to report somewhat ruefully, it is not easy for a status quo power to support even moderate radicalism. The Latin American oligarchies resisted land and tax reform; the terms of trade turned against the Continent; the rich took their money to Europe; and the people were not reached. "One sometimes felt," Schlesinger wrote, "that the communists, operating on a shoe string in city universities or back-country villages, were reaching the people who mattered for the future—the students, the intellectuals, the labor leaders, the nationalist militants—while our billions were bringing us into contact with government of doubtful good faith and questionable life expectancy.''[23]

In saying these things, it is important to be very clear about the role of the Communists. The rank-and-file were, and are, unquestionably sincere. Their dedication, their willingness to fight and die for the cause, were reasons why they were able to win leadership. But once the struggling, underground Communist movement achieved power during this period—in China, in Cuba, in Vietnam—it moved to repress all of its foes and to set up a totalitarian society. Moreover, Communists in power behaved remarkably like capitalists in power; the Soviets invaded Hungary, Czechoslovakia, and Afghanistan, the Chinese attacked India and Vietnam, the Vietnamese overthrew the Cambodian government. Indeed, in one of the most critical policy reversals in history, China invited Richard Nixon to Bejing and made its peace with its old foe, the United States. Therefore, to be critical of American policy in this regard is hardly to become an apologist for the Communists.

More importantly for the future, it is necessary, as Arthur Schlesinger demonstrates, to understand how difficult it is for America to shed not simply the image but the reality of being a status quo power. Yet that remains the

Richard Nixon, shown shaking hands with Mao Tse-tung, renewed America's ties with the People's Republic of China during his visit there in 1972.

precondition of breaking the pattern of unrealistic *Realpolitik* which puts American democracy in the service, not just of dictators, but of unstable dictators—which is impolitic as well as immoral. But if that task is difficult, it is necessary or this country will remain locked in the pattern which had such a tragic outcome in Vietnam.

There is no one solution to changing the course of the history we have been analyzing. America's role in the Cold War, we have seen, was profoundly influenced by a whole series of developments in American political life: by a traditional moralism and universalism; by a sophisticated school of crisis managers who countered some of the moralism but brought their own dangerous arrogance into play; by the growth of state power, sometimes as a quasi-autonomous force, and the attack on civil liberties waged in the name of defending democracy; by economic considerations which cannot be precisely related to specific decisions but which formed the broad framework of policy; and so on.

It is necessary to understand how difficult it is for America to shed not simply the image but the reality of being a status quo power. Yet that remains the precondition of breaking the pattern of unrealistic Realpolitik which puts American democracy in the service, not just of dictators, but of unstable dictators—which is impolitic as well as immoral.

If fear was also a factor, as President Carter contended in 1977, perhaps our national innocence had a role in generating our national paranoia. Since we knew that we were not colonialist and that the communists were totalitarians, and since we did not understand how much our status quo economic position made us conservatives in a revolutionary world, we therefore did not understand the appeal of communism as a genuine social movement capturing the leadership of authentic popular insurrections. Rather, we viewed it as merely a subversive phenomenon and thus looked for spies and traitors and ignored a revolutionary change in the structure of the world.

The last point leads to a brief consideration of the epochal event noted at the outset of this chapter: the decolonialization of the Third World.

NORTH AND SOUTH

The conflict between East and West was the central preoccupation of the first phase of American policy in the post–World War II period. But soon another theme asserted itself: the relationship between North and South, between the rich countries of the world—the United States, the richest of them all—and the poor nations, most of which are found in the Southern portion of the globe.

It is not mere portentous rhetoric to say that an era of four hundred years began to end in the period following World War II. In the sixteenth century, Western Europe was in many respects inferior to the civilizations of China, India, and Islam. Indeed, in its "take-off," Europe borrowed inventions and ideas—not only technology but the zero concept, Arabic numerals, and the like—from non-Europeans and then utilized those innovations to subjugate the innovators.

It is impossible to even sketch this enormously complex process here. For our purposes, suffice it to say that one of the principal results was a global division of labor in which poor countries specialized in the least profitable economic pursuits, like mining, agriculture, and the employment of used industrial revolutions from the West, while the advanced powers engaged in the most profitable investments. As we have seen, there are complications in this scheme—agriculture, a "primary" industry, exists as a high-technology sector in the United States—but it roughly describes the consequences of world economic development from the sixteenth to the twentieth century.[24]

In the nineteenth century, Western economic domination of the planet led to an imperialist "scramble" among the major powers. As Henry Kissinger described the situation:

> In the nineteenth century, the Industrial Revolution gave birth to improved communications, technological innovations and new forms of business organization which immeasurably expanded man's capacity to exploit the frontiers and territories of the entire globe. In less than one generation one fifth of the land area of the planet and one tenth of its inhabitants were gathered into the domain of imperial powers in an unrestrained scramble for colonies. The costs—in affront to human dignity, in material waste and deprivation, and in military conflict and political turbulence—haunt us still.[25]

In the years after World War II, two relevant developments took place. First, there was political decolonialization. The achievement of political independence in the ex-colonies did not, however, mean that economic independence was at hand. For the most part, the newly free nations took over impoverished economies which were in a structurally inferior position in the world market. By the sixties, they had learned that formal independence and economic dependence contradicted one another. They were, the spokespeople for the Third World began to say, suffering from "neo-colonialism"—not from outright political domination but from indirect economic dependency which kept them in an inferior position more subtly than the occupying troops did before World War II.

The conflict between East and West was the central preoccupation of the first phase of American policy in the post–World War II period. But soon another theme asserted itself: the relationship between North and South, between the rich countries of the world—the United States, the richest of them all—and the poor nations, most of which are found in the Southern portion of the globe.

The United Nations has increasingly become a forum for the concerns of Third World countries in recent years.

In the sixties, that consciousness was formulated into a program by the United Nations Conference on Trade and Development (UNCTAD) and the Group of 77 (the caucus of poor countries, named when it had seventy-seven members but now with adherents from over a hundred nations). At the Seventh Special Session of the United Nations General Assembly in 1976, this attempt to deal with neo-colonialism was approved under the heading of a New International Economic Order (NIEO). The underlying analysis concentrated on the unfavorable terms of trade for the poor countries—that throughout almost all of the postwar years they have been selling cheap and buying dear—and the fact that industry tended to be concentrated in the North and agriculture and raw materials production in the South. This was not, it should be noted, a very radical approach, even though the rhetoric which accompanied it sometimes was quite apocalyptic.

If, the Third World was saying, the world market could be structured more fairly, then they could and would compete in it and improve their lot by using this very capitalist mechanism. There were four main changes urged which were supposed to transform that market: the advanced countries would increase their aid for the poor countries and help them industrialize; the nations in the South would get control over sophisticated technology; the debts owed by the underdeveloped countries would be renegotiated and even forgiven; and, above all, there would be a "common fund" which would smooth out the fluctuations in export earnings that make it so hard for these powers to engage in rational planning.

That last point sounds very complicated, but it really isn't, particularly if one remembers that there has been just such a "common fund" for agriculture *within* the United States since the New Deal. Agriculture and raw materials prices are very unpredictable. One year, coffee or sugar or rubber will be in tremendous demand; the next year the demand can plummet. A common fund—the idea was first proposed by John Maynard Keynes, a firm believer in capitalism—would buy those commodities when world demand was low and thus keep the prices up; it would sell its stocks when there was high demand and thus help keep prices from soaring into the stratosphere. The producers would get stable returns from their efforts. The buyers in the rich countries would benefit, too, because they would be able to schedule their purchases without having to be fearful of roller-coaster prices.

Thus, although the NIEO was sometimes described as a revolutionary assault on the very structure of the international economy, it was actually rather moderate. Indeed, in 1980 an international commission headed by Willy Brandt, and including an American businessman, Peter Peterson, a former Conservative prime minister of Britain, Edward Heath, and a Chilean Christian Democrat, Eduardo Frei, argued that such steps were in the national interests of the affluent countries as well as those of the poor.[26]

How did the United States react to decolonialization? On the political level, Washington's response was ambiguous. It hailed the independence of India—and supported French colonialism in North Africa and Indochina. The difference in attitude is, of course, explained by the fact that America wanted to maintain good relations with both Britain and France and endorsed the contradictory policies of those two powers. More broadly, as the last section demonstrated, the United States associated itself with anticommunist dictators in the poor countries and opposed most of the national liberation movements. To cite but a few instances, this was true in China in the forties, in Cuba in the Fifties, in Vietnam in the sixties, and in Nicaragua in the seventies. There were, as we have seen, efforts to break this pattern, most notably Alliance for Progress, but they did not succeed.

On the economic level, at least, the United States naively thought that it could repeat the achievements of the Marshall Plan in the Third World. After his surprise election in 1948, President Truman proposed a "Point Four" program in which America would provide money and technology for the rapid transformation of the poor economies. The assumptions behind this approach were to be spelled out much later by Walt W. Rostow in *The Stages of Economic Growth*, but Truman clearly acted on them in the late forties.[27]

Western capitalism in general and American capitalism in particular were seen as the models for the underdeveloped world. This theory held that communism was totalitarian; socialism was inefficient and perhaps only a prelude to communism; capitalism was the answer. And just as the Western economies had gone through "stages" of growth—accumulation, take-off, mass consumption—the Third World economies would follow the same, obviously successful, progression.

That did not happen. More to the point, it could not happen. When the United States funded the restoration of capitalism in Western Europe after World War II, it was dealing with societies that had been through the capitalist social and cultural revolution. Their populations had long been schooled in the skill and discipline of industrial production; their nations still remained in a privileged position in the world economy. The "only" problem was to remove the wreckage and devastation of the war. These countries either had strong democratic traditions, like Britain, or were determined not to repeat the anti-democratic patterns of the past, like West Germany. Thus, U. S. capital could accomplish a miracle in an area which lacked only U. S. capital.

The Third World was, and is, an entirely different situation. One of the preconditions of the stages of Western growth was that the Western powers were the first to ascend that ladder. That is, there was no preexisting division of labor working to keep them backward. But the poor nations of the post–World War II period were only liberated from the political control of the Western powers; they remained economically dependent. And the West was not going to let new countries up the ladder it had built, not the least because there was already much pushing and shoving at the top. In 1969, Gabriel Valdes, a Chilean Christian Democrat, tried to explain this point to Richard Nixon at a White House meeting. He said:

> It is generally believed that our continent is receiving real aid in financial matters. The figures demonstrate the contrary. We can affirm that Latin America is contributing to financing the development of the United States and the other industrial nations. Private investments have signified, and signify today, for all of Latin America that the funds which are taken out of our continent are many times greater than those which are invested in it. . . . The so-called aid, with all of the conditions we know so well, means trade and more development for the advanced economies but certainly has not succeeded in compensating us for the sums which leave Latin America in paying foreign debt and as a result of the profits which direct foreign investment generates. In a word, we are becoming conscious that Latin America gives more than it receives.[28]

The "conditions" on American foreign aid, cited by Valdes, deserve a moment of comment. During this period, foreign aid was normally "tied"— the recipient country was required to spend the funds in the United States even if it could buy higher quality goods at a cheaper price somewhere else. Therefore, aid, among many other things, helped to enforce the monopoly prices of some suppliers and probably did at least as much for the American economy as it did for the underdeveloped nation.

This is not to suggest, as some overly enthusiastic partisans of the Third World have done, that the post–World War II affluence of the United States was primarily a product of the exploitation of the poor lands. In these years, as we saw in the discussion of imperialism, American direct investment shifted toward Europe and Canada and, in relative terms, away from the Third

A meeting of OPEC ministers in 1978. OPEC, a cartel of oil-producing nations, has been able to control the production and the price of its oil.

World. And the boom of 1945–69 had many sources besides foreign trade. In a sense, this makes the American position even more questionable: the exploitation of the Third World was not a necessity of the system but merely a convenience for some of its members.

Truman proposed Point Four in 1949; the OPEC embargo occurred in 1973. During those twenty-four years, America became progressively disillusioned with its commitment to the Third World, largely because it had begun with such unrealistic expectations. In the process, the U.S. government decreased its foreign-aid contributions, computed as a percentage of Gross National Product, to less than two-tenths of a percent (countries like Sweden and Holland met the United Nations recommendations for three to four times that percentage). Here, again, the moralism and universalism of American policies were, and are, at work. Many people naively thought that solutions which worked here could be exported overseas. They ignored an economic structure, the world division of labor, which was the result of some four hundred years of development. So our innocence and excessive hopes turned into indifference, our moralizing into callousness.

In 1973, a new era began. With the formation of OPEC, at least one group of Third World countries found a way of getting tens of billions of dollars from the advanced economies. But, as geographical chance would have it, the countries most richly endowed with oil were only thinly populated. The monopoly prices they charged Americans also applied in the poor countries, where they had infinitely more devastating consequences. In the late 1970s, poor or small countries were carrying 90 percent of the deficit caused by the OPEC increases.[29] Moreover, there are limits to how much investment a poor country can absorb in a short period of time even when, as is the case in Saudi Arabia, there is no capital shortage. When such transformations are accomplished from the top down, shattering the traditional society, they can also lead to social revolutions, as the overthrow of the Shah of Iran demonstrated.

During this period, American foreign aid was normally "tied"—the recipient country was required to spend the funds in the United States even if it could buy higher quality goods at a cheaper price somewhere else. Therefore, aid probably did at least as much for the American economy as it did for the underdeveloped nation.

So, OPEC probably worsened the lot of most of the people of the Third World. It also caused a reassessment of policy in the United States. Washington clearly feared the possibility of the interruption of vital supplies from the poor lands. The right of "access" became a major consideration for American policy planners. Immediately after the OPEC embargo of 1973, Henry Kissinger took a hard line, threatening Third World powers which engaged in such tactics and seeking to split the oil and the non-oil factions among the non-aligned powers. When that did not work, Kissinger briefly flirted with some kind of concessions—he proposed, for instance, some limited American aid for international development of the resources of the ocean—but soon abandoned that policy as the West absorbed the OPEC shock more easily than had been anticipated.

In 1973, a new era began. With the formation of OPEC, at least one group of Third World countries found a way of getting tens of billions of dollars from the advanced economies.

By the 1980s, American public sympathy with the poor countries was at a low ebb. For most people, the Third World was personified by OPEC price-fixers, by militant students holding Americans hostage in Iran, and by unstable and demagogic dictators like Colonel Qadaffi of Lybia. Few Americans sensed how much those upheavals—which were often humiliating and wrong-headed (as in the case of the hostages in Teheran) and which almost always increased the instability of a precarious world—were the inevitable consequences of a structure of Western domination which could no longer survive.

The proposals for a New International Economic Order were more and more ignored in Washington. In the period right after the OPEC embargo of 1973, as we have seen, the United States made some gestures in the direction of supporting such an undertaking, seeking guaranteed right of access to the Third World in return for its help in industrializing those nations. So, as the eighties began, this country's relationship with the majority living in under-developed nations was correct but unsympathetic.

The United States was wary of the automatic Third World majorities in the UN General Assembly, which were sometimes mobilized for mere propaganda victories or for worse purposes, as in the shrill denunciation of Jewish self-determination in Israel as "racist." Washington even moved against a proposal to declare outer space the common heritage of humankind on the grounds that such an international treaty might keep corporations from developing the resources of the heavens. Thus, if the Leninist theory does not hold in general or in particular, it remains true that the United States has not transcended the limits of being a rich, "have" power on a planet in which the poor majority is, after more than four centuries of subjugation, demanding justice.

In late 1979 and in 1980, Iranians held frequent demonstrations to show their support for the militants holding the American hostages in Iran.

After fourteen months of captivity, the hostages were released on Jan. 20, 1981.

AMERICA AND THE WORLD IN THE 1980s

Political decades rarely follow the regular calendar. However, in many ways January 1, 1980, seemed to mark a turning point in America's relations with the world.

On that day, the President of the United States was immersed in a basic reconsideration of U.S. foreign policy in the wake of the Soviet invasion of Afghanistan. And the nation as a whole was feeling the impact of economic changes that had shifted the position of America in the global economy. In a sense, the experience of decline, of the slippage of American power, was inevitable. In 1945, this country was the only atomic power on the face of the earth. Its economy towered over the devastated industrial plants of Western Europe and Japan. In the classic phase of the Cold War, from 1945 to 1956, America had clearly been in charge of the entire Western alliance. The dollar had become the reserve currency of international trade, a kind of paper gold which commanded almost as much confidence as the precious metal itself.

Clearly, however, those conditions could not endure for long. Russia, and then other countries, soon broke the atomic monopoly. West Germany and Japan became competitors in the world market. And a globe which had seemed to gravitate around two poles, Washington and Moscow, became politically much more complex.

Richard Nixon had been the first President to define the new complexity. In a speech delivered at Kansas City in July, 1971, Nixon had said that a world of "five great economic superpowers" was in the making: the United States, Western Europe, Japan, the Soviet Union, and China. Indeed, Henry Kissinger reports that this statement had a considerable impact upon the Chinese Communists and was one of the reasons why they decided to invite Nixon to Bejing in 1972.[30]

That trip, and the recognition of the Peoples' Republic of China which followed it, was itself evidence of the change that had taken place over the years. At the height of the Cold War, between 1946 and 1956, most Americans, and both Democratic and Republican Presidents, believed that communism was a monolithic international conspiracy. With the events of 1956, including the Hungarian Revolution and the Polish stand against the Russians, it became clear that this concept was seriously flawed.

Then the Sino-Soviet dispute of the sixties revealed how profoundly disunited the communist world was. That development eventually led to America playing the "China card" by trying to frighten Moscow with a Bejing alliance and Bejing with a Moscow alliance. That somewhat Machiavellian strategy was one more indication of the distance American foreign policy had traveled from the days of Cold War moralizing, when John Foster Dulles refused to shake hands with Chou En-lai. After all, the representative of the forces of Light did not socialize with a leader of the forces of Darkness.

A mere sixteen years after that snub, a conservative American President was toasting the Chinese Communist leadership in Bejing.

President Carter and Chinese Vice Premier Deng Xiaoping at a ceremony on the White House lawn in January 1979. The Chinese leader's visit to the United States followed the establishment of full diplomatic relations between the two countries on January 1, 1979.

In his study of nineteenth-century European politics, Henry Kissinger distinguished between a Burkean conservatism—named for Edmund Burke, the English foe of the French Revolution—and a Metternichian conservative—after Metternich, the Austrian statesman who created the post-Napoleonic peace structure in Europe. The Burkean approach, Kissinger said, was moralistic; the Metternichian, which was just as conservative, was willing to make deals with enemies if that would serve the purpose of stability in an unstable world. Kissinger developed that theory as a scholar long before he became a presidential adviser. Yet Nixon clearly acted on it in the momentous rapprochement with the Chinese. Here is a sign of how profoundly the world had changed during the period under discussion and above all, how much more complex it had become.

What, then, is the position of this nation as it enters the 1980s: How much of its strength has eroded? Is that development a necessity or the result of poor policy choices by American leaders? Clearly, these are open-ended questions. The times are so turbulent that no serious analyst can hazard exact predictions. We can, however, talk of some of the forces and trends that are at work in this new period.

On the economic level, the greatest single problem arises from a singular American success: the Marshall Plan—as well as aid to Japan—brilliantly brought capitalism to life in those countries. Though dependent on the United States in the late '40s and early '50s, they began to pull even in the late '50s and early '60s and now are competitive in a number of significant sectors. Ironically, there are advantages to having an industrial plant destroyed in a war, for when it is replaced one is able to install the most modern equipment. Steel factories in West Germany and Japan, for example, are much more productive than their aging counterparts in the U.S.[31]

In 1945, this country was the only atomic power on the face of the earth. Its economy towered over the devastated industrial plants of Western Europe and Japan. Clearly, however, those conditions could not endure for long. Russia, and then other countries, soon broke the atomic monopoly; West Germany and Japan became competitors in the world market; and a globe which had seemed to gravitate around two poles, Washington and Moscow, became politically much more complex.

The results of this and related developments were reported by the Council of Economic Advisers in 1979: "The U.S. share of total manufactured exports of 15 industrial nations," it said, "fell from almost 30 percent in the late 1950s to 19.2 percent in 1972." In the first quarter of 1978, the U.S. share was at 18.9 percent.[32] By then, the problems were not confined to the competition between this country and the most advanced nations. In machine-tool production, for instance, the United States was matched, not simply against Japan, but against Taiwan and Spain as well. In 1978, for the first time in its history, this country imported more machine tools than it exported.[33] The fact of the matter is that a technologically innovative society loses its advantage over time. In the "product cycle," new products are invented in the most affluent, scientifically progressive countries. But their production then becomes routinized and it becomes cheaper to carry it out in an underdeveloped area. In order to maintain its relative position, a nation has to move relentlessly forward. And this the United States did not do during the postwar period.

Some of the most alarmed comments about this trend come not from radical critics of the society, but from the pro-business press. In 1979, for instance, *Business Week* wrote of the steel industry: "Sometimes it is possible to see a disaster in the making a decade before it occurs. A case in point is the willingness of U.S. Steel Corporation to let a large part of its steel business die of old age while it concentrated on new investments in such areas as chemicals, transportation, and resource development." The United States, *Business Week* said, could become dependent on foreign steel just as it had become dependent on foreign oil.[34] Indeed, two weeks earlier, in a fiftieth-anniversary survey of the economy, the same magazine had speculated that the United States might lose the steel, textile, auto, shoe, and apparel industries "to producers in other countries because American corporations are unable or unwilling to compete."[35] And in the same period, the New York *Times* commented that Japanese companies were much more willing to invest profits in long-term and planned gains, while the Americans wanted a higher yield right away.[36]

One measure of the impact of this on the U.S. economy was the Gross National Product. From 1960 to 1967—one of the most successful periods in the history of the economy—America's GNP increased an average of 4.6 percent per year. From 1967 to 1976, the increases averaged only 2.5 percent per year. One result was a shrinking standard of living in the United States: real wages in 1979 had *less* buying power than in 1972. Of course, America was not alone in experiencing these problems. But while other advanced economies may have faltered, they did not drop as dramatically.[37]

It must be carefully understood, however, that these figures do not prove that the United States is no longer a great economic power. In some areas—aircraft production, computers, semiconductors—America retains its lead. Even when one takes into account the industries in which it is less competitive, it is still the biggest economy in the world. Further, as we noted earlier, some of this decline was inevitable: the unique conditions surrounding America's dominance in the first postwar years could not possible last. Still, this relative shift in economic position obviously has political and military implications. As the '80s begin, what are the American prospects in the world in those areas?

To begin with, economic and political-military power are not equivalent. The Soviet Union, to cite a famous example, is much stronger militarily than it is economically because, in totalitarian fashion, it has committed proportionally greater resources to the arms sector than the United States. Indeed, there are serious analysts who believe the Soviet belligerence is partly due to the fact that it is *only* in the military sphere that it can even begin to compete with the United States.[38] Moreover, in this area, too, it was not possible for

U.S. missile warheads stockpiled in West Germany.

America's predominance after 1945 to last. For one thing, the atomic monopoly was going to be broken sooner or later. Indeed, the crisis managers came to believe that rough Russian equivalence in the arms race was a factor making for peace. If, they said, the Soviets were utterly outclassed, they might try to make a preemptive strike. But if they were secure in the knowledge that a Third World War would lead to "mutually assured destruction" (or MAD, as the acronym puts it), they might come to accept the balance of terror and even agree to a phased reduction of armaments on both sides.

But the question remains: Is the strategic situation radically different, from the American point of view, at the beginning of the 1980s as compared, say, to the '60s? Almost everyone is agreed that a new phase in the East-West relationship is at hand. Samuel P. Huntington, a scholar who served on the National Security Council staff in 1977–78 and who is known as being hawkish in attitude, argues that from 1945 to the mid-1960s American-Soviet relations were characterized by intense competition. Then, from the late 1960s until 1973, there was a period of cooperation. Beginning in 1973 there was a new period, less cooperative than the prior phase but not quite as competitive as the opening phase.

Soviet tanks and troops in Afghanistan.

Some would question Huntington's dates, but few would challenge the assertion that a shift has been, and is, taking place. President Carter's militant response to the Russian invasion of Afghanistan in early 1980—the proclamation of a "Carter Doctrine" defining the Persian Gulf as an area of such vital interest for the U.S. that Soviet intervention there could call forth a military response—only served to underline this fact.

But there were, and are, serious differences as to what was happening. One school, which includes Henry Kissinger and Zbigniew Brzezinski, Carter's national security adviser, believes that the Soviets have taken the offensive in a decidedly new way. As Kissinger put this thesis, the Russians are responding to an America in which a "rapid succession of domestic crises over a decade culminated in recent years in foreign policies that gave up major geopolitical positions and permitted the Soviets to extend their sphere without challenge."

Kissinger argues that this Soviet drive began with the Cuban expeditionary force in Angola, which acted as a surrogate for Moscow:

> The global offensive then continued in 1977 with Cuban troops in Ethiopia, Cuban troops in Yemen, East German forces all over Africa, two invasions of Zaire. This was one side of the pincer. The other started with a Communist coup in April 1978 in Afghanistan which overthrew a pro-Soviet neutralist government. It has now been completed by the application of the Brezhnev doctrine to a country which has never been in the Communist sphere.[40]

A contrasting view comes from Stanley Hoffman, who wrote, shortly before the invasion of Afghanistan:

> Is Soviet policy a deliberate, planned and masterly march toward world domination? More plausibly, it is a relentless attempt at achieving equality with the United States—at breaking the American monopoly of control of the high seas or of means to intervene all over the world—and at imposing Soviet participation in the settlement of all major disputes. It is also the skillful exploitation of opportunities, many of which arise spontaneously or through the independent efforts of a Soviet client or ally. The USSR has moved, but with considerable caution. The Litany of Angola, the Horn of Africa, South Yemen, and Vietnam ties together disparate events, tied by two threads: low risks and opportunities provided by previous Western mistakes, defeats, or (as in Afghanistan) indifference.[41]

CONCLUSIONS

Clearly, there is a new phase in American international politics as the '80s begin. It cannot be described or analyzed since it is still very much in motion. But a broad generalization can be derived from these recent events as well as from the whole period surveyed in this chapter. In a very real sense, the creation of the world began in the sixteenth century. There was, of course, a planet Earth before that time, but it was subdivided into geographical areas with little or no contact between them. Only with the rise of capitalism and the insatiable Western expansionist drive did the world start to become an economic, political, and social unit.

Now, four hundred years later, the particular power configuration which resulted from that capitalist creation of the world—with the Western powers in total command, even if they warred with one another—is being transformed. We live, in a sense, in the midst of the second creation of the world, a time of enormous instability and danger. We live during a time which, if Earth does not blow itself up in the process, may well set the patterns of the next four hundred years.

Footnotes

1. David Halberstam, *The Best and the Brightest* (New York: Fawcett Crest, 1972), p. 101.
2. Lenin, *Collected Works,* Vol. 22 (Moscow: Progress Publishers, 1964).
3. *Ibid.,* p. 266.
4. *Ibid.,* p. 241.
5. Michael Harrington, *The Vast Majority* (New York: Simon & Schuster, 1978), Ch. 4.
6. Harry Magdoff, *The Age of Imperialism* (New York: Monthly Review Press, 1969), p. 16.
7. *Ibid.,* p. 14.
8. Franz Schurmann, *The Logic of World Power* (New York: Pantheon, 1974), pp. xxvi–xxvii.
9. Noam Chomsky, *For Reasons of State* (New York: Random House), p. 43.
10. William Shawcross, *Side Show* (New York: Pocket Books, 1979).
11. Henry Kissinger, *White House Years* (Boston: Little, Brown, 1979), p. 240.
12. Shawcross, *Side Show,* p. 77.
13. John Lukacs, *A History of the Cold War* (New York: Doubleday, 1961), p. 143ff.
14. *Ibid.,* pp. 190–91.
15. For a review of the literature, see Daniel Bell, *The Coming of Post-Industrial Society* (New York: Basic Books, 1973), pp. 112–113, and especially footnote 91, which contains a short bibliography on this subject.
16. William Appleman Williams, *The Contours of American History* (Chicago: Quadrangle, 1966).
17. Harrington, *Vast Majority.*
18. Tony Thomas, "World Champions: A Survey of American Farming," *The Economist* (London), January 5, 1980.
19. Andre Fontaine, *History of the Cold War,* Vol. 2 (New York: Pantheon Books, 1968), p. 401.
20. Henry Kissinger, *White House Years,* p. 117.
21. Stanley Hoffmann, "Muscle and Brains," *Foreign Policy,* 37 (Winter 1979–1980): 9.
22. Arthur Schlesinger, Jr., *A Thousand Days* (Cambridge: Houghton Mifflin, 1963), Ch. 7.
23. Schlesinger, pp. 789ff and 792.
24. Harrington, *Vast Majority,* Ch. 4.
25. Henry Kissinger, *The Law of the Sea* (Washington, D.C.: State Dept., April 1976), p. 2.

26. Willy Brandt, et al., *North-South* (Cambridge: MIT Press, 1980).
27. Walt W. Rostow, *The Stages of Economic Growth* (Cambridge: Cambridge University Press, 1966).
28. Quoted in Harrington, *The Vast Majority,* p. 142.
29. *Ibid.,* p. 243.
30. Kissinger, *White House Years,* p. 749.
31. Michael Harrington, *Decade of Decision* (New York: Simon & Schuster, 1980), Ch. 1.
32. Council of Economic Advisers, *Report* (1979), p. 161.
33. "Machine Tools Lose an Export Edge," *Business Week,* February 5, 1979.
34. "Editorial," *Business Week,* September 17, 1979.
35. "The End of Industrial Society," *Business Week,* September 3, 1979.
36. "Myopia Incorporated," New York *Times,* November 25, 1979.
37. Theotonio Dos Santos, "La Crisis International del Capitalismo: Balance Y Perspectivas," *Nueva Sociedad* (Caracas), 44 (September-October 1979).
38. Miles Kahler, "Rumors of War," *Foreign Affairs.*
39. Samuel P. Huntington, "Trade, Technology, and Leverage: Economic Diplomacy," *Foreign Policy,* 32 (Fall 1978).
40. Henry Kissinger, *Wall Street Journal,* January 21, 1980.
41. Hoffmann, "Muscle and Brains," p. 5.

> If I am not for myself,
>   who will be for me?
> If I am only for myself,
>   then what am I for?
>
> Hillel

21

Cooperative public interactions dedicated to creating a prosperous, just, and civilized society have been impossible to achieve in most nations, modestly successful in many others, and less successful than they need to be in even the most successful of societies, such as our own. The seemingly simple goal of pooling community talents and resources to create a good society for all has eluded most nations throughout history. A variety of factors has been responsible, but the most frequent has been the seizure or dominance of power by a small segment of the population. These groups have used their position to enhance their own well-being at the expense of the larger population and have created a social, economic, and/or political philosophy to justify their actions.

Epilogue: On Sanity and Self-Government

These rationalizing philosophies, which are accepted by a large enough proportion of society to make them successful, have such familiar names as the divine right of kings, the gospel of wealth, capitalism, and communism. Authoritarian regimes often supplement their power by control of the police and the militia. But acceptance of the rationalizing ideology used by rulers and their agents—often the church, business leaders, intellectuals, and the media—to justify ignoring or suppressing the needs of large segments of the population has played as large a role in retarding the development of just societies as violence and its threat.

The struggle to achieve a just and prosperous society for all in America has been long, often violent, and incomplete. America has passed through various political periods. It has experienced several types of elite rule supported by rationalizing philosophies based in some way on the myth of laissez-faire capitalism. During the nineteenth century only a very small percentage of the total population (mostly white males from middle to upper income groups) had any political power. Women and minorities struggled far into the twentieth century to gain the franchise and some measure of political power. By the end of the 1960s, most Americans had formal political rights, but for many reasons they continue to play only a very modest role in the political process

The Washington Monument looms above the Capitol Building in this view of the nation's capital at night.

today. As earlier chapters documented, the public's limited political role—and the consequent power of elites—creates severe problems while retarding progress.

The direction our system will take in the future and its progress toward achieving a good society are not easy to predict, but a number of predictions can be made.

MORE GOVERNMENT

Our system of government will continue to increase in size and complexity, making it even more difficult to understand and control. It will grow because the population to be served, the demands placed on government, and expectations about the responsibilities of government and society will all increase. Modern technology, which spawns products and chemicals that have both the potential to improve and destroy life, and urbanization, which concentrates large populations in small geographic areas, create problems which produce greatly increased public demands for safeguards and services.

The public increasingly thinks of government as the natural problem-solving agent in our society. As populations increase and problems become more complex, only the government seems large enough and authoritative enough to even begin to tackle issues such as mass transit, pollution control, and literally hundreds of other problems. The number of groups locating or working in the national and state capitals to convince the government to provide new services or safeguards increases yearly. Twenty years ago few groups lobbied for environmental and consumer protection laws, antidiscrimination statutes for women and minorities, barrier-free environments for the handicapped, and dozens of other policies that increase the size, responsibilities, and authority of government.

Along with increases in demands have come increases in public expectations. A much larger proportion of our society now expects to be able to live comfortably, and standards of societal obligation to those in need have changed. Fewer Americans today than thirty years ago accept poverty, hunger, medical neglect, or lack of consideration for the needs of the aged as just; they now expect society to play a role in reversing and preventing such conditions. The aged increasingly do not expect to live out the last years of their lives in want, neglect, economic insecurity, or immobility. They expect to enjoy their latter years, and expect government to protect them from the ravages of inflation, medical bankruptcy, inadequate housing, and other threats to their happiness and security.

Similarly, the poor are less inclined to accept responsibility for their condition and increasingly expect the government to either eradicate conditions that cause poverty or adequately provide for its victims. The handicapped no longer expect to spend their years as shut-ins, outcasts, and dependents. As these and other groups articulate their views and needs and accomplish some part of their goals, the legitimacy of their demands is accepted by larger proportions of the population, establishing new expectations about government services and obligations. As other groups raise questions about product safety and serviceability, additional issues become the focus of articulation, investigation, and policy. Thus, government grows. To a large extent, then, big government is a consequence of our society's struggle to become more just and civilized.

CONTINUED SOCIAL INJUSTICE

Despite the increased size and obligations of government, many people will continue to be poorly served or neglected. As earlier chapters have attempted to make clear, the biases inherent in the political system give disproportionate power to a few, the institutional designs make effective responses to policy needs difficult or impossible, and the deficiencies of capitalism have always spawned poverty and economic insecurity for millions. These problems have not been overcome and certainly are not likely to be in the immediate future. They will continue because the public understands them so poorly. And they will persist because attention is directed away from such problems by an economic ideology which legitimizes disproportionate influence by some and fixes blame for social problems such as poverty and economic insecurity not on the system but on the victims of these problems.

The continuation of poverty, illiteracy, urban blight, congestion, pollution, and dozens of other social ills will continue to be the source of social tensions, and could easily lead to more social uprisings like the riots of the 1960s.

Our system of government will continue to increase in size and complexity, making it even more difficult to understand and control. It will grow because the population to be served, the demands placed on government, and expectations about the responsibilities of government and society will all increase.

PUBLIC ALARM ABOUT THE SIZE OF GOVERNMENT

Despite the fact that the public increasingly expects the government to meet its needs, there will continue to be concern, even protest, about the ever larger size, cost, complexity, authority, and intrusiveness of government. The reason is that larger and larger government *is* intrusive, expensive, and more difficult to control and influence. However, reduction in the scope of governmental activities is difficult because the public does not want reductions in their services or standard of living. Since all groups try to preserve the benefits they receive from government—and even try to get them expanded—and since our political system is more inclined to defend the status quo rather than to institute change, it is unlikely that the size of government will decrease.

A special report of the American Enterprise Institute's *Public Opinion* in January 1980, confirms this judgment. The Institute is a conservative "think tank," so if it were biased it would be in the direction of showing that government programs are unpopular. In fact, *Public Opinion* found that the people have a "love-hate" relationship to Washington. Some 84 percent of the respondents thought that the federal government was spending too much, and 76 percent believed that it had become too powerful. But 57 percent were *for* that very same government controlling wages and prices; 57 percent supported existing regulations or wanted to see them expanded; and the same percentage thought too little had been done to protect the nation's health.[1] These findings corroborate similar patterns dating as far back as the mid-1960s. Under these circumstances, it is clear that big government will be around for the foreseeable future.

Big government, however, is not necessarily good, as we saw clearly in the analysis of the urban crisis and the description of contemporary capitalism. Washington can make problems worse rather than better. That is obviously the case with policies which touch upon the cities.

As the economy and society become much more complex, as the political decisions require technical expertise, people feel that they really can't make a difference in their own country. Indeed, in a late twentieth-century nation, a monopoly over the means of technical information—computers, statistical definitions, the educated technocrats—can be as potentially undemocratic as monopoly control over prices and resources. And if the various proposals suggested in this book are to be adopted, one further reform is needed: public funds and structures to see to it that there is really effective grass-roots representation in the making of basic decisions.

When, for instance, a presidential commission reported on nuclear safety in the aftermath of the accident at Three Mile Island, most citizens had to take its findings as true. They did not have the ability to challenge the commissioners in this area of great technological complexity. Yet the President's panel did not contain a single opponent of nuclear power, even though there are a significant number of responsible scientists with this point of view. Shouldn't public funds have been available for anti-nuclear thinkers like Ralph Nader and Barry Commoner, so that they could produce an equally authoritative report? More broadly, if big government is going to stay because the people—even those critical of it in the abstract—want it to carry out a whole range of functions, then the democratization of political structures and information becomes a central priority for the future.

THE CLASH: CAPITALISM VS. DEMOCRACY

Americans tend to think that capitalism and democracy go hand in hand. In fact, they conflict in many ways; and this conflict will continue. Capitalism is an economic philosophy that gives great power, prestige, and independence to economic elites. The influence of economic elites has many significant impacts on the political, economic, and social systems. Some of these impacts, such as disproportionate control over public officials and major economic investment decisions, were discussed in earlier chapters.

Capitalism also affects the values of society, often in ways that conflict with democratic values. For example, capitalism puts great emphasis on accumulation of material wealth as the measure of a successful life. Democracy, on the other hand, is based on more humanistic values stressing equality, human dignity, liberty, and solidarity.[2] But the benefits of material wealth and the values that underlie justification for accumulation and consumption are more immediately attractive and more easily socialized than democratic values. The clash of values is generally resolved, therefore, on the side of materialism, making it considerably more influential in our lives than many of the values inherent in democratic theory.

Along with increases in demands have come increases in public expectations. A much larger proportion of our society now expects to be able to live comfortably.

The result is a kind of business civilization in which material accumulation and self-aggrandizement are primarily emphasized. This emphasis provides a justification for behavior that often robs citizens of human dignity, such as employer exploitation, suppression, and even abuse of workers. Throughout American history, employer abuse has created a subclass of Americans too poor and too dependent on the propertied class to have the luxury of a full, secure, and satisfying life. While the proportion of the American population in this category has declined during the twentieth century, America's 25 to 40 million poor and the millions of other Americans who live just above the poverty level are testimony enough that the problem continues in very severe form.

The capitalist emphasis on material accumulation often conflicts with the need for societal cooperation or solidarity—the need to consider the group impact of actions and the necessity of public co-operation to solve problems. Businesses that pollute the air or water without regard for the societal impact of their actions are an all-too-familiar example; so, too, are people who litter the streets. Special interests that struggle for policy preferences that aid them to the detriment of others—whether the interest involved is a pharmaceutical company, a labor union, or the AMA—are also obvious examples. The critical point is that in a truly democratic society there must be a sense of public solidarity, a sense that only through responsible personal cooperation can citizens hope to live in a truly civilized society.

Capitalism also creates conditions that conflict with the democratic concept of equality. Political and individual equality are threatened or even denied by class barriers. Capitalism creates differentials in economic rewards that are so large that social classes result. The data in Tables 7.3 and 7.4 reveal how severely income and wealth are maldistributed in America, and several chapters have documented the power of wealth and class in the political and economic systems.

As long as severe maldistribution of wealth is created by the economic system, and as long as wealth can be translated into power in the political system, equality and thus genuine democracy will remain a goal rather than a reality. In a true democracy the public must genuinely control their political leaders and participate in the formulation of public policies. Control of policy formulation must include public control over economic institutions, including major investment decisions, such as long-run energy plans, that affect the broader society.

Capitalism and democracy conflict in many ways; and this conflict will continue. Capitalism puts great emphasis on accumulation of material wealth as the measure of a successful life. Democracy, on the other hand, is based on more humanistic values stressing equality, human dignity, liberty and solidarity.

Thus, the cumulative impact of the biases and distortions created by capitalism is to undermine many of the fundamental tenets of democracy. Capitalism not only creates conditions that frequently suppress human dignity, equality, and solidarity, but it also retards democracy by being economically inefficient. Democracy can genuinely flourish only in a society that is sufficiently prosperous to provide a decent standard of living for all citizens.

To compensate for the flaws of capitalism, all Western democracies have assumed a larger role in the economic system since World War II. The increased public role has not replaced capitalism in any Western democracy, but nations have attempted in varying degrees to overcome the deficiencies of capitalism and make it more compatible with democratic principles. Although the public role has been expanded significantly in America, this nation has been much more resistant to economic innovations than most other Western democracies. The result can be clearly seen in the current economic malaise in the United States and in the slippage of America's economic position in the world. A critical challenge of the future, therefore, will be for America to be more pragmatic in its attempts to create an efficient, prosperous, publicly controlled, and socially responsible economy that will serve the needs of all citizens and allow democracy to flourish to its full potential.

The eighties, as we have seen, witness a double crisis of American society. The liberal economic orthodoxy which has guided both liberals and conservatives for a generation has collapsed, and a shift in American power has occurred. This country remains the mightiest nation in the world but has lost its total dominance of advanced Western capitalism. It must face turbulent times in the Third World as well as a hostile communist totalitarianism. In each case, this decade will be a time of redefinition and reorientation. The 1990s are likely to differ from 1980 as much as 1940 did from 1930.

In this context, American democracy is both a remarkable achievement and a problem. It is an achievement in that this society has preserved and expanded individual freedom while undergoing momentous transformations from being a small, thinly populated agrarian nation to an industrial—some would say post-industrial—superpower on a global scale. It is a problem in that our democracy is indeed unfinished. In the last fifty years workers, blacks, and women have, by means of democratic social movements, made significant strides forward. But they and those who remain behind in the slums, ghettos, and impoverished rural areas have discovered that economic and social power wields autocratic power within this country.

To solve the structural challenges of the economy and world in a progressive way will require the involvement of millions of Americans in shaping new departures. Can a computerized and interdependent globe be mastered by free men and women in a democratic fashion? That is the question on the agenda of our unfinished democracy in the 1980s.

Footnotes

1. *Public Opinion,* AEI, Washington, D.C. Dec.-Jan. 1980, pp. 20–21.
2. For an excellent discussion of democratic values, see Norman Furniss and Timothy Tilton, *The Case For The Welfare State* (Bloomington, Indiana: Indiana University Press, 1979), pp. 28–39.

> *"I'd rather vote for what I want and not get it than vote for what I don't want and get it."*
>
> Eugene V. Debs

The 1980 presidential election reflected the public's continuing displeasure with the nation's political leaders and the people's concern over the nation's domestic and international problems. The public's evaluation of President Carter's performance was so low, in fact, that a major member of his own party, Senator Edward Kennedy, was encouraged to run against him for the Democratic nomination. Carter's unpopularity with the electorate stemmed from his failure to alleviate the economic problems he promised to redress in the 1976 election and from his turnaround on many of his 1976 campaign pledges. In 1976 Carter attacked President Ford for allowing unemployment and inflation to get out of hand. He also accused Ford of allowing unemployment to rise as a method of fighting inflation. Instead of resolving these problems, Carter allowed both to worsen.

Postscript

The 1980 Presidential Campaign and Election: A Swing to the Right

In fact, Carter, who sounded like a populist in 1976, turned out to be the most conservative Democratic President since Grover Cleveland. Many of those who suffered the most under Carter's economic policies were blue-collar workers and minorities, the backbone of the Democratic party. Carter's attempts to fight inflation with high interest rates and tight money cost 1.8 million workers their jobs, resulting in an unemployment rate of 7.8 percent in August 1980. Double-digit inflation eroded income. "At the beginning of the 1980's real discretionary income per worker had declined 9 percent since 1970 and 18 percent since 1973."[1]

Carter also backed away from his campaign support for tax reform, national health insurance, a genuine full-employment policy, and low-cost energy. His foreign policy impressed much of the public and many opinion leaders as being erratic and amateurish. Many, in fact, thought ineptness and amateurism good descriptions of Carter's overall performance. As late in the campaign as July, only 20 percent of the public approved of the way he was doing his job as President.[2]

THE DEMOCRATIC PRIMARIES AND THE CONVENTION

Within the Democratic party, dissatisfaction with Carter was so intense, especially among liberals, that Senator Edward Kennedy decided to run for the party nomination. In the fall of 1979 the polls showed Kennedy with a 30-point lead over Carter. But then an event occurred that eroded much of Kennedy's support. A few hundred militant students (perhaps 300) seized the American embassy in Iran, holding the embassy employees as hostages. The militants demanded the return of the deposed Shah, and much of the nation's wealth that had been secreted out of the nation by the Shah, in return for the embassy employees.

The public responded by rallying around the President. The embassy seizure began to dominate the news, relegating opposition political campaigns to the back pages. While Kennedy struggled to keep his campaign afloat, a second international crisis occurred when the Russians invaded their neighboring nation of Afghanistan. This second crisis involved much more than just the nation's prestige being bruised by militant students. The invasion of Afghanistan raised the very serious issue of Russian efforts to dominate by military aggression all the nations that surround it, including the oil-rich Middle East. President Carter reacted by issuing a sharp verbal attack, and again the people rallied around their President. Kennedy's lead in the polls evaporated.

As the primaries began in early 1980, Carter and Kennedy were running close in the polls. Carter further used the nation's international problems to his advantage. He took the position that he would not debate Kennedy or any other candidate while the hostages were being held. This denied Kennedy the opportunity to debate issues such as inflation, unemployment, and health care with the President. Carter's people also raised the issue of Chappaquiddick, suggesting that Kennedy lacked the moral character necessary for the Presidency. Carter also kept many Democratic leaders in control by using his influence over federal programs and grants to reward supporters and punish defectors.

The result was that while Kennedy and Carter continued to run fairly close in the polls, Carter was the top vote-getter in the thirty-four presidential primaries. Carter received about 10 million votes to Kennedy's 7.3 million, giving him 1,971 delegates (59 percent) out of a total of 3,311. Even though Carter had more than the required simple majority before the convention began, Kennedy refused to bow out of the race.

Kennedy hoped that Carter's public support would drop so low that he would decide not to continue his run for reelection. Kennedy also hoped that by the time of the convention in August many delegates would decide that Carter could not win reelection and would shift their allegiance to him. To clear the way for Carter delegates to vote for Kennedy, a party rule binding

Ronald Reagan won the 1980 presidential election by a wide electoral margin.

Reagan/Bush Headquarters

delegates to vote on the first ballot for the candidate they represented would have had to be overturned. Kennedy's supporters tried to get the convention to overturn the rule. When this move failed, Kennedy announced his withdrawal from the race. Carter, then, officially won the nomination on the first ballot.

While Kennedy failed to win the nomination, he and his supporters did manage to influence the party platform. The Kennedy supporters centered most of this attention on Carter's economic priorities. They emphasized that Carter's decision to relegate unemployment to a secondary role behind the fight against inflation constituted a break with decades of Democratic tradition. Kennedy also criticized Carter's refusal to support national health insurance, his decision not to use wage-and-price controls, and his lack of commitment to a genuine full-employment policy. In response, the Platform Committee voted in favor of a clause stating that the President should never take actions to increase unemployment, and it voted to support a Kennedy proposal to spend an additional $12 billion on job programs.

THE REPUBLICAN PRIMARIES AND THE CONVENTION

The Republican primaries were not as closely contested as the Democratic primaries. While six major candidates announced their candidacy and launched campaigns, the race rather quickly boiled down to a contest between former California Governor Ronald Reagan, former CIA Director George Bush, and Illinois Congressman John Anderson. Reagan's supporters controlled the party in most states, giving him an early and decisive edge. Reagan received 7.6 million votes (60 percent) in the primaries, to 3 million for Bush, his closest competitor. Out of a total of 1,994 Republican delegates, Reagan won 1,580 (79 percent).

Reagan's dominance of the Republican party resulted from its recent misfortunes. The Watergate scandal and Ford's defeat in the 1976 election had greatly reduced its popularity and support. As Burnham notes, ''One of the regular dynamics of politics seems to be that as a party shrinks, the influence of its hard-core elements grow within it. The hard-core Republicans are very, very conservative.''[3] Thus, the hard-core representatives in the party had the power to win the nomination for Reagan, the most conservative of the major Republican candidates.

Immediately upon winning the nomination, Reagan proved that he understood that to win the election he needed to broaden his appeal. To do so he decided to choose a vice-presidential running mate from the center of his party, rather than from the far right. Initially Reagan tried to entice Ford into accepting the vice-presidential position, but Ford wanted Reagan to guarantee him a major role in the administration by turning over specified important duties to him. Ford's demands were more than Reagan could agree to, so he turned to George Bush, a moderate and the second most popular vote-getter in the Republican primaries. The choice of Bush gave Reagan a broader base of support in the Republican party and broadened his public appeal.

THE ANDERSON CAMPAIGN

Independent candidate
John Anderson.

One of the most interesting events in the 1980 campaign was the independent (non-party) candidacy of John Anderson, a member of the House from Illinois. Anderson, a moderate-to-liberal Republican, originally tried to win the Republican nomination. After failing there, he decided to run as an independent. Anderson's reasons for staying in the campaign were based on his belief that neither Reagan nor Carter was presidential material and on evidence that a significant percentage of the voters were not pleased with a choice between them. Several major polls during the spring and summer of 1980 showed that about half of the public was either "somewhat unsatisfied" or "very unsatisfied" with a choice between Reagan and Carter.[4] It was often said that the major party contest was a race between a second-rate actor and a third-rate President. At one point Anderson hinted to the press that he would withdraw from the contest if Kennedy won the Democratic nomination; but when Kennedy's efforts failed, Anderson stayed in the race.

Bruce Hoertel/Camera 5

Anderson's positions on the issues were quite moderate. He favored a gradual reduction in federal spending, new job training programs, and increased incentives for businesses to hire the unemployed. He rejected the idea that a tax cut was necessary, arguing that it would be inflationary. His most controversial proposal was for a 50¢ tax on each gallon of gasoline. The tax, Anderson argued, would force conservation without being inflationary, because the revenues could be used to pay part of the cost of Social Security. In foreign affairs, Anderson found both Carter and Reagan to be overly hawkish. He favored Salt II, and proposed that negotiations on Salt III begin. He favored more cooperation with our allies, and nuclear parity, rather than superiority, with the Russians.

Anderson and his supporters had to struggle mightly just to get him on the ballot in many states, but eventually he managed to win a position on the ballot in every state. He also won a ruling from the Federal Election Commission that his independent candidacy qualified him to receive public financing.

Some of Anderson's financial problems reflected the hardships placed on third-party candidates by the Federal Election Campaign Act of 1974 (See Chapter 6). The act provides matching funds for any qualifying candidate during the primaries (with an upper limit of $14.7 million in expenditures in 1980). During the general election, however, the law favors major party candidates. In 1980 both Carter and Reagan opted for public financing and accepted $29.4 million each to run their general election campaigns. A third-party candidate, however, does not receive a grant. Instead, a third-party candidate who appears on the ballot in at least 10 states and draws at least 5 percent of the national popular vote can be reimbursed for part of his/her election expenses *after* the November election. Thus, Anderson had to attempt to finance his campaign with the hope of obtaining federal funds after the election. Financially, then, he was at a severe disadvantage.

The polls never showed major support for Anderson. During the summer and fall of 1980, 11 to 14 percent of the voters expressed a preference for him.

Anderson's support came mostly from moderates and liberals in both of the parties. He had almost no support in the South. For the most part, Anderson seemed to draw about as many voters away from Carter as Reagan. In two key states, however, Anderson drew important support away from each candidate. In Illinois, Anderson drew significant support from moderate Republicans, and in New York he won the endorsement of the Liberal party, reducing Carter's strength there.

Given the significant percentage of the public expressing reservations about both Carter and Reagan, Anderson's failure to win more than modest support might seem surprising. Anderson's lack of broader support seemed to result from the feeling on the part of many liberals and moderates that he did not significantly differ from the major candidates on the issues, from his inability to raise sufficient funds to finance a more vigorous campaign, and from a feeling on the part of many voters that a vote for Anderson would be wasted. Many voters also seemed to have a psychological block toward support for a third party. Such parties are so rare in our electoral system that many voters felt that to support one would be a rather radical act. The other third-party candidates, such as Ed Clark of the Libertarian party and Barry Commoner of the Citizen's party, encountered similar problems.

THE CANDIDATES, THE ISSUES, AND CAMPAIGN STRATEGIES

By election time, all three candidates had taken basically conservative to moderate positions on the issues. All the candidates expected the government to continue to play a large and important role in society, and each intended to use government power to solve social problems. Similarly, each expected the government to asisst business in making profits. Reagan was considerably more conservative than Carter or Anderson, but as the election neared he moderated many of his stands.

Reagan

Reagan began his campaign for the Republican nomination as the darling of the party's right wing. On domestic policy he supported the controversial Kemp-Roth proposal to slash federal taxes by 30 percent over a three-year period. He proposed reducing business taxes by accelerating the depreciation rate for plant and equipment. He also promised to cut federal spending, balance the budget, and reduce business regulation. Reagan argued that a drastic reduction in taxes and spending would promote economic growth, thereby basically solving the nation's unemployment problems.

Reagan supported the adoption of three constitutional amendments: (1) to ban abortions; (2) to allow prayers in the public schools; and (3) to require a balanced budget. While claiming support for women's rights, he opposed the ratification of the Equal Rights Amendment. He also favored the repeal of all gun registration laws and the 55 mile-an-hour speed limit. He opposed national health insurance, a guaranteed income for the poor, most federal regulation of education, and forced busing of school children.

On energy, Reagan believed that the oil companies could be trusted to solve the problem if they were given enough profits. To aid the oil companies, he supported decontroling the price of oil and gas at the wellhead and repealing the windfall profits tax on new oil and hard-to-get oil. He also proposed the repeal of "overly stringent" sections of the Clean Air Act and advocated greater reliance on nuclear power.

Reagan's foreign policy proposals were decidedly hawkish. He argued that America had become weak and indecisive in foreign affairs and that America had fallen behind the Russians militarily. He proposed a significant increase in military spending to achieve "military superiority" over the Russians. He voiced disapproval of both the Salt I and Salt II treaties, arguing that both involved too many concessions and too little verification of Russia's arsenal. He argued for a program of foreign aid to nations that support America, without regard for their record on human rights.

As the campaign progressed, Reagan decided that to win he had to broaden his appeal to moderates in both parties, convince the public that he was not a "mad bomber" who would start World War III, and convince the public that he understood the issues. To broaden his appeal, he recanted a proposal to make the Social Security program voluntary, a suggestion that had frightened many older persons. He recanted his long-held position that unemployment is necessary to control infaltion and that unemployment compensation is nothing more than a paid vacation. He campaigned heavily in areas with high unemployment, and rescinded his opposition to aid for Chrysler Corporation. He promised to seek only a 2 percent reduction in federal spending, rather than the large reductions he had called for earlier. Campaigning in New York, he rescinded his earlier opposition to aid for that city.

On foreign policy, he emphasized his interest in peace and openly confronted the issue of his militancy by telling audiences that he was not "triggerhappy." He dropped his proposal to blockade Cuba in retaliation for Russia's invasion of Afghanistan, stopped calling for the repeal of the Panama Canal Treaties, and reversed his call for an end to our recognition of China in favor of Taiwan. Finally, he argued that Carter's weak and inconsistent policies put the nation in more danger than his "peace through strength" approach.

Questions about Reagan's understanding of the issues and his temperance were raised because he frequently made statements that were factually incorrect or inflammatory. He frequently cited incorrect program and budget figures, often revealing an ignorance of legislation and government policies. He also created controversies by doubting the theory of evolution, by calling the Vietnam War an "act of moral courage," by calling the Russians monsters, and by accusing Carter of being a racist for giving a speech in a Southern city with a Klu Klux Klan history.

Reagan's corrective strategies revealed that he understood that the American people expect a President to be well-informed and reasoned in his behavior. In fact, during the last two months of the campaign his aides attempted to keep Reagan away from the press so that he could not make hasty, off-the-cuff comments that would cause new controversies. His aides also prepared small cue cards on various subjects for him, hoping that it would reduce the number of factual errors.

His attempts to broaden his appeal revealed that he also understood that a candidate on the far right could not appeal to enough voters to win the Presidency. Since only about 22 percent of the public identified with the Republican party in 1980, any Republican candidate would have to appeal to a very broad electorate, including millions of people who normally vote Democratic. Barry Goldwater's 1964 campaign had shown that there is no conservative majority just waiting for a chance to elect a candidate who will turn the clock backwards. As noted in Chapter 2, even citizens who identify themselves as conservatives tend to expect the government to play a substantial role in solving and preventing social problems.

Reagan's strategy, then, was to convince a majority of the public that his policies would benefit all Americans and that he was a reasoned and strong leader running against a weak and inept incumbent.

Carter

Carter's approach to the issues and to his opponents was defensive. Arguing that his approach to the nation's economic problems had been basically correct, he claimed that recovery had been slow because of the severity of the problems he had inherited from the Nixon and Ford administrations. He also argued that Anderson was not a viable candidate and implied that Reagan was incompetent and dangerous. Carter's campaign aides relished pointing out Reagan's errors and rapidly changing policy shifts; they predicted that a Reagan administration would divide the nation at home and provoke war abroad.

Carter maintained that progress was being made in controlling inflation, arguing that continued fiscal prudence would bring it under control. He saw no need for a constitutional amendment requiring a balanced budget. Unemployment, Carter said, would be alleviated by a modest tax cut, countercyclical and antirecessionary fiscal policies, increased spending for job training, and a new tax relief program for business.

Although he opposed constitutional amendments prohibiting abortions and allowing prayers in public schools, he supported the ratification of the Equal Rights Amendment. He defended existing grants to education and supported busing as a last resort to achieve racial desegregation. He felt that the nation could not currently afford national health insurance but believed that the welfare system should be reformed to provide a guaranteed floor of income for the nation's poorest families.

President Jimmy Carter.

Doug Bruce/Camera 5

On energy, Carter supported a continued strategy of exploration, development of synthetic fuels, coal production, and conservation. He also favored a 10¢-a-gallon increase in gasoline taxes to encourage more conservation. Nuclear energy plants would be retired as alternative fuels become available.

Carter favored an increase of at least 4 percent a year in military spending and development of the MX missile, the Trident submarine, and the cruise missile. But since he believed that attempts to achieve a clear superiority in military strength over the Russians would only set off another arms race, he thought a more sensible strategy was to maintain nuclear equivalency. He also proposed Salt II as a method of "restraining the Russians."

Carter further promised to enhance the nation's international position by strengthening ties with Western Europe and Japan. He argued that the Camp David accord was an excellent step toward peace in the Middle East, and he promised to use military force to protect the Persian Gulf nations from outside aggression. He defended the grain embargo against the Soviet Union and his Human Rights policy as being in the best long-term interests of the nation.

THE FINAL THREE WEEKS

In late October, Carter and Reagan finally agreed to a debate. Carter had earlier refused to debate because the sponsors (The League of Women Voters) had insisted that Anderson had to be included, and Carter had maintained that this format pitted him against two Republicans. As the campaign neared its end, however, the League agreed to exclude Anderson, and the other two candidates met. Carter hammered at Reagan's hawkish foreign policy and attacked his domestic proposals. Reagan emphasized Carter's failed economic policies, his indecisive foreign policy, and sought again to assure the public that he was interested in world peace. While neither candidate made any serious blunders during the debate, Reagan was more relaxed and confident, and clearly came across better than Carter did. Most importantly, however, Reagan managed to dispel much of his image as a rash and war-prone candidate. His edge in the debate clearly boosted his campaign.

Events in Iran also worked to Reagan's advantage. Losing in a war with Iraq, the Iranian leaders finally concluded that the hostage issue should be resolved. Iran hoped to free its assets in America and gain much-needed military equipment in return for the hostages. Some Iranian leaders sparked rumors that the release was imminent, raising public hopes that the hostages would be home before the election. Instead, the issue peaked and fizzled during the last two weeks of the campaign, and by election day it was still dragging on. Carter's failure to resolve the issue before the election clearly cost him voter support. The inconclusive nature of the hostage crisis simply struck much of the public as reflecting a pattern of unsuccessful and failed foreign policy during the Carter administration.

Electoral Vote by States: The 1980 Presidential Election

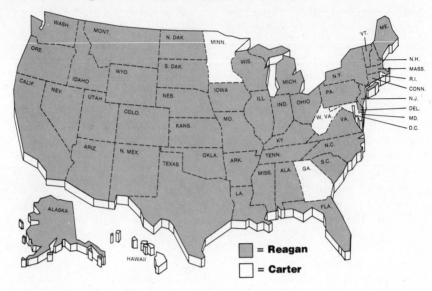

= Reagan
= Carter

THE ELECTION

The election proved to be a disaster for both President Carter and the Democratic party. Despite the closeness of the race in the polls, Reagan won a decisive electoral victory. Carter became the first incumbent Democratic president in eighty years to be denied a second term. Millions of voters who had been undecided until the last days and hours of the campaign cast their votes for Reagan, and often also voted for other Republican candidates. Reagan won 489 Electoral College votes, Carter won only 49 votes, and Anderson won none. Reagan won in every region of the country, including the once solidly Democratic South. He won by one of the largest electoral margins in American history.

Reagan's victory resulted from many factors, but two were particularly important. The first, quite simply, was Carter's dismal economic and foreign policy record. Inflation, unemployment, and the loss of American prestige abroad seriously concerned the public. By the summer of 1980, polls showed that only a small percentage of the American people believed that Carter had been a good President. The public clearly wanted a change. The second factor was Reagan's decision to moderate and broaden his appeal. By election day, Reagan had managed to convince a majority of the voters that he was a safe and viable alternative to Carter. He had convinced the public that he was neither an extremist nor a man who would precipitously get the country into a war.

As part of his winning coalition, Reagan was able to convince millions of white blue-collar and lower-middle-income workers that he would represent them better than Carter had. Reagan had campaigned hard against Carter in the industrial North, hard-hit by a high unemployment rate. These traditionally Democratic voters will, of course, stick with the Republican party in the future only if Reagan is able to significantly improve the economy. If Reagan fails to bring unemployment and inflation down substantially, the Democratic party will have an excellent chance of attracting these workers back to the Democratic party in 1984. Thus, it is not yet clear whether a genuine relignment of voters has taken place or whether many voters have simply opted to deviate from their normal position in this election.

Reagan's victory also helped many Republican candidates win against major Democratic opponents. Eight incumbent Democratic senators, including some of the party's most powerful, were defeated. In addition, five Republican senatorial candidates won open seats. This produced a Republican majority in the Senate (fifty-two Republicans, forty-seven Democrats, and one independent, Harry F. Byrd of Virginia), allowing the Republican party to take over the committee chairs and the leadership positions. The House remained in Democratic control, but its membership became more conservative as the Republicans gained thirty-three seats. For the first time since 1916, the House and Senate came under the control of different parties. Wealthy, right-wing groups such as the Moral Majority and the National Conservative Political Action Committee contributed to the defeat of many incumbent Democrats in the Senate and House. In well-planned campaigns, these groups raised and spent enormous sums of money, managing to outspend targeted incumbents by margins of as much as three to one.

The nation, then, had clearly made its decision. It had opted for a more conservative approach to domestic issues and a more aggressive stance in foreign policy. The Democratic party was left to regroup and rebuild for the future. A majority of the 52 percent of the eligible voters who turned out (the lowest in thirty-two years) clearly felt that the Democratic party was not offering them a viable choice. The New Deal consensus, especially on economic policy, seemed to be breaking up. The remaining question is how extensive and how permanent the shifts in voting coalitions will be.

Footnotes

1. Walter Dean Burnham, "American Politics in the 1980s," *Dissent* (Spring 1980), p. 155.
2. *Congressional Quarterly,* September 13, 1980, p. 2704.
3. Burnham, "American Politics in the 1980s," p. 151.
4. *Congressional Quarterly,* June 24, 1980, p. 1114.

THE CONSTITUTION OF THE UNITED STATES OF AMERICA

We the People of the United States, in Order to form a more perfect Union, establish justice, insure domestic Tranquility, provide for the common defence, promote the general Welfare, and secure the Blessings of Liberty to ourselves and our Posterity, do ordain and establish this Constitution for the United States of America.

ARTICLE 1

Section 1.

All legislative Powers herein granted shall be vested in a Congress of the United States, which shall consist of a Senate and House of Representatives.

Section 2.

The House of Representatives shall be composed of Members chosen every second Year by the People of the several States, and the Electors in each State shall have the Qualifications requisite for Electors of the most numerous Branch of the State Legislature.

No Person shall be a Representative who shall not have attained to the Age of twenty five Years, and been seven Years a Citizen of the United States, and who shall not, when elected, be an Inhabitant of that State in which he shall be chosen.

Representatives and direct Taxes shall be apportioned among the several States which may be included within this Union, according to their respective Numbers, which shall be determined by adding to the whole Number of free Persons, including those bound to Service for a Term of Years, and excluding Indians not taxed, three fifths of all other Persons.[1] The actual Enumeration shall be made within three years after the first Meeting of the Congress of the United States, and within every subsequent Term of ten Years, in such Manner as they shall by Law direct. The Number of Representatives shall not exceed one for every thirty Thousand, but each State shall have at Least one Representative; and until such enumeration shall be made, the State of New Hampshire shall be entitled to chuse three, Massachusetts eight, Rhode-Island and Providence Plantations one, Connecticut five, New-York six, New Jersey four, Pennsylvania eight, Delaware one, Maryland six, Virginia ten, North Carolina five, South Carolina five, and Georgia three.

When vacancies happen in the Representation from any State, the Executive Authority thereof shall issue Writs of Election to fill such Vacancies.

The House of Representatives shall chuse their Speaker and other Officers; and shall have the sole Power of Impeachment.

Section 3.

The Senate of the United States shall be composed of two Senators from each State, chosen by the Legislature thereof, for six Years; and each Senator shall have one Vote.

Immediately after they shall be assembled in Consequence of the first Election, they shall be divided as equally as may be into three Classes. The Seats of the Senators of the first Class shall be vacated at the Expiration of the second Year, of the second Class at the Expiration of the fourth Year, and of the third Class at the Expiration of the Sixth Year, so that one third may be chosen every second Year; and if Vacancies happen by Resignation, or otherwise, during the Recess of the Legislature of any State, the Executive thereof may make temporary Appointments until the next Meeting of the Legislature, which shall then fill such Vacancies.[2]

No Person shall be a Senator who shall not have attained to the Age of thirty Years, and been nine Years a Citizen of the United States, and who shall not, when elected, be an Inhabitant of that State for which he shall be chosen.

The Vice President of the United States shall be President of the Senate, but shall have no Vote, unless they be equally divided.

The Senate shall chuse their other Officers, and also a President pro tempore, in the Absence of the Vice President, or when he shall exercise the Office of President of the United States.

The Senate shall have the sole Power to try all impeachments. When sitting for that Purpose, they shall be on Oath or Affirmation. When the President of the United States is tried the Chief Justice shall preside: And no Person shall be convicted without the Concurrence of two thirds of the Members present.

Judgment in Cases of Impeachment shall not extend further than to removal from Office, and disqualification to hold and enjoy any Office of honor, Trust or Profit under the United States: but the Party convicted shall nevertheless be liable and subject to Indictment, Trial, Judgment and Punishment, according to Law.

Section 4.

The Times, Places and Manner of holding Elections for Senators and Representatives, shall be prescribed in each State by the Legislature thereof; but the Congress may at any time by Law make or alter such Regulations, except as to the Places of chusing Senators.

The Congress shall assemble at least once in every Year, and such Meeting shall be on the first Monday in December, unless they shall by Law appoint a different Day.[3]

Section 5.

Each House shall be the Judge of the Elections, Returns and Qualifications of its own Members, and a Majority of each shall constitute a Quorum to do Business; but a smaller Number may adjourn from day to day, and may be authorized to compel the Attendance of absent Members, in such Manner, and under such Penalties as each House may provide.

Each House may determine the Rules of its Proceedings, punish its Members for disorderly Behaviour, and, with the Concurrence of two thirds, expel a Member.

Each House shall keep a Journal of its Proceedings, and from time to time publish the same, excepting such Parts as may in their Judgment require Secrecy; and the Yeas and Nays of the Members of either House on any question shall, at the Desire of one fifth of those Present, be entered on the Journal.

Neither House, during the Session of Congress, shall, without the Consent of the other, adjourn for more than three days, nor to any other Place than that in which the two Houses shall be sitting.

Section 6.

The Senators and Representatives shall receive a Compensation for their Services, to be ascertained by Law, and paid out of the Treasury of the United States. They shall in all Cases, except Treason, Felony and Breach of the Peace, be privileged from Arrest during their Attendance at the Session of their respective Houses, and in going to and returning from the same; and for any Speech or Debate in either House, they shall not be questioned in any other Place.

No Senator or Representative shall, during the Time for which he was elected, be appointed to any civil Office under the Authority of the United States, which shall have been created, or the Emoluments whereof shall have been encreased during such time; and no Person holding any Office under the United States, shall be a Member of either House during his Continuance in Office.

Section 7.

All Bills for raising Revenue shall originate in the House of Representatives; but the Senate may propose or concur with Amendments as on other Bills.

Every Bill which shall have passed the House of Representatives and

---

[1] "Other Persons" being black slaves. Modified by Amendment XIV, Section 2.
[2] Provisions changed by Amendment XVII.

[3] Provision changed by Amendment XX, Section 2.

the Senate, shall, before it become a Law, be presented to the President of the United States; If he approve he shall sign it, but if not he shall return it, with his Objections to that House in which it shall have originated, who shall enter the Objections at large on their Journal, and proceed to reconsider it. If after such Reconsideration two thirds of that House shall agree to pass the Bill, it shall be sent, together with the Objections, to the other House, by which it shall likewise to be reconsidered, and if approved by two thirds of that House, it shall become a Law. But in all such Cases the Votes of both Houses shall be determined by yeas and Nays, and the Names of the Persons voting for and against the Bill shall be entered on the Journal of each House respectively. If any Bill shall not be returned by the President within ten Days (Sundays excepted) after it shall have been presented to him, the Same shall be a Law, in like Manner as if he had signed it, unless the Congress by their Adjournment prevent its Return, in which Case it shall not be a Law.

Every Order, Resolution, or Vote to which the Concurrence of the Senate and House of Representatives may be necessary (except on a question of Adjournment) shall be presented to the President of the United States; and before the Same shall take Effect, shall be approved by him, or being disapproved by him, shall be repassed by two thirds of the Senate and House of Representatives, according to the Rules and Limitations prescribed in the Case of a Bill.

Section 8.

The Congress shall have Power To lay and collect Taxes, Duties, Imposts and Excises, to pay the Debts and provide for the common Defence and general Welfare of the United States; but all Duties, Imposts and Excises shall be uniform throughout the United States;

To borrow Money on the credit of the United States;

To regulate Commerce with foreign Nations, and among the several States, and with the Indian Tribes;

To establish an uniform Rule of Naturalization, and uniform Laws on the subject of Bankruptcies throughout the United States;

To coin Money, regulate the Value thereof, and of foreign Coin, and fix the Standard of Weights and Measures;

To provide for the Punishment of counterfeiting the Securities and current Coin of the United States;

To establish Post Offices and post Roads;

To promote the Progress of Science and useful Arts, by securing for limited Times to Authors and Inventors the exclusive Right to their respective Writings and Discoveries;

To constitute Tribunals inferior to the supreme Court;

To define and punish Piracies and Felonies committed on the high Seas, and Offences against the Law of Nations;

To declare War, grant Letters of Marque and Reprisal, and make Rules concerning Captures on Land and Water;

To raise and support Armies, but no Appropriation of Money to that Use shall be for a longer Term than two Years;

To provide and maintain a Navy;

To make Rules for the Government and Regulation of the land and naval Forces;

To provide for calling forth the Militia to execute the Laws of the Union, suppress Insurrections and repel Invasions;

To provide for organizing, arming, and disciplining, the Militia, and for governing such Part of them as may be employed in the Service of the United States, reserving to the States respectively, the Appointment of the Officers, and the Authority of training the Militia according to the discipline prescribed by Congress;

To exercise exclusive Legislation in all Cases whatsoever, over such District (not exceeding ten Miles square) as may, by Cession of particular States, and the Acceptance of Congress, become the Seat of the Government of the United States, and to exercise like Authority over all Places purchased by the Consent of the Legislature of the State in which the Same shall be, for the Erection of Forts, Magazines, Arsenals, dock-Yards, and other needful Buildings;—And

To make all Laws which shall be necessary and proper for carrying into Execution the foregoing Powers, and all other Powers vested by this Constitution in the Government of the United States, or in any Department or Officer thereof.

Section 9.

The Migration or Importation of such Persons as any of the States now existing shall think proper to admit, shall not be prohibited by the Congress prior to the Year one thousand eight hundred and eight, but a Tax, or duty may be imposed on such Importation, not exceeding ten dollars for each Person.

The Privilege of the Writ of Habeas Corpus shall not be suspended, unless when in Cases of Rebellion or Invasion the public Safety may require it.

No Bill of Attainder or ex post facto Law shall be passed.

No Capitation, or other direct, Tax shall be laid, unless in Proportion to the Census or Enumeration herein before directed to be taken.

No Tax or Duty shall be laid on Articles exported from any State.

No Preference shall be given by any Regulation of Commerce or Revenue to the Ports of one State over those of another; nor shall Vessels bound to, or from, one State, be obliged to enter, clear, or pay Duties in another.

No Money shall be drawn from the Treasury, but in Consequence of Appropriations made by Law; and a regular Statement and Account of the Receipts and Expenditures of all public Money shall be published from time to time.

No Title of Nobility shall be granted by the United States: And no Person holding any Office of Profit or Trust under them, shall, without the Consent of the Congress, accept of any present, Emolument, Office, or Title, of any kind whatever, from any King, Prince, or foreign State.

Section 10.

No State shall enter into any Treaty, Alliance, or Confederation; grant Letters of Marque and Reprisal; coin Money; emit Bills of Credit; make any Thing but gold and silver Coin a Tender in Payment of Debts; pass any Bill of Attainder, ex post facto Law, or Law impairing the Obligation of Contracts, or grant any Title of Nobility.

No State shall, without the Consent of the Congress, lay any Imposts or Duties on Imports or Exports, except what may be absolutely necessary for executing its inspection Laws: and the net Produce of all Duties and Imposts, laid by any State on Imports or Exports, shall be for the Use of the Treasury of the United States; and all such Laws shall be subject to the Revision and Controul of the Congress.

No State shall, without the Consent of Congress, lay any Duty of Tonnage, keep Troops, or Ships of War in time of Peace, enter into any Agreement or Compact with another State, or with a foreign Power, or engage in War, unless actually invaded, or in such imminent Danger as will not admit of delay.

ARTICLE II

Section 1.

The executive Power shall be vested in a President of the United States of America. He shall hold his Office during the Term of four Years, and, together with the Vice President, chosen for the same Term, be elected, as follows:

Each State shall appoint, in such Manner as the Legislature thereof may direct, a Number of Electors, equal to the whole Number of Senators and Representatives to which the State may be entitled in Congress: but no Senator or Representative, or Person holding an Office of Trust or Profit under the United States, shall be appointed an Elector.

The Electors shall meet in their respective States, and vote by Ballot for two Persons, of whom one at least shall not be an Inhabitant of the same State with themselves. And they shall make a List of all the Persons voted for, and of the Number of Votes for each; which List they shall sign and certify, and transmit sealed to the Seat of the

Government of the United States, directed to the President of the Senate. The President of the Senate shall, in the Presence of the Senate and House of Representatives, open all the Certificates, and the Votes shall then be counted. The Person having the greatest Number of Votes shall be the President, if such Number be a Majority of the whole Number of Electors appointed; and if there be more than one who have such Majority, and have an equal Number of Votes, then the House of Representatives shall immediately chuse by Ballot one of them for President; and if no Person have a Majority, then from the five highest on the List the said House shall in like Manner chuse the President. But in chusing the President, the Votes shall be taken by States, the Representation from each State having one Vote; A quorum for this Purpose shall consist of a Member or Members from two thirds of the States, and a Majority of all the States shall be necessary to a Choice. In every Case, after the Choice of the President, the Person having the greatest Number of Votes of the Electors shall be the Vice President. But if there should remain two or more who have equal Votes, the Senate shall chuse from them by Ballot the Vice President.[4]

The Congress may determine the Time of chusing the Electors, and the Day on which they shall give their Votes; which Day shall be the same throughout the United States.

No Person except a natural born Citizen, or a Citizen of the United States, at the time of the Adoption of this Constitution, shall be eligible to the Office of President; neither shall any Person be eligible to that Office who shall not have attained to the Age of thirty five Years, and been fourteen Years a Resident within the United States.

In Case of the Removal of the President from Office, or of his Death, Resignation, or Inability to discharge the Powers and Duties of the said Office, the Same shall devolve on the Vice President, and the Congress may by Law provide for the Case of Removal, Death, Resignation or Inability, both of the President and Vice President, declaring what Officer shall then act as President, and such Officer shall act accordingly, until the Disability be removed, or a President shall be elected.

The President shall, at stated Times, receive for his Services, a Compensation, which shall neither be encreased nor diminished during the Period for which he shall have been elected, and he shall not receive within that Period any other Emolument from the United States, or any of them.

Before he enter on the Execution of his Office, he shall take the following Oath or Affirmation:—"I do solemnly swear (or affirm) that I will faithfully execute the Office of President of the United States, and will to the best of my Ability, preserve, protect and defend the Constitution of the United States."

Section 2.

The President shall be Commander in Chief of the Army and Navy of the United States, and of the Militia of the several States, when called into the actual Service of the United States; he may require the Opinion, in writing, of the principal Officer in each of the executive Departments, upon any Subject relating to the Duties of their respective Offices, and he shall have Power to grant Reprieves and Pardons for Offences against the United States, except in Cases of Impeachment.

He shall have Power, by and with the Advice and Consent of the Senate, to make Treaties, provided two thirds of the Senators present concur; and he shall nominate, and by and with the Advice and Consent of the Senate, shall appoint Ambassadors, other public Ministers and Consuls, Judges of the supreme Court, and all other Officers of the United States, whose Appointments are not herein otherwise provided for, and which shall be established by Law: but the Congress may by Law vest the Appointment of such inferior Officers, as they think proper in the President alone, in the Courts of Law, or in the Heads of Departments.

The President shall have Power to fill up all Vacancies that may happen during the Recess of the Senate, by granting Commissions which shall expire at the end of their next Session.

Section 3.

He shall from time to time give to the Congress Information of the State of the Union, and recommend to their Consideration such Measures as he shall judge necessary and expedient; he may, on extraordinary Occasions, convene both Houses, or either of them, and in Case of Disagreement between them, with Respect to the Time of Adjournment, he may adjourn them to such Time as he shall think proper; he shall receive Ambassadors and other public Ministers; he shall take Care that Laws be faithfully executed, and shall Commission all the Officers of the United States.

Section 4.

The President, Vice President and all civil Officers of the United States, shall be removed from Office on Impeachment for, and Conviction of, Treason, Bribery, or other high Crimes and Misdemeanors.

ARTICLE III

Section 1.

The judicial Power of the United States, shall be vested in one supreme Court, and in such inferior Courts as the Congress may from time to time ordain and establish. The Judges, both of the supreme and inferior Courts, shall hold their Offices during good Behaviour, and shall, at stated Times, receive for their Services, a Compensation, which shall not be diminished during their Continuance in Office.

Section 2.

The judicial Power shall extend to all Cases in Law and Equity, arising under this Constitution, the Laws of the United States, and Treaties made, or which shall be made, under their Authority;—to all Cases affecting Ambassadors, other public Ministers and Consuls;—to all Cases of admiralty and maritime Jurisdiction;—to Controversies to which the United States shall be a Party;—to Controversies between two or more states;—between a State and Citizens of another State;—between Citizens of different States;—between Citizens of the same State claiming Lands under Grants of different States, and between a State, or the Citizens thereof, and foreign States, Citizens or Subjects.[5]

In all Cases affecting Ambassadors, other public Ministers and Consuls, and those in which a State shall be Party, the supreme Court shall have original Jurisdiction. In all the other Cases before mentioned, the supreme Court shall have appellate Jurisdiction, both as to Law and Fact, with such Exceptions, and under such Regulations as the Congress shall make.

The Trial of all Crimes, except in Cases of Impeachment, shall be by Jury; and such Trial shall be held in the State where the said Crimes shall have been committed, but when not committed within any State, the Trial shall be at such Place or Places as the Congress may by Law have directed.

Section 3.

Treason against the United States, shall consist only in levying War against them, or in adhering to their Enemies, giving them Aid and Comfort. No person shall be convicted of Treason unless on the Testimony of two Witnesses to the same overt Act, or on Confession in open Court.

The Congress shall have Power to declare the Punishment of Treason, but no Attainder of Treason shall work Corruption of Blood, or Forfeiture except during the Life of the Person attainted.

ARTICLE IV

Section 1.

Full Faith and Credit shall be given in each State to the public Acts, Records, and judicial Proceedings of every other State. And the Congress may by general Laws prescribe the Manner in which such Acts, Records and Proceedings shall be proved, and the Effect thereof.

---

[4]Provisions superseded by Amendment XII.

[5]Clause changed by Amendment XI.

Section 2.

The Citizens of each State shall be entitled to all Privileges and Immunities of Citizens in the several States.

A Person charged in any State with Treason, Felony, or other Crime, who shall flee from Justice, and be found in another State, shall on Demand of the executive Authority of the State from which he fled, be delivered up, to be removed to the State having Jurisdiction of the Crime.

No Person held to Service or Labour in one State, under the Laws thereof, escaping into another, shall, in Consequence of any Law or Regulation therein, be discharged from such Service or Labour, but shall be delivered up on Claim of the Party to whom such Service or Labour may be due.

Section 3.

New States may be admitted by the Congress into this Union; but no new State shall be formed or erected within the jurisdiction of any other State; nor any State be formed by the Junction of two or more States, or Parts of States, without the Consent of the Legislatures of the States concerned as well as of the Congress.

The Congress shall have Power to dispose of and make all needful Rules and Regulations respecting the Territory or other Property belonging to the United States; and nothing in this Constitution shall be so construed as to Prejudice any Claims of the United States, or of any particular State.

Section 4.

The United States shall guarantee to every State in this Union a Republican Form of Government, and shall protect each of them against Invasion; and on Application of the Legislature, or of the Executive (when the Legislature cannot be convened) against domestic Violence.

ARTICLE V

The Congress, whenever two thirds of both Houses shall deem it necessary, shall propose Amendments to this Constitution, or, on the Application of the Legislatures of two thirds of the several States, shall call a Convention for proposing Amendments, which, in either Case, shall be valid to all Intents and Purposes, as Part of this Constitution, when ratified by the Legislatures of three fourths of the several States, or by Conventions in three fourths thereof, as the one or the other Mode of Ratification may be proposed by the Congress; Provided that no Amendment which may be made prior to the Year One thousand eight hundred and eight shall in any Manner affect the first and fourth Clauses in the Ninth Section of the first Article; and that no State, without its Consent, shall be deprived of its equal Suffrage in the Senate.

ARTICLE VI

All Debts contracted and Engagements entered into, before the Adoption of this Constitution, shall be as valid against the United States under this Constitution, as under the Confederation.

This Constitution, and the Laws of the United States which shall be made in Pursuance thereof; and all Treaties made, or which shall be made, under the Authority of the United States, shall be the supreme Law of the Land; and the Judges in every State shall be bound thereby, any Thing in the Constitution or Laws of any State to the Contrary notwithstanding.

The Senators and Representatives before mentioned, and the Members of the several State Legislatures, and all executive and judicial Officers, both of the United States and of the several States, shall be bound by Oath or Affirmation, to support this Constitution; but no religious Test shall ever be required as a Qualification to any Office or public Trust under the United States.

ARTICLE VII

The Ratification of the Conventions of nine States shall be sufficient for the Establishment of this Constitution between the States so ratifying the Same.

done in Convention by the Unanimous Consent of the States present the Seventeenth Day of September in the Year of our Lord one thousand seven hundred and Eighty seven and of the Independence of the United States of America and the Twelfth[6] IN WITNESS whereof We have here unto subscribed our Names.

---

[6]The Constitution was submitted on September 17, 1787, by the Constitutional Convention, was ratified by the conventions of several states at various dates up to May 29, 1790, and became effective on March 4, 1789.

AMENDMENTS TO THE CONSTITUTION

[AMENDMENT I]

Congress shall make no law respecting an establishment of religion, or prohibiting the free exercise thereof; or abridging the freedom of speech, or of the press, or the right of the people peaceably to assemble, and to petition the Government for a redress of grievances.

[AMENDMENT II]

A well regulated Militia being necessary to the security of a free State, the right of the people to keep and bear Arms, shall not be infringed.

[AMENDMENT III]

No Soldier shall, in time of peace be quartered in any house, without the consent of the Owner, nor in time of war, but in a manner to be prescribed by law.

[AMENDMENT IV]

The right of the people to be secure in their persons, houses, papers, and effects, against unreasonable searches and seizures, shall not be violated, and no Warrants shall issue, but upon probable cause, supported by Oath or affirmation, and particularly describing the place to be searched, and the persons or things to be seized.

[AMENDMENT V]

No person shall be held to answer for a capital, or otherwise infamous crime, unless on a presentment or indictment of a Grand Jury, except in cases arising in the land or naval forces, or in the Militia, when in actual service in time of War or public danger; nor shall any person be subject for the same offense to be twice put in jeopardy of life or limb; nor shall be compelled in any criminal case to be a witness against himself, nor be deprived of life, liberty, or property, without due process of law; nor shall private property be taken for public use, without just compensation.

[AMENDMENT VI]

In all criminal prosecutions, the accused shall enjoy the right to a speedy and public trial, by an impartial jury of the State and district wherein the crime shall have been committed, which district shall have been previously ascertained by law, and to be informed of the nature and cause of the accusation; to be confronted with the witnesses against him; to have compulsory process for obtaining witnesses in his favor, and to have the Assistance of Counsel for his defence.

[AMENDMENT VII]

In Suits at common law, where the value in controversy shall exceed twenty dollars, the right of trial by jury shall be preserved, and no fact tried by a jury, shall be otherwise re-examined in any court of the United States, than according to the rules of the common law.

[AMENDMENT VIII]

Excessive bail shall not be required, nor excessive fines imposed, nor cruel and unusual punishments inflicted.

[AMENDMENT IX]

The enumeration in the Constitution, of certain rights, shall not be construed to deny or disparage others retained by the people.

[AMENDMENT X]

The powers not delegated to the United States by the Constitution, nor prohibited by it to the States, are reserved to the States respectively, or to the people.[7]

[AMENDMENT XI]

The Judicial power of the United States shall not be construed to extend to any suit in law or equity, commenced or prosecuted against one of the United States by Citizens of another State, or by Citizens or Subjects of any Foreign State.[8]

[AMENDMENT XII]

The Electors shall meet in their respective states, and vote by ballot for President and Vice-President, one of whom, at least, shall not be an inhabitant of the same state with themselves; they shall name in their ballots the person voted for as President, and in distinct ballots the person voted for as Vice-President, and they shall make distinct lists of all persons voted for as President, and of all persons voted for as Vice-President, and of the number of votes for each, which lists they shall sign and certify, and transmit sealed to the seat of the government of the United States, directed to the President of the Senate;—The President of the Senate shall, in the presence of the Senate and House of Representatives, open all the certificates and the votes shall then be counted;—The person having the greatest number of votes for President, shall be the President, if such number be a majority of the whole number of Electors appointed; and if no person have such majority, then from the persons having the highest numbers not exceeding three on the list of those voted for as President, the House of Representatives shall choose immediately, by ballot, the President. But in choosing the President, the votes shall be taken by states, the representation from each state having one vote; a quorum for this purpose shall consist of a member or members from two-thirds of the states, and a majority of all the states shall be necessary to a choice. And if the House of Representatives shall not choose a President whenever the right of choice shall devolve upon them, before the fourth day of March next following, then the Vice-President shall act as President, as in the case of the death or other constitutional disability of the President.—The person having the greatest number of votes as Vice-President, shall be the Vice-President, if such number be a majority of the whole number of Electors appointed, and if no person have a majority, then from the two highest numbers on the list, the Senate shall choose the Vice-President; a quorum for the purpose shall consist of two-thirds of the whole number of Senators, and a majority of the whole number shall be necessary to a choice. But no person constitutionally ineligible to the office of President shall be eligible to that of Vice-President of the United States.[9]

[AMENDMENT XIII]

Section 1.

Neither slavery nor involuntary servitude, except as a punishment for crime whereof the party shall have been duly convicted, shall exist within the United States, or any place subject to their jurisdiction.

Section 2.

Congress shall have power to enforce this article by appropriate legislation.[10]

[AMENDMENT XIV]

Section 1.

All persons born or naturalized in the United States and subject to the jurisdiction thereof, are citizens of the United States and the State wherein they reside. No State shall make or enforce any law which shall abridge the privileges or immunities of citizens of the United States; nor shall any State deprive any person of life, liberty, or property, without due process of law; nor deny to any person within its jurisdiction the equal protection of the laws.

Section 2.

Representatives shall be apportioned among the several States according to their respective numbers counting the whole number of

---

[7]The first ten amendments were all proposed by Congress on September 25, 1789, and were ratified and adoption certified on December 15, 1791.

[8]Proposed by Congress on March 4, 1794, and declared ratified on January 8, 1798.

[9]Proposed by Congress on December 9, 1803; declared ratified on September 25, 1804; supplemented by Amendments XX and XXIII.

[10]Proposed by Congress on January 31, 1865; declared ratified on December 18, 1865.

persons in each State, excluding Indians not taxed. But when the right to vote at any election for the choice of electors for President and Vice-President of the United States, Representatives in Congress, the Executive and Judicial officers of a State, or the members of the Legislature thereof, is denied to any of the male inhabitants of such State being twenty-one years of age and citizens of the United States, or in any way abridged, except for participation in rebellion or other crime, the basis of representation therein shall be reduced in the proportion which the number of such male citizens shall bear to the whole number of male citizens twenty-one years of age in such State.

Section 3.

No person shall be a Senator or Representative in Congress, or elector of President and Vice President or hold any office, civil or military, under the United States or under any State, who, having previously taken an oath, as a member of Congress, or as an officer of the United States, or as a member of any State legislature or as an executive or judicial officer of any State to support the Constitution of the United States, shall have engaged in insurrection or rebellion against the same, or given aid or comfort to the enemies thereof. But Congress may by a vote of two-thirds of each House, remove such disability.

Section 4.

The validity of the public debt of the United States authorized by law, including debts incurred for payment of pensions and bounties for services in suppressing insurrection or rebellion, shall not be questioned. But neither the United States nor any State shall assume or pay any debt or obligation incurred in aid of insurrection or rebellion against the United States, or any claim for the loss or emancipation of any slave; but all such debts, obligations and claims shall be held illegal and void.

Section 5.

The Congress shall have power to enforce, by appropriate legislation, the provisions of this article.[11]

[AMENDMENT XV]

Section 1.

The right of citizens of the United States to vote shall not be denied or abridged by the United States or by any State on account of race, color, or previous condition of servitude.

Section.

The Congress shall have power to enforce this article by appropriate legislation.[12]

[AMENDMENT XVI]

The Congress shall have power to lay and collect taxes on incomes, from whatever source derived, without apportionment among the several States, and without regard to any census or enumeration.[13]

[AMENDMENT XVII]

The Senate of the United States shall be composed of two Senators from each State, elected by the people thereof, for six years; and each Senator shall have one vote. The electors in each State shall have the qualifications requisite for electors of the most numerous branch of the State legislatures.

When vacancies happen in the representation of any State in the Senate, the executive authority of such State shall issue writs of election to fill such vacancies: *Provided*, That the legislature of any State may empower the executive thereof to make temporary appointments until the people fill the vacancies by election as the legislature may direct.

This amendment shall not be so construed as to affect the election or term of any Senator chosen before it becomes valid as part of the Constitution.[14]

[AMENDMENT XVIII]

Section 1.

After one year from the ratification of this article the manufacture, sale, or transportation of intoxicating liquors within, the importation thereof into, or the exportation thereof from the United States and all territory subject to the jurisdiction thereof for beverage purposes is hereby prohibited.

Section 2.

The Congress and the several States shall have concurrent power to enforce this article by appropriate legislation.

Section 3.

This article shall be inoperative unless it shall have been ratified as an amendment to the Constitution by the legislatures of the several States, as provided in the Constitution, within seven years from the date of the submission hereof to the States by the Congress.[15]

[AMENDMENT XIX]

The right of citizens of the United States to vote shall not be denied or abridged by the United States or by any State on account of sex.

Congress shall have power to enforce this article by appropriate legislation.[16]

[AMENDMENT XX]

Section 1.

The terms of the President and Vice President shall end at noon on the 20th day of January, and the terms of Senators and Representatives at noon on the 3d day of January, of the years in which such terms would have ended if this article had not been ratified; and the terms of their successors shall then begin.

Section 2.

The Congress shall assemble at least once in every year, and such meeting shall begin at noon on the 3d day of January, unless they shall by law appoint a different day.

Section 3.

If, at the time fixed for the beginning of the term of the President, the President elect shall have died, the Vice President elect shall become President. If a President shall not have been chosen before the time fixed for the beginning of his term, or if the President elect shall have failed to qualify, then the Vice President elect shall act as President until a President shall have qualified; and the Congress may by law provide for the case wherein neither a President elect nor a Vice President elect shall have qualified, declaring who shall then act as President, or the manner in which one who is to act shall be selected, and such person shall act accordingly until a President or Vice President shall have qualified.

Section 4.

The Congress may by law provide for the case of the death of any of the persons from whom the House of Representatives may choose a President whenever the right of choice shall have devolved upon them, and for the case of the death of any of the persons from whom the Senate may choose a Vice President whenever the right of choice shall have devolved upon them.

Section 5.

Sections 1 and 2 shall take effect on the 15th day of October following the ratification of this article.

---

[11]Proposed by Congress on June 13, 1866; declared ratified on July 28, 1868.
[12]Proposed by Congress on February 26, 1869; declared ratified on March 30, 1870.
[13]Proposed by Congress on July 12, 1909; declared ratified on February 25, 1913.

---

[14]Proposed by Congress on May 13, 1912; declared ratified on May 31, 1913.
[15]Proposed by Congress on December 18, 1917; declared ratified on January 29, 1919; repealed by Amendment XXI.
[16]Proposed by Congress on June 4, 1919; declared ratified on August 26, 1920.

Section 6.

This article shall be inoperative unless it shall have been ratified as an amendment to the Constitution by the legislatures of three-fourths of the several States within seven years from the date of its submission.[17]

[AMENDMENT XXI]
Section 1.

The eighteenth article of amendment to the Constitution of the United States is hereby repealed.

Section 2.

The transportation or importation into any States, Territory, or possession of the United States for delivery or use therein of intoxicating liquors, in violation of the laws thereof, is hereby prohibited.

Section 3.

This article shall be inoperative unless it shall have been ratified as an amendment to the Constitution by conventions in the several States, as provided in the Constitution, within seven years from the date of the submission hereof to the States by the Congress.[18]

[AMENDMENT XXII]
Section 1.

No person shall be elected to the office of the President more than twice, and no person who has held the office of President, or acted as President, for more than two years of a term to which some other person was elected President shall be elected to the office of the President more than once. But this Article shall not apply to any person holding the office of President when the Article was proposed by the Congress, and shall not prevent any person who may be holding the office of President, or acting as President, during the term within which this Article becomes operative from holding the office of President or acting as President during the remainder of such term.

Section 2.

This article shall be inoperative unless it shall have been ratified as an amendment to the Constitution by the legislatures of three-fourths of the several States within seven years from the date of its submission to the States by the Congress.[19]

[AMENDMENT XXIII]
Section 1.

The District constituting the seat of Government of the United States shall appoint in such manner as the Congress shall direct:

A number of electors of President and Vice President equal to the whole number of Senators and Representatives in Congress to which the District would be entitled if it were a State, but in no event more than the least populous State; they shall be in addition to those appointed by the States, but they shall be considered, for the purposes of the election of President and Vice President, to be electors appointed by a State; and they shall meet in the District and perform such duties as provided by the twelfth article of amendment.

Section 2.

The Congress shall have power to enforce this article by appropriate legislation.[20]

[AMENDMENT XXIV]
Section 1.

The right of citizens of the United States to vote in any primary or other election for President or Vice President, for electors for President or Vice President, or for Senator or Representative in Congress, shall not be denied or abridged by the United States or any state by reason of failure to pay any poll tax or other tax.

Section 2.

The Congress shall have the power to enforce this article by appropriate legislation.[21]

[AMENDMENT XXV]
Section 1.

In case of the removal of the President from office or his death or resignation, the Vice President shall become President.

Section 2.

Whenever there is a vacancy in the office of the Vice President, the President shall nominate a Vice President who shall take the office upon confirmation by a majority vote of both houses of Congress.

Section 3.

Whenever the President transmits to the President pro tempore of the Senate and the Speaker of the House of Representatives his written declaration that he is unable to discharge the powers and duties of his office, and until he transmits to them a written declaration to the contrary, such powers and duties shall be discharged by the Vice President as Acting President.

Section 4.

Whenever the Vice President and a majority of either the principal officers of the executive departments or of such other body as Congress may by law provide, transmit to the President pro tempore of the Senate and the Speaker of the House of Representatives their written declaration that the President is unable to discharge the powers and duties of his office, the Vice President shall immediately assume the powers and duties of the office as Acting President.

Thereafter, when the President transmits to the President pro tempore of the Senate and the Speaker of the House of Representatives his written declaration that no inability exists, he shall resume the powers and duties of his office unless the Vice President and a majority of either the principal officers of the executive department or of such other body as Congress may by law provide, transmit within four days to the President pro tempore of the Senate and the Speaker of the House of Representatives their written delcaration that the President is unable to discharge the powers and duties of his office. Thereupon Congress shall decide the issue, assembling within 48 hours for that purpose if not in session. If the Congress, within 21 days after receipt of the latter written declaration, or, if Congress is not in session, within 21 days after Congress is required to assemble, determines by two-thirds vote of both houses that the President is unable to discharge the powers and duties of his office, the Vice President shall continue to discharge the same as Acting President; otherwise, the President shall resume the powers and duties of his office.[22]

[AMENDMENT XXVI]
Section 1.

The right of citizens of the United States, who are 18 years of age or older, to vote shall not be denied or abridged by the United States or any state on account of age.

Section 2.

The Congress shall have the power to enforce this article by appropriate legislation.[23]

[17]Proposed by Congress on March 2, 1932; declared ratified on February 6, 1933.
[18]Proposed by Congress on February 20, 1933; declared ratified on December 5, 1933.
[19]Proposed by Congress on March 24, 1947; declared ratified on March 1, 1951.
[20]Proposed by Congress on June 16, 1960; declared ratified on April 3, 1961.
[21]Proposed by Congress on August 27, 1962; declared ratified on January 23, 1963.
[22]Proposed by Congress on July 6, 1965; declared ratified on February 10, 1967.
[23]Proposed by Congress on March 23, 1971; declared ratified on June 30, 1971.

Glossary

Adjudication The process of resolving conflict through the courts (p. 369).

Appellate jurisdiction The power of one court to review the rulings of other (lower) courts (p. 370).

Appropriation An act of Congress allowing a specified amount of money to be spent on an authorized program (p. 292).

Authorization An act of Congress permitting a government program to begin or continue and specifying an upper limit of funds to support the program (p. 292).

Bad tendency doctrine A doctrine stating that speech can be limited if it can be demonstrated that the speech might endanger public health, safety, or morals (p. 374).

Bill of Rights The first ten amendments to the Constitution (p. 388).

Brown v. Board of Education A landmark 1954 case in which the Supreme Court ruled that public schools segregated on the basis of race were in violation of the Fourteenth Amendment's equal protection clause (p. 462).

Budget Control and Impoundment Act A law passed by Congress in 1974 in an attempt to restrain presidential power. The act outlines specific procedures for establishing the federal budget, provides for greater congressional involvement in the budget process, and limits the President's ability to impound funds (p. 332).

Bureaucracy A term used to refer collectively to government agencies, regulations, and services (p. 338).

Cabinet The heads of executive departments (e.g., secretary of agriculture) in the national government. These are among the President's principal advisers (p. 301).

Capitalism An economic system characterized by private ownership of the means of production. Capitalism originally operated under the principle of total competition. However, in modern times the system has been characterized by increased concentration of wealth accompanied by greater government regulation and subsidization (p. 171).

Caucus A meeting of party activists to nominate candidates for office and to agree on party policy (p. 233).

Checks and balances An organizational arrangement in which each branch of government has some power over actions of the other branches (p. 75).

Civil disobedience The nonviolent violation of laws with which one disagrees. One important purpose of this activity is to test the constitutionality of the law in the courts (p. 463).

Civil rights   Protections afforded citizens from potentially harmful actions by both government and other individuals. Voting is one important example of a U.S. citizen's civil rights. Government remedies are provided for the correction of civil-rights violations (p. 460).

Clear and present danger doctrine   The doctrine stating that speech can be limited only if a direct relationship can be demonstrated between the speech and an action that endangers public health, safety, or morals that the government has a right to regulate (p. 374).

Closed primary   A primary election in which only party members may vote. Membership is determined by state laws and party rules (p. 230).

Cloture   A vote taken in the Senate to end debate. This is the method used to stop a filibuster. To be successful, a motion to invoke cloture must receive a three-fifths majority (p. 160).

Cold War   A term used to describe the post–World War II period of confrontation between the United States and the Soviet Union (p. 518).

Colonialism   The direct political domination of a foreign territory by a country (p. 548).

Constituency   The electoral base of an elected public official. Voters and organized interests that make up this base are known as constituents (p. 282).

Constitution   The basic principles and laws of a state or governing body. A constitution outlines the structure of government and describes the relationship between individuals and their government (p. 2).

Containment   The post–World War II American response to communist movements in Europe and elsewhere. The aim of the policy was to prevent further communist expansion (p. 522).

De facto segregation   Racial segregation resulting from neighborhood racial patterns (p. 474).

De jure segregation   Racial segregation created by law (p. 474).

Defendant   The individual accused of a crime in a criminal case or sued by a plaintiff in a civil case (p. 389).

Deficit   An excess of government expenditures over government revenues (p. 355).

Deficit financing (spending)   A budgetary practice in which expenditures exceed revenues. Under this practice, the government spends more money than it takes in. This policy is designed to stimulate the economy (p. 181).

Democracy   A political system based on a belief in the equality of all people. In a democracy, all individuals are allowed a voice in their own government. Ideally, this results in majority rule, either directly or through representatives, with protection afforded the rights of minorities (p. 15).

Détente   A term used to describe the 1970s period of relative conciliation between the United States and the Soviet Union (p. 543).

Direct primary   An election in which candidates run for their party's nomination for a particular office. The voters of the party select the party's nominee (p. 230).

Due process clause   That portion of the Fourteenth Amendment requiring states to treat their citizens in such a manner that no person is deprived of life, liberty, or property unfairly. The limitations placed on the national government by the Bill of Rights have largely been incorporated under the due process clause and applied to the states (p. 389).

Electoral College   The formal structure, consisting of a body of electors, through which the President is elected. Each state has one elector for each representative and senator. The candidate with the most popular votes in a state wins all of that state's electoral votes. See Article II, Section 1 of the Constitution (p. 75).

Electorate   That portion of the population eligible to vote (p. 22).

Elitism   A political theory which views society as being divided into two classes—the masses, and the few who rule society (elites) (p. 85).

Equal protection clause   That portion of the Fourteenth Amendment prohibiting action by states that would deny citizens equal protection under the law (p. 462).

Exclusionary rule   A court ruling prohibiting the use of illegally seized evidence in a prosecution (p. 392).

Executive privilege   The doctrine which protects the confidentiality of discussions, advice, and memoranda between the President and his major aides (p. 315).

Federal budget   The statement of all anticipated revenues, expenditures, and programs of the federal government (p. 354).

Federal Election and Campaign Act of 1974   A law establishing a presidential election campaign fund to cover the election expenses of major presidential candidates. The income for the fund comes from the voluntary income tax check-off system that allows taxpayers to allocate one dollar of their tax to the fund each year (p. 156).

Federal reserve system   A group of twelve district reserve banks created by an act of Congress in 1913. These banks serve as reserve and discount banks for their affiliated members, which include all national banks. The policies and regulations of the system serve to control the amount of money available in the economy (p. 7).

Filibuster   The practice of talking a bill to death. The Senate's rule of unlimited debate allows an individual senator or small group of senators to continue to speak until business is disrupted and members will agree to table the objectionable bill. A filibuster can be stopped by a cloture vote (p. 159).

Fiscal policy   A governmental policy designed to control the economy through taxation and spending. Under fiscal policy, the federal budget is used as a tool to promote a prosperous private economic sector (p. 5).

Franchise   The right to vote (p. 22).

Frontier thesis   The historical argument that America's greatness resulted from the westward expansion of the frontier. This supposedly created the economic basis for American democracy (p. 555).

Grandfather clause   A provision of law used to give voting rights only to citizens whose ancestors ("grandfathers") had possessed that right. This was one of several means used to prevent blacks from voting in many Southern states (p. 126).

Gross national product (GNP) The sum of all goods and services produced in a nation during a given period of time (normally one year). This also includes consumer and government expenditures and private investment. GNP is a traditional measure of national economic well-being (p. 11).

Habeas corpus A principle of common law, protected by the Constitution, which provides a means of determining whether sufficient legal grounds exist for holding an individual in custody. This right affords citizens a protection against an abuse of the police's arresting power (p. 393).

Hatch Act A congressional law designed to limit political activity on the part of federal employees (p. 344).

Ideology A set of ideas designed to legitimize a particular philosophy or group of leaders and their stated policies (p. 214).

Impeachment A formal accusation by the House of Representatives of wrong-doing by a federal official. This act is somewhat analogous to indictment by a grand jury (p. 319).

Imperialism The economic domination of one country by another (p. 548).

Impoundment The President's refusal to spend money authorized and appropriated by Congress for a particular government project (p. 312).

Incorporation The inclusion of Bill of Rights protections into the Fourteenth Amendment's restrictions on activity by the states (p. 389).

Incumbency The sphere of action, power, and influence associated with holding public office. An incumbent is someone who holds an elective office (p. 44).

Independent agencies Executive agencies located outside the major executive departments. These agencies report directly to the President (p. 340).

Independent regulatory commissions Institutions created by Congress to regulate areas of the public sector. They have executive, legislative, and judicial powers. Members are appointed by the President for fixed terms. However, the commissions report to Congress rather than to the President (p. 342).

Inflation An economic situation in which prices increase rapidly (p. 5).

Initiative A practice in several states allowing citizens to place a policy question on the election ballot by petition (p. 219).

Injunction A court order prohibiting some action by an individual or organization (p. 116).

Interest group (special interest group; public interest group) Any group organized on the basis of common interests to influence the actions of public officials and government policies. Their efforts are known collectively as lobbying (p. 244).

Interlocking directorate A business practice in which individuals serve as directors of two or more often competing companies (p. 196).

Judicial review The power of the courts to determine the constitutionality of a government act (p. 366).

Laissez faire An economic theory based largely on the principle of government noninterference in the economy. In a laissez-faire economy, business and industry determine the rules of competition and labor without government regulation (p. 173).

Lobbying   Efforts by individuals and groups to influence the actions of public officials and government policies (p. 244).

Logrolling   A strategy used by individuals, groups, and legislators to strengthen their position and broaden support. Under this strategy, a mutual support alliance is formed whereby diverse groups or individuals agree to support each other in certain policy areas (p. 258).

Majority   Fifty percent plus one (p. 216).

Majority leader   The floor leader of the majority party in a legislative body. The majority leader is elected by the members of the majority party (p. 280).

Majority whip   An assistant to the majority leader in a legislative body. This person works to obtain support from other legislators of the same party for party legislative proposals (p. 280).

Marshall Plan   The multi-billion-dollar American plan for the post–World War II economic reconstruction of Europe (p. 530).

Media   Mass communications networks such as radio, television, wire services, and newspapers (p. 312).

Merit system   The practice of hiring, promoting, and rewarding federal employees on the basis of competitive exam and/or job performance (p. 343).

Minority leader   The floor leader of the minority party in a legislative body who is elected by the members of the minority party (p. 280).

Minority whip   An assistant to the minority leader in a legislative body. This individual's job is to convince other minority party legislators to support the party position on legislation (p. 280).

Monetary policy   A governmental policy designed to control the economy by regulating the supply of money. The purpose of the policy is to maintain a stable private economic sector (p. 5).

Monopoly   One company's control of the majority of sales in an economic area (p. 200).

Monroe Doctrine   Doctrine espoused by President Monroe declaring a dominant role for the United States in Latin America (p. 516).

Multiplier effect   The effect resulting from the investment of additional money in the economy. The Keynesian economic view of this is essentially that the availability of "extra" dollars in the economy will result in additional profits and increased buying power at all levels (p. 182).

National debt   The sum of all debts owed by the federal government. This includes both long and short term obligations (p. 361).

Negative Income Tax (NIT)   A tax plan designed to provide income subsidies to those individuals whose annual income falls below some stated figure. This plan would provide a guaranteed annual income (p. 436).

New Deal   The reform movement begun during Franklin Roosevelt's administration in response to the Great Depression. In part, the federal government intervened in the economy to promote full employment and economic stability (p. 4).

Oligopoly   The control by a few (four or fewer) companies of the majority of sales in an economic area (p. 200).

Ombudsman An agency created to aid the public in dealing with the bureaucracy. It is supposed to help prevent bureaucratic abuses. Developed in Europe, it is best known in the Scandinavian countries (p. 350).

One person, one vote rule A rule first stated by the Supreme Court requiring that congressional districts within a state be nearly equal in population. This rule was later extended to state and local elections (p. 398).

Open Door Policy Policy proposed by the United States at the turn of the century calling for all nations to have equal access to China (p. 518).

Original jurisdiction Jurisdiction, or authority to hear a case, in the first instance. A court with original jurisdiction will be the court in which a case is first heard (p. 370).

Out-party The political party not holding political power. This can refer either to Congress or the Presidency (p. 36).

Oversight The act of reviewing the actions and budgets of government agencies. This is normally carried out by congressional committees (p. 349).

Parliamentary political system A form of government in which the executive and legislature do not have separate terms and may not exist as separate branches. The executive is elected by the legislature (p. 59).

Plaintiff The individual bringing the initial complaint to court in a legal action (p. 370).

Platform A statement by a national political party outlining its view of contemporary society and stating the party goals (p. 214).

Plea bargaining The practice of allowing defendants in criminal cases to plead guilty to lesser offenses than those with which they were originally charged. This practice is often followed in courts with crowded dockets (p. 448).

Pluralism A political theory which views political influence as being widely dispersed among competing interests. This theory sees the public as having a stronger voice in politics than does elitism (p. 86).

Plurality In an election, the person or party who receives more votes than any other competitor, but not necessarily a majority of the votes cast (p. 218).

Pocket veto A form of presidential veto of a bill. A pocket veto takes place if the President takes no action on a bill within ten working days of receiving it and if Congress adjourns during that time (p. 292).

Political action committee (PAC) An organization created by groups, unions, and professional organizations to collect campaign funds for candidates or to spend money on behalf of candidates (p. 147).

Political efficacy The feeling on the part of citizens that they can exert some control and influence over their government (p. 13).

Political machine The highly organized leadership of a local political party, often associated with corrupt political practices (p. 136).

Political patronage A system under which the winning political party can award certain government jobs to the party faithful, regardless of merit. Prior to the creation of the U.S. Civil Service in 1883, this was the standard method for filling jobs in the federal government (p. 343).

Polity Another term for a national political system (p. 74).

Poll tax   A fee charged for registering to vote. This tax was used in some areas to prevent or discourage segments of the population from voting. It is no longer legal (p. 52).

Positive state   A government that adopts an activist posture in relation to the citizens. Government provides numerous services to the people beyond such acts as police protection and plays a major role in shaping social, economic, and political structures (p. 336).

Preferred position doctrine   The legal concept that the rights protected by the First Amendment are the most important in a free society (p. 375).

President pro tempore   The presiding officer of the Senate in the absence of the Vice-President. The president pro tempore is elected by the majority party. It is normally an honorary position held by the member of the majority party with the longest continuous service (p. 280).

Prior restraint   The suppression of speech or writing prior to its utterance or publication (p. 381).

Proportional representation   A system of representation in which a party's membership in the legislative body is based on the proportion of the entire national vote its candidates receive in an election. This system is used in some Western European nations (p. 59).

Proposition 13   A state tax initiative approved by California voters which limited property tax collection by local jurisdictions (p. 433).

Quorum   The minimum number of members needed in attendance for a legislative body to conduct business (p. 289).

Recall   A practice in some states allowing voters to determine whether a public official should be removed from office before that official's elected term expires. The question is placed on the ballot by petition (p. 219).

Recession   A temporary decline in economic activity. It is generally recognized as resulting from two successive quarters of negative growth in the economy (p. 191).

Red tape   A term, often critical, used to describe the regulations and procedures of government agencies (p. 348).

Referendum   An election in which voters decide on a particular policy option. Bond issues are fairly common examples of referenda (p. 219).

Regressive tax   A tax which places a proportionately greater burden on those with the lowest incomes (p. 190).

Roll-call vote   A vote in a legislative body in which each member's vote is recorded (p. 68).

Seniority system   A system granting status and authority in Congress to those members with long and continuous service. In the twentieth century, prior to 1971, both parties in Congress followed a strict seniority system in committee assignments and selection of committee chairmen. Chairmanships were always held by the member of the majority party with the longest continuous service on the committee (p. 278).

Separation of powers   An organizational arrangement in which political power is legally dispersed among the branches of government—the legislative, the judiciary, and the executive (p. 75).

Social contract An agreement among the people as to how they shall be governed (p. 2).

Social determinism The theory that general trends in social behavior are determined largely by the social and economic environment (p. 497).

Social mobility Upward or downward movement by individuals between social classes (p. 497).

Speaker of the House The presiding officer of the House of Representitives. The individual holding this position is the acknowledged leader of the majority party and is elected by the membership of the House (p. 280).

Spoils system The system of political patronage used prior to the creation of the U.S. Civil Service (p. 343).

Stagflation A phenomenon occurring when both unemployment and inflation are high at the same time. This situation, although at odds with conventional economic wisdom, prevailed throughout the 1970s (p. 6).

Structural theory of power The doctrine that political choices can be made only from a narrow range of options that are predetermined by political, economic, and social structures (p. 88).

Sunset laws Laws requiring that government agencies and commissions will cease to exist unless their charters are renewed by a positive act of the legislature (p. 350).

Sunshine laws Laws designed to open the activities of government institutions to public scrutiny. Examples include open meetings and open records laws (p. 76).

Surplus An excess of government revenues over government expenditures (p. 355).

Target pricing A practice typical of concentrated industries in which a product's price is set to guarantee a certain level of profit, regardless of supply or demand (p. 201).

Trickle-down theory The view that government aid to business will benefit the entire economy. The masses will be aided as the economy expands and benefits "trickle down" the socioeconomic ladder (p. 33).

Truman Doctrine Doctrine presented by President Truman in 1947 that committed the United States to resist communist movements in Greece and Turkey (p. 527).

Urban blight The decline and deterioration of neighborhoods in poverty-stricken central cities (p. 494).

Veto The power of the President to reject a bill passed by Congress. Congress can override a presidential veto by a two-thirds vote in both houses (p. 292).

War Powers Act A law passed by Congress in 1973 that limits the President's ability to commit American troops to action (p. 332).

White-collar crime A nonviolent form of crime often committed by middle- and upper-class individuals. Although usually thought of in terms of employee thefts, white-collar crime also includes a variety of fraudulent business practices (p. 448).

Acknowledgments

FIGURES AND TABLES

Figure 1.1, p.9; 1976 Survey, p. 13; 1978 Survey, p. 14; Table 2.1, p. 29; Figure 2.4, p. 41; and Table 8.1, p. 224: Data made available by the Inter-university Consortium for Political and Social Research from the University of Michigan SRC/CPS American National Election Studies, 1952–1978.

Figure 2.1, p. 23; and Figure 2.3, p. 27: Data made available by the Inter-university Consortium for Political Research from the University of Michigan Center for Political Studies/American National Election Study, 1976.

Figure 2.1, p. 23: After Table 2–1 (p. 31) in *Participation in Democracy: Political Democracy and Social Equality* by Sidney Verba and Norman H. Nie. Copyright © 1972 by Sidney Verba and Norman H. Nie. Reprinted by permission of Harper & Row, Publishers, Inc.

Figure 2.3, p. 27: From Norman H. Nie, et al., "The Sequence of Changes," from *The Changing American Voter*, p. 273. Copyright © 1976, Harvard University Press. Reprinted by permission.

Figure 2.5, p. 42: © 1978 by the New York Times Company. Reprinted by permission.

Table, p. 148: From "Interest Group Gifts to 1976 Congressional Campaigns," *Congressional Quarterly Weekly Report*, Vol. 35, no. 16, p. 710. Copyright 1977 Congressional Quarterly Inc.

Figure 7.1, p. 176: Reprinted by permission of the publisher, from Douglas F. Dowd, *Modern Economic Problems in Historical Perspective* (Lexington, Mass.: D. C. Heath and Company, 1965).

Table 7.1, p. 189: From Philip M. Stern, *The Rape of the Taxpayer*, p. 11. Copyright © 1972, 1973 by Philip M. Stern. Published by Random House, Inc.

Table 7.3, p. 202: From Edward C. Budd, "Introduction," from *Inequality and Poverty*, p. 22. Copyright © 1967 by W. W. Norton and Company, Inc.

Table 8.3, p. 230: From "Politics-6," *Congressional Quarterly Weekly Report*, Vol. 34, no. 51, pp. 3335–3336. Copyright 1976, Congressional Quarterly Inc.

Table 8.4, p. 238: From "Official 1976 Presidential Vote," *Congressional Quarterly Weekly Report*, Vol. 34, no. 51, p. 3334. Copyright 1976 Congressional Quarterly Inc.

Table 10.1, p. 281: From *Congress Reconsidered*, edited by Lawrence C. Dodd and Bruce I. Oppenheimer. Copyright © 1977 by Praeger Publishers, a division of Holt, Rinehart and Winston. Reprinted by permission of Holt, Rinehart and Winston.

Table, p. 482: © 1978 by the New York Times Company. Reprinted by permission.

PHOTOGRAPHS AND CARTOONS

Chapter 14: 367, Paul Conklin; 373, Yoichi R. Okamoto/Photo Researchers; 377, UPI; 380, Photoworld; 384, Richard Stromberg; 387, © 1980 Sidney Harris; 390, Flip Schulke/Black Star; 396, Martin A. Levick/Black Star; 397, Ken Regan/Camera 5; 400, © 1980 Sidney Harris.

Chapter 15: 407, Arthur Grace/Stock Boston; 412, Sidney Harris, permission from *The Wall Street Journal;* 415, UPI; 418, © 1972, Norris, Vancouver Sun/Rothco; 419, George W. Gardner; 429, Plus 4; 433, Michael D. Sullivan; 438, Christopher Vail.

Chapter 16: 443, Stephen Feldman; 447, James H. Karales/Magnum; 451, Michael Abramson/ Black Star; 453, from *The Herblock Gallery* (Simon & Schuster, 1968); 455, John Crawford, *Alabama Journal.*

Chapter 17: 461, Bruce Davidson/Magnum; 463, John Tweedle; 465, Matt Herron/Black Star; 466, Bruce Roberts/Photo Researchers; 472, Martin A. Levick/Black Star; 483, Sipa Press/Black Star; 486, Claude Salhani/Gamma-Liaison.

Chapter 18: 491, Brian Alpert/Keystone; 495, Jean-Claude Lejeune; 495, Bruce Davidson/Magnum; 500, UPI; 501, Courtesy Whisler-Patri/Jeremiah O. Bragstad; 503, Ellis Herwig/Stock Boston; 506, from *The Herblock Gallery* (Simon & Schuster, 1968); 508, John Loengard/*Life* Magazine, © Time, Inc.; 510, Wide World.

Chapter 19: 517, UPI; 519, William Graham/Camera 5; 521, Wide World; 523, by permission of Bill Mauldin & Wil-Jo Associates, Inc.; 527, Walter Sanders/*Life* Magazine, © Time, Inc.; 530, Wide World; 534, George Skadding/*Life* Magazine, © Time, Inc.; 537, Photoworld; 539, UPI; 540, Erich Lessing/Magnum.

Chapter 20: 547, Photoworld; 549, Wide World(L), Terry Arthur/Camera 5(C), Michael D. Sullivan(R); 554, Jim Moore/Gamma-Liaison; 557, Corky Trinidad/*Honolulu Star-Bulletin;* 559, Magnum; 562, United Nations/T. Chen; 565, Francois Lochon/Gamma-Liaison; 567, Wide World; 569, Jim Moore/Gamma-Liaison; 571 Cornell Capa/Magnum; 572, Francois Lochon/Gamma-Liaison.

Chapter 21: 577, Paul Conklin; 579, © 1980 Sidney Harris.

Part One, pages 18–19 (left to right): UPI; Patricia Hollander Gross/Stock, Boston; Library of Congress; Puck; Wayne State University Archives of Labor & Urban Affairs; **Part Two,** pages 212–213 (left to right): A. Pierce Bounds/Uniphoto; UPI; UPI; Wide World; Paul Conklin; **Part Three,** pages 404–405 (left to right): Matt Heron/Black Star; Arthur S. Grace/Stock, Boston; Jean-Claude Lejeune; Walter Sanders/Life Magazine © *Time,* Inc.; Bruce Davidson/Magnum; Jim Moore/Gamma-Liaison.

Index